KT-547-411

The Design and Implementation of the

4.3BSD UNIX Operating System

The Design and Implementation of the

4.3BSD UNIX Operating System

Samuel J. Leffler
Silicon Graphics, Inc.

Marshall Kirk McKusick
University of California, Berkeley

Michael J. Karels
University of California, Berkeley

John S. Quarterman
Texas Internet Consulting

Addison-Wesley Publishing Company

Reading, Massachusetts • Menlo Park, California • New York
Don Mill, Ontario • Wokingham, England • Amsterdam • Bonn
Sydney • Singapore • Tokyo • Madrid • San Juan

This book is in the Addison-Wesley Series in Computer Science

Michael A. Harrison: Consulting Editor

Keith Wollman: Sponsoring Editor
Carolyn Berry: Marketing Manager
Karen Myer: Production Supervisor
Hugh Crawford: Manufacturing Supervisor
Patsy DuMoulin: Production Coordinator
Jean Seal: Cover Designer
Jean Hammond: Book Designer
Jaap Akkerhuis: Troff Macro Designer
Lyn Dupré: Copy Editor

John Lasseter created the cover art.

Library of Congress Cataloging-in-Publication Data

The Design and implementation of the 4.3 BSD UNIX operating / system by Samuel J. Leffler ... [et al.].
p. cm
Includes bibliographies and index.
ISBN 0-201-06196-1
1. UNIX (Computer operating system) I. Leffler, Samuel J.

QA76.76.063D474 1988
005.4'3--dc19 88-22809
CIP

Reprinted with corrections October, 1990

13 14 15-MA-97 96 95 94

Dedication

This book was inspired by Elliot Organick's book, *The Multics System*.

This book is dedicated to the UNIX community. Without the contributions of its members, there would be nothing about which to write.

Preface

This book is the first authoritative and full-length description of the design and implementation of the research versions of the UNIX system developed at the University of California at Berkeley. Most detail is given about 4.3BSD, which incorporates the improvements of the previous Berkeley versions.

The UNIX System

The UNIX system runs on computers ranging from personal home systems to the largest supercomputers. It is the operating system of choice for most multiprocessor, graphics, and vector-processing systems, and is widely used for its original purpose of timesharing. It is the most portable operating system ever developed. This portability is due partly to its implementation language, C [Kernighan & Ritchie, 1978] (which is itself one of the most widely ported languages), and partly to the elegant design of the system. Many of the system's features are imitated in other systems [O'Dell, 1987].

Since its inception in 1969 [Ritchie & Thompson, 1978], the UNIX system has developed in a number of divergent and rejoining streams. The original developers continue to advance the state of the art with their Ninth Edition UNIX inside AT&T Bell Laboratories. Meanwhile, AT&T licenses UNIX System V as a product. Both of those systems have been strongly influenced by the Berkeley Software Distributions produced by the Computer Systems Research Group (CSRG) of the University of California at Berkeley.

Berkeley Software Distributions

These Berkeley systems have introduced a number of useful programs and facilities to the UNIX community, such as the text editor **vi** in 2BSD (the Berkeley PDP-11 system), demand-paged virtual-memory support in 3BSD (the first Berkeley VAX system), performance improvements in 4.0BSD, job control, autoconfiguration, and long C identifiers in 4.1BSD, as well as reliable signals, improved networking, sophisticated interprocess-communication (IPC) primitives, a fast filesystem, and more performance improvements in 4.2BSD and 4.3BSD. 4.2BSD and 4.3BSD are the bases for the UNIX systems of many vendors, and are used internally by the development groups of many other vendors. Many of these developments have also been incorporated by System V or added by vendors whose products are otherwise based on System V.

The implementation of the TCP/IP networking protocol suite in 4.2BSD and 4.3BSD and the availability of those systems explain why the TCP/IP networking protocol suite is so widely implemented throughout the world. Numerous vendors have adapted the Berkeley networking implementations, whether their base system is 4.2BSD, 4.3BSD, System V, or even VMS.

4BSD has also been a strong influence on the POSIX (IEEE Std 1003.1) operating-system interface standard, and on related standards. Several features—such as reliable signals, job control, multiple access groups per process, and the routines for directory operations—have been adapted from 4.3BSD for POSIX.

Material Covered in this Book

Except in the introductory historical material, the word "UNIX" is used in this book to refer to 4.3BSD. Where particular hardware is relevant, the book refers to the Digital Equipment Corporation (DEC) VAX. Although many vendors sell systems derived from 4.2BSD or 4.3BSD that run on numerous processors and computer systems (such as the Motorola 68020, the National Semiconductor 32032, or the Intel 80386), 4BSD was originally developed on the VAX. Because that machine is one of those on which the current Berkeley software distribution runs, it still provides a convenient point of reference.

This book is about the *internal* structure of 4.3BSD [Quarterman *et al.*, 1985], and about the concepts, data structures, and algorithms used in implementing 4.3BSD's system facilities. Its level of detail is similar to that of Bach's book about System V UNIX [Bach, 1986]; however, this text focuses on the facilities, data structures, and algorithms used in the Berkeley variant of the UNIX operating system. The book covers 4.3BSD from the system-call level down—from the interface to the kernel to the hardware itself. The kernel includes system facilities, such as process management, memory management, the I/O system, the filesystem, the *socket* IPC mechanism, and network-protocol implementations. Material above the system-call level—such as libraries, shells, commands, programming languages, and other user interfaces—is excluded, except for some material related to the terminal interface and to system startup. Like Organick's book about Multics [Organick, 1975], it is an in-depth study of a contemporary operating system.

Readers who will benefit from this book include operating-system implementors, system programmers, UNIX application developers, administrators, and curious users. The book may be read as a companion to the source code of the system, falling as it does between the manual [CSRG, 1986] and the code in detail of treatment. But the book is specifically neither a UNIX programming manual nor a user tutorial (for a tutorial see [Libes & Ressler, 1988]). Familiarity with the use of some version of the UNIX system (see, for example [Kernighan & Pike, 1984]), and with the C programming language (see, for example [Kernighan & Ritchie, 1988]), would be extremely useful.

Use in Courses on Operating Systems

This book is suitable for use as a reference text to provide background for a primary textbook in a second-level course on operating systems. It is not intended for use as an introductory operating-system textbook; the reader should have already encountered terminology such as *memory management*, *process scheduling*, and *I/O systems* [Peterson & Silberschatz, 1985]. Familiarity with the concepts of network protocols will be useful in some of the later chapters [Tanenbaum, 1988; Stallings, 1985; Schwartz, 1987].

Exercises are provided at the end of each chapter. The exercises are graded into three categories indicated by zero, one, or two asterisks. The answers to exercises without any asterisks can be found in the text. Exercises with a single asterisk require a step of reasoning or intuition beyond a concept presented in the text. Exercises with two asterisks present major design projects or open research questions.

Organization

This text discusses both philosophical and design issues, as well as details of the actual implementation. Often, the discussion starts at the system-call level and descends into the kernel. Tables and figures are used to clarify data structures and control flow. Pseudocode similar to the C language is used to display algorithms. Boldface font is used to identify program names and filesystem pathnames. Italics font is used to introduce terms that appear in the glossary, and to identify the names of system calls, variables, routines, and structure names. Routine names (other than system calls) are further identified by following the name with a pair of parenthesis (e.g., *malloc*() is the name of a routine while *argv* is the name of a variable).

The book is divided into five parts, organized as follows:

- **Part 1, Overview** Three introductory chapters provide the context for the complete operating system and for the rest of the book. Chapter 1, *History and Goals*, sketches the historical development of the system, emphasizing its research orientation. Chapter 2, *Design Overview of 4.3BSD*, describes the nature of the services offered by the system, and outlines the internal organization of the kernel. It also discusses the design decisions that were made as the system was developed. Chapter 3, *Kernel Services*, explains how system calls are performed, and describes in detail some of the basic services of the kernel.

- **Part 2, Processes** The first chapter in this part—Chapter 4, *Process Management*—lays the foundation for subsequent chapters by describing the structure of a process, the algorithms used for scheduling the execution of processes, and the synchronization mechanisms used by the system to ensure consistent access to kernel-resident data structures. In Chapter 5, *Memory Management*, the virtual-memory–management system is discussed in detail.

- **Part 3, I/O System** First, Chapter 6, *I/O System Overview*, explains the system interface to I/O and describes the structure of the facilities that support this interface. Following this introduction are three chapters that describe the details of the three main parts of the I/O system. Chapter 7, *The Filesystem*, describes the data structures and algorithms that implement the filesystem. Chapter 8, *Device Drivers*, explains block and character device drivers, including the method of autoconfiguration used by the system to determine what physical devices are attached. A detailed example of a disk device driver is given. Chapter 9, *Terminal Handling*, describes support for character terminals and provides a description of a character-oriented device driver.

- **Part 4, Interprocess Communication** Chapter 10, *Interprocess Communication*, describes the mechanism for providing communication between related or unrelated processes. Chapters 11 and 12, *Network Communication* and *Network Protocols*, are closely related, as the facilities described in the former are largely implemented in terms of specific protocols, such as the TCP/IP protocol suite, described in the latter.

- **Part 5, System Operation** Chapter 13, *System Startup*, discusses system startup, shutdown, and configuration, and explains system initialization at the process level, from kernel initialization to user login.

The book is intended to be read in the order that the chapters are presented, but the parts other than Part 1 are relatively independent of one another and may be read separately. Chapter 13 should be read after all the others, but knowledgeable readers may find it useful independently.

At the end of the book are a *Glossary* with brief definitions of major terms, and an *Index*. Each chapter contains a *Reference* section, with citations of related material.

Acknowledgments

We thank the following people, all of whom read and commented on early drafts of the book: Wayne Hathaway (Ultra Network Technologies), Maurice Herlihy (Carnegie-Mellon University), Thomas LeBlanc (University of Rochester), Larry Peterson (University of Arizona), Robert Elz (University of Melbourne), Peter Collinson (University of Kent), Dennis Ritchie (AT&T Bell Laboratories), Matt Koehler (Sun Microsystems), Eric Allman (International Computer Science Institute), Mike Hibler (University of Utah), Robert Gingell (Sun Microsystems), Joseph Moran (Legato Systems), Christopher Torek (University of Maryland), Kevin Fall (University of California, Berkeley), Peter Salus (Usenix Association), Evi Nemeth (University of Colorado), Jim Lawson (Pixar), Mike Paquette (Pixar),

Mike Russell (Pixar), Donn Seeley (University of Utah), Jay Lepreau (University of Utah), Bill Shannon (Sun Microsystems), Donald Coleman (Unisoft Corporation), Michael O'Dell (Prisma, Incorporated), Michel Gien and associates (Chorus Systèmes).

This book was produced using **pic**, **tbl**, **eqn**, and **ditroff**. The index was generated by **awk** scripts derived from indexing programs written by Jon Bentley and Brian Kernighan [Bentley & Kernighan, 1986]. Most of the art was created with **cip** to produce **pic** input that had to be hand-tuned to clean up ragged lines and improperly centered text. Figure placement and widow elimination were handled by the **ditroff** macros, but orphan elimination and production of even page bottoms had to be done by hand. In the end, we concluded that there must be a better way!

The authors encourage readers to send suggested improvements or comments about typographical or other errors found in the book by electronic mail to **bsdbook-bugs@berkeley.edu**.

References

Bach, 1986.
M. J. Bach, *The Design of the UNIX Operating System,* Prentice-Hall, Englewood Cliffs, NJ (1986).

Bentley & Kernighan, 1986.
J. Bentley & B. Kernighan, ''Tools for Printing Indexes,'' Computing Science Technical Report 128, AT&T Bell Laboratories, Murray Hill, NJ (1986).

CSRG, 1986.
CSRG, ''UNIX Programmer's Manual, 4.3 Berkeley Software Distribution, Virtual VAX-11 Version,'' Six Volumes and an Index Volume, University of California Computer Systems Research Group, Berkeley, CA (April 1986).

Kernighan & Ritchie, 1978.
B. W. Kernighan & D. M. Ritchie, *The C Programming Language,* Prentice-Hall, Englewood Cliffs, NJ (1978).

Kernighan & Pike, 1984.
B. W. Kernighan & R. Pike, *The UNIX Programming Environment,* Prentice-Hall, Englewood Cliffs, NJ (1984).

Kernighan & Ritchie, 1988.
B. W. Kernighan & D. M. Ritchie, *The C Programming Language,* 2nd ed, Prentice-Hall, Englewood Cliffs, NJ (1988).

Libes & Ressler, 1988.
D. Libes & S. Ressler, *Life with UNIX,* Prentice-Hall, Englewood Cliffs, NJ (1988).

O'Dell, 1987.
M. O'Dell, ''UNIX: The World View,'' *Proceedings of the 1987 Winter USENIX Conference*, pp. 35–45 (January 1987).

Organick, 1975.
E. I. Organick, *The Multics System: An Examination of Its Structure,* MIT Press, Cambridge, MA (1975).

Peterson & Silberschatz, 1985.
J. Peterson & A. Silberschatz, *Operating System Concepts,* Addison-Wesley, Reading, MA (1985).

Quarterman *et al.*, 1985.
J. S. Quarterman, A. Silberschatz, & J. L. Peterson, "4.2BSD and 4.3BSD as Examples of the UNIX System," *ACM Computing Surveys* **17**(4), pp. 379–418 (December 1985).

Ritchie & Thompson, 1978.
D. M. Ritchie & K. Thompson, "The UNIX Time-Sharing System," *Bell System Technical Journal* **57**(6 Part 2), pp. 1905–1929 (July-August 1978). The original version [*Comm. ACM* **7**(7), pp. 365–375 (July 1974)] described the 6th edition; this citation describes the 7th edition.

Schwartz, 1987.
M. Schwartz, *Telecommunication Networks,* Addison-Wesley, Reading, MA (1987).

Stallings, 1985.
R. Stallings, *Data and Computer Communications,* Macmillan, New York, NY (1985).

Tanenbaum, 1988.
A. S. Tanenbaum, *Computer Networks,* 2nd ed, Prentice-Hall, Englewood Cliffs, NJ (1988).

Contents

Part 1 Overview 1

Chapter 1 History and Goals 3

1.1 History of the UNIX System 3
- Origins 3
- Research UNIX 4
- AT&T UNIX System III and System V 6
- Other Organizations 7
- Berkeley Software Distributions 7
- UNIX in the World 8

1.2 BSD and Other Systems 8
- The Influence of the User Community 9

1.3 Design Goals of 4BSD 10
- 4.2BSD Design Goals 11
- 4.3BSD Design Goals 12
- Future Berkeley Releases 12

1.4 Release Engineering 14
- References 15

Chapter 2 Design Overview of 4.3BSD 19

2.1 UNIX Facilities and the Kernel 19
- The Kernel 20

2.2 Kernel Organization 20

2.3 Kernel Services 23

2.4 Process Management 23
- Signals 25
- Process Groups 26

2.5 Memory Management 26
BSD Memory-Management Design Decisions 27
Memory Management Inside the Kernel 28
2.6 I/O System 29
Descriptors and I/O 30
Descriptor Management 31
Files 32
Devices 33
Socket IPC 33
Scatter/Gather I/O 34
2.7 Filesystem 34
2.8 Devices 37
2.9 Terminals 38
2.10 Interprocess Communication 38
2.11 Network Communication 39
2.12 Network Implementation 40
2.13 System Operation 40
Exercises 41
References 41

Chapter 3 Kernel Services 43

3.1 Kernel Organization 43
System Activities 43
Run-Time Organization 44
System Processes 45
Entry to the Kernel 46
Return from the Kernel 47
3.2 System Calls 47
Result Handling 47
Returning from a System Call 48
3.3 Traps and Interrupts 49
I/O Device Interrupts 49
Software Interrupts 50
3.4 Clock Interrupts 50
Timeouts 51
Process Scheduling 53
3.5 Timing 53
Real Time 53
Adjusting the Time 53
External Representation 54
Interval Time 55
Profiling 55
3.6 Process Management 55
3.7 User and Group Identifiers 58
Host Identifier 60
3.8 Resource Controls 60
Process Priorities 60

Resource Utilization 61
Resource Limits 61
Filesystem Quotas 62
3.9 System Operation 62
Accounting 62
Exercises 63
References 64

Part 2 Processes 67

Chapter 4 Process Management 69

4.1 Introduction 69
Multiprogramming 70
Scheduling 71
4.2 Process State 72
The Proc Structure 72
The User Structure 77
Memory 79
The Text Structure 79
4.3 Context Switching 79
Process State 80
Low-Level Context Switching 80
Voluntary Context Switching 81
Intraprocess Context Switching 83
Synchronization 84
4.4 Process Scheduling 86
Calculations of Process Priority 87
Process-Priority Routines 88
Process Run Queues and Context Switching 89
4.5 Process Creation 91
4.6 Process Termination 93
4.7 Signals 94
Process Groups 96
Comparison with Other Systems 97
Changes to 4.3BSD Signals in POSIX 99
Posting a Signal 99
Delivering a Signal 101
Job Control 102
4.8 Process Debugging 103
Exercises 105
References 107

Chapter 5 Memory Management 109

5.1 Terminology 109
Processes and Memory 110

Paging 111
Replacement Algorithms 112
Working-Set Model 113
Swapping 113
Secondary Storage 114
Advantages of Virtual Memory 114
Hardware Requirements for Virtual Memory 114
5.2 Evolution of 4.3BSD Memory Management 115
Version 7 UNIX 115
UNIX 32V 116
3BSD 116
4.1BSD 117
4.3BSD 118
5.3 VAX Memory-Management Hardware 118
VAX Virtual Address Space 118
VAX Page Tables 119
System-Address Translation 120
User-Address Translation 121
Page Faults 122
Translation Buffers 124
5.4 Management of Main Memory: The Core Map 124
Physical-to-Virtual Translation 126
Memory Free List 126
Synchronization 126
Text-Page Cache 127
Core-Map Limits 127
Memory-Allocation Routines 127
5.5 Management of Swap Space 128
5.6 Per-Process Resources 129
4.3BSD Process Virtual Address Space 129
Page Tables 129
Types of Page-Table Entries 131
Modified Pages 134
Text Page Tables 134
Swap Space 134
5.7 Creation of a New Process 136
Duplicating Kernel Resources 136
Duplicating the User Address Space 137
Implementation Issues 138
Creating a New Process Without Copying 138
5.8 Execution of a File 140
5.9 Change Process Size 142
5.10 Termination of a Process 144
5.11 Demand Paging 145
Fill-on-Demand Pages 146
Fill-on-Demand Klustering 146
Interaction with the Filesystem Cache 147
Pagein of Swapped Pages 147

5.12 Page Replacement 149
Global CLOCK Algorithm 150
The Paging Daemon 151
Paging Parameters 151
Two-Handed Clock 153
Operation of Pageout 153
5.13 Swapping 155
The Swapping Process 156
Choosing a Process to Swap In 156
Involuntary Swapping 157
Choosing a Process to Swap Out 158
Swapout 158
Swapin 159
Swapping of Text Images 160
Exercises 161
References 163

Part 3 I/O System 167

Chapter 6 I/O System Overview 169

6.1 I/O Mapping from User to Device 169
Character Devices 170
Block Devices 171
Socket-Interface Buffering 172
6.2 Descriptor Management and Services 172
Open File Table 173
Management of Descriptors 175
Descriptor Locking 177
Implementation of Locking 178
Multiplexing I/O on Descriptors 179
Implementation of Select 181
Moving Data Inside the Kernel 184
Exercises 185
References 186

Chapter 7 The Filesystem 187

7.1 Structure and Overview 187
Directories 187
Links 189
Quotas 191
7.2 Overview of the Internal Filesystem 191
Allocating and Finding the Blocks on the Disk 193
7.3 Internal Structure and Redesign 195
New Filesystem Organization 196
Optimizing Storage Utilization 198

Filesystem Parameterization 200
Layout Policies 201
7.4 Filesystem Data Structures 203
Inode Management 205
Finding File Blocks 206
File-Block Allocation 207
7.5 Buffer Management 208
Implementation of Buffer Management 211
7.6 Quotas 213
7.7 Allocation Mechanisms 217
7.8 Translation of Filesystem Names 219
Exercises 221
References 223

Chapter 8 Device Drivers **225**

8.1 Overview 225
8.2 Device Drivers 227
I/O Queueing 228
Interrupt Handling 229
8.3 Block Devices 229
8.4 Character Devices 230
Raw Devices and Physical I/O 231
Character-Oriented Devices 233
Entry Points for Character Device Drivers 233
8.5 Autoconfiguration 234
Probing for Devices 235
Attaching a Device 236
Device Naming 236
8.6 UNIBUS Devices 237
The *up* Device Driver 238
Autoconfiguration Support 239
Logical-to-Device Mapping of I/O Requests 242
I/O Strategy 243
Disksort 244
Drive-Positioning Algorithm 245
Initiating an I/O Operation 246
Interrupt Handling 247
UNIBUS Adapter Support Routines 249
8.7 MASSBUS Devices 253
Autoconfiguration 253
I/O Strategy 253
Interrupt Handling 254
Exercises 256

Chapter 9 Terminal Handling **259**

9.1 Terminal Processing Modes 259
9.2 Line Disciplines 260

9.3 User Interface 262
9.4 The *tty* Structure 263
9.5 Process Groups and Terminal Control 265
9.6 C-lists 266
9.7 RS-232 and Modem Control 267
9.8 Terminal Operations 268
Open 268
Output Line Discipline 268
Output Top Half 270
Output Bottom Half 271
Input Bottom Half 271
Input Top Half 273
The *stop* Routine 273
The *ioctl* Routine 274
Modem Transitions 275
Closing Terminal Devices 275
9.9 Other Line Disciplines 276
Berknet 276
Serial Line IP Discipline 276
Graphics Tablet Discipline 277
9.10 Summary 277
Exercises 277
References 278

Part 4 Interprocess Communication 279

Chapter 10 Interprocess Communication 281

10.1 Interprocess-Communication Model 282
Using Sockets 284
10.2 Implementation Structure and Overview 288
10.3 Memory Management 289
Mbufs 289
Storage-Management Algorithms 291
Mbuf Utility Routines 292
10.4 Data Structures 292
Communication Domains 293
Sockets 294
Socket Addresses 296
10.5 Connection Setup 298
10.6 Data Transfer 300
Transmitting Data 301
Receiving Data 302
Passing Access Rights 304
Access Rights in the UNIX Domain 305
10.7 Socket Shutdown 306
Exercises 307
References 309

Chapter 11 Network Communication **311**

11.1 Internal Structure 312
Data Flow 312
Communication Protocols 314
Network Interfaces 315
11.2 Socket-to-Protocol Interface 318
Protocol User-Request Routine 318
Internal Requests 321
Protocol Control-Output Routine 322
11.3 Protocol–Protocol Interface 322
pr_output 323
pr_input 323
pr_ctlinput 323
11.4 Protocol–Network-Interface Interface 324
Packet Transmission 324
Packet Reception 325
11.5 Routing 327
Routing Tables 328
Routing Redirects 329
Routing-Table Interface 330
User-Level Routing Policies 330
11.6 Buffering and Congestion Control 331
Protocol Buffering Policies 331
Queue Limiting 332
11.7 Raw Sockets 332
Control Blocks 332
Input Processing 333
Output Processing 334
11.8 Additional Network Subsystem Topics 334
Out-of-Band Data 334
Address Resolution Protocol 335
VAX UNIBUS Interfaces 336
Trailer Protocols 338
Exercises 340
References 341

Chapter 12 Network Protocols **343**

12.1 DARPA Internet Network Protocols 343
Internet Addresses 345
Subnets 346
Broadcast Addresses 347
Internet Ports and Associations 348
Protocol Control Blocks 348
12.2 User Datagram Protocol (UDP) 350
Initialization 350
Output 350

Input 351
Control Operations 352
12.3 Internet Protocol (IP) 352
Output 353
Input 354
Forwarding 356
12.4 Transmission Control Protocol (TCP) 357
TCP Connection States 358
Sequence Variables 360
12.5 TCP Algorithms 362
Timers 363
Estimation of Round-Trip Time 365
Connection Establishment 366
Connection Shutdown 367
12.6 TCP Input Processing 368
12.7 TCP Output Processing 371
Sending Data 371
Avoidance of the Silly-Window Syndrome 372
Avoidance of Small Packets 373
Window Updates 374
Retransmit State 375
Source-Quench Processing and Congestion Control 375
Slow Start 376
Avoidance of Congestion with Slow Start 377
12.8 Internet Control Message Protocol (ICMP) 378
12.9 ARPANET Host Interface 380
12.10 Xerox Network Systems Communication Domain (XNS) 381
XNS Control Operations 383
12.11 Summary 384
Creating a Communication Channel 384
Sending and Receiving Data 385
Terminating Data Transmission and/or Reception 386
Exercises 387
References 389

Part 5 System Operation 391

Chapter 13 System Startup 393

13.1 Overview 393
13.2 Bootstrapping 394
The **boot** Program 394
VAX Console Media 396
13.3 Kernel Initialization 396
Assembly-Language Startup 397
Machine-Dependent Initialization 398
Message Buffer 399

System Data Structures 399
Memory Allocator 400
Autoconfiguration 400
Machine-Independent Initialization 403
13.4 User-Level Initialization 405
/etc/init 406
/etc/rc 406
/etc/getty 407
/bin/login 407
13.5 System Startup Topics 407
Kernel Configuration 408
System Shutdown and Autoreboot 409
System Debugging 410
Exercises 410
References 411

Glossary **413**

Index **451**

PART 1

Overview

CHAPTER 1

History and Goals

1.1 History of the UNIX System

The UNIX system is one of the older of the widely used operating systems, with a history of almost 20 years, but many of its most distinctive and useful facilities are relatively recent developments.

Origins

The first version of the UNIX system was developed at Bell Laboratories in 1969 by Ken Thompson as a private research project to use an otherwise idle PDP-7. Thompson also designed the language B, in which much of the early system was soon rewritten. He was joined shortly thereafter by Dennis Ritchie, who not only contributed to the design and implementation of the system, but also invented the C programming language in which later versions are written. The original elegant design of the system [Ritchie, 1978] and developments [Ritchie, 1984a] of the past 15 years [Compton, 1985] have made the UNIX system an important and powerful operating system [Ritchie, 1987].

Ritchie, Thompson, and other early Research UNIX developers had previously worked on the Multics project [Peirce, 1985; Organick, 1975], which had a strong influence on the newer operating system. Even the name ''UNIX'' is merely a pun on Multics; in areas where Multics attempted to do many things, UNIX tried to do one thing well. The basic organization of the UNIX filesystem, the idea of the command interpreter (the shell) being a user process, the general organization of the filesystem interface, and many other system characteristics, come directly from Multics.

Ideas from various other operating systems, such as the Massachusetts Institute of Technology's (MIT's) CTSS, also have been used. The *fork* operation to create new processes comes from Berkeley's GENIE (SDS-940, later XDS-940) operating system. Allowing a user to create processes inexpensively led to using one process per command, rather than running commands as procedure calls, as is done in Multics.

There are at least three major streams of development of the UNIX system. Figure 1.1 sketches their evolution, especially of those branches leading to 4.3BSD and to System V [Chambers & Quarterman, 1983; Uniejewski, 1985]. The dates given are approximate, and there is no attempt to show all influences. Some of the systems named in the figure are not mentioned in the text, but are included to show more clearly the relations among the ones that we shall examine.

Research UNIX

The first major editions were the Research systems from Bell Laboratories. In addition to the earliest versions of the system, these include **UNIX Time-Sharing System, Sixth Edition**, commonly known as **V6**, which, in 1976, was the first version widely available outside Bell Laboratories. Systems are identified by the edition numbers of the UNIX Programmer's Manual that were current when the distributions were made.

The system was distinguished from other operating systems in three important ways:

1. The system was written in a high-level language
2. The system was distributed in source form
3. The system provided powerful primitives normally found in only those operating systems that ran on much more expensive hardware

Most of the system source was written in C rather than in assembly language. The prevailing belief at the time was that an operating system had to be written in assembly language to provide reasonable efficiency and to get access to the hardware. The C language itself was at just a high enough level to allow it to be easily compiled for a wide range of computer hardware, without its being so complex or restrictive that systems programmers had to revert to assembly language to get reasonable efficiency or functionality. Access to the hardware was provided through assembly-language stubs for the 3 percent of the operating-system functions—such as context switching—that needed them. Although the success of UNIX does not stem solely from the fact that it was written in a high-level language, the use of C was a critical first step [Ritchie *et al.*, 1978; Kernighan & Ritchie, 1978; Kernighan & Ritchie, 1988]. Ritchie's C language is descended [Rosler, 1984] from Thompson's B language, which was itself descended from BCPL [Richards & Whitby-Strevens, 1982]. C continues to evolve [Tuthill, 1985; X3J11, 1988], and there is a variant, C++, that more readily permits data abstraction [Stroustrup, 1984; USENIX, 1987].

The second important distinction of UNIX was its early release from Bell Laboratories to other research environments in source form. By providing source, the system's founders ensured that other organizations would be able not only to

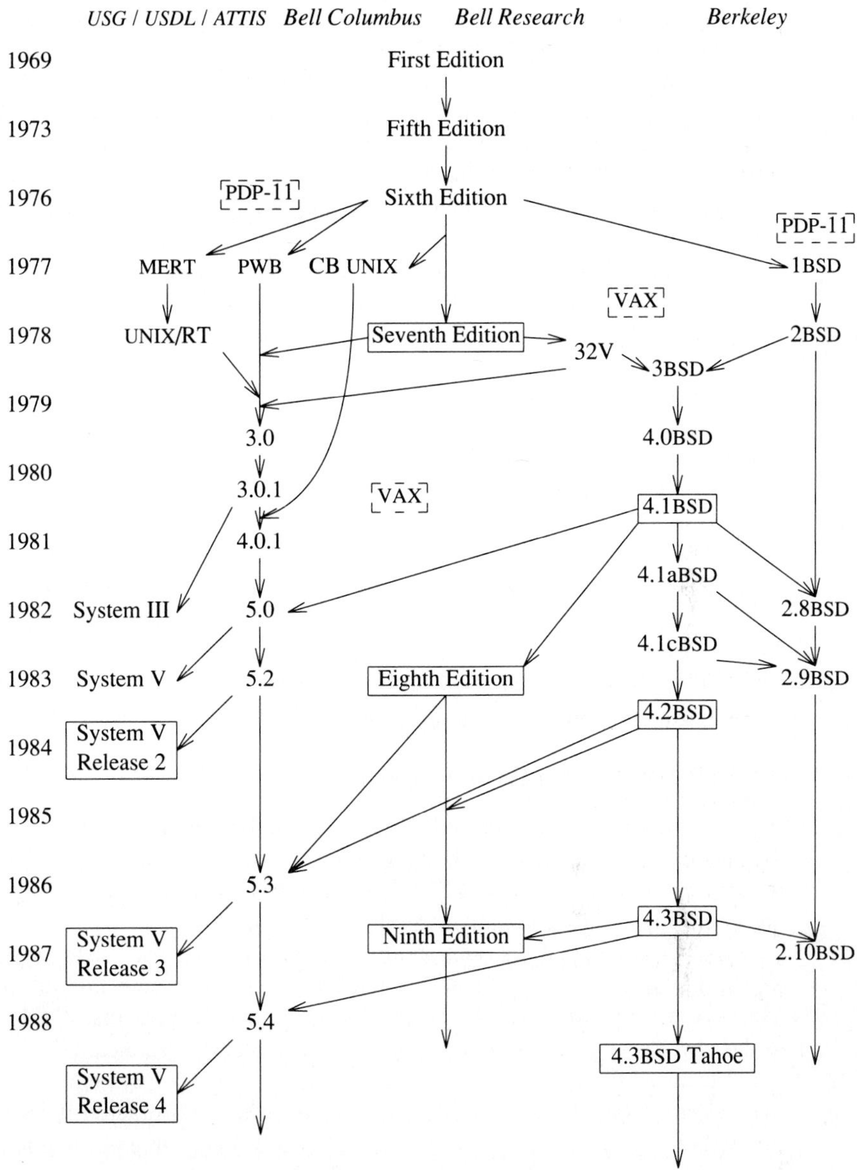

Figure 1.1 The UNIX system family tree.

use the system, but also to tinker with its inner workings. The ease with which new ideas could be adopted into the system always has been key to the changes that have been made to it. Whenever a new system that tried to upstage UNIX came along, somebody would dissect the newcomer and clone its central ideas into UNIX. The unique ability to use a small, comprehensible system, written in a high-level language, in an environment swimming in new ideas led to a UNIX system that evolved far beyond its humble beginnings.

The third important distinction of UNIX was that it provided individual users with the ability to run multiple processes concurrently and to connect these processes into pipelines of commands. At the time, only operating systems running on large and expensive machines had the ability to run multiple processes, and the number of concurrent processes usually was tightly controlled by a system administrator.

Most early UNIX systems ran on the PDP-11, which was inexpensive and powerful for its time. Nonetheless, there was at least one early port of Sixth Edition UNIX to a machine with a rather different architecture [Miller, 1978]. The PDP-11 also had an inconveniently small address space. The introduction of machines with 32-bit address spaces, especially the VAX-11/780, provided an opportunity for UNIX to expand its services to include virtual memory and networking. Earlier experiments by the Research group in providing UNIX-like facilities on different hardware had led to the conclusion that it was as easy to move the entire operating system as it was to duplicate its services under another operating system. The first UNIX system with portability as a specific goal was **UNIX Time-Sharing System, Seventh Edition** (**V7**), which ran on the PDP-11 and the Interdata 8/32, and had a VAX variety called **UNIX/32V Time-Sharing, System Version 1.0** (**32V**). The Research group at Bell Laboratories has also developed **UNIX Time-Sharing System, Eighth Edition** (**V8**). Their current system is **UNIX Time-Sharing System, Ninth Edition** (**V9**).

AT&T UNIX System III and System V

After the distribution of Seventh Edition in 1978, the Research group turned over external distributions to the UNIX Support Group (USG). USG had previously distributed such systems as the **UNIX Programmer's Work Bench** (**PWB**) internally, and sometimes externally as well [Mohr, 1985].

Their first external distribution after Seventh Edition was **UNIX System III (System III)**, in 1982, which incorporated features of Seventh Edition, of 32V, and also of several UNIX systems developed by groups other than the Research group. Features of UNIX/RT (a real-time UNIX system) were included, as well as many features from PWB. USG released **UNIX System V (System V)** in 1983; that system is largely derived from System III. The court-ordered divestiture of the Bell Operating Companies from AT&T has left AT&T in a position to market System V aggressively [Wilson, 1985; Bach, 1986].

USG metamorphosed into the UNIX System Development Laboratory (USDL), which released **UNIX System V, Release 2** in 1984. System V, Release 2, Version 4 introduced paging [Miller, 1984; Jung, 1985] , including copy-on-write and shared memory, to System V. The System V implementation was not based on the Berkeley paging system. USDL was succeeded by AT&T Information Systems (ATTIS), which distributed **UNIX System V, Release 3** in 1987. That system included STREAMS, an IPC mechanism adopted from V8 [Presotto & Ritchie, 1985].

Other Organizations

The ease with which the UNIX system can be modified has led to development work at numerous organizations, including the Rand Corporation, responsible for the Rand ports mentioned in Chapter 10; Bolt Beranek and Newman (BBN), who produced the direct ancestor of the 4.2BSD networking implementation discussed in Chapter 12; the University of Illinois, which did earlier networking work; Harvard; Purdue; and Digital Equipment Corporation (DEC).

Probably the most widespread version of the UNIX operating system, according to the number of machines on which it runs, is XENIX by Microsoft Corporation. XENIX was based originally on Seventh Edition, but later on System V. More recently, Microsoft and AT&T have agreed to merge the two systems.

Berkeley Software Distributions

The most influential of the non–Bell Laboratories and non–AT&T UNIX development groups has been the University of California at Berkeley [McKusick, 1985]. UNIX software from Berkeley is released in **Berkeley Software Distributions** (BSD); for example, as 4.3BSD. The first Berkeley VAX UNIX work was the addition to 32V of virtual memory, demand paging, and page replacement in 1979 by William Joy and Özalp Babaoğlu to produce **3BSD** [Babaoğlu & Joy, 1981]. The large virtual-memory space of 3BSD was motivated by the development of very large programs, such as Berkeley's own *Franz* LISP. This memory-management work convinced the Defense Advanced Research Projects Agency (DARPA) to fund the Berkeley team for the later development of a standard UNIX system (4BSD) for DARPA's contractors to use.

One of the goals of this project was to provide support for the DARPA Internet networking protocols, TCP/IP [Cerf & Cain, 1983]. The networking implementation was general enough to communicate among diverse network facilities, ranging from local networks, such as Ethernets and token rings, to long-haul networks, such as DARPA's ARPANET.

We refer to all the Berkeley VAX UNIX systems following 3BSD as 4BSD, although there were actually several releases—4.0BSD, 4.1BSD, 4.2BSD, 4.3BSD, and 4.3BSD Tahoe. 4BSD was the operating system of choice for VAXes from the time the VAX first became available in 1977 until the release of System III (1979 to 1982), and it remains so for many research or networked installations. Most organizations would buy a 32V license, but order 4BSD from Berkeley. Many installations inside the Bell System ran 4.1BSD (many now run 4.3BSD).

The 4BSD work for DARPA was guided by a steering committee that included many notable people from both commercial and academic institutions. The culmination of the original Berkeley DARPA UNIX project was the release of **4.2BSD** in 1983; further research at Berkeley has already produced **4.3BSD**—and work still proceeds.

UNIX in the World

Dozens of computer manufacturers,[1] including almost all the ones usually considered ''major'' by market share, have either announced or introduced computers that run the UNIX system or close derivatives, and numerous other companies sell related peripherals, software packages, support, training, documentation, or combinations of these. The hardware packages involved range from micros through minis, multis, and mainframes to supercomputers. Most of these use ports of System V, 4.2BSD, 4.3BSD, or mixtures, although there is still a variety of machines running software based on System III, 4.1BSD, and Seventh Edition. There are PDP-11s running 2BSD and other UNIX variants. There are even some Sixth Edition systems still in regular operation.

The UNIX system is also a fertile field for academic endeavor. Thompson and Ritchie were given the Association for Computing Machinery Turing award for the design of the system [Ritchie, 1984b]. It and related, specially designed teaching systems—such as Tunis [Ewens *et al.*, 1985; Holt, 1983], XINU [Comer, 1984], and MINIX [Tanenbaum, 1987]—are widely used in courses on operating systems. The UNIX system is ubiquitous in universities and research facilities throughout the world, and is ever more widely used in industry and commerce.

1.2 BSD and Other Systems

The Computer Systems Research Group (CSRG) incorporated features not only from UNIX systems, but also from other operating systems. Many of the features of the 4BSD terminal drivers are from TENEX/TOPS-20. Job control (in concept, not implementation) is derived from that of TOPS-20 and from the MIT Incompatible Timesharing System (ITS). The virtual-memory interface first proposed for 4.2BSD, and since implemented by several commercial vendors, was based on the file-mapping and page-level interfaces that first appeared in TENEX/TOPS-20. Multics has often been a reference point in the design of new facilities.

The quest for efficiency has been a major factor in much CSRG work. Some efficiency improvements have been made due to comparisons with the proprietary operating system for the VAX, VMS [Kashtan, 1980;].

Other UNIX variants have adopted several 4BSD features. Both AT&T UNIX System V [AT&T, 1987] and the IEEE 1003.1 POSIX standard [P1003.1, 1988] have adopted these filesystem system calls (see Chapter 6):

---

[1] These manufacturers include Altos, Alliant, Amdahl, Apollo, Apple, Ardent Computer, AT&T, Bull, Callan, Celerity, Codata, Convergent Technologies, Convex, COSI, Cray, Cromemco, Data General, DEC, Dual Systems, ELXSI, Encore, Ericsson, Fairchild, Flexible, Gould, Heurikon, Hewlett-Packard, Honeywell, IBM, ICON, ICL, Integrated Business Computers, Integrated Solutions, Intel, Interactive Systems, Locus, Logical MicroComputer, Medical Informatics, Microsoft, MIPS, NBI, NCR, National Semiconductor, NeXT, Nixdorf, Olivetti, Onyx, Pacific Computer, Parallel, Perkin-Elmer, Philips, Plexus, Prime, Pyramid, R Systems, Ridge, Sequent, Siemens, Silicon Graphics, Sony, Stellar, Sun Microsystems, Symmetric, Tandy, Tektronix, Unisys, Visual Technology, and WICAT.

- *rename* for renaming files and directories
- *mkdir* and *rmdir* for directory creation and deletion

Both have also adopted the directory-access routines.

In addition, POSIX and the related National Bureau of Standards (NBS) Federal Information Processing Standard (FIPS) have adopted

- Reliable signals (Chapter 4)
- Job control (Chapter 2)
- Multiple file-access permission groups (Chapter 6)

The X/OPEN Group, originally solely European vendors, but now including several U.S. companies, produced the X/OPEN Portability Guide [X/OPEN, 1987], a document that specifies both the kernel interface and many of the utility programs available to UNIX system users. X/OPEN has adopted many of the POSIX facilities. Other, similar, standards and guides are expected to adopt them, as well. The IEEE 1003.1 standard is also an ISO Draft International Standard, named SC22 WG15. Thus, the POSIX facilities will probably be accepted in most UNIX-like systems worldwide.

The 4BSD *socket* interprocess-communication mechanism (see Chapter 10) was designed for portability and was immediately ported to AT&T System III, although it was never distributed with that system. The 4BSD implementation of the TCP/IP networking protocol suite (see Chapter 12) is widely used as the basis for further implementations on systems ranging from AT&T 3B machines running System V to VMS to IBM PCs.

CSRG also continues to cooperate closely with vendors whose systems are based on 4.2BSD and 4.3BSD. This simultaneous development contributes to the ease of further ports of 4.3BSD, and to ongoing development of the system.

The Influence of the User Community

Much of the Berkeley UNIX development work was done in response to the user community. Ideas and expectations came not only from DARPA, the principal direct-funding organization, but also from many of the users of the system at companies and universities worldwide.

The Berkeley researchers accepted not only ideas from the user community, but also actual software. Contributions to 4BSD came from numerous universities and other organizations in Australia, Canada, Europe, and the United States. These contributions included major features, such as autoconfiguration and disk quotas. A few ideas, such as the *fcntl* system call, were taken from System V, although licensing and pricing considerations have prevented the use of any actual code from System III or System V in 4BSD. In addition to contributions that are included in the distributions proper, CSRG also distributes a set of user-contributed software.

An example of a community-developed facility is the public-domain time-zone–handling package that was adopted with the 4.3BSD Tahoe release. It was designed and implemented by an international group, including Arthur Olson, Robert Elz, and Guy Harris, partly due to discussions in the USENET newsgroup **comp.std.unix**. This package takes time-zone–conversion rules completely out of the C library, putting them in files that require no system-code changes in order to change time-zone rules; this change is especially useful with binary-only distributions of UNIX. The method also allows individual processes to choose rules, rather than keeping one ruleset specification systemwide. The distribution includes a large database of rules used in many areas throughout the world, from China to Australia to Europe. Distributions of the UNIX system are thus simplified, because it is not necessary to have the software set up differently for different destinations, as long as the whole database is included.

Berkeley accepts mail about bugs and their fixes at a well-known electronic address, **4bsd-bugs@berkeley.edu**, and the UNIX software house MT XINU distributes a bug list compiled from such submissions. Many of the bug fixes are incorporated in future distributions. There is constant discussion of UNIX in general (including 4.3BSD) in the DARPA Internet mailing list UNIX-WIZARDS, which appears on the USENET network as the newsgroup **comp.unix.wizards**; both the Internet and USENET are international in scope. There is another USENET newsgroup dedicated to 4BSD bugs: **comp.bugs.4bsd**. Few ideas have been accepted by Berkeley directly from these lists and newsgroups, because of the difficulty of sifting through the voluminous submissions. But there is now a moderated newsgroup dedicated to CSRG-sanctioned fixes to such bugs, called **comp.bugs.4bsd.bug-fixes**, and discussions in these newsgroups sometimes lead to new facilities being written that are later accepted.

1.3 Design Goals of 4BSD

4BSD is a research system developed for and partly by a research community, and, more recently, a commercial community. The developers considered many design issues as they wrote the system. There were nontraditional considerations in and inputs into the design, which nevertheless yielded results with commercial importance.

The early systems were technology-driven. They took advantage of current hardware that was unavailable in other UNIX systems. This new technology included

- Virtual-memory support
- Device drivers for third-party (non-DEC) peripherals
- Terminal-independent support libraries for screen-based applications; numerous applications were developed that used these libraries, including the screen-based editor *vi*.

4BSD's support of a huge number of popular third-party peripherals, compared to the AT&T distribution's meager offerings in 32V, was an important factor in 4BSD popularity. Until other vendors began providing their own support of 4.2BSD-based systems, there was no alternative for universities that had to minimize hardware costs.

Terminal-independent screen support, although it may now seem rather pedestrian, was at the time very important in Berkeley software's popularity.

4.2BSD Design Goals

DARPA wanted Berkeley to develop 4.2BSD as a standard research operating system for the VAX. Many new facilities were designed for inclusion in 4.2BSD. These facilities included a completely revised virtual-memory system to support processes with large sparse address space, a much higher-speed filesystem, interprocess communication facilities, and networking support. The high-speed filesystem and revised virtual-memory system were needed by researchers doing computer-aided design and manufacturing (CAD/CAM), image processing, and artificial intelligence (AI). The interprocess communication facilities were needed by sites doing research in distributed systems. The networking support was primarily motivated by DARPA's interest in connecting their researchers through the 56-Kbit per second ARPA Internet (although Berkeley was also interested in getting good performance over higher-speed local-area networks).

No attempt was made to provide a true distributed operating system [Popek, 1981]. Instead, the traditional ARPANET goal of resource sharing was used. There were three reasons that a resource-sharing design was chosen:

- The systems were widely distributed and demanded administrative autonomy. At the time, a true distributed operating system required a central administrative authority.
- The known algorithms for tightly coupled systems did not scale well.
- Berkeley's charter was to incorporate current, proven software technology, rather than to develop new, unproven technology.

Therefore, easy means were provided for remote login (*rlogin*, *telnet*), file transfer (*rcp*, *ftp*), and remote command execution (*rsh*), but all host machines retained separate identities that were not hidden from the users.

Due to time constraints, the system that was released as 4.2BSD did not include all the facilities that were originally intended to be included. In particular, the revised virtual-memory system was not part of the 4.2BSD release. CSRG did, however, continue its ongoing effort to track fast-developing hardware technology in several areas. The networking system supported a wide range of hardware devices, including multiple interfaces to 10-Mbit/s Ethernet, to ring networks, and to NSC's Hyperchannel. The kernel sources were modularized and rearranged to ease portability to new architectures, including to microprocessors and to larger machines.

4.3BSD Design Goals

Problems with 4.2BSD were among the motivations for 4.3BSD. Because 4.2BSD included many new facilities, there were bugs in some of them, particularly in the TCP protocol implementation. There was a loss of performance, partly due to the introduction of symbolic links. Some facilities were not included due to lack of time. Others, such as TCP/IP subnet and routing support, were not specified soon enough by outside parties for them to be incorporated in the 4.2BSD release.

Commercial systems usually maintain backward compatibility for many releases so as not to make existing applications obsolete. Maintaining compatibility is increasingly difficult, however, so most research systems maintain little or no backward compatibility. As a compromise to other researchers, the BSD releases are usually backward compatible for one release, but have the deprecated facilities clearly marked. This approach allows for an orderly transition to the new interfaces without constraining the system from evolving smoothly. In particular, backward compatibility of 4.3BSD with 4.2BSD was considered highly desirable for application portability.

The C language interface to 4.3BSD differs from that of 4.2BSD in only a few commands to the terminal interface and in the use of one argument to one IPC system call (*select*: see Section 6.2). A flag was added in 4.3BSD to the system call that establishes a signal handler to allow a process to request the 4.1BSD semantics for signals, rather than the 4.2BSD semantics (see Section 4.7). The sole purpose of the flag was to allow existing applications that depended on the old semantics to continue working without being rewritten.

The implementation changes between 4.2BSD and 4.3BSD often are not visible to users, but they are numerous. For example, changes were made to improve support for multiple network-protocol families, such as XEROX NS, in addition to TCP/IP. Since 4.3BSD retains the advances of the earlier Berkeley systems, this book's examination of 4.3BSD is an investigation of the major features of the Berkeley systems.

The second release of 4.3BSD, hereafter referred to as 4.3BSD Tahoe, added support for the Computer Consoles, Inc. (CCI) Power 6 (Tahoe) series of minicomputers in addition to the VAX. Although generally similar to the original release of 4.3BSD for the VAX, it includes many modifications and new features.

Future Berkeley Releases

4.3BSD is not perfect. In particular, the virtual-memory system needs to be completely replaced. The new virtual-memory system needs to provide algorithms that are better suited to the large memories and slow disks currently available, and needs to be less VAX architecture dependent. The terminal driver has been carefully kept compatible not only with Seventh Edition, but even with Sixth Edition. This feature has been useful, but is less so now, especially considering the lack of orthogonality of its commands and options. CSRG plans to distribute a POSIX-compatible terminal driver; since System V will be compliant with POSIX, the terminal driver will also be compatible with System V. POSIX compatibility in general is a goal.

Other currently planned BSD work includes development of an implementation of networking protocols in the International Organization for Standardization (ISO) suite, further TCP/IP performance improvements and enhancements, and the implementation of other networking protocols.

The most critical shortcoming of 4.3BSD is the lack of a distributed filesystem. As with networking protocols, there is no single distributed filesystem that provides enough speed and functionality for all situations. It is frequently necessary to support several different distributed filesystem protocols, just as it is necessary to run several different network protocols. Thus, a standard interface to filesystems somewhat more general than but very similar to Sun Microsystems' framework for their Network File System (NFS) is being developed so that multiple local and remote filesystems can be supported, much as multiple networking protocols are supported by 4.3BSD [Sandberg, 1985].

Original work on the flexible configuration of IPC processing modules was done at Bell Laboratories in UNIX Eighth Edition [Presotto & Ritchie, 1985]. This *stream I/O system* was based on the UNIX character I/O system. It allowed a user process to open a raw terminal port and then to insert appropriate kernel-processing modules, such as one to do normal terminal line editing. Modules to process network protocols also could be inserted. Stacking a terminal-processing module on top of a network-processing module allowed flexible and efficient implementation of *network virtual terminals* within the kernel. A problem with stream modules, however, is that they are inherently linear in nature, and thus they do not adequately handle the fan-in and fan-out associated with multiplexing in datagram-based networks; such multiplexing is done in device drivers, below the modules proper. The Eighth Edition stream I/O system was adopted in System V, Release 3 as the STREAMS system.

The design of the networking facilities for 4.2BSD took a different approach, based on the *socket* interface and a flexible multilayer network architecture. This design allows a single system to support multiple sets of networking protocols with stream, datagram, and other types of access. Protocol modules may deal with multiplexing of data from different connections onto a single transport medium, as well as with demultiplexing of data for different protocols and connections received from each network device.

There are plans to redesign the internal protocol layering using ideas from the V8 stream I/O system. A socket interface will be used, rather than a character-device interface, and demultiplexing will be handled internally by the network protocols in the kernel. However, like streams, the interfaces between kernel protocol modules above the multiplexed layers will follow a uniform convention. This convention will allow the incorporation of terminal-processing modules into a network stream, producing efficient network virtual-terminal connections. It will also allow kernel support for remote-procedure protocols based on standard transport protocols. Finally, this interface will provide a mechanism to extend the kernel protocol framework into user processes, to allow prototyping of new protocols and to do network-monitoring functions.

1.4 Release Engineering

CSRG has always been a small group of software developers. This resource limitation requires careful software-engineering management. Careful coordination is needed not only of CSRG personnel, but also of members of the general community who contribute to the development of the system. Major distributions usually alternate between

- Major new facilities: 3BSD, 4.0BSD, 4.2BSD
- Bug fixes and efficiency improvements: 4.1BSD, 4.3BSD

This alternation allows release in a timely manner, while providing for refinement and correction of the new facilities and the elimination of performance problems produced by the new facilities. The timely followup of releases that include new facilities reflects the importance CSRG places on providing a reliable and robust system on which its user community can depend.

Developments from CSRG are released in three steps: alpha, beta, and final, as shown in Table 1.1. Alpha and beta releases are not true distributions—they are test systems. Alpha releases are normally available to only a few sites, most of those within the University. More sites get beta releases, but they do not get them directly; a tree structure is imposed to allow bug reports, fixes, and new software to be collected, evaluated, and checked for redundancies by first-level sites before forwarding to CSRG. For example, 4.1aBSD ran at more than 100 sites, but there were only about 15 primary beta sites. The beta-test tree allowed the developers at CSRG to concentrate on actual development rather than sifting through details from every beta-test site. This book was reviewed for technical accuracy by a similar process.

Many of the primary beta-test personnel not only had copies of the release running on their own machines, but also had login accounts on the development machine at Berkeley. Such users were commonly found logged in at Berkeley over the ARPA Internet, or sometimes via telephone dialup, from places far away, such as Massachusetts, Utah, Maryland, Texas, and Illinois, and from closer places, such as Stanford. For the 4.3BSD release, certain accounts and users had permission to modify the master copy of the system source directly. A number of

Table 1.1 Release test steps.

	Release Steps			
Description	**alpha**	**internal**	**beta**	**final**
name:	4.1aBSD	4.1bBSD	4.1cBSD	4.2BSD
major new facility:	networking	fast filesystem	IPC	revised signals

facilities, such as the Fortran and C compilers, as well as important system programs, such as *telnet* and *ftp*, include significant contributions from people who did not work for CSRG. One important exception to this approach was that changes to the kernel were made by only CSRG personnel, although the changes often were suggested by the larger community.

People given access to the master sources were carefully screened beforehand, but were not closely supervised. Their work was checked at the end of the beta-test period by CSRG personnel, who did a complete comparison of the source of the previous release with the current master sources—for example, of 4.3BSD with 4.2BSD. Facilities deemed inappropriate, such as new options to the directory-listing command or a changed return value for the *fseek*() library routine, were removed from the source before final distribution.

4BSD releases have usually included a pair of documents detailing changes to every user-level command [McKusick *et al.*, 1986] and to every kernel source file [Karels, 1986]. These documents are delivered with the final distribution. A user can look up any command by name and see immediately what has changed, and a developer can similarly look up any kernel file by name and get a summary of that file's changes.

This process illustrates an *advantage* of having a small number of principal developers: The developers all know the whole system thoroughly enough to be able to coordinate their own work with that of other people to produce a coherent final system. Companies with large development organizations find this result difficult to duplicate.

There is no CSRG marketing division. Thus, technical decisions are made largely for technical reasons, and are not driven by marketing promises. The Berkeley developers have been fanatical about this, and are well known for never promising delivery on a specific date.

References

AT&T, 1987.

AT&T, *The System V Interface Definition (SVID)*, Issue 2, American Telephone and Telegraph, Murray Hill, NJ (January 1987).

Babaoğlu & Joy, 1981.

Ö. Babaoğlu & W. N. Joy, "Converting a Swap-Based System to Do Paging in an Architecture Lacking Page-Referenced Bits," *Proceedings of the Eighth Symposium on Operating Systems Principles*, pp. 78–86 (December 1981).

Bach, 1986.

M. J. Bach, *The Design of the UNIX Operating System*, Prentice-Hall, Englewood Cliffs, NJ (1986).

Cerf & Cain, 1983.

V. G. Cerf & E. Cain, *The DoD Internet Architecture Model*, Elsevier Science, Amsterdam, Netherlands (1983).

Chambers & Quarterman, 1983.
J. B. Chambers & J. S. Quarterman, ''UNIX System V and 4.1C BSD,'' *USENIX Association Conference Proceedings*, pp. 267–291 (June 1983).

Comer, 1984.
D. Comer, *Operating System Design: The Xinu Approach,* Prentice-Hall, Englewood Cliffs, NJ (1984).

Compton, 1985.
M. Compton, editor, ''The Evolution of UNIX,'' *UNIX Review* **3**(1) (January 1985).

Ewens *et al.*, 1985.
P. Ewens, D. R. Blythe, M. Funkenhauser, & R. C. Holt, ''Tunis: A Distributed Multiprocessor Operating System,'' *USENIX Association Conference Proceedings*, pp. 247–254 (June 1985).

Holt, 1983.
R. C. Holt, *Concurrent Euclid, the UNIX System, and Tunis,* Addison-Wesley, Reading, MA (1983).

Joy, 1980.
W. N. Joy, ''Comments on the Performance of UNIX on the VAX,'' Technical Report, University of California Computer System Research Group, Berkeley, CA (April 1980).

Jung, 1985.
R. S. Jung, ''Porting the AT&T Demand Paged UNIX Implementation to Microcomputers,'' *USENIX Association Conference Proceedings*, pp. 361–370 (June 1985).

Karels, 1986.
M. J. Karels, ''Changes to the Kernel in 4.3BSD,'' pp. 13:1–32 in *UNIX System Manager's Manual, 4.3 Berkeley Software Distribution, Virtual VAX-11 Version*, USENIX Association, Berkeley, CA (1986).

Kashtan, 1980.
D. L. Kashtan, ''UNIX and VMS: Some Performance Comparisons,'' Technical Report, SRI International, Menlo Park, CA (February 1980).

Kernighan & Ritchie, 1978.
B. W. Kernighan & D. M. Ritchie, *The C Programming Language,* Prentice-Hall, Englewood Cliffs, NJ (1978).

Kernighan & Ritchie, 1988.
B. W. Kernighan & D. M. Ritchie, *The C Programming Language,* 2nd ed, Prentice-Hall, Englewood Cliffs, NJ (1988).

McKusick, 1985.
M. K. McKusick, ''A Berkeley Odyssey,'' *UNIX Review* **3**(1), p. 30 (January 1985).

McKusick *et al.*, 1986.
M. K. McKusick, J. M. Bloom, & M. J. Karels, ''Bug Fixes and Changes in 4.3BSD,'' pp. 12:1–22 in *UNIX System Manager's Manual, 4.3 Berkeley Software Distribution, Virtual VAX-11 Version*, USENIX Association, Berkeley, CA (1986).

Miller, 1978.
R. Miller, ''UNIX—A Portable Operating System,'' *ACM Operating System Review* **12**(3), pp. 32–37 (July 1978).

Miller, 1984.
R. Miller, ''A Demand Paging Virtual Memory Manager for System V,'' *USENIX Association Conference Proceedings*, pp. 178–182 (June 1984).

Mohr, 1985.
A. Mohr, ''The Genesis Story,'' *UNIX Review* **3**(1), p. 18 (January 1985).

Organick, 1975.
E. I. Organick, *The Multics System: An Examination of Its Structure*, MIT Press, Cambridge, MA (1975).

P1003.1, 1988.
P1003.1, *IEEE P1003.1 Portable Operating System Interface for Computer Environments (POSIX)*, Institute of Electrical and Electronic Engineers, Piscataway, NJ (1988).

Peirce, 1985.
N. Peirce, ''Putting UNIX In Perspective: An Interview with Victor Vyssotsky,'' *UNIX Review* **3**(1), p. 58 (January 1985).

Popek, 1981.
B. Popek, ''Locus: A Network Transparent, High Reliability Distributed System,'' *Proceedings of the Eighth Symposium on Operating Systems Principles*, pp. 169–177 (December 1981).

Presotto & Ritchie, 1985.
D. L. Presotto & D. M. Ritchie, ''Interprocess Communication in the Eighth Edition UNIX System,'' *USENIX Association Conference Proceedings*, pp. 309–316 (June 1985).

Richards & Whitby-Strevens, 1982.
M. Richards & C. Whitby-Strevens, *BCPL: The Language and Its Compiler*, Cambridge University Press, Cambridge, UK (1980, 1982).

Ritchie, 1978.
D. M. Ritchie, ''A Retrospective,'' *Bell System Technical Journal* **57**(6), pp. 1947–1969 (July–August 1978).

Ritchie *et al.*, 1978.
D. M. Ritchie, S. C. Johnson, M. E. Lesk, & B. W. Kernighan, ''The C Programming Language,'' *Bell System Technical Journal* **57**(6), pp. 1991–2019 (July–August 1978).

Ritchie, 1984a.
D. M. Ritchie, ''The Evolution of the UNIX Time-Sharing System,'' *AT&T Bell Laboratories Technical Journal* **63**(8), pp. 1577–1593 (October 1984).

Ritchie, 1984b.
D. M. Ritchie, ''Reflections on Software Research,'' *Comm ACM* **27**(8), pp. 758–760 (1984).

Ritchie, 1987.
D. M. Ritchie, ''Unix: A Dialectic,'' *USENIX Association Conference Proceedings*, pp. 29–34 (January 1987).

Rosler, 1984.
L. Rosler, ''The Evolution of C—Past and Future,'' *AT&T Bell Laboratories Technical Journal* **63**(8), pp. 1685–1699 (October 1984).

Sandberg, 1985.
R. Sandberg, ''The Design and Implementation of the Sun Network File System,'' *USENIX Association Conference Proceedings*, pp. 119–130 (June 1985).

Stroustrup, 1984.
B. Stroustrup, ''Data Abstraction in C,'' *AT&T Bell Laboratories Technical Journal* **63**(8), pp. 1701–1732 (October 1984).

Tanenbaum, 1987.
A. S. Tanenbaum, *Operating Systems: Design and Implementation*, Prentice-Hall, Englewood Cliffs, NJ (1987).

Tuthill, 1985.
B. Tuthill, ''The Evolution of C: Heresy and Prophecy,'' *UNIX Review* **3**(1), p. 80 (January 1985).

USENIX, 1987.
USENIX, *Proceedings of the C++ Workshop*, USENIX Association, Berkeley, CA (November 1987).

Uniejewski, 1985.
J. Uniejewski, *UNIX System V and BSD4.2 Compatibility Study*, Apollo Computer, Chelmsford, MA (March 1985).

Wilson, 1985.
O. Wilson, ''The Business Evolution of the UNIX System,'' *UNIX Review* **3**(1), p. 46 (January 1985).

X/OPEN, 1987.
X/OPEN, *The X/OPEN Portability Guide (XPG)*, Issue 2, Elsevier Science, Amsterdam, Netherlands (1987).

X3J11, 1988.
X3J11, *X3.159 Programming Language C Standard*, Global Press, Santa Ana, CA (1988).

CHAPTER 2

Design Overview of 4.3BSD

2.1 UNIX Facilities and the Kernel

The UNIX kernel provides four basic facilities: processes, a filesystem, communications, and system startup. This section outlines where each of these four basic services is described in this book.

1. Processes constitute a thread of control in an address space. Mechanisms for creating, terminating, and otherwise controlling processes are described in Chapter 4. The system multiplexes separate virtual-address spaces for each process; this memory management is discussed in Chapter 5.

2. The user interface to the filesystem and devices is similar; common aspects are discussed in Chapter 6. The filesystem is a set of named files, organized in a tree-structured hierarchy of directories, and of operations to manipulate them, as presented in Chapter 7. Files reside on physical media such as disks, and there are device drivers to access them, as set forth in Chapter 8. Terminals are used to access the system; their device drivers are the subject of Chapter 9.

3. Communication mechanisms provided by traditional UNIX systems include device I/O (Chapters 8 and 9), simplex reliable byte streams between related processes (see pipes, Section 10.1), and notification of exceptional events (see signals, Section 4.7). 4.3BSD also has a general interprocess-communication facility; this is described in Chapter 10. This facility uses access mechanisms distinct from those of the filesystem, but, once a connection is set up, it is possible to access it as though it were a pipe. There is a general networking framework, discussed in Chapter 11, that is normally used as a layer underlying the IPC facility. Chapter 12 describes a particular networking implementation in detail.

4. Any real operating system has operational issues, such as how to start it running, as described in Chapter 13.

Sections 2.4 through 2.13 present introductory material related to Chapters 4 through 13. We shall define terms, mention basic system calls, and explore historical developments. Finally, we shall give the reasons for many major design decisions.

The Kernel

The *kernel* is the part of the system that provides the basic system facilities; it creates and manages processes, and provides functions to access the filesystem and communication facilities. These functions, called *system calls*, appear to user processes as library subroutines like any others. These system calls are the only interface processes have to these facilities. Details of the system-call mechanism are given in Chapter 3, as are descriptions of some kernel mechanisms that do not execute as the direct result of a process doing a system call.

Users ordinarily interact with the system through a command-language interpreter, called a *shell*, and perhaps through additional user application programs. Such programs and the shell are implemented as sets of processes. Details of such programs are beyond the scope of this book, which instead concentrates almost exclusively on the kernel.

A *kernel* in traditional operating-system terminology is a small nucleus of software that provides only the minimal facilities necessary for implementing additional operating-system services. In contemporary research operating systems such as Accent [Fitzgerald & Rashid, 1986], Tunis [Ewens *et al.*, 1985], and the V Kernel [Cheriton, 1988], this division of functionality is more than just a logical one. Services such as filesystems and networking protocols are implemented as client application processes of the nucleus or kernel.

The 4.3BSD kernel is not partitioned into multiple processes. This was a basic design decision in the earliest versions of UNIX. The first two implementations by Ken Thompson had no memory mapping at all, and thus made no hardware-enforced distinction between user and kernel space [Ritchie, 1988]. A message-passing system could have been implemented as readily as the actually implemented model of kernel and user processes. The latter was chosen for simplicity. And the early kernels were small. It has been largely the introduction of more and larger facilities (such as networking) into the kernel that has made their separation into user processes an attractive prospect—one that is being pursued in, for example, Mach [Accetta *et al.*, 1986].

The following sections describe the services provided by the 4.3BSD kernel, and give an overview of the services design. Later chapters describe the detailed design and implementation of these services as they appear in 4.3BSD.

2.2 Kernel Organization

In this section, we view the organization of the UNIX kernel in two ways:

- As a static body of software, categorized by the functionality offered by the modules that make up the kernel
- By its dynamic operation, categorized according to the services provided to users

The largest part of the kernel implements the system services that applications access through system calls. In 4.3BSD, this software has been organized according to

- Basic kernel facilities: timer and system clock handling, descriptor management, and process management
- Memory-management support: paging and swapping
- Generic system interfaces: the I/O, control, and multiplexing operations performed on descriptors
- The filesystem: files, directories, pathname translation, file locking, and I/O buffer management
- Terminal-handling support: the terminal-interface driver and terminal line disciplines
- Interprocess-communication facilities: sockets
- Support for network communication: communication protocols and generic network facilities, such as routing

Most of the software in these categories is machine independent and is portable across different hardware architectures. One major exception is the memory-management support that was originally written for the VAX. Although it can be ported to other architectures (basically by emulating VAX memory management), rewriting it for a target architecture is generally a better idea. This has been done numerous times by vendors who have ported the system to non-VAX architectures.

The machine-dependent aspects of the kernel are isolated from the mainstream code. The software that is machine dependent includes

- Lowest-level system-startup actions
- Trap and fault handling
- Low-level manipulation of the run-time context of a process
- Configuration and initialization of hardware devices
- Run-time support for I/O devices

Table 2.1 summarizes the software that constitutes the 4.3BSD kernel for the VAX. The numbers in column 2 are for lines of C source code, header files, and

Table 2.1 Machine-independent software in the 4.3BSD kernel.

Category	Lines of Code	Percentage
headers	6,240	5.4
initialization	580	0.5
kernel facilities	5,440	4.7
generic interfaces	1,340	1.2
filesystem	6,650	5.7
filesystem disk quotas	1,430	1.2
interprocess communication	3,500	3.0
network communication	13,440	11.5
terminal handling	3,410	2.9
virtual memory	4,990	4.3
other machine independent	1,250	1.1
total machine independent	48,270	41.5

assembly language. Virtually all the software in the kernel is written in the C programming language; less than 3 percent is written in assembly language. As the statistics in Table 2.2 show, the machine-dependent software, excluding device support, accounts for a minuscule 4.3 percent of the kernel.

Only a small part of the kernel is devoted to initializing the system. This code is used when the system is *bootstrapped* into operation and is responsible for setting up the kernel hardware and software environment (see Chapter 13). Some operating systems (especially those with limited physical memory) discard or *overlay* the software that performs these functions after they have been executed. The 4.3BSD kernel does not reclaim the memory used by the startup code because

Table 2.2 VAX-dependent software in the 4.3BSD kernel.

Category	Lines of Code	Percentage
input/output device headers	5,725	4.9
input/output device support	36,800	31.6
network device headers	2,450	2.1
network device support	14,800	12.7
routines in assembly language	3,400	2.9
other machine dependent	5,025	4.3
total machine dependent	68,200	58.5

that memory space is only a small fraction of the overall resources available on a typical machine. Also, the startup code does not appear in one place in the kernel—it is scattered throughout, and it usually appears in places logically associated with what is being initialized. DEC's Ultrix, a 4.2BSD-derived system, does recover this code, however.

2.3 Kernel Services

The boundary between the kernel- and user-level code is enforced by hardware-protection facilities provided by the underlying hardware. The kernel operates in a separate address space that is inaccessible to user processes. Privileged operations such as starting I/O and halting the central processing unit (CPU) are available to only the kernel. Applications request services from the kernel with *system calls*. System calls are used to cause the kernel to execute complicated operations, such as writing data to secondary storage, and simple operations, such as returning the current time of day. All system calls appear *synchronous* to applications: While the kernel does the actions associated with a system call, the application is not permitted to run.

A system call usually is implemented as a hardware trap that changes the CPU's execution mode and the current address-space mapping. Parameters supplied by users in system calls are validated by the kernel before they are used to ensure the integrity of the system. All parameters passed into the kernel are copied into the kernel's address space. Parameters are copied to ensure that validated parameters are not changed as a side effect of the system call. System-call results are returned by the kernel either in hardware registers or by their values being copied into user-supplied buffers. Like parameters passed into the kernel, user buffers used for the return of results must also be validated to ensure that they are part of an application's address space. If the kernel encounters an error while processing a system call, it returns an error code to the user. For the C programming language, this error code is stored in the global variable *errno*, and the function call used to start the system call returns the value −1.

User applications and the kernel operate independently of each other. UNIX does not infringe on an application by placing I/O control blocks or other operating-system–related data structures in the application's address space. Each user-level application is provided an independent address space in which it executes. The kernel makes most state changes, such as suspending a process while another is running, invisible to the processes involved.

2.4 Process Management

UNIX supports a multitasking environment. Each task or thread of execution is termed a *process*. The *context* of a UNIX process consists of user-level state, including the contents of its address space and the run-time environment, and kernel-level state, which includes scheduling parameters, resource controls, and identification information. The context includes everything used by the kernel in providing services for the process. Users can create processes, control the processes' execution, and receive notification when the processes' execution status changes. Every process is assigned a unique value, termed a *process identifier* (PID). This value is used by the kernel to identify a process when reporting status changes to a user, and by a user when referencing a process in a system call.

The kernel creates a process by duplicating the context of another process. The new process is termed a *child process* of the original *parent process*. The context duplicated in process creation includes both the user-level execution state of the process and the process's system state managed by the kernel. Important components of the kernel state are described in Chapter 4.

The process lifecycle is depicted in Fig. 2.1. A process may create a new process that is a copy of the original by using the *fork* system call. The *fork* call returns twice, once in the parent process, where the return value is the process identifier of the child, and once in the child process, where the return value is 0. The parent–child relationship induces a hierarchical structure on the set of processes in the system. The new process shares all its parent's resources, such as file descriptors, signal-handling status, and memory layout.

Normally, when a new process is created, it is to execute a program different from the one its parent is executing. A process can overlay itself with the memory image of another process, passing to the newly created process a set of parameters, using the system call *execve*. One parameter is the name of a file whose contents are in a format recognized by the system—either a binary-executable file, or a file that causes the execution of a specified interpreter program to process its contents.

A process may terminate by executing an *exit* system call, returning eight bits of exit status to its parent. If a process wants to communicate more than a single byte of information with its parent, it must either set up an interprocess-communication channel using pipes or sockets, or use an intermediate file. Interprocess communication is discussed more extensively in Chapter 10.

Figure 2.1 Process-management system calls.

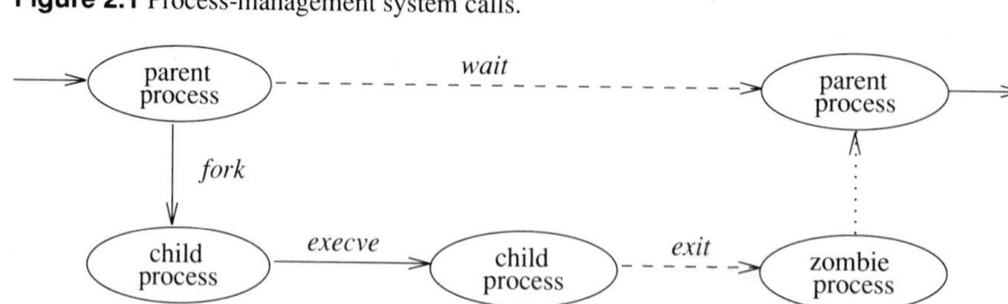

A process can suspend execution until any of its child processes terminate using the *wait* system call, which returns its PID and exit status. A parent process can arrange to be notified by a signal when a child process exits or terminates abnormally. Using the *wait3* system call, the parent can retrieve information about the event that caused termination of the child process, and about resources consumed by the process during its lifetime. If a process is orphaned because its parent exits before it is finished, then the kernel arranges for its exit status to be passed back to a special system process (*init*: see Section 3.1 and Section 13.4).

The details of how the kernel creates and destroys processes are described in Chapter 5.

Processes are scheduled for execution according to a *process-priority* parameter. This priority is managed by a kernel-based scheduling algorithm. Users can influence the scheduling of a process by specifying a parameter (*nice*) that weights the overall scheduling priority, but in general are obligated to share the underlying CPU resources according to the kernel's scheduling policy.

Signals

The system defines a set of *signals* that may be delivered to a process. Signals in 4.3BSD are modeled after hardware interrupts. A process may specify a user-level subroutine to be a *handler* to which a signal should be delivered. When a signal is generated, it is blocked from further occurrence while it is being *caught* by the handler. Catching a signal involves saving the current process context and building a new one in which to run the handler. The signal is then delivered to the handler, which can either abort the process or return to the executing process (perhaps after setting a global variable). If the handler returns, the signal is unblocked and can be generated (and caught) again.

A process may instead specify that a signal is to be *ignored* or that a default action as determined by the kernel is to be taken. The default action of some signals is to terminate the process. This termination may be accompanied by creation of a *core file* that contains the current memory image of the process for use in postmortem debugging.

Some signals cannot be caught or ignored. These include SIGKILL, which is used to kill runaway processes, and the job-control signal SIGSTOP.

A process may choose to have signals delivered on a special stack so that sophisticated software stack manipulations are possible. For example, a language supporting coroutines needs to provide a stack for each coroutine. The language run-time system can allocate these stacks by dividing up the single stack provided by UNIX. If the kernel does not support a separate signal stack, the space allocated for each coroutine must be expanded by the amount of space required to catch a signal.

All signals have the same *priority*. If multiple signals are pending simultaneously, the order in which signals are delivered to a process is implementation-specific. Signal handlers execute with the signal that caused their invocation blocked, but other signals may yet occur. Mechanisms are provided that processes may use to protect critical sections of code against the occurrence of specified signals.

The detailed design and implementation of signals is described in Section 4.7.

Process Groups

Processes are organized into *process groups*. Process groups are used to control access to terminals and to provide a means of distributing signals to collections of related processes. A process inherits its process group from its parent process. Mechanisms are provided by the kernel to allow a process to alter its process group or the process group of any of its descendents. Creating a new process group is easy; the value of a new process group is ordinarily that of the process identifier of the creating process.

The group of processes in a process group is sometimes referred to as a *job* and is manipulated by high-level system software, such as the shell. A common kind of job created by a shell is a *pipeline* of several processes connected by pipes such that the output of the first process is the input of the second, the output of the second is the input of the third, and so forth. The shell creates such a job by forking, setting the process-group identifier of the child process to the child's PID, then building up the rest of the pipeline by creating the rest of the processes in the job and setting their process-group identifiers to the same PID.

A user process can send a signal to each process in a process group as well as to a single process. A process in a specific process group may receive software interrupts affecting the group, causing the group to suspend or resume execution or to be interrupted or terminated.

A terminal has a process-group identifier assigned to it. This identifier is normally set to the identifier of a process group associated with the terminal. A job-control shell may create a number of process groups associated with the same terminal; the terminal is the *controlling terminal* for each process in these groups. A process may read from a descriptor for its controlling terminal only if the terminal's process-group identifier matches that of the process. If the identifiers do not match, the process will be blocked if it attempts to read from the terminal. By changing the process-group identifier of the terminal, a shell can arbitrate a terminal among several different jobs. This is called *job control* and is described along with process groups in Section 4.7.

2.5 Memory Management

Each process has its own private address space. The address space is divided into three logical segments: *text*, *data*, and *stack*. The text segment is read-only and contains the machine instructions of a program. The data and stack segments are both readable and writable. The data segment contains the initialized and uninitialized data portions of a program, whereas the stack segment holds the application's run-time stack. On most machines, the stack segment is automatically extended by the kernel as the process executes. A data segment may be explicitly expanded or contracted by a system call being made, whereas the size of the text segment can be changed only when its contents are overlaid with data from the filesystem, or when debugging takes place. The initial contents of the segments of a child process are duplicates of the segments of a parent process.

The entire contents of a process address space need not be resident for a process to execute. If a process references a part of its address space that is not resident in main memory, the system *pages* the necessary information into memory. When system resources are scarce, the system uses a two-level approach to maintain available resources. If a modest amount of memory is available, the system will take memory resources away from processes if these resources have not been used recently. Should there be a severe resource shortage, the system resorts to *swapping* the entire context of a process to secondary storage. The *demand paging* and *swapping* performed by the system is effectively transparent to processes. A process may, however, advise the system about expected future memory utilization as a performance aid.

BSD Memory-Management Design Decisions

A requirement for 4.2BSD was that it support large sparse address spaces, mapped files, and shared memory. An interface was specified, called *mmap*(), that allowed unrelated processes to map a file into their address space. If multiple processes mapped the same file into their address space, changes to the address space by one process would be reflected in the area mapped by the other processes as well as in the file itself. Ultimately, 4.2BSD was shipped without the *mmap*() interface because of the pressures to make other features, such as networking, available.

Further development of the *mmap*() interface continued during the work on 4.3BSD. Over 40 companies and research groups participated in the discussions leading to the revised architecture that was described in the Berkeley Software Architecture Manual [Joy *et al.*, 1986]. Several of the companies have implemented the revised interface [Gingell *et al.*, 1987].

Once again, time pressures prevented 4.3BSD from providing an implementation of the interface. Although the latter could have been built into the existing 4.3BSD virtual-memory system, the developers decided not to do so because that implementation was nearly 10 years old. Furthermore, the original virtual-memory design was based on the assumption that computer memories were small and expensive, whereas disks were locally connected, fast, large, and inexpensive. Thus, the virtual-memory system was designed to be frugal with its use of memory at the expense of generating extra disk traffic. In addition, the 4.3BSD implementation was riddled with VAX memory-management hardware dependencies that impeded its portability to other computer architectures. Finally, the virtual-memory system was not designed to support the tightly coupled multiprocessors that are becoming increasingly common and important today.

Attempting to improve the old implementation incrementally seemed doomed to failure. A completely new design, on the other hand, could take advantage of large memories, conserve disk transfers, and have the potential to run on multiprocessors. At the time of 4.3BSD's release, few of the implementations of virtual memory had been completed. Thus, the design alternatives were not yet tested and the optimal choices were still unknown. The hope is that the correct choices will become clear, and that a new virtual-memory system can be crafted for the next Berkeley UNIX system from the work of the new implementations.

Another issue with the virtual-memory system is the way that information is passed into the kernel when a system call is made. UNIX always copies data from the process address space into a buffer in the kernel. For read or write operations that are transferring large quantities of data, doing the copy can be time consuming. An alternative to doing the copying is to remap the process memory into the kernel. The 4.3BSD kernel always copies the data for several reasons:

- Often, the user data are not page aligned and are not a multiple of the hardware page length.
- If the page is taken away from the process, it will no longer be able to reference that page. Some programs depend on the data remaining in the buffer even after the latter have been written.
- If the process is allowed to keep a copy of the page (as with current 4.3BSD semantics), the page must be made *copy-on-write*. A copy-on-write page is one that is protected against being written by its being made read-only. If the process attempts to modify the page, the kernel gets a write fault. The kernel then makes a copy of the page that the process can modify. Unfortunately, the typical process will immediately try to write new data to the buffer, forcing the data to be copied anyway.
- The 4.3BSD virtual-memory design does not have provision for doing copy-on-write.
- When pages are remapped to new virtual-memory addresses, most memory-management hardware requires that the hardware address-translation cache be purged selectively. The cache purges are often slow. The net effect is that remapping is slower than copying for blocks of data less than 4 to 8 Kbyte.

The biggest incentive for memory mapping is the need for accessing big files and for passing large quantities of data between processes. The *mmap*() interface will provide a way for both of these tasks to be done without copying.

Memory Management Inside the Kernel

The 4.3BSD kernel has at least 10 different memory allocators. Some of them handle large blocks, some of them handle small, chained data structures, and others include information to describe I/O operations. Often, the allocations are for pieces of memory that are needed only for the duration of a single system call. In a user process, such short-term memory would be allocated on the run-time stack. Because the kernel has a limited run-time stack, it is not feasible to allocate even moderate-sized blocks of memory on it. Consequently, such memory must be allocated through a more dynamic mechanism. For example, when the system must translate a pathname, it must allocate a 1-Kbyte buffer to hold the name.

Other blocks of memory must be more persistent than a single system call and thus could not be allocated on the stack even if there was space. An example is protocol-control blocks that remain throughout the duration of a network connection.

Demands for dynamic memory allocation in the kernel have increased as more services have been added. Each time a new type of memory allocation has been required, developers have written a specialized memory-allocation scheme to handle it. Often, the new memory-allocation scheme has been built on top of an older allocator. For example, the block-device subsystem provides a crude form of memory allocation through the allocation of empty buffers. The allocation is slow because of the implied semantics of finding the oldest buffer, pushing its contents to disk if they are dirty, and moving physical memory into or out of the buffer to create the requested size (see Section 7.5). To reduce the overhead, a ''new'' memory allocator is built for name translation that allocates a pool of empty buffers. It keeps them on a free list, so they can be quickly allocated and freed [McKusick *et al.*, 1985].

This memory-allocation method has three drawbacks. First, the new allocator can handle only a limited range of sizes. Second, it depletes the buffer pool as it steals memory intended to buffer disk blocks. Third, it creates yet another interface of which the kernel programmer must be aware.

A generalized memory allocator reduces the complexity of writing code inside the kernel. Rather than providing many semispecialized ways of allocating memory, the kernel provides a single, general-purpose allocator. With only a single interface, programmers need not concern themselves with trying to figure out the most appropriate way to allocate memory. A good general-purpose allocator helps to avoid the syndrome of inventing new special-purpose allocators.

The 4.3BSD Tahoe release introduced a memory allocator with an interface similar to the C library routines *malloc*() and *free*() that provide memory allocation to application programs [McKusick & Karels, 1988]. Like the C library interface, the allocation routine takes a parameter specifying the size of memory that is needed. The range of sizes for memory requests is not constrained; however, physical memory is allocated and is not paged. The free routine takes a pointer to the storage being freed, but does not require the size of the piece of memory being freed.

2.6 I/O System

The basic model of the UNIX I/O system is a sequence of bytes that can be accessed either randomly or sequentially. There are no *access methods* and no *control blocks* in a typical UNIX user process.

Different programs expect various levels of structure, but the kernel does not impose structure on I/O. For instance, the convention for text files is lines of

ASCII characters separated by a single newline character (the ASCII line-feed character), but the kernel knows nothing about this convention. For the purposes of most programs, the model is further simplified to being a stream of data bytes, or an *I/O stream*. It is this single common data form that makes the characteristic UNIX tool-based approach work [Kernighan & Pike, 1984]. An I/O stream from one program can be fed as input to almost any other program. (This kind of traditional UNIX I/O stream should not be confused with the Eighth Edition stream I/O system or with the System V, Release 3 STREAMS derived from them; both of those latter objects can be accessed in those systems as traditional I/O streams.)

Descriptors and I/O

UNIX processes use *descriptors* to reference I/O streams. A descriptor is a small unsigned integer. A *read* or *write* system call can be applied to a descriptor to transfer data. The *close* system call can be used to deallocate any descriptor.

Descriptors represent underlying objects supported by the kernel, and are created by system calls specific to the type of object. In 4.3BSD, three kinds of objects may be represented by descriptors: files, pipes, and sockets.

- A *file* is a linear array of bytes with at least one name. A file exists until all its names are explicitly deleted and no process holds a descriptor for it. A descriptor for a file is produced by opening that file's name with the *open* system call. I/O devices are accessed as files.

- A *pipe* is a linear array of bytes, as is a file, but it is used solely as an I/O stream, and it is unidirectional. It also has no name, and thus cannot be opened with *open*. Instead, it is created by the *pipe* system call, which returns two descriptors, one of which accepts input that is sent to the other descriptor reliably, without duplication, and in order.

- A *socket* is a transient object that is used for interprocess communication; it exists only as long as some process holds a descriptor referring to it. A socket is created by the *socket* system call, which returns a descriptor for it. There are different kinds of sockets that support various communication semantics, such as reliable delivery of data, preservation of message ordering, and preservation of message boundaries.

In UNIX systems prior to 4.2BSD, pipes are implemented using the filesystem; when sockets were introduced in 4.2BSD, pipes were reimplemented as sockets.

The kernel keeps a *descriptor table* for each process; this is a table that the kernel uses to translate the external representation of a descriptor—a small unsigned integer—into an internal representation. (The descriptor is merely an index into this table.) The descriptor table of a process is inherited from its parent, and thus access to the objects to which the descriptors refer also is inherited. The main ways a process can obtain a descriptor are by opening or creation of an object and by inheritance from the parent process. In addition, socket IPC allows passing descriptors in messages between unrelated processes.

Every valid descriptor-table entry in turn refers to a *file structure*, which contains a *file offset* in bytes from the beginning of the object. Read and write operations start at this offset, which is updated after each data transfer. For objects that permit random access, the file offset also may be set with the *lseek* system call. Ordinary files permit random access, and some devices do, as well. Pipes and sockets do not.

When a process terminates, the kernel reclaims all the descriptors that were in use by that process. If the process was holding the last reference to an object, the object's manager is notified so that it can do any necessary cleanup actions, such as final deletion of a file or deallocation of a socket.

Descriptor Management

Most processes expect three descriptors to be open already when they start running. These are descriptors 0, 1, 2, more commonly known as *standard input*, *standard output*, and *standard error*, respectively. Usually, all three are associated with the user's terminal by the login process (see Section 13.4) and are inherited through *fork* and *exec* by processes run by the user. Thus, a program can read what the user types by reading standard input, and the program can send output to the user's screen by writing to standard output. The standard error descriptor also is open for writing and is used for error output, whereas standard output is used for ordinary output.

These (and other) descriptors can be mapped to objects other than the terminal; this is called *I/O redirection*, and all the standard shells permit users to do it. The shell can direct the output of a program to a file by closing descriptor 1 (standard output) and opening the desired output file to produce a new descriptor 1. Standard input may similarly be redirected to come from a file by closing descriptor 0 and opening the file.

Pipes allow the output of one program to be input to another program without rewriting or even relinking of either program. Instead of descriptor 1 (standard output) of the source program being set up to write to the terminal, it is set up to be the input descriptor of a pipe. Similarly, descriptor 0 (standard input) of the sink program is set up to reference the output of the pipe instead of the terminal keyboard. The resulting set of two processes and the connecting pipe is known as a *pipeline*. Pipelines can be arbitrarily long series of processes connected by pipes.

The *open*, *pipe*, and *socket* system calls produce new descriptors with the lowest unused number usable for a descriptor. For pipelines to work, some mechanism must be provided to map such descriptors into 0 and 1. The *dup* system call creates a copy of a descriptor that points to the same file-table entry. The new descriptor is also the lowest unused one, but if the desired descriptor is closed first, *dup* can be used to do the desired mapping. Care must be taken, however, because if descriptor 1 is desired, and descriptor 0 happens also to have been closed, descriptor 0 will be the result. To avoid this problem, the *dup2* system call is provided; it is like *dup*, but it takes an additional argument specifying the number of the desired descriptor (if it was already open, *dup2* closes it before reusing it).

Files

A regular file in UNIX is a sequence of bytes with one or more names. The *open* system call takes as arguments the name of a file and a permission mode to specify whether the file should be open for reading, writing, or both. This system call also may be used to create a new, empty file (and there is also a system call *creat* for that purpose). The *read* and *write* system calls can be applied to the resulting descriptor, if the appropriate mode was set with *open*. A descriptor can be closed with the *close* system call.

The *link* system call takes the name of a file and makes another name for it. A filename may be removed with the *unlink* system call. When the last name for a file is removed (and the last process that has the file open closes it), the file is deleted.

Files are organized hierarchically in *directories*. A directory is a type of file, but, in contrast to regular files, a directory has a structure imposed on it by the system. A process can read a directory as it would an ordinary file, but only the system is permitted to modify a directory. Directories are created by the *mkdir* system call and are removed by the *rmdir* system call. Before 4.2BSD, the *mkdir* and *rmdir* system calls were implemented by a series of *link* and *unlink* system calls being done. There were three reasons for adding systems calls explicitly to create and delete directories:

- The operation could be made atomic. If the system crashed, the directory would not be left half constructed, as could happen when using a series of link operations.
- When a networked filesystem is being run, the creation and deletion of files and directories need to be specified atomically so that they can be serialized.
- Non-UNIX filesystems may not support link operations. Although they might support the concept of directories, they probably would not create and delete the directories with links, as the UNIX filesystem does. Consequently, they could create and delete directories only if explicit directory create and delete requests were presented.

The *chown* system call sets the owner and group of a file, and *chmod* changes protection attributes. *Stat* applied to a filename can be used to read back such properties of a file. The *fchown*, *fchmod*, and *fstat* system calls are applied to a descriptor instead of to a filename to do the same set of operations. The *rename* system call may be used to give a file a new name in the filesystem, replacing one of the file's old names. Like the directory-creation and directory-deletion operations, the *rename* system call was added to 4.2BSD to provide atomicity to name changes in the local filesystem. Later, it proved useful explicitly to export renaming operations to foreign filesystems and over the network.

The *truncate* system call was added to 4.2BSD to allow files to be shortened to an arbitrary offset. The call was added primarily in support of the Fortran runtime library which has the semantics such that the end of a random-access file is set to be wherever the program last accessed that file. Without the *truncate* system call, the only way to shorten a file was to copy the part that was desired to a new file, delete the old file, then rename the copy to the original name. Besides being slow, the library could potentially fail on a full filesystem.

Once the filesystem had the ability to shorten files, the kernel took advantage of that ability to shorten large empty directories. The advantage of shortening empty directories is that it reduces the time spent in the kernel searching them when names are being created or deleted.

Some other UNIX systems provide *FIFO*s. A FIFO is essentially a pipe that has a name in the filesystem and that does not vanish when the last descriptor referring to it is closed. Because POSIX has FIFOs, future 4BSD releases may also include them. See Section 1.2 for filesystem facilities adopted by POSIX *from* 4.3BSD.

Devices

Hardware devices have filenames, and may be accessed by the user by the same system calls as are used for regular files. The kernel can distinguish a *device special file* or *special file* and determine to what device it refers, but most processes do not need to do this. Terminals, printers, and tape drives are all accessed as though they were streams of bytes, like UNIX disk files. Thus, device dependencies and peculiarities are kept in the kernel as much as possible, and even in the kernel most of them are segregated in the device drivers.

Device special files are created by the *mknod* system call. There is an additional system call, *ioctl*, for manipulating the underlying device parameters of special files. The operations that can be done differ for each device. This system call allows the special characteristics of devices to be accessed, rather than overloading the semantics of other system calls. For example, there is an *ioctl* on a tape drive to write an end-of-tape mark instead of there being a special or modified version of *write*.

Socket IPC

The 4.2BSD kernel introduced an IPC mechanism more flexible than pipes, based on *sockets*. A socket is an endpoint of communication referred to by a descriptor, just like a file or a pipe. Two processes can each create a socket, and then connect those two endpoints to produce a reliable byte stream. Once connected, the descriptors for the sockets can be read or written by processes, just as the latter would do with a pipe. The transparency of sockets allows the kernel to redirect the output of one process to the input of another process residing on another machine. A major difference between pipes and sockets is that pipes require a common parent process to set up the communications channel. A connection between sockets can be set up by two unrelated processes, possibly residing on different machines.

The socket mechanism requires extensions to the traditional UNIX I/O system calls to provide the associated naming and connection semantics. Rather than overloading the existing interface, the developers used the existing interfaces to the extent that the latter worked without being changed, and designed new interfaces to handle the added semantics. The *read* and *write* system calls were used for byte-stream type connections, but six new system calls were added to allow sending and receiving addressed messages such as network datagrams. The system calls for writing messages include *send*, *sendto*, and *sendmsg*. The system calls for reading messages include *recv*, *recvfrom*, and *recvmsg*. In retrospect, the first two in each class are special cases of the others; *recvfrom* and *sendto* probably should have been added as library interfaces to *recvmsg* and *sendmsg* respectively.

Scatter/Gather I/O

In addition to the traditional *read* and *write* system calls, 4.2BSD introduced the ability to do scatter/gather I/O. Scatter input uses the *readv* system call to allow a single read to be placed in several different buffers. Conversely, the *writev* system call allows several different buffers to be written in a single atomic write. Instead of passing a single buffer and length parameter, as is done with *read* and *write*, the process passes in a pointer to an array of buffers and lengths, along with a count describing the size of the array.

This facility allows buffers in different parts of a process address space to be written atomically without the need to copy them to a single contiguous buffer. Atomic writes are necessary in the case where the underlying abstraction is record-based, such as tape drives that output a tape block on each write request. It is also convenient to be able to read a single request into several different buffers (such as a record header into one place and the data into another). Although the ability to scatter data can be entirely simulated by reading the data into a large buffer and then copying the pieces to their intended destinations, the cost of memory-to-memory copying in such cases often would more than double the running time of the affected program.

Just as *send* and *recv* could have been implemented as library interfaces to *sendto* and *recvfrom*, it would have also been possible to simulate *read* with *readv* and *write* with *writev*. However, *read* and *write* are used so much more frequently that the added cost of simulating them would not have been worthwhile.

2.7 Filesystem

A regular file is a linear array of bytes, and can be read and written starting at any byte in the file. The kernel distinguishes no record boundaries in regular files, although many programs recognize line-feed characters as distinguishing the ends of lines, and other programs may impose other structure. No system-related information about a file is kept in the file itself, but the filesystem stores a small amount of ownership, protection, and usage information with each file.

A *filename* component is a string of up to 255 characters. These filenames are stored in a type of file called a *directory*. The information in a directory about a file is called a *directory entry* and includes, in addition to the filename, a pointer to the file itself. Directory entries may refer to other directories as well as to plain files. A hierarchy of directories and files is thus formed, and is called a *filesystem*; a small one is shown in Fig. 2.2. Directories may contain subdirectories, and there is no inherent limitation to the depth with which directory nesting may occur. To protect the consistency of the filesystem, the kernel does not permit processes to write directly into directories. A filesystem may include not only plain files and directories, but also references to other objects, such as devices and sockets.

The filesystem forms a tree, the beginning of which is the *root directory*, sometimes referred to by the name **slash**, spelled with a single solidus character (/). The root directory contains files—in our example in Fig. 2.2, **vmunix**, a copy of the kernel-executable object file. It also contains directories—in this example, the **usr** directory. Within the **usr** directory is the **bin** directory, which mostly contains executable object code of programs, such as the files **ls** and **vi**.

A process identifies a file by specifying that file's *pathname*, a string composed of zero or more *filenames* separated by slash (/) characters. The kernel associates two directories with each process for use in interpreting pathnames. A process's *root directory* is the topmost point in the filesystem that the process can access; it is ordinarily set to the root directory of the entire filesystem. A pathname beginning with a slash is called an *absolute pathname* and is interpreted by the kernel starting with the process's root directory.

A pathname that does not begin with a slash is called a *relative pathname* and is interpreted relative to the *current working directory* of the process. (This directory is also known by the shorter names *current directory* or *working directory*.)

Figure 2.2 A small filesystem tree.

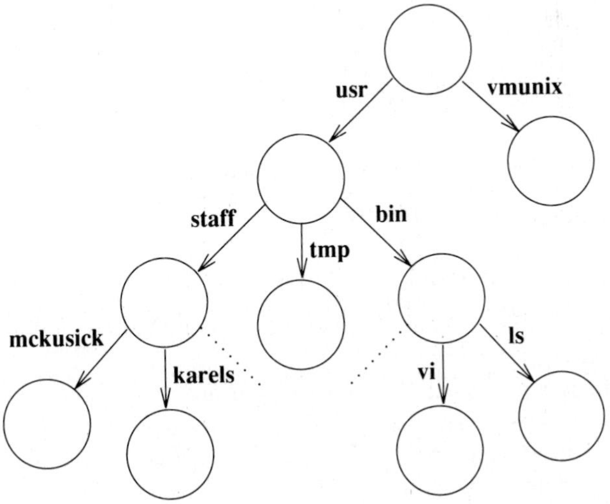

The current directory itself may be referred to directly by the name *dot*, spelled with a single period (**.**). The filename *dot-dot* (**..**) refers to a directory's parent directory. The root directory is its own parent.

A process may set its root directory with the *chroot* system call, and its current directory with the *chdir* system call. Any process may do *chdir* at any time, but *chroot* is permitted only to the superuser, and is normally used in setting up restricted access to the system.

Using the filesystem shown in Fig. 2.2, if a process has the root of the filesystem as its root directory, and **/usr** as its current directory, it can refer to the file **vi** either from the root with the absolute pathname **/usr/bin/vi**, or from its current directory with the relative pathname **bin/vi**.

System utilities and databases are kept in certain well-known directories. Part of the well-defined hierarchy includes a directory that contains the *home directory* for each user; for example, **/usr/staff/mckusick** and **/usr/staff/karels** in Fig. 2.2. When users log in, the current working directory of their shell is set to the home directory. Within their home directories, users can create directories as easily as they can regular files. Thus, a user can build arbitrarily complex subhierarchies.

The user usually knows of only one filesystem, but the system may know that this one virtual filesystem is really composed of several physical filesystems, each on a different device. A physical filesystem may not span multiple hardware devices. Since most physical disk devices are divided into several logical devices, there may be more than one filesystem per physical device, but no more than one per logical device. One filesystem—the filesystem that anchors all absolute pathnames—is called the *root filesystem*, and is always available. Others may be mounted; that is, they may be integrated into the directory hierarchy of the root filesystem. References to a directory that has a filesystem mounted on it are transparently converted by the kernel into references to the root directory of the mounted filesystem.

Newly created files are assigned the user identifier of the process that created them and the group identifier of the directory in which they were created. A three-level access-control mechanism is provided for the protection of files. These three levels specify the accessibility of a file to

- The user who owns the file
- The group that owns the file
- Everyone else

Each level of access has separate indicators for read permission, write permission, and execute permission.

Files are created with zero length and may grow when they are written. While a file is open, the system maintains a pointer into the file indicating the current location in the file associated with the descriptor. This pointer can be moved about in the file in a random-access fashion. Files may have *holes* in them.

Holes are void areas in the linear extent of the file where data have never been written. A process can create these holes by positioning the pointer past the current end-of-file and writing. When read, holes are treated by the system as zero-valued bytes.

Earlier UNIX systems had a limit of 14 characters per filename component. This limitation was often a problem. For example, besides the natural desire of users to give files long descriptive names, a common way of forming filenames is as **basename.extension**, where the extension (indicating the kind of file, such as **.c** for C source or **.o** for intermediate binary object) is one to three characters, leaving 10 to 12 characters for the basename. Source-code–control systems and editors usually take up another two characters, either as a prefix or a suffix, for their purposes, leaving eight to 10 characters. It is easy to use 10 or 12 characters in a single English word as a basename (e.g., ‘‘multiplexer’’).

It is possible to keep within these limits, but it is inconvenient or even dangerous, because other UNIX systems accept strings longer than the limit when creating files, but then *truncate* to the limit. A C language source file named **multiplexer.c** (already 13 characters) might have a source-code–control file with **s.** prepended, producing a filename **s.multiplexer** that is indistinguishable from the source-code–control file for **multiplexer.ms**, a file containing **troff** source for documentation for the C program. The contents of the two original files could easily get confused with no warning from the source-code–control system. Careful coding can detect this problem, but the long filenames first introduced in 4.2BSD practically eliminate it.

2.8 Devices

Hardware devices can be categorized as either *structured* or *unstructured*; these are known as *block* or *character* devices, respectively. Processes typically access devices through *special files* in the filesystem. I/O operations to these files are handled by kernel-resident software modules termed *device drivers*. Most network-communication hardware devices are accessible only through the interprocess-communication facilities and do not have special files in the filesystem name space. This is because the *raw-socket* interface provides a more natural interface than does a special file.

Structured or block devices are typified by disks and magnetic tapes, and include most random-access devices. The kernel supports read-modify-write–type buffering actions on block-oriented structured devices to allow the latter to be read and written in a totally random byte-addressed fashion, like regular files. Filesystems are created on block devices.

Unstructured devices are those devices that do not support a block structure. Familiar unstructured devices are communication lines, raster plotters, and unbuffered magnetic tapes and disks. Unstructured devices typically support large block I/O transfers.

Unstructured files are called *character devices* because the first of these to be implemented were terminal device drivers. The kernel interface to the driver for these devices proved convenient for other devices that were not block structured.

2.9 Terminals

Terminals support the standard system I/O operations as well as a collection of terminal-specific operations to control input-character editing and output delays. At the lowest level are the terminal device drivers that control the hardware terminal ports. Terminal input is handled according to the underlying communication characteristics, such as baud rate, and a set of software-controllable parameters, such as parity checking.

Layered above the terminal device drivers are line disciplines that provide various degrees of character processing. The default line discipline usually is used when a port is being used for an interactive login. The default line discipline has three modes: *raw*, *cbreak*, or *cooked*. In raw mode, input is passed through to the reading process immediately and without interpretation. In cbreak mode, the terminal handler interprets only input characters that cause the generation of signals or output flow control; all other characters are passed through to the process as in raw mode. In cooked mode, input is processed to provide standard line-oriented editing functions, and input is presented to a process on a line-by-line basis.

On output, the terminal handler provides some simple formatting services. These services include

- Converting the line-feed character to the two-character return–line-feed sequence
- Inserting delays after certain standard control characters
- Expanding tabs
- Providing translation for uppercase-only terminals
- Displaying echoed nongraphic ASCII characters as a two-character sequence of the form ‘‘^X’’ (i.e., the ASCII caret character followed by a printable ASCII character related to the control character)

Each of these formatting services can be disabled individually by a process through control requests.

2.10 Interprocess Communication

Interprocess communication in 4.3BSD is organized in *communication domains*. Domains currently supported include the *UNIX domain*, for communication between processes executing on the same machine; the *internet domain*, for communication between processes using the TCP/IP protocol suite (perhaps within the DARPA Internet or NSFnet); and the *XNS domain*, for communication between processes using the XEROX Network Systems (XNS) protocols.

Within a domain, communication takes place between communication endpoints known as *sockets*. As mentioned in Section 2.6, the *socket* system call creates a socket and returns a descriptor; other IPC system calls are described in Chapter 10. Each socket has a type that defines its communications semantics; these include properties such as reliability, ordering, and prevention of duplication of messages.

Each socket has a *communication protocol* associated with it. This protocol provides the semantics required by the socket type. Applications may request a specific protocol when creating a socket, or may allow the system to select a protocol that is appropriate for the type of socket being created.

Sockets may have addresses bound to them. The form and meaning of socket addresses are dependent on the communication domain in which the socket is created. Binding a name to a socket in the UNIX domain causes a file to be created in the filesystem.

Normal data transmitted and received through sockets are untyped. Data-representation issues are the responsibility of libraries built on top of the interprocess-communication facilities. In addition to normal data, communication domains may support the transmission and reception of specially typed data, termed *access rights*. The UNIX domain, for example, uses this facility to pass descriptors between processes.

Networking implementations on UNIX before 4.2BSD usually worked by overloading the character device interfaces. One goal of the socket interface was that it should be possible for naive programs to work without change on stream-style connections. Such programs can work only if the *read* and *write* systems calls are unchanged. Consequently, the original interfaces were left intact and were made to work on stream-type sockets. A new interface was added for more complicated sockets, such as those used to send datagrams, with which a destination address must be presented with each *send* call.

Another benefit of the new interface is that it is highly portable. Shortly after a test release was available from Berkeley, the socket interface had been ported to System III by a UNIX vendor (although AT&T never adopted the socket interface or implementation, deciding instead to use the Eighth Edition stream mechanism). The socket interface was also ported to run in many Ethernet boards by vendors such as Excelan and Interlan that were selling into the PC market, where the machines were too small to run networking in the main processor.

2.11 Network Communication

Some of the communication domains supported by the *socket* IPC mechanism provide access to network protocols. These protocols are implemented as a separate software layer logically below the socket software in the kernel. The kernel provides many ancillary services, such as buffer management, message routing, standardized interfaces to the protocols, and interfaces to the network interface drivers for the use of the various network protocols. These services and interfaces are described in Chapter 11.

At the time that 4.2BSD was being implemented, there were many networking protocols in use or under development, each with its own strengths and weaknesses. There was no clearly superior protocol or protocol suite. By supporting multiple protocols, 4.2BSD could provide interoperability and resource sharing among the diverse set of machines that was available in the Berkeley environment. Multiple protocol support also provides for future changes. Today's protocols designed for 10 Mbit/s Ethernets are likely to be inadequate for tomorrow's 100 Mbit/s fiber-optic nets. Consequently, the network-communication layer is designed to support multiple protocols. New protocols are added to the kernel without the support for older protocols being affected. Older applications can continue to operate using the old protocol over the same physical network as is used by newer applications running with a newer network protocol.

2.12 Network Implementation

The first protocol suite implemented in 4.2BSD was DARPA's Transmission Control Protocol/Internet Protocol (TCP/IP). CSRG chose TCP/IP as the first network to incorporate into the socket IPC framework because a 4.1BSD-based implementation was publicly available from a DARPA-sponsored project at Bolt, Beranek, and Newman (BBN). That was an influential choice: The 4.2BSD implementation is the main reason for the extremely widespread use of this protocol suite. Subsequent performance and capability improvements to the TCP/IP implementation have also been widely adopted. The TCP/IP implementation is described in detail in Chapter 12.

The release of 4.3BSD added the Xerox Network Systems (XNS) protocol suite, partly building on work done at the University of Maryland and Cornell University. This suite was needed to connect isolated machines that could not communicate using TCP/IP.

The ISO protocol suite will be the next network implementation added to future versions of 4.3BSD because of its increasing visibility both within and outside the United States.

2.13 System Operation

Bootstrapping mechanisms are used to start the system running. First, the UNIX kernel must be loaded into the main memory of the processor. Once loaded, it must go through an initialization phase to set the hardware into a known state.

Next, the kernel must do autoconfiguration, a process that finds and configures the peripherals that are attached to the processor. The system begins running single-user while a start-up script does disk checks and starts the accounting and quota checking. Finally, the start-up script starts the general system services and brings up the system to full multiuser operation.

During multiuser operation, processes wait for login requests on the terminal lines and network ports that have been configured for user access. When a login request is detected, a login process is spawned and user validation is done. When the login validation is successful, a login shell is created from which the user can run additional processes.

Exercises

2.1 How does a user process request a service from the kernel?

2.2 How are data transferred between a process and the kernel? What alternatives are available?

2.3 How does a process access an I/O stream? List three types of I/O streams.

2.4 What are the four steps in the lifecycle of a process?

2.5 Why are process groups provided in 4.3BSD?

2.6 What are the machine-dependent functions of the kernel?

2.7 Describe the difference between an absolute and a relative pathname.

2.8 List the three system calls that were required to create a new directory **foo** in the current directory before the addition of the *mkdir* system call. Give three reasons why the *mkdir* system call was added to 4.2BSD.

2.9 Define scatter-gather I/O. Why is it useful?

2.10 What is the difference between a block and a character device?

2.11 List five functions provided by a terminal driver.

2.12 What is the difference between a pipe and a socket?

2.13 Describe how to create a group of processes in a pipeline.

*2.14 Explain the difference between interprocess communication and networking.

References

Accetta *et al.*, 1986.
M. Accetta, R. Baron, D. Golub, R. Rashid, A. Tevanian, & M. Young, "Mach: A New Kernel Foundation for UNIX Development," Technical Report, Carnegie Mellon University, Pittsburgh, PA (August 1986).

Cheriton, 1988.
D. R. Cheriton, ``The V Distributed System,'' *Comm ACM* **31**(3), pp. 314–333 (March 1988).

Ewens *et al.*, 1985.
P. Ewens, D. R. Blythe, M. Funkenhauser, & R. C. Holt, ``Tunis: A Distributed Multiprocessor Operating System,'' *USENIX Association Conference Proceedings*, pp. 247–254 (June 1985).

Fitzgerald & Rashid, 1986.
R. Fitzgerald & R. F. Rashid, ``The Integration of Virtual Memory Management and Interprocess Communication in Accent,'' *ACM Transactions on Computer Systems* **4**(2), pp. 147–177 (May 1986).

Gingell *et al.*, 1987.
R. A. Gingell, J. P. Moran, & W. A. Shannon, ``Virtual Memory Architecture in SunOS,'' *USENIX Association Conference Proceedings*, pp. 81–94 (June 1987).

Joy *et al.*, 1986.
W. N. Joy, R. S. Fabry, S. J. Leffler, M. K. McKusick, & M. J. Karels, ``Berkeley Software Architecture Manual, 4.3BSD Edition,'' pp. 6:1–43 in *UNIX Programmer's Supplementary Documents, Volume 1, 4.3 Berkeley Software Distribution, Virtual VAX-11 Version*, USENIX Association, Berkeley, CA (1986).

Kernighan & Pike, 1984.
B. W. Kernighan & R. Pike, *The UNIX Programming Environment,* Prentice-Hall, Englewood Cliffs, NJ (1984).

McKusick *et al.*, 1985.
M. K. McKusick, M. Karels, & S. Leffler, ``Performance Improvements and Functional Enhancements in 4.3BSD,'' *USENIX Association Conference Proceedings*, pp. 519–531 (June 1985).

McKusick & Karels, 1988.
M. K. McKusick & M. J. Karels, ``Design of a General Purpose Memory Allocator for the 4.3BSD UNIX Kernel,'' *USENIX Association Conference Proceedings*, pp. 295–304 (June 1988).

Ritchie, 1988.
D. M. Ritchie, ``Early Kernel Design,'' private communication (March 1988).

CHAPTER 3

Kernel Services

3.1 Kernel Organization

The UNIX kernel provides services to user processes. Processes access most services directly through system calls. Other services, such as process scheduling and memory management, are implemented as UNIX processes that execute in kernel mode or as routines that execute periodically within the kernel. In this chapter, we shall describe how kernel services are provided to user processes, and explain the ancillary processing that is performed by the kernel in normal operation. Following this description, we shall introduce some of the basic kernel services and shall describe their implementation.

System Activities

Each entry into the kernel is termed a *system activity*. These activities can be categorized according to the event or action that initiates them:

- System calls
- Hardware interrupts
- Hardware traps
- Software-initiated traps or interrupts

System calls usually are a special case of the last category—the machine instruction used to initiate a system call typically causes a hardware trap that is treated specially by the kernel. Hardware interrupts arise from external events, such as an I/O device needing attention. The kernel depends on the presence of a real-time clock or interval timer to maintain the current time of day, to drive process scheduling, and to initiate the execution of system timeout functions. Hardware interrupts occur *asynchronously* and rarely relate to the context of the process that is currently executing. Hardware traps, on the other hand, usually are unexpected, but *are* related to the current executing process. Examples of hardware traps are those generated as a result of incorrect arithmetic calculations, such as dividing by zero. Finally, software-initiated traps or interrupts are used by the system to force the scheduling of a system activity at an opportune time. An example of this type of event is the *asynchronous system trap* (AST) that is posted by the system while it is executing in kernel mode, but that is not delivered until user mode is reentered. (ASTs are used to force process rescheduling.)

Run-Time Organization

The run-time structure of the kernel is divided into a *top half* and a *bottom half*, as shown in Fig. 3.1. The top half of the kernel provides services to applications in response to system calls or traps. This software can be thought of as a library of routines that are shared among all UNIX processes. The top half of the kernel executes in a privileged execution mode in which it has access both to kernel data structures and to the context of the user-level process that it supports. Each process has an area of memory reserved for process-specific information used by the kernel when the process accesses system services. This information includes a small stack for use by the kernel while executing system calls for the process. Below this stack is the *user area* that contains long-term information about the state of the process. This information includes the unique identifiers associated with the process. It also records information about the maximum and current resource utilization and about the rights and privileges associated with the

Figure 3.1 Run-time structure of the kernel.

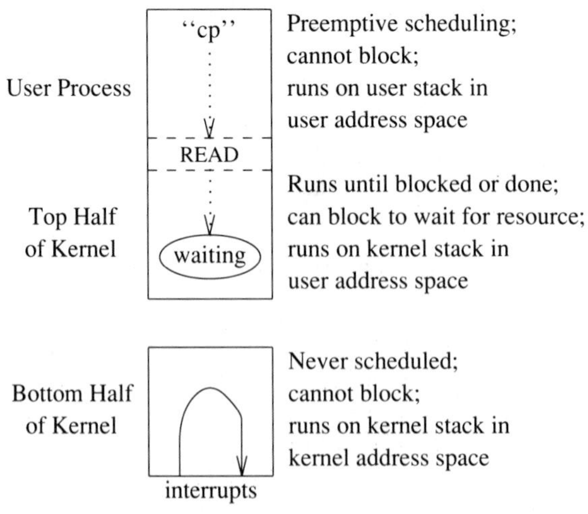

process. Pending and future external events are recorded in the user area, along with the action to take when they are ready to be delivered to the process. Finally, the user area records all the descriptors held by the process.

The bottom half of the kernel is a collection of routines that are invoked to handle hardware interrupts and traps that are unrelated to the current process. Interrupts may be delivered by I/O devices or by other hardware devices, such as a real-time clock. The kernel assumes that interrupts are prioritized at least to the extent that hardware facilities are available to block the delivery of interrupts. Whereas the VAX assumes there are distinct hardware priority levels for different kinds of interrupts, 4BSD also runs on architectures such as the Perkin Elmer, where interrupts are all at the same priority, or the ELXSI, where there are no interrupts in the traditional sense.

Activities in the bottom half of the kernel occur *asynchronously*, and the software cannot depend on having a specific process running at the time of an interrupt. In particular, some per-process state may not be available, and the run-time stack used by the top half of the kernel should not be altered by routines in the bottom half. Instead, the bottom half of the kernel typically runs on a system-wide *interrupt stack*.

The kernel is never preempted to run another process while executing the code to do a system call. Its execution may be interrupted, however, by activities done by the bottom half of the kernel. It must explicitly give up the processor to wait for a resource or run to completion. The top half can block entry to routines in the bottom half of the kernel by setting the *processor priority level* to a value that blocks out the appropriate interrupts. This mechanism is used, for example, to ensure the consistency of data structures shared between the top and bottom halves.

Processes cooperate in the sharing of system resources, such as the CPU. The top half of the kernel can voluntarily relinquish control of the processor when it must wait for an event or for access to a shared resource. The top and bottom halves of the kernel also work together in implementing certain system operations, such as I/O. Typically, the top half will start an I/O operation, relinquish the processor, and then wait for notification from the bottom half when the I/O request has completed.

System Processes

All UNIX processes originate from a single process that is handcrafted by the kernel at startup. Three processes are always expected to exist. Two of these processes, termed *kernel processes*, function wholly within the kernel. Kernel processes execute code that is compiled into the kernel's load image and operate with the kernel's privileged execution mode. The third process is the first process to execute a program in user mode; it serves as the parent process to all subsequent processes.

The two kernel processes are termed the *swapper* and the *pagedaemon*. The *swapper*, historically process 0, is responsible for scheduling the transfer of whole processes between main memory and secondary storage when system resources are low. The *pagedaemon*, process 2, is specific to Berkeley versions of UNIX and is responsible for writing parts of the address space of a process to secondary storage in support of the paging facilities of the virtual-memory system. The third process created by the system is the *init* process (process 1). This process performs administrative tasks such as spawning login processes for each terminal on a machine and handling the orderly shutdown of a system from multiuser to single-user operation. The actions of the *init* process are embodied in a program that is independent of the kernel (see Section 13.4).

Entry to the Kernel

When a process enters the kernel through a system call, a trap, or an interrupt, the kernel must first ensure that it saves all the machine state before it begins to service the event. For the VAX, the machine state that must be saved includes the 16 general-purpose registers and the processor status longword. If the machine state were not fully saved, the kernel would change values in the currently executing program in unexpected and improper ways. Since interrupts may occur between any two user-level instructions, and because they may be completely unrelated to the currently executing process, incompletely saved state would cause otherwise correct programs to fail in mysterious and unreproduceable ways even while not doing system calls.

The exact sequence of events required to save the process state is highly machine-dependent, although the VAX provides a good example of the general procedure. When a trap or system call occurs, the following events occur:

- The hardware switches into kernel mode, so that memory-access checks are made with kernel privilege, references to the stack pointer use the kernel's stack pointer, and privileged instructions can be executed.
- The program counter and processor status longword are pushed onto the per-process kernel stack.
- A code showing the type of trap (or system call number) is pushed onto the stack.
- An assembly-language routine saves the general-purpose registers.

This preliminary state saving allows the kernel then to call a C routine that can freely use the machine registers as any other C routine would, without concern about destroying an unsuspecting process's state. There are several major kinds of handlers, corresponding to particular kinds of kernel entries:

- *Syscall*() for a system call
- *Trap*() for a trap
- An appropriate device-driver interrupt handler for a device interrupt

The parameters to the handler include the user's stack pointer, the program counter, and the code showing the trap type.

Return from the Kernel

On completion of its task, the handler returns. An assembly-language routine then restores the register state and executes a *return from interrupt* instruction. The *return from interrupt* instruction reverses the process of entering the kernel by

- Restoring the program counter and program status longword previously pushed onto the stack
- Changing to user mode, so that future references to the stack pointer use the user's stack pointer, privileged instructions may not be executed, and memory-access checks are done with user-level privilege

Execution resumes at the next instruction in the user's process.

3.2 System Calls

The most frequent trap into the kernel (after clock processing) is a request to do a system call. Good performance requires the kernel to minimize the overhead in fielding and dispatching a system call. The system-call dispatcher must do the following work to initiate a system call:

- Look up the number of parameters in the system call
- Verify that the parameters are located at a valid user address, then copy them from the user process into the kernel
- Prepare for the possibility of an interrupted system call
- Call a specific kernel routine to do the system call

Result Handling

Eventually, a system call returns to the calling process, either successfully or unsuccessfully. On the VAX, success or failure is indicated by the carry bit in the user process's program status longword: If it is zero, the return was successful; else, it was unsuccessful. On the VAX and many other machines, return values of C functions are passed back through general-purpose register 0. On a successful system call, the kernel system-call handler replaces the saved value of that register with a return value. On an unsuccessful call, the system-call handler takes an error code from the kernel variable *u.u_error* (where it has been left by deeper kernel routines for that system call) and puts that code in the register—this is a place where the kernel deliberately modifies the state of a process. The system call C library routine moves that value to the global variable *errno* and sets the register to −1. The calling process is supposed to notice the value of the register and then examine *errno* on an error. This mechanism involving the carry bit and the global variable *errno* exists for historical reasons derived from the PDP-11.

There are two kinds of unsuccessful returns from a system call: those where kernel system-call–handling routines discover an error, and those where a system call is interrupted. A system call can be interrupted when it has relinquished the processor to wait for an event that may not occur for a long time (such as waiting for terminal input), and a signal arrives in the interim. Before the signal can be posted, the system call must be aborted by doing a nonlocal goto back to the dispatcher. When signal handlers are set up by a process, they must specify whether system calls that they interrupt should be restarted, or aborted with an *interrupted system call* error.

The dispatcher determines what to do when the nonlocal goto occurs, by examining a per-process global variable. If the process has requested that the system call be aborted, the dispatcher arranges to return an error, as described previously. If the system call is to be restarted, however, the dispatcher calculates how to make the process's program counter point to the machine instruction that caused the system-call trap into the kernel. This calculation is necessary because the program-counter value that was saved when the system-call trap was done is for the beginning of the system-call result-handling code. The dispatcher replaces the saved program-counter value with the newly calculated value. The next time the process is scheduled, it will be forced to handle the signal. When it returns from its signal handler, it will then resume at the program-counter value that the dispatcher provided, so the process will reexecute the same system call.

Restarting a system call by backing up the program counter has certain implications. Most important is that the kernel must ensure that it does not modify any of the input parameters. Second, it must ensure that the system call has not partially completed. For example, if a partial line has been read from the terminal, the read must return with a short count. If the call were restarted, the partially read line would be inappropriately overwritten.

Returning from a System Call

While the system call is running, a signal may be posted to the process, or another process may attain a higher scheduling priority. After the system call completes, the dispatcher checks to see whether either of these events has occurred.

The dispatcher first checks for a posted signal. These include signals that caused the system call to abort, as well as signals that arrived while a system call was in progress, but were held pending while the system call completed. Signals that are ignored either by default or by an explicit setting are never posted to the process. Signals that have a default action have that action taken before the process is able to run again (i.e., the process is killed or stopped as appropriate). If a signal is to be caught (and is not currently blocked), the dispatcher arranges to have the appropriate signal handler called rather than have the process return directly from the system call. Only after the handler returns normally will the process resume execution at system-call return (or system-call execution, if the system call is to be restarted).

After checking for posted signals, the dispatcher checks to see whether another process has a higher priority than does the currently running one. If such a process exists, the dispatcher calls the context-switch routine to arrange to have the higher-priority process run. At a later time, the current process will attain the highest priority, and will resume execution by returning from the system call to the user process.

If a process has requested the system to do profiling, the dispatcher calculates the amount of time that has been spent in the system call. The time is calculated by taking the difference in system time accounted to the process between its entry and exit from the dispatcher. The system time is charged to the routine in the user's process that did the system call.

3.3 Traps and Interrupts

Traps, like system calls, occur synchronously for a process. Traps can occur because of unintentional errors, such as division by zero, or because of indirection through an invalid pointer; the process is made aware of the problem either by catching a signal or by being terminated. Traps can also occur because of a page fault, in which case the system arranges to make the page available and then restarts the process without the process ever being aware that the fault occurred.

The trap handler is invoked like the system-call dispatcher. First, the process state is saved. Next, the trap handler determines the trap type, then arranges to post a signal or to cause a page-in as appropriate. Finally, it checks for pending signals and exits identically to the system-call handler.

I/O Device Interrupts

Interrupts from I/O devices are handled by *device-driver* modules that are included in the kernel at the time a system is built. Interrupts from other devices are handled by interrupt routines that are a standard part of the kernel. These routines handle a console terminal interface, a real-time clock, and several software-initiated interrupts used by the system for low-priority clock processing and for the networking facilities.

Unlike traps and system calls that are executed synchronously by a process, device interrupts occur asynchronously. Usually, the process that started the operation that eventually caused the interrupt is not even running. As with traps and system calls, the entire machine state must be saved, since any inadvertent changes would cause irreproducible errors in the currently running process. Notification to the process that requested the service must be done by requesting that it be run; it will then notice that the operation that it started has finished.

Device-interrupt handlers run only on demand; they are never scheduled by the kernel. Unlike system calls, interrupt handlers do not have a per-process context. Interrupt handlers cannot depend on using any of the context of the currently running process (i.e., the process's user structure). The stack normally used by the kernel is part of a process context. On some systems, interrupts are caught on the unused part of the kernel stack of whichever process is currently running. This approach requires that all the per-process kernel stacks be large enough to handle both a system call and the deepest nesting of interrupts. On the VAX, there is a single interrupt stack used by all device interrupts. When an interrupt occurs, the hardware switches to the interrupt stack before beginning to handle the interrupt. Having a separate interrupt stack allows the per-process kernel stacks to be sized based on only the requirements for handling a synchronous trap or system call.

Whether the interrupt is handled on the current per-process stack or on a separate interrupt stack, the interrupt handler cannot use that stack to save state between invocations. An interrupt handler must obtain and save all needed information from its global work queue. Because it does not have a per-process context, it cannot relinquish the processor to wait for resources, and must instead run to completion and return.

Software Interrupts

Many events in the kernel are driven by hardware interrupts. For high-speed devices such as network controllers, these interrupts occur at a high priority. For a network controller, it is important to acknowledge receipt of a packet and quickly to reenable the controller to accept another packet, to avoid losing closely spaced packets. However, the further processing of passing the packet to its destination process, although often time consuming, need not be done quickly. Thus, a lower priority is desirable for the further processing, so that critical operations are not blocked from executing for too long.

The mechanism for doing lower-priority processing is called a *software-interrupt process*. Typically, a high-priority interrupt creates a queue of work to be done at a lower-priority level. After queueing a work request, the high-priority interrupt posts a request for a function to be run at the lower-priority level. When the machine priority drops below the lower priority, an interrupt is generated that calls the requested function. If a higher-priority interrupt comes in while the function is executing, the function is preempted while the high-priority event occurs.

The delivery of network packets to destination processes is handled by a packet-processing function that runs at low priority. As packets come in, they are put onto a work queue and the controller is reenabled. Between packet arrivals, the packet-receiving function works to deliver the packets. Thus, the controller can accept new packets without having to wait for the previous packet to be delivered. In addition to network processing, software interrupts are used to handle time-related events and process rescheduling.

3.4 Clock Interrupts

The system is driven by a clock that interrupts at regular intervals. Each interrupt is referred to as a *tick*. On the VAX, the clock ticks 100 times per second. These ticks are used to force context switches so that all processes can get a share of the

CPU. At each tick, the system collects statistics about what is happening at that instant, which can be used to do accounting, to monitor what the system is doing, and to determine future scheduling priorities. These interrupts are also used to drive timers both within the system and externally in user processes.

Interrupts for clock ticks are posted at a high hardware-interrupt priority. After the process state has been saved, the *hardclock*() routine is called. It is important that the *hardclock*() routine finish its job quickly.

- If *hardclock*() runs for more than 0.01 second, it will miss its next interrupt.
- Since *hardclock*() maintains the time of day for the system, lost ticks mean that the system will slowly lose track of time.
- Because of the high interrupt priority, while *hardclock*() is running, nearly all other activity on the system is blocked. This blocking can cause network controllers to miss packets, or a disk controller to miss the transfer of a sector coming under a disk drive's head.

To minimize the time spent in *hardclock*(), time-consuming but less time critical processing is handled by a lower-priority software-interrupt handler called *softclock*().

The work done by *hardclock*() is as follows:

- Charge the currently running process with a tick; if the process has accumulated four ticks, recalculate its priority. If it has a real-time timer or a profiling timer (see Section 3.5), decrement the timer and post a signal if expired. If the current process is over its CPU time limit, post a SIGXCPU signal to the process.
- Increment the time-of-day clock.
- Collect statistics on what the system was doing at the time of the tick (idle, executing in user mode, or executing in system mode).

The remaining time-related processing involves processing timeout requests and periodically reprioritizing processes that are ready to run. These functions are handled by the *softclock*() routine. When *hardclock*() finishes, it checks to see whether there are any *softclock*() functions to be done. If there are, it schedules a softclock interrupt. As an optimization, *hardclock*() checks to see whether the state of the processor is such that the *softclock*() interrupt will occur as soon as the hardclock interrupt returns. If so, *hardclock*() explicitly lowers the processor priority and calls *softclock*() directly, thus avoiding the cost of returning from one interrupt and immediately reentering another interrupt. Because interrupts are expensive, and because these interrupts occur 100 times per second, the savings add up substantially over time.

Timeouts

The primary task of the *softclock*() routine is to arrange for the execution of periodic events, such as

- Network retransmission timers
- Watchdog timers on peripherals that require constant monitoring
- System-scheduling events

The data structure that describes the set of events is called the *callout queue*. Figure 3.2 shows a snapshot of the callout queue. When a process wishes to request a future event, it specifies a function to be called, an argument to be passed to the function when the event occurs, and the number of clock ticks in the future that the event should occur.

The queue is sorted in the order that the events are to occur; events to happen soonest are at the front, and the most distant events are at the end. The time for each event is kept as a difference from the time of the previous event on the queue. Thus, the *hardclock*() routine needs only to decrement the time to expire of the first element of the queue to decrement time for all events. The *softclock*() routine removes events from the front of the queue whose time has decremented to zero until it finds an event with a still-future (positive) time. Events are typically posted much less frequently than 100 times per second that ticks must be processed and the queue checked to see whether any events are to occur. Thus, it is more efficient to identify the proper location to place an event when that event is posted than it would be to scan the entire queue to determine which events should occur.

The reason for providing an argument as well as a function to be called is to allow a single function to be used by multiple processes. For example, the real-time timer function may be used by several different processes. There is a single function that receives acknowledgment that a timer has expired and that sends a signal to a process. Each process that has a real-time timer running will post a timeout request for this function. The argument that is passed to the function is a pointer to the process-table entry for the process requesting the timeout. This pointer enables the timeout function to post the signal properly. The alternative would require a unique function name for each process that wished to post a real-time timeout.

Timeout processing is more efficient when the timeouts are specified in ticks. Time updates require only an integer decrement, and checks for timer expiration require only a comparison against zero. If the timers contained time values, the comparing and decrementing would be more complex, at least in requiring the

Figure 3.2 Timer events in the callout queue. Ms—milliseconds.

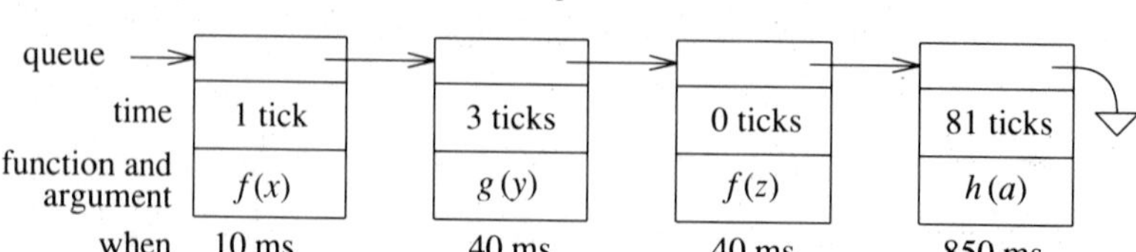

decrement to be by some constant other than one. When the number of events that must be managed gets large, the cost of linear searching to place new events can dominate the simple linear queue used in 4.3BSD. Other possible approaches include maintaining a heap with the next occurring event at the top, and maintaining separate queues of short-, medium- and long-term events [Barkley & Lee, 1988; Varghese & Lauck, 1987].

Process Scheduling

The clock routine is responsible for accumulating CPU time to processes. In addition, it is responsible for periodically running the scheduler that raises and lowers the CPU priority for each process in the system based on the processes recent CPU usage (see Section 4.4). The rescheduling calculation is done once per second. The scheduler is started at boot time. Each time that it runs, it posts itself onto the timeout queue 1 second in the future.

On a heavily loaded system with many processes, the scheduler may take a long time to complete its job. Its timeout is posted 1 second after the completion of the scheduling task. On such a system, the scheduling will occur less frequently than once per second. Since the scheduler is not responsible for any time-critical functions, such as maintaining the time of day, this is not a problem.

3.5 Timing

The kernel provides several different timing services to processes. These services include timers that run in real time and timers that run only while a process is executing.

Real Time

The system's notion of the current Universal Coordinated Time (UTC) and the current time zone is returned by the system call *gettimeofday*. Most processors today, including all the VAX processors, maintain a battery-backup time-of-day register. This clock continues to run even if the processor is powered down. When the system boots, it consults the processor's time-of-day register to find out the current time. The system's time is then maintained by the hardclock interrupts. At each interrupt, the system increments its global time variable by an amount equal to the number of microseconds per tick. For the VAX running at 100 ticks per second, each tick represents 10,000 microseconds. If the system loses hardclock interrupts, its internal clock will slow. For this behavior to be avoided, the clock must interrupt at high priority, and must finish its job quickly.

Adjusting the Time

Often, it is desirable to maintain the same time on all the machines on a network. It is also possible to have more accurate time than that available from the basic processor clock. For example, devices are readily available that listen to WWV, the set of radio stations that broadcast UTC synchronization signals in the United States. A set of processes communicating over the network can arrange to agree on a common time. They then wish to change the clock on their host processor to agree with the networkwide timebase. One alternative is to set the system time to the network time using the *settimeofday* system call. For machines whose clocks were fast, this would result in time running backward. This would confuse user programs (such as **make**) that expect time to be nondecreasing. To avoid this problem, the system provides an *adjtime* system call to adjust the time [Gusella *et al.*, 1986]. The system call takes a time delta either positive or negative, and changes the rate at which time advances by 10 percent, faster or slower, respectively, until the adjustment has been effected. The speedup is done through incrementation of the global time by 11,000 microseconds on each hardclock tick; the slowdown is done through incrementation of the global time by 9000 microseconds on each hardclock tick. In either case, time monotonically increases, so user processes that depend on ordering of file-modification times are not adversely affected. Time changes that take tens of seconds to adjust will affect programs that are measuring time intervals by using repeated calls to *gettimeofday*.

External Representation

The kernel maintains its internal time as microseconds since January 1, 1970, UTC. Time is always exported from the system as microseconds rather than as clock ticks, to provide a resolution-independent format. Internally, the kernel is free to select whatever tick rate is desirable to trade off clock overhead with timer resolution. As the tick rate per second increases, the time spent in fielding hardclock interrupts increases. However, the higher the tick rate, the finer the resolution of the system timers. As processors become faster, the tick rate can be increased to provide finer resolution without adversely affecting any existing user applications.

The system has a compiled-in value that specifies in what time zone the machine resides, and a magic number specifying whether and what algorithm to use to calculate daylight saving time. Internally, all timestamps are maintained in UTC. Conversion to local time is handled externally to the system in the C library. There is a library routine that requests the time zone and daylight-saving-time algorithm number from the kernel. This C library routine is responsible for converting kernel timestamps according to local conventions.

There are problems with traditional UNIX time-zone handling, including that in 4.3BSD. Because the rules are compiled into the C library, they are unchangeable on binary distributions, and are difficult to change in source distributions. The compiled-in ruleset is not complete or accurate for many places where UNIX systems are used. In 4.3BSD, it is also not possible for a user to set the desired time zone per process.

The Olson time-zone–handling method (see Section 1.2) that CSRG first released in the 4.3BSD Tahoe release avoids these problems by putting the rules in database files and allowing individual processes to select a set of rules by specifying a ruleset. This method is extremely flexible, being able to account for multiple rule changes in the same year (e.g., the proposed U.S. presidential election time, by which the West Coast moves ahead 3 hours for 1 day only), for offsets of more than 1 hour (double daylight saving time, as used in World War II) or less (as in Newfoundland), and even for solar time (as in Saudi Arabia). Offsets are still done in seconds, however, as even solar time does not require higher precision. Missing rules can be added at the destination, as can later real-world changes to time-zone rules (which happen frequently and with little notice).

Interval Time

The system provides each process with three interval timers. The *real* timer decrements in real time. It could be used by a library routine to maintain a wakeup-service queue. A SIGALRM signal is delivered when this timer expires. As discussed in Section 3.1, the real-time timer is run from the timeout queue maintained by the *softclock*() routine.

Profiling

The *profiling* timer decrements both in process virtual time (when running in user mode) and when the system is running for the process. It is designed to be used by processes to profile their execution statistically. A SIGPROF signal is delivered when the profiling timer expires. The profiling timer is implemented by the *hardclock*() routine. Each time it is run, it checks to see whether the currently running process has requested a profiling timer; if so, *hardclock*() increments the timer, and, if the timer interval is reached, sends the process a signal.

The *virtual* timer decrements in process virtual time. It runs only when the process is executing in user mode. A SIGVTALRM signal is delivered when it expires. The virtual timer is implemented in *hardclock*() exactly as the profiling timer is, except that it increments the timer for the current process only if it is executing in user mode, not if it is running in the kernel.

Normally, all time-oriented events in the system run off the same clock. Thus, statistics gathering occurs at the same time as rescheduling. This can lead to anomalous statistics, particularly for processes that are driven off system-generated timer events. To allow the collection of more accurate statistics, the kernel supports a second profiling clock. When a second clock is available, it is set to run at a tick rate that is relatively prime to the main system clock (109 ticks per second on the VAX). The statistics gathering is then done by the alternate clock, whereas the timing and scheduling are still done by the original clock.

3.6 Process Management

The memory organization and layout associated with a UNIX process is shown in Fig. 3.3. Each process begins execution with three memory segments, called text, data, and stack. The data segment is divided into initialized data and uninitialized

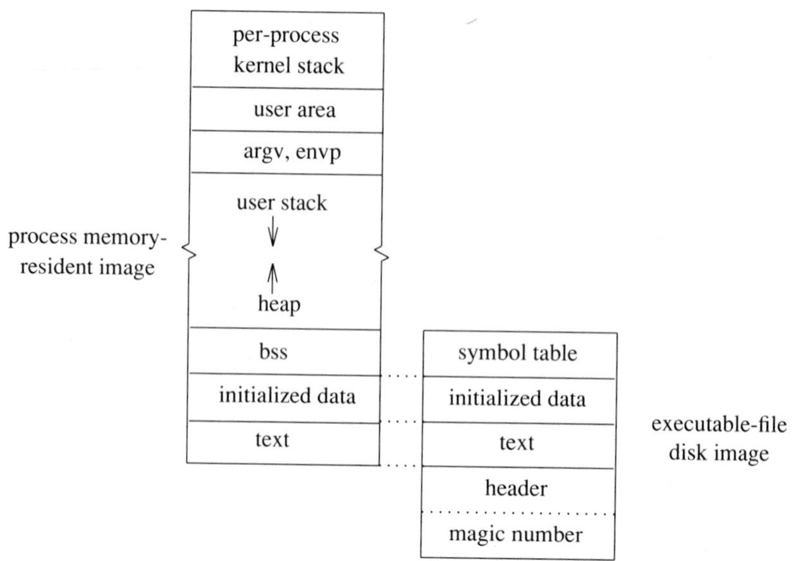

Figure 3.3 Layout of a UNIX process in memory and on disk.

data (bss). The text is read-only and is shared while the data and stack areas are private to the process.

The text and initialized data for the process are taken from the file named when the process is executed. An executable file is distinguished by its being a plain file (not a directory, special file, or symbolic link) and by its having one or more execute bits set. The first few bytes of the file (the first four bytes on the VAX) contain a *magic number* that specifies what type of executable file that file is. Executable files fall into two major classes:

1. Files that are directly executable

2. Files that must be executed by an interpreter

For interpreted files, the magic number is the two-character sequence **#!** followed by a string specifying the pathname of the interpreter to be used. For example, **#!/bin/sh** might refer to the Bourne shell. The kernel executes the named program, passing the name of the file that is to be interpreted as an argument. To prevent loops, only one level of interpretation is allowed; a file's interpreter may not itself be interpreted.

Other files are directly executable. The magic number of such a file specifies whether it can be paged and whether the text part of the file can be shared among multiple processes. Following the magic number is an *exec* header that specifies the sizes of text, initialized data, uninitialized data, and some additional information for debugging. Following the header is an image of the text followed by an image of the initialized data. Uninitialized data are not contained in the executable file, as they can be created with zero-filled memory. The debugging information is not used by the kernel or by the executing program.

To begin execution, the kernel arranges to have the text portion of the file mapped into the low part of the process address space. The initialized data portion of the file is mapped into the address space following the text. An area equal to the uninitialized data region is created with zero-filled memory after the initialized data region. The stack is also created from zero-filled memory. Although the stack should not need to be zero filled, early UNIX systems made it so. In an attempt to save some startup time, the kernel was modified to skip the zero filling of the stack, leaving the random previous contents of the page instead. Numerous programs stopped working because they depended on the local variables in their *main* procedure being initialized to zero. Consequently, the zero filling of the stack was restored.

Copying the entire text and initialized data portion of a large program into memory causes a long startup latency. We can avoid this startup time by *demand paging* the program into memory rather than preloading it. In demand paging, the program is loaded in small pieces (pages) as it is needed, rather than all at once before it begins execution. The system does demand paging by dividing up the address space into equal-sized pages. For each page, the kernel records the offset into the executable file of the corresponding data. The first access to an address on each page causes a page-fault trap into the kernel. The page-fault handler reads the correct page of the executable file into the process memory. Thus, the kernel loads only those parts of the executable file that are really needed. Chapter 5 explains paging details.

The uninitialized data area may be extended with zero-filled pages through use of the system call *sbrk*, although most user processes use the library routine *malloc*() for this purpose (*malloc*() calls *sbrk*). This newly allocated memory, starting from the top of the original data segment, is called the *heap*. On the VAX, the stack grows down from the top of memory, whereas the heap grows up from the bottom of memory.

Above the user stack is an area of memory that is created by the system when the process is started. Directly above the user stack is the process environment vector (*envp*) and the argument vector (*argv*) set up when the program was executed. At the top of user memory is the user area (**u.**) and the per-process kernel stack. In 4.3BSD, the user address space also contains the user-mode execution state of a process. The execution state is saved on each entry into the kernel, and is restored on each exit. The user area is visible at the top of the user address space because it is used in the implementation of signal handling on the VAX; ports of 4BSD to other hardware may not have this arrangement.

In addition to the information maintained in the user area, a process also requires the use of some global system resources. The kernel maintains a *process table* that contains an entry for each process created in the system. Among other things, the process table records information on scheduling and on virtual-memory allocation. Because the entire process address space, including the user area, may be swapped out of main memory, the process table must record enough information to be able to locate the user area and to bring the latter back into memory. The scheduling information is maintained in the process table rather than in the user area to avoid swapping in the process only to decide that it is not at a high-enough priority to be run. Similarly, information about events that the process wants to ignore are stored in the process table.

Other global resources associated with a process include space in tables to record information about descriptors, page tables that record information about physical-memory utilization, and space in the text table that coordinates the sharing of common texts.

3.7 User and Group Identifiers

There are a number of objects in a UNIX system that must be identifiable so that the kernel can implement access-control mechanisms. The most important of these objects is a *user*. Users are identified by a 16-bit number termed a *user identifier* (UID). UIDs are not assigned by the kernel—they are assigned by an outside administrative authority. UIDs are the basis for accounting, for controlling the use of disk space, for accessing the filesystem, and for restricting access to sundry privileged kernel operations, such as the request used to reboot a running system. A single user, termed the *superuser* (also known by the user name *root*), is trusted by the system and is permitted to do any kernel operation it requests (with certain exceptions—even the superuser cannot write to a directory or link to an existing file). The superuser has a UID of zero.

Users are organized into *groups*. Each group is assigned a 16-bit number called a *group identifier* (GID), presumably by the same authority that assigns UIDs. GIDs, like UIDs, are used in the access-control facilities provided by the filesystem. UIDs are also used in deciding to what processes a signal may be sent, and in accounting. GIDs are normally used only in determining filesystem-access permissions.

Every UNIX process is associated with a user. The state of the process includes a UID and a set of GIDs. A process's filesystem-access privileges are completely defined by the UID and GIDs of the process (for the filesystem hierarchy beginning at the process's root directory). Normally, these identifiers are inherited automatically from the parent process when a new process is created. Only the superuser is permitted to alter the UID and GID of a process. This scheme by itself enforces a strict compartmentalization of privileges and ensures that no user other than the superuser can *gain* privileges.

Groups may be used in file-access validation. Each file has three sets of permission bits, for read, write, or execute permission for each of user, group, and other. These are checked in order:

1. If the UID of the file is the same as the UID of the process, only the owner permissions apply; the group and other permissions are not checked.

2. If the UIDs do not match, but the GID of the file matches one of the GIDs of the process, the group permissions must allow the requested operation. The other permissions are not checked.

3. Only if the UID and GIDs of the process fail to match those of the file are the permissions for all others checked. These permissions must allow the requested operation.

The UID and GIDs for a process are inherited from that process's parent. When a user logs in, the login program (see Section 13.4) sets the UID and GIDs before performing the *exec* system call to run the user's login shell. All processes run from the login shell therefore inherit the appropriate identifiers. The UID and GIDs are maintained in the user area.

GIDs are implemented as one distinguished GID and a supplementary array of GIDs. The supplementary array is of a fixed size (16 in 4.3BSD), that is settable at the time the system is compiled. Two separate data structures were used to avoid changing existing source code; logically, they are treated as one set of GIDs.

Often, it is desirable to grant a user certain privileges in a constrained manner. For example, a user who wants to send mail must be able to append the mail to another user's mailbox. Making the target mailbox writable by all users would permit a user other than its owner to destroy messages in it (whether maliciously or unintentionally). To solve this problem, the kernel allows the creation of programs that are granted additional privileges when they are run. Programs that run with an additional group privilege are called *set-group-identifier* (setgid) programs; programs that run with a different UID are called *set-user-identifier* (setuid) programs [Ritchie, 1979]. When a setuid program is executed, the permissions of the process are augmented to include those of the UID associated with the program. The UID of the program is termed the *effective UID* of the process, whereas the original UID of the process is termed the *real UID*. Similarly, executing a setgid program augments a process's permissions with those of the program's GID and the *effective GID* and *real GID* are defined accordingly.

Setuid and setgid programs can be used, for example, to provide controlled access to files or services. The program that delivers mail runs with the privileges of the superuser that can write to any file in the system. Thus, users need not be given the privilege to write other users' mailboxes, but can still do so by running this program, which has been carefully written to append data to mailboxes without colliding with other mail deliveries and without deleting any existing messages.

The setgid capability is implemented by addition of the group of the file to the supplementary groups of the process that executed the setgid program. Permissions can then be checked as with a normal process. Because of the additional group, the setgid program usually will be able to access more files than can a user process that runs a program without the special privilege.

The setuid capability is implemented by the effective UID of the process being changed from that of the user to that of the program being executed. As with setgid, the protection mechanism will now permit access without any change or special knowledge that the program is running setuid. Since a process can have only a single UID at a time, it may lose some privilege in running setuid. The previous UID is still held as the real UID when the new effective UID is installed. The real UID, however, is not used for any validation checking. Processes that need to use both the original UID privilege and the setuid privilege can ask the system to swap the real and effective UIDs. The protection mechanism uses whichever identifier is currently installed as the effective UID.

Host Identifier

Two additional identifiers are defined by the kernel for use on machines operating in a networked environment. A 32-bit *host identifier* and a string specifying a host's name are maintained by the kernel. These values are intended to be defined uniquely for each machine in a network. Use of the host identifier permits applications easily to craft networkwide unique identifiers for objects such as processes, files, and users, by concatenating the local identifier for the object with the host identifier. The ability to generate networkwide unique identifiers can be useful in the construction of distributed applications [Gifford, 1981]. The host identifier and host name for a machine are defined outside the kernel.

3.8 Resource Controls

All systems have limits imposed by their hardware architecture and configuration; to ensure reasonable operation, these limits must not be exceeded. At a minimum, the hardware limits must be imposed on processes that run on the system. Sometimes, it may be desirable to limit processes further, below these hardware-imposed limits. The system measures resource utilization and allows limits to be imposed on consumption either at or below the hardware-imposed limits.

Process Priorities

The system gives CPU scheduling priority to processes that have not used CPU time recently. This priority scheme tends to favor interactive processes and processes that execute for only short periods. The priority selected for each process is maintained internally by the kernel. The calculation of the priority is affected by the per-process *nice* variable. Positive *nice* values mean that the process is willing to receive less than its share of the processor. Negative values of *nice* mean that the process should be given more than its share of the processor. Most processes run with the default *nice* of zero which gives neither higher nor lower access to the processor. It is possible to determine or change the *nice* currently assigned to a process, to a process group, or to the processes of a specified user. There are many other factors besides the *nice* that affect scheduling. These include the amount of CPU time that the process has used recently, the amount of memory that the process has used recently, and the current load on the system. The exact algorithms that are used are described in Section 4.4.

Resource Utilization

As a process executes, it uses system resources, such as the CPU and memory. The kernel tracks the resources used by each process and compiles statistics describing this usage. The statistics managed by the kernel are available to a process while the latter is executing; when the process terminates, the statistics are made available to its parent.

The resources used by a process are returned by the system call *getrusage*. The resources used by the current process, or by all the terminated children of the current process, may be requested. This information includes

- The amount of user and system time used by the process
- The memory utilization of the process
- The paging and disk I/O activity of the process
- The number of voluntary and involuntary context switches taken by the process
- The amount of interprocess communication done by the process

The resource-usage information is collected at locations throughout the kernel. The CPU time is collected at each tick in *hardclock*(). The kernel calculates memory utilization by sampling the amount of memory an active process is using each second. The scheduler does memory sampling at the same time that it is recomputing process priorities. The *pagein*() routine recalculates the paging activity each time it starts a disk transfer to fulfill a paging request (see Section 5.11). The I/O activity statistics are collected each time the process has to start a transfer to fulfill a file or device I/O request. The IPC communication activity is counted each time a packet is sent through the socket interface.

Resource Limits

The kernel controls the usage of certain per-process resources. These controls include

- The maximum amount of CPU time that can be accumulated
- The maximum size of a file that can be created
- The maximum size of a process's data segment
- The maximum size of a process's stack segment
- The maximum size of a core file
- The maximum amount of physical memory a process may use at any given moment.

For each resource controlled by the kernel, two limits are maintained: a *soft limit* and a *hard limit*. Only the superuser can raise a hard limit. Other users may alter a soft limit within the range from 0 to the corresponding hard limit, or (irreversibly) may only lower the hard limit. If a process exceeds some soft limits, the kernel delivers a signal to the process to notify it that a resource limit has been exceeded. Normally, this signal causes the process to terminate, but the process may elect to catch or ignore the signal.

The limits are enforced at the same locations that the resource statistics are collected. The CPU time limit is enforced in *hardclock*(). The physical-memory limit is enforced by *pageout*(). While a process exceeds its limit for physical memory, the *pageout*() routine will take any page that it finds away from the process. The stack and data-segment limits are enforced by a return of allocation failure once those limits have been reached. The file-size limit is enforced by the filesystem. Once the file-size limit is reached, the process is sent a signal. The default action is to kill the process. If the process catches or ignores the signal and attempts to continue writing, it will get error returns.

Filesystem Quotas

In addition to limits on the size of individual files, the kernel will also enforce limits on the total amount of space that a user can utilize on a filesystem. Our discussion of the implementation of these limits is deferred to Section 7.6.

3.9 System Operation

There are several operational functions having to do with system startup and shutdown. The bootstrapping operations are described in Section 13.2. System shutdown is described in Section 13.5.

Accounting

The system supports a simple form of resource accounting. As each process terminates, an accounting record describing the resources used by that process is written to a systemwide accounting file. The information supplied by the system comprises

- The name of the command that ran
- The amount of user and system CPU time that was used
- The elapsed time the command ran
- The average amount of memory used
- The number of disk I/O operations done
- The UID and GID of the process
- The terminal from which the process was started

The information in the accounting record is drawn from the run-time statistics that were described in Section 3.8. The granularity of the time fields is in sixty-fourths of a second. To conserve space in the accounting file, the times are stored in a 16-bit word as a *floating-point* number using three bits as a base-8 exponent, and the other 13 bits as the fractional part. For historic reasons, the same floating-point conversion routine processes the count of disk operations. Thus, the number of disk operations is multiplied by 64 before it is converted to the floating-point representation.

There are also Boolean flags that tell how the process terminated, whether it used superuser privileges, and whether it used *exec* after *fork*.

The superuser requests accounting by passing a name for the accounting file to the kernel. As part of terminating a process, the kernel appends an accounting record to the accounting file. The kernel makes no use of the accounting records; the records' summaries and usage are entirely the domain of user-level accounting programs. As a guard against running out of space on a filesystem due to unchecked growth of the accounting file, the system suspends accounting when the filesystem is reduced to only 2 percent free space. Accounting resumes when the filesystem has at least 4 percent free space.

The accounting information has certain limitations. The information on run time and memory usage is only approximate, because it is gathered statistically. Accounting information is written only when a process exits, so processes that are still running when a system is shut down unexpectedly do not show up in the accounting file. These unaccounted processes include all the long-lived system daemons. Finally, the accounting records fail to include much information that is needed to do accurate billing. The missing information includes usage of other resources, such as tape drives, printers, and network communication.

Exercises

3.1 Describe three types of system activity.

3.2 When can a routine executing in the top half of the kernel be preempted? When can it be interrupted?

3.3 Why are routines executing in the bottom half of the kernel precluded from using information located in the user area?

3.4 Why does the system defer as much work as possible from high-priority interrupts to lower-priority software-interrupt processes?

3.5 What determines the shortest (nonzero) time period that a user process can request when setting a timer?

3.6 How does the kernel determine the system call for which it has been invoked?

3.7 How are initialized data represented in an executable file? How are uninitialized data represented in an executable file? Why are the representations different?

3.8 Why is the conversion from UTC to local time done by user processes, rather than in the kernel?

3.9 Describe the security implications of not zero filling the stack region at program startup.

3.10 Describe how the "#!" mechanism can be used to make programs that require emulation appear as though they were normal executables.

3.11 Is it possible for a file to have permissions set such that its owner cannot read it, even though a group can? Is this possible if the owner is a member of the group that can read the file?

*3.12 What is the advantage of having the kernel, rather than an application, restart an interrupted system call?

*3.13 Describe a scenario in which the sorted-difference algorithm used for the callout queue does not work well. Suggest an alternative data structure that runs more quickly than does the sorted difference algorithm for your scenario.

*3.14 The SIGPROF profiling timer was originally intended to replace the *profil* system call to collect a statistical sampling of a program's program counter. Give two reasons why the *profil* facility had to be retained.

*3.15 Should a setuid program that swaps its effective and real UIDs be allowed to swap them back again? Why or why not?

**3.16 What weakness in the process-accounting mechanism makes the latter unsuitable for use in a commercial environment?

References

Barkley & Lee, 1988.
R. E. Barkley & T. P. Lee, "A Heap-Based Callout Implementation to Meet Real-Time Needs," *USENIX Association Conference Proceedings*, pp. 213–222 (June 1988).

Gifford, 1981.
D. Gifford, "Information Storage in a Decentralized Computer System," PhD Thesis, Electrical Engineering Department, Stanford University, Stanford, CA (1981).

Gusella *et al.*, 1986.
R. Gusella, S. Zatti, & J. M. Bloom, "The Berkeley UNIX Time Synchronization Protocol," pp. 22:1–10 in *UNIX System Manager's Manual, 4.3*

Berkeley Software Distribution, Virtual VAX-11 Version, USENIX Association, Berkeley, CA (1986).

Ritchie, 1979.
D. M. Ritchie, ''Protection of Data File Contents,'' *United States Patent* (4,135,240), United States Patent Office (January 16, 1979). Assignee: Bell Telephone Laboratories, Inc., Murray Hill, NJ, Appl. No.: 377,591, Filed: Jul. 9, 1973.

Varghese & Lauck, 1987.
G. Varghese & T. Lauck, ''Hashed and Hierarchical Timing Wheels: Data Structures for the Efficient Implementation of a Timer Facility,'' *Proceedings of the Eleventh Symposium on Operating Systems Principles*, pp. 25–38 (November 1987).

PART 2

Processes

CHAPTER 4

Process Management

4.1 Introduction

A *process* is a program in execution. A process must have system resources, such as memory and the underlying CPU. UNIX supports the illusion of concurrent execution of multiple processes by scheduling system resources among the set of processes that are ready to execute. In this chapter, we describe the composition of a process, the method the system uses to switch between processes, and the scheduling policy used to promote sharing of the CPU. In later sections, we study process creation and termination, the signal facilities, and process-debugging facilities.

Two months after the beginning of the first implementation of the UNIX operating system, there were two processes, one for each of the terminals of the PDP-7. At age 10 months, and still on the PDP-7, UNIX had many processes, the *fork* operation, and something like the *wait* system call. A process executed a new program by reading a new program in on top of itself. The first PDP-11 system (First Edition UNIX) saw the introduction of *exec*. All these systems allowed only one process in memory at a time. When a PDP-11 with memory management (a KS-11) was obtained, the system was modified to permit several processes to remain in memory simultaneously, in order to reduce swapping. But this modification did not apply to multiprogramming, because disk I/O was synchronous. This state of affairs persisted into 1972 and the first PDP-11/45 system. True multiprogramming was finally introduced when the system was rewritten in C. Disk I/O for one process could then proceed while another process ran. The basic structure of process management in UNIX has not changed since that time [Ritchie, 1988].

A UNIX process operates in either *user mode* or *kernel mode*. In user mode, a process executes application code with the machine in a nonprivileged protection mode. When a process requests services from the operating system with a system call, it switches into the machine's privileged protection mode and operates in kernel mode.

The resources used by a process are similarly split into two parts. The resources needed for execution in user mode are defined by the CPU architecture and typically include the CPU's general-purpose registers, the program counter, the processor-status register, and the stack-related registers, as well as the contents of the memory segments that constitute the UNIX notion of a program (the text, data, and stack segments).

Kernel-mode resources include those required by the underlying hardware—such as registers, program counter, and stack pointer—but also by the state required for the UNIX kernel to perform system services for a process. This *kernel state* includes parameters to the current system call, the current process's user identity, scheduling information, and so on. UNIX divides the kernel state for each process into two separate data structures: the *proc structure* and the *user structure*.

The proc structure contains information that must always remain resident in main memory, whereas the user structure contains information that needs to be resident only when the process is executing (although user structures of other processes also may be resident). User structures are allocated dynamically through the memory-management facilities. The user structure of the currently running process is mapped to a fixed location in the kernel's virtual address space, so that kernel software may refer to it as a static C language structure. Proc structures are allocated from a fixed-sized table created by the kernel at system startup. The proc structure for the current process is referenced through a pointer in the current process's user structure.

Multiprogramming

UNIX supports transparent multiprogramming—the illusion of concurrent execution of multiple processes or programs. This is done by *context switching*; that is, by switching between the execution context of processes. A mechanism is also provided for *scheduling* the execution of processes; that is, for deciding which one to execute next. Facilities are provided for ensuring consistent access to data structures that are shared among processes.

Context switching is a hardware-dependent operation whose implementation is influenced by the underlying hardware facilities. Some architectures provide machine instructions that save and restore the hardware-execution context of the process, but the software state used by the kernel must be switched as well.

Context switching is done frequently, so increasing the speed of a context switch noticeably decreases time spent in the kernel and provides more time for executing user applications. Since most of the work of a context switch is expended in saving and restoring the operating context of a process, reducing the amount of the information required for that context is an effective way of producing faster context switches. Many UNIX systems avoid copying the context states of resident processes by using memory-management hardware (if available) to map the user structure of the new running process into the user structure's expected location. This mapping could also be done in software by using an indirect structure reference, but that approach would be less efficient.

Scheduling

Fair scheduling of processes is an involved task that is dependent on the types of executable programs and on scheduling policy goals. Programs are characterized according to the amount of computation and the amount of I/O that they do. Scheduling policies typically attempt to balance resource utilization against the time it takes for a program to complete. A process's priority is periodically recalculated based on parameters such as the amount of CPU time it has used, the amount of memory resources it holds or requires for execution, and so on.

UNIX uses a priority-based scheduling policy that is biased to favor *interactive programs*, such as text editors, over long-running batch-type jobs. Interactive programs tend to exhibit short bursts of computation followed by periods of inactivity or I/O. The scheduling policy initially assigns each process a high execution priority and allows that process to execute for a fixed *time slice*. Processes that execute for the duration of their slice have their priority lowered, whereas processes that give up the CPU (usually because they do I/O) are allowed to remain at their priority. Processes that are inactive have their priority raised. Thus, jobs that use large amounts of CPU time sink rapidly to a low priority, whereas interactive jobs that are mostly inactive remain at a high priority so that, when they are ready to run, they will preempt the long-running lower-priority jobs. An interactive job, such as a text editor searching for a string, may become compute bound briefly, and will get a lower priority, but it will return to a high priority when it is inactive again.

The system also needs a scheduling policy to deal with problems that arise from not having enough main memory to hold the execution contexts of all processes that want to execute. The major goal of this scheduling policy is to minimize *thrashing*—a phenomenon that occurs when memory is in such short supply that more time is spent in the system handling page faults and scheduling processes than in executing application code in user mode.

The system must both detect and eliminate thrashing. It detects thrashing by observing the amount of free memory and the rate of memory requests. When the system has few free memory pages and a high rate of new memory requests, it considers itself to be thrashing. The system eliminates thrashing by finding the four largest processes and swapping out the one that has been resident in memory the longest. The memory freed by swapping out the process can then be distributed to the remaining processes, which usually can then proceed. This selection criterion is chosen to favor small interactive jobs over large batch jobs. If the thrashing continues, additional processes are selected for swapping out until enough memory becomes available for other processes to run effectively. Eventually, enough processes complete and free their memory that swapped-out processes can return to main memory to run. However, even if there is not enough memory, the swapped-out processes are allowed to return after about 20 seconds. Usually, the thrashing condition will return. But the swapped-in process

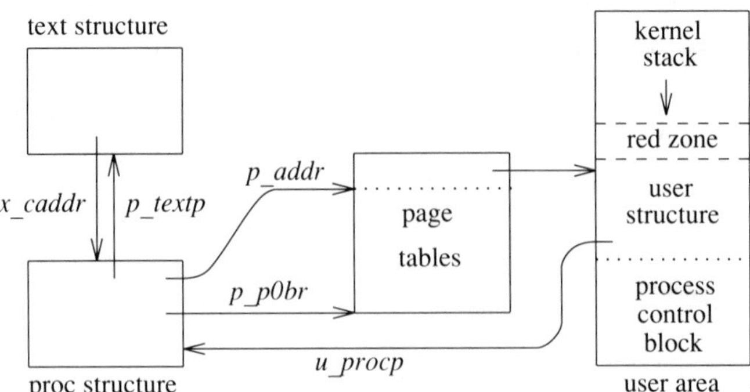

Figure 4.1 Process state.

will no longer have the longest memory-resident time, so some other process will be selected for swapping out.

The orientation of the scheduling policy toward an interactive job mix reflects the original design of UNIX for use in a time-sharing environment. Numerous papers have been written about alternative scheduling policies, such as those used in batch-processing environments or real-time systems. Usually, these policies require changes to the system in addition to alteration of the scheduling policy.

Section 4.2 details the state of a process, including the proc and user structures. Section 4.3 describes the facilities for context switching and for synchronizing access to system data structures used by both the top and bottom halves of the kernel. Section 4.4 explains the implementation of the priority-based scheduling algorithm described previously. Section 4.5 covers process creation, and Section 4.6 describes process termination.

4.2 Process State

There are several data structures that describe the state of a process, as shown in Fig. 4.1. Some of the structures must remain resident in main memory, whereas others may be moved to secondary storage when memory resources are low. The *proc structure* and *text structure* are the two data structures that must always remain in main memory. The *user structure* and process page tables are needed only when a process is resident and running. The following sections describe the portions of these structures that are relevant to process management. The text structure and page tables are described more fully in Chapter 5.

The Proc Structure

A *proc structure* contains the process state that must remain in memory at all times, as shown in Table 4.1. This state is logically divided into several categories of information having to do with the following:

Table 4.1 Process data structure.

Category	Name	Description
scheduling	*p_pri*	current priority; negative is high
	p_usrpri	user priority based on *p_cpu* and *p_nice*
	p_nice	user-requested scheduling priority
	p_cpu	recent CPU usage
	p_slptime	amount of time sleeping
identifiers	*p_pid*	unique process identifier
	p_ppid	parent-process identifier
	p_uid	user identifier
memory management	*p_textp*	pointer to description of executable file
	p_p0br	pointer to process page tables
	p_szpt	size of process page tables
	p_addr	location of user area page tables
	p_swaddr	location of user area when swapped out
synchronization	*p_wchan*	event process is awaiting
signals	*p_sig*	mask of signals pending delivery
	p_sigignore	mask of signals being ignored
	p_sigcatch	mask of signals being caught
	p_pgrp	process-group identifier
resource accounting	*p_rusage*	pointer to *rusage* structure
	p_quota	pointer to disk-quota structure
timer management	*p_time*	amount of real time until timer expires

- **Scheduling**. The process priority, user-mode scheduling priority, recent CPU utilization, and amount of time spent sleeping
- **Identification**. The process identifier, the parent-process identifier, and the real user identifier
- **Memory management**. A pointer to a text-table entry used in managing shared text segments, a pointer to the page tables for the process, the size of the set of pages currently resident in main memory, and an address for the user structure and page tables when they are swapped to secondary storage
- **Synchronization**. The *wait channel*, a description of the event for which the process is waiting (see the next section)
- **Signals**. Signals pending delivery and the action to take when a signal is posted to a process, as well as the process group
- **Resource accounting**. The *rusage* structure that describes the utilization of the many resources provided by the system (see Section 3.8), and a pointer to any disk quotas

Table 4.2 Process states.

State	Description
SSLEEP	awaiting an event
SRUN	runnable
SIDL	intermediate state in process creation
SZOMB	intermediate state in process termination
SSTOP	process stopped or being traced

- **Timer management**. The time until a real-time timer is to expire

A process's state has a value, as shown in Table 4.2. When a process is first created with a *fork* system call, it is initially marked as SIDL. The state is changed to SRUN when enough resources are allocated to the process for the latter to begin execution. From that point onward, a process's state will fluctuate between SRUN (runnable), SSLEEP (waiting for an event), and SSTOP (stopped by a signal or the parent process), until the process terminates. A deceased process is marked as SZOMB until its termination status is communicated to its parent process.

The system organizes proc structures into three lists to speed lookups based on process state. These lists are threaded by the *p_nxt* field of the proc structure. Process-table entries that are in use are either on the *zombproc* list if the process is in the SZOMB state, or on the *allproc* list. Process-table entries that are not in use are found on the *freeproc* list.

Most processes, except the currently executing process, are also in one of two queues: a *run queue* or a *sleep queue*. Processes that are in a runnable state are placed on a run queue, whereas processes that are blocked awaiting an event are located on a sleep queue. Stopped processes not also awaiting an event are on neither type of queue. Both queues are organized as an array of doubly linked lists, using the *p_link* and *p_rlink* fields in the proc structure. The run queues are organized according to process-scheduling priority, and described in Section 4.4. The sleep queues are organized in a hashed data structure that optimizes finding a sleeping process by the event number (wait channel) for which the process is waiting. The sleep queues are described in Section 4.3.

Flags in the *p_flag* field of the proc structure show additional information about a process's *operational* state, as shown in Table 4.3. Most of these flags are used by the kernel to mark transient states during operations that may involve one or more context switches. Other flags are used to record information communicated by a user (SSEQL, SUANOM, SOUSIG) or deduced by the system (SSYS). We shall describe the purpose of each flag as we encounter it in later sections (see Section 13.4 for SLOGIN).

Every process in the system is assigned a unique identifier termed the *process identifier*, or *PID*. PIDs are the common mechanism used by applications and by

Table 4.3 Process flags.

Flag	Description
SLOAD	process loaded in main memory
SSYS	process created by system (e.g., swapper or page daemon)
SLOCK	process is being swapped out
SSWAP	alternate return after swap
STRC	process is being debugged
SWTED	another debugging flag
SOUSIG	process using old signal mechanism
SULOCK	user requested that process not be swapped
SPAGE	process waiting for page to be retrieved
SKEEP	kernel requires process in memory
SOWEUPC	process collecting system-call timing information
SOMASK	restore old mask after taking signal
SWEXIT	process is exiting
SPHYSIO	process doing physical I/O
SVFORK	process resulted from *vfork*( )
SNOVM	child has parent's virtual memory during a *vfork*( )
SVFDONE	child returned virtual memory to parent during a *vfork*( )
SPAGI	page in data space from filesystem on demand
SSEQL	user advised of sequential virtual-memory behavior
SUANOM	user advised of random virtual-memory behavior
STIMO	timing out during sleep
SSEL	process selecting; clear if wakeup occurs
SLOGIN	a login process
SPTECHG	page tables for process have changed

the kernel to reference processes. PIDs are used by applications when sending a signal to a process and when receiving the exit status from a deceased process. Two PIDs are of special importance to each process: the process's own PID, and the PID of the process's parent process.

The *p_pgrp* field and related links (*p_pptr*, *p_cptr*, *p_osptr*, and *p_ysptr*) are used in locating descendent processes, as shown in Fig. 4.2. When a process spawns a child process, a forward link is created from the parent to the child in the *p_cptr* field, and a backward link from the child to the parent is kept in the *p_pptr* field. If a process has more than one child process active at a time, the children are linked together, with the oldest child process forward-linked to its younger sibling processes through *p_ysptr* and backward-linked through *p_osptr*. In Fig. 4.2, process B is a direct descendent of process A, whereas processes C, D, and E are descendents of process B and are siblings of one another. Process B typically

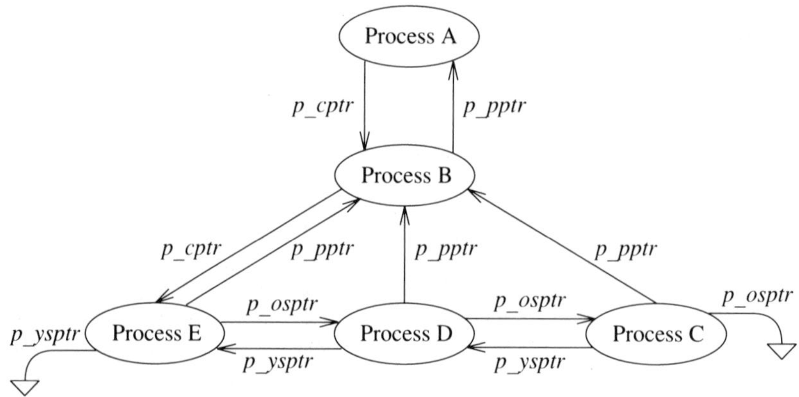

Figure 4.2 Process-group hierarchy.

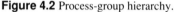

would be a shell that started a pipeline (see Sections 2.4 and 2.6), including processes C, D, and E. Process A probably would be the system-initialization process *init* (see Sections 3.1 and 13.4).

A *process group* is a collection of related processes, such as a pipeline, that have been assigned the same *process-group identifier*. Process groups are an integral part of the signal facilities. The *killpg* system call can be used to *broadcast* a signal to all the processes in a process group. In Fig. 4.2, processes C, D, and E usually would be placed in a process group separate from that of processes A and B. This separation would allow the job represented by processes C, D, and E to be started, stopped, brought into the foreground, or put into the background as a group. The terminal I/O system (described in Chapter 9) synchronizes access to a terminal by permitting only a single process group to be associated with a terminal at any time. This synchronization facility, combined with the process-group and signal mechanisms, provides the foundation for the job-control facilities described in Section 4.7.

CPU time is made available to processes according to their *scheduling priority*. A process has two scheduling priorities; one for scheduling user-mode execution, and one for scheduling kernel-mode execution. The *p_usrpri* field in the proc structure contains the user-mode scheduling priority, whereas the *p_pri* field holds the current kernel-mode scheduling priority. The current priority may be different from the user-mode priority when the process is executing in kernel mode. Priorities range between 0 and 127, with a lower value interpreted as a higher priority (see Table 4.4). User-mode priorities range from PUSER (50) to 127; priorities less than PUSER are used only when a process is *asleep*—that is, awaiting an event in the kernel—and immediately after such a process is awakened. A kernel process that is asleep with a priority in the range PZERO to PUSER may be awakened by a signal. But a process asleep at a priority below PZERO will never be awakened by a signal; this rule is necessary to prevent signals from

Table 4.4 Process-scheduling priorities.

Priority	Value	Description
PSWP	0	priority while swapping process
PINOD	10	priority while waiting for file control information
PRIBIO	20	priority while waiting on disk I/O completion
PZERO	25	baseline priority
PWAIT	30	base priority for waiting on resources
PLOCK	35	base priority for waiting on resource locks
PSLEP	40	base priority for waiting for an event
PUSER	50	base priority for user-mode execution

interfering with operations such as disk transfers that must be completed atomically.

The ordering of the priorities has remained unchanged since the Sixth Edition. All kernel priorities must be better than those assigned to user processes. Because priorities encode whether a system call may be aborted by a signal, the assignment of values above or below PZERO is important. The use of priorities to specify whether a system call can be interrupted by a signal was implemented to save text space in early UNIX kernels. Instead of adding an additional parameter to the *sleep*() routine, which is called in many places in the kernel, the value was encoded in the priority.

The User Structure

The *user structure*, (also called the *u-dot* (**u.**) *structure* because all references in C are of the form *u.*), contains the process state that may be swapped to secondary storage. This state includes

- The user- and kernel-mode execution states
- The state related to system calls
- The descriptor table
- The accounting information
- The resource controls
- The per-process execution stack for the kernel

For the VAX, the current execution state of a process is encapsulated in a VAX *process control block* (PCB). This structure, shown in Fig. 4.3, is defined by the VAX machine architecture and includes the general-purpose registers, stack pointers,

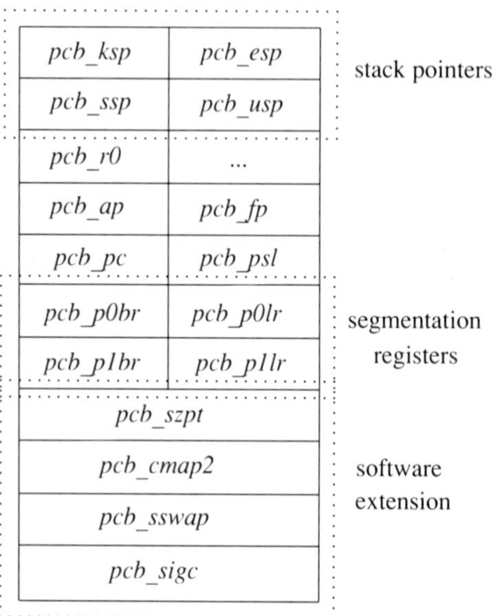

Figure 4.3 VAX process control block (PCB).

program counter, processor status longword, and segment base and length registers. In addition to the information required by the hardware, four fields that are manipulated by the kernel have been added. These fields specify the size of the process page table, two pointers used in context switching and segment copying, and a chunk of code used in implementing the delivery of signals.

The user structure is mapped to a fixed location in the VAX virtual-address space and is marked readable in user mode. Having the user structure readable in user mode permits signal delivery to be implemented more efficiently (see Section 4.7).

The location of the kernel stack in the user structure simplifies context switching by localizing all a process's kernel-mode state in a single structure. This design, however, restricts the stack to a fixed size and requires implementors to be careful when writing code that executes in the kernel. That is, kernel code must avoid using large local variables and deeply nested subroutine calls to avoid overflowing the run-time stack. In the 4.3BSD system for the VAX, 10 pages of 512 bytes each are allocated for each user structure. The kernel stack grows down from the top of the user structure. The fixed-size portion of the user structure, including the PCB, is about 2300 bytes. The page above the end of the fixed-size portion is marked invalid. Thus, overflowing the kernel stack will cause a kernel-access fault instead of overwriting the fixed-sized portion of the user structure, which would cause disastrous results. These uses leave about 2050 bytes for the kernel's run-time stack. Because interrupt processing takes place on a separate *interrupt stack*, the size of the kernel stack in the user structure restricts only that code executed as a result of traps and system calls.

Memory

The memory used by a process is described by fields in the proc and user structures. A process's user-mode execution state is described by the information in the PCB and in the *page tables* that describe which pages of the process's memory are currently resident in main memory. Before a process can execute, the process's page tables must be loaded into memory and the appropriate VAX memory-management registers must be set to point at them. For the purposes of discussing process management, we shall ignore most of the details of memory management and assume that memory resources are available. Chapter 5 discusses how memory is managed by the system and details memory-related actions that are required to perform a context switch.

The Text Structure

4.3BSD supports the sharing of memory that holds *pure* code; that is, code that cannot be modified. Each of these memory regions, called a *shared text segment*, is described by a *text structure*. When a program image is loaded with an *execve* system call, if the code segment is marked as *pure*, the system will load the text segment of the image separately from the initialized and uninitialized data segments and will create a text structure that describes the loaded image. (The image may not be brought completely into memory; instead, it may be paged into memory on demand.) Future executions of the same image may then share the text segment by referencing the resources described in the text structure. Process creation and context switching of shared texts are discussed in this chapter; memory management of shared texts is presented in Chapter 5.

4.3 Context Switching

The kernel switches among processes in an effort to share the CPU effectively; this is termed *context switching*. When a process executes for the duration of its time slice or when it blocks because it requires a resource that is currently unavailable, the kernel finds another process to run and context switches to it. The system can also interrupt the currently executing process to service an asynchronous event such as a device interrupt. Although both scenarios involve switching the execution context of the CPU, switching between processes occurs *synchronously* with respect to the currently executing process, whereas servicing interrupts occurs *asynchronously* with respect to the current process. In addition, interprocess context switches are classified as *voluntary* or *involuntary*. A voluntary context switch occurs when a process blocks because it requires a resource that is unavailable. An involuntary context switch takes place when a process executes for the duration of its time slice or when the system identifies a higher-priority process to run.

Each type of context switching is performed through a different interface. Voluntary context switching is initiated with a call to the *sleep*() routine, whereas an involuntary context switch is forced by direct invocation of the low-level context-switching mechanism embodied in the *swtch*() and *resume*() routines. Asynchronous event handling is managed by the underlying hardware and is effectively transparent to the system. Our discussion of asynchronous event handling shall focus on how it relates to synchronizing access to kernel data structures.

Process State

Context switching between processes requires that both the kernel- and user-mode context be changed; to facilitate this, the system ensures that all of a process's user-mode state is located in one data structure: the user structure (some kernel state is kept elsewhere). The following conventions apply to this localization:

- **Kernel-mode hardware-execution state**. Context switching can take place in only kernel mode. Thus, the kernel's hardware-execution state is defined by the contents of the PCB that is located at the beginning of the user structure.
- **User-mode hardware-execution state**. When execution is in kernel mode, the user-mode state of a process (such as copies of program counter, stack pointer, and general registers) always resides on the kernel's execution stack that is located in the user structure. The kernel ensures this location of user-mode state by requiring that the system call and trap handlers save the contents of the user-mode execution context each time the kernel is entered (see Section 3.1).
- **The proc structure**. The proc structure always remains resident in memory; thus, a pointer to the structure can be held safely in the user structure.
- **The text structure**. Likewise, any shared text used by the process is defined by an entry in the text table that is also a permanently resident data structure. This permits a pointer to the text structure to be held in the proc structure.
- **Memory resources**. Finally, memory resources of a process are effectively described by the contents of the base and length registers located in the PCB and by the values present in the proc structure. As long as the process remains in memory, these values will remain valid, and context switches can be performed without the associated page tables being saved and restored. After a process is swapped to secondary storage, however, these values need to be recalculated when the process returns to main memory.

Low-Level Context Switching

The localization of the context of a process in its user structure permits the kernel to do context switching simply by switching the notion of the current user structure. To make switching user structures as efficient as possible on the VAX, the system maps the physical memory associated with each process's user structure to a fixed location at the top of the user-mode virtual-address space. (This location is also at a fixed virtual address in the kernel's address space.) Since the user-mode virtual-memory mapping is defined by values maintained in a process's PCB, switching between processes, and between user structures, simply becomes a matter of swapping PCBs. The VAX architecture includes two instructions and a privileged register specifically designed for swapping PCBs. The *Process Control Block Base* (PCBB) register contains the physical address of the PCB for the current process. The *svpctx* instruction *saves* the current machine state in the current PCB, whereas the *ldpctx* instruction *loads* the current machine state from the current PCB. Swapping between two processes is then performed with

svpctx	# save current state in current PCB
...	# load address of a new PCB, and...
ldpctx	# ... establish state from the PCB

These low-level details are hidden inside the *swtch*() and *resume*() routines. Whenever a context switch is required, a call to the *swtch*() routine causes the highest-priority process to run. *Swtch*() first selects the appropriate process from the scheduling queues, then invokes *resume*() with the information needed to load the PCBB register. Once *resume*() has performed a *ldpctx* instruction to restore the execution state of the new process, it must also check the state of the new process for a nonlocal return request (such as when a process first starts execution after a *fork*; see Section 4.5).

Voluntary Context Switching

A *voluntary* context switch occurs whenever a process must await the availability of a resource or the arrival of an event. Voluntary context switches happen frequently in normal system operation. For example, a process typically blocks each time it requests data from a slow input device, such as a terminal. In UNIX, voluntary context switches are initiated through the *sleep*() routine. When a process no longer needs the CPU, it invokes *sleep*() with a *wait channel* and a scheduling priority. The wait channel is typically the address of some data structure that identifies the resource or event for which the process is waiting. Some conventional addresses used for wait channels are

lbolt	wait for up to 1 second
proc	wait for a child process to terminate
u	wait for a signal
buf	wait for a block I/O operation to complete

The priority specified in a *sleep*() call is the priority that should be assigned to the process when that process is awakened. This priority does not affect the user-level scheduling priority. Sleeping processes are organized in an array of queues

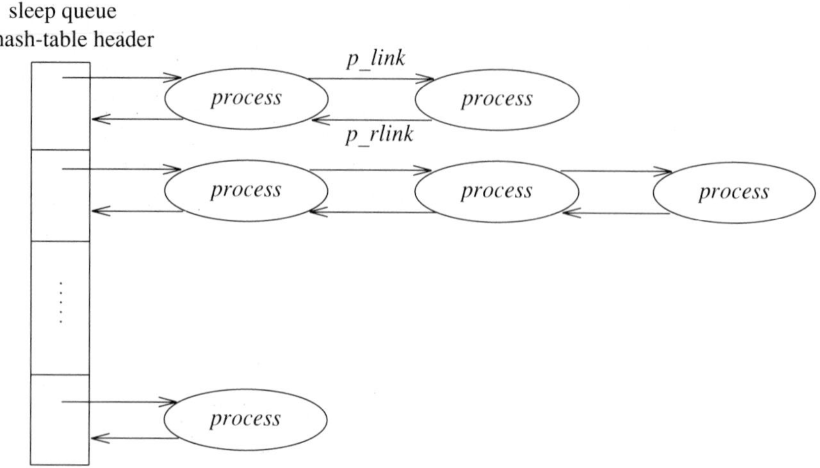

Figure 4.4 Queueing structure for sleeping processes.

(see Fig. 4.4). The *sleep*() and *wakeup*() routines hash wait channels to calculate an index into the sleep queues.

The *sleep*() routine performs the following steps in its operation:

1. Prevent interrupts that might cause process-state transitions by raising the hardware-processor priority level to *splhigh*

2. Record the wait channel in the proc structure and hash the wait-channel value to locate a sleep queue for the process

3. Set the process's priority to the priority the process will have when the process is awakened

4. Place the process at the *end* of the sleep queue selected in step 2

5. Call *swtch*() to request that a new process be scheduled; the hardware priority level is implicitly reset as part of switching to the other process

A sleeping process is not selected to execute until it is removed from a sleep queue and marked runnable. This operation is performed by the *wakeup*() routine. A process that puts itself to sleep with a priority between PZERO and PUSER is interruptible; that is, it may be awakened and marked runnable if a signal is posted to it. For example, a process waiting for input from a terminal will wait at an interruptible priority. Otherwise, a sleeping process is uninterruptible; that is, it will not be scheduled to run until the event for which it is waiting occurs. For example, a process waiting for disk I/O will sleep at an uninterruptible priority.

Processes usually sleep at uninterruptible priorities so that they can hold kernel resources while they wait. Processes that sleep at interruptible priorities may abort their system call because of a signal arriving before the event for which they are waiting has occurred. To avoid holding a kernel resource permanently, these processes must release any resources that they hold before going to sleep. Because of the extra work that must be done to prepare for an interruptible sleep, the only time that these sleeps are used is when a process must wait for events that may not occur for a long time. Occasionally, an event that is supposed to occur quickly, such as a tape I/O, will get held up because of a hardware failure. Because the process is sleeping in the kernel at an uninterruptible priority, it will be impervious to any attempts to send it a signal, even one that should cause it to exit unconditionally.

The *wakeup*() routine is called to signal that an event has occurred or that a resource is available. *Wakeup*() is invoked with a wait channel, and it awakens *all* processes sleeping on that wait channel. A *wakeup*() operation processes entries on a sleep queue from *front* to *back*. For each process that needs to be awakened, *wakeup*()

1. Removes the process from the sleep queue

2. Recomputes the user-mode scheduling priority if the process has been sleeping longer than 1 second

3. Makes the process runnable if it is in a SSLEEP state and places it on the run queue if it is not swapped out of main memory; if the process has been swapped out, the *swapin* process will be awakened to load it back into memory (see Section 5.13); if the process is in a SSTOP state, it is left on the queue until it is explicitly restarted by a user-level process, either by a *ptrace* system call or by a *continue* signal (see Section 4.7)

If *wakeup*() moved any processes to the run queue and one of them had a higher scheduling priority than does the currently executing process, it will also request that the CPU be rescheduled as soon as possible.

The most common use of *sleep*() and *wakeup*() is in scheduling access to shared data structures; this use is described in the section on *synchronization*, later in this chapter.

Intraprocess Context Switching

In addition to the interprocess context-switching mechanism, a mechanism is also provided for performing *nonlocal gotos*. This facility permits a routine to transfer control to a calling routine at some place *up* the execution stack, as shown in Fig. 4.5. Nonlocal gotos normally are used to handle an exceptional condition that should abort an operation in progress. For example, if a signal is received while the kernel is processing a system call, the kernel may abort the system call and return control to the system-call handler where an error code can be returned to the application.

Nonlocal gotos are implemented with the *setjmp*() and *longjmp*() routines, which work analogously to the C library routines *setjmp*() and *longjmp*(). The *setjmp*() routine saves the minimal amount of information about the current stack

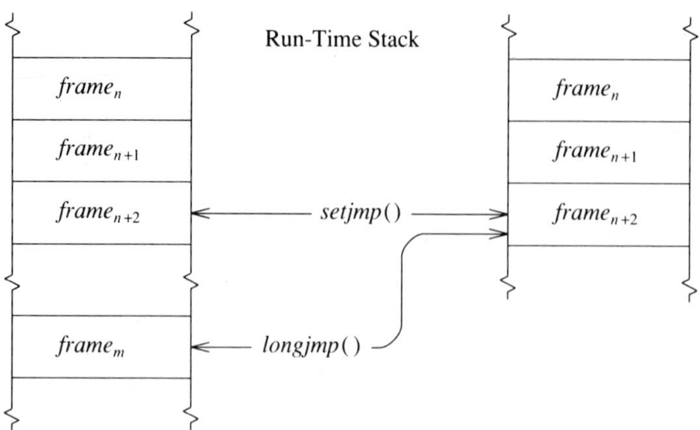

Figure 4.5 Stack-frame management for a nonlocal goto.

frame to allow a later *longjmp*() call to unwind the execution stack to the point at which the *setjmp*() call was taken. When *setjmp*() is first called, its return value is zero. A call to *longjmp*() causes *setjmp*() to return a second time with a nonzero value. The state saved by a call to *setjmp*() typically includes the kernel-mode frame pointer and program counter. When a process is swapping out itself, the last operation that it does is to request that its u-dot area (including its kernel stack) be written out to backing store. The I/O operation may begin (from a disk interrupt) before the process has had a chance to call the *sleep*() routine. Thus, it is necessary to save the contents of all the general-purpose registers before making the I/O request, so that the process can be started successfully when it is swapped back in from secondary storage. The *savectx*() and *ldctx*() routines are used for these situations.

Nonlocal gotos are used sparingly in the system and are never nested. Two entries in the user structure, *u_qsave* and *u_ssave*, are used to hold the state required to do nonlocal gotos when a signal interrupts a system call and when execution context is being restored after being swapped in from secondary storage, respectively. A more general, nestable, exception-handling facility would be useful in reducing the complexity of some parts of the system.

Synchronization

Interprocess synchronization to a resource typically is implemented by the association with the resource of two flags; a *locked* flag and a *wanted* flag. When a process wants to access a resource, it first checks the locked flag. If the resource is not currently in use by another process, this flag should not be set, and the process can simply set the locked flag and use the resource. If the resource is in use, however, the process should set the wanted flag and call *sleep*() with a wait channel associated with the resource (typically the address of the data structure used to describe the resource). When a process no longer needs the resource, it clears the

Table 4.5 VAX interrupt-priority assignments.

Name	Priority	Blocks
spl0()	0	nothing (normal operating mode)
splsoftclock()	8	low-priority clock processing
splnet()	12	network protocol processing
spl4()	20	low-priority devices
spltty()	21	terminal multiplexers
splbio()	21	disk and tape controllers
splimp()	22	network device controllers
splclock()	24	high-priority clock processing
splhigh()	31	all interrupt activity

locked flag and, if the wanted flag is set, invokes *wakeup*() to awaken all the processes that called *sleep*() to await access to the resource.

Routines that run in the bottom half of the kernel do not have a context and consequently cannot wait for a resource to become available by calling *sleep*(). When the top half of the kernel accesses resources that are shared with the bottom half of the kernel, it cannot use the locked flag to ensure exclusive use. Instead, it must prevent the bottom half from running while it is using the resource. Synchronizing access with routines that execute in the bottom half of the kernel requires knowledge about when these routines may run. Although machine-dependent, most implementations of UNIX order interrupt priorities according to Table 4.5. To block interrupt routines at and below a certain priority level, an appropriate *set-priority-level* call must be made. For example, when a process needs to manipulate a terminal's data queue, the code that accesses the queue is written in the following style:

```
s = spltty();        /* raise priority to block tty processing */
 ...                 /* manipulate tty */
splx(s);             /* reset priority level to previous value */
```

Processes must take care to avoid deadlocks when locking multiple resources. Suppose two processes, A and B, require two resources, R_1 and R_2, to perform some operation. If process A acquires R_1 and process B acquires R_2, then a deadlock occurs when process A tries to acquire R_2 and process B tries to acquire R_1. Since a UNIX process executing in kernel mode is never preempted by another process, locking multiple resources is relatively simple, although it must be done carefully. If a process knows that multiple resources are required to perform an operation, then it can safely lock one or more of these resources in any order, as long as it never voluntarily relinquishes control of the CPU. If, however, a process cannot acquire all the resources it needs, it must release any resources it holds before calling *sleep*() to wait for the currently inaccessible resource to become available.

Alternatively, if resources can be partially ordered, it is necessary only that they be allocated in an increasing order. For example, as the *namei*() routine traverses the filesystem name space, it must lock the next component of a pathname before it relinquishes the current component. A partial ordering of pathname components exists from the root of the name space to the leaves. Thus, translations down the name tree can request a lock on the next component without concern for deadlock. However, when it is traversing up the name tree (i.e., following a pathname component of dot-dot (**..**)), the kernel must take care to avoid sleeping while holding any locks.

Raising the processor priority level to guard against interrupt activity works for a uniprocessor architecture, but not for a shared-memory multiprocessor machine. Similarly, much of the UNIX kernel implicitly assumes that kernel processing will never be done concurrently. Numerous vendors—such as Sequent, AT&T, Encore, and Alliant—have redesigned the synchronization schemes and eliminated the uniprocessor assumptions implicit in the standard UNIX kernel, so that UNIX will run on tightly coupled multiprocessor architectures.

4.4 Process Scheduling

4.3BSD uses a process-scheduling algorithm based on *multilevel feedback queues*. All processes that are runnable are assigned a scheduling priority that determines in which *run queue* they are placed. In selecting a new process to run, the system scans the run queues from highest to lowest priority and chooses the first process on the first nonempty queue. If multiple processes reside on a queue, the system runs them *round robin*; that is, it runs them in the order that they are found on the queue, with equal amounts of time allowed. If a process blocks, it is not put back onto any run queue. If a process uses up the *time quantum* (or *time slice*) allowed it, it is placed at the end of the queue from which it came, and the process at the front of the queue is selected to run.

The shorter the time quantum, the better the interactive response. However, longer time quanta provide higher overall system throughput, because the system will have less overhead from doing context switches, and processor caches will be flushed less often. The time quantum used by 4.3BSD is one-tenth of a second. This value was empirically found to be the longest quantum that could be used without loss of the desired response for interactive jobs such as editors.

The system adjusts the priority of a process dynamically to reflect resource requirements (e.g., being blocked awaiting an event) and the amount of resources consumed by the process (e.g., CPU time). Processes are moved between run queues based on changes in their scheduling priority (hence, the word *feedback* in the name *multilevel feedback queue*). When a process other than the currently running process attains a higher priority, the system switches to that process when the time quantum for the first process expires; if a sleeping process is awakened, the current process is preempted after any current system call. The system tailors this *short-term scheduling algorithm* to favor interactive jobs by raising the scheduling priority of processes that are blocked for a *long time* waiting for I/O, and by lowering the priority of processes that accumulate significant amounts of CPU time.

Short-term process scheduling is broken up into two parts. The next section describes when and how a process's scheduling priority is altered; the section after describes the management of the run queues and the interaction between process scheduling and context switching.

Calculations of Process Priority

A process's scheduling priority is directly determined by two values contained in the proc structure: *p_cpu* and *p_nice*. The value of *p_cpu* provides an estimate of the recent CPU utilization of the process. The value of *p_nice* is a user-settable weighting factor that ranges numerically between −20 and 20. The normal value for *p_nice* is 0. Negative values increase a process's priority, whereas positive values decrease its priority.

A process's user-mode scheduling priority is calculated every four clock ticks (40 milliseconds on a VAX) by this equation:

$$p\_usrpri = PUSER + \left\lceil \frac{p\_cpu}{4} \right\rceil + 2 \cdot p\_nice \qquad \text{(Eq. 4.1)}$$

Values must be at least PUSER (see Table 4.4); values greater than 127 are clamped to 127. This calculation causes the priority to decrease linearly based on recent CPU utilization. The user-controllable *p_nice* parameter acts as a limited weighting factor. Negative values retard the effect of heavy CPU utilization by offsetting the additive term containing *p_cpu*. Otherwise, if one ignores the second term, *p_nice* simply shifts the priority by a constant factor.

The CPU utilization, *p_cpu*, is incremented each time the system clock ticks and the process is found to be executing. In addition, *p_cpu* is adjusted once per second using a digital decay filter. The decay causes about 90 percent of the CPU usage accumulated in a 1-second interval to be forgotten over a period of time that is dependent on the system *load average*. To be exact, *p_cpu* is adjusted according to

$$p\_cpu = \frac{(2 \cdot load)}{(2 \cdot load + 1)} p\_cpu + p\_nice \qquad \text{(Eq. 4.2)}$$

where the *load* is a sampled average of the length of the run queue over the previous 1-minute interval of system operation.

To understand the effect of the decay filter, we can consider the case where a single compute-bound process monopolizes the CPU. The process's CPU utilization will accumulate clock ticks at a rate dependent on the clock frequency. The load average will be effectively 1, resulting in a decay of

$$p\_cpu = 0.66 \cdot p\_cpu + p\_nice$$

If we assume the process accumulates T_i clock ticks over time interval i, and that *p_nice* is zero, then the CPU utilization for each time interval will count into the current value of *p_cpu* according to

$$\begin{aligned}
p_cpu &= 0.66 \cdot T_0 \\
p_cpu &= 0.66 \cdot (T_1 + 0.66 \cdot T_0) = 0.66 \cdot T_1 + 0.44 \cdot T_0 \\
p_cpu &= 0.66 \cdot T_2 + 0.44 \cdot T_1 + 0.30 \cdot T_0 \\
p_cpu &= 0.66 \cdot T_3 + \cdots + 0.20 \cdot T_0 \\
p_cpu &= 0.66 \cdot T_4 + \cdots + 0.13 \cdot T_0
\end{aligned}$$

Thus, after five decay calculations, only 13 percent of T_0 remains present in the current CPU utilization value for the process. Since the decay filter is applied once per second, another way of saying this is that about 90 percent of the CPU utilization is forgotten after 5 seconds.

Processes that are runnable have their priority adjusted periodically as just described. However, the system ignores processes blocked awaiting an event: These processes cannot accumulate CPU usage, so an estimate of their filtered CPU usage can be calculated in one step. This optimization can significantly reduce a system's scheduling overhead when many blocked processes are present. The system recomputes a process's priority when that process is awakened and has been sleeping for longer than 1 second. The system maintains a value, *p_slptime*, that is an estimate of the time a process has spent blocked waiting for an event. The value of *p_slptime* is set to 0 when a process calls *sleep*(), and is incremented once per second while the process remains in an SSLEEP or SSTOP state. When the process is awakened, the system computes the value of *p_cpu* according to

$$p\_cpu = \left[\frac{(2 \cdot load)}{(2 \cdot load + 1)} \right]^{p\_slptime} p\_cpu \qquad \text{(Eq. 4.3)}$$

and then recalculates the scheduling priority using Eq. 4.1. This analysis ignores the influence of *p_nice*; also, the *load* used is the current load average, not the load average at the time the process blocked.

Process-Priority Routines

The priority calculations used in the short-term scheduling algorithm are spread out in several areas of the system. Two routines, *schedcpu*() and *roundrobin*(), run periodically. *Schedcpu*() recomputes process priorities once per second, using Eq. 4.2, and updates the value of *p_slptime* for processes blocked by a call to *sleep*(). The *roundrobin*() routine runs 10 times per second and causes the system to reschedule the processes in the highest-priority (nonempty) queue in a round-robin fashion, and allows each process a 100-millisecond time quantum.

The CPU usage estimates are updated in the system clock-processing module, *hardclock*(), which executes 100 times per second. Each time a process accumulates four ticks in its CPU usage estimate, *p_cpu*, the system recalculates the priority of the process. This recalculation uses Eq. 4.1 and is done by the *setpri*() routine. The decision to recalculate after four ticks is related to the management of the run queues described in the next section. In addition to the call from *hardclock*(), each time *setrun*() places a process on a run queue, it also calls *setpri*() to recompute the process's scheduling priority. This call from *wakeup*() to *setrun*() operates on a process other than the currently running process. Accordingly, *wakeup*() invokes *updatepri*() to recalculate the CPU usage estimate according to Eq. 4.3 before calling *setpri*().

Process Run Queues and Context Switching

The scheduling-priority calculations are used to order the set of runnable processes. The scheduling priority ranges between 0 and 127, with 0 to 49 reserved for scheduling processes executing in kernel mode, and 50 to 127 reserved for scheduling processes executing in user mode. The number of queues used to hold the collection of runnable processes affects the cost of managing the queues. If only a single (ordered) queue is maintained, then selecting the next runnable process becomes simple, but other operations become expensive. Using 128 different queues can significantly increase the cost of identifying the next process to run. The system uses 32 run queues, selecting a run queue for a process by dividing the process's priority by four. The selection of 32 different queues is a compromise based mainly on the availability of certain VAX machine instructions that permit the lowest-level scheduling algorithm to be implemented efficiently.

The run queues contain all the runnable processes in main memory except the currently running process. Figure 4.6 shows how each queue is organized as a doubly linked list of proc structures. The head of each run queue is kept in an array, *qs*[ ], and associated with this array is a bit vector, *whichqs*, that is used in identifying the nonempty run queues. Two routines, *setrq*() and *remrq*(), are used to place a process at the tail of a run queue, and to take a process off the head

Figure 4.6 Queueing structure for runnable processes.

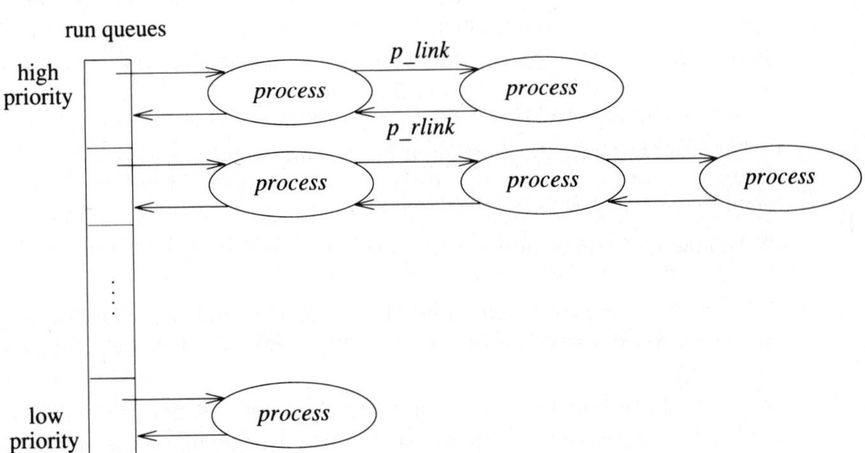

of a run queue. The heart of the scheduling algorithm is the *swtch*() routine. *Swtch*() is responsible for selecting a new process to run; it operates as follows:

1. Look for a nonempty run queue. This is easy to do on the VAX through use of the *ffs* (find first bit set) instruction on the *whichqs* bit vector. If *whichqs* is zero, there are no processes to run and *swtch*() will unblock interrupts and loop; this is the *idle loop*.

2. Given a nonempty run queue, remove the first process on the queue. On the VAX, this can be done with a single instruction, *remque*.

3. If this run queue is now empty as a result of removing the process, reset the appropriate bit in *whichqs*.

4. Reset the *noproc* and *runrun* flags. The *noproc* flag is a global flag used to show that *no process is currently running*. The *runrun* flag shows that a context switch should take place; this is described later.

5. Set the new process running with a call to *resume*().

On the VAX, the *swtch*() routine is coded in assembly language for efficiency.

Given the *swtch*() routine and the process-priority calculations, the only missing piece in the scheduling facility is how the system forces an involuntary context switch. Remember that voluntary context switches occur when a process calls the *sleep*() routine. *Sleep*() can be invoked by only a runnable process, so it need only place the process on a sleep queue and invoke *swtch*() to schedule the next process to run. The *swtch*() routine, however, cannot be called from code that executes at interrupt level, because the VAX architecture does not permit context switching from the interrupt stack.

An alternative mechanism must exist. This mechanism is to set a global *reschedule request* flag, named *runrun*, and then to post an *asynchronous system trap* (AST) for the current process. An AST is a trap that is delivered to a process the next time that process returns to user mode. The VAX architecture directly supports ASTs in hardware; other systems emulate ASTs by, for example, forcing memory faults. The system interrogates the *runrun* flag and forces a context switch by calling *swtch*() in each of these situations:

- After returning from an interrupt, if the system was idling
- At the end of a system call or trap
- When the AST trap occurs

The *wakeup*(), *setpri*(), *roundrobin*(), *schedcpu*(), and *setrun*() routines all set *runrun* and post an AST to force rescheduling and, possibly, an involuntary context switch.

It should be noted that, because UNIX does not preempt processes executing in kernel mode, real-time response to events is dependent on the amount of time spent in each system activity. In addition, processes have no way to determine which of their pages are resident, so they have no way of ensuring that they will be able to execute a sequence of instructions without incurring one or more page faults. Since the system guarantees no upper bounds on the duration of a system activity, UNIX is decidedly not a real-time system. Attempts to retrofit UNIX with real-time process scheduling have addressed this problem in different ways [Ferrin & Langridge, 1980; Sanderson *et al.*, 1986].

4.5 Process Creation

In UNIX, new processes are created with the *fork* system call. There is also a *vfork* system call that differs from *fork* in how the virtual-memory resources are treated; *vfork* is described in Chapter 5.

The process created by a *fork* is termed a *child process* of the original *parent process*. From a user's point of view, the child process is an exact duplicate of the parent process except for two values: the PID, and the parent PID. A call to *fork* returns the child PID to the parent and zero to the child process. Thus, a program can identify whether it is the parent or child process after a fork by checking this return value.

A *fork* involves three main steps:

1. Allocating and initializing a new proc structure for the child process
2. Duplicating the context of the parent (including the user structure and virtual-memory resources) for the child process
3. Scheduling the child process to run

The second step is intimately related to the operation of the memory-management facilities described in Chapter 5. Consequently, only those actions related to process management will be described here.

The system maintains a linked list of free process-table entries, so an unused entry can be found by examining the head of the list, *freeproc*.

While creating a new process, the system initializes most of the child's proc structure from that of the parent. One value that is not propagated, however, is the PID, which must be unique among all processes. Early versions of UNIX verified the uniqueness of a PID by performing a linear search of the process table. This search became infeasible on large systems with many processes. 4.3BSD maintains a range of unallocated PIDs between *mpid* and *pidchecked*. A new PID is allocated by using the value of *mpid*, and *mpid* is then incremented. When *mpid* reaches *pidchecked*, the system calculates a new range of unused PIDs by making a single scan of all existing processes (not just the active ones—zombie and swapped processes also are checked).

The child process inherits all the privileges and limitations of its parent. In addition to the open files and other information contained in the u-dot area, the proc entry of a child process inherits the following information from the parent:

- The signal state—the UID for delivering signals, process group, and signal actions
- The *p_nice* scheduling parameter
- Program-segment information—the size of each segment and the page tables, and, if a shared text segment is being used, a pointer to the associated text table entry
- The in-core disk-quota information (see Section 7.6)

To duplicate a process's image, the memory-management facilities are invoked through a call to *procdup*(). The *procdup*() routine is passed a pointer to the initialized proc structure for the child process and is expected to allocate all the resources that the child will need to execute. A call to *procdup*() returns a value of 1 in the child process and of 0 in the parent process. The kernel returns different values by arranging for a nonlocal goto when the child process is first set running. When *procdup*() is called, it fills in the *pcb_sswap* field in the child's PCB, and invokes *savectx*(), passing the address of *u_ssave* in the user structure of the child process:

```
procdup(p, isvfork)
     struct proc *p;
{
     ...                /* allocate and initialize child u */
     childu.u_pcb.pcb_sswap = &childu.u_ssave;
     if (savectx(&childu.u_ssave))
          return (1);   /* return 1 in child process */
     ...                /* duplicate process image */
     return (0);
}
```

The *resume*() routine checks the *pcb_sswap* field in the software extension to the PCB after each context switch. If this field is nonzero, *resume*() invokes the *ldctx*() routine, passing it the value found in *pcb_sswap* as the location for a nonlocal goto, returning control to the *procdup*() routine at the point where the original *savectx*() call was made, but with an alternate return value. This series of actions permits *procdup*() to return different values to its caller, depending on whether it is executing in the context of the child or parent process.

Finally, the new child process is made known to the scheduler by its being placed on the run queue, and the return value from *procdup*() is passed back to become the return value of the *fork* system call.

4.6 Process Termination

Processes terminate either voluntarily through an *exit* system call, or involuntarily as the result of a signal. In either case, process termination causes a status code to be returned to the parent of the terminating process (if it still exists). This termination status is returned through the *wait* or *wait3* system calls. The *wait3* call is a variant of the standard *wait* call that permits an application to request the status of both stopped and terminated processes. *Wait3* can also request statistics describing the resource utilization of a terminated child process. Also, unlike *wait*, *wait3* allows a process to request status codes without blocking.

Within the kernel, a process terminates by calling the *exit*() routine. *Exit*() first cleans up the process's kernel mode execution state by

- Canceling any pending timers
- Releasing virtual-memory resources
- Closing open descriptors
- Handling stopped or traced child processes

With the kernel-mode state reset, the process is then removed from the list of active processes—the *allproc* list—and is placed on the list of *zombie processes* pointed to by *zombproc*, as shown in Fig. 4.7. The process state is changed and the global flag *noproc* is marked to show that no process is currently running. The *exit*() routine then

- Records the termination status in the *p_xstat* field of the proc structure
- Bundles up a copy of the process's accumulated resource usage (for accounting purposes) and hangs this structure from the *p_ru* field of the proc structure

Figure 4.7 Management of the proc structure during process termination.

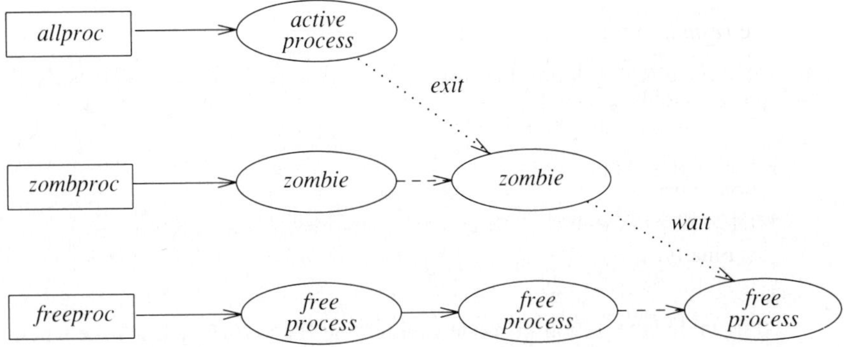

• Notifies the deceased process's parent

Finally, after the parent has been notified, the CPU is rescheduled directly through a call to *swtch*().

The *wait* and *wait3* calls both work by searching a process's descendant processes for processes that have terminated. If a process in SZOMB state is found, the system will copy the termination status from the deceased process and then reclaim the associated process structure, reinitializing it to a state suitable for future use. In particular, the process-table entry is taken off the zombie list and is returned to the free list pointed to by *freeproc*. Note that resources used by children of a process are accumulated only as a result of a *wait* system call. When trying to analyze the behavior of a long-running program, users would find it useful to be able to obtain this information before the termination of a process.

4.7 Signals

UNIX defines a set of *signals* for software and hardware conditions that may arise during the normal execution of a program; these signals are listed in Table 4.6. Signals may be delivered *asynchronously* to a process through application-specified *signal handlers*, or may result in *default* actions, such as process termination, carried out by the system. 4.3BSD signals are designed to be software equivalents of hardware interrupts or traps.

Each signal has an associated *action* that defines how a signal should be handled when it is delivered to a process. Each signal has a *default* action that may be any one of

• Ignoring the signal

• Terminating the process

• Terminating the process after generating a *core file* that contains the process's execution state at the time the signal was delivered

• Stopping the process

An application program may use the *sigvec* system call to specify an action for a signal, including

• Taking the default action

• Ignoring the signal

• Catching the signal with a *handler*

A signal handler is a user-mode routine that the system will invoke when the signal is received by the process. The handler is said to *catch* the signal, which is

Table 4.6 Signals defined in 4.3BSD.

Name	Default Action	Description
SIGHUP	terminate process	terminal line hangup
SIGINT	terminate process	interrupt program
SIGQUIT	create core image	quit program
SIGILL	create core image	illegal instruction
SIGTRAP	create core image	trace trap
SIGIOT	create core image	I/O trap instruction executed
SIGEMT	create core image	emulate instruction executed
SIGFPE	create core image	floating-point exception
SIGKILL	terminate process	kill program
SIGBUS	create core image	bus error
SIGSEGV	create core image	segmentation violation
SIGSYS	create core image	bad argument to system call
SIGPIPE	terminate process	write on a pipe with no one to read it
SIGALRM	terminate process	real-time timer expired
SIGTERM	terminate process	software termination signal
SIGURG	discard signal	urgent condition on I/O channel
SIGSTOP	stop process	stop signal not from terminal
SIGTSTP	stop process	stop signal from terminal
SIGCONT	discard signal	a stopped process is being continued
SIGCHLD	discard signal	notification to parent on child stop or exit
SIGTTIN	stop process	read on terminal by background process
SIGTTOU	stop process	write to terminal by background process
SIGIO	discard signal	I/O possible on a descriptor
SIGXCPU	terminate process	CPU time limit exceeded
SIGXFSZ	terminate process	file-size limit exceeded
SIGVTALRM	terminate process	virtual timer expired
SIGPROF	terminate process	profiling timer expired
SIGWINCH	discard signal	window size changed
SIGUSR1	terminate process	user-defined signal 1
SIGUSR2	terminate process	user-defined signal 2

thus *caught*. The two signals, SIGSTOP and SIGKILL, may not be ignored or caught; this restriction ensures that a software mechanism exists for stopping and killing runaway processes. It is not possible for a user process to decide which signals would cause the creation of a core file by default, but it is possible for a process to prevent the creation of such a file by ignoring, blocking, or catching the signal.

Signals are *posted* to a process by the system when it detects a hardware event such as an illegal instruction, or a software event such as a stop request from the terminal. A signal may also be posted by another process through the *kill* or *killpg* system calls. A sending process may post signals only to receiving processes that have the same effective user identifier (unless the sender is the superuser). A single exception to this rule is the *continue signal*, SIGCONT, which may always be sent to any descendent of the sending process. The reason for this exception is to allow users to restart a setuid program that they have stopped from their keyboard.

Like hardware interrupts, the delivery of signals may be *masked* by a process. The execution state of each process contains a set of signals currently masked from delivery. If a signal posted to a process is being masked, the signal is recorded in the process's set of pending signals, but no action is taken until the signal is unmasked. The *sigblock* and *sigsetmask* system calls modify a set of masked signals for a process. The *sigblock* call *adds* to the set of masked signals, whereas the *sigsetmask* call *replaces* the set of masked signals.

The system does not allow the SIGKILL, SIGSTOP, or SIGCONT signals to be masked. Preventing SIGCONT from being masked is necessary in 4.3BSD only because the delivery of this signal is required to resume stopped processes. POSIX, for example, specifies alternative semantics for SIGCONT that permit users to mask the signal without causing problems.

Two other signal-related system calls are *sigpause* and *sigstack*. The *sigpause* call permits a process to relinquish the processor until it receives a signal. This facility is similar to the system's *sleep*() routine. The *sigstack* call allows a process to specify a run-time stack to use in signal delivery. By default, the system will deliver signals to a process on its normal run-time stack. In some applications, however, this is unacceptable. For example, if an application is running on a stack that the system does not automatically expand, and the stack overflows, the signal handler must execute on an alternate stack. This facility is similar to the *interrupt-stack* mechanism provided by VAX hardware.

The final signal-related facility is the *sigreturn* system call. *Sigreturn* is the equivalent of a user-level load-processor-context operation. A pointer to a (machine-dependent) context block that describes the user-level execution state of a process is passed to the kernel. This state is used to restore state and to resume execution after a normal return from a user's signal handler.

Process Groups

A *process-group identifier* is a 16-bit number used to identify a collection of processes, a *process group*, such as a pipeline set up by the shell. Process-group identifiers are used by the *killpg* and *setpriority* system calls as a means of identifying a collection of processes, and by the terminal handler as an identification mechanism when multiplexing access to a terminal. A process inherits its process group from its parent process. The system never changes the process group of a proce˜ that has one; only user programs (usually shells) do this with the *setpgrp* system call. For process-group initialization, see Section 13.4.

Within the system, the two main users of process groups are the terminal handler (Chapter 9) and the interprocess-communication facilities (Chapter 10). Both facilities record process-group identifiers in private data structures and use them in delivering signals. The terminal handler, in addition, uses process groups to multiplex access to a terminal. When a process attempts to *read* from or *write* to a terminal, or otherwise to alter the state of a terminal with an *ioctl* call, and the process's process-group identifier is different from the terminal's process-group identifier, the terminal handler will *stop* the process by posting a signal that causes the process to enter an SSTOP state. This facility is the basic mechanism used in implementing *job control*; it is described in more detail later in this chapter.

Comparison with Other Systems

UNIX signals were originally designed to model exceptional events, such as an attempt by a user to kill a runaway program. They were not intended to be used as a general interprocess-communication mechanism, and thus no attempt was made to make them reliable. In earlier systems, whenever a signal was caught, its action was reset to the default action. The introduction of job control brought much more frequent use of signals, and made more visible a problem that faster processors also exacerbated: If two signals were sent rapidly, the second could cause the process to die, even though a signal handler had been set up to catch the first signal. Thus, reliability became desirable, and there was pressure from the user community for it. Rather than trying to fit the necessary major changes into the existing signal mechanism, the developers designed a completely new framework to contain the old capabilities as a subset while accommodating new mechanisms.

4.3BSD signal facilities differ radically from the facilities found in other versions of UNIX. In particular, 4.3BSD signals address the following problems:

- On older systems, the action associated with a signal is reset to the default action when the signal is received by a process. Thus, a process that wants to handle receipt of multiple instances of a given signal must reinstall the handler after each signal is received. This produces a race condition: Another instance of the signal may be received before the handler is reinstalled, causing the default action to take place, rather than what the programmer intended. In 4.3BSD, signal handlers are permanently installed with a single *sigvec* system call.
- On older systems, the currently handled signal is not masked while it is being handled by an application. This permits a later signal to terminate a process, as described previously. In addition, the signal not being masked means recursive interrupts may occur unless the signal handler marks the signal to be ignored. In 4.3BSD, the signal currently being handled is automatically masked from delivery while an application's signal handler is invoked.
- Previous UNIX systems did not permit user processes to mask the delivery of signals. The only mechanism provided to an application that needed to guard a critical region against signals was the ability to disable delivery of those signals.

Further, because only one signal at a time could be disabled, it was not possible to guarantee that a collection of signals could be disabled before one was delivered to the process. In 4.3BSD, sets of signals can be masked with the *sigblock* and *sigsetmask* system calls. If a signal is posted to a process that has it currently masked, the delivery of the signal is postponed until the signal is unmasked.

- In previous UNIX systems, signals were always delivered on the normal run-time stack of a process. In 4.3BSD, an alternate stack may be specified for delivering signals with the *sigstack* system call. Signal stacks permit programs that manage fixed-sized run-time stacks to handle signals reliably.

- On older UNIX systems, system calls interrupted by a signal caused the call to be terminated prematurely and an EINTR error code to be returned. In 4.3BSD, system calls interrupted by a signal are automatically restarted whenever possible and reasonable. Automatic restarting of system calls permits programs to service signals without having to check the return code from each system call to determine whether the call should be restarted. 4.3BSD (but not 4.2BSD) contains a flag for *sigvec* that will cause the old semantics to apply.

The signal facilities found in 4.3BSD are designed around a UNIX *virtual-machine* model, in which UNIX system calls are considered the parallel of machine's hardware instruction set. Signals are the software equivalent of traps or interrupts, and signal-handling routines perform the equivalent function of interrupt or trap service routines. Just as machines provide a mechanism for blocking hardware interrupts so that consistent access to data structures can be performed, the signal facilities allow software signals to be masked. Finally, because complex run-time stack environments may be required, signals, like interrupts, may be handled on an alternate run-time stack. These machine models are summarized in Table 4.7.

Table 4.7 Comparison of hardware machines and software virtual machines.

Hardware machine	Software virtual machine
instruction set	set of system calls
restartable instructions	restartable system calls
interrupts/traps	signals
interrupt/trap handlers	signal handlers
blocking interrupts	masking signals
interrupt stack	signal stack

Changes to 4.3BSD Signals in POSIX

4.3BSD signals have been adopted by POSIX, except for signal stacks. There have been some syntax changes in the signal functions, however, and because of them all the names have been changed, as summarized in Table 4.8. The only function found in POSIX that has no equivalent in 4.3BSD is *sigpending*; this routine determines what signals have been posted but have not yet been delivered.

Posting a Signal

The implementation of signals is broken up into two parts: posting a signal to a process, and recognizing the signal and delivering it to the target process. Signals may be posted by any process or by code that executes at interrupt level. Signal delivery normally takes place within the context of the receiving process. But when a signal forces a process to be stopped, the action is instead sometimes carried out when the signal is posted.

A signal is posted to a single process with the *psignal*() routine, or to a group of processes with the *gsignal*() routine. The *gsignal*() routine invokes *psignal*() for each process in the specified process group. The actions associated with posting a signal are straightforward, but the details are messy. In theory, posting a signal to a process simply causes the appropriate signal to be added to the set of pending signals for the process, and the process is then set to run (or is awakened if it was sleeping at an interruptible priority level). The *p_cursig* field in the proc structure, if nonzero, contains the signal currently being delivered to a process. The *p_sig* field contains the set of signals pending delivery to a process. Each time a process returns from a call to *sleep*() (with the process priority less than PZERO), or prepares to exit the system after processing a system call or trap, it checks to see whether a signal is pending delivery. If a signal is pending and must be delivered in the process's context, it is moved from the pending set to *p_cursig*,

Table 4.8 4.3BSD and POSIX signal-handling facilities.

4.3BSD	POSIX
sigmask()	sigsetopts functions
sigblock()	*sigprocmask*()
sigsetmask()	*sigprocmask*()
sigpause()	*sigsuspend*()
sigvec()	*sigaction*()
sigstack()	(none)
sigreturn()	(none)
(none)	*sigpending*()
signal()	*signal*()

and the process invokes the *psig*() routine to carry out the appropriate action.

The work of *psignal*() is a patchwork of special cases required by the process-debugging and job-control facilities, and by intrinsic properties associated with signals. The steps involved in posting a signal are as follows:

1. Determine the action that the receiving process will take when the signal is delivered. This information is kept in the *p_sigignore*, *p_sigmask*, and *p_sigcatch* fields of the process's proc structure. If a process is not ignoring, masking, or catching a signal, the default action is presumed to apply. If a process is being traced by its parent—that is, by a debugger—the parent process is always permitted to intercede before the signal is delivered. If the process is ignoring the signal, *psignal*()'s work is done and the routine may return.

2. Given an action, *psignal*() adds the signal to the set of pending signals, *p_sig*, and then does any implicit actions specific to that signal. For example, if the signal is a *continue signal*, SIGCONT, any pending signals that would normally cause the process to stop, such as SIGTTOU, are removed.

3. Next, *psignal*() checks whether the signal is being masked. If the process is currently masking delivery of the signal, *psignal*()'s work is complete and it may return.

4. If, however, the signal is not being masked, *psignal*() must either perform the action directly, or arrange for the process to execute so that it will carry out the action associated with the signal. To get the process running, *psignal*() must interrogate the state of the process.

SSLEEP The process is blocked awaiting an event. If the process is sleeping at a negative priority, then nothing further can be done. Otherwise, the action can be applied, either directly, or indirectly by waking up the process. There are two actions that can be applied directly. For signals that cause a process to stop, the process is placed in an SSTOP state, and the parent process is notified of the state change by posting of a SIGCHLD signal to it. For signals that are ignored by default, the signal is removed from *p_sig* and the work is complete. Otherwise, the action associated with the signal must be performed in the context of the receiving process, and the process is placed onto the run queue with a call to *setrun*().

SSTOP The process is stopped by a signal or because it is being debugged. If the process is being debugged, then there is nothing to do until the controlling process permits it to run again. If the process is stopped by a signal and the posted signal would cause the process to stop again, then there is nothing to do and the posted signal is discarded. Otherwise, the signal is either a *continue signal*, or a signal that would normally cause the process to terminate (unless caught). If the signal is SIGCONT, then the process is set running again unless it is blocked waiting on an event; if the process is blocked, it is returned to SSLEEP state. If the signal is SIGKILL, then the process is set running again no matter what, so that it can terminate the next time it is scheduled to run. Otherwise, the signal causes the process to be made *runnable*, but the process is not placed on the run queue, as it must wait for a continue signal.

SRUN, SIDL, SZOMB
: If the process is not the currently executing process, an AST is posted so that the signal will be noticed by the receiving process as soon as possible.

The implementation of *psignal*() is complicated, mostly because *psignal*() controls the process-state transitions that are part of the job-control facilities and because it interacts strongly with process-debugging facilities.

Delivering a Signal

Most actions associated with delivering a signal to a process are carried out within the context of that process. A process checks its proc structure for pending signals at least once each time it enters the system, by calling the *issig*() routine.

Issig() takes the first signal it encounters in the set of pending signals, *p_sig*, and places that signal in the *p_cursig* field. If delivering the signal causes a signal handler to be invoked or a core dump to be performed, the caller is notified that a signal is pending, and actual delivery is done by a call to *psig*(). That is,

```
if (issig())
    psig();
```

Otherwise, the action associated with the signal is performed within *issig*() (these actions mimic the actions carried out by *psignal*()).

The *psig*() routine has two cases to handle:

1. Producing a core dump

2. Invoking a signal handler

The former task is performed by the *core*() routine and is always followed by a call to *exit*() to force process termination. To invoke a signal handler, *psig*() first calculates a set of masked signals and installs it in *p_sigmask*. This set normally includes the signal being delivered, so that the signal handler will not be invoked recursively by the same signal. Any signals specified in the *sigvec* system call at the time the handler was installed also will be included. *Psig*() then calls the *sendsig*() routine to arrange for the signal handler to execute immediately after the process returns to user mode. Finally, the signal in *p_cursig* is cleared and *psig*() returns, presumably to be followed by a return to user mode.

The implementation of the *sendsig*() routine is machine-dependent. Figure 4.8 shows the flow of control associated with signal delivery on the VAX. For the VAX, an argument list and the process's current user-mode execution context are stored on the signal stack (possibly different from the normal run-time stack), and the state of the process is manipulated so that, on return to user mode, a call will be immediately made to a body of code stored in the process's user structure. (The u-dot area must be readable by the user process for this to work.) This code, termed the *signal-trampoline code*, invokes the signal handler with the appropriate argument list, and, if the handler returns, makes a *sigreturn* system call to reset the process's signal state to what it was prior to the signal.

Job Control

Job control is a facility provided by the C shell [Joy, 1986] and by the Korn shell [Korn, 1983; Korn, 1984] that permits a user to control the operation of groups of processes termed *jobs*. The most important facility provided by job control is multiplexing access to the user's terminal, so that only one job at a time may read from and/or write to the terminal. This facility provides some of the advantages of window systems, although job control is sufficiently different that it is often used in combination with windows on those systems that have them. Job control is implemented on top of the process group and signal facilities.

Figure 4.8 Delivering a signal to a process.

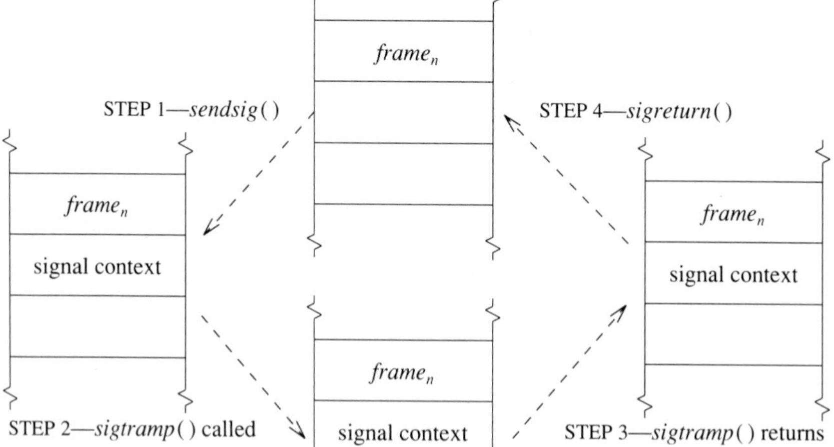

Each job is a collection of processes that are assigned the same process-group identifier. Processes organized in a pipeline (see Sections 2.4 and 2.6) are placed in a single process group, typically defined by the PID of the process at the head of the pipeline. Jobs are manipulated by posting of signals to the job's process group with the *killpg* system call. For example, to force a job to stop,

```
killpg(pgrp, SIGSTOP)
```

would be used.

Several jobs may compose a *session*, which is intuitively all the processes started during a single login session. A session usually has an associated *controlling terminal* that is used by default for communicating with the user. Certain characters typed at the keyboard of this terminal produce signals that are sent to all processes in one job in the session; that job is in the *foreground*, while all other jobs in the session are in the *background*. A shell may change the foreground job by using the TIOCSPGRP *ioctl* on the controlling terminal. Background jobs will be automatically stopped by a signal if they attempt to access the terminal by performing a *read*, *write*, or *ioctl* system call (with the last enforced only if the call would alter the state of the terminal).

The job-control facilities were added to the Berkeley UNIX systems in 1980. Their design was based on similar facilities included in the TENEX operating system [Bobrow *et al.*, 1972]. The original UNIX implementation was done on a PDP-11/70 by Jim Kulp at the International Institute for Applied Systems Analysis (IIASA) in Laxenburg, Austria. There is more to job control than has been described here; Chapter 9 covers the material related to terminal handling.

The job-control facilities found in AT&T System V, Release 3 attempt to provide equivalent functionality, but use a scheme based on pseudoterminals and process groups [AT&T, 1987]. POSIX has adopted job control very much like that in 4.3BSD, and the corresponding FIPS requires it. Thus, it is likely that most UNIX future systems will have job control derived from 4BSD.

4.8 Process Debugging

4.3BSD, like most UNIX systems, provides a simplistic facility for controlling and debugging the execution of a process. This facility, accessed through the *ptrace* system call, permits a parent process to control a child process's execution by manipulating user- and kernel-mode execution state. In particular, with *ptrace*, a parent process can perform the following operations on a child process:

- Read and write address space and registers
- Intercept signals posted to the process
- Single step and continue the execution of the process
- Terminate the execution of the process

The *ptrace* call is used almost exclusively by program debuggers, such as **adb** and **dbx**.

When a process is being traced, any signals posted to a process cause the process to enter the SSTOP state. The parent process is notified with a SIGCHLD signal and may interrogate the status of the child with the *wait* and *wait3* system calls. On most machines, *trace traps*, generated when a process is single stepped, and *breakpoint faults*, caused by a process executing a breakpoint instruction, are translated by UNIX into SIGTRAP signals. Because signals posted to a traced process cause it to stop and result in the parent being notified, a program's execution can be controlled easily.

To start a program that is to be debugged, the debugger first creates a child process with a *fork* system call. After the fork, the child process uses a *ptrace* call that causes the process to be flagged as *traced* by setting the STRC bit in the *p_flag* field of the proc structure. The child process then sets the *trace trap* bit in the process's processor status word and calls *execve* to load the image of the program that is to be debugged. Setting this bit ensures that the first instruction executed by the child process after the new image is loaded will result in a hardware trace trap, which is translated by the system into a SIGTRAP signal. As the parent process is notified about all signals to the child, it can intercept the signal and gain control over the program before it executes a single instruction.

All the operations provided by *ptrace* are carried out in the context of the process being traced. When a parent process wants to perform an operation, it places the parameters associated with the operation into a data structure named *ipc*, clears the SWTED flag in the proc structure of the child process, and sleeps on the address of *ipc*. The next time the child process encounters a signal (immediately if it is currently stopped by a signal), it retrieves the parameters from the *ipc* structure and performs the requested operation. The child process then places a return result in the *ipc* structure and does a *wakeup*() call with the address of *ipc* as the wait channel.

The *ptrace* facility is *very* inefficient for three reasons. First, *ptrace* uses a single global data structure for passing information back and forth between all the parent and child processes in the system. As there is only one structure, it must be interlocked to ensure that only one parent–child process pair will use it at a time. Second, because the data structure has a small, fixed size, the parent process is limited to reading or writing 32 bits at a time. Finally, since each request by a parent process must be performed in the context of the child process, two context switches need to be done for each request—one from the parent to the child to send the request, and one from the child to the parent to return the result of the operation.

The debugging facilities included in the /**proc** filesystem, found in UNIX Eighth Edition [Killian, 1984], address all these problems. In the /**proc** system, the address space of another process can be accessed with *read* and *write* system calls, which allows a debugger to access a process being debugged with much greater efficiency. The data structure used to pass messages back and forth between processes has been replaced by a mechanism that eliminates contention for the *ipc* structure, as well as the context switches between the parent and child processes.

Exercises

4.1 Why is the user structure separate from the proc structure?

4.2 What are the implications of not having the user structure mapped at a fixed virtual address in the kernel's address space?

4.3 Why is the performance of the context-switching mechanism critical to the performance of a highly multiprogrammed system?

4.4 What effect would increasing the time quantum have on the system's interactive response and overall throughput?

4.5 What effect would reducing the number of run queues from 32 to 16 have on the scheduling overhead and on overall system performance?

4.6 Give three reasons for the system to select a new process to run.

4.7 What type of scheduling policy does 4.3BSD use? What type of jobs does the policy favor? Propose an algorithm for identifying these favored jobs.

4.8 Is job control still a useful facility, now that window systems are widely available? Why or why not?

4.9 When and how does process scheduling interact with the memory-management facilities?

4.10 Define the properties of a real-time system. Give two reasons why 4.3BSD is not a real-time system.

4.11 After a process has exited, it may enter the state of being a zombie, SZOMB, before disappearing from the system entirely. What is the purpose of the SZOMB state? What event causes a process to exit from SZOMB?

4.12 Suppose the data structures shown in Fig. 4.2 did not exist. What is the minimal information that the system would need to maintain to identify all the descendents of a process? Compare the costs in space and time to support each of the following operations:

a. creation of a new process

b. lookup of the process's parent

c. lookup of all of a process's siblings

d. lookup of all of a process's descendents

e. destruction of a process

4.13 The system raises the hardware priority to *splhigh* in the *sleep*() routine before altering the contents of a process's proc structure. Why?

4.14 A process blocked with a priority less than PZERO may never be awakened by a signal. Describe problems this situation may cause if a disk becomes unavailable while the system is running.

4.15 For each state listed in Table 4.2, list the system queues on which a process in that state might be found.

*4.16 In 4.3BSD, the signal SIGTSTP is delivered to a process when a user types a ‘‘suspend character.’’ Why would a process want to catch this signal before it is stopped?

*4.17 Before the 4.3BSD signal mechanism was added, signal handlers to catch the SIGTSTP signal were written as

```
catchstop()
{
        prepare to stop;
        signal(SIGTSTP, SIG_DFL);
        kill(getpid(), SIGTSTP);
        signal(SIGTSTP, catchstop);
}
```

This code causes an infinite loop in 4.3BSD. Why? How should the code be rewritten?

*4.18 The process-priority calculations and accounting statistics are all based on sampled data. Describe hardware support that would permit more accurate statistics and priority calculations.

*4.19 What are the implications of adding a fixed-priority scheduling algorithm to 4.3BSD?

*4.20 Why are signals a poor interprocess-communication facility?

**4.21 A *kernel-stack-invalid* trap occurs when an invalid value for the kernel-mode stack pointer is detected by the hardware. Assume this trap is received on an interrupt stack in kernel mode. How might the system gracefully terminate a process that receives such a trap while executing on the kernel's run-time stack contained in the user structure?

**4.22 Describe a synchronization scheme that would work in a tightly coupled multiprocessor hardware environment. Assume the hardware supports a *test-and-set* instruction.

**4.23 Describe alternatives to the *test-and-set* instruction that would allow you to build a synchronization mechanism for a multiprocessor UNIX system.

**4.24 A *lightweight process* is a thread of execution that operates within the context of a normal UNIX process. Multiple lightweight processes may exist in a single UNIX process and share memory, but each is able to do blocking operations, such as system calls. Describe how lightweight processes might be implemented entirely in user mode.

**4.25 Describe new kernel facilities that would be useful in implementing lightweight processes. How does the existing UNIX process context organization make kernel support for lightweight processes difficult?

References

AT&T, 1987.
AT&T, *The System V Interface Definition (SVID)*, Issue 2, American Telephone and Telegraph, Murray Hill, NJ (January 1987).

Bobrow *et al.*, 1972.
D. G. Bobrow, J. D. Burchfiel, D. L. Murphy, & R. S. Tomlinson, ''TENEX, a Paged Time Sharing System for the PDP-10,'' *Comm ACM* **15**(3), pp. 135–143, Association for Computing Machinery (March 1972).

Ferrin & Langridge, 1980.
T. E. Ferrin & R. Langridge, ''Interactive Computer Graphics with the UNIX Time-Sharing System,'' *Computer Graphics* **13**, pp. 320–331 (1980).

Joy, 1986.
W. N. Joy, ''An Introduction to the C Shell,'' pp. 4:1–46 in *UNIX User's Supplementary Documents, 4.3 Berkeley Software Distribution, Virtual VAX-11 Version*, USENIX Association, Berkeley, CA (1986).

Killian, 1984.
T. J. Killian, ''Processes as Files,'' *USENIX Association Conference Proceedings*, pp. 203–207 (June 1984).

Korn, 1983.
D. Korn, ''KSH—A Shell Programming Language,'' *USENIX Association Conference Proceedings*, pp. 191–202 (June 1983).

Korn, 1984.
D. Korn, *Introduction to the Korn Shell*, Issue 2, AT&T Bell Laboratories, Murray Hill, NJ (November 1984).

Ritchie, 1988.
D. M. Ritchie, ''Multi-Processor UNIX,'' private communication (April 25, 1988).

Sanderson *et al.*, 1986.
T. Sanderson, S. Ho, N. Heijden, E. Jabs, & J. L. Green, ''Near-Realtime Data Transmission During the ICE-Comet Giacobini-Zinner Encounter,'' *ESA Bulletin* **45**(21) (1986).

CHAPTER 5

Memory Management

5.1 Terminology

A central component of any operating system is the *memory-management system*. As the name implies, memory-management facilities are responsible for the management of memory resources available on a machine. These resources are typically layered in a hierarchical fashion, with memory access times inversely related to their proximity to the CPU, as shown in Fig. 5.1. The primary memory system is termed *main memory*; the next level of storage is referred to as *secondary storage* or *backing storage*. Main-memory systems usually are constructed from random-access memories, whereas secondary stores are placed on moving-head disk drives. In some workstation environments, the common two-level hierarchy is

Figure 5.1 Hierarchical layering of memory.

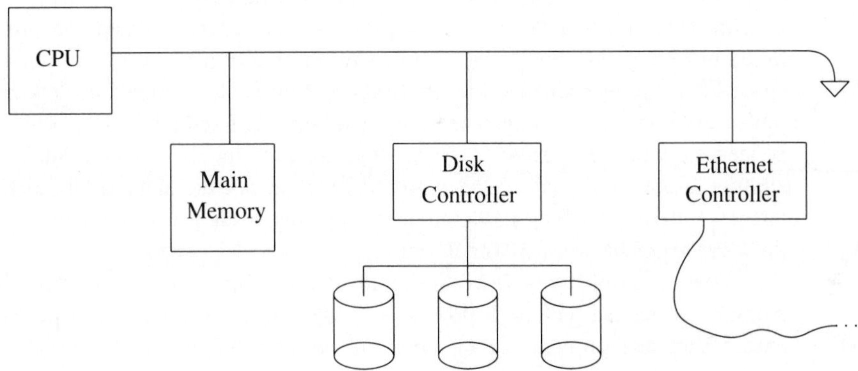

becoming a three-level hierarchy, with the addition of file-server machines connected to a workstation via a local-area network [Gingell *et al.*, 1987].

In a multiprogrammed environment, it is critical for the operating system to share available memory resources effectively among the processes. The operation of any memory-management policy is directly related to the memory required for a process to execute. That is, if a process must reside entirely in main memory in order for it to execute, then a memory-management system must be oriented toward allocating large units of memory. On the other hand, if a process can execute when it is only partially resident in main memory, then memory-management policies are likely to be very different. Memory-management facilities usually try to optimize the number of runnable processes that are resident in main memory. This goal must be considered together with the goals of the process scheduler (Chapter 4), in order to avoid conflicts that can adversely affect overall system performance.

Although the availability of secondary storage permits more processes to exist than can be resident in main memory, it also requires additional algorithms that can be complicated. Space management typically requires algorithms and policies different from those used for main memory, and a policy must be devised for deciding when to move processes between main memory and secondary storage.

Processes and Memory

Each process operates on a *virtual machine* that is defined by the architecture of the underlying hardware on which it executes. We are interested in only those machines that include the notion of a *virtual address space*. A virtual address space is a range of memory locations that a process references independently of the physical memory present on the hardware. References to the virtual address space—*virtual addresses*—are translated by hardware into references to physical memory. This operation, termed *address translation*, permits programs to be loaded into memory at any location without requiring position-dependent addresses in the program to be changed. Address translation and virtual addressing are also important in efficiently sharing a CPU, because position-independence usually permits context switching to be done very quickly.

Most machines provide a contiguous virtual address space for processes. Some machines, however, choose to partition visibly a process's virtual address space into regions termed *segments* [Intel, 1984]; such segments usually must be physically contiguous in main memory and begin at fixed addresses. We shall be concerned with only those systems that do not visibly segment their virtual address space. This use of the word *segment* is not the same as its earlier use when we were describing UNIX process segments, such as text and data segments; the latter segments are variable in size.

When multiple processes are coresident in main memory, the physical memory associated with each process's virtual address space must be protected to ensure that one process cannot alter the contents of another process's virtual address space. This protection is implemented in hardware and is usually tightly coupled with the implementation of address translation. Consequently, the two operations usually are defined and implemented together as hardware termed the *memory-management unit*.

When the effective range of addressable memory locations provided to a process is independent of the size of main memory, we say the machine supports *virtual memory*. Another way of saying this is that the virtual address space of a process is independent of the physical address space of the CPU. For a machine to support virtual memory, we also require that the whole of a process's virtual address space need not be resident in main memory for that process to execute.

Virtual memory can be implemented in many ways, some of which are software-based, such as *overlays*. Most effective virtual-memory schemes are, however, hardware-based. In these schemes, the virtual address space is divided into fixed-sized units, termed *pages*, as shown in Fig. 5.2. Virtual-memory references are resolved by the address-translation unit to a page in main memory and an offset within that page. Hardware protection is applied by the memory-management unit on a page-by-page basis.

Some systems provide a two-tiered virtual memory system in which pages are grouped into segments [Organick, 1975]. In these systems, protection is usually at the segment level. In the remainder of this chapter, we shall be concerned with only those virtual-memory systems that are page-based.

Paging

Address translation handles the first requirement of virtual memory by decoupling the virtual address space of a process from the physical address space of the CPU. To satisfy the second requirement, each page of virtual memory is marked as *resident* or *nonresident* in main memory. If a process references a location in virtual memory that is not resident, a hardware trap termed a *page fault* is generated.

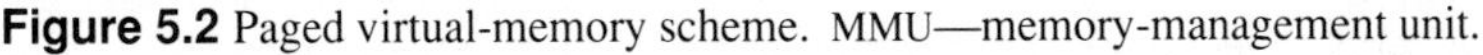

Figure 5.2 Paged virtual-memory scheme. MMU—memory-management unit.

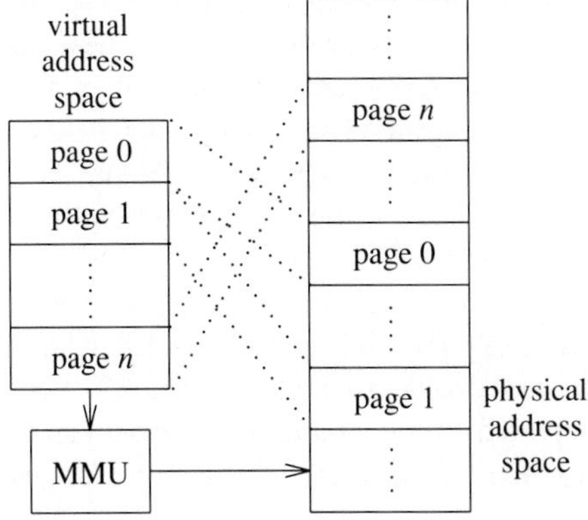

The servicing of page faults, or *paging*, permits processes to execute even if they are only partially resident in main memory.

Coffman and Denning [1973] characterize paging systems by three important policies:

1. When the system loads pages into memory (the *fetch policy*)
2. Where the system places pages in memory (the *placement policy*)
3. How the system selects pages to be removed from main memory when pages are unavailable for a placement request (the *replacement policy*)

In normal circumstances, all pages of main memory are equally good and the placement policy has no effect on the performance of a paging system. Thus, a paging system's behavior is dependent on only the fetch policy and the replacement policy. Under a *pure demand-paging* system, a demand-fetch policy is used, in which only the missing page is fetched and replacements occur only when main memory is full. Consequently, the performance of a pure demand-paging system depends on only the system's replacement policy. In practice, paging systems do not implement a pure demand-paging algorithm. Instead, the fetch policy often is altered to do *prepaging*—the fetching pages of memory other than the one that caused the page fault—and the replacement policy is invoked before main memory is full.

Replacement Algorithms

The replacement policy is the most critical aspect of any paging system. There is a wide range of algorithms from which we can select in designing a replacement strategy for a paging system. Much research has been carried out in evaluating the performance of different page-replacement algorithms [Belady, 1966; King, 1971; Marshall, 1979]. In preparation for our discussion of the replacement algorithm used in 4.3BSD, we shall introduce some basic terminology.

A process's paging behavior for a given input is described in terms of the pages referenced over the time of the process's execution. This sequence of pages, termed a *reference string*, represents the behavior of the process at discrete times during the process's lifetime. Corresponding to the sampled references that constitute a process's reference string are real-time values that reflect whether or not the associated references resulted in a page fault. A useful measure of a process's behavior is the *fault rate*, which is the number of page faults encountered while processing a reference string, normalized by the length of the reference string.

Page-replacement algorithms typically are evaluated in terms of their effectiveness on reference strings that have been collected from executing real programs. Formal analysis can also be used, although it is difficult to perform unless many restrictions are applied to the execution environment. The most common metric used in measuring the effectiveness of a page-replacement algorithm is the fault rate.

Page-replacement algorithms are defined in terms of the criteria they use for selecting pages to be reclaimed. For example, the *Optimal Replacement Policy* [Denning, 1970] states that the "best" choice of a page to replace is the one with the longest expected time until its next reference. Clearly, this policy is not applicable to dynamic systems, as it requires a priori knowledge of the paging characteristics of a process. The policy is useful for evaluation purposes, however, as it provides a yardstick for comparing the performance of other page-replacement algorithms.

Practical page-replacement algorithms require a certain amount of state information that is used in selecting replacement pages. This state typically includes the reference pattern of a process, sampled at discrete time intervals. On some systems, this information can be expensive to collect [Babaoğlu & Joy, 1981]. As a result, the "best" page-replacement algorithm may not be the most efficient.

Working-Set Model

The working-set model assumes that processes exhibit a slowly changing locality of reference. For a period of time, a process operates in a set of subroutines or loops, causing all its memory references to refer to a fixed subset of its address space, termed the *working set*. The process periodically changes its working set, abandoning certain areas of memory and beginning to access new ones. After a period of transition, the process defines a new set of pages as its working set. In general, if the system can provide the process with enough pages to hold the pages in that process's working set, the process will experience a low page-fault rate. If the system cannot provide the process with enough pages for the working set, the process will run slowly and will have a high page-fault rate.

Precisely calculating the working set of a process is impossible without a priori knowledge of that process's memory reference pattern. However, the working set can be approximated by various means. One method of approximation is to track the number of pages held by a process and that process's page-fault rate. If the page-fault rate increases above a high watermark, the working set is assumed to have increased and the number of pages held by the process is allowed to grow. Conversely, if the page-fault rate drops below a low watermark, the working set is assumed to have decreased and the number of pages held by the process is contracted.

Swapping

Swapping is the term used to describe a memory-management policy in which entire processes are moved to and from secondary storage when main memory is in short supply. Swap-based memory-management systems usually are less complicated than are demand-paged systems, since there is less bookkeeping to do. However, pure swapping systems are typically less effective than are paging systems, since the degree of multiprogramming is lowered by the requirement that processes be fully resident to execute. Swapping is sometimes combined with paging in a two-tiered scheme, whereby paging is used to satisfy memory demands until a severe memory shortfall requires drastic action, in which case swapping is used.

Secondary Storage

In this chapter, a portion of secondary storage that is used for paging and/or swapping is termed a *swap area* or *swap space*. The hardware devices on which these areas reside are termed *swap devices*.

Advantages of Virtual Memory

There are several advantages to the use of virtual memory on computers capable of supporting this facility properly. Virtual memory allows large programs to be run on machines with main memory configurations that are smaller than the program size. On machines with a moderate amount of memory, it allows more programs to be resident in main memory to compete for CPU time, as the programs need not be completely resident. When programs use sections of their program or data space for some time, leaving other sections unused, the unused sections need not be present. Also, the use of virtual memory allows programs to start up faster, as they generally require only a small section to be loaded before they begin processing arguments and determining what actions to take. Other parts of a program may not be needed at all during individual runs. As a program runs, additional sections of its program and data spaces are paged in on demand (*demand paging*). Finally, there are many algorithms that are more easily programmed by sparse use of a large address space than by careful packing of data structures into a small area. Such techniques are too expensive for use without virtual memory, but may run much faster when that facility is available, without using an inordinate amount of real memory.

On the other hand, the use of virtual memory can degrade performance. It is more efficient to load a program all at one time than to load it entirely in small sections on demand. There is a finite cost for each operation, including saving and restoring state and determining which page must be loaded. So, some systems use demand paging only for programs larger than some minimum size.

Hardware Requirements for Virtual Memory

Nearly all versions of UNIX have required some form of memory-management hardware to support transparent multiprogramming. To protect processes from modification by other processes, the memory-management hardware must prevent programs from changing their own address mapping. The UNIX kernel runs in a privileged mode (*kernel mode* or *system mode*) in which memory mapping may be controlled, whereas processes run in an unprivileged mode (*user mode*). There are several additional architectural requirements for support of virtual memory. The first and most obvious is that the CPU must distinguish between resident and nonresident portions of the address space, must suspend programs when they refer to nonresident addresses, and must resume their operation once the operating system has placed the required section in memory. As the CPU may discover missing data at various times during the execution of an instruction, it must provide a mechanism to save the machine state so that the instruction can be continued or restarted later. The CPU may implement restarting by saving enough state when an instruction begins that the state can be restored when a fault is discovered. Alternatively, instructions could delay any modifications or side effects until after any faults would be discovered, so that the instruction execution need not back up before restarting. On some computers, instruction backup requires the assistance of the operating system.

Most machines designed to support demand-paged virtual memory include hardware support for the collection of information on program references to memory. When the system selects a page for replacement, it must save the contents of that page if they have been modified since the page was brought into memory. The hardware usually maintains a per-page flag showing whether the page has been modified. Many machines also include a flag recording any access to a page for use by the replacement algorithm.

5.2 Evolution of 4.3BSD Memory Management

The 4.3BSD memory-management system has evolved from early releases of UNIX on the PDP-11 minicomputer. Before we present the 4.3BSD memory-management system, we shall review aspects of some of its predecessors.

Version 7 UNIX

Version 7 was the last version of UNIX that was released from Bell Laboratories for the PDP-11, a 16-bit minicomputer. The PDP-11 uses a segmented memory architecture. The virtual-address space of a process is divided into eight segments that can be up to 8 Kbyte each. This virtual-address–space limit of 64 Kbyte (2^{16} bytes) applies not only to each user process but also to the kernel (which executes in a separate, privileged protection mode).

Early PDP-11s supported a maximum of 248 Kbyte of main memory; later models, such as the PDP-11/70, allowed nearly 4 Mbyte of memory. Some models also supported separate instruction and data spaces, a feature that effectively doubled the maximum program size.

The limited virtual-address range of the PDP-11 inspired developers at Case Western Reserve, Purdue University, the University of California at Berkeley, and several European universities to create software-overlay schemes for both user programs and the kernel. Overlays for the kernel were especially useful because the limited address space was usually the biggest problem with providing facilities such as networking on the PDP-11. Even with software overlays, however, the maximum size of individual programs on the PDP-11 was small in comparison to the amount of main memory that was usually available. And overlays extended only the effective text space, not the data space (at least, not without losing addressing transparency). Larger data space is what many programs, such as those written in LISP, really need.

UNIX memory-management techniques were particularly simple, as befitted this class of machine. Programs were loaded contiguously in physical memory and in their entirety. Memory sharing was limited to read-only sharing of text segments in suitably marked programs. Memory management was swap-based, with the secondary storage used for swapping limited to a single dedicated area of a disk. Finally, swap space for processes was allocated at the time a process was created, to ensure its availability.

UNIX 32V

The VAX-11/780 was introduced in 1978. This 32-bit minicomputer has a 4-gigabyte (2^{32}-byte) virtual-address space and was designed to support demand-paged virtual memory.

The first UNIX system that ran on a VAX was called 32V; it was a straightforward port of the existing PDP-11 version of UNIX. The developers created this port initially by emulating PDP-11 hardware memory-management facilities on the VAX's paged virtual-memory architecture [London & Reiser, 1978]. Processes were still fully resident and contiguous in main memory. The only restriction that was eased was the maximum size of a program; this limit was increased from 64 Kbyte to a tunable limit that was, by default, 192 Kbyte. Although programs could be larger than on the PDP-11, they still had to be fully resident. Therefore, programs were limited in size by the amount of physical memory present on a machine (0.5 to 2 Mbyte, although part of that memory was occupied by the UNIX kernel, which was permanently resident).

The original port also followed Version 7 in that entire processes were still swapped to secondary storage when main memory was in short supply. In addition, the only memory sharing among processes was accomplished through pure text segments.

Subsequent revisions to the memory-management system before release of 32V expanded on this initial scheme in two ways. First, contiguous layout of programs in main memory was replaced by a *scatter-loading* scheme whereby a process's virtual-address space was loaded into main memory on a page-by-page basis. Second, when main memory was needed, parts of a process, instead of entire processes, could be swapped to secondary storage. Although these two facilities avoided memory fragmentation and provided a higher degree of multiprogramming than was available on the PDP-11, respectively, they did not fully support the VAX's virtual-memory architecture. It still was not possible to create a process whose virtual memory was larger than the physical memory available on a machine, because the entire process was required to be resident in order for that process to execute.

3BSD

The 3BSD release replaced the scatter loading and partial swapping found in 32V with a demand-paged virtual-memory–management system. The design of this system was motivated by a need to run very large processes (larger than the available physical memory), and to provide an accessible environment for carrying out performance evaluation studies related to virtual-memory management [Babaoğlu *et al.*, 1979].

The 3BSD paging system used

- A demand-paging fetch policy (i.e., only those pages that were faulted were fetched by the system)
- A page-by-page placement policy
- A replacement algorithm that approximated global least recently used (LRU)

The replacement algorithm considered all available physical memory as a loop of pages, scanning the loop to collect reference information, and selecting replacements according to least recent use. In addition, memory-utilization statistics maintained by the paging system were used by the process scheduler to vary dynamically the degree of multiprogramming.

As in previous systems, all of the kernel text and most of the kernel data resided permanently in main memory. The structure of the virtual-address space of a process (text, data, and stack segments) remained unchanged, although the space's maximum size was no longer limited by the available memory. Memory sharing among processes also was unchanged, due mainly to an underlying design decision to minimize user-visible changes to the system.

Secondary-storage management was not significantly different in 3BSD from that in 4.3BSD. Storage was preallocated for the entire address space of a process at the time the process was created. This policy was mainly a result of the large amount of secondary storage in comparison to main memory.

4.1BSD

The memory-management system in the 4.0BSD and 4.1BSD releases was the result of concentrated performance-tuning work [Kashtan, 1980; Joy, 1980]. The fundamental algorithms and data structures introduced in 3BSD remained virtually unchanged. Alterations were made, however, to address specific performance problems and to track hardware changes, such as the introduction of the VAX-11/750.

4.1BSD contained five changes of note:

1. The paging system was altered such that, instead of manipulating hardware pages, it dealt with a logical page, termed a *cluster*. Clusters were required to be multiples of the underlying hardware page size and were added to reduce the cost of page-related operations, such as page-fault handling. The use of clustering also reduced the size of certain system data structures, thereby permitting larger virtual memories to be supported in the same amount of physical memory.

2. A limited amount of prepaging was added to the fetch policy. Part of the prepaging was a consequence of the addition of clustering. Instead of fetching a single page in response to a fault, the system fetched as many pages as were in the cluster.

3. The overhead associated with moving dirty pages to secondary storage was reduced by multiple clusters being written in a single operation whenever possible.

4. The device and block numbers of pages from text images were stored with the descriptions of free pages, caching text pages that had been used recently in memory.

5. Processes were provided a minimal amount of control over the page-replacement and prepaging policies used by the system. This control took the form of a system call that a process could use to notify the system when it was expecting to exhibit sequential or random memory reference patterns. The system then used this information to disable prepaging (in the case of random accesses), or to mark pages as likely candidates for replacement.

4.3BSD

The changes to the virtual-memory system that appeared in 4.3BSD were oriented toward adapting to changes in hardware technology.

- The text images and page tables of all programs were retained in a cache after *exit*, much as in the older *sticky-bit* mechanism that was used to force pages of heavily used programs to be retained in swap space.
- The page-replacement algorithm was modified to be independent of the size of main memory; this change improved the performance of the paging system on machines with large main memories.
- Workstations that utilized remote file servers, combined with larger main memories, made it worthwhile to expand the amount of prepaging.

5.3 VAX Memory-Management Hardware

This section provides an overview of the VAX memory-management architecture, on which the design of the 4.3BSD virtual-memory system is heavily dependent. Further information on the VAX hardware can be found in the VAX *Hardware Handbook* [DEC, 1980]. Memory management on the Tahoe processor is similar to that on the VAX.

VAX Virtual Address Space

The VAX memory-management hardware supports a two-level mapping mechanism for doing address translation. The first-level page tables reside in the system's virtual address space and map user page tables. These tables in turn, map the user virtual address space. The 32-bit virtual address space of the VAX is divided into four equal-sized blocks, as shown in Fig. 5.3.

Two of these blocks, known as the *P0* and *P1 regions*, are used for the address space of a user process. The third block, known as the *system region*, contains the shared kernel virtual address space; the fourth region (marked *reserved*) is not supported by current VAX hardware. The P0 region starts at virtual address 0 and grows toward higher addresses. The P1 region on the other hand, starts at the top of the user virtual address space and grows toward lower addresses. The regions are described by two per-process base-length register pairs. The address space on the Tahoe uses all four regions, with the system in the top region.

On the VAX, the virtual address space of the current user process is directly addressable by the kernel. In general, the system takes advantage of this accessibility in only low-level parts of the kernel—for example, in the *copyin*() and *copyout*() routines that move data between user and kernel space. Use in such clearly defined routines provides efficiency benefits, while avoiding more widespread use that would inhibit portability. The efficiency advantages are large enough that some non-VAX implementations, such as Sun Microsystems MC68000 machines, also map user space into the kernel.

VAX Page Tables

The VAX page size is fixed at 512 bytes. Each VAX *page-table entry (PTE)* consists of four bytes of mapping and protection information, as shown in Fig. 5.4. If the hardware attempts to translate an address through a PTE that has the *valid* bit

Figure 5.3 Layout of VAX virtual address space.

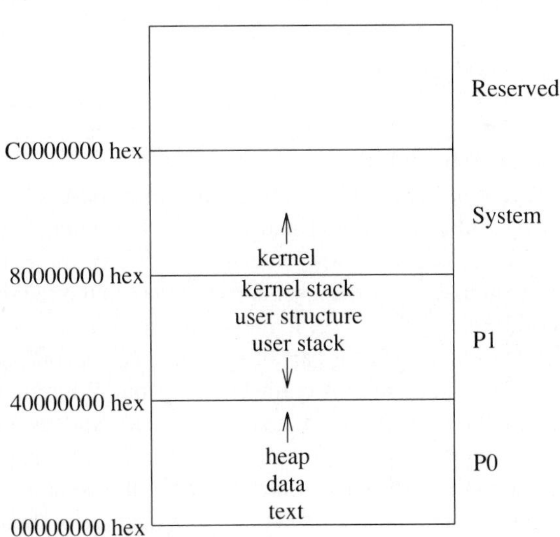

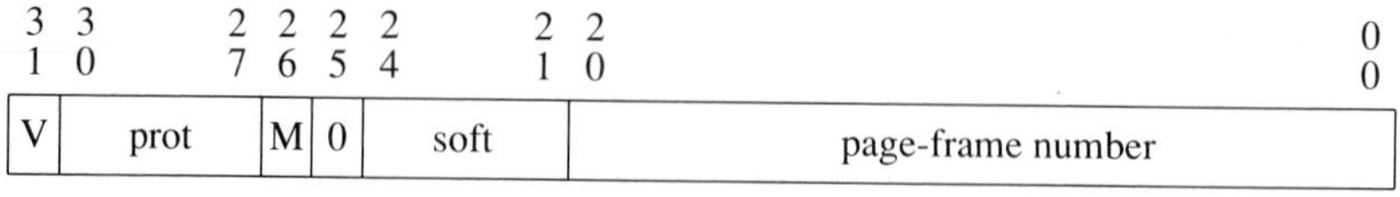

31	30–27	26	25	24–21	20–00
V	prot	M	0	soft	page-frame number

Figure 5.4 Format of a VAX page-table entry (PTE). V—page valid bit; prot—protection-mode field; M—page-modified bit; soft—software defined field.

off, a *translation-not-valid fault* (i.e., a *page fault*) is generated. Whereas most architectures that support virtual memory, including the Tahoe, provide a per-page *reference bit* that is automatically set by the hardware when the corresponding page is referenced, the VAX has no such mechanism. The mechanism used by 4.3BSD to simulate a reference bit is discussed in Section 5.12.

The fields in a PTE contain the physical page address that holds the data for that address, as well as access modes that specify whether a page may be read and/or written. A four-bit portion of each PTE is reserved for use by software; it is not interpreted by the VAX memory-management hardware. Finally, one bit of the PTE, the *modify* bit, is set by the hardware each time the page is modified.

VAX page tables reside in main memory when they are being used. The hardware supports paging of page tables, but this facility is not utilized by 4.3BSD.

System-Address Translation

Each region of the address space is mapped by a separate page table. System space is mapped by the system page table, which is physically contiguous in main memory. Two hardware registers are set to the address and length of the system page table once it has been set up at boot time. The *system base register* (SBR) contains the physical address of the *system page table*, and the *system length register* (SLR) contains the number of entries in the page table. In 4.3BSD, the system page table is statically allocated, and the size of the system map is thus set when the kernel is compiled.

Since the 32-bit VAX address space is divided into four equal-sized regions, the two most significant bits of the address determine the region into which an address falls (see Table 5.1).

Once a region has been selected, the remaining address bits are interpreted as a page number within the region and a byte offset within the page. Since the pages are 512 bytes each, the low-order nine bits give the byte offset within the page. The remaining 21 bits specify the page index in the region.

Virtual-address translation for kernel addresses is shown in Fig. 5.5. Once an address has been identified as a part of system space according to bits 30 and 31 of the address, the page index is extracted from bits 9 through 29. The index is checked against the system length register, and, if valid, is added to the system base register to find the PTE. As the memory-management hardware translates the address, it locates the PTE, checks that the page is resident and that the desired access is allowed, and then extracts the physical page number. Finally, the

Table 5.1 Mapping of high-order bits to regions.

High-order address bits	Region
11	reserved
10	system
01	P1
00	P0

physical page number is combined with the byte offset within the page to generate a physical-memory address.

User-Address Translation

Unlike the system page tables, the user page tables (mapping the P0 and P1 regions) are located in virtual rather than physical memory. Because a four-byte entry is needed to map each 512-byte page of address space, a map for one of these 1-gigabyte regions would require 8 Mbyte of page tables if all the entries

Figure 5.5 System virtual-address translation. SLR—system length register; SBR—system base register.

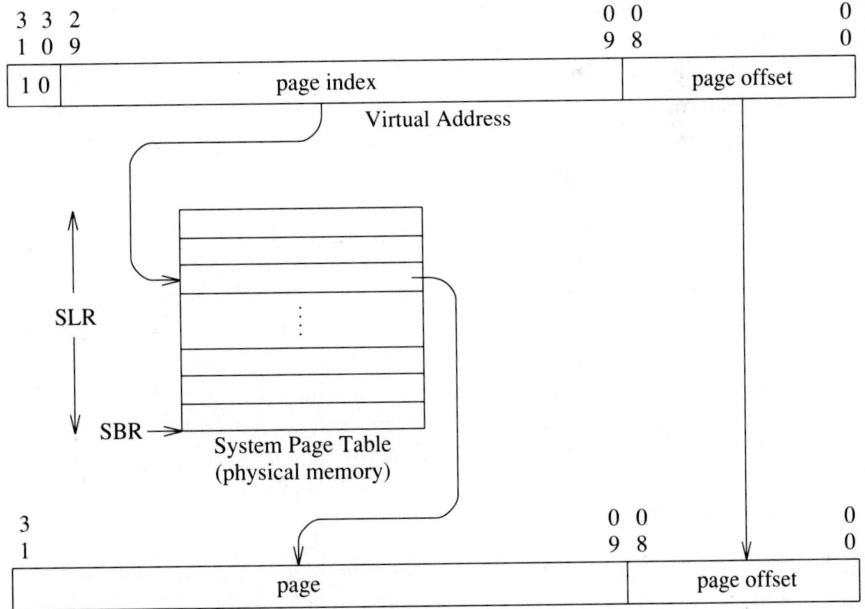

mapping the region were created. However, the hardware locates these page tables in kernel virtual memory, and therefore not all pages of the page table need to be resident simultaneously (although the system does not take advantage of this capability). As a result, the virtual-address–translation process for user addresses is a two-step translation using a two-level page table.

Like the system page table, the P0 page table is described by two hardware registers. The *P0 base register* (*P0BR*) is the system virtual address of the start of the page table for the P0 region for the current process. The *P0 length register* (*P0LR*) contains the number of entries in the P0 table. These registers are set from the PCB on each context switch, as they are generally different for each process. The P1 region is described in a similar way by the *P1 base register* (*P1BR*), and by the *P1 length register* (*P1LR*). Both base registers point to the beginning of the map for a 1-gigabyte region. However, whereas the P0LR specifies the number of PTEs present in the P0 map, the P1 length register specifies the number of entries that are *outside* the region. This scheme is optimized for segment growth, since expansion requires only a change in the length register.

The procedure for virtual-address translation for a reference to a P0 or P1 address is similar to the procedure for system-address translation, except for the location of the page tables. The high-order bits of the address select a region. Then, as with a system address, the page index is extracted from bits 9 through 29 of the address. This index is compared with the appropriate length register. If the index is less than the value of the length register for P0 space (greater than or equal to the length register for P1 space), the page value is valid. The index is then combined with the base register to yield a system virtual address for the PTE. Figure 5.6 shows the translation that indexes into the table to find the entry for the desired page. This system address is translated as described previously to calculate a physical address from which to fetch the user PTE. Finally, the PTE is checked for validity and protection of the page, and to obtain the physical page number. The page offset is added to the page address to produce the final physical address.

Note that the location of user (P0 and P1) page tables in kernel virtual memory means that two translations are needed to find a user physical address: one translation using the system page table and one using the P0 or P1 page table. This translation mechanism can be regarded as a two-level page table for user addresses. Because the user page tables are allocated in pages and are mapped by the system page table, the page index (bits 9 through 29 of the user virtual address) can be considered to have two parts. Bits 16 through 29 select a page of PTEs, and bits 9 through 15 select a PTE in the page. Thus, one kernel PTE maps one 512-byte page of kernel memory containing 128 user PTEs, which, in turn, map 64 Kbyte of user memory. System-address translation uses only one page table, however, so the system page table has only a single level of translation.

Page Faults

While translating a virtual address, the memory-management hardware may discover a PTE that does not have the valid bit set. When such a PTE is found, the

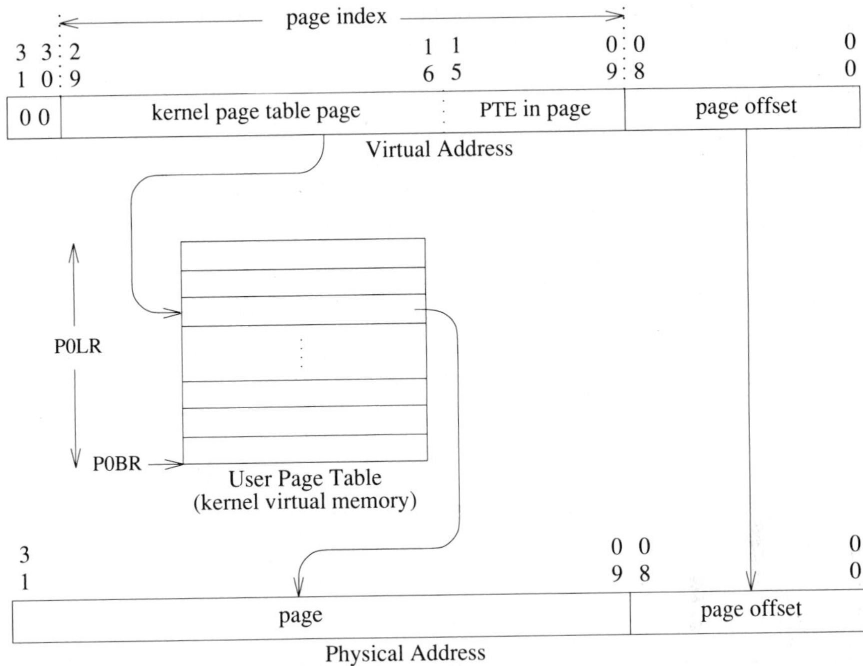

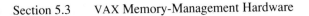

Figure 5.6 User virtual-address translation. P0LR—process length register; P0BR—process base register.

current instruction cannot be completed until the needed page is brought into memory and the PTE is marked valid. The memory-management hardware initiates a *page fault* by executing a trap sequence to system mode. The pending instruction is backed up to its beginning, so that it can be restarted. Restarting requires that any side effects, such as register or memory modifications, be undone so that they will be performed only once. (A few complex instructions, such as string moves, may set the state, so that the instruction can be resumed rather than restarting.) When a fault occurs, the operating system gains control and analyzes the fault. In the normal case, a page is fetched from disk or a new page is allocated for the process. After updating the PTE, the system returns from the trap. The return to user mode allows the CPU to reattempt execution of the original instruction.

The memory-management hardware may discover other conditions that prevent an address translation from completing successfully. A page index may be outside the range specified by the appropriate length register, or an access may not be allowed by the protection field of a PTE. If the hardware detects either of these conditions, it causes a trap to the kernel instead of completing the address translation. Most such traps cause the kernel to deliver a signal (SIGSEGV or SIGBUS) to the process rather than to continue execution. There is one exception:

When the stack pointer is below the current stack segment but still within the P1 region, the kernel automatically extends the stack and returns to the user program.

Translation Buffers

The use of a two-level page table and the table's location in main memory imply that as many as three memory references may be required to fetch the contents of a virtual address. As this process would be prohibitive if it were required on each memory reference, a hardware cache of PTEs, termed a *translation lookaside buffer*, is maintained. When an address translation is performed, the translation buffer is checked for a matching entry, thus avoiding memory accesses. If the required translation is not already in the cache, it is fetched and is placed in the cache, possibly displacing an older entry.

The presence of the translation cache requires that the operating system purge any *stale translations* when PTEs are modified in memory. Purges may be done on the VAX through invalidation of the entire cache by moving a zero to the *translation buffer invalidate all* (TBIA) register, or through invalidation of an entry for a single virtual address by moving the address to the *translation buffer invalidate single* (TBIS) register.

5.4 Management of Main Memory: The Core Map

In 4.3BSD, main memory is logically divided into two parts. The kernel is permanently resident in memory and uses memory to hold its text segment and most of its data segment. In addition, certain kernel data structures, such as the process table, that also must remain resident are allocated at the time the kernel is initialized. The remainder of main memory is allocated to processes according to demand (see Fig. 5.7). (A small area at the top of memory is used to hold the last few messages that were printed on the console; this arrangement allows postmortem debugging after a system crash.)

The *core map* is the central data structure used to manage main memory. It consists of an array of structures, one entry for each cluster of pages in main memory, excluding those allocated to the kernel text and data. The core map is allocated at boot time as one of the last steps in the bootstrap procedure. The core map manages a contiguous section of main memory from *firstfree* at the end of the kernel data segment to *maxfree*, as shown in Fig. 5.7. This contiguous region is the part of main memory available to user processes.

Figure 5.7 Physical memory available to processes. Msgs—messages.

Kernel	User memory	msgs

0 *firstfree* *maxfree*

The core map is maintained as a contiguous array of structures, one per page cluster. Although the elements are small (16 bytes in 4.3BSD), if there are many of them, the overall size may be large. Thus, it is desirable for the page-cluster size to be large to reduce the number of elements and the size of the array. The definition of the core-map structure is given in Fig. 5.8.

Because there is a one-to-one correspondence between the core-map array and the page clusters of main memory available for allocation, it is simple to locate a page cluster given a core-map structure, and vice versa. Thus, it is common for the memory-management routines in 4.3BSD to use core-map structures as a means of referencing portions of main memory.

A core-map structure is used for several different functions:

- The structure records information about the current use of a page cluster. This information can be used to map physical-memory addresses to virtual-memory addresses.
- Core-map elements for free pages are linked to form the memory free list.
- Locking and synchronization on a per-cluster basis is done through core-map structures.

Figure 5.8 Definition of the core-map structure.

```
struct cmap {
unsigned short c_next,       /* index of next free-list
                                entry */
               c_prev,       /* index of previous
                                free-list entry */
               c_hlink;      /* hash link for <blkno,mdev> */
unsigned short c_ndx;        /* index of owner proc or text */
unsigned int   c_page:21,    /* virtual page number
                                in segment */
               c_lock:1,     /* locked for raw i/o or pagein */
               c_want:1,     /* wanted */
               c_intrans:1,  /* intransit bit */
               c_free:1,     /* on the free list */
               c_gone:1,     /* associated page has
                                been released */
               c_type:2,     /* type CSYS or CTEXT or CSTACK
                                or CDATA */
               :4,           /* to longword boundary */
               c_blkno:24,   /* disk block this is a copy of */
               c_mdev:8;     /* which mounted dev
                                this is from */
};
```

- Free pages with useful contents are located using the core map.

The next few sections elaborate on each of these functions.

Physical-to-Virtual Translation

The first function of the core map is to store information about the current usage of the corresponding pages. This information is stored in a compact form to minimize space. The type of a page in its core-map entry is any one of system, text, data, or stack. Core-map entries for system pages need not contain other information, as they are immune to the operations done on the core map. Otherwise, the entry contains an index into the text table (for text pages) or into the process table (for data and stack pages and executables with writeable text segments) to identify the current user of a page cluster. The core-map entry also contains a page index describing the position of the page in the virtual segment that contains that page. These two items are sufficient to locate the PTEs for the process(es) using the memory associated with a core-map structure. Thus, information in the core-map structure permits translation of physical address to virtual address, much as the page tables support translation in the other direction.

Memory Free List

The second use of the core map is in creating the *memory free list*. All unallocated clusters of main memory are chained together using a doubly linked list formed from two fields of the core-map structure. To save space, the kernel constructs these chains using 16-bit indices, instead of 32-bit pointers (at least on the VAX).

The free list is kept in least-recent-use (LRU) order, and acts as a cache of potentially useful data. That is, clusters with useful contents may be reclaimed from the free list until they are overwritten. Because of its use as a cache, the free list is maintained as a doubly linked list. A flag in each core-map structure, *c_free*, indicates whether the cluster is on the free list.

Synchronization

The core map serves as the point of synchronization for virtual-memory functions that operate on individual page clusters. Hence, two synchronization flags (*c_lock* and *c_want*) are stored there. Memory pages are locked during the service of a page fault while I/O is being done; they are also locked during *raw* I/O operations that read or write directly to or from the user-process pages. The page-replacement algorithm (yet to be described) must write *dirty pages* to the swap area before freeing them; the page-replacement daemon locks such pages during the operation to avoid confusion with the page-fault handler, *pagein*().

An additional flag is used during page-fill operations for synchronization among processes sharing a page. This flag, the *in-transit flag*, (*c_intrans*), is set between the time that a read is initiated on a page cluster and the time that the cluster is ready for use. If multiple users of a nonresident cluster attempt to use that cluster at nearly the same time, this flag prevents any process but the first from starting the read.

Text-Page Cache

As mentioned in the previous section, free pages may hold useful data. One particular case—pages of a pure text segment—requires special-purpose information to be maintained. This information is used to identify the file from which pages were originally obtained. File information is recorded in a core-map structure as a <device, block number> pair. The device information specifies either a mounted filesystem, using the associated index in the filesystem mount table, or a pseudo–mounted-device index reserved for the swap device. The block number is the filesystem block number from which the data were obtained.

Core-Map Limits

The dense packing of the core-map structure forces many fields to be limited in size. As a result, the core-map structure is the major limitation on the sizes of other objects that may be supported by the system. The core map places limits on

- The amount of main memory that can be supported (through the link fields)
- The number of mounted filesystems (through the filesystem index used for identifying the origin of an associated page cluster)
- The size of filesystems, including interleaved swap space (through the filesystem block-number field)
- The number of processes and shared text images (through the field used to index in the process and shared text tables)

Memory-Allocation Routines

Main memory is allocated through one of two routines, *memall*() and *vmemall*(). These routines differ in only one respect: *memall*() will return failure if there is not enough main memory available, whereas *vmemall*() will wait for memory to be freed, so that it always succeeds; the latter uses *memall*() to do the actual allocation. As newly allocated memory must always be mapped into some virtual address before it can be used, these routines operate by filling in a virtual-address range. The *memall*() routine is called with a pointer to a PTE mapping the start of the range, a page count, and a process and type for use in setting up core-map entries. For each page cluster in the range, *memall*() finds memory by removing the first core-map entry from the memory free list. If a previous user of the page still has a reference to the page, the corresponding PTEs are located and cleared. The page numbers are then recorded in each PTE in the cluster, and the core-map entry is initialized with the information supplied by the caller.

Two interfaces are provided for freeing memory. The *memfree*() routine reclaims all memory assigned to a range of virtual addresses, presuming all the pages are resident. An alternate interface, provided by *vmemfree*(), reclaims only that memory that is associated with resident pages in a range of virtual addresses; it ignores nonresident pages.

The main-memory pool is initialized at boot time to include all pages not used statically by the kernel. Pages for user processes and for page tables are allocated from this pool. Certain parts of the kernel, such as the network, also allocate memory from this pool. However, because the network often needs to allocate memory at interrupt level, it is important that memory be available to avoid losing packets. For this reason, and for reasons that are described in Section 5.12, the kernel attempts to maintain at least a minimal amount of free memory (the amount is a configurable parameter). The current amount of free memory is kept in a global variable, *freemem*, that can be checked by routines that need memory and cannot block. This variable is also used for synchronization: Processes may sleep on the address of *freemem* awaiting more memory; they will be awakened when memory is freed after a shortage.

5.5 Management of Swap Space

Early versions of UNIX reserved a single area of one disk as a swap area. Processes were swapped to and from this area if all active processes could not fit into main memory. In general, swap activity was low; systems were configured to avoid swapping, because system performance was unacceptable when active processes had to be swapped. The addition of virtual memory placed new demands on the swap device. Larger programs demanded larger swap areas, and constant paging generated more transfers to and from the swap device. To gain higher performance from the disks for paging, 4BSD uses swap areas on multiple disks. A single logical swap device is interleaved among the available swap partitions on the disks. The devices are interleaved on *dmmax*-block boundaries so that a maximally sized allocation will never span devices. *Dmmax* has a value that depends on the virtual-memory limit configured for the system; it ranges from 0.5 to 2 Mbyte. The swap devices to be used are configured into the kernel ahead of time; the size of each is computed during autoconfiguration. Swap areas need not be the same size; the interleaving is computed using the maximum size of the available devices. The ordering of the swap blocks on the interleaved devices is illustrated in Fig. 5.9; each square represents *dmmax* blocks, with virtual block numbers increasing in the order shown.

Figure 5.9 Swap-block interleaving.

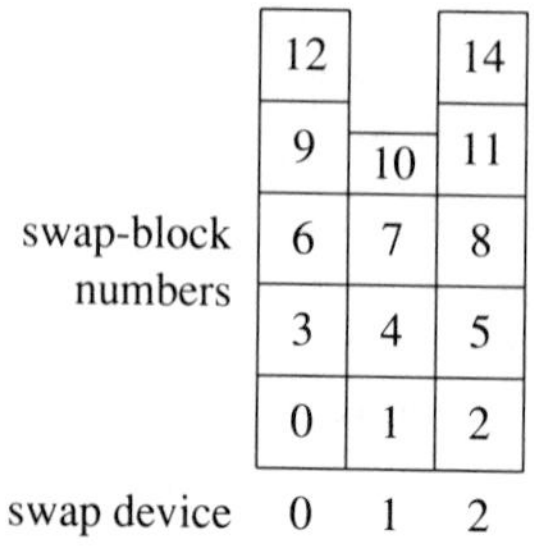

<table>
<tr><td></td><td>12</td><td></td><td>14</td></tr>
<tr><td></td><td>9</td><td>10</td><td>11</td></tr>
<tr><td>swap-block numbers</td><td>6</td><td>7</td><td>8</td></tr>
<tr><td></td><td>3</td><td>4</td><td>5</td></tr>
<tr><td></td><td>0</td><td>1</td><td>2</td></tr>
<tr><td>swap device</td><td>0</td><td>1</td><td>2</td></tr>
</table>

As the system must have at least one swap device available immediately, the first swap device is enabled at boot time; the virtual swap blocks that map to it are placed in a swap-resource map. The other swap devices are enabled by a *swapon* system call at system startup, and their sections of the interleaved swap device are made available at that time.

Swap space for each process segment is allocated when the segment grows. The resource allocator does not return swap blocks that span devices because of interleaving. Thus, individual chunks for a segment map to a single disk device. The use of interleaving rather than concatenation of the swap devices tends to distribute the allocation of space evenly on the swap devices so as to spread the transfers among the disks used for swapping and paging.

5.6 Per-Process Resources

In Chapter 4, we discussed several of the components of a UNIX process. Each process is described by a proc structure, which is allocated from an array of such entries in the kernel data segment, and by a user structure, which is allocated dynamically. In this section, we examine the memory utilization of UNIX processes in 4.3BSD. We start by examining how a process's page tables describe the process's virtual memory. This presentation is followed by a discussion of the various types of PTEs that may exist during the lifetime of a process. Finally, the shared resources associated with shared text segments and the space allocated on secondary storage for each process are considered.

4.3BSD Process Virtual Address Space

In 4.3BSD on the VAX, the P0 region is used to hold the text segment of a process, followed by the data segment. The kernel stack and user structure are stored at the top of the P1 region, with the user stack growing downward below them. The set of page tables for the P0 and P1 regions for each VAX process are saved and restored during process-context switches. The placement of the kernel stack and user structure in the P1 region allows those objects to be placed at fixed addresses, and also allows them to be remapped quickly as part of the user address space at each context switch. The pages at the top of the P1 region that hold the user structure and kernel run-time stack are made read-only to the user process. One advantage of having these pages readable to the user is that the signal-trampoline code stored in the user structure is readily available (see Section 4.7).

Page Tables

As we saw in looking at the VAX memory-management architecture in Section 5.3, each process must have a set of page tables that describes the memory associated with the process. The two-level translation process implies that processes hold two types of resources: *user page tables* to map P0 and P1 regions, and a portion of the *system page table* to map the user page tables.

System map
Alternate mappings
Utility maps
I/O map
User page-table map

Figure 5.10 Layout of the system page table.

In 4.3BSD, the system page table is statically allocated as the concatenation of a number of smaller page tables (see Fig. 5.10). The static entries in the map are filled in at boot time, and others are filled in as they are used. The first section (*Sysmap*) maps the fixed part of the kernel code, data, and tables allocated at boot time. This section also maps the filesystem's buffer cache (see Section 7.5).

The second area of the system page table is divided into sections that are used by different parts of the kernel to map in the user structures of processes that are not currently executing. The third area contains maps for dynamic allocation of kernel memory and temporary access of main memory pages. The fourth section of the map is set up to address I/O space rather than main memory, so that device drivers and autoconfiguration procedures can access peripheral-device registers directly. The last piece of the system page table, the user page-table map, or *Usrptmap*, is used to map user-process page tables into the kernel's address space. Because of the difficulty in allocating additional physically contiguous memory to expand the system page table, the *Usrptmap* has a fixed size. The standard size is 32 pages, enough to map 4096 pages of user page tables, which in turn map 524,288 pages of memory. A standard configuration thus supports page tables for resident processes whose virtual memory sizes total up to 256 megabytes.

A process needs several contiguous system PTEs to map its own page tables. The allocation of *Usrptmap* entries is managed with a *resource map* called *kernelmap*. Resource maps are ordered arrays of <base, size> pairs describing the free segments of a resource (see Fig. 5.11). A segment of a given size is allocated from a resource map by *rmalloc*(), using a first-fit algorithm, and is subsequently freed with *rmfree*(). The kernelmap is initialized at boot time to contain all the *Usrptmap* entries. An index into the kernelmap at which space has been allocated is used both as the index into the array of PTEs and as the index into the

Figure 5.11 A kernel resource map.

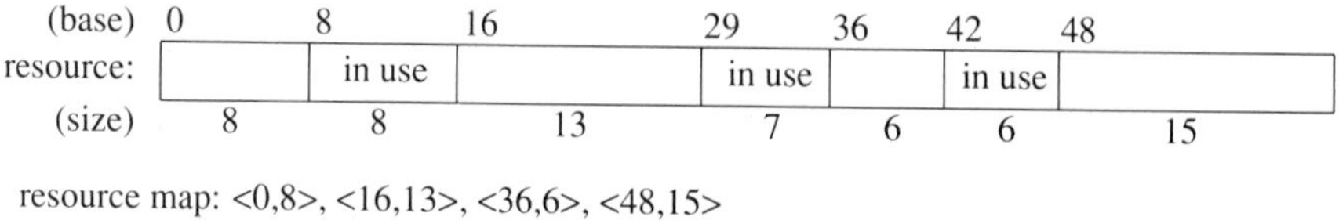

(base)	0	8	16	29	36	42	48
resource:		in use		in use		in use	
(size)	8	8	13	7	6	6	15

resource map: <0,8>, <16,13>, <36,6>, <48,15>

corresponding array of virtual addresses that corresponds to these pages. The P0 and P1 page tables are placed in adjacent areas using one set of kernelmap entries.

Reserving an area of the user page-table map provides a process with a virtual-address range in which to store its page tables. However, pages of physical memory still must be assigned to this virtual-address range. These pages are allocated with either *vmemall*() or *memall*(), both of which were described in Section 5.4.

Note that all a process's user page tables are allocated during this procedure, even though the corresponding system PTEs could have remained invalid. 4BSD does this because it does not support paging of the page tables; it always allocates memory for all a process's page tables. This policy is a holdover from previous versions of the system, but has become rather costly as the maximum size of a process has grown over time.

Figure 5.12 shows the arrangement of the page tables for a process. The page tables for the process illustrated occupy four pages of memory, which are mapped by four kernel PTEs in *Usrptmap*. The first section of the process's page tables is the P0 page table, with P0BR pointing to its start. The value of P0BR is stored in the PCB for use by the VAX hardware, and is also stored in the proc structure as *p_p0br*. The P1 page tables are placed after the P0 tables, ending on a page boundary. An additional pointer into this area is maintained; the proc structure contains a field, *p_addr*, that points to the first PTE for the user structure (near the end of the P1 map). A gap between the two sections allows for a small amount of expansion in place. Expansion is complicated; it is dealt with in Section 5.9.

Types of Page-Table Entries

When a process is created, its address space is empty, so its PTEs are set up with the valid bit off. As the process executes, memory references to the text segment cause page faults that result in pages being brought in from the

Figure 5.12 Layout of page tables for a process.

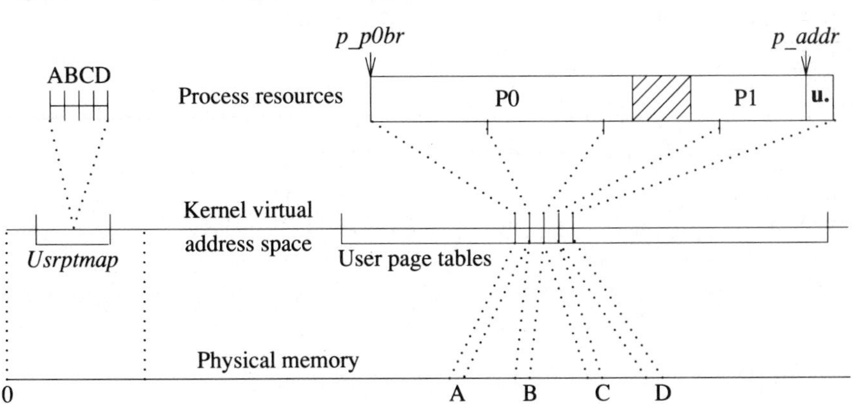

associated object file image that resides on disk. These page faults are termed *fill-on-demand page faults*, and, thus, the associated PTEs in this initial state are called *fill-on-demand PTEs*.

When the valid bit is off in a PTE, only the protection field is examined by the hardware. The other parts of the entry may be used in any way by software. 4.3BSD takes advantage of this fact by storing precomputed information in the unused part of the PTE that will be needed during the processing of an initial page fault. All user-process PTEs are initialized in this fashion. As there are several possible reasons for the valid bit to be turned off later in execution, a software-only bit is defined to show whether a page is still a fill-on-demand page. If so, the alternate interpretation of the PTE information is still valid.

The structure definition for a normal PTE, *struct pte*, is given in Fig. 5.13. The fill-on-demand PTE, *struct fpte*, is shown in Fig. 5.14. The valid bit and protection bits are identical in both structures, as required by the hardware. The fill-on-demand bit is also common, and distinguishes which of the two structures should be used to interpret a given PTE.

The rules for distinguishing PTEs are summarized in Table 5.2. In the next four paragraphs, we describe the PTEs in each of these states.

A fill-on-demand page may be of one of two types: either fill-from-file, or fill-with-zeros. Text and initialized data pages are filled from the executable text image file, whereas uninitialized data (*bss*), dynamically extended heap, and stack areas are filled with zeros. These types are distinguished by the *pg_fileno* field in the *fpte* structure, which has a value of either PG_TEXT or PG_ZERO. When a page should be filled from the text file, the precomputed disk block number of the appropriate page will be found in the *pg_blkno* field and the disk device number will be available from the text-table entry. These values are computed all at once, at the time the page tables are initially created for a shared text file. This precomputing of the block numbers is done because the calculation usually requires many accesses to secondary storage and thus is relatively slow. Precomputation guarantees that all the necessary filesystem structures will be found in the buffer cache after their first access.

When a page is valid, it is assumed to be resident in main memory. Valid PTEs always contain a nonzero page number, which is the physical-memory page number of the page to which this address is mapped.

Figure 5.13 Normal page-table entry (*struct pte*).

```
struct pte {
unsigned int   pg_pfnum:21,   /* page frame number */
               :4,
               pg_fod:1,      /* fill-on-demand */
               pg_m:1,        /* modified */
               pg_prot:4,     /* protection */
               pg_v:1;        /* valid */
};
```

```
struct fpte {
unsigned int  pg_blkno:24,    /* filesystem block number */
              pg_fileno:1,    /* fill-from-text or with-zeros */
              pg_fod:1,       /* fill-on-demand */
              :1,
              pg_prot:4,      /* protection */
              pg_v:1;         /* valid */
};
```

Figure 5.14 Fill-on-demand page-table entry (*struct fpte*).

An invalid page with a nonzero page number recorded in its PTE has a page of main memory allocated to it. In this situation, one of the following is true:

1. The page is filling from the disk: A page-in operation is in progress.

2. The page is in transit to the disk: A page-out operation is in progress.

3. A reference bit on the page is being simulated.

The last case is peculiar to the VAX. When the page-replacement algorithm would clear the reference bit on a page (if it were present), it clears the valid bit instead. After the valid bit is cleared, the process cannot use the page without causing a page fault. The page-fault service routine will note that the page is otherwise valid, and that this fault serves only to note that the page is still in use. The page-fault service routine can simply restore the valid bit, marking the page as both valid and *referenced*. Section 5.12 discusses the operation of the page-replacement algorithm in detail.

The last possible state for a PTE is that where both valid and fill-on-demand bits are clear, and the page number is zero. This state represents a PTE whose page has been created and brought into memory, but whose page has since been moved to swap space.

Table 5.2 Types of page-table entries.

Valid *(pg_v)*	Fill-on-demand *(pg_fod)*	Page number *(pg_pfnum)*	Structure type, usage
0	1	(none)	*struct fpte*; fill-on-demand page
1	0	nonzero	*struct pte*; valid, resident page
0	0	nonzero	*struct pte*; invalid, resident page
0	0	zero	*struct pte*; invalid, nonresident page
1	1	(none)	unused

Modified Pages

The last field in the PTE that is used for valid pages is the modified bit. This bit is set on the VAX by the hardware when a translation is done for the page during a write operation. When a page marked as modified is to be moved from memory, the page must be saved in swap space before it is freed. When a page is first created and filled, the modified bit is set to force the page to be saved the first time it is released. Text pages could be refilled from the filesystem, but their filesystem location is overwritten by the physical page number. It is faster to save them on swap space than to recalculate the disk block location, as the latter may require reading indirect blocks (see Section 7.2).

Text Page Tables

The only memory shared among processes in 4.3BSD is the instruction area of a pure text-executable program (except for *vfork*, which is described in Section 5.7). On the VAX, the most efficient way to implement this sharing is to have one set of page tables for each shared text segment, and then to have each process sharing a text segment simply reference these page tables. This was not done, however, because it would have required the text section to start and end on 64-Kbyte boundaries, resulting in an incompatible user-visible change for binary sites. Instead, processes sharing a text segment maintain individual copies of page tables that reference the physical pages of a text segment, and the system ensures that these tables remain consistent by propagating changes that result from loading, invalidating, or paging out text pages.

Swap Space

In a virtual-memory operating system, programs may run with less than their full address space resident in physical memory. But the system must be able to obtain or create the contents of any section of the address space at any time. With demand paging, a process initially has nothing in its address space. Some portions of the address space are mapped to the executable image in a file, whereas other portions are marked to be filled with zeros on first reference. Later, some pages that have already been created and used may need to be removed from memory to make room for other pages. The pages that are removed must be saved on secondary storage if their contents cannot be reproduced. The 4BSD virtual-memory system never attempts to reproduce the contents of a page once that page has been brought into memory (for example, by paging the page from the executable image again if both the file and the page are unmodified). Instead, such pages are stored in swap space. Swap space uses reserved areas of the disks. These areas contain no filesystem structures, and are usually 16 or 32 Mbyte per area on one or more disks. To avoid running out of swap space at an inconvenient time, the system allocates enough swap space for each program, so that all a program's pages can be written to swap space if necessary. The decision to preallocate swap space was reasonable when the system was originally designed. VAX systems of the day generally had no more than 4 Mbyte of main memory, but usually had several disks totaling hundreds of Mbyte. However, memory sizes of 16 to 128 Mbyte have become more common, while disk sizes have grown much less rapidly.

The allocation and mapping of swap space for a process is described by a data structure called a *swap map*. Each process has two swap maps, one describing the swap area for its data and heap segment (P0 space excluding text) and one describing its stack segment. A swap map describing the text segment of a shared text image may also be referenced by a process. The shared text swap map is maintained separately from the per-process swap maps, and is described later.

Each per-process area may grow dynamically and independently, and may occupy a wide range of sizes, from a few Kbyte to many Mbyte. If a swap map used fixed-sized blocks, either large processes would require large maps, or small processes would have to overallocate, losing much space because of internal fragmentation. The small-process problem could be solved by reducing the last swap block to the actual size required. However, such a reduction would make growth of a segment expensive, as it might require a disk-to-disk copy of a small swap block to a larger one.

The solution to this problem in 4.3BSD is the use of a fixed-size swap map that contains swap addresses for varying sizes of blocks. Figure 5.15 shows the swap map for a 140-Kbyte process. The size of each block is determined by its index in the map. The first block is of size *dmmin*; standard 4.3BSD configurations set *dmmin* to 32 sectors (16 Kbyte). Succeeding blocks are each larger than their predecessor by a factor of two until they reach size *dmmax*. Each block used by a process is fully allocated, so growth to the end of the block is simple. Growth past the end of the last block is done by allocation of a new block. Small processes thus consist entirely of small swap blocks, minimizing fragmentation, whereas large processes can still be described by a map of moderate size. The actual process-segment swap map, called a *dmap* structure, contains the amount of swap space allocated to the segment, the amount currently used, and a fixed-size array of swap block addresses for the blocks that are allocated. The user structure of each process holds maps for the data portion of P0 space (*u_dmap*) and the stack portion of P1 space (*u_smap*).

Swap space for the text segment is handled differently; only one copy needs to be stored on disk, and its size is constant. The text structure holds an array of

Figure 5.15 The *dmap* structure.

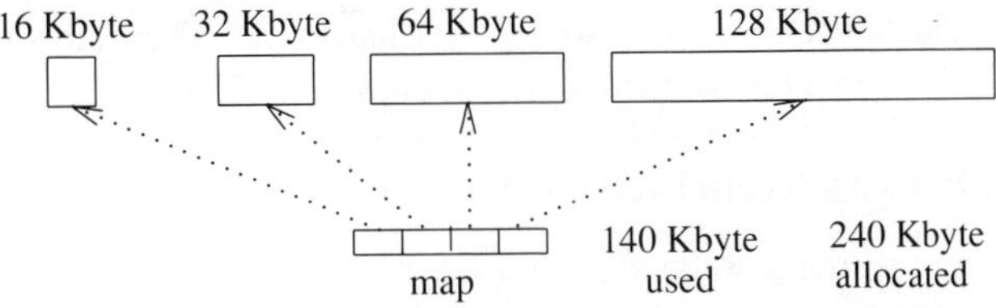

block pointers to map the swap image. Each block but the last has a fixed size, *dmtext*, ordinarily 512 Kbyte; the last block holds just the number of 1-Kbyte clusters needed for the remainder of the text image.

5.7 Creation of a New Process

UNIX processes are created with a *fork* system call. The *fork* is usually followed shortly thereafter by an *exec* system call that overlays the virtual address space of the child process with the contents of an executable image that resides in the filesystem. The process then executes until it terminates by exiting, either voluntarily, or involuntarily by receiving a signal. In the next few sections, we trace the management of memory resources used at each step in this cycle.

A *fork* system call duplicates the address space of an existing process, creating an identical child process. *Fork* is the only way that new processes are created in UNIX (except for its variant, *vfork*, which is described later). The 4.3BSD implementation of *fork* duplicates all the resources of the original process and copies that process's address space.

The virtual-memory resources of the process that must be allocated for the child include the proc structure, the secondary storage used to back the process, the kernel page tables and user page tables, the user structure, and the kernel stack. Main memory is allocated for many of the pages of the new process (those that are not still fill-on-demand in the parent process), although it may need to be paged out by the time the process first runs. The general outline of the implementation of a *fork* is as follows:

- Allocate secondary storage for the child process
- Allocate a proc entry for the child process and fill it in
- Allocate page tables for the child process
- Allocate a new user structure, copying the current one to initialize it
- Duplicate the address space, copying fill-on-demand PTEs and duplicating the contents of all other pages
- Arrange for the return to the child process, to distinguish it from the parent process

The allocation and initialization of the proc structure and the arrangement of the return value were covered in Chapter 4. The remainder of this section discusses the other steps involved in duplicating a process.

Duplicating Kernel Resources

The first resource to be allocated when an address space is duplicated is the swap area. Swap space is allocated first, because it is the resource most likely to be unavailable. As the existing process already has swap maps for its own swap space, the new allocation must be recorded in *shadow swap maps* in the user structure until they can be installed in the child-process user structure. These swap maps, *u_cdmap* and *u_csmap*, are also used during *exec*; their treatment is described later. The kernel allocates swap space by zeroing the shadow maps, then expanding these maps to the full size of the process data and stack segment sizes. The process then holds enough swap space for two complete copies of itself, one copy of which has no contents.

The next step in *fork* is to allocate and initialize a new proc structure. This operation must be done before the address space of the current process is duplicated, because it records state in the proc structure. To duplicate the address space in the new process, the kernel must allocate page tables and pages of main memory. Allocation of the page tables is done by *vgetpt*(), which allocates system PTEs from *kernelmap* to map the user page tables, then allocates memory pages to contain the user page tables from the free memory pool with *vmemall*(). If space is not available in the system page table, the allocation request will cause the process to block. Lack of space in the system page table is usually due to fragmentation. When this occurs, the system resorts to the *swapping* of processes as a means of reclaiming resources; this mechanism is described in Section 5.13.

Between the time that space is allocated in the system page table and the time that user page tables are allocated, the parent process is locked against swapping to avoid deadlock. The child is in an inconsistent state, and cannot yet run or be swapped, and the parent is needed to complete the duplication of page tables. To ensure that the child process is ignored by the scheduler, the kernel sets the process's state to SIDL during the entire fork procedure.

With the virtual-memory resources allocated, the system sets up the kernel- and user-mode state of the new process, including the hardware memory-management registers and the user structure. Creating a copy of the user structure requires that a consistent copy of the VAX process control block be obtained. The parent process does this by simulating a context switch to itself:

```
resume(pcbb(u.u_procp));
```

Then, so that the current and the new user structures can be accessed simultaneously, the new user structure is mapped into a special window in kernel virtual memory using a special page map named *Forkmap*. With both parent and child user structures addressable in the kernel's virtual address space, the current user structure can then be copied to the new one, and the virtual-memory section of the new user structure can be updated to reflect the child's page tables and swap-space allocation.

Duplicating the User Address Space

The remainder of the user address space may be duplicated once the kernel state of the child process has been created. The text portion is easy; the reference count on the text structure is incremented to show that there is another process sharing it, and the page tables are copied from a current process using that text segment.

Finally, the data and stack areas are duplicated one page at a time. For pages that are still fill-on-demand, only the PTEs need to be duplicated. The kernel copies all other pages by allocating memory for the new process and copying the data from the current process to the new memory page. The copy is done from a user virtual address to a physical address, because the new address space is not accessible to the parent process. The machine-language routine *copyseg*() does this copy by using a reserved system map entry to map in the destination page before copying the data. If the source page is not resident in memory, the copy will cause a page fault; the fault is serviced normally, and the copy proceeds on return. (Note that this situation is one of the few places in the kernel where a fault in kernel mode is not treated as a system failure.) The new PTE is validated and marked as modified, as the corresponding swap block does not yet have the correct contents.

Implementation Issues

When large processes fork, copying the entire user address space is expensive. All the pages that are on secondary storage must be read back into memory to be copied. If there is not enough free memory for both complete copies of the process, this memory shortage will cause the system to begin paging to create enough memory to do the copy (see Section 5.12). This may result in parts of the parent and child processes being paged out, as well as in the paging of parts of unrelated processes. Other ways to create processes without this overhead have been considered.

One technique that was considered for inclusion in 4.2BSD, but that was not implemented, is called *copy-on-write*. Rather than each page of a process that forks being copied, each process resulting from the fork is given references to the same physical pages. The page tables are changed to prevent either process from modifying a shared page. Instead, when a process attempts to modify a page, the kernel is entered with a protection fault. On discovering that the fault was caused by an attempt to modify a shared page, the kernel simply copies the page and changes the protection field for the page to allow modification once again. Only pages modified by one of the processes need to be copied. Because processes that fork typically overlay the child process with a new image with *exec* shortly thereafter, this technique can significantly improve performance.

Copy-on-write was not part of the original design of the virtual-memory system for various pragmatic reasons. It requires that reference counts be maintained on a per-page basis—which is most important for pages resident on secondary storage. More important, at the time, microcode problems with one model of the VAX made it unclear whether copy-on-write could be implemented reliably. As a result, the *vfork* system call, described in the next section, was included instead.

Creating a New Process Without Copying

A different scheme used to avoid the memory copy implied in a *fork* eliminates the copy altogether. When a process (such as a shell) wishes to start another program, it will generally *fork*, do a few simple operations such as redirecting I/O descriptors and changing signal actions, and then start the new program with an *exec*. In the meantime, the parent shell suspends itself with *wait* until the new program completes. For such operations, it is not necessary for both parent and child to run simultaneously, and therefore only one copy of the address space is required. This frequently arising situation led to the implementation of the *vfork* system call. Although it is extremely efficient, *vfork* has peculiar semantics and is generally considered to be an architectural blemish.

Most of the implementation of *vfork* is shared with *fork*. The major difference is that, instead of copying the address space for the child, the parent simply *passes* its address space to the child and suspends itself. The child process needs to allocate only new proc and user structures, receiving everything else from the parent. The child process returns from the *vfork* system call with the parent still suspended. The child does the usual activities in preparation for starting a new program, then calls *exec*. Now the address space is passed back to the parent process, rather than being abandoned as in a normal *exec*. Alternatively, if the child process encounters an error and is unable to execute the new program, it will *exit*. Again, the address space is passed back to the parent instead of being abandoned. This sequence of events is illustrated in Fig. 5.16.

The child process in a *vfork* is created initially with just a user structure and enough page tables to map that structure. The parent then exchanges address spaces with the child. Most of the work is in exchanging pointers, maps, and counters in the proc and user structures that describe the address space. The exchange of the page tables is complicated, because the active kernel stack is contained in the user structure that is being passed. The transfer is done in the context of the parent process by mapping the child's user structure using the *Forkmap*, then copying the parent's PTEs for the user structure into the child's page tables. When the page tables are really swapped by changing the hardware page-table base registers, the user structure for the parent retains the correct mapping. The page map for the child's user structure is restored from the copy in *Forkmap*.

After passing its resources to the child, the parent process marks its own process-table entry with the flag SNOVM (has no virtual memory resources), so that it will be ignored during page reclamation, and also marks the child's entry with SVFORK. The parent then blocks until the child finishes its use of the parent's resources. When the child calls either *exec* or *exit*, it clears the SVFORK flag, awakens the parent, and sleeps until the parent has taken back its address space. The reverse transfer is done in an identical fashion to the first transfer, with care taken to retain the correct mapping for the user structure. When the parent has completed the transfer, it marks the child with the flag SVFDONE and awakens it. When the child sees that the transfer is complete, it continues with its system call; in either case, it has fewer resources to release than in a normal process.

This description of *vfork* shows that neither the pages of the address space nor the page maps themselves need to be copied. *Vfork* is likely to remain more efficient than copy-on-write or other schemes that must duplicate the process' virtual address space. The architectural quirk of the *vfork* call is that the child process may modify the contents and even the size of the parent's address space while the child has control. Although modification of the parent's address space

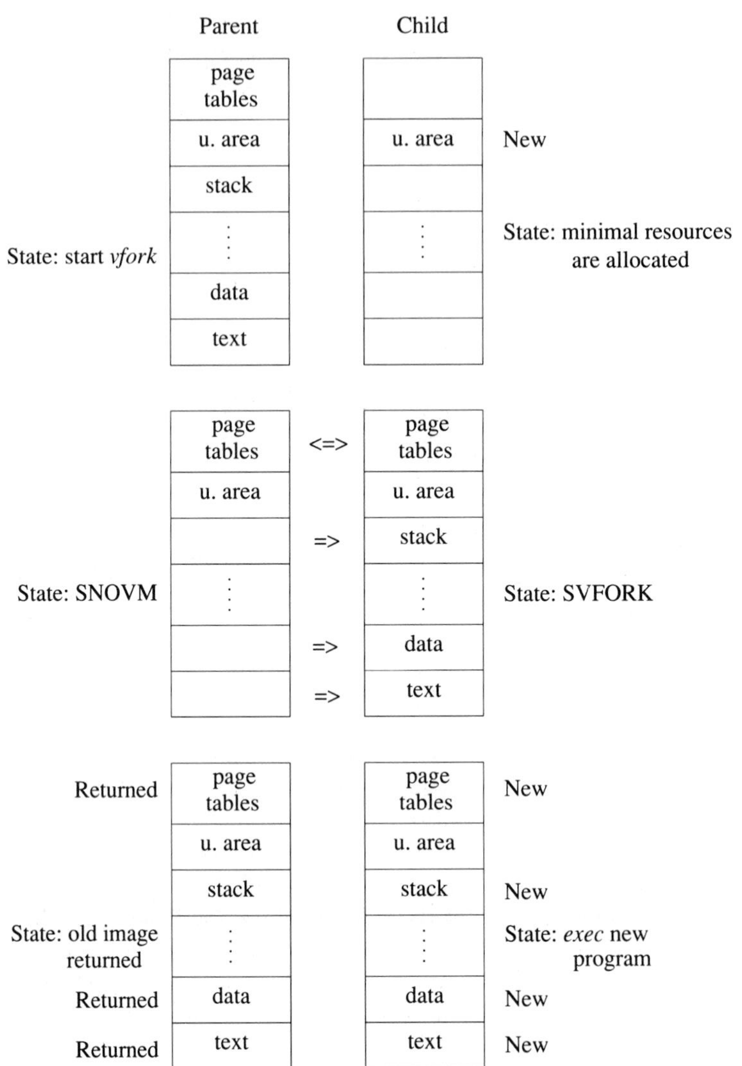

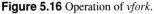

Figure 5.16 Operation of *vfork*.

is bad programming practice, some programs have been known to take advantage of this quirk.

5.8 Execution of a File

The *execve* system call was described in Sections 2.4 and 3.6; it replaces the address space of a process with the contents of a new program obtained from an executable file. During an *exec*, the target executable image is validated, then the arguments and environment are copied from the current process image into a temporary area.[1]

To perform an *exec*, the system must allocate resources to hold the new contents of the virtual address space, set up the mapping for this address space to reference the new image, and release the resources being used for the existing virtual memory. This procedure is complicated by the possibility of the process being swapped to secondary storage if resources, such as the system page tables, are in short supply.

The first step is to allocate swap space for the new data and stack sections. *Exec*() does this allocation without first releasing the currently assigned space, because the system must always have a place on secondary storage to which the process can be swapped (see Section 5.13). If the system were to release the current swap space, and the swap allocation failed, the *exec* would be unable to return to the original process. The duplicate swap space that is allocated is recorded in *shadow swap maps* in the process' user structure, and the address space and virtual-memory resources of the current process are then freed as though the process were exiting; this mechanism is described later.

Now, the process has only a user structure and kernel stack, plus page tables that map only the user structure. The shadow swap maps that hold the new swap area are moved to their normal locations, and resources are arranged for the new text, data, and stack sizes of the process. This arrangement is done by expansion of the page tables to the new size and updating of the hardware registers. The PTEs for the stack segment are set to be fill-with-zeros and, if the image about to be executed is not demand-loaded (an uncommon case), the initialized data are read into the data space, faulting in the required pages as the read proceeds.

The kernel sets up the text portion of the new address space by locating the text structure for the text file if that file is already in memory, or by allocating and initializing a new text structure if the text file is not in memory. When a new text structure is being set up, swap space is allocated for the text segment and for a swap image of the page table for the text. Otherwise, the process is added to the list of processes sharing the text. The text page tables are initialized in one of three ways:

1. If another process using this text is present in memory, the page tables for the text region are simply copied from those of the other process.

2. Otherwise, if a copy of the page tables for text are on swap space, the swap copy is read into place.

3. If neither of these shortcuts is possible, the page tables are set up as fill-from-file.

The third case represents the largest overlap of information between the filesystem and the virtual-memory system; text PTEs are initialized with the disk

[1] A section of the first swap device, called *argdev*, is reserved for argument processing. Enough disk blocks to hold a maximal argument list are allocated and arguments are copied into I/O buffers identified with the disk blocks for that area. In normal operation, these buffers are never written to disk, as their contents are retrieved before any write operation occurs.

block number for each page cluster. For each filesystem block that is mapped, the disk block number must be found using *bmap*(), and must be recorded in the block numbers for the page clusters that map the block. This mapping is an expensive operation, since *bmap*() may need to read through indirect blocks to find the location of some of the filesystem blocks. It is thus more efficient to do all these mappings at one time, so that indirect blocks will remain in the buffer cache during the operation. (See Chapter 7 for more of the details of filesystem operation.) Following the initialization of the text structure and page tables, the page tables for initialized data are set to fill-from-file.

No further operations are needed to create a new address space during an *exec* system call; the remainder of the work comprises copying the arguments and environment out to the top of the new stack. Initial values are set for the registers: The program counter is set to the entry point and the stack pointer is set to point to the argument vector. The new process image is then ready to run.

5.9 Change Process Size

A process may change its size during execution by explicitly requesting with the *sbrk* system call that the size of the data (heap) region be changed. Also, the stack segment will be expanded automatically if a protection fault is encountered because of growth of the stack below the end of the stack region. In either case, the size of the process address space must be changed. Hence, the size of the appropriate page table and swap map must be changed. If the change is to reduce the size of the data segment, the operation is easy: Any memory allocated to the pages that will no longer be part of the address space is freed, and the excess PTEs are cleared. Future references to these addresses will result in protection faults, as access is disallowed when the protection field is zero.

More commonly, the direction of change is to enlarge one of the two process segments, data or stack. New pages are marked fill-with-zeros, as there are no contents initially associated with new sections of the address space. The first step is to check whether the new size would violate the size limit for the process segment involved. If the new size is in range, the swap map for the segment is enlarged as needed. Recall that the swap maps for these segments are allocated in blocks of fixed sizes according to their indices in the map, and that both the current size and current allocation are maintained. If the current allocation is large enough for the new size, only the size needs to be changed; no new allocation is necessary. If the size has exceeded the current allocation, new full-sized blocks are added to the map in succeeding slots until enough space has been allocated. This process is identical to the one that occurs when a process is created by *exec*.

Once enough swap space has been obtained, the address space is adjusted through alteration of the region sizes in the proc and user structures, and then computation of the new size of the page tables. The size of the page tables is always rounded up to the end of the next page cluster, with any unused entries between the P0 and P1 page tables. There may be enough room for the additional entries. If not, the page tables for the process must be expanded. The page tables are always expanded by allocation of a complete new section of the system page table and copying of the page table PTEs; for simplicity, the growth is never done in place by allocation of adjoining free entries. As discussed in Section 5.6, a process page table requires several contiguous system PTEs allocated from the kernel map, as well as physical memory mapped by the system PTEs.

Figure 5.17 indicates how a new set of system PTEs is allocated in the user page-table map so that enough pages can be mapped for the new page map. Rather than allocating new kernel memory for the user page tables and copying the tables, the kernel maps the page-table pages into the new area by copying the system PTEs in the user page-table map. The pages containing only stack or u-dot page tables are moved to the end of the new area, and the remaining pages are moved to the beginning of the new area, as shown in step 1. The new page(s) between these sections are allocated and are cleared so that unused portions will have their protection fields set to zero. Any stack (P1) entries that were sharing a page with the P0 map are copied to their correct locations at the end of the new pages, as shown in step 2. During this period, the user page tables are doubly mapped at both the new and old addresses; the kernel is running on a stack in P1 space, and it is important that the stack page tables not become invalid during this manipulation. Once the new user page tables are ready, the hardware and software page-table base and length registers are updated, and the old system PTEs can be freed. The new PTEs mapping the portion of the address space that was specifically requested are initialized to be read-write, fill-with-zeros; the other new entries are left uninitialized until a new request requires their use.

If either the system page-map allocation from the kernel map or the memory allocation for the new page-table pages fails, the kernel swaps out the process to await enough page-map space. Because the new sizes are already set up (in the process structure), when the process is swapped in it will have the correct size. The growth process will complete with the initialization of the new PTEs. A process would therefore be required to swap to expand its page tables if it grew large enough to require one-half of the system page table.

Figure 5.17 Page-table expansion.

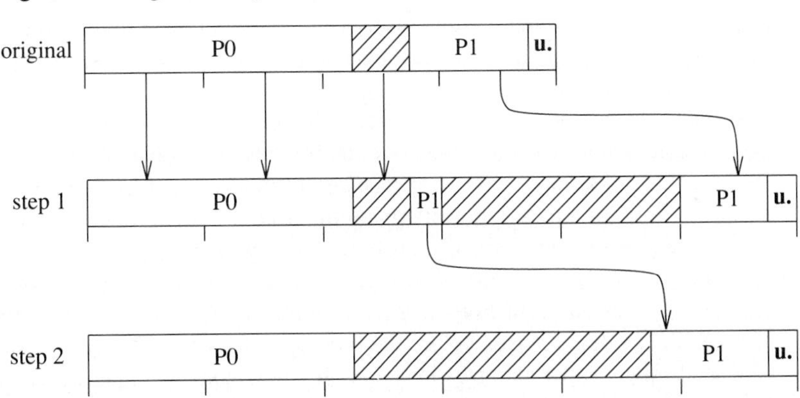

5.10 Termination of a Process

The final change in process state that relates to the operation of the virtual-memory system is *exit*; this system call terminates a process, as described in Chapter 4. The part of *exit* that is discussed here is the release of the virtual-memory resources of the process. The release is done in three steps:

1. The user portions of the address space are freed, both in memory and on swap space

2. The user structure is freed

3. The page-table resources are freed

The latter two operations are somewhat complicated because the user structure and its map must be used until the process relinquishes the processor for the last time.

The first step, freeing the user address space, is identical to the one that occurs during *exec* to free the old address space. In either case, this step is not needed if the process is the child process of a *vfork*; instead, the address space is passed back to the process's parent. First, the text section of the process is released. If other processes in memory are still attached to the text, the reference count is simply decremented and the text pointer in the process structure is cleared. If there are no other users of the text image in memory, the text image is freed; it is swapped out first if it has not yet been written to swap. The image is saved for any swapped-out processes attached to the text, or for possible reattachment if the image is used again soon. The pages of the text region are freed and any pages that might be involved in page-out operations at the time are marked as *gone*, rather than their being freed immediately; the dirty-page–cleanup routine will note that the pages are gone and will place the pages on the free list when their I/O operations complete (see Section 5.12). The data and stack pages are freed similarly. The swap space is next to be freed, but this step must wait if any of the process pages were being paged out. Otherwise, the swap blocks involved might be reallocated and reused before the page-out operation occurred, destroying the new user's swap image. For this purpose, the system keeps in its proc structure a counter of the number of page-out operations in progress for each process. When any pageouts have completed, the swap blocks in the data and stack swap maps are freed.

Next the memory used by the user structure must be freed. This begins the problematical time when the process must free resources that it is not yet finished using. This condition causes two changes from the usual procedure of freeing memory. First, the page tables mapping the user structure are copied into a temporary area, so that when memory is freed with *vmemfree*(), the valid and protection bits on the page tables that map the user structure will not be cleared. Second, it would be disastrous if a page from the user structure or kernel stack were reallocated and reused before the process had finished the *exit*(). Memory is allocated either synchronously by the page-fault handler, or asynchronously by the network from interrupt level when packets arrive (see Chapter 11). To block any allocation of memory, it is necessary to delay network interrupts by raising the processor interrupt-priority level. The process may then free the pages of its user structure, safe from having them reused until it has relinquished the processor. The next context switch will lower the priority so that interrupts may resume.

The final step in freeing the resources of the process is to free the page tables. The memory containing the page tables is freed with *vmemfree*(), using the address of the system PTEs mapping those page tables. The system PTEs are then returned to their resource map, *kernelmap*, with *rmfree*().

With all its resources free, the exiting process finishes its manipulation of its proc entry to detach the process from its process group, and notifies its parent of its completion. The process has now become a zombie process—one with no resources, not even a kernel stack. Its parent will collect its exit status with a *wait* call, and will free its process structure.

There is nothing for the virtual-memory system to do when *wait* is called: The pages and page tables of a process are removed when *exit* is performed. On *wait*, the system just returns the process status to the caller, and deallocates the process-table entry and the small amount of space in which that resource usage information was kept.

5.11 Demand Paging

When the memory-management hardware detects an invalid PTE while translating a virtual address, it generates a trap to the system. This page-fault trap can occur for several reasons. Most 4BSD programs are created in a format that permits the executable image to be paged into main memory directly from the filesystem. When a program in a demand-paged format is first run, the kernel marks the PTEs for the text and initialized data regions of the executing process as invalid and as fill-on-demand from the filesystem. As each page of the text region is first referenced, a page fault occurs. Page faults can also occur when a process first references a page in the uninitialized data region of a program. Here, the system automatically allocates memory to the process and initializes the newly assigned page to zero. Other types of page fault arise from the simulation of reference bits and when previously resident pages have been reclaimed by the system in response to a memory shortage.

The handling of page faults centers around the *pagein*() routine; this is the routine that services all page faults. Each time *pagein*() is invoked, it is provided the virtual address that caused the fault. The first actions of *pagein*() are to find the PTE for the faulting address and to categorize the page as text, data, or stack, then to determine the state of the page. The possible states are

- Fill-on-demand
- Resident but not valid
- Paged out

Once the type and state of the page have been determined, *pagein*() must fetch the needed data, validate the PTE associated with the faulted page, and return to restart the process. The following sections describe the actions of *pagein*() for each of the possible types of pages that can be fetched.

Fill-on-Demand Pages

For a fault on a fill-on-demand page, the paging system must first determine the source of the data that the page should contain. If the page is fill-from-file, the memory free list might contain a copy of the desired page, allowing the read from disk to be avoided; see Section 5.4. If the page is found on the free list, *pagein*() reclaims it by removing it from the free list and using it for the current process. Otherwise, *pagein*() must allocate a page of main memory, fill it with the correct contents, and then record the identity of the physical page in the appropriate PTE. Zero-fill pages are simply cleared, whereas the contents of fill-from-text pages must be obtained from secondary storage. The secondary-storage location of each fill-from-text page is either specified by the disk block number and device identifier that are present in the PTE (when paging in from the filesystem), or is derived from the process swap map (for pages that have been paged out). These items and a page count fully identify the source of the disk data to be paged in. The identity of the process and the virtual address of the start of the page describe the destination of the paging operation.

To complete the page-fault servicing of a fill-on-demand page, the page needs to be marked as valid and as modified. The page is marked as modified to indicate that the swap page allocated to it does not yet have the correct contents; if the page is selected to be replaced, it will be written to swap space before being reused.

Fill-on-Demand Klustering

Servicing a fill-from-text page fault can involve significant work. Fortunately, most programs tend to exhibit some degree of *locality of reference*; that is, their memory references are localized within their virtual address space over short periods of time. If a process exhibits locality of reference, then a process's fault rate can be reduced by *prefetching* of pages that are adjacent to the one that faulted.

Whenever a fill-from-file page fault is serviced, the paging system attempts to read any pages of the file adjacent to the faulted page that may also be needed. This operation is termed *fill-on-demand klustering* and is implemented by *fodklus-ter*(); its name is spelled as it is to distinguish it from page clustering (described in Section 5.2). The read of the prefetched pages is piggybacked on the disk transfer that is already needed. The small additional cost of prefetching is outweighed by the improvement in service times for future page faults. Prefetched pages are placed at the tail of the free list, from which they may be reclaimed if the process uses them soon.

Kluster calculations form a set of page clusters that include a desired page and any clusters that are adjacent both in virtual memory and on the disk and are

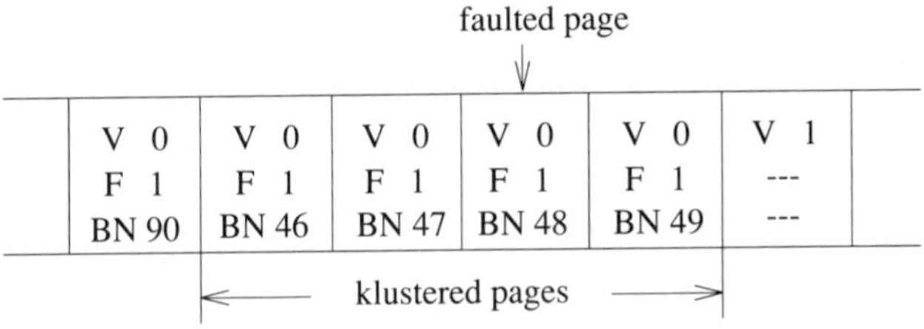

faulted page

V 0	V 0	V 0	V 0	V 0	V 1
F 1	F 1	F 1	F 1	F 1	---
BN 90	BN 46	BN 47	BN 48	BN 49	---

← klustered pages →

Figure 5.18 The operation of fill-on-demand klustering. V—valid bit; F—fill-on-demand bit; BN—block number on disk.

still fill-on-demand (see Fig. 5.18). No more than 16 clusters (32 pages on a VAX) will be included in a kluster set. When reading of a fill-on-demand page from the filesystem is performed, klustering will typically result in a read of an entire filesystem block (usually 4 or 8 Kbyte) instead of a single page cluster (1 Kbyte).

Interaction with the Filesystem Cache

The executable image of a program is always paged from the filesystem directly into the pages of the process, bypassing the filesystem cache. Because the filesystem uses a write-back cache (see Chapter 7), the disk blocks of an executable file might not contain the correct data soon after the file is created; instead, the data may still be in the filesystem buffer cache. There are two possible solutions to this problem. One is to check the filesystem cache before paging data in from the disk, copying the data from the cache if they are present; the other is to flush write-behind blocks from the filesystem cache before reading them in from the disk. The kernel uses the latter approach, forcing any write-behind blocks to disk before paging in data. The selection of this alternative is historic; the VAX computers on which the system was developed were CPU limited but had excess I/O capacity. Better system throughput could be obtained by having the disk controller use DMA to do the memory-to-memory copy from the buffer cache to the process text page (via the disk), than by tieing up the overworked CPU doing the memory-to-memory copy. The tradeoff is reversed today, when I/O is usually the limiting factor. At an extreme is a diskless workstation; copying the data via the disk implies two transfers across a network.

Pagein of Swapped Pages

After a page has been resident in memory, it can be paged out and invalidated. Another reference to the page by the process will then generate a page fault. Here, the work to be done differs from that done for the initial fault. Whereas the first step is still to locate the PTE for the page that faulted, if the page is not fill-on-demand and the page number in the PTE is nonzero, the corresponding core-map entry must be consulted to determine the state of the page.

There are four possible states for a page that is not marked fill-on-demand, and is not valid:

1. The page was invalidated in order to sample references to it. The page number in the PTE is nonzero (valid), the core-map entry for the page is not locked, and the page is not on the free list; *pagein*() can simply mark the page as valid and return control to the process. This operation is called a *reclaim*.

2. The page has been freed but has not yet been reused. The page number in the PTE is nonzero, and the core-map entry is not locked but is on the free list. The page must be unlinked from the free list before it is validated. This operation is termed a *reclaim from free*.

3. A text page may not be resident, but another process may already have faulted the same page and started a read operation to bring the page into memory. The page number will be nonzero, and the core-map entry will be marked as locked and in transit. For pages of this type, *pagein*() must wait until the transfer finishes. The associated core-map structure is marked to indicate that some process is waiting on the page, and then *pagein*() sleeps on the address of the text structure for the page. If the page is valid when the process awakens, the pagein is complete. Otherwise, the page service must restart from the beginning, as the page may have changed state; the process may have been suspended for any length of time, or may even have been swapped out.

4. The page may not be resident in memory. The page may have been reused if it was freed by *pageout*() and then allocated for another purpose. For pages of this type, the page number in the PTE will have been set to zero when the page was reallocated.

If a missing page is a text page, it is possible that the page may still be in memory, in the text page cache described in Section 5.4. The page may be in memory at either of two times: when the PTE is marked fill-on-demand, and the page is still in memory from a previous invocation, or when the text page was swapped out at the time the current process attached to the text. The latter case occurs after users release a text, causing the image and page table to be swapped out and saved as a *sticky text*. 4.3BSD saves all text images for possible reuse, but previous versions of UNIX provided a save-text or *sticky bit* in the mode of an executable file to cause the image to be saved. When a new process attaches to the text and reloads the page tables, some of the pages are still present in memory, although the page tables contain no reference. These pages are located by a search of the free list for pages associated with the block numbers of allocated swap space. If the page is found, it will be marked *gone* because the text page table no longer holds a reference to the page. To reclaim the page, *pagein*() needs only to remove it from the free list, to place the page number in the PTE, and to mark the entry valid. This PTE must also be distributed to other processes sharing the page.

If a page that has been faulted is no longer in memory, a new page must be allocated. The usual mechanism to allocate memory cannot be used in *pagein*()

because, if the process is blocked, the state of the page might change (requiring the page-fault service to restart). Thus, *pagein*() explicitly checks for enough memory. If there is free memory, it allocates the page clusters it needs; otherwise, it sleeps on the global variable *freemem* until more memory is available, then restarts its operation.

Once memory has been allocated to hold a page that has been paged out, the remaining work is to retrieve the contents of the page from swap space. As occurs when *pagein*() is filling from the filesystem or when swapping out, adjacent pages are considered for inclusion in the transfer. Here, adjacent pages that were also swapped out are eligible for inclusion, although the size of the block considered is smaller (normally 4 Kbyte for text pages and 8 Kbyte for data pages) because the locality for data references is assumed to be larger than is the locality for text references.

If the swapped-out page is a text page, other processes sharing the text image must be able to tell that the swap has been initiated. Therefore, the changed PTEs are propagated to the other processes after the page number is filled in; this will allow them to find the core-map entry for the new page.

The memory allocator returns the core-map entry locked; *pagein*() marks the pages *in-transit*. The PTE is validated after the page has been read. For text pages, the PTE is distributed again to validate all the copies, and any processes waiting for the page are awakened. Pages that were prepaged as a result of the klustering are not validated. Instead, text pages are left reclaimable, whereas data or stack pages are freed but are left reclaimable from the free list. If the pages are used soon, they will be found in memory. Otherwise, they will be reallocated if they have not been used by the time they reach the front of the free list.

5.12 Page Replacement

The service of page faults and other demands for memory may be satisfied from the free list for some time, but eventually memory must be reclaimed for reuse. Some pages are reclaimed when processes exit. On systems with a large amount of memory and low memory demand, exiting process may provide enough free memory to fill demand. This situation arises when there is enough memory for the kernel and for all pages that have ever been used by any current process. Obviously, many computers do not have enough main memory to retain all pages in memory. Thus, it eventually becomes necessary to move some pages to secondary storage—to the swap space. Unlike paging in a page, which is demand-driven, there is no immediate indication when a page is no longer needed by a process. The kernel must implement some strategy for deciding which pages to move out of memory so that it can replace these pages with the ones that are currently needed in memory. Ideally, the strategy will choose pages for replacement that will not be needed soon. An approximation to this strategy is to find pages that have not been recently used. On the VAX, finding a page that has not been recently used is complicated by the lack of a *reference bit* in the PTEs to mark pages that have been used. Many other virtual-memory architectures, including the Tahoe, provide such a facility.

The design of the paging system is based on results of extensive trace-driven simulation [Babaoğlu, 1981]. Accordingly, the system implements demand paging with a page-replacement algorithm that approximates global LRU. The complete per-process address space is pageable, although it maintains the familiar UNIX structure of text, data, and stack segments.

Global CLOCK Algorithm

The page-replacement policy used in 4BSD UNIX is a variant of the *CLOCK algorithm* [Corbato, 1968; Easton & Franaszek, 1979] in which reference bits are simulated in software (at least on the VAX). It is an example of a *global replacement algorithm*, one in which the choice of a page for replacement is made according to systemwide criteria; a *local replacement algorithm* would choose a process for which to replace a page, and then chose a page based on per-process criteria. The general notion of the CLOCK algorithm is to scan physical memory on a regular basis, considering pages for replacement. The part of main memory that is used by pageable processes is treated as a circular *loop* of pages, and a pointer or *clock hand* rotates around the loop one page cluster at a time. When the clock hand first reaches a cluster, the cluster is marked as unreferenced. On the next revolution, the clock hand examines the cluster to see whether the latter has been referenced in the intervening time. If the cluster has not been used, it is a strong candidate for replacement. The cluster is written to swap space if necessary, then is placed on the free list.

On a machine with a reference bit, the first pass would clear the bit and the second pass would check to see whether the reference bit had been set again. To simulate a reference bit on the VAX, 4BSD clears the valid bit on the first pass. If a process attempts to use the page that is being checked for reference (i.e., one for which the valid bit is off), the page-fault handler just sets the valid bit and returns. The second pass examines the valid bit as though it were a reference bit. The 4.3BSD Tahoe release includes revisions to the page-replacement routines to use the reference bit when it is supported by the hardware.

The simulation of reference bits on the VAX adds to the cost of operation of the CLOCK algorithm, as additional page faults occur due solely to the collection of reference information. The page-fault handler recognizes that the state of the invalid page is normal except for the simulation of the reference bit on that page. The initial cost to simulate reference bits on the VAX was about 10 percent of the total time spent in paging. On a system with a severe memory shortfall, up to 30 percent of the CPU time is spent in paging. Thus, the initial cost to simulate reference bits consumed up to 3 percent of the CPU time. To reduce the cost of reference-bit simulation, the code to handle initial page-fault characterization and revalidation was rewritten in assembly language. The result was a 70-percent drop in the time spent simulating reference bits and a reduction in the maximum simulation cost to about 1 percent of the CPU time.

The use of a single loop of pages forces all processes to compete for memory on an equal basis. This algorithm was selected based on simulations. It is interesting to note that it is also consistent with the way that UNIX treats other resources provided by the system. A common alternative to allowing all processes to compete equally for memory is to partition memory into multiple independent areas, each localized to a collection of processes that compete with one another for memory. This scheme is used, for example, by the VMS operating system [Kenah & Bate, 1984]. With this scheme, system administrators can guarantee that a process, or collection of processes, will always have a minimal percentage of memory. Unfortunately, this scheme can be difficult to administer. Setting the loop sizes too small can result in underutilization of memory and excessive I/O activity to secondary-storage devices, whereas setting them too high can result in swapping [Lazowska & Kelsey, 1978].

The 4.3BSD virtual-memory system does not use the working-set model because it lacks accurate information about the reference pattern of a process. It does track the number of pages held by a process (the *resident-set size*), but it does not know which of the resident pages constitute the working set; the count of resident pages is used only in making decisions on whether there is sufficient memory for a process to be swapped in when that process wants to run.

The system handles excessive paging by swapping out one of the processes holding the largest amounts of memory; see Section 5.13. Swapping is invoked only when paging is unable to keep up with memory needs, or when short-term resource needs warrant swapping a process. In general, the swap-scheduling mechanism does not perform well under heavy load; system performance is much better when memory scheduling can be done by the page-replacement algorithm than it is when the swap algorithm is used.

The Paging Daemon

Page replacement is done in the *pageout*() routine. When *pageout*() reclaims pages that have been modified, it is responsible for writing them to the swap area. Thus, *pageout*() must be able to use normal kernel synchronization mechanisms such as *sleep*(). It therefore runs as a separate process, the *pagedaemon*, with its own proc structure, user structure, and kernel stack. Like *init*, the *pagedaemon* is created by an internal *fork* operation during system startup (see Section 13.3); unlike *init*, however, it remains in kernel mode after the fork. The *pagedaemon* simply enters *pageout*(), which never returns. For convenience, the *pagedaemon* has a large address space into which it maps the pages that it writes to swap. Unlike other users of the disk I/O routines, the pageout process needs to do its disk operations asynchronously, so it can continue scanning in parallel with disk writes.

Paging Parameters

The memory-allocation needs of processes, through the page-fault handler, constantly compete with the overall system goal of maintaining a minimum threshold of pages in the free list. As the system operates, it monitors main-memory

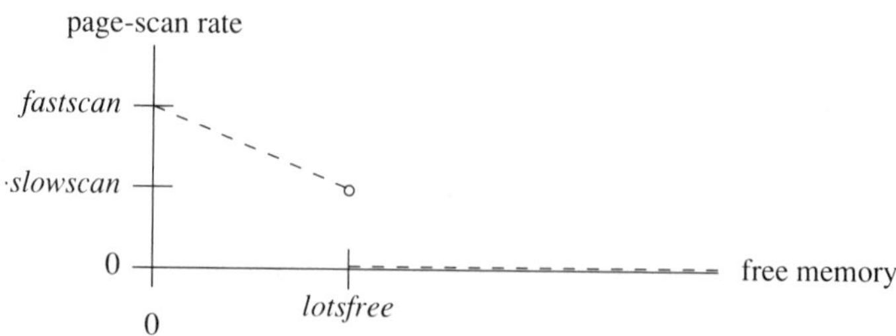

Figure 5.19 Page-scan rate.

utilization, attempting to run the *pagedaemon* frequently enough to keep the amount of free memory at or above the minimum threshold. The *pagedaemon* remains dormant until memory needs cause it to be awakened. The work of the *pagedaemon* is controlled by a number of parameters that are calculated in the *schedpaging*() routine. In general, the goal of this policy is to maintain free memory at, or above, a minimum threshold. The policy is implemented by the CLOCK algorithm, which reclaims pages for the free list. The number of pages to be reclaimed by the *pagedaemon* is a function of the memory needs of the system. As more memory is needed by the system, more pages are scanned, and the time between sampling references to pages becomes shorter. This in turn causes the number of pages freed to increase.

Four times per second, the system checks to see whether there is any need for memory. If there is, a paging rate is determined and the *pagedaemon* is awakened. The paging rate is given as the number of page clusters to scan in each quarter-second interval. *Schedpaging*() determines the need for memory by comparing the number of free memory clusters against several parameters. The first parameter, *lotsfree*, specifies a threshold (in Kbyte) for stopping the *pagedaemon*. When available memory is above this threshold, no pages will be scanned or paged out by the *pagedaemon*. *Lotsfree* is normally 512 Kbyte, and is at most one-fourth of user memory. The other interesting limits specify the desired amount of free memory that should be maintained, *desfree*, and the minimum free memory considered tolerable before involuntary swapping begins, *minfree*. *Desfree* usually is set to 200 Kbyte, and is at most one-eighth of memory; *minfree* usually is 64 Kbyte, and is at most one-sixteenth of memory. The rate at which pages are scanned for replacement varies linearly from 200 pages (or at most 20 percent of memory) per second when completely out of memory to 100 pages per second when free memory is equal to *lotsfree* (see Fig. 5.19).

The desired values for the paging parameters are communicated to the *pagedaemon* through global variables. Likewise, the *pagedaemon* records its progress, in terms of pages scanned over each time interval it runs, through a global variable.

Two-Handed Clock

The paging parameters can be used to determine the amount of time that it takes the clock hand to revolve once around the memory. With 2 Mbyte of memory divided into 1-Kbyte clusters, the hand traverses all of memory in less than 10 seconds. On a machine with 16 Mbyte of memory, a complete revolution takes 80 seconds. The length of time allowed a process to prove its need for a page is therefore highly dependent on memory size when the normal CLOCK algorithm is used. If a sudden memory shortfall caused paging to begin after a period without scanning, the clock would require a full revolution before the first page was freed. For this reason, the CLOCK algorithm was modified in 4.3BSD to support large-memory machines more effectively. The new algorithm uses two clock hands moving through memory, with the front hand clearing reference bits and the back hand sampling the reference bits, as shown in Fig. 5.20.

The two-handed CLOCK algorithm is a generalization of the original CLOCK algorithm; in it, the distance between the hands is implicitly the size of main memory available to user processes. The reference-sampling time is proportional to the distance between the two hands and is inversely proportional to the scan rate. For simplicity, the spread between the hands is fixed at 2 Mbyte or the size of the entire memory, whichever is smaller. With the two-handed CLOCK algorithm in use, the time for sampling a page's use is independent of memory size.

Operation of Pageout

We now have enough information to examine the operation of *pageout*(), the routine that implements the page-replacement policy. *Pageout*() begins by setting the pointers for the two clock hands to be the proper distance apart. The pointers are really indices into the core map, which is treated as a circular array. The scan through memory avoids those pages used statically by the kernel. *Pageout*() then goes to sleep until free memory becomes low. It is awakened at least four times

Figure 5.20 Two-handed clock.

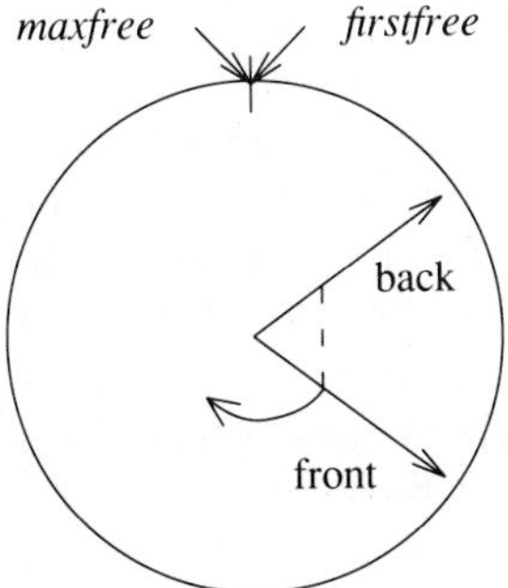

per second while free memory is less than *lotsfree*. Each time *pageout*() runs, it sweeps the clock hands through the core map until the desired number of page clusters have been examined, or the desired amount of free memory has been reached. At each iteration in the sweep, it examines the two page clusters, one cluster at the front hand and one at the back hand, then advances each hand by one cluster.

Clusters at the first hand are examined to determine what their state is and to see whether they are candidates for replacement. If a cluster is not free, *pageout*() invalidates the PTEs for the cluster and, if the cluster is in a shared text segment, propagates the changed PTEs to the other processes sharing the page.

When *pageout*() is examining an entry at the back hand, it checks to see whether the cluster has been used since the front hand passed. If it has been used, the valid bit will have been set again, and the cluster is left in memory. Otherwise, the cluster is selected to be freed. If any of the pages have been modified (or have not yet been written to swap), they must be ''pushed'' to swap before they are freed. If the pages have not been modified, they are freed immediately.

The procedure for writing process pages to the swap device, a *page push*, is somewhat complicated. The preallocated swap space for the process is described in the process's user structure. However, the push is done in the context of the pageout process, which has its own user structure. Therefore, a private page table (*Pushmap*) is used to map the user structure of the process owning the page into the kernel-address space.

As long as a pageout is needed to save the current page, adjacent pages of the process that are resident and dirty are klustered together and are written to secondary storage. If they are freed before they are next modified, they will not require separate page-out operations. No more than *dmmin* pages, normally 32, beginning on a *dmmin*-page boundary, are klustered together (*dmmin* is used to ensure that all the pages in such a block would be contiguous on swap space).

The mechanism used by *pageout*() to write pages to the swap area differs from normal I/O in two important ways:

1. The dirty pages are mapped into the virtual address space of the *pagedaemon*, rather than being part of the virtual address space of the process.

2. The write operation is performed asynchronously.

Both these operations are done by the *swap*() routine, which recognizes a dirty page push by a special flag that is passed to it. The buffer header used to describe the I/O operation is then initialized correctly for a page push. The PTEs for the dirty pages are copied to the *pagedaemon*'s page table; the address of the page that is to be freed is recorded in the swap buffer in the field *b_pfcent*. Also, because *pageout*() does not sleep while the push is done, it would not normally regain control after the I/O operation completed. Therefore, *swap*() marks the buffer with a call-back flag and sets the routine for the call back to be *swdone*(). When the push completes, *swdone*() is called; it places the buffer on the list of completed pageouts and awakens *pageout*().

The write being done asynchronously allows *pageout*() to continue examining pages, possibly starting additional pushes. Because the number of swap buffers is constant, care must be taken to ensure that a buffer is available before a commitment to a new page push is made. If *pageout*() has used all the swap buffers, it waits for at least one write operation to complete before it continues. As usual, blocking at this point requires that state be recomputed when *pageout*() resumes; the page at hand might have been freed or reused in the meantime. When pageout operations complete, the buffers are added to the list of completed pageouts and, if *pageout*() was blocked awaiting a buffer, it is awakened.

The list of completed pageouts is processed by *cleanup*() each time *pageout*() is awakened and just prior to another swap header being used. For each pageout operation on the list, the page cluster to be freed is placed on the memory free list unless some process has reclaimed and revalidated it. Any other pages that were included in a pageout due to klustering are unlocked, and any processes that were waiting for the locked pages are awakened. If the process using a page has abandoned that page, the *c_gone* flag will have been set in the core map, but the page will not have been freed; the page is freed at this time. Also, a count of *pageouts in progress* is kept for each process (*p_poip* in the proc entry) and for each shared text segment (*x_poip* in the text entry); this count is decremented when the pageout completes, and, if the count goes to zero, a *wakeup*() is issued. This operation is done so that exiting processes can wait for the completion of all pageout operations before freeing their references to the associated swap space.

5.13 Swapping

Although swapping is generally avoided, there are several times when it is used in 4.3BSD to address a problem not easily solved by the paging system. This problem is either a serious resource shortage, or an operation that can be most efficiently implemented with swapping. Swapping is done in 4.3BSD when any of the following occurs:

- The system becomes so short of memory that the paging process cannot free memory fast enough to satisfy the demand. For example, a memory shortfall may happen when multiple large processes are run on a machine lacking enough memory for the minimum working sets of the processes.
- The system page map becomes fragmented, preventing new or growing processes from allocating space for their page tables. Page tables do not normally shrink; however, if a process is swapped out and back in again, any extra space will be reclaimed.
- Processes are completely inactive for more than 20 seconds. Otherwise, such processes would retain a few pages of memory as well as pages for page tables.

Swapping occurs voluntarily or involuntarily. When swapping is voluntary, such as when the system page map is fragmented, it is initiated by the process that is to be swapped. When swapping is involuntary, however, it is initiated by a process called the *swapper*.

Swap operations completely remove a process from main memory, including the process page tables, the pages of the data and stack segments that are not already in swap space, the user structure, and the text segment. The text segment is handled differently from the data and stack segments because it is potentially shared by other processes.

The Swapping Process

Involuntary swapping operations are done by the swapping process, process 0. This process is the first one created by the system when it is started. The swapping policy of the *swapper* is embodied in the *sched*() routine. This routine swaps out processes when necessary, and also swaps processes back in when memory is available and they are ready to run. At any time, the swapper is in one of three states:

1. **Idle**: No swapped-out processes are ready to be run, and there is no reason to swap out anything. This is the normal state.
2. **Swapping in**: At least one runnable process is swapped out, and *sched*() attempts to find memory for it.
3. **Swapping out**: The system is short of memory or system page-table space, or there is not enough memory to swap in a process. Under these circumstances, *sched*() chooses processes and swaps them out until the memory shortage abates.

Under normal circumstances, when paging is able to keep an adequate level of free memory, the swapping process is inactive. If a process must swap itself out, or when free memory becomes low, the *swapper* is awakened.

Choosing a Process to Swap In

If more than one swapped-out process is runnable, the first task of the *swapper* is to decide which process to swap in. This decision may affect the decision whether to swap out another process. Each swapped-out process is assigned a priority based on

- The length of time it has been swapped out
- Its size when it was swapped out
- Its *nice* value, and the amount of time it was asleep since it last ran

In general, the process that has been swapped out longest or was swapped out because it was not runnable will be brought in first. Larger processes receive lower priority, to account for the greater length of time required to swap them in and out. Having gone to the effort required to swap out a large process to free memory, it is important to keep that process out long enough to derive some benefit. Once a process is selected, the *swapper* checks to see whether there is enough memory free to swap in the process. At first, as much memory is required as was occupied by the process before it was swapped (*p_swrss*) in the process-table entry. After a process has been swapped for over 10 seconds, it will be swapped in if one-half that amount of memory is available. If there is enough memory available, the process is brought back into memory. The user structure and page tables are swapped in immediately, but the process loads the rest of its working set by demand paging from the swap device. Thus, not all the memory that was committed to the process is really used immediately. To reserve memory for processes that have been swapped in, the *swapper* creates an artificial demand for memory by setting a global variable called *deficit* to the number of pages reserved for processes that have been swapped in recently. The deficit is designed to account for the expected amount of memory that a process will need to restart; it is intended to prevent all the swapped-out processes from returning when a block of memory big enough for only one of them becomes available. The amount of memory considered to be free for the purposes of scheduling swapping and paging is therefore *freemem* minus *deficit*. As these processes will gradually bring pages into memory, *deficit* must be decreased accordingly. Rather than attempting to account for such pages brought into memory, the system reduces *deficit* gradually, by 10 percent per second, until the value reaches zero.

Involuntary Swapping

If the system does not have enough memory to swap in a process, or if it is otherwise short of memory, it will consider swapping out a process from memory. Under any of the following conditions, the system will begin to swap out processes:

- The system page map has become too fragmented to allocate page tables for some process.
- There are at least two runnable processes, the average amount of free memory has been less than that desired (*desfree*; see Section 5.12, paging parameters) over the last 5 and 30 seconds, and either the paging rate is excessive or the short-term average memory is less than *minfree*.
- A swapped-out process is ready to run, and a process is found in memory that has been sleeping for at least 20 seconds; or the swapped-out process has been out for at least 10 seconds, and the process chosen for swapping out has been in memory at least 20 seconds.

These criteria attempt to avoid swapping entirely until the *pagedaemon* is clearly unable to keep enough memory free. Once swapping has begun, an attempt is made to swap out sleeping or large, low-priority jobs. If swapping continues to be necessary, processes that are chosen for swapping must be left out long enough to make the swap worthwhile. Finally, the processes eligible for swapping should take turns in memory, so that no process is frozen out entirely.

Many of these criteria, as well as those described in the next section, are the result of tuning on large (50 to 80 simultaneous users) timesharing systems in an academic environment.

Choosing a Process to Swap Out

When the *swapper* has committed to swapping out a process involuntarily from memory, it must choose a process to be swapped. Two criteria are used: the length of time that a process has been asleep in memory, and the size of the process. If any processes can be found that have been sleeping for more than 20 seconds (*maxslp*, the cutoff for considering the time sleeping to be "a long time"), the one sleeping for the longest time will be swapped out. Such processes have the least likelihood of making good use of the memory they occupy; thus, they are swapped out even if they are small. Otherwise, a runnable or recently run process must be swapped. The object of swapping is to free memory; thus, process size is the major criterion for choosing a process to swap. The algorithm used selects the four largest processes in memory that are eligible to be swapped. (A process may be locked into memory if it is doing raw I/O directly from its address space, or if it is doing operations on its address space, such as expanding or exiting.) Of the four processes identified, the one that has been resident in memory the longest is chosen for swapping. If free memory remains low, the system will swap out each of the four largest processes in turn, swapping another out each time one of them is swapped in. Of course, if the memory shortage abates, all the processes will be swapped in back to memory, and paging will be used to control memory use.

Swapout

Processes are swapped out of memory according to the following steps:

1. Map the user structure of the process into kernel virtual memory
2. Allocate swap space for the user structure and page tables
3. Release the text portion of the image
4. Forcibly page out all resident pages in the data and stack sections of the process
5. Write out the page tables to swap space
6. Write out the user structure and kernel stack to swap space
7. Release the user structure
8. Free the page tables

We described many of these operations in our examination of *exit* (see Section 5.10). We discussed the use of a virtual-memory window to map another process's user structure in Sections 5.7 and 5.12. For swap operations, there are two such windows, mapped by *Xswapmap* and *Xswap2map*. These windows are locked when in use, as more than one swapout could happen at the same time.

Except when a process is swapped out, its user structure and page tables remain in memory at all times. Swap space for the entire process virtual image is preallocated, but the area for the user structure and page tables is allocated only when the process is swapped out. A swapout may fail if space cannot be allocated, and therefore swap allocation is done early in the procedure. A single, contiguous block of swap space is allocated, large enough for the user structure, the data page tables, and the stack page tables. The address of the swap area is stored in the proc-structure element *p_swaddr*. The user structure is placed at the beginning of the area, followed by the page tables. Note that the page tables for the text are handled separately, as there may be at most one copy of the text page table.

When the process is eventually swapped back in, it is useful to know how much memory the process is likely to consume. Therefore, the current resident-set size of the process is recorded in the proc structure before the swap. The removal of the process then proceeds. The only subtle part of this process is related to the handling of the page tables. A process that needs to expand its page tables but is unable to do so because of fragmentation of the system page tables assumes that its page tables will be rearranged to reflect its new size when it returns to memory. Similarly, a process doing an *exec* may need to have its page tables compressed if the new size is smaller than the original one was. In both these cases, the swapping code must carefully rearrange and/or compress page tables as needed.

After the page tables have been swapped out, the user structure is written to swap space and is freed. As in *exit*(), freeing the user structure of the current process requires that the system block memory allocation by raising the processor priority until the next process-context switch. When the swapout is done by the *swapper*, no special precautions are necessary. Finally, the page-table resources for the process are freed in the same way as they are in *exit*(). If the current process is swapping itself out, the processor priority is still high enough that the page-table pages cannot be reallocated. Once the processor has switched to a new process, the priority will be lowered, and memory allocation can resume. The swapped-in process flag SLOAD is cleared to show that the process is not resident in memory, and if necessary the process is removed from the runnable process queue. The swapped out process cannot be run until after it is swapped back into memory.

Swapin

Processes that are swapped out are swapped in back to memory under the control of the *swapper*. The procedure is the reverse of the swapout. It is simpler in that it does not have to concern itself with pages in the user address space; instead, the process reloads its pages on demand by paging them in. The procedure is as follows:

1. Any shared text for the process is locked against change.
2. Resources are allocated for page tables.
3. Memory is allocated for the user structure, and the user structure is read back from swap space.
4. The page tables are read into memory.
5. Swap space for the user structure and page tables is freed.
6. The text area is attached, the text page tables being swapped in if necessary.
7. The process is returned to the run queue if it is runnable.

If the process is runnable, it was removed from the run queue when it was swapped out, or was not added due to a call to *wakeup*(), as the run queue contains only runnable processes that are resident in memory. Thus, the process just swapped in must be added to the run queue if it is now runnable. The process is also marked as resident once more. If the process swapped itself out during page-table expansion, it will have marked itself with the flag SSWAP to show that it should take an alternate return when it first runs. This alternate return is necessary because the program counter saved before the swapout does not show that the swap has completed, and that the process is again ready to run. When this flag is set, the location of the alternate return (*u.u_ssave*) is marked before the SSWAP flag is cleared. When the process first runs, the *resume*() routine will arrange for a nonlocal goto (*longjmp*()).

After the swapin completes, the process is ready to run like any other, except that it has no resident pages. It will bring in the pages that it needs by faulting them, similar to operation after an *exec*, except that most of the pages are likely to be paged in from the swap device.

Swapping of Text Images

The text portion of a process being swapped in or out is handled differently from the data or stack sections, as it is potentially shared with other processes. To some degree, the text-image manipulation during swapping follows the actions during *exit* and *exec*. When a process is swapped out, it releases its use of the text image, but other processes using that image in memory may prevent it from being swapped out. A text image has two reference counts, one for the number of processes holding a reference to the text image, and the other to count the number of those processes that are currently resident in memory—the in-core reference count. When a process is swapped out, only the number of in-core references to the image is decremented. If the in-core reference count is still nonzero after this decrement, the current process needs only to be unlinked from the list of processes using the image. If the in-core count has reached zero, however, no process using the image remains in memory, and the text image can be swapped out. The resident pages that are "modified" (have not yet been written to swap space) are pushed to the text swap area in the same way that dirty data and stack pages are swapped out. If the page tables have not yet been written to swap space, they also are swapped out; this swapout is done only once.

When a process sharing a text is swapped back into memory, the text is reattached as for an *exec*: Either the text will be in memory already and the page tables can simply be copied, or the page tables may be swapped into memory from the copy on swap space. The pages of a text image are faulted in on demand. They may be paged back from the swap space if they were resident before the text page table was swapped out; otherwise, they are paged in from the filesystem. In either case, the pages of a text image may be found in the text page cache if they have not been reused since they were freed.

Exercises

5.1 What does it mean for a machine to support virtual memory? What hardware facilities are typically required for a machine to support virtual memory?

5.2 What is the relationship between paging and swapping on a demand-paged virtual-memory system? Is it desirable to provide both mechanisms in the same system? Can you suggest an alternative to providing both mechanisms?

5.3 What three policies characterize paging systems? Which of these policies usually has no effect on the performance of a paging system?

5.4 Why is the virtual-memory system in 4.3BSD poorly suited to supporting processes with very large sparse address spaces?

5.5 What change in technology made it reasonable for 4.3BSD to cache more data in main memory than was done in previous systems?

5.6 Why does 4.3BSD simulate reference bits on PTEs on the VAX? How does it simulate them?

5.7 Name three functions of the core map.

5.8 Why were the kernel stack and user structure explicitly placed in the P1 region of the VAX virtual address space?

5.9 How are PTEs for pages that are to be filled from a load image identified? What information specific to this type of entry is stored in the PTE?

5.10 If an invalid page has a nonzero page number in its PTE, which of the following statements is certain to be true?

a. The page is a fill-on-demand page.

b. The page may be in transit to the disk.

c. There is main memory allocated to the page.

d. The reference bit on the page is being simulated.

5.11 Why does 4.3BSD keep separate copies of a text segment's page tables, rather than just referencing a single copy?

5.12 Describe a disadvantage of the scheme used for the management of swap space that holds the dynamic per-process segments. *Hint*: Consider what happens when a process with a large virtual-memory size expands in small increments.

5.13 What are shadow swap maps? How are they used in the implementation of the *fork* system call?

5.14 What is *copy-on-write*? In most UNIX applications, the *fork* system call is followed almost immediately by an *exec* system call. Why does this behavior make it particularly attractive to use copy-on-write in implementing *fork*?

5.15 Explain why the *vfork* system call will always be more efficient than a clever implementation of the *fork* system call will be.

5.16 When a process expands the size of its data segment, does it actually get more main memory? What type of PTEs are created for the new pages in the virtual address space?

5.17 When a process exits, all its pages may not be immediately placed on the memory free list; explain why this is true.

5.18 The 4.3BSD virtual-memory system assumes that the overhead of memory-to-memory copy and of direct reads from the filesystem are similar. When a block to be paged in from the filesystem might be present in the filesystem buffer cache, the buffer is written to disk before the pagein. This assumption might be far from true for some current classes of virtual-memory computers. Name at least one such class. What other assumptions might be different for such computers?

5.19 What is klustering? Where is it used in the virtual-memory system?

5.20 Why was the global CLOCK algorithm modified in 4.3BSD to use two clock hands?

5.21 What purpose does the *pagedaemon* process serve in the virtual-memory system? What facility is used by the *pagedaemon* that is not available to a normal user process?

5.22 Why is the *sticky bit* no longer useful in 4.3BSD?

5.23 Give two reasons for swapping to be initiated.

5.24 Why is the current resident set size of a process recorded just before the process is swapped out?

5.25 Give two conditions under which a process will be swapped out when it attempts to expand its page tables.

*5.26 Why are process's page tables never contracted except during a swap operation?

*5.27 Consider the modifications to the global CLOCK algorithm to use two clock hands. Would it be desirable to vary the distance between the clock hands? If it would be, describe an algorithm for doing so; if it would not be, explain why not. What precautions would be necessary while the spread between the hands was being changed? How would the algorithm be affected by a limitation in the scan rate by excessive load on the paging devices?

*5.28 What are the factors affecting the choice of software page size (or clustering factor)? On what machines would a larger page size be most efficient? On what machines would a smaller page size be more efficient?

*5.29 Consider swap space that is spread across multiple disk partitions. What effect do widely varying partition sizes have on the swap-block interleaving scheme? Describe an alternative scheme to the one used in 4.3BSD that makes better use of disk space in this situation.

**5.30 The 4.3BSD virtual-memory system allocates enough swap space for the full address space of a process. On some machines (such as workstations), more physical memory than swap space is available, making preallocation of swap space undesirable. Design a per-process swap map that allows swap space to be allocated as it is needed. What problems can arise from such a scheme?

**5.31 Discuss the implementation of a virtual-memory system similar to the one in 4.3BSD on a computer with a virtual-memory architecture radically different from that of the VAX. For example, consider a machine with an ''inverted page table''—a page table that has a register for each hardware page that contains the virtual address represented by the page.

References

Babaoğlu *et al.*, 1979.
Ö. Babaoğlu, W. N. Joy, & J. Porcar, ''Design and Implementation of the Berkeley Virtual Memory Extensions to the UNIX Operation System,'' Technical Report, CS Division, EECS Dept., University of California, Berkeley, CA (December 1979).

Babaoğlu, 1981.
Ö. Babaoğlu, "Virtual Storage Management in the Absence of Reference Bits," PhD Thesis, CS Division, EECS Dept., University of California, Berkeley, CA (1981).

Babaoğlu & Joy, 1981.
Ö. Babaoğlu & W. N. Joy, "Converting a Swap-Based System to Do Paging in an Architecture Lacking Page-Referenced Bits," *Proceedings of the Eighth Symposium on Operating Systems Principles*, pp. 78–86 (December 1981).

Belady, 1966.
L. A. Belady, "A Study of Replacement Algorithms for Virtual Storage Systems," *IBM Systems Journal* **5**(2), pp. 78–101 (1966).

Coffman & Denning, 1973.
E. G. Coffman, Jr. & P. J. Denning, *Operating Systems Theory*, Prentice-Hall, Englewood Cliffs, NJ (1973).

Corbato, 1968.
F. J. Corbato, "A Paging Experiment with the Multics System," Project MAC Memo MAC-M-384, Massachusetts Institute of Technology, Boston, MA (July, 1968).

DEC, 1980.
DEC, *VAX Hardware Handbook*, Digital Equipment Corporation, Maynard, MA (1980).

Denning, 1970.
P. J. Denning, "Virtual Memory," *Computer Surveys* **2**(3), pp. 153–190 (September, 1970).

Easton & Franaszek, 1979.
M. C. Easton & P. A. Franaszek, "Use Bit Scanning in Replacement Decisions," *IEEE Transactions on Computing* **28**(2), pp. 133–141 (February, 1979).

Gingell *et al.*, 1987.
R. A. Gingell, J. P. Moran, & W. A. Shannon, "Virtual Memory Architecture in SunOS," *USENIX Association Conference Proceedings*, pp. 81–94 (June 1987).

Intel, 1984.
Intel, "Introduction to the iAPX 286," Order Number 210308, Intel Corporation, Santa Clara, CA (1984).

Joy, 1980.
W. N. Joy, "Comments on the Performance of UNIX on the VAX," Technical Report, University of California Computer System Research Group, Berkeley, CA (April 1980).

Kashtan, 1980.
D. L. Kashtan, "UNIX and VMS: Some Performance Comparisons," Technical Report, SRI International, Menlo Park, CA (February 1980).

Kenah & Bate, 1984.
L. J. Kenah & S. F. Bate, *VAX/VMS Internals and Data Structures*, Digital Press, Bedford, MA (1984).

King, 1971.
W. F. King, ''Analysis of Demand Paging Algorithms,'' *IFIP*, pp. 485–490, North Holland (1971).

Lazowska & Kelsey, 1978.
E. D. Lazowska & J. M. Kelsey, ''Notes on Tuning VAX/VMS.,'' Technical Report 78-12-01, Department of Computer Science, University of Washington, Seattle, WA (December 1978).

London & Reiser, 1978.
T. B. London & J. F. Reiser, ''A UNIX Operating System for the DEC VAX-11/780 Computer,'' Technical Report TM-78-1353-4, Bell Laboratories, Murray Hill, NJ (July 1978).

Marshall, 1979.
W. T. Marshall, ''A Unified Approach to the Evaluation of a Class of 'Working Set Like' Replacement Algorithms,'' PhD Thesis, Department of Computer Engineering, Case Western Reserve University, Cleveland, OH (May 1979).

Organick, 1975.
E. I. Organick, *The Multics System: An Examination of Its Structure,* MIT Press, Cambridge, MA (1975).

PART 3

I/O System

CHAPTER 6

I/O System Overview

6.1 I/O Mapping from User to Device

Many hardware device peculiarities are hidden from the user by high-level kernel facilities, such as the filesystem (Chapter 7) and the socket interface (Chapter 10). Other such peculiarities are hidden from the bulk of the kernel itself by the I/O system. The I/O system consists of buffer caching systems, general device-driver code, and drivers for specific hardware devices that must finally address peculiarities of the specific devices. The various I/O systems are summarized in Fig. 6.1.

There are four main kinds of I/O in 4.3BSD; the *filesystem*, the *character-device* interface, the *block-device* interface, and the *socket* interface with its

Figure 6.1 Kernel I/O structure.

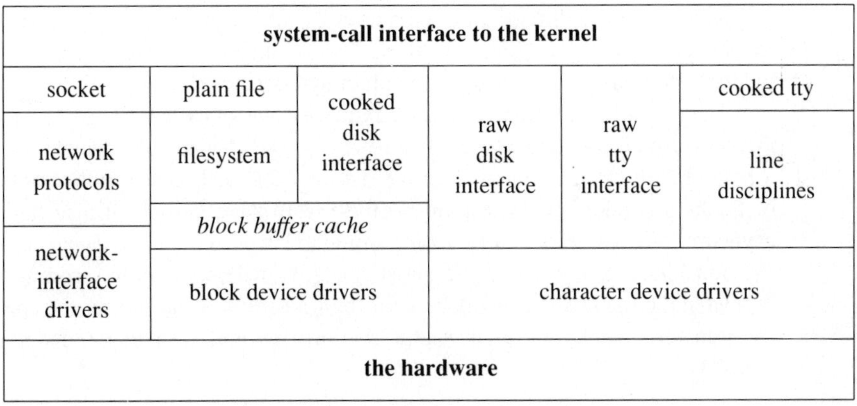

system-call interface to the kernel

socket
network protocols
network-interface drivers

plain file
filesystem
cooked disk interface
block buffer cache
block device drivers

raw disk interface
raw tty interface
cooked tty
line disciplines
character device drivers

the hardware

related network devices. The character and block interfaces appear in the filesystem name space. The character interface provides *unstructured* access to the underlying hardware, whereas the block device provides *structured* access to the underlying hardware. The network devices do not appear in the filesystem, but are accessible only through the socket interface.

For the character and block devices, there is an array of entry points for the various drivers. A device is distinguished by a class and by a *device number*. The device number has two parts. The *major device number* indexes the array appropriate to the class to find entries into the appropriate device driver. The *minor device number* is interpreted by the device driver as, for example, a logical disk partition or a terminal line.

All device drivers are connected to the rest of the kernel only by the entry points recorded in the array for their class, by their use of common buffering systems, and by their use of common low-level hardware-support routines and data structures. This segregation is important for portability, and also for configuring systems.

Character Devices

Almost all peripherals on the system except network interfaces have a character-device interface. A character device usually maps the hardware interface into a byte stream, similar to that of the UNIX filesystem. Character devices of this type include terminals (e.g., **/dev/tty00**), line printers (e.g, **/dev/lp0**), an interface to physical main memory (**/dev/mem**), and a bottomless sink for data and an endless source of end-of-file markers (**/dev/null**). Some of these, such as terminal devices, may have special behavior on line boundaries, but are still in general treated as byte streams.

Terminallike devices use *C-lists*, buffers that are smaller than those used for disks and tapes. This buffering system involves small (usually 64-byte) blocks of characters kept in linked lists. Although all free character buffers are kept in a single free list, most device drivers that use them limit the number of characters that may be queued at one time for a single terminal port.

Devices such as high-speed graphics interfaces may have their own buffers or may always do I/O directly into the address space of the user; they too are classed as character devices. Some of these drivers may recognize special types of records, and thus be further from the plain byte-stream model.

The character interface for disks and tapes is also called the *raw device interface*; it provides an unstructured interface to the device. Its primary task is to arrange for direct I/O to and from the device. The disk driver isolates the details of tracks, cylinders, and the like from the rest of the kernel. It also handles the asynchronous nature of I/O by maintaining and ordering an active queue of pending transfers. Each entry in the queue specifies whether it is for reading or writing, what the main-memory address for the transfer is, what the device address for the transfer (usually the disk sector number) is, and what the transfer size (in bytes) is.

All other restrictions of the underlying hardware are passed through the character interface to its clients, making these character-device interfaces the furthest from the byte-stream model. Thus, the user process must abide by the sectoring restrictions imposed by the underlying hardware. For magnetic disks, the file offset and transfer size must be a multiple of the sector size. The character interface does not copy the user data into a kernel buffer before putting them on an I/O queue. It arranges to have the I/O done directly to or from the address space of the process. The size and alignment of the transfer is limited by the physical device. However, the transfer size is not restricted by the maximum size of the internal buffers of the system, since these buffers are not used. The software does restrict the size of a single transfer to 65,535 bytes; this restriction is an artifact of the PDP-11 derivation of many of the devices themselves.

The character interface is typically used by only those system utility programs that have an intimate knowledge of the data structures on the disk or tape. The character interface also allows user-level prototyping; for example, the 4.2BSD filesystem implementation was written and largely tested as a user process that used a raw disk interface before the code was moved into the kernel.

Block Devices

Block devices include disks and tapes. The task of the block-device interface is to convert from the user abstraction of a disk as an array of bytes to the structure imposed by the underlying physical medium. Although the user may wish to write a single byte to a disk, the hardware can read and write only in multiples of sectors. Hence, the system must arrange to read in the sector containing the byte to be modified, to replace the affected byte, and to write the sector back to the disk. This operation of converting random access to an array of bytes to reads and writes of disk sectors is known as *block I/O*. Block devices are accessible directly through appropriate device special files, but are more commonly accessed indirectly through the filesystem, see (Chapter 7). The kernel also uses the block device interface for disk drivers when doing swapping and paging transfers.

Processes may read data in sizes smaller than a disk block. The first time a small read is required from a particular disk block, the block will be transferred from the disk into a kernel buffer. Succeeding reads of parts of the same block then usually require only copying from the kernel buffer to the memory of the user process. Multiple small writes are treated similarly. A cache buffer is allocated when the first write to a disk block is made, and succeeding writes to the part of the same block are then likely to require only copying into the kernel buffer, and no disk I/O.

In addition to providing the abstraction of arbitrary alignment of reads and writes, the block buffer cache reduces the number of disk I/O transfers required by accesses to the filesystem. Because system parameter files, commands, and directories are read repeatedly, their data blocks are usually in the buffer cache when they are needed. Thus, the kernel does not need to read them from the disk every time that they are requested.

If the system crashes while data for a particular block are in the cache but have not yet been written to disk, the filesystem on the disk will be incorrect and those data will be lost.[1] To alleviate this problem, writes are periodically forced for dirty buffer blocks. These forced writes are done (usually every 30 seconds) by a user process, *update*, doing a *sync* system call. There is also a system call, *fsync*, that may be used to force all blocks of a single file to be written to disk immediately; this synchronization is useful for database consistency.

Most magnetic tape accesses are done, in practice, through the appropriate raw tape device, bypassing the block buffer cache. When the cache is used, tape blocks must still be written in order, so the tape driver forces synchronous writes for them.

Socket-Interface Buffering

Interprocess communication and networking use the *memory buffering system*, or simply *mbufs*. Mbufs are fully described in Chapter 10; they hold moderately sized (usually 112-byte) blocks of characters kept in linked lists. Although all free mbufs are kept in a single free list, most interprocess-communication facilities limit the number of characters that may be queued at one time for a single connection.

A *write* (or *send*) system call on a socket descriptor puts characters on an output queue for the connection. For a network connection, an initial transfer on the network often is started. For intramachine connections, if a process is waiting for data on the connection, it is made runnable or is notified that the data can be read. In either event, further activity related to delivery is handled asynchronously by the kernel, independently of user processes. If there is not enough space on the output queue for all the data supplied by a *write* system call, the system call may block until space becomes available when the network or the other process has accepted enough characters from the output queue.

Input is driven by the arrival of data from the network or from other processes on the same machine. This collecting of arriving data is done asynchronously; the user process does not have to do a *read* (or *recv*) system call first. If there is not enough space in the receiving queue when input arrives, the sending process is put to sleep until the receiver has read some of the data.

When a user process uses a *read* system call to request data from the input queue, any data in the queue are returned immediately. If there are no data in the input queue, the *read* system call may block until data are put on the queue.

6.2 Descriptor Management and Services

For user processes, all I/O is done through descriptors. The user interface to descriptors was described in Section 2.6. This section describes how the kernel

[1] Critical system data, such as the contents of directories, however, are written synchronously to disk to ensure filesystem consistency; this is described in Chapter 7.

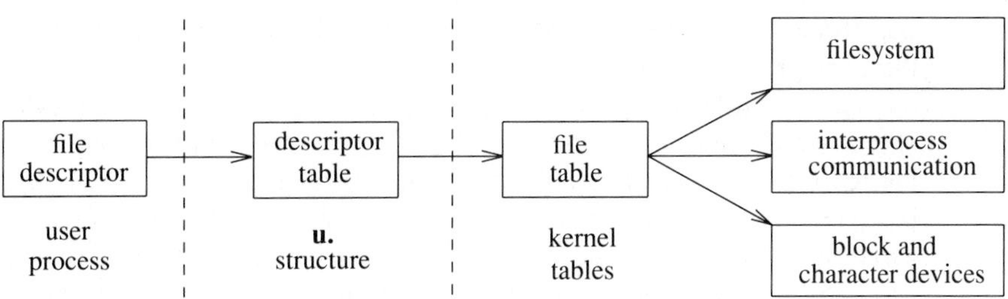

Figure 6.2 File descriptor reference to file table.

manages descriptors and how it provides descriptor services, such as locking and selecting.

System calls that refer to open files take a file descriptor as an argument to specify the file. The file descriptor is used by the kernel to index the *descriptor table* for the current process (kept in the user structure of the process) to locate a *file-table entry*, or *file structure*. The relations of these data structures are shown in Fig. 6.2.

The file-table entry provides a file type and a pointer to an underlying object for the descriptor. For data files, the file-table entry points to a table containing filesystem specific information that is described in Chapter 7. Special files do not have data blocks allocated on the disk. The kernel notices these file types and calls appropriate drivers to handle I/O for them. The 4.3BSD file-table entry may also reference a *socket* instead of a file. Sockets have a different file type, and the file-table entry points to a system block that is used in doing interprocess communication.

Open File Table

The file table is the focus of activity for file descriptors. It contains the information necessary to access the underlying objects and to maintain common information.

The file table is an object-oriented data structure. Each entry in the table contains a type and an array of function pointers that translate the generic operations on file-table descriptors into the specific actions associated with their type. In 4.3BSD, there are two descriptor types, files and sockets. The operations that must be implemented for each type are as follows:

- A function to read and write the descriptor
- A function to select on the descriptor
- A function to do *ioctl* operations on the descriptor
- A function to close, and possibly to deallocate, the object associated with the descriptor

Note that there is no open routine defined in the object table. 4.3BSD treats descriptors in an object-oriented fashion only after they are created. This was done because sockets and files have very different characteristics, and combining these at open time would have overloaded an otherwise simple interface.

Each file-table entry has a pointer to a data structure that contains information specific to the instance of the underlying object. The data structure is opaque to the routines that manipulate the file table. A reference to the data structure is passed on each call to a function that implements a file-table operation. All state associated with an instance of an object must be stored in that instance's data structure; the underlying objects are not permitted to manipulate the file table themselves.

The *read* and *write* system calls do not take an offset in the file as an argument. Instead, each read or write updates the current *file offset* in the file according to the number of data transferred. The offset determines the position in the file for the next read or write. The offset can be set directly by the *lseek* system call. Since more than one process may open the same file, and each such process needs its own offset for the file, the offset cannot be stored in the per-object data structure. Thus, each *open* system call allocates a new file-table entry, and the open file table contains the offset.

Semantics associated with all file descriptors are enforced at the descriptor level before the system calls through the function entries. These semantics are maintained in a set of flags associated with the descriptor. For example, the flags record whether the descriptor is open for reading and/or writing. If a descriptor is marked as open only for reading, an attempt to write it will be caught by the descriptor code. Thus, the functions defined for doing reading and writing need not check the validity of the request; we can implement them knowing that they will never receive an invalid request.

Other information maintained in the flags includes

- The *no-delay* (NDELAY) flag. If a read or a write would cause the process to block, the system call returns an error (EWOULDBLOCK) instead.
- The *asynchronous* (ASYNC) flag. The kernel watches for a change in the status of the descriptor and arranges to send a signal (SIGIO) when a read or write becomes possible.

Other information that is specific to regular files also is maintained in the flags field:

- Information on whether the descriptor holds a shared or exclusive lock on the underlying file. Although the locking primitives could be extended to work on sockets as well as files, the descriptors for a socket usually refer to the same file-table entry.
- The *append* flag. Each time a write is made to the file, the offset pointer is first set to the end of the file. This feature is useful when, for example, multiple processes are writing to the same log file.

Each entry in the file table has a reference count. A single process may have multiple references to the entry because of calls to the *dup* or *fcntl* system calls. Also, file structures are inherited by the child process after a *fork*, so several different processes may reference the same file-table entry. Thus, a read or write by either process on the twin descriptors will advance the file offset. This allows two processes to read the same file or to interleave output to the same file alternately, while another process that has independently opened the file will refer to that file through a different file structure with a different file offset. This capability was the original reason for the existence of the file structure; the file structure provides a place for the file offset intermediate between the descriptor and the underlying object.

Each time a new reference is created, the reference count is incremented. When a descriptor is closed (either explicitly with a *close*, or implicitly after an *exec* because the descriptor has been marked as close-on-exec, or on exit), the reference count is decremented. When the reference count finally drops to zero, the file-table entry can be freed.

The UNIX domain interprocess-communication facility allows descriptors to be sent between processes. While a descriptor is in transit between processes, it may not have any explicit references. It must not be deallocated as it will be needed when the message is received by the destination process. However, the message might never be received; thus, the file table also holds a *message count* for each entry. The message count is incremented for each descriptor that is in transit, and is decremented when the descriptor is received. The file-table entry might need to be reclaimed when all the remaining references are in messages. For more details on message passing in the UNIX domain, see Section 10.6.

The close-on-exec flag is kept in the descriptor table rather than in the file table. This flag is not shared among all the references to the file table, as it is an attribute of the file descriptor itself. The close-on-exec flag is the only piece of information that is kept in the descriptor table rather than being shared in the file table.

Management of Descriptors

The *fcntl* system call manipulates the file structure. It can be used to make the following changes to a descriptor:

- Duplicate a descriptor as if by a *dup* system call.
- Get or set the close-on-exec flag. When a process *fork*s, all the parent's descriptors are duplicated in the child. The child process then *exec*s a new process. Any of the child's descriptors that were marked close-on-exec are closed. The remaining descriptors are available to the newly executed process.
- Set the descriptor into nonblocking mode. If any data are available for a read operation, or any space is available for a write operation, an immediate partial read or write is done. If no data are available for a read operation, or a write operation would block, the system call returns an error showing that the operation would block, instead of putting the process to sleep. This facility was never implemented for regular files in 4.3BSD.

- Force all writes to append data to the end of the file, instead of at the descriptor's current location in the file.
- Send a signal to the process when it is possible to do I/O.
- Send a signal to a process when an exception condition arises, such as when urgent data arrive on an interprocess-communication channel.
- Set or get the process identifier or process-group identifier to which the two I/O related signals in the previous steps should be sent.

The implementation of the *dup* system call is easy. The kernel scans the descriptor table for the current process, starting at descriptor zero, until it finds an unused entry. If no unused entries exist, the kernel returns an error. Otherwise, the kernel allocates the entry to point to the same file-table entry as does the descriptor it has been asked to duplicate. The kernel then increments the reference count on the file-table entry, and returns the index of the allocated descriptor-table entry. The *fcntl* system call provides a similar function, except that it specifies a descriptor from which to start the scan.

Sometimes, a process wants to allocate a specific descriptor-table entry. Such a request is made with *dup2*. The process specifies the descriptor-table index into which the duplicated reference should be placed. The kernel implementation is the same as for *dup*, except that the scan to find a free entry is changed to close the requested entry if it is open, and then to allocate it as before. No action is taken if the new and old descriptors are the same.

The system implements getting or setting the close-on-exec flag via the *fcntl* system call by doing the appropriate action to the flags field of the associated descriptor-table entry. Other attributes that *fcntl* can get or set manipulate the flags in the file table. However, the implementation of the various flags cannot be handled by the generic code that manages the file table. Instead, the file-table flags must be passed through the object interface to the type-specific routines to do the appropriate operation on the underlying object. For example, manipulation of the nonblocking flag for a socket must be done by the socket layer, since the flag resides in a socket structure and the socket structure is opaque to the routines that operate on the file table.

The implementation of the *ioctl* system call is broken into two major parts. The upper level handles the system call itself. The *ioctl* call includes a descriptor, a command, and pointer to a data area. The command argument encodes the size of the data area for the parameters and whether the parameters are input and/or output. The upper level is responsible for decoding the command argument, allocating a buffer, and copying in any input data. If a return value is to be generated and there is no input, the buffer is zeroed. Finally, the *ioctl* is dispatched through the file-table *ioctl* function, along with the I/O buffer, to the lower-level routine that implements the requested operation.

The lower level does the requested operation. Along with the command argument, it receives a pointer to the I/O buffer. The upper level has already checked for valid memory references, but the lower level must do more precise argument validation because it knows more about the expected nature of the arguments. However, it does not need to copy the arguments in or out of the user process. If the command is successful and produces output, the lower level places the results in the buffer provided by the top level. When the lower level returns, the upper level copies the results to the process.

Descriptor Locking

Early UNIX systems had no provision for locking files. Processes that needed to synchronize the updates of a file had to use a separate *lock file*. A process would try to create a *lock file*. If the creation succeeded, then the process could proceed with its update; if the creation failed, the process would wait and then try again. This mechanism had three drawbacks:

1. Processes consumed CPU time by looping over attempts to create locks.
2. Locks left lying around because of system crashes had to be manually removed (normally in a system startup command script).
3. Processes running as the special system-administrator user, the *superuser*, are always permitted to create files, and so were forced to use a different mechanism.

Although it is possible to get around all these problems, the solutions are not straightforward, so a mechanism for locking files was added in 4.2BSD.

The most general locking schemes allow multiple processes to update a file concurrently. Several of these techniques are discussed in [Peterson, 1983]. A simpler technique is to serialize access to a file with locks. To attain reasonable efficiency, certain applications require the ability to lock pieces of a file. Locking facilities for UNIX that support a byte-level granularity are well understood [Bass, 1981] and even appear in System V. However, for the standard system applications, a mechanism that locks at the granularity of a file is sufficient.

Locking schemes can be classified according to the extent that they are enforced. A scheme in which locks are enforced for every process without choice is said to use *mandatory locks*, whereas a scheme in which locks are enforced for only those processes that request them is said to use *advisory locks*. Clearly, advisory locks are effective only when all programs accessing a file use the locking scheme. With mandatory locks, there must be some override policy implemented in the kernel. With advisory locks, the policy is left to the user programs. In the UNIX system, programs with superuser privilege are allowed to override any protection scheme. Because many of the programs that need to use locks must also run as the superuser, 4.2BSD implemented advisory locks rather than creating an additional protection scheme that was inconsistent with the UNIX philosophy or that could not be used by privileged programs.

The 4.2BSD file-locking facilities allow cooperating programs to apply advisory *shared* or *exclusive* locks on files. Only one process may have an exclusive lock on a file, whereas multiple shared locks may be present. Both shared and exclusive locks cannot be present on a file at the same time. If any lock is requested when another process holds an exclusive lock, or an exclusive lock is requested when another process holds any lock, the lock request will block until the lock can be obtained. Because shared and exclusive locks are only advisory, even if a process has obtained a lock on a file, another process may access the file if it ignores the locking mechanism.

Locks are applied or removed on only open files. Thus, a process can manipulate locks without needing to close and reopen a file. This feature is useful, for example, when a process wishes to apply a shared lock, read some information, determine whether an update is required, then apply an exclusive lock and update the file.

A request for a lock will cause a process to block if the lock cannot be obtained immediately. In certain instances, this is unsatisfactory. For example, a process that wants only to check whether a lock is present would require a separate mechanism to find out this information. Consequently, a process may specify that its locking request should return with an error if a lock cannot be obtained immediately. Being able to request a lock conditionally is useful to *daemon* processes that wish to service a spooling area. If the first instance of the daemon locks the directory where spooling takes place, later daemon processes can easily check to see whether an active daemon exists. Since locks exist only while the locking processes exist, lock files can never be left active after the processes exit or if the system crashes.

Implementation of Locking

The implementation of advisory locks is shown in Fig. 6.3. A process requesting either type of lock must first wait for any exclusive locks to clear. Whenever the kernel is about to put a process to sleep, the kernel must first check to see whether it is processing a nonblocking request. For nonblocking requests, the kernel must return an error, rather than putting the process to sleep. If the process wants a shared lock, it can proceed. If the process wants an exclusive lock, it must wait for any shared locks to clear. Since several processes may want an exclusive lock, they may all be waiting at line 20 in Fig. 6.3. Only one of them can get the lock; the rest must wait. Since all processes waiting at line 20 are awakened when the shared lock clears, they must all start over at the first line of Fig. 6.3. One process will make it through the code and acquire the lock; the rest will be blocked at line 9.

The processes waiting at lines 9 and 20 are awakened when other processes release their locks. When the last shared lock is released, all processes waiting for the shared lock to clear (line 20) are started. When an exclusive lock is released, all processes waiting for the exclusive lock to clear (line 9) are started.

Any resource-allocation scheme with two or more resources that allow exclusive use can create an allocation deadlock. In general, detection of deadlock is difficult [Shaw, 1974]. The 4.3BSD locking code makes a cursory attempt at preventing deadlock. The code at lines 3 through 5 ensures that a process seeking a shared lock will not deadlock against an exclusive lock that it already holds.

```
1   top:
2   while (an exclusive lock exists) {
3       if (current process has an exclusive lock) {
4           free its exclusive lock
5       }
6       if (any process holds an exclusive lock) {
7           if (nonblocking request)
8               return EWOULDBLOCK
9           wait for exclusive lock to clear
10      }
11  }
12  if (current process wants an exclusive lock) &&
13     (any process holds a shared lock) {
14      if (current process has a shared lock) {
15          free its shared lock
16      }
17      if (any process holds a shared lock) {
18          if (nonblocking request)
19              return EWOULDBLOCK
20          wait for shared lock to clear
21      }
22      goto top
23  }
24  acquire requested lock type
```

Figure 6.3 Algorithm to acquire a lock.

The code at lines 14 through 16 ensures that a process seeking an exclusive lock will not deadlock against a lock that it already holds.

The decision not to put deadlock detection into the kernel is pragmatic. Doing deadlock detection in all situations is complex and time consuming [Kenah & Bate, 1984]. The locking mechanism is designed to be fast and simple. Most locks (mailbox locks, for example) are used on only a single resource at a time, and consequently have no possibility of deadlock. More complex applications can more efficiently develop their own specialized strategies for doing deadlock detection, rather than depending on a slow generalized mechanism that is implemented in the kernel.

Multiplexing I/O on Descriptors

A process sometimes wants to handle I/O on more than one descriptor. For example, a remote login program wants to read data from the keyboard and send them through a socket to a remote machine. The program also wants to read data from the socket connected to the remote end and to write them to the screen. If a process makes a read request when there are no data available, it is normally blocked in the kernel until the data become available. In our example, blocking is unacceptable. If the process reads from the keyboard and blocks, it will be unable to read data from the remote end that are destined for the screen. The user cannot type any input until more data have arrived from the remote end; hence, the session deadlocks. Conversely, if the process reads from the remote end when there are no data for the screen, it will block and will be unable to read from the terminal. Again, deadlock would occur if the remote end were waiting for output before sending any data. There is an analogous set of problems to blocking on the writes to the screen or to the remote end. If users have stopped output to their screens by typing the stop character, the write will block until they type the start character. In the meantime, the process cannot read from the keyboard to find out that the users want to flush the output.

Traditional UNIX systems have handled the multiplexing problem by using multiple processes that communicate through pipes or some other interprocess-communication facility, such as shared memory. This approach, however, can result in significant overhead as a result of context switching between the processes if the cost of processing input is small relative to the cost of a context switch. Furthermore, it is often more straightforward to implement applications of this sort in a single process. For these reasons, 4.3BSD provides two mechanisms that permit multiplexing I/O on descriptors: *nonblocking I/O* and *signal-driven I/O*. Operations on nonblocking descriptors complete immediately, partially complete an input or output operation and return a partial count, or return an error that indicates the operation could not be completed at all. Descriptors that have signaling enabled cause the associated process or process group to be notified when the I/O state of the descriptor changes.

There are four possible alternatives that avoid the blocking problem:

1. Set all the descriptors into nonblocking mode. The process can then try operations on each descriptor in turn to find out which descriptors are ready to do I/O. The problem with this approach is that the process must run continuously to discover whether there is any I/O to be done.

2. Enable all descriptors of interest to signal when I/O can be done. The process can then wait for a signal to discover when it is possible to do I/O. The drawback to this approach is that signals are expensive to catch. Hence, signal driven I/O is impractical for applications that do moderate to large amounts of I/O.

3. Have the system provide a method for asking which descriptors are capable of doing I/O. If none of the requested descriptors is ready, the system can put the process to sleep until a descriptor becomes ready. This approach avoids the problem of deadlock, since the process will be awakened whenever it is possible to do I/O, and will be told which descriptor is ready. It does have the drawback that the process must do two system calls per operation: one to poll for the descriptor that is ready to do I/O, and another to do the operation itself.

4. Have the process notify the system of all the descriptors that it is interested in reading, then do a blocking read on that set of descriptors. When the read returns, the process is notified on which descriptor the read completed. The benefit of this approach is that the process does a single system call to specify the set of descriptors, then loops doing only reads [Accetta *et al.*, 1986].

The third approach is used in 4.3BSD through the *select* system call. Although less efficient than the fourth approach, it is a more general interface. In addition to handling reading from multiple descriptors, it handles writes to multiple descriptors, notification of exceptional conditions, and timeout when no I/O is possible.

The *select* interface takes three masks of descriptors to be polled, corresponding to interest in reading, writing, and exceptional conditions. In addition, it takes a timeout value for returning from *select* if none of the requested descriptors becomes ready before a specified amount of time has elapsed. The *select* call returns the same three masks of descriptors after modifying them to show the descriptors that are able to do reading, to do writing, or to provide an exceptional condition. If none of the descriptors has become ready in the timeout interval, select returns indicating that no descriptors are ready for I/O.

Implementation of Select

The implementation of *select*, like that of many other kernel functions, is divided into a generic top layer and many device- or socket-specific bottom pieces.

At the top level, *select* decodes the request of the user and then arranges to call the appropriate lower-level select functions. The top level proceeds by taking several steps:

1. Fetch and validate the descriptor masks for read, write, and exceptional conditions. Validation requires checking that each requested descriptor is currently open by the process.

2. Set the *selecting* flag for the process.

3. For each descriptor in each mask, poll the device by calling its select routine. If the descriptor is not able to do the requested I/O operation, the select routine is responsible for recording that the process wants to do I/O. When I/O becomes possible for the descriptor, usually as a result of an interrupt from the underlying device, a notification must be issued for the selecting process.

4. If the process is no longer marked as selecting, mark the process as selecting and poll all the specified devices again. Because the selection process may take a long time, the kernel does not want to block out I/O during the time it takes to poll all the requested descriptors. Instead, the kernel arranges to detect the occurrence of I/O that may affect the status of the descriptors being polled. When such I/O occurs, the select-notification routine, *selwakeup*(), clears the *selecting* flag. If the top-level select code finds that the *selecting* flag for the

process has been cleared while it has been doing the polling, then the top level knows that the polling results may be invalid and must be repeated. The other condition that requires the polling to be repeated is caused by a *collision*. Collisions arise when multiple processes attempt to select on the same descriptor at the same time. Because the select routines have only enough space to record a single process identifier, they cannot track multiple processes that need to be awakened when I/O is possible. In such rare instances, all processes that are selecting must be awakened. If no descriptors are ready and the *select* specified a timeout, the kernel posts a timeout for the requested amount of time. The timeout function, *unselect*(), takes a pointer to the process-table entry for the process. The process goes to sleep, giving the address of the kernel global variable *selwait*. Normally, a descriptor will become ready and the process will be notified by *selwakeup*(). If none of the descriptors becomes ready before the timer expires, *unselect*() gets called and awakens the process. When the process is awakened, it repeats the polling process and returns the available descriptors. If it is awakened because of a timeout, the available descriptor list will be empty.

Each of the low-level polling routines in the terminal drivers and the network protocols follows roughly the same set of steps. A piece of the select routine for a terminal driver is shown in Fig. 6.4. The steps involved in a polling device are as follows:

1. The socket or device select entry is called with flag of FREAD, FWRITE, or 0 (exceptional condition). The example in Fig. 6.4 shows the FREAD case; the others cases are similar.

2. The poll returns success if the requested operation is possible. In Fig. 6.4, it is possible to read a character if the number of unread characters is greater than zero. In addition, if the carrier has dropped, it is possible to get a read error: A

Figure 6.4 Select for reading in a terminal driver.

```
struct tty *tp;

case FREAD:
    if (nread > 0 || (tp->t_state & TS_CARR_ON) == 0)
        return (1);
    if (tp->t_rsel &&
        tp->t_rsel->p_wchan == (caddr_t)&selwait)
        tp->t_state |= TS_RCOLL;
    else
        tp->t_rsel = u.u_procp;
    return (0);
```

return from select does not necessarily mean that there are data to read; rather, it means that a read will not block.

3. If the requested operation is not possible, the process identifier is recorded with the socket or device for later notification. In Fig. 6.4, the second **if** statement is false and the process identifier (a pointer to the process table entry for the process) is saved in *t_rsel*.

4. If multiple processes are selecting on the same socket or device, a collision is recorded for the socket or device because the structure has only enough space for a single process identifier. In Fig. 6.4, a collision occurs when the second **if** statement is true.

There is a *tty* structure for each terminal line (or pseudoterminal) on the machine. Normally, only one process at a time is selecting to read from the terminal. The second **if** statement in Fig. 6.4 detects the case when more than one process is selecting at the same time. The check for a collision is as follows. The first part of the conjunctive checks to see whether any process identifier is recorded already. If there is none, then there is no collision. If there is a process identifier recorded, it may remain from an earlier call on select by a process that is no longer selecting because one of its other descriptors became ready. If that process is still selecting, it will be sleeping on *selwait* (when sleeping, the address of the sleep event is stored in *p_wchan*). If it is sleeping on some other event, its *p_wchan* will have a value different from that of *selwait*. If it is running, its *p_wchan* will be zero. Usually, *t_rsel* is set to the current process, but, since the current process is running (in the select code), the value for its *p_wchan* will be zero and no collision will occur.

Selecting processes must be notified when I/O becomes possible. The steps involved in detecting and awakening a process are as follows:

1. The device or socket detects a change in status. Status changes normally occur because of an interrupt (for example, a character coming in from a keyboard or a packet coming in from the network).

2. *Selwakeup*() is called with the process identifier and a flag showing whether a collision occurred.

3. If the process is sleeping on *selwait*, it is made runnable (or is marked ready if it is stopped). If the process is sleeping on some event other than *selwait*, it is not made runnable. A spurious call to *selwakeup*() can occur when the process returns from *select* to begin processing one descriptor and then another descriptor on which it had been selecting also becomes ready.

4. If the process has its *selecting* flag set, the flag is cleared so that it will know that its polling results are invalid and must be recomputed.

5. If a collision has occurred, all sleepers on *selwait* are awakened to rescan to see whether one of their descriptors became ready. Awakening all selecting

processes is necessary because the low-level select routine could not record all the processes that needed to be awakened. Hence, it has to wake up all processes that could possibly have been interested. Empirically, collisions occur very infrequently. If they were a frequent occurrence, it would be worthwhile to design a more complex data structure to hold multiple process identifiers.

Moving Data Inside the Kernel

Within the kernel, I/O data are described by an array of vectors. Each vector has a base address and a length, and is called an *I/O vector* or *iovec*. The I/O vectors are identical to the I/O vectors used by the *readv* and *writev* system calls.

The kernel maintains another structure that holds additional information about the I/O operation called a *uio* structure. A sample *uio* structure is shown in Fig. 6.5; it contains

- A pointer to the *iovec* array
- The size of the *iovec* array
- The file offset at which the operation should start
- A flag showing whether the source and destination are both within the kernel, or whether the source and destination are split between the user and the kernel
- The sum of the lengths of the I/O vectors

Figure 6.5 A *uio* structure.

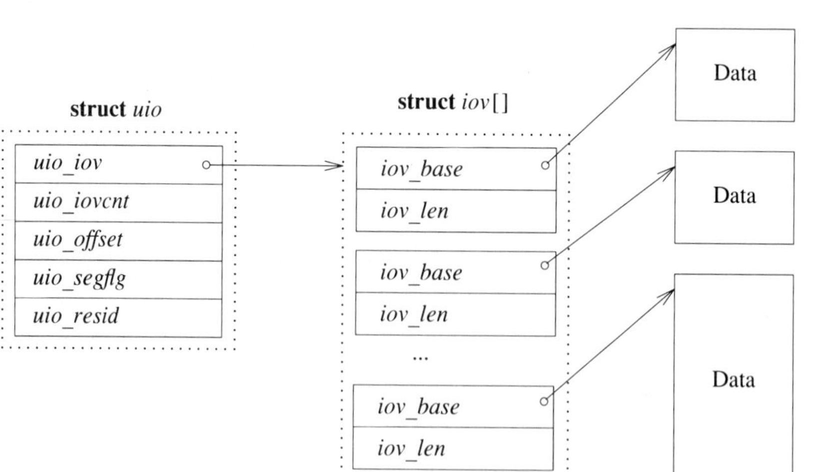

All I/O within the kernel is described with *iovec* and *uio* structures. System calls such as *read* and *write* that are not passed an *iovec* create a *uio* to describe their arguments; this *uio* structure is passed to the lower levels of the kernel to specify the parameters of an I/O operation. Eventually, the *uio* structure reaches the part of the kernel responsible for moving the data to or from the process address space—the filesystem, the network, or a device driver. In general, these parts of the kernel do not interpret *uio* structures directly. Instead, they arrange a kernel buffer to hold the data, then use *uiomove*() to copy the data to or from the buffer(s) described by the *uio* structure. The *uiomove*() routine is called with a pointer to a kernel data area, a data count, and a *uio* structure. As it moves data, it updates the counters and pointers of the *iovec* and *uio* structures by a corresponding amount. If the kernel buffer is not as large as the areas described by the *uio* structure, the *uio* structure will point to the part of the process address space just beyond the last location completed. Thus, while servicing a request, the kernel may call *uiomove*() multiple times, each time giving a pointer to a new kernel buffer for the next block of data.

Character device drivers that do not copy data from the process generally do not interpret the *uio* structure themselves either. Instead, there is one low-level kernel routine that arranges a direct transfer to or from the address space of the process. Here, a separate I/O operation is done for each *iovec* element, calling back to the driver with one piece at a time.

Traditional UNIX systems use global variables in the user area to describe I/O. This approach has several problems. The lower levels of the kernel are not reentrant, since there is exactly one context to describe an I/O operation. The system cannot do scatter-gather I/O, since there is only a single base and size variable per process. Finally, the bottom half of the kernel cannot do I/O, since it does not have a user area.

The one part of the 4.2BSD kernel that does not use *uio* structures is the block device drivers. The decision not to change these interfaces to use *uio* structures was largely pragmatic. The developers would have had to change many drivers. The existing buffer interface was already decoupled from the user structure; hence, the interface was already reentrant and could be used by the bottom half of the kernel. The only gain was to allow scatter-gather I/O. The kernel does not need scatter-gather operations on block devices, however, and user operations on block devices are done through the buffer cache.

Exercises

6.1 Where are the read and write attributes of an open file descriptor stored?

6.2 Why is the close-on-exec bit located in the per-process descriptor table instead of in the system file table?

6.3 Why are the file-table entries reference counted?

6.4 What shortcomings of lock files are addressed by the 4.3BSD descriptor-locking facilities?

6.5 What problems are raised by mandatory locks?

6.6 Why is the implementation of *select* split between the descriptor-management code and the lower-level routines?

6.7 Describe how the *process selecting flag* is used in the implementation of *select*.

6.8 The *update* program is usually started shortly after the system is booted. Once every 30 seconds, it does a *sync* system call. What problems could arise if this program were not run?

6.9 The special device **/dev/kmem** provides access to the kernel's virtual address space. Would you expect it to be a character or a block device? Explain your answer.

6.10 Many tape drives provide a block-device interface. Is it possible to support a filesystem on a such a tape drive?

*6.11 True asynchronous I/O is not supported in 4.3BSD. What problems arise with providing asynchronous I/O in the existing read–write interface?

**6.12 Describe an alternative scheme to the per-process descriptor table that does not impose an upper bound on the number of open files that a process may have. What problems are created for your scheme by the requirement that open file descriptors be inherited across a *fork*?

References

Accetta *et al.*, 1986.
M. Accetta, R. Baron, D. Golub, R. Rashid, A. Tevanian, & M. Young, "Mach: A New Kernel Foundation for UNIX Development," Technical Report, Carnegie Mellon University, Pittsburgh, PA (August 1986).

Bass, 1981.
J. Bass, *Implementation Description for File Locking*, Onyx Systems Inc., 73 E. Trimble Road, San Jose, CA (January 1981).

Kenah & Bate, 1984.
L. J. Kenah & S. F. Bate, *VAX/VMS Internals and Data Structures*, Digital Press, Bedford, MA (1984).

Peterson, 1983.
G. Peterson, "Concurrent Reading while Writing," *ACM Transactions on Programming Languages and Systems* **5**(1), pp. 46–55 (January 1983).

Shaw, 1974.
A. C. Shaw, *The Logical Design of Operating Systems*, Prentice-Hall, Englewood Cliffs, NJ (1974).

CHAPTER 7

The Filesystem

7.1 Structure and Overview

4.3BSD organizes data in filesystems that reside on mass-storage media such as disk drives. Each disk drive is divided into one or more subdivisions, or partitions. Each such partition may contain only one filesystem, and a filesystem never spans multiple partitions.

Within the filesystem are files, most of which contain ordinary data. Certain files are distinguished as directories and contain pointers to files that may themselves be directories. This hierarchy of directories and files is organized into a tree structure; Fig. 7.1 shows a small filesystem tree.

Directories

Directories are allocated in units called *chunks*; Fig. 7.2 shows a typical directory chunk. The size of a chunk is chosen such that each allocation can be transferred to disk in a single operation; the ability to change a directory in a single operation allows directory updates to be atomic. Chunks are broken up into variable-length directory entries to allow filenames to be of nearly arbitrary length. No directory entry is allowed to span multiple chunks. The first three fields of a directory entry are fixed length and contain

1. A pointer to an on-disk data structure describing the file; the contents of this on-disk data structure, which is called an *inode*, are described in Section 7.2

2. The size of the entry

3. The length of the filename contained in the entry

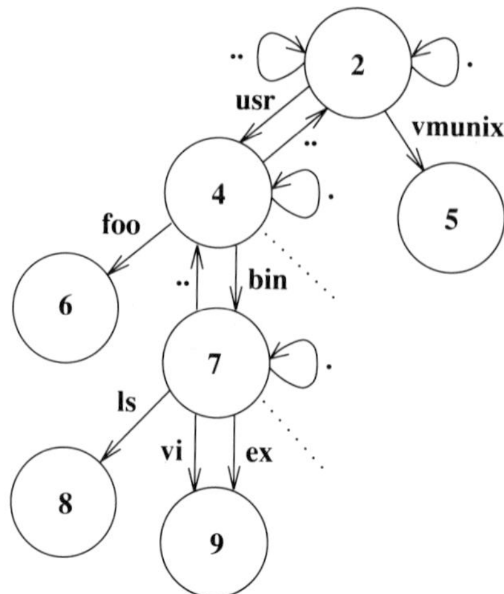

Figure 7.1 A small filesystem tree.

The remainder of an entry is variable length and contains a null-terminated filename, padded to a 4-byte boundary. The maximum length of a filename in a directory is 255 characters.

Available space in a directory is recorded by having one or more entries accumulate the free space in their size fields. This results in directory entries that are larger than required to hold the entry name plus fixed-length fields. Space allocated to a directory should always be completely accounted for by the total of the sizes of its entries. When an entry is deleted from a directory, the system coalesces its space into the previous entry in the same directory chunk by increasing the size of the previous entry by the size of the deleted entry. If the first entry of a directory chunk is free, then the pointer to the entry's inode is set to zero to show that it is unallocated.

Figure 7.2 Format of directory entries.

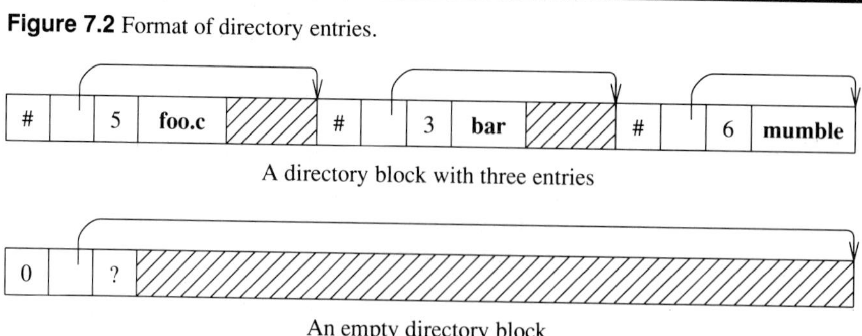

The new directory structure was introduced in 4.2BSD. Other UNIX systems use 14-character filenames. Directories consist of arrays of 16-byte entries: The first two bytes are the inode number; the remaining 14 bytes are the filename. Programs scan directories by reading the latter as ordinary files with *open*, *read*, *lseek*, and *close*. 4.2BSD introduced a new library interface that could be used to access either the new or the old directory structure. The *opendir*() function returns a structure pointer that is used by *readdir*() to obtain the next directory entry, by *rewinddir*() to reset the read position to the beginning, and by *closedir*() to close the directory. In addition, there is *seekdir*(), which returns to a position previously obtained with *telldir*().

Another benefit of using directory-access routines is that they can be emulated over a network, or even for a non-UNIX filesystem such as MS-DOS.

Links

Every file has an associated inode that contains information describing access permissions, ownership of the file, timestamps marking last modification and access times for the file, and an array of indices that point to the data blocks for the file. Each file has a single inode, but may have multiple directory entries in the same filesystem to reference it (i.e., multiple names). Each directory entry creates a *hard link* of a filename to the inode that describes its contents. The link concept is fundamental; inodes do not reside in directories, but exist separately and are referenced by links. When all the links to an inode are removed, the inode is deallocated. If one link to a file is removed and the filename is recreated with new contents, the other links will continue to point to the old inode. Figure 7.3 shows two different directory entries, **foo** and **bar**, that reference the same file; thus, the inode for the file shows a reference count of two.

Figure 7.3 Hard links to a file.

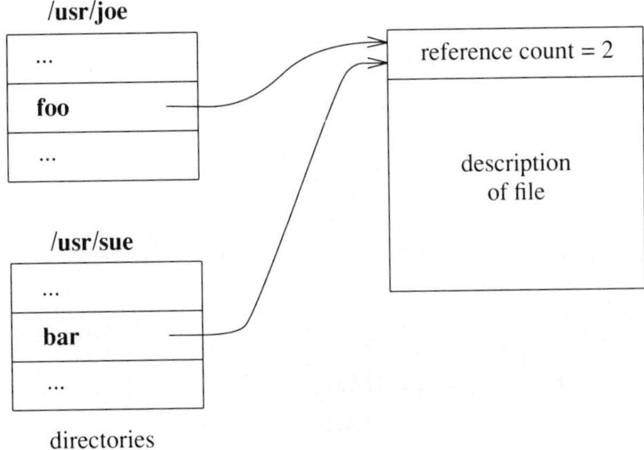

The system also supports a *symbolic link*, or *soft link*. A symbolic link is implemented as a file that contains a pathname. When the system encounters a symbolic link while interpreting a component of a pathname, the contents of the symbolic link are prepended to the rest of the pathname, and this name is interpreted to yield the resulting pathname. If a symbolic link contains an absolute pathname, that absolute pathname is used; otherwise, the contents of the symbolic link are evaluated relative to the location of the link in the file hierarchy (not according to the current working directory of the calling process).

An example symbolic link is shown in Fig. 7.4. Here there is a hard link, **foo**, that points to the file. The other reference, **bar**, points to a different inode whose contents is a pathname of the referenced file. When a process opens **bar**, the system interprets the contents of the symbolic link as a pathname to find the file the link references. Symbolic links are treated like data files by the system, rather than as part of the filesystem structure; thus, they can point at directories or files on other filesystems. If a filename is removed and replaced, any symbolic links that point to it will access the new file. Finally, if the filename is not replaced, the symbolic link will point at nothing and any attempt to access it will cause an error to be returned.

When *open* is applied to a symbolic link, it returns a file descriptor for the file pointed to, not for the link itself. Otherwise, it would be necessary to use some sort of indirection to access the file pointed to—and that file, not the link, is what is usually wanted. For the same reason, most other system calls that take pathname arguments also follow symbolic links. The *stat* system call is an exception to this rule, because it is sometimes useful to be able to detect a symbolic link when traversing a filesystem or when making an archive tape. So another variant

Figure 7.4 Symbolic link to a file.

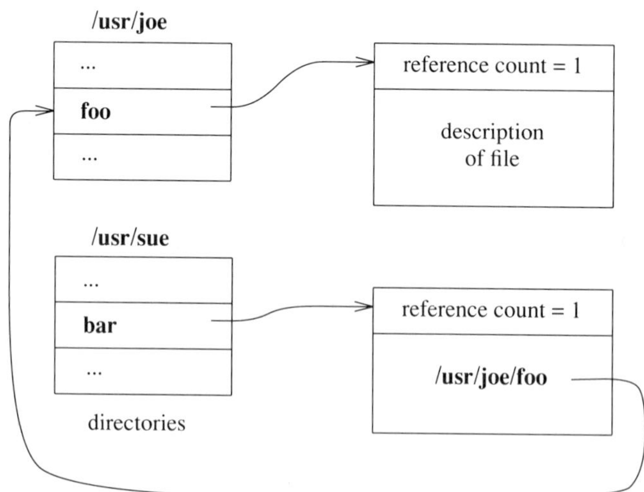

of *stat*, *lstat*, is available to get the status of a symbolic link instead of the object at which that link points.

A symbolic link has several advantages over a hard link. Specifically, a symbolic link can refer to a directory or to a file on a different filesystem. A hard link is not permitted to refer to a directory, to prevent loops in the filesystem hierarchy. The implementation of hard links prevents them from referring to files on a different filesystem.

There are some interesting implications of symbolic links. Consider a process that has current working directory **/usr/sue** and does *cd* **src**, where **src** is a symbolic link to directory **/usr/src**. If the process then does a *cd* **..**, then it will end up in **/usr** instead of in **/usr/sue**, as it would have done if **src** was a normal directory instead of a symbolic link. The kernel could be changed to keep track of the symbolic links that a process had traversed, and to interpret **..** differently if the directory had been reached through a symbolic link. There are two problems with this implementation. First, the kernel would have to maintain a potentially unbounded amount of information. Second, no program could depend on being able to use **..**, since it could not be sure how the name would be interpreted.

Since symbolic links may cause loops in the filesystem, the kernel checks for a large number (eight) of symbolic link traversals in a single pathname translation. If the limit is reached, the kernel produces an error (ELOOP).

Quotas

Resource sharing traditionally has been a design goal for the UNIX system. In some implementations, any single user can allocate all the available space in the filesystem. In certain environments, this is unacceptable. Consequently, 4.3BSD includes a quota mechanism to restrict the amount of filesystem resources that a user can obtain. The quota mechanism sets limits on both the number of files and the number of disk blocks that a user may allocate. Quotas can be set separately for each user on each filesystem.

Resources are given both a hard and a soft limit. When a process exceeds a soft limit, a warning is printed on the user's terminal; the offending process is not terminated unless it exceeds its hard limit. The idea is that users should stay below their soft limit between login sessions, but may use more resources while they are working actively. To encourage this behavior, the system warns users when they log in if they are over any of their soft limits. If a user fails to correct the problem for too many login sessions, the soft limit starts being enforced as the hard limit. These quotas are derived from a larger resource-limit package that was developed at the University of Melbourne in Australia by Elz [Elz, 1984].

7.2 Overview of the Internal Filesystem

The filesystem implementation converts from the user abstraction of a file as an array of bytes to the structure imposed by the underlying physical medium. Consider a typical medium of a magnetic disk with fixed-sized sectoring. Although the user may wish to write a single byte to a file, the disk can read and write only in multiples of sectors. Here, the system must arrange to read in the sector containing the byte to be modified, to replace the affected byte, and to write the sector back to the disk. This operation of converting random access to an array of bytes to reads and writes of disk sectors is known as *block I/O*.

First, the system breaks the user's request into a set of operations to be done on each *logical block* of the file. Logical blocks describe block-sized pieces of a file. The system calculates the logical blocks by dividing the array of bytes into filesystem-sized pieces. Thus, if a filesystem's block size is 8192 bytes, then logical block 0 would contain bytes 0 to 8191, logical block 1 would contain bytes 8192 to 16,383, and so on.

Figure 7.5 shows the flow of information and work required to access the filesystem on the disk. The abstraction shown to the user is an array of bytes. These bytes are collectively described by a file descriptor that refers to some location in the array. The user can request a write operation on the file by presenting the system with a pointer to a buffer, along with a request for some number of bytes to be written. Figure 7.5 shows that the requested data need not be aligned with the beginning or end of a disk sector. Further, the size of the request is not constrained to a single disk sector. In the example shown, the user has requested data to be written to parts of logical blocks 1 and 2.

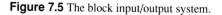

Figure 7.5 The block input/output system.

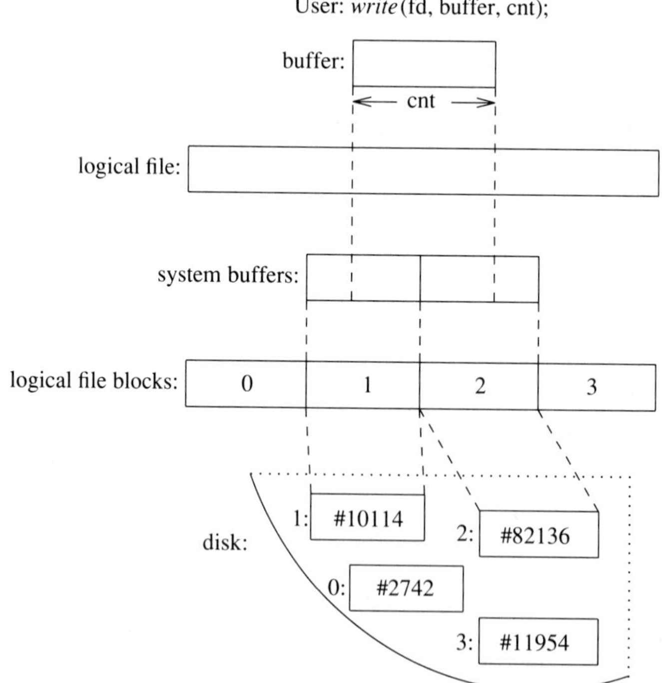

The data in each logical block are stored in a *physical block* on the disk. A physical block is the location on the disk to which the system maps a logical block. A physical disk block is constructed from one or more contiguous sectors. For a disk with 512-byte sectors, an 8192-byte filesystem block would be built up from 16 contiguous sectors. Although the contents of a logical block are contiguous on disk, the logical blocks of the file need not be laid out contiguously. The next section describes the data structure used by the system to convert from logical blocks to physical blocks.

Returning to our example in Fig. 7.5, we have now figured out which logical blocks are to be updated. Since the disk can transfer data only in multiples of sectors, the filesystem must first arrange to read in the data for the part of the block that is to be left unchanged. The system must arrange an intermediate staging area for the transfer. This staging is done through one or more system buffers.

In our example, the user wishes to modify data in logical blocks 1 and 2. The operation iterates over five steps:

1. Allocate a buffer

2. Determine the location of the corresponding physical block on the disk

3. Request the disk controller to read the contents of the physical block into the system buffer and wait for the transfer to complete

4. Do a memory-to-memory copy from the beginning of the user's I/O buffer to the appropriate portion of the system buffer

5. Write the block to the disk

If the user's request is incomplete, the process is repeated with the next logical block of the file. In our example, the system fetches logical block 2 of the file and is able to complete the user's request. Had an entire block been written, the system could have skipped step 3 and have simply written the data to the disk without first reading in the old contents. This incremental filling of the write request is transparent to the user's process because that process is blocked from running during the whole filling procedure. The filling is transparent to other processes; since the inode is locked during the whole process, any attempted access by any other process will be blocked until the initial write has completed.

Allocating and Finding the Blocks on the Disk

The filesystem also handles the allocation of new blocks to files as the latter grow. Simple filesystem implementations, such as those used by early microcomputer systems, allocate files contiguously, one after the next, until the files reach the end of the disk. As files are removed, holes occur. To reuse the freed space, the system must compact the disk to move all the free space to the end. Files can be created only one at a time; for the size of a file other than the last one on the disk to be increased, the file must be copied to the end, then expanded.

To allow both multiple file allocation and random access, most UNIX systems use the concept of an *index node*, or *inode*. Figure 7.6 shows that the inode contains an array of pointers to the blocks in the file. The system can convert from a logical block number to a physical sector number by indexing into the array using the logical block number. A null array entry indicates that no block has been allocated, and will cause a block of zeros to be returned on a read. On a write of such an entry, a new block is allocated, the array entry is updated with the new block number, and the data are written to the disk.

Inodes are statically allocated and most files are small, so the array of pointers must be small for efficient use of space. The first 12 array entries are allocated in the inode itself. For typical filesystems, this allows the first 48 or 96 Kbyte of data to be located directly using a simple indexed lookup.

For somewhat larger files, Fig. 7.6 shows that the inode contains a *single indirect pointer* that points to a *single indirect block* of pointers to data blocks. To find the one-hundredth logical block of a file, the system first fetches the block identified by the indirect pointer, then indexes into the eighty-eighth block (100 – 12 direct pointers), and fetches that data block.

For files that are bigger than a few Mbytes, the single indirect block is eventually exhausted; these files must resort to using a *double indirect block*, which is a pointer to a block of pointers to pointers to data blocks. Finally, the system leaves provision for a *triple indirect block*, although such a block is not used in existing implementations.

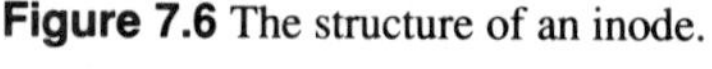

Figure 7.6 The structure of an inode.

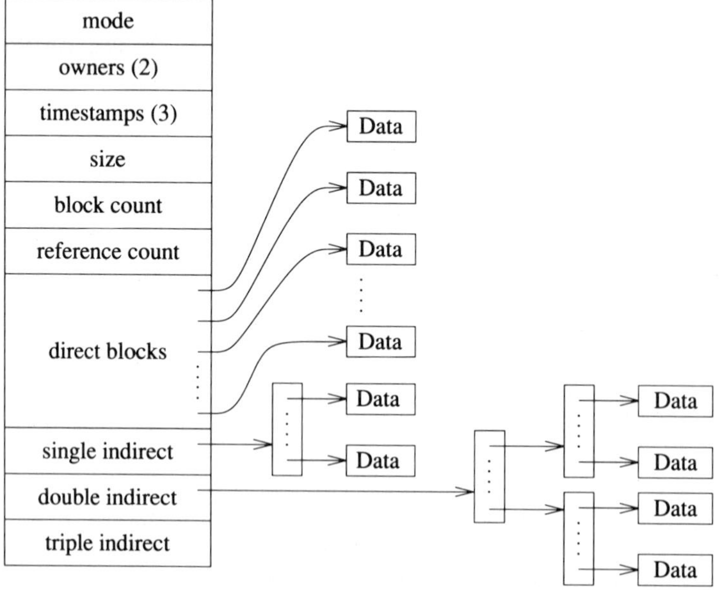

Although single and double indirect blocks appear to double or triple the number of disk accesses required to get a block of data, the overhead of the transfer is typically much lower. In Section 7.5, we shall discuss the management of the filesystem cache that holds recently used disk blocks. The first time that a block of indirect pointers is needed, it is brought into the filesystem cache. Further accesses to the indirect pointers find the block already resident in memory; thus, they require only a single disk access to get the data.

In addition to the logical-to-physical block mapping, the inode contains the other information about the contents of the file. This information includes

- The type and access mode for the file
- The file's owner
- The group-access identifier
- The number of references to the file
- The time the file was last read and written
- The time that the inode was last updated by the system
- The size of the file in bytes
- The number of physical blocks used by the file (including blocks used to hold indirect pointers)

Notably missing in the inode is the filename. Filenames are maintained in directories rather than in inodes because a file may have many names, or links, and the name of a file may be large (up to 255 bytes in length).

To create a new name for a file, the system increments the count of the number of names referring to that inode. Then, the new name is entered in a directory, along with the number of the inode. Conversely, when a name is deleted, the entry is deleted from a directory and the name count for the inode is then decremented. When the name count reaches zero, the system deallocates the inode by putting all the inode's blocks back on a list of free blocks and putting the inode back on a list of unused inodes.

7.3 Internal Structure and Redesign

A traditional UNIX filesystem, such as that of System V, is described by its superblock, which contains the basic parameters of the filesystem. These parameters include the number of data blocks in the filesystem, a count of the maximum number of files, and a pointer to the *free list*, which is a list of all the free blocks in the filesystem.

A 150-Mbyte traditional UNIX filesystem consists of 4 Mbyte of inodes followed by 146 Mbyte of data. That organization segregates the inode information from the data; thus, accessing a file normally incurs a long seek from the file's inode to its data. Files in a single directory typically are not allocated consecutive slots in the 4 Mbyte of inodes, causing many nonconsecutive disk blocks to be read when many inodes in a single directory are accessed.

The allocation of data blocks to files also is suboptimal. The traditional filesystem implementation uses a 512-byte physical block size. But the next sequential data block often is not on the same cylinder, so seeks between 512-byte data transfers are required frequently. This combination of small block size and scattered placement severely limits filesystem throughput.

The first work on the UNIX filesystem at Berkeley attempted to improve both the reliability and the throughput of the filesystem. The developers improved reliability by staging modifications to critical filesystem information so that the modifications could be either completed or repaired cleanly by a program after a crash [McKusick & Kowalski, 1986]. They improved the performance of the filesystem by a factor of more than two between 3BSD and 4.0BSD by doubling the block size. This doubling caused each disk transfer to access twice as many data and eliminated the need for indirect blocks for many files. We shall refer to the filesystem with these changes in the rest of this section as the *old filesystem*.

The performance improvement in the old filesystem gave a strong indication that increasing the block size was a good method for improving throughput. Although the throughput had doubled, the old filesystem was still using only about 4 percent of the maximum disk throughput. The main problem was that the order of blocks on the free list quickly became scrambled as files were created and removed. Eventually, the free-list order became entirely random, causing files to have their blocks allocated randomly over the disk. This forced a seek before every block access. Although the old filesystem provided transfer rates of up to 175 Kbyte per second when it was first created, the scrambling of the free list caused this rate to deteriorate to an average of 30 Kbyte per second after a few weeks of moderate use. There was no way of restoring the performance of an old filesystem except to recreate the system.

New Filesystem Organization

In the 4.3BSD filesystem organization (as in the old filesystem organization), each disk drive contains one or more filesystems. A 4.3BSD filesystem is described by its *superblock*, located at the beginning of the filesystem's disk partition. Because the superblock contains critical data, it is replicated to protect against catastrophic loss. This replication is done when the filesystem is created; since the superblock data do not change, the copies need not be referenced unless a disk failure causes the default superblock to be corrupted.

To ensure that files as large as 2^{32} bytes may be created with only two levels of indirection, the minimum size of a filesystem block is 4096 bytes. The block size can be any power of two greater than or equal to 4096. The block size is recorded in the filesystem's superblock, so it is possible for filesystems with different block sizes to be accessible simultaneously on the same system. The block size must be selected at the time that the filesystem is created; it cannot be changed subsequently without rebuilding of the filesystem.

The new filesystem organization divides a disk partition into one or more areas, each of which is called a *cylinder group*. Figure 7.7 shows a set of cylinder groups, each comprising one or more consecutive cylinders on a disk. Each cylinder group contains bookkeeping information that includes a redundant copy of the superblock, space for inodes, a bit map describing available blocks in the cylinder group, and summary information describing the usage of data blocks within the cylinder group. The bit map of available blocks in the cylinder group replaces the traditional filesystem's free list. For each cylinder group, a static number of inodes is allocated at filesystem creation time. The default policy is to allocate one inode for each 2048 bytes of space in the cylinder group, with the expectation that this amount will be far more than will ever be needed.

The motivation for cylinder groups is to create clusters of inodes that are spread over the disk, instead of them all being located at the beginning of the disk. The filesystem attempts to allocate file blocks close to the inodes that describe them to avoid long seeks between getting the inode and getting its associated data. Also, when the inodes are spread out, there is less chance of losing all of them in a single disk failure.

All the bookkeeping information could be placed at the beginning of each cylinder group. If this approach were used, however, all the redundant information would be on the same platter of a disk. A single hardware failure could then destroy all copies of the superblock. Thus, the bookkeeping information begins at a varying offset from the beginning of the cylinder group. The offset for each successive cylinder group is calculated to be about one track farther from the

Figure 7.7 Layout of cylinder groups.

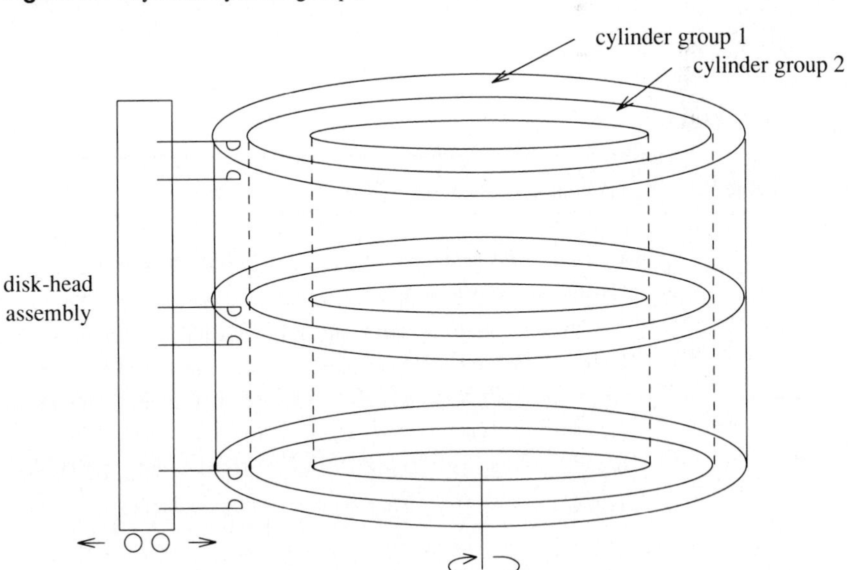

beginning than is the preceding cylinder group. In this way, the redundant information spirals down into the pack so that any single track, cylinder, or platter can be lost without all copies of the superblock also being lost. Except for the first cylinder group, the space between the beginning of the cylinder group and the beginning of the cylinder-group information is used for data blocks.

Optimizing Storage Utilization

Data are laid out so that larger blocks can be transferred in a single disk operation, greatly increasing filesystem throughput. A file in the new filesystem might be composed of 4096-byte data blocks, as compared to the 1024-byte blocks of the old filesystem: Disk accesses would thus transfer up to four times as much information per disk transaction. In large files, several blocks may be allocated from the same cylinder, so that even larger data transfers are possible before a seek is required.

The main problem with larger blocks is that most UNIX filesystems contain primarily small files. A uniformly large block size wastes space. Table 7.1 shows the effect of filesystem block size on the amount of wasted space in the filesystem. The files measured to obtain these figures reside on a time-sharing system at Berkeley that has roughly 1.2 gigabytes of on-line storage. The measurements are based on the active user filesystems containing about 920 Mbyte of formatted space. The space wasted is calculated to be the percentage of disk space not containing user data. As the block size increases, the waste rises quickly to an intolerable 45.6 percent waste with 4096-byte filesystem blocks.

For large blocks to be used without significant waste, small files must be stored more efficiently. The developers obtained this efficiency by allowing the division of a single filesystem block into one or more *fragments*. The fragment size is specified at the time that the filesystem is created; each filesystem block optionally can be broken into two, four, or eight fragments, each of which is

Table 7.1 Amount of space wasted as a function of block size.

Space used (Mbyte)	Percent waste	Organization
775.2	0.0	Data only, no separation between files
807.8	4.2	Data only, each file starts on 512-byte boundary
828.7	6.9	Data + inodes, 512-byte block UNIX filesystem
866.5	11.8	Data + inodes, 1024-byte block UNIX filesystem
948.5	22.4	Data + inodes, 2048-byte block UNIX filesystem
1128.3	45.6	Data + inodes, 4096-byte block UNIX filesystem

bits in map	----	--11	11--	1111
fragment numbers	0-3	4-7	8-11	12-15
block numbers	0	1	2	3

Figure 7.8 Example of the layout of blocks and fragments in a 4096/1024 filesystem.

addressable. The lower bound on the fragment size is constrained by the disk-sector size, which is typically 512 bytes. The block map associated with each cylinder group records the space available in a cylinder group in fragments; to determine whether a block is available, the system examines aligned fragments. Figure 7.8 shows a piece of a block map from a filesystem with 4096-byte blocks and 1024-byte fragments, hereinafter referred to as a 4096/1024 filesystem. Each bit in the map records the status of a fragment; an ‘‘-’’ shows that the fragment is in use, whereas a ‘‘1’’ shows that the fragment is available for allocation. In this example, fragments 0 through 5, 10, and 11 are in use, whereas fragments 6 through 9 and 12 through 15 are free. Fragments of adjacent blocks cannot be used as a full block, even if they are large enough. In this example, fragments 6 through 9 cannot be allocated as a full block; only fragments 12 through 15 can be coalesced into a full block.

On a filesystem with a block size of 4096 bytes and a fragment size of 1024 bytes, a file is represented by zero or more 4096-byte blocks of data, possibly plus a single fragmented block. If a block must be fragmented to obtain space for a small number of data, the remaining fragments of the block are made available for allocation to other files. As an example, consider an 11000-byte file stored on a 4096/1024 filesystem. This file would use two full-sized blocks and one three-fragment portion of another block. If no block with three aligned fragments were available at the time the file was created, a full-sized block would be split, yielding the necessary fragments and a single unused fragment. This remaining fragment could be allocated to another file as needed.

Each time a process does a *write* system call, the system checks to see whether the size of the file has increased. A process may overwrite data in the middle of an existing file, in which case space would have been allocated already. If the file needs to be expanded, the request is rounded up to the next fragment size and only that much space is allocated. Many small write requests may expand the file one fragment at a time. The problem with expanding a file one fragment at a time is that data may be copied many times as a fragmented block expands to a full block. Fragment reallocation can be minimized if the user process writes a full block at a time, except for a partial block at the end of the file. Since filesystems with different block sizes may reside on the same system, the filesystem interface provides application programs with the optimal size for a read or write. This facility is used by the standard I/O library that many application programs use, and by certain system utilities, such as archivers and loaders, that do their own I/O management.

The amount of wasted space in the 4096/1024 new filesystem organization is empirically observed to be about the same as that in the old 1024-byte filesystem organization. A filesystem with 4096-byte blocks and 512-byte fragments has about the same amount of wasted space as the 512-byte block UNIX filesystem. The new filesystem uses less space than the 512-byte or 1024-byte filesystems for indexing information for large files, and the same amount of space for small files. These savings are offset by the need to use more space for keeping track of available free blocks. The net result is about the same disk-space utilization when a new filesystem's fragment size is equal to an old filesystem's block size.

For the layout policies (described at the end of this section) to be effective, a filesystem cannot be kept completely full. A parameter, termed the *free-space reserve*, gives the minimum percentage of filesystem blocks that should be kept free. If the number of free blocks drops below this level, only the superuser is allowed to allocate blocks. This parameter may be changed at any time. When the number of free blocks approaches zero, the filesystem throughput tends to be cut in half, because the filesystem is unable to localize blocks in a file. If a filesystem's throughput drops because of overfilling, it may be restored by removal of files until the amount of free space once again reaches the minimum acceptable level. Users can restore access rates for files created during periods of little free space by moving the file's data when enough space is available. We must add the free-space reserve to the percentage of waste when comparing the organizations given in Table 7.1. Thus, the percentage of waste in an old 1024-byte UNIX filesystem is roughly comparable to a new 4096/512 filesystem with the free-space reserve set at 5 percent. (Compare 11.8 percent wasted with the old filesystem to 6.9 percent waste + 5 percent reserved space in the new filesystem.)

Filesystem Parameterization

Except for the initial creation of the free list, the old filesystem ignores the parameters of the underlying hardware. It has no information about either the physical characteristics of the mass-storage device, or the hardware that interacts with the filesystem. A goal of the new filesystem is to parameterize the processor capabilities and mass-storage characteristics so that blocks can be allocated in an optimum configuration-dependent way. Important parameters include the speed of the processor, the hardware support for mass-storage transfers, and the characteristics of the mass-storage devices. Disk technology is constantly improving, and a given installation can have several different disk technologies running on a single processor. Each filesystem is parameterized so that it can be adapted to the characteristics of the disk on which it is located.

For mass-storage devices such as disks, the new filesystem tries to allocate a file's new blocks on the same cylinder and rotationally well positioned. The distance between *rotationally optimal* blocks varies greatly; optimal blocks can be consecutive or rotationally delayed, depending on system characteristics. For disks attached to a dedicated I/O processor, two consecutive disk blocks often can be accessed without time lost because of an intervening disk revolution. For processors without a dedicated I/O processor, the main processor must field an interrupt and prepare for a new disk transfer. The expected time to service this interrupt and to schedule a new disk transfer depends on the speed of the main processor.

The physical characteristics of each disk include the number of blocks per track and the rate at which the disk spins. The allocation routines use this information to calculate the number of milliseconds required to skip over a block. The characteristics of the processor include the expected time to service an interrupt and to schedule a new disk transfer. Given a block allocated to a file, the allocation routines calculate the number of blocks to skip over such that the next block in the file will come into position under the disk head in the expected amount of time that it takes to start a new disk-transfer operation. For sequential access to large numbers of data, this strategy minimizes the amount of time spent waiting for the disk to position itself.

The parameter that defines the minimum number of milliseconds between the completion of a data transfer and the initiation of another data transfer on the same cylinder can be changed at any time. If a filesystem is parameterized to lay out blocks with a rotational separation of 2 milliseconds, and the disk is then moved to a system that has a processor requiring 4 milliseconds to schedule a disk operation, the throughput will drop precipitously because of lost disk revolutions on nearly every block. If the target machine is known, the filesystem can be parameterized for that machine even though it is initially created on a different processor. Even if the move is not known in advance, the rotational-layout delay can be reconfigured after the disk is moved, so that all further allocation is done based on the characteristics of the new device.

Layout Policies

The filesystem layout policies are divided into two distinct parts. At the top level are global policies that use summary information to make decisions regarding the placement of new inodes and data blocks. These routines are responsible for deciding the placement of new directories and files. They also calculate rotationally optimal block layouts, and decide when to force a long seek to a new cylinder group because there is insufficient space left in the current cylinder group to do reasonable layouts. Below the global-policy routines are the local-allocation routines. These routines use a locally optimal scheme to lay out data blocks. The original intention was to bring out these decisions to user level, so that they could be ignored or replaced by user processes. They are thus definitely policies, not simple mechanisms.

Two methods for improving filesystem performance are to increase the locality of reference to minimize seek latency [Trivedi, 1980], and to improve the layout of data to make larger transfers possible [Nevalainen & Vesterinen, 1977]. The global layout policies try to improve performance by clustering related information. They cannot attempt to localize all data references, but must instead try to spread unrelated data among different cylinder groups. If too much localization is attempted, the local cylinder group may run out of space, forcing the data to be scattered to nonlocal cylinder groups. Taken to an extreme, total localization can result in a single huge cluster of data resembling the old filesystem. The global policies try to balance the two conflicting goals of localizing data that are concurrently accessed while spreading out unrelated data.

One allocatable resource is inodes. Inodes of files in the same directory frequently are accessed together. For example, the list-directory command, **ls**, may access the inode for each file in a directory. The inode layout policy tries to place all the inodes of files in a directory in the same cylinder group. To ensure that files are distributed throughout the filesystem, the system uses a different policy to allocate directory inodes. New directories are placed in cylinder groups with a greater than average number of free inodes, and with the smallest number of directories. The intent of this policy is to allow inode clustering to succeed most of the time. The allocation of inodes within a cylinder group is done using a next-free strategy. Although this method allocates the inodes randomly within a cylinder group, all the inodes for a particular cylinder group can be accessed with eight to 16 disk transfers. (At most 16 disk transfers are required because a cylinder group may have no more than 2048 inodes.) This allocation strategy puts a small and constant upper bound on the number of disk transfers required to access the inodes for all the files in a directory. In contrast, the old filesystem typically requires one disk transfer to fetch the inode for each file in a directory.

The other major resource is data blocks. Because data blocks for a file typically are accessed together, the policy routines try to place data blocks for a file in the same cylinder group, preferably at rotationally optimal positions in the same cylinder. The problem with allocating all the data blocks in the same cylinder group is that large files quickly use up available space, forcing a spillover to other areas. Further, using all the space causes future allocations for any file in the cylinder group also to spill to other areas. Ideally, none of the cylinder groups should ever become completely full. The heuristic solution chosen is to redirect block allocation to a different cylinder group after every 1 Mbyte of allocation. The spillover points are intended to force block allocation to be redirected when a file has used about 25 percent of the data blocks in a cylinder group. In day-to-day use, the heuristics appear to work well in minimizing the number of completely filled cylinder groups.

The newly chosen cylinder group for block allocation is selected from the next cylinder group that has a greater-than-average number of free blocks left. Although big files tend to be spread out over the disk, 1 Mbyte of data is typically accessible before a long seek must be performed, and the cost of one long seek per Mbyte is small. It is also important to force large files to move before using up all the available blocks in a cylinder group, because the last few blocks will be scattered around the cylinder group and thus will require many small seeks to access.

The global-policy routines call local-allocation routines with requests for specific blocks. The local-allocation routines will always allocate the requested block if it is free; otherwise, they will allocate a free block of the requested size that is rotationally closest to the requested block. If the global layout policies had complete information, they could always request unused blocks and the allocation routines would be reduced to simple bookkeeping. However, maintaining complete information is costly; thus the global layout policy uses heuristics that employ only partial information.

If a requested block is not available, the local allocator uses a four-level allocation strategy:

1. Use the next available block rotationally closest to the requested block on the same cylinder. It is assumed that head-switching time is zero. On disk controllers where this is not the case, it may be possible to incorporate the time required to switch between disk platters when the rotational layout tables are constructed. This, however, has not yet been attempted.
2. If no blocks are available on the same cylinder, use a block within the same cylinder group.
3. If the cylinder group is full, quadratically hash the cylinder group number to choose another cylinder group to look for a free block.
4. Finally, if the hash fails, apply an exhaustive search to all cylinder groups.

Quadratic hash is used because of its speed in finding unused slots in nearly full hash tables [Knuth, 1975]. Filesystems that are parameterized to maintain at least 10 percent free space rarely use this strategy. Filesystems used without free space typically have so few free blocks available that almost any allocation is random; the most important characteristic of the strategy used under such conditions is that it be fast.

7.4 Filesystem Data Structures

We are now ready to look at the filesystem data structures in more detail. The small filesystem introduced in Fig. 7.1 is expanded to show its internal structure in Fig. 7.9. Each of the files in Fig. 7.1 is shown expanded into its constituent inode and data blocks. As an example of how these data structures work, consider how the system finds the file **/usr/bin/vi**. It must first search the root directory of the filesystem to find the directory **usr**. To do this, it must first find the inode that describes the root directory. By convention, inode 2 is always reserved for the root directory; therefore, the system finds and brings inode 2 into memory. This inode shows where the data blocks are for the root directory; these data blocks must also be brought into memory so that they can be searched for the entry **usr**. Having found the entry for **usr**, the system finds that the contents of **usr** are described by inode 4. Returning once again to the disk, the system fetches inode 4 to find where the data blocks for **usr** are located. Searching these blocks, it finds the entry for **bin**. The **bin** entry points to inode 7. Next the system brings in inode 7 and its associated data blocks from the disk, to begin searching for the entry for **vi**. Having found that **vi** is described by inode 9, the system can fetch this inode and discover the set of blocks that describe the **vi** binary.

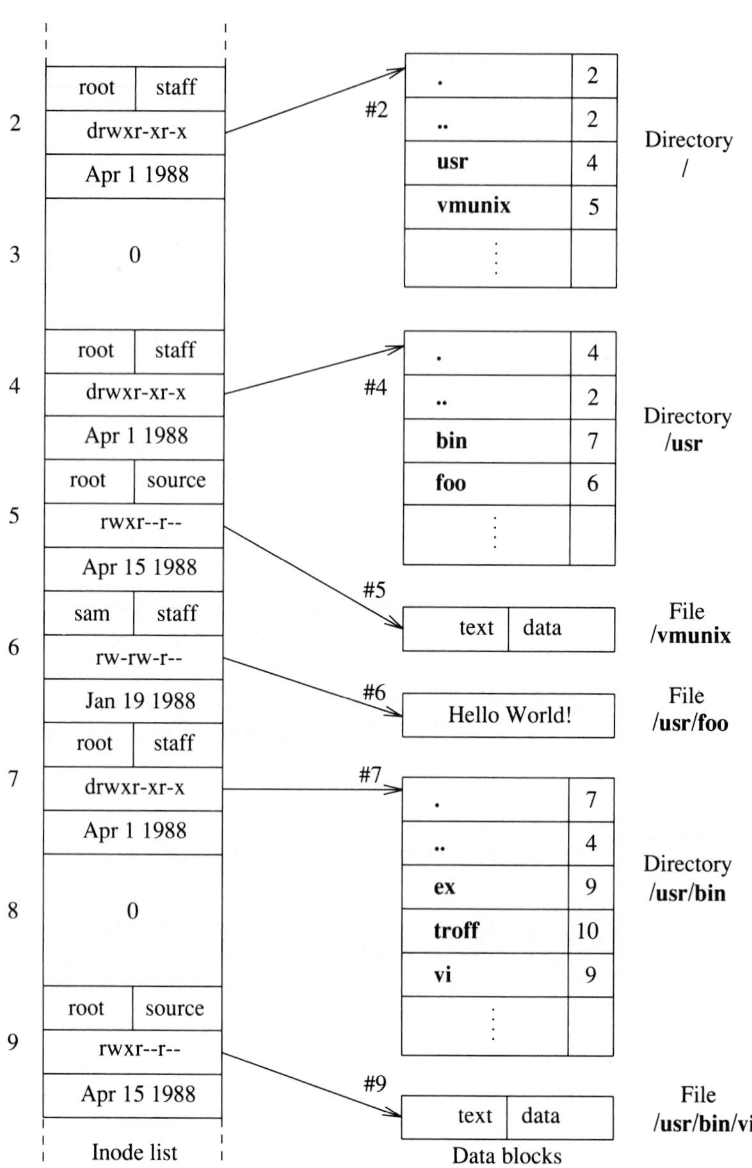

Figure 7.9 Internal structure of a small filesystem.

This whole process implies an enormous amount of disk I/O for even such trivial tasks as executing system utilities. To obtain reasonable performance, the system must cache frequently used information to reduce the number of disk requests. This section describes the inode table that holds recently used inodes, Section 7.5 discusses the system buffer pool that holds recently used disk blocks, and Section 7.8 discusses the name-translation cache that holds recent name translations for the inodes held in the inode table. By using these caches, the system typically finds over 85 percent of the information that it needs without having to bring in the data from disk.

Inode Management

Most of the activity in the filesystem revolves around inodes. The kernel keeps a table of active and recently accessed inodes. Figure 7.10 shows the location of the inode table within the system.

As described in Section 6.2, each process has a *process open file table* that has slots for up to a reasonable number (such as 64) of file descriptors; this table is maintained as part of the process state. When a user process opens a file (or socket), an unused slot is located in its open file table; the small integer file descriptor that is returned on a successful *open* is the value that indexes into this table.

The per-process file-table entry points into the *system open file table*, each entry of which contains information about the underlying file or socket represented by the descriptor. For files, the file table points to the inode representing the open file. The active and recently used inodes are stored in another systemwide table called the *inode table*, shown in Fig. 7.11.

The first step in opening a file is to find the file's associated inode. First, the kernel searches the inode table to see whether the requested inode is already in memory. To avoid doing a linear scan of all the entries in the table, the system keeps a set of hash chains keyed on inode number and filesystem identifier. Even with an inode table containing hundreds of entries, the kernel needs to inspect only about five entries to determine whether a requested inode is already in the table. If the inode is not in the table, such as the first time a file is opened, the system must allocate a new inode-table slot and read in the inode from disk. The new inode-table slot is allocated from the least recently used inode in the inode table. To quickly find the oldest inode, the system keeps unused inodes linked together in an LRU chain. When the last reference to a file is closed, the system puts the inode onto the end of the LRU chain. Thus, the inode on the front of the LRU chain yields the least recently used inode. Frequently used inodes will be

Figure 7.10 Layout of kernel tables.

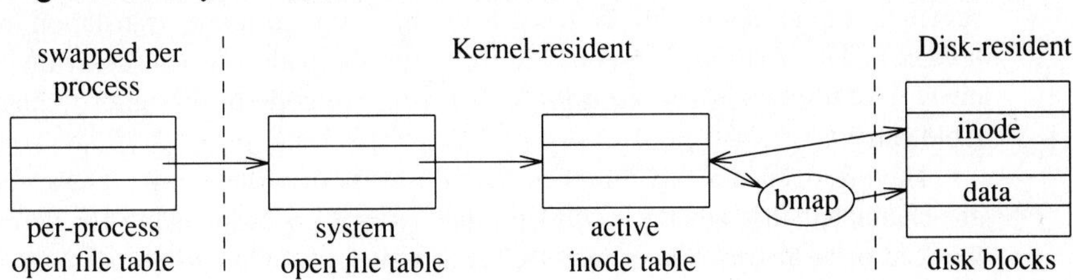

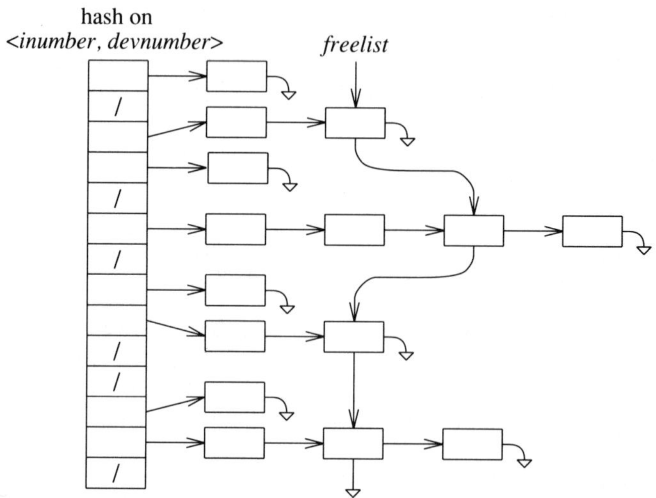

Figure 7.11 Structure of the inode table.

reclaimed from the middle of the LRU chain and will be replaced at the end after use. This algorithm reduces the probability of reuse of the inode slots.

The next step is to locate the disk block containing the inode and to read that block into a buffer in system memory. When the disk I/O completes, the inode is copied from the disk buffer into its slot in the inode table. In addition to the information contained in the disk portion of the inode, the inode table itself maintains supplemental information while the inode is in memory. This information includes the hash and use chains described previously, as well as flags showing the inode's status, reference counts on its use, and information to manage locks. The information also contains pointers to other kernel data structures of frequent interest, such as the superblock for the filesystem containing the inode.

Finding File Blocks

Once an inode has been brought into memory, the system can locate the data blocks associated with the file. It locates the physical data blocks associated with a file by interpreting the block pointers in the inode. The task of interpreting and allocating these pointers is managed by the *block-mapping* routine called *bmap*(). Figure 7.12 shows the procedural access path through the kernel. The pathname specified in an *open* call is passed to the name-to-inode translation routine *namei*(). This routine is responsible for doing the path traversal described previously, and ultimately for returning either a failure code or a pointer to an inode-table entry.

Having opened a file, a process can do reads or writes on it. These requests are channeled through the *rwip*() routine. *Rwip*() is responsible for converting the read or write into one or more reads or writes of logical file blocks. A logical

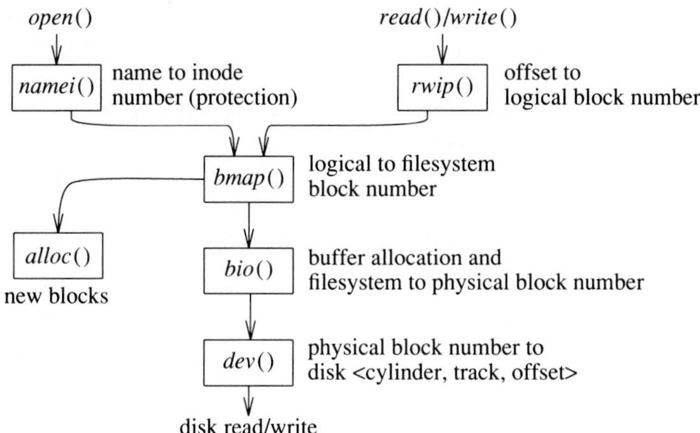

Figure 7.12 Procedural access through the filesystem.

block request is then handed off to *bmap*(). *Bmap*() is responsible for converting a logical block number to a physical block number by interpreting the direct and indirect block pointers in an inode. If a read is requested, *rwip*() requests the block I/O system to return a buffer filled with the contents of the disk block. If two or more logically sequential blocks are read from a file, the process is assumed to be reading the file sequentially. Here, *bmap*() returns two values, first the requested block, and second the number of the next block in the file. The system makes two disk requests, one for the requested block and a second for the read-ahead block in anticipation that the process will soon want that block.

If a write is requested, *rwip*() allocates a buffer to hold the contents of the block. The user's data are copied into the returned buffer, and the buffer is marked as dirty. If the buffer has been completely filled, it is queued to be written to the disk. If the buffer has not been completely filled, it is not immediately queued. The buffer is held in the expectation that the process will soon want to add more data to it. It is not released until it is needed for some other block; that is, until it has reached the head of the free list, or until a user process does a *sync* system call. There is normally a user process called *update* running that does a *sync* every 30 seconds.

File-Block Allocation

The task of managing block and fragment allocation is done by *bmap*(). If the file is being written and a block pointer is zero or points to a fragment that is too small to hold the additional data, *bmap*() calls the allocation routines to obtain a new block. If the file needs to be expanded, one of two conditions exists:

1. The file contains no fragmented blocks (and the last block in the file contains insufficient space to hold the new data). If space exists in a block already

allocated, the space is filled with new data. If the remainder of the new data consists of more than a full block, a full block is allocated and the first full block of new data is written there. This process is repeated until less than a full block of new data remains. If the remaining new data to be written will fit in less than a full block, a block with the necessary fragments is located; otherwise, a full block is located. The remaining new data are written into the located space. However, to avoid excessive copying for slowly growing files, the filesystem allows only direct blocks of files to refer to fragments.

2. The file contains one or more fragments (and the fragments contain insufficient space to hold the new data). If the size of the new data plus the size of the data already in the fragments exceeds the size of a full block, a new block is allocated. The contents of the fragments are copied to the beginning of the block and the remainder of the block is filled with new data. The process then continues as in step 1. Otherwise, a block big enough to hold the data is located; if enough of the rest of the current block is free, that block is used to avoid copying. The contents of the existing fragments, appended with the new data, are written into the allocated space.

Bmap() is also responsible for allocating blocks to hold indirect pointers. It must also deal with the special case in which a process seeks out past the end of a file and begins writing. Because of the constraint that only the last block of a file may be a fragment, *bmap*() must first ensure that any previous fragment has been upgraded to a full-sized block.

On completing a successful allocation (Section 7.7), the allocation routines return the block or fragment number to be used; *bmap*() then updates the appropriate block pointer in the inode. Having allocated a block, the system is ready to allocate a buffer to hold the block's contents so that the block can be written to disk.

7.5 Buffer Management

The semantics of the UNIX filesystem imply much disk I/O. If every implied disk transfer really had to be done, the CPU would spend most of its time waiting for I/O to complete. The task of the buffer cache is two-fold. One task is to manage the memory that buffers data being transferred to and from the disk. The second, and more important, task is to act as a cache of recently used disk blocks. On a typical UNIX system, over 85 percent of the implied disk transfers can be skipped because the requested block already resides in the buffer cache. Depending on available memory, a system may be configured with anything from a hundred to a thousand buffers. The larger the number of buffers, the longer a given disk block can be retained in memory, and the greater the chance that disk I/O can be avoided.

Figure 7.13 shows the format of a buffer. The buffer is composed of two parts. The first part is the buffer header, which contains information used to find

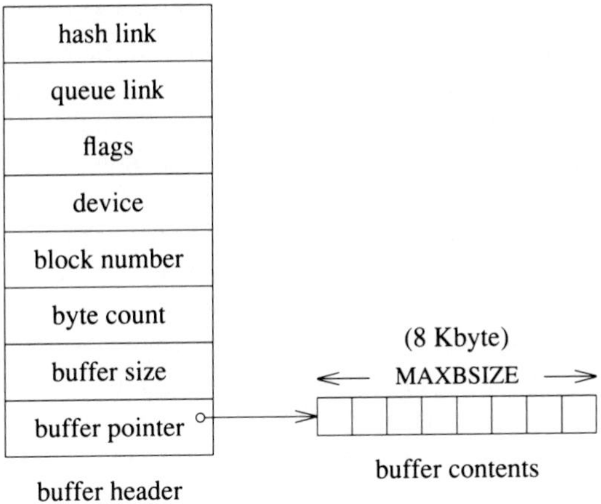

Figure 7.13 Format of a buffer.

the buffer and to describe its contents. The content information includes the device (i.e., disk and partition on that disk), the starting physical block number (counting from the beginning of the partition), and the number of bytes contained in the buffer. The flags entry tracks status information about the buffer, such as whether the buffer contains useful data, whether the buffer is in use, and whether the data must be written back to the disk before the buffer can be reused.

The second part is the actual buffer contents. Rather than the header being prepended to the data area of the buffer, as is done with mbufs (see Section 10.2), the data areas are maintained separately. Thus, there is a pointer to the data and a field that shows the size of the data buffer. The buffer size is always at least as big as the fragment size. Data are maintained separately from the header to allow easy manipulation of the buffer sizes with the page-mapping hardware. If the headers were prepended, either each header would have to be on a page by itself or the kernel would have to avoid remapping buffer pages that contained headers.

The size of buffer requests from the filesystem range from 512-byte fragments up to 8192-byte full-sized blocks. If many small files are being accessed, then many small buffers are needed. Alternatively, if several large files are being accessed, then fewer large buffers are needed. To allow the system to adapt efficiently to these changing needs, each buffer is allocated 8192 bytes of virtual memory, but the address space is not fully populated with physical memory. Initially, each buffer is assigned 2048 bytes of physical memory. As smaller buffers are allocated, they give up their excess physical memory to other buffers that need to hold more than 2048 bytes. The algorithms for managing the physical memory are described later.

The internal kernel interface to the buffer pool is simple. The filesystem allocates and fills buffers by calling the *bread*() routine. *Bread*() takes a device, a block number, and a size, and returns a pointer to a locked buffer. Any other process that tries to access the buffer will be put to sleep until the buffer is released.

A buffer can be released in one of four ways. If the buffer has not been modified, it can simply be released through use of *brelse*(). If the buffer has been modified, it is called *dirty*. Dirty buffers must eventually be written back to the disk. Three routines are available based on the urgency with which the data must be written to disk. In the typical case, *bdwrite*() is used; it assumes that the buffer probably will be modified again soon, so should be marked as dirty, but should not be immediately written to disk. The heuristic is that, if the buffer will be modified again soon, the disk I/O would be wasted. Because the buffer is held for an average of 15 seconds before it is written, a process doing many small writes will not repeatedly access the disk. If the buffer has been completely filled, then it is unlikely to be written again soon, so it should be released with *bawrite*(). *Bawrite*() schedules a write to disk, but allows the caller to continue running while the output completes. The final case is *bwrite*(), which ensures that the disk write is complete before proceeding. Because this mechanism can introduce a long latency to the requester, it is used only when the process explicitly requests the behavior (such as the *fsync* system call), or when the operation is critical to ensure the consistency of the filesystem in case of a system crash.

Figure 7.14 shows a snapshot of the buffer pool. A buffer with valid contents is contained on exactly one *bufhash* hash chain. The hash chains are used to determine quickly whether a disk block is contained in the buffer pool, and, if the block is, to locate it. A buffer is removed only when it becomes invalid or is reused for a different block. Thus, even if the buffer is in use by one process, it can still be found by another process, although the *busy* flag will be set so that it will not be used until its contents are consistent.

In addition to the hash list, each buffer not currently in use appears on exactly one free list. The first free list is the locked list. Buffers on this list may not be

Figure 7.14 Snapshot of the buffer pool.

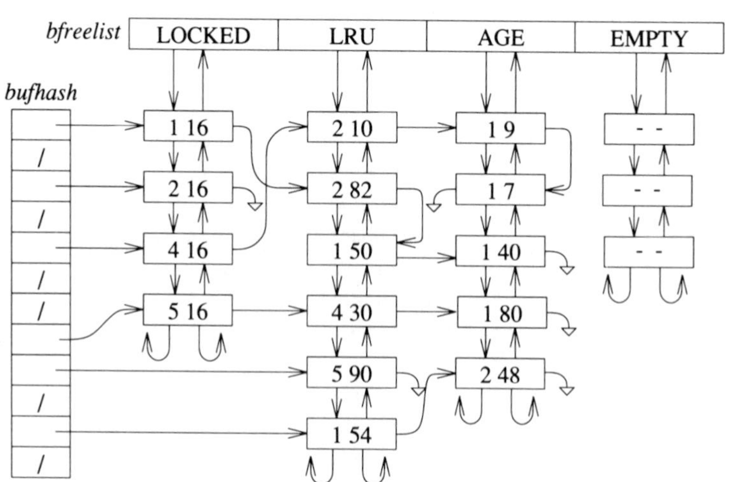

flushed from the cache; the list is currently unused. The LOCKED queue was intended to hold the superblocks of mounted filesystems, but deadlock with a process trying to access the same disk block through the block device forced the superblocks to be copied to private system memory instead.

The second list is the *LRU* list. When a buffer is found, typically on the LRU list, it is removed and used. The buffer is then returned to the end of the LRU list. When buffers must be recycled from the LRU list, they are taken from the front. Thus, buffers that are used repeatedly will continue to be migrated to the end of the LRU list and are not likely to be recycled for new blocks. As the name suggests, this list implements an LRU algorithm.

The third free list is the *AGE* list. This list holds blocks that have not proven their usefulness, but are expected to be used soon, or have already been used and are not likely to be reused. Buffers can be pushed onto either end of this list: Buffers containing no useful data are pushed on the front (where they will be reclaimed quickly) and other buffers are pushed on the end (where they might remain long enough to be used again). The list typically is used to hold read-ahead blocks. If a requested block is found on the AGE list, it is returned to the end of the LRU list, as it has proven its usefulness. When a new buffer is needed, the AGE queue is searched first; only when the list is empty is the LRU list used.

The final list is the list of empty buffers, the *EMPTY* list. The empty buffers have had all their physical memory stripped away by other buffers. They are held on this list awaiting some other buffer to be reused for a smaller block and thus to give up its extra physical memory.

Implementation of Buffer Management

Having looked at the function and algorithms used to manage the buffer pool, we shall now turn our attention to the actual implementation requirements for ensuring the consistency of the data in the buffer pool. Figure 7.15 shows the support

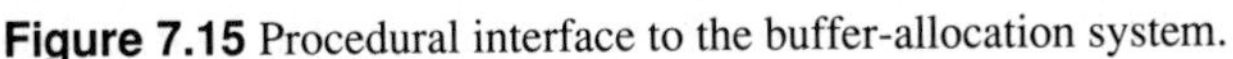

Figure 7.15 Procedural interface to the buffer-allocation system.

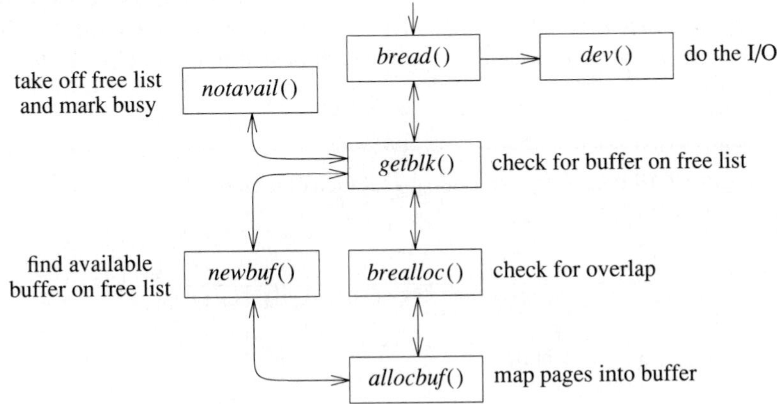

routines that implement the interface for getting buffers. The primary interface to getting a buffer is through *bread*(), which is called with a request for a data block of a specified size on a specified disk. *Bread*() first calls *getblk*() to find out whether the data block is available in a buffer that is already in memory. If the block is available in a buffer, *getblk*() calls *notavail*() to take the buffer off whichever free list it is on and to mark it busy; *bread*() can then return the buffer to the caller.

If the disk block is not already in memory, *getblk*() calls *newbuf*() to allocate a new buffer. The new buffer is then passed to *brealloc*() to ensure that there will not be any overlap with other buffers. Next, the buffer is passed to *allocbuf*(), which ensures that the buffer has the right amount of physical memory. *Getblk*() then returns the buffer to *bread*() marked busy and unfilled. Noticing that the buffer is unfilled, *bread*() passes it to the disk driver to have the data read in. When the disk read completes, the buffer can be returned.

To maintain the consistency of the filesystem, *brealloc*() ensures that a disk block is mapped into at most one buffer. If the same disk block were present in two buffers, and both buffers were marked dirty, the system would be unable to determine which buffer had valid information. Figure 7.16 shows a sample allocation. In the middle of the figure are the blocks on the disk. Above the disk is shown an old buffer containing a 4096-byte fragment for a file that presumably has been removed or shortened. The new buffer is going to be used to hold a 3072-byte fragment for a file that is presumably being created and that will reuse part of the space previously held by the old file. If the old buffer is marked dirty, it must first be written, then marked invalid, so that it cannot be found in the buffer pool again. After being marked invalid, the buffer is put at the front of the AGE queue so that it will be used before any buffers with potentially useful data. The system can then allocate the new buffer knowing that that buffer uniquely maps the corresponding disk blocks.

The final task in allocating a buffer is to ensure that the buffer has enough physical memory allocated to it; this task is handled by *allocbuf*(). Figure 7.17 shows the virtual memory for the data part of a buffer. The data area for each buffer is allocated 8192 bytes of virtual address space. The *bufsize* field in the buffer header shows how much of the virtual address space really is backed by physical memory. *Allocbuf*() compares the size of the intended data block with the amount of physical memory already allocated to the buffer. If there is excess

Figure 7.16 Potentially overlapping allocation of buffers.

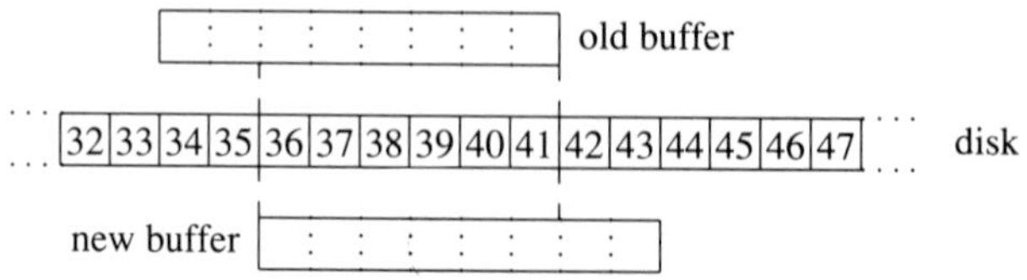

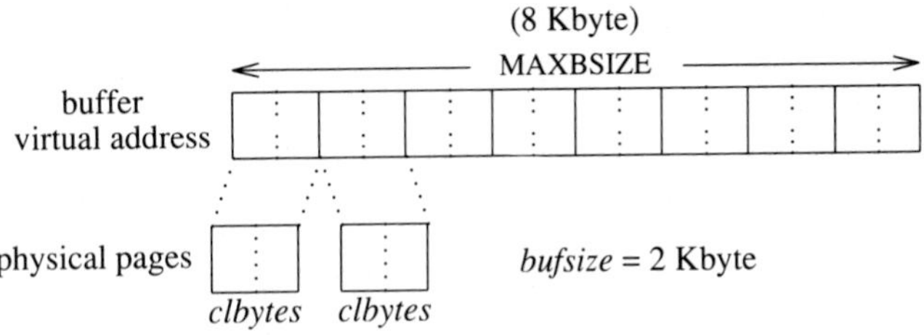

Figure 7.17 Allocation of buffer memory.

physical memory and there is a buffer available on the EMPTY queue, a buffer is taken off the EMPTY queue, the excess memory is put into the empty buffer, and it is then released onto the front of the AGE queue. If there are no buffers on the EMPTY queue, the excess physical memory is retained in the original buffer.

If the buffer has insufficient memory, *allocbuf*() takes memory from other buffers. *Allocbuf*() does the allocation by calling *newbuf*() to allocate another buffer and then transferring the physical memory in the new buffer to the buffer under construction. As before, if there is excess memory, it is released to the front of the AGE queue; otherwise, it is released to the EMPTY queue. If the new buffer still does not have enough physical memory, the process is repeated. *Allocbuf*() ensures that each physical-memory page is mapped into exactly one buffer at all times.

7.6 Quotas

The quota system allows administrators to control the number of inodes and data blocks that can be allocated by any user on each filesystem. Quotas for each user are maintained on a per-filesystem basis.

Quotas hook into the system primarily as an adjunct to the allocation routines. Figure 7.18 shows that, when the allocation routines are passed a request for a new block from *bmap*(), the request is first validated by *quotachk*(). *Quotachk*() consults the quota associated with the owner of the file. If the owner is below quota, its request is permitted and the request is added to their usage statistics. If the owner has reached or exceeded its limit, the request is denied and the allocator returns a failure to *bmap*() as though the filesystem were full.

Quotas are assigned to a filesystem after it has been mounted. A system call associates a file containing the quotas with the mounted filesystem. By convention, the file is named **quotas** and lives in the root of the mounted filesystem. The system opens the **quotas** file and holds a reference to it in the mount-table entry associated with the mounted filesystem; Fig. 7.19 shows the mount-table reference. As quotas for different users are needed, they can be fetched from the **quotas** file.

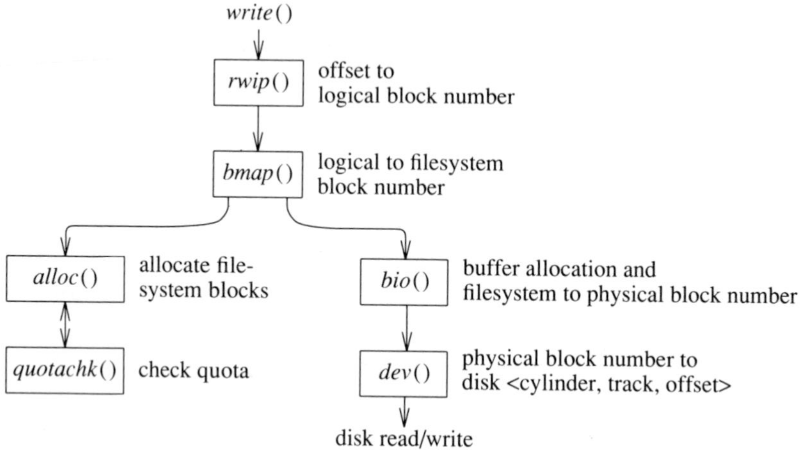

Figure 7.18 Procedural interface to quota control.

The **quotas** file is maintained as an array of quota records indexed by user identifiers; Fig. 7.20 shows a typical record. To find the quota for user identifier *i*, the system seeks to location $i \times$ **sizeof**(quota structure) in the quota file and reads the quota structure at that location. Each quota structure contains the limits imposed on the user for the associated filesystem. These limits include the hard and soft limits on the number of blocks and inodes that the user may have, the number of blocks and inodes the user currently has allocated, and the number of warnings that the user has left before the soft limit is enforced as the hard limit.

Quotas are maintained in a system table called the *dquot table*; Fig. 7.21 shows two typical entries. As with the inode table, the dquot table maintains additional information about the quota information while that information is resident to allow faster access and identification. Since quotas may have to be updated on every write to a file, *quotachk*() must be able to find and manipulate them quickly. Thus, the task of finding the dquot structure associated with a file is done once

Figure 7.19 Access to quotas files.

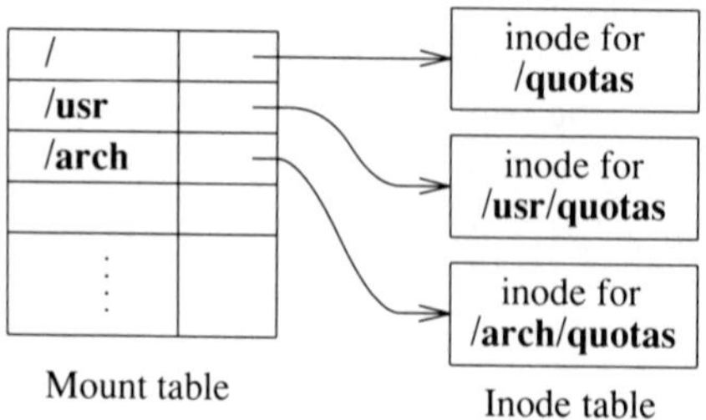

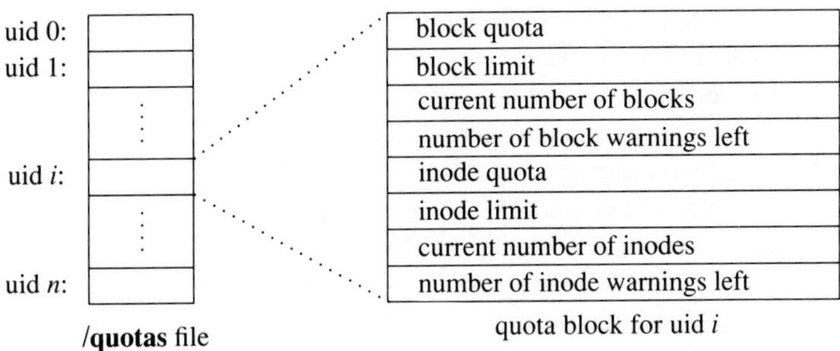

Figure 7.20 Contents of a quota record.

when the file is first opened. When the inode associated with a file is first entered into the inode table, the system checks to see whether there is a quota associated with it. If a quota exists, the inode is set up to hold a reference to the dquot structure as long as the inode is resident. The *quotachk*() routine can determine that a file has a quota by simply checking whether the dquot pointer is nonnull. If it is nonnull, all the necessary information can be accessed directly. If a user has multiple files open on the same filesystem, all inodes describing those files point to the same dquot entry. Thus, the number of blocks allocated to a particular user can always be easily and consistently known.

Figure 7.21 The dquot table.

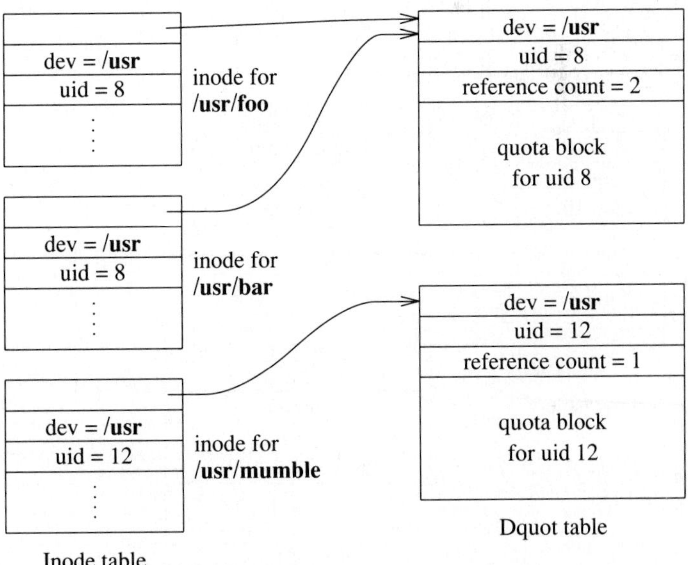

The number of entries in the dquot table can grow large. To speed access, a hashed lookup scheme is used. In the dquot table, the hash is keyed on the filesystem and user identifier. The hashing structure and free list are set up in the same way as is the inode table shown in Fig. 7.11. When the reference count on a dquot structure drops to zero, the entry is linked onto the free list. The dquot structure is not removed from its hash chain, so if the structure is needed again soon it can still be located. Only when a dquot structure is recycled with a new quota record is it removed and relinked into the hash chain.

The hashing structure allows recently used dquot structures to be found quickly. However, it does not solve the problem of how to discover that a user has no quota on a particular filesystem. If a user has no quota, a lookup for the quota will fail. The cost of going to disk and reading the quota file to discover that the user has no quota imposed would be prohibitive. To avoid this work each time a new file is accessed, a *quota table* is maintained that has an entry per active user identifier; Fig. 7.22 shows a typical quota table. When an inode owned by a user that does not already have an entry in the quota table is first accessed, an entry for that user is made in the quota table. At that time, the system checks each filesystem that has quotas enabled to determine whether the user has quotas on

Figure 7.22 The quota table.

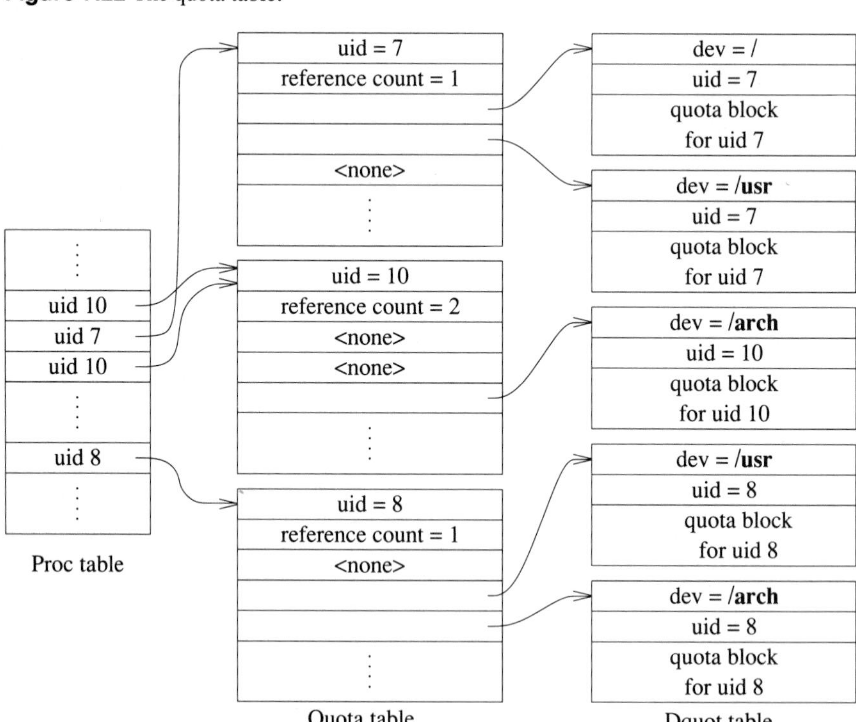

that filesystem. If quotas exist, a pointer to the dquot table is held for that filesystem. If quotas do not exist, the entry is marked to show that they do not. To further speed the usual case of users opening one of their own files, the system maintains a pointer from each proc-table entry to the quota-table entry for each user. When a process opens a file owned by the user running that process, the system follows the pointer to the structure for the user. If the user has a quota on the affected filesystem, the system can increment the reference count on the associated dquot structure and can store the reference in the inode. If the process opens a file of some other user, the system must hash into the quota table to find the entry for the other user; once that entry is found, the same procedure can be followed.

7.7 Allocation Mechanisms

We shall now turn our attention to the details of allocating a data block. The procedural description of the allocation process is shown in Fig. 7.23. *Bmap*() is the routine responsible for determining when a new block must be allocated. It first calls the layout-policy routine *blkpref*() to select the most desirable block based on the preference from the global-policy routines that were described in Section 7.3. If a fragment has already been allocated and needs to be extended, *bmap*() calls *realloccg*(). If nothing has been allocated yet, *bmap*() calls *alloc*().

Realloccg() first tries to extend the current fragment in place. Consider the sample block of an allocation map with two fragments allocated from it, shown in Fig. 7.24. The first fragment can be extended from a size 2 fragment to a size 3 fragment, since an adjacent piece is unused. The second fragment cannot be extended, as it occupies a full block, and fragments are not allowed to span blocks. If *realloccg*() is able to expand the current fragment in place, the map is updated appropriately and it returns. If the fragment cannot be extended,

Figure 7.23 Procedural interface to block allocation.

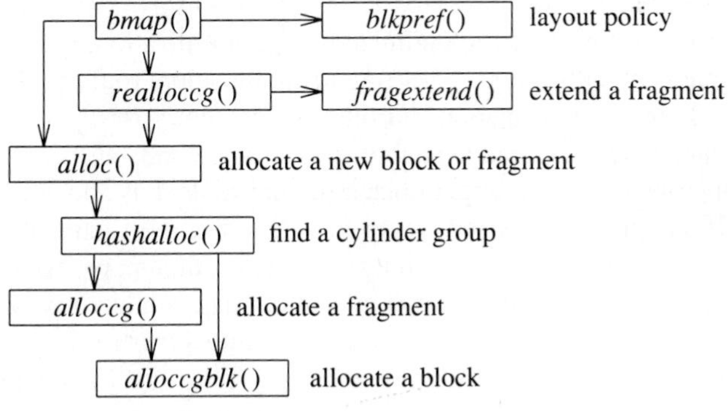

entry in table	1	-	-	1	-	-	-	-
allocated fragments		size 2				size 4		

Figure 7.24 Sample block with two allocated fragments.

realloccg() calls the *alloc*() routine, described later, to get a new fragment. The old fragment is copied to the beginning of the new fragment, and the old fragment is freed.

The bookkeeping tasks of allocation are handled by *alloc*(). It first verifies that a block is available in the desired cylinder group by checking the filesystem summary information. If the summary information shows that the cylinder group is full, *alloc*() will quadratically rehash through the summary information looking for a cylinder group with free space. Having found a cylinder group with space, *alloc*() will call either the fragment-allocation routine or the block-allocation routine to acquire a fragment or block.

The block-allocation routine is given a preferred block. If that block is available, it is returned. If the block is unavailable, the allocation routine tries to find another block on the same cylinder that is rotationally closest to the requested block. To simplify the task of locating rotationally optimal blocks, the summary information for each cylinder group includes a count of the available blocks at different rotational positions. Eight rotational positions are distinguished, so the resolution of the summary information is 2 milliseconds for a 3600 revolution-per-minute drive. The superblock contains a vector of lists called the *rotational-layout table*. The vector is indexed by rotational position. Each component of the vector lists the index into the block map for every data block contained in its rotational position. When looking for an allocatable block, the system first looks through the summary counts for a rotational position with a nonzero block count. It then uses the index of the rotational position to find the appropriate list of rotationally optimal blocks. This list enables the system to limit its scan of the free block map to only those parts that contain some free, rotationally well-placed blocks.

The fragment-allocation routine is given a preferred fragment. If that fragment is available, it is returned. If the requested fragment is not available, and the filesystem is configured to optimize for space utilization; it uses a best-fit strategy for fragment allocation. The fragment-allocation routine checks the cylinder-group summary information, starting with the entry for the desired size and scanning larger sizes until an available fragment is found. If there are no fragments of the appropriate size or larger, then a full-sized block is allocated and is broken up.

If an appropriate-sized fragment is listed in the fragment summary, then the allocation routine expects to find it in the allocation map. To speed up the process of scanning the potentially large allocation map, a table-driven algorithm is used. Each byte in the map is treated as an index into a *fragment-descriptor table*. Each entry in the fragment-descriptor table describes the fragments that are free for that corresponding map entry. Thus, by doing a logical AND with the bit

Bits in map	Decimal value
-111--11	115

Figure 7.25 Map entry for an 8192/1024 filesystem.

corresponding to the desired fragment size, the allocator can quickly determine whether the desired fragment is contained within a given allocation-map entry. As an example, consider the following entry from an allocation map for the 8192/1024 filesystem shown in Fig. 7.25. The map entry shown has already been fragmented, with a single fragment allocated at the beginning and a size 2 fragment allocated in the middle. Remaining unused is another size 2 fragment, and a size 3 fragment. Thus, if we look up entry 115 in the fragment table, we find the entry shown in Fig. 7.26. If we were looking for a size 3 fragment, we would inspect the third bit and find that we had been successful; if we were looking for a size 4 fragment, we would inspect the fourth bit and find that we needed to continue. The C code that implements this algorithm is as follows:

```
for (i = 0; i < MAPSIZE; i++)
    if (fragtbl[allocmap[i]] & (1 << (size - 1)))
        break;
```

Using a best-fit policy has the benefit of minimizing disk fragmentation; however, it has the undesirable property that it maximizes the number of fragment-to-fragment copies that must be made when a process writes a file in many small pieces. To avoid this behavior, the system can configure filesystems to optimize for time rather than for space. The first time a process does a small write on a filesystem configured for time optimization, it is allocated a best-fit fragment. On the second small write, however, a full-sized block is allocated, with the unused portion being freed. Later small writes are able to extend the fragment in place, rather than requiring additional copy operations. Under certain circumstances, this policy can cause the disk to become heavily fragmented. The system tracks this condition, and automatically reverts to optimizing for space if the fragmentation gets within 2 percent of the minimum free-space limit.

7.8 Translation of Filesystem Names

Profiling studies show that nearly one-quarter of the time in the kernel is spent in the pathname-translation routine, *namei*(), translating pathnames to inodes. *Namei*() is responsible for doing access checks on each component of the name to verify that the current process has the necessary permissions to search the intervening directories, and to access the target file in the way that the process has requested. *Namei*() consists of two nested loops. The outer loop is traversed once per pathname component. The inner loop performs a linear search through a directory looking for a particular pathname component.

entry in table	0	0	0	0	0	1	1	0
available fragment size	8	7	6	5	4	3	2	1

Figure 7.26 Fragment-table entry for entry 115.

Two caching techniques are used to reduce the cost of name translation. The first technique is to reduce the number of iterations around the inner loop of *namei*() by observing that many programs sequentially scan a directory. To improve performance for processes exhibiting this behavior, the directory offset of the last component of the most recently translated pathname is maintained for each process. If the next name that the process requests to be translated is in the same directory, the search is started from the offset at which the previous name was found (instead of from the beginning of the directory). Changing directories invalidates the cache. For programs that step sequentially through a directory with n files, search time decreases from $Order(n^2)$ to $Order(n)$.

A quick benchmark to show the maximum effectiveness of the cache is *ls –l* on a directory containing 600 files. Adding the per-process cache reduces the amount of system time for this test by 85 percent. Unfortunately, the maximum effectiveness is much greater than the average effectiveness. Although the cache is 90 percent effective when hit, it is usable on only about 25 percent of the names being translated. An additional reason for the improvement being small is that, although the amount of time spent in *namei*() itself decreases substantially, more time is spent in the routines that it called, because cache misses cause a directory to be accessed twice—once to search from the middle to the end, and once to search from the beginning to the middle.

Frequent requests for a small set of names are best handled with a cache of recent name translations. 4.3BSD uses a cache keyed on a name and the inode and device number of the directory that contains the name. Associated with each entry is a pointer to the corresponding entry in the inode table. This cache has the effect of eliminating the inner loop of *namei*(). For each pathname component, *namei*() first looks in its cache of recent translations for the needed name. If the name exists, the directory search can be eliminated.

An issue to be considered is how the name cache should hold references to the inode table. Normally, processes hold *hard references* by incrementing the reference count in the inode they reference. Since the system reuses only inodes with zero reference counts, a hard reference ensures that the inode pointer will remain valid. However, if the name cache holds hard references, its size is limited to some fraction of the size of the inode table, since some inodes must be left free for new files. Holding of hard references also makes it impossible for other parts of the kernel to verify sole use of a device or file. These are reasons why it is impractical to use hard references without affecting the behavior of the inode-caching scheme. Thus, *soft references* are kept, protected by a *capability*—a 32-bit number guaranteed to be unique. When all the numbers have been exhausted, all outstanding capabilities are purged, and numbering restarts from scratch.

Purging is possible, as all capabilities are easily found in kernel memory. When an entry is made in the name cache, the capability of its inode is copied to the name-cache entry. When an inode is reused, it is issued a new capability. When a name-cache hit occurs, the capability of the name-cache entry is compared with the capability of the inode that the entry references. If the capabilities do not match, the name-cache entry is invalid. Since the name cache holds only soft references, it may be sized independent of the size of the inode table. A final benefit of using capabilities is that all cached names for an inode can be invalidated without a search through the entire cache; instead, it is necessary only to assign a new capability to the inode.

In 1984, on a general time-sharing system at Berkeley during the 12-hour period from 8:00 A.M. to 8:00 P.M., the system did 500,000 to 1,000,000 name translations. Statistics on the performance of both caches showed that the large performance improvement was caused by the high hit ratio. The name cache had a hit rate of 70 to 80 percent; the directory offset cache hit rate was 5 to 15 percent. The combined hit rate of the two caches almost always was 85 percent. With the addition of the two caches, the percentage of system time devoted to name translation dropped from 25 percent to less than 10 percent. Although the systemwide cache reduced both the amount of time in the routines that *namei*() calls and the amount in *namei*() itself (since fewer directories needed to be accessed or searched), it is interesting to note that the actual percentage of system time spent in *namei*() itself increased even though the actual time per call decreased. This increase occurred because less total time was being spent in the kernel; hence, a smaller absolute time became a larger total percentage.

Exercises

7.1 Why are directory entries not allowed to span chunks?

7.2 Why are hard links not permitted to span filesystems?

7.3 Describe the difference in interpretation of a symbolic link containing an absolute pathname from that of a symbolic link containing a relative pathname.

7.4 Explain why unprivileged users are not permitted to make hard links to directories, but are permitted to make symbolic links to directories.

7.5 How can hard links be used to gain access to files that could not be accessed if a symbolic link were used instead?

7.6 How does the system recognize loops caused by symbolic links? Suggest an alternative scheme for doing loop detection.

7.7 How many blocks and fragments are allocated to a 31,200-byte file on a filesystem with 4096-byte blocks and 1024-byte fragments? How many blocks and fragments would be allocated to this file on a filesystem with

4096-byte blocks and 512-byte fragments? Answer these two questions assuming that an inode had only six direct block pointers, instead of 12.

7.8 What is the difference between a logical block and a physical block? Why is this distinction important?

7.9 How do quotas differ from the file-size resource limits described in Section 3.8?.

7.10 Why is the per-cylinder group information placed at varying offsets from the beginning of the cylinder group?

7.11 Why are triple indirect blocks not commonly useful on machines with a 32-bit word size and a 512-byte minimum fragment size?

7.12 What is a quadratic hash? Describe what it is used for in the filesystem, and why it is used for that purpose.

7.13 Explain why the 4.3BSD filesystem maintains a 5 to 10 percent reserve of free space. What problems would arise if the free-space reserve were set to zero?

7.14 Why are the allocation policies for inodes different from those for data blocks?

7.15 Why are the buffer headers allocated separately from the memory that holds the contents of the buffer?

7.16 How does the maximum filesystem block size affect the buffer cache?

7.17 Give two reasons why increasing the basic block size in the old filesystem from 512 bytes to 1024 bytes more than doubled the system's throughput.

7.18 Describe the two methods used to improve the performance of the traditional UNIX filesystem in 4.2BSD.

*7.19 Why is there an AGE list and an LRU list, instead of all buffers being managed on the LRU list?

*7.20 Filenames can be up to 255 characters long. How can the systemwide name cache be implemented to avoid allocating 255 bytes for each entry?

*7.21 If a process reads a large file, the blocks of the file will fill the buffer cache completely, flushing out all other contents. All other processes in the system then will have to go to disk for all their filesystem accesses. Describe an algorithm to control the purging of the buffer cache.

*7.22 Discuss the tradeoff between dedicating memory to the buffer cache and making the memory available to the virtual-memory system for use in fulfilling paging requests. Give a policy for moving memory between the buffer pool and the virtual-memory system.

*7.23 Which filesystem operations must be done synchronously to ensure that the filesystem can always be recovered deterministically after a crash (barring unrecoverable hardware errors)?

*7.24 What problems would arise if files had to be allocated in a single contiguous piece of the disk? Consider the problems created by multiple processes, random access, and files with holes.

**7.25 Inodes could be allocated dynamically as part of a directory entry. Instead, inodes are statically allocated when the filesystem is created. Why is the latter approach used?

References

Elz, 1984.

K. R. Elz, "Resource Controls, Privileges, and Other MUSH," *USENIX Association Conference Proceedings*, pp. 183–191 (June 1984).

Knuth, 1975.

D. Knuth, *The Art of Computer Programming, Volume 3—Sorting and Searching*, Addison-Wesley, Reading, MA (1975).

McKusick & Kowalski, 1986.

M. K. McKusick & T. J. Kowalski, "Fsck—The UNIX File System Check Program," pp. 5:1–22 in *UNIX System Manager's Manual, 4.3 Berkeley Software Distribution, Virtual VAX-11 Version*, USENIX Association, Berkeley, CA (1986).

Nevalainen & Vesterinen, 1977.

O. Nevalainen & M. Vesterinen, "Determining Blocking Factors for Sequential Files by Heuristic Methods," *The Computer Journal* **20**(3), pp. 245–247 (August 1977).

Trivedi, 1980.

K. Trivedi, "Optimal Selection of CPU Speed, Device Capabilities, and File Assignments," *Journal of the ACM* **27**(3), pp. 457–473 (July 1980).

CHAPTER 8

Device Drivers

A *hardware device* is a peripheral such as a disk or tape drive, terminal multiplexer, or network controller. For each hardware device supported by UNIX, a software module termed a *device driver* is required. Device drivers provide a consistent interface to varying hardware devices by hiding device-specific details from the rest of the UNIX kernel and user applications.

UNIX provides three internal interfaces that a device driver may support. These interfaces permit a device to be used in three different ways: as a block-oriented device suitable for holding one or more filesystems, as a message-oriented channel through which network communication may take place, or as an unstructured device that is potentially suitable for use by the terminal I/O system. A device driver may provide any or all of these interfaces to the system. Most device drivers provide one interface, although some device drivers provide more. This chapter examines how UNIX supports hardware devices and how device drivers operate within the framework of the I/O system. The network-related aspects of handling hardware devices are discussed in Chapter 11, together with the networking facilities.

8.1 Overview

Computers store and retrieve data through supporting peripheral I/O devices. These devices typically include mass-storage devices, such as moving-head disk drives, magnetic-tape drives, and network interfaces. Storage devices such as disks and tapes are accessed through I/O controllers that manage the operation of their *slave* devices according to I/O requests from the CPU.

On the VAX machines supported by 4.3BSD, most peripheral devices are connected to the *UNIBUS* or to the *MASSBUS*. These buses are, in turn, connected to a VAX's main system bus through *bus adapters*. The UNIBUS and MASSBUS are relatively old buses that were originally designed for PDP-11 computers. DEC used bus adapters to these buses in the original VAX machines to provide backward hardware compatibility and to allow customers to upgrade their hardware systems while still using existing peripherals.

I/O devices are accessed through memory locations in the physical address space of the CPU. That is, the VAX uses a *memory-mapped I/O architecture*. Since the UNIX kernel runs with the memory management enabled, the physical addresses associated with hardware devices must be *mapped* into the virtual address space of the kernel.

In addition to mapping the memory locations at which I/O devices reside, the system must also be prepared to field *interrupts* from devices and to invoke the appropriate device-driver software to *service* the interrupt. All UNIBUS and MASSBUS I/O devices utilize *vectored interrupts*. That is, when a device needs to interrupt the CPU, it transmits an *interrupt vector* along with its interrupt request. When the interrupt request is honored, the interrupt vector is used to index into an *interrupt-vector table* to extract the address of the interrupt service routine that should process the interrupt. For each I/O device present on a machine, UNIX must initialize the appropriate entries in the interrupt-vector tables. As we shall see later, the interrupt service routines for a device driver are not invoked directly from the interrupt-vector tables. Instead, UNIX interposes a small layer of code that saves machine state and establishes *context* for the device driver. This context includes the identity of the device that is interrupting.

Under UNIX, applications cannot directly access most I/O devices. Instead, the system interposes one or more layers of software between the device and the application to promote a uniform interface across all devices of the same type. For example, disk drives are typically accessed only through the filesystem, whereas network interface controllers are utilized only through the interprocess-communication facilities described in Chapter 10. In some cases, however, user applications need direct, or almost direct, access to I/O devices. In these instances, UNIX supports two standard interfaces to hardware devices through block and character special device files. Devices that are accessed through a block (character) device special file are referred to as *block devices* (*character devices*) or as having a *block-device interface* (*character-device interface*).

A block-device interface, as the name indicates, supports only block-oriented I/O operations. The block-device interface uses the buffer cache to minimize the number of I/O requests that actually require an I/O operation, and to synchronize with filesystem operations on the same device. All I/O is done to or from I/O buffers that reside in the kernel's address space. This approach requires at least one memory-to-memory copy operation to satisfy a user request, but also allows UNIX to support I/O requests of nearly arbitrary size and alignment.

A character-device interface comes in two styles that depend on the characteristics of the underlying hardware device. For some character-oriented hardware devices, such as terminal multiplexers, the interface is truly character-oriented, although higher-level software such as the terminal driver may provide a line-oriented interface to applications. However, for block-oriented devices such as disks and tapes, a character device interface is actually a very *unstructured* or *raw* interface. For this interface, I/O operations do not go through the buffer cache; instead, they are made directly between the device and buffers in the application's virtual address space. Consequently, the size of the operations must be a multiple of the underlying *block size* required by the device and, on some machines, the application's I/O buffer must be aligned on a suitable boundary.

Internal to the system, I/O devices are accessed through a fixed set of entry points provided by each device's *device driver*. The set of entry points varies according to whether the I/O device supports a block- or character-device interface. For a block-device interface, a device driver is described by a *bdevsw* structure, whereas for character-device interface, it accesses a *cdevsw* structure. All the *bdevsw* structures are collected in the *block-device table*, whereas *cdevsw* structures are similarly organized in a *character-device table*.

Devices are identified by a *device number* that is constructed from a *major* and a *minor* device number. The *major device number* uniquely identifies the type of device (really the device driver) and is the index of the device's entry in the block- or character-device table. Devices that support both block- and character-device interfaces have two major device numbers, one for each table. The *minor device* number is interpreted solely by the device driver and is used by the driver to identify to which, of potentially many, hardware devices an I/O request refers. For magnetic tapes, for example, minor device numbers are used to identify a specific controller and tape transport. The minor device number may also specify a section of a device; for example, a channel of a multiplexed device, or optional handling parameters.

The remainder of this chapter describes the structure and operation of device drivers. The next section examines the general structure of a device driver and discusses the data structures shared between the I/O system and device drivers. Following this examination, the interaction between device drivers and the autoconfiguration facilities is considered. Finally, the operation of device drivers for hardware devices that reside on a UNIBUS and a MASSBUS are discussed.

8.2 Device Drivers

A device driver is divided into three main sections:

1. Autoconfiguration and initialization routines
2. Routines for servicing I/O requests (the top half)
3. Interrupt service routines (the bottom half)

The autoconfiguration portion of a driver is responsible for *probing* for a hardware device to see whether the latter is present and to initialize the device and any associated software state that is required by the device driver. This portion of the driver is typically called only once, when the system is initialized.

The section of a driver that services I/O requests by the system is invoked as a result of system calls or on behalf of the virtual-memory system. This portion of the device driver executes synchronously in the top half of the kernel and is permitted to block by calling the *sleep*() routine. We commonly refer to this body of code as the *top half* of a device driver.

Interrupt service routines are invoked when the system fields an interrupt from a device. Consequently, these routines cannot depend on any per-process state and cannot block. On the VAX, interrupt routines execute on the interrupt stack. We commonly refer to a device driver's interrupt services routines as the *bottom half* of a device driver.

In addition to these three sections of a device driver, an optional *crash-dump* routine may be provided. This routine, if present, is invoked when the system recognizes an unrecoverable error and wishes to record the contents of physical memory for use in postmortem analysis. Most device drivers for disk controllers, and some for tape controllers, provide a crash-dump routine. The use of the crash-dump routine is described in Chapter 13.

I/O Queueing

Device drivers typically manage one or more queues of I/O requests in their normal operation. As an input or output request is received by the top half of the driver, it is recorded in a data structure that is placed on a per-device queue for processing. When an input or output operation completes, the device driver receives an interrupt from the controller. The interrupt service routine removes the appropriate request from the device's queue, notifies the requester that the command has completed, and then initiates another request from the queue. The I/O queues are the primary means of communication between the *top* and *bottom* halves of a device driver. Block-oriented devices construct their I/O queues from *buf* structures, whereas character-oriented devices use *C-list* structures.

As I/O queues are shared among asynchronous routines, access to the queues must be synchronized. Routines that make up the top half of a device driver must raise the processor priority level (using *splbio*(), *spltty*(), etc.) to prevent the bottom half from being entered as a result of an interrupt while a top-half routine is manipulating an I/O queue. Synchronization among multiple processes initiating I/O requests must also be done. This synchronization is done using the mechanisms described at the end of Chapter 4.

In addition to per-device I/O queueing, on the VAX, device drivers must also interact with the support routines for the bus adapter on which a device resides. For example, a device driver for a UNIBUS-based disk controller must schedule access to the UNIBUS through the UNIBUS adapter-support routines. This scheduling is required because limited resources are available in each adapter for doing I/O operations. In addition, certain I/O devices require exclusive use of the bus for reliable operation. To handle these problems, device drivers package each I/O request, then pass the request to a bus-adapter routine that schedules the I/O operation. When resources are available for the operation to be done, the device driver is *called back* and the I/O operation is started. This scheduling may involve additional queueing beyond that provided by the device driver.

Interrupt Handling

Interrupts are generated by devices to signal that an operation has completed or that a change in status has occurred. On receiving a device interrupt, the system invokes the appropriate device-driver interrupt service routine with one or more parameters that uniquely identify the device that requires service. These parameters are needed because device drivers typically support multiple devices of the same type. If the interrupting device's identity were not supplied with each interrupt, the driver would be forced to poll all the potential devices to identify the device that interrupted.

Interrupt routines for UNIBUS devices are passed a *physical unit number* that is defined at the time the system is configured. Interrupt routines for MASSBUS devices are actually invoked indirectly from the MASSBUS adapter interrupt service routines. The MASSBUS adapter interrupt service routines are passed a *MASSBUS unit number* that is defined at the time the system is configured. The system arranges, in each case, for the appropriate parameter to be passed to the interrupt service routine for each device by installing the address of an auxiliary glue routine in the interrupt vector table. This glue routine, rather than the actual interrupt service routine, is invoked to service the interrupt; it takes the following actions:

1. Save all volatile registers
2. Update statistics on device interrupts
3. Call the interrupt service routine with the appropriate unit number parameter
4. Restore the volatile registers saved in step 1
5. Return from the interrupt

Because a glue routine is interposed between the interrupt-vector table and the interrupt service routine, device drivers do not need to be concerned with saving and restoring machine state. In addition, special-purpose instructions that cannot be generated from C, but that are needed by the hardware to support interrupts, can be kept out of the device driver; this permits device drivers to be written without assembly language.

8.3 Block Devices

Device drivers for block devices are described by an entry in the *bdevsw* table. Block devices are most commonly associated with disk drives and tape transports. Each *bdevsw* structure contains the following entry points:

open Open the device in preparation for I/O operations. A device's open entry point will be called for each *open* system call on a block special device file, or, internally, when a device is prepared for mounting a filesystem with the *mount* system call. The *open*() routine will commonly verify the integrity of the associated medium. For example, it will verify that the device was identified during the autoconfiguration phase and, for tape and disk drives, that a medium is present and on-line.

strategy Initiate a read or write operation and return immediately. I/O requests to or from filesystems located on a device are translated by the system into calls to the block I/O routines *bread*() and *bwrite*(). These block I/O routines in turn call the device's strategy routine to read or write data not in the cache. Each call to the strategy routine specifies a pointer to a *buf* structure containing the parameters for an I/O request. If the request is synchronous, the caller must sleep (on the address of the *buf* structure) until I/O completes.

close Close a device. The *close*() routine is called after the last client interested in using the device terminates. These semantics are defined by the higher-level I/O facilities. Disk devices have nothing to do when a device is closed, and thus use a null *close*() routine. Devices that support access to only a single client must mark the device as available once again. Closing a tape drive that was open for writing typically causes end-of-file marks to be written on the tape and the tape to be rewound.

dump Write all of physical memory to the device. The dump entry point is used to save the contents of memory on secondary storage. The system automatically takes a dump when it detects an unrecoverable error and is about to *crash*. The dump is used in a postmortem analysis of the problem that caused the system to crash. The dump routine is invoked with the processor priority at its highest level; thus, the device driver must poll for device status, rather than wait for interrupts. All disk devices are expected to support this entry point; some tape devices do as well.

psize Return the size of a disk-drive partition. The driver is supplied a logical unit and is expected to return the size of that unit, typically a disk-drive partition, in DEV_BSIZE blocks. This entry point is used during the bootstrap procedure to calculate the location at which a crash dump should be placed and to determine the sizes of the swap devices.

8.4 Character Devices

Character devices are described by entries in the *cdevsw* table. The entry points in this table (see Table 8.1) are used to support raw access to block-oriented devices as well as normal access to character-oriented devices through the terminal driver. Because of the diverse requirements of these two types of devices, the set of entry points is really the union of two disjoint sets. Raw devices support a subset of the entry points that correspond to those entry points found in a block device driver, whereas character devices support the full set of entry points. Each is described in the following sections.

Table 8.1 Entry points for character and raw device drivers.

Entry point	Function
open()	open the device
close()	close the device
ioctl()	perform an I/O control operation
mmap()	map device contents into memory
read()	perform an input operation
reset()	reinitialize device after a bus reset
select()	poll device for I/O readiness
stop()	stop output on the device
write()	perform an output operation

Raw Devices and Physical I/O

Most raw devices differ from block devices only in the way they do I/O. Whereas block devices read and write data to and from the system buffer cache, raw devices transfer data to and from user data buffers. Bypassing the buffer cache eliminates the memory-to-memory copy that must be done by block devices, but also denies applications the benefits of data caching. In addition, for devices that support both raw- and block-device access, applications must take care to preserve consistency between data in the buffer cache and data written directly to the device; the raw device should be used only when the block device is idle. Raw-device access is used by many filesystem utilities such as the filesystem check program, **fsck**, and by programs that read and write magnetic tapes—for example, **tar**, **dump**, and **restore**.

Because raw devices bypass the buffer cache, they are responsible for managing their own buffer structures. Each raw-device driver maintains a static set of buffer structures, one for each unit on which raw I/O is supported. The read and write routines use the *physio*() routine to initiate a raw I/O operation (see Fig. 8.1). The *strategy* parameter identifies a block-device strategy routine that is used to initiate I/O operations on the device. The buffer indicated by *bp* is used by *physio*() in constructing the request(s) made to the strategy routine. The device, read-write flag, and *uio* parameters completely specify the I/O operation that should be done. The *minphys*() routine is called by *physio*() to adjust the size of each I/O transfer before the latter is passed to the strategy routine; this allows the transfer to be done in sections, according to the maximum transfer size supported by the device.

The operation of *physio*() includes synchronizing access to the buffer structure used in doing the I/O operation. This synchronization is required because each device maintains only a single buffer for doing raw I/O operations. There are checks to ensure that only one process at a time will execute the section of code using the raw buffer. There is no other particular reason to restrict raw I/O

```
physio(strategy, bp, dev, flags, minphys, uio)
    int strategy();
    buffer *bp;
    device dev;
    int flags;
    int minphys();
    struct uio *uio;
{
    check user read/write access to the data buffer;
    raise the processor priority to splbio;
    while (the buffer is marked busy) {
        mark the buffer wanted;
        wait until the buffer is available;
    }
    lower the priority level;
    set up the fixed part of the buffer for a transfer;
    while (there are data to transfer and no I/O error) {
        mark the buffer busy for physical I/O;
        set up the buffer for a maximum sized transfer;
        call minphys to bound the transfer size;
        lock the part of the user address space
            involved in the transfer;
        call strategy to start the transfer;
        raise the priority level to splbio;
        wait for the transfer to complete;
        unlock the part of the address space previously
            locked;
        lower the priority level;
        deduct the transfer size from the total number
            of data to transfer;
    }
    clean up the state of the buffer;
    if (another process is waiting for the raw I/O buffer)
        wake up processes waiting to do physical I/O;
}
```

Figure 8.1 Algorithm for physical I/O.

operations for each device to be single threaded since, as we shall see, the device drivers queue I/O operations to a controller as needed. The 4.3BSD Tahoe release avoids this single threading of raw I/O requests by borrowing swap buffer structures instead of using per-device buffers.

Raw-device I/O operations request the hardware device to transfer data directly to or from the data buffer in the user program's address space described by the *uio* parameter. Thus, unlike I/O operations that do direct memory access

(DMA) from buffers in the kernel address space, raw I/O operations must check that the user's buffer is accessible by the device, and must lock it into memory for the duration of the transfer.

Character-Oriented Devices

Character-oriented I/O devices are typified by terminal multiplexers, although they also include printers and other character- or line-oriented devices. These devices are usually accessed through the terminal driver, described in Chapter 9. The close tie to the terminal driver has heavily influenced the structure of character device drivers. For example, several entry points in the *cdevsw* structure exist for communication between the generic terminal handler and the terminal multiplexer hardware drivers. This interface is described fully in Chapter 9.

Entry Points for Character Device Drivers

A device driver for a character device is defined by an entry in the *cdevsw* table. This structure contains many of the same entry points found in an entry in the *bdevsw* table.

open
close The *open*() and *close*() entry points provide similar functions to those of a block device driver. In fact, for character devices that simply provide raw access to a block device, these entry points are usually the same. But some block devices do not have these entry points, whereas most character devices do have them.

read Read data from a device. For raw devices, this entry point normally just calls the *physio*() routine with device-specific parameters. For terminal-oriented devices, a read request is passed immediately to the terminal driver. For other devices, a read request requires that the specified data be copied into the kernel's address space, typically with the *uiomove*() routine, and then be passed to the device.

write Write data to a device. This entry point is a direct parallel of the read entry point: Raw devices utilize *physio*(), terminal-oriented devices call the terminal driver to do this operation, and other devices handle the request internally.

ioctl Perform an operation other than a read or write. This entry originally provided a mechanism to get and set device parameters for terminal devices, and its use has expanded to other types of devices as well. Historically, *ioctl*() operations have varied widely from device to device. 4.3BSD, however, defines a set of operations that are supported by all tape devices. These operations position tapes, return unit status, write end-of-file marks, and place a tape drive off-line.

select Check the device to see whether data are available for reading and/or space is available for writing data. The select entry point is used by the *select* system call in checking file descriptors associated with device special files. For raw devices, a select operation is meaningless, since data are not buffered. In this case, the entry point is set to *seltrue*(), a routine that returns true for any select request. For devices used with the terminal driver, this entry point is set to *ttselect*(), a routine described in Chapter 9.

stop Stop output on a device. The stop routine is meaningful only for devices used with the terminal driver. For these devices, the stop routine is used to halt transmission on a line when the terminal driver receives a *stop character*—for example, ''^S''—or when it prepares to flush its output queues.

mmap Map a device's contents into memory. This entry point was added in preparation for the *mmap* system call; its semantics are currently undefined.

reset Reset device state after a bus reset. The reset routine is called from the bus-adapter support routines after a bus reset is made. The device driver is expected to reinitialize the hardware, and to reset any driver state related to the adapter. For example, if a device does DMA transfers, it must allocate resources to map the data buffer into the address space of the I/O bus. When a bus reset occurs, the bus-adapter routines revoke the allocation of all such resources and, consequently, a device driver must reallocate the resources it needs. If a transfer was in progress, the driver must then restart it. This routine is specific to the VAX architecture.

8.5 Autoconfiguration

Some hardware devices, such as the interface to the console terminal, are required for system operation. Other devices, however, may not be needed and their inclusion in the system may needlessly utilize system resources. Devices that might be present in different numbers, at different addresses, or in different combinations are difficult to configure in advance, however, and the system must support them if they are present and must fail gracefully if they are not present. To address these problems, 4.3BSD supports both a static *configuration procedure* that is done when a bootable system image is created, and a dynamic *autoconfiguration phase* that is done when the system is bootstrapped.

The static configuration procedure is done by the **/etc/config** program. A configuration file is created by the system administrator that defines the set of hardware devices that might be present on a machine. This file identifies not only the types of devices, but also where each device might be located on the machine. For example, a system might be configured with two disk controllers and four disk drives that are connected in any of the configurations shown in Fig. 8.2. The configuration procedure generates several files that define the hardware topology. These files are compiled into the system for use in the autoconfiguration phase.

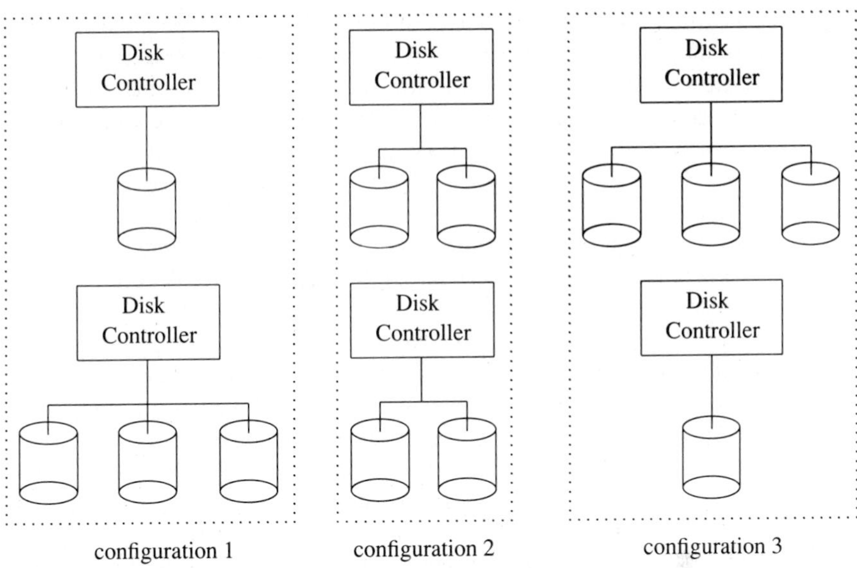

Figure 8.2 Drive configuration on the VAX.

The autoconfiguration phase is done during system initialization to identify the set of configured devices that are actually present on a machine. Autoconfiguration works by *probing* for configured devices at each of the possible locations where the device might be attached to the machine. Devices that are recognized during the autoconfiguration phase are *attached* and are made available for use. Devices that are present but not recognized remain unavailable until the system is rebooted.

Although this scheme requires that all the device drivers for hardware devices that might potentially be present on a machine be configured into a system, it permits device drivers to allocate system resources for only those devices that are present in a running system. It allows the physical device topology to be changed without requiring the system load image to be regenerated. It also prevents crashes resulting from attempts to access a nonexistent device. In the remainder of this section, we consider the autoconfiguration facilities from the point of view of the device-driver writer. We examine the device-driver support required to identify hardware devices that are present on a machine and the steps needed to *attach* a device once its presence has been identified. The internal structures of the configuration and autoconfiguration phases are left to Chapter 13.

Probing for Devices

During the autoconfiguration phase, a device-driver *probe routine* is called for each configured hardware device controller that responds to a memory access. The system passes to the probe routine the address of the controller's I/O registers and expects the routine both to verify that the device is present and, if possible, to force the device to interrupt the host. If the probe routine is successful in forcing an interrupt, then the system will trap the interrupt and use the value of the vector to initialize the appropriate entries in the interrupt-vector table, so that the interrupt service routines for the device driver will be invoked on subsequent interrupts. For some hardware devices, it is impossible to force an interrupt reliably. In these instances, the system allows the probe routine to force a device to be configured by returning a known interrupt vector. If no interrupt is received and none is returned, the system assumes that the controller is not present at the supplied location.

In addition to probing for device controllers, a device driver may also be asked to probe for devices that may be attached to a controller. For example, the system will first probe to see whether a disk controller is present. For each controller found, the system will then probe for each possible disk drive that might be attached. Devices attached to a controller are termed *slave devices*. Disk drives and tape transports are the two types of slave devices. Device drivers that may have slave devices attached to their controller must provide a *slave routine* to probe for slave devices. The slave routine does not have to force an interrupt for each slave device; it needs only to return an indication of whether or not the slave device is present.

Attaching a Device

Once a device is found by a probe, the autoconfiguration code must *attach* it. Attaching a device is separated from probing to allow the system to initialize data structures used by the bus-adapter routines. Most device drivers use the attach routine to initialize the hardware device and any software state. For disk devices, for example, the attach routine is used to identify the geometry of the disk drive and to initialize the partition table that defines the placement of filesystems on the drive.

Device Naming

The autoconfiguration facilities support flexible placement of hardware on a machine by imposing a level of indirection in the naming of devices. Applications reference devices through block and character special files placed in the filesystem. The inode associated with a special file contains the major and minor device numbers of the associated hardware device. The major device number identifies the type of the device, whereas the minor device number identifies a *logical device unit*. For example, suppose the file **/dev/up1a** was created with the command

/etc/mknod /dev/up1a b 2 8

This file would refer to a block device with major device number 2 and minor device number of 8. Internally, the major device number would indicate a disk drive supported by the *up* device driver. The minor device number would be passed to the device driver, where it would be interpreted according to the formula

$$minor = (8 \cdot logical\ unit) + logical\ partition$$

or, in this instance, partition 0 on logical unit (drive) 1. The *logical unit* for each device is assigned during the autoconfiguration phase and is distinct from hardware unit numbers used to identify devices. That is, whereas a tape unit or disk drive might have a hardware unit plug that identifies the device as physical unit x on a controller, to the system that device would be identified by a possibly different logical unit y. A logical unit may refer to different hardware devices each time a system is initialized or, more interesting, a specific hardware device may map to the same logical unit no matter where it is placed on the machine. This logical-to-physical mapping of device names within the system permits, for example, a disk drive to be shifted from one disk controller to another without rebuilding of the operating system. Flexibility in device naming is important in simplifying system maintenance in environments where redundant hardware is maintained for reliability. It also allows logical numbering to span controllers: There may be more than one hardware unit 0, whereas there can be only one logical unit 0.

8.6 UNIBUS Devices

The UNIBUS is an asynchronous bidirectional I/O bus that supports a wide variety of devices and moderate data-transfer rates; it is the original PDP-11 I/O bus. Each UNIBUS on a VAX is connected to the system bus through a *UNIBUS adapter*. Many devices may be attached to a UNIBUS. Several UNIBUS adapters may be attached to a VAX's system bus. The entire 18-bit address space of each UNIBUS is present in the VAX physical address space, and is mapped into the kernel's 32-bit virtual address space. This allows the kernel to access directly the whole address space on all UNIBUSes. The inverse mapping problem—providing a UNIBUS device access to VAX memory—is handled with a set of mapping registers in each UNIBUS adapter. These registers permit up to 248 Kbyte of VAX memory to be mapped into the address space of a UNIBUS at any one time. (The last 8 Kbyte of each UNIBUS address space, the *I/O page*, are reserved for device control register access.)

Many UNIBUS device controllers support DMA operations. In a DMA operation, the device controller moves data between main memory and the device without the assistance of the CPU. For a DMA operation to be done, the associated I/O buffer must be mapped into the address space of the UNIBUS using the mapping registers. In addition, a *data path* through the UNIBUS adapter must be allocated for use during the operation. Data paths act as a conduit for data transferred between a UNIBUS and the VAX's system bus. UNIBUS adapters support two types of data paths: *buffered* and *unbuffered*. The UNIBUS supports 8- and 16-bit data transfers, whereas the system bus on a VAX uses 32- or 64-bit transfers.

Buffered data paths collect the data from multiple UNIBUS transfers into single operations on the system bus, whereas unbuffered data paths do one system-bus transfer for each unit of data transferred on a UNIBUS. The use of a buffered data path reduces the number of system-bus transfers required during a DMA operation, which in turn reduces the load on the system bus and on the system as a whole. Each UNIBUS adapter provides a number of buffered data paths (from three to 15) that must be scheduled, along with the mapping registers, for each DMA transfer. Unbuffered data paths can be shared by devices, as they maintain no state.

In the next sections, we examine the structure and operation of device drivers for UNIBUS-based devices. The operation of the *up* device driver, a driver for an Emulex SC-21V disk controller, will be used as an example. Following our examination of the *up* device driver, we shall discuss the operation of the UNIBUS adapter-support routines.

The *up* Device Driver

The *up* device driver supports both raw and block-oriented access to multiple disk drives on the SC-21V controller. A variety of drives may be used with the controller; the driver automatically determines the identity and geometry of the drives during autoconfiguration. Aside from the more straightforward tasks of initiating and tracking I/O operations, the device driver also provides a number of reasonably sophisticated features:

- Overlapping seek operations with I/O operations
- Doing ECC correction on data transfers
- Automatically replacing sectors that have been marked as having uncorrectable media flaws with good sectors that are reserved as replacements

The *up* driver is described by entries in the block- and character-device tables. The *bdevsw* entry looks like the following:

```
{ upopen,       /* device open routine */
  nulldev,      /* device close routine */
  upstrategy,   /* i/o strategy routine */
  updump,       /* crash-dump routine */
  upsize        /* partition size routine */
},
```

The close entry point is not needed, so the default system null routine, *nulldev*(), is supplied in its place.

The *cdevsw* entry is similar:

```
{ upopen,   /* device open routine */
  nulldev,  /* device close routine */
  upread,   /* device read routine */
```

```
        upwrite,    /* device write routine */
        nodev,      /* device ioctl routine */
        nodev,      /* device stop routine */
        upreset,    /* device bus-reset routine */
        seltrue,    /* device select routine */
        nodev       /* device mmap routine */
    },
```

It makes use of the kernel default routines *nulldev*() (which returns a success indication) and *nodev*() (which returns an error indication).

Our look at the *up* driver is broken into the three areas described in Section 8.2: autoconfiguration support, routines for servicing I/O requests, and interrupt service routines. We shall concentrate initially on the block-oriented interface to the device, then shall return to consider the simple additions required to support a raw (character-device) interface.

Autoconfiguration Support

The *up* driver supports multiple disk controllers, each of which may have up to four disk drives attached. For the autoconfiguration phase, the driver must supply a *probe routine* to check for the presence of a disk controller, a *slave routine* to check for the presence of a disk drive on a controller, and an *attach routine* to attach each disk drive as that drive's presence is confirmed. To understand how these routines work, we must first understand a little about how the device itself functions.

The SC-21V controller is a DMA device that resides on the UNIBUS. The controller is manipulated through a bank of registers that is located in the UNIBUS I/O page and, through the autoconfiguration facilities, is made directly accessible to the device driver in the kernel's address space. The two most important registers on the controller, for the purposes of our discussion, are the *control status* register and the *drive status* register. The control status register contains controller-related status bits such as *controller ready* and is also used to select a specific drive on a controller when the driver is passing commands such as *start-read-operation* to the controller. The drive status register contains drive-related status information such as *drive on-line*. The content of the drive status register is meaningful only after the completion of a controller command. A no-operation command that completes immediately can be used by the host to poll for a drive's status.

To probe for a controller, the autoconfiguration routines test for the presence of a register at the beginning of the register bank. If a register is present, the autoconfiguration routines call the *upprobe*() routine, passing the address of a controller's register bank. The probe routine sets the controller ready with interrupts enabled and then pauses for a moment to allow the controller time to interrupt the CPU (see Fig. 8.3). After this delay, controller interrupts are disabled and the probe routine returns the size of the controller's register bank. If the controller is present, this sequence will cause it to interrupt the host. The system will

```
int upprobe(devaddr)
    device memory location *devaddr;
{
    force controller interrupt;
    delay 10 milliseconds to allow device interrupt;
    turn off controller interrupt;
    return (size of up register bank);
}
```

Figure 8.3 Algorithm for *up* driver controller probe.

trap the interrupt and will use the interrupt vector to install the *up* interrupt service routine, *upintr*(), in the appropriate entry in the interrupt-vector table. If the address at the beginning of the register bank does not happen to have anything plugged in, the UNIBUS adapter will note the error, and the autoconfiguration code will detect and handle it. If some other device happens to be at that address, the code that forces an interrupt is unlikely to make the other device interrupt.

Presuming that a controller is recognized, it will be assigned a logical unit number, and the bank of registers in the UNIBUS address space associated with the device will be marked as *in-use* (this is the reason *upprobe*() returns the size of its register bank). The autoconfiguration facilities keep track of the portions of the UNIBUS address space that have been allocated to devices to avoid allocation of overlapping regions by two devices.

To probe for a disk drive, the *upslave*() routine, shown in Fig. 8.4, is called. The drive to be checked is indicated by the value of *ui_slave*, a number specified at the time the system was configured. This value is given to the controller and the drive's status is requested from the controller. Depending on the controller's response, *upslave*() returns a value that indicates whether the disk drive was present.

The final routine associated with the autoconfiguration phase is the attach routine, *upattach*(), shown in Fig. 8.5. Attaching a drive involves some minor

Figure 8.4 Algorithm for *up* driver slave probe.

```
boolean upslave(ui, devaddr)
    unibus device *ui;
    device memory location *devaddr;
{
    select drive ui->ui_slave;
    request drive status;
    return (drive is present ? true : false);
}
```

```
upattach(ui)
    unibus device *ui;
{
    set up mapping between unibus device and
        <controller,slave>;
    increment number of drives attached to this controller;
    call upmaptype to figure out type of disk drive;
}
```

Figure 8.5 Algorithm for *up* driver attach.

bookkeeping tasks and one major task—figuring out the type of the drive. The *up* driver maintains a table that it uses to map <*controller*, *slave*> pairs to logical devices. This table is necessary because the *up* driver must be able to locate the data structures associated with a particular drive at interrupt time, given only the controller and slave numbers. In addition to setting up this mapping, the driver counts the number of drives attached to a controller. If two or more drives are found on a controller, then the driver will automatically overlap seek operations with I/O requests.

To deduce the type of disk drive attached to a controller, either the driver requests drive-geometry information from the controller, or, in the 4.3BSD Tahoe release, the driver tries to read a label from the disk with the geometry information in it. If the disk label is read correctly, no further information is needed from the controller. If the label cannot be read successfully, the geometry is deduced from a *personality PROM* on the controller, and is matched against a table of known geometries. If the geometry supplied by the controller matches a known drive's geometry, the drive presumes the associated drive type. Otherwise, a default drive type is supplied—most likely an incorrect one.

The drive type deduced in the attach routine is used to determine several important pieces of information either from the disk label, or, if no disk label exists, from tables compiled into the driver.

- The complete disk geometry: sectors per track, tracks per cylinder, and cylinders per drive. This information is needed to map a logical drive location into a cylinder, track, and sector for each I/O or positioning operation. (Some drives supply all this information directly, but no changes have been made to the general historical procedure for those drives.)
- The drive-partitioning information. Default drive partitions are defined on a per–drive-type basis because they start and end on cylinder boundaries for performance reasons.
- The seek optimization parameters. These parameters are dependent on a drive's physical characteristics; they are described later.

Historically, the drive-dependent information was compiled into the device driver. Recently, many vendors began using disk labels. The 4.3BSD Tahoe distribution has a comprehensive disk label that includes most of the parameters provided in the disk labels of the vendors. Disk labels have many advantages, not the least of which is that removable disk packs and fixed disk drives would be portable. That is, users could take media from one machine to another, or from just one type of controller to another, without having to depend on the software configuration for proper operation. Disk labels also allow each drive to use its own partition layout.

Logical-to-Device Mapping of I/O Requests

All I/O requests to the *up* driver are made through calls to the *upstrategy*() routine. For block-device access, each request to read or write data is encapsulated in a buffer structure allocated from the buffer pool. The block I/O system specifies requests in terms of logical blocks on a logical device. The *up* driver is responsible for mapping these *logical* units into units specific to the destination disk drive. The mapping of logical devices to physical hardware devices is done with data structures created during autoconfiguration. The minor device number specified in the buffer is used to index into a table of pointers to structures, each of which describe a disk drive. This data structure in turn contains a pointer to the structure describing the controller to which the drive is attached (see Fig. 8.6).

To map the logical disk block specified in an I/O request into a physical location on the disk drive, the driver consults partition tables associated with the drive.

Figure 8.6 Mapping of logical units to the physical device.

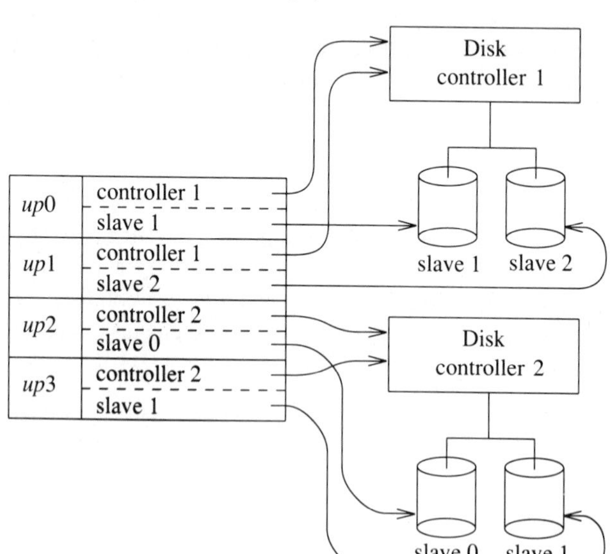

The partition tables define the base and extent of *logical drive partitions* in terms of sectors. The minor device encoding includes a drive partition. To calculate the physical location on the drive at which an I/O operation should commence, the driver simply adds the base offset of the indicated partition to the logical block specified in the buffer. The driver can further specify this location by using the drive-geometry information to calculate the cylinder, track, and sector of the start of the I/O transfer.

I/O Strategy

The *up* driver's strategy routine is passed I/O requests as they arise in normal system operation. The system does not order these requests in any way; it depends on the driver to stage them to the devices in an optimal fashion. Optimal scheduling of disk I/O traffic can be difficult. For most moving-head disk drives, the time to position a drive's read–write head at or near the location of an I/O transfer is normally much longer than the time it takes to transfer the data between the physical medium and memory in the controller. Consequently, the *up* driver strategy routine is mainly concerned with minimizing the time a controller spends waiting to position its read–write heads. When positioning time is minimized, one controller can most effectively be shared among multiple drives. An additional factor here is the implicit assumption that the disk controller is capable of overlapping positioning operations with data-transfer operations. The *up* driver and the Emulex SC-21V are typical: They allow multiple positioning operations to be carried out in parallel with a single transfer operation.

The staging of I/O requests is implemented with a collection of request queues, one per drive and one per controller. As requests come into the driver, they are sorted into the request queue for each drive by the *disksort*() routine, a systemwide utility routine that is used by most disk device drivers. The driver attempts to keep the controller as busy as possible by positioning drives at or near the location of a transfer in an operation separate from the actual transfer. That is, operations on each drive's request queue are first used to initiate a positioning operation on that drive; then, when the drive is positioned, the drive is moved onto the controller queue so that the I/O transfer can be done. Use of this strategy can be costly, however, if all I/O requests require two separate commands be given to the controller, because the completion of each command may require a separate interrupt to the host, and interrupt processing is a relatively costly operation. Consequently, the driver does not do positioning operations for all I/O requests. Instead, only those requests that are likely to allow additional concurrent requests are initiated.

The *upstrategy*() algorithm is shown in Fig. 8.7. The strategy routine utilizes two driver-specific routines, *upustart*() and *upstart*(), and the system's *disksort*() routine. The *upustart*() routine is responsible for deciding whether to initiate a positioning command for a drive and for adding the drive to the controller's request queue when the next I/O request is ready to start its transfer. The *upstart*() routine is responsible for initiating I/O transfers; it simply starts the

```
upstrategy(bp)
    buffer *bp;
{
    validate logical unit;
    check that transfer is within a drive's partition;
    calculate cylinder for transfer;
    raise priority to block upintr;
    call disksort to sort request into drive queue;
    if (drive is inactive) {
        call upustart to start drive;
        if (controller is inactive and drive is ready)
            call upstart to start controller;
    }
    lower priority;
}
```

Figure 8.7 Algorithm for *up* driver I/O strategy.

transfer operation specified by the request for the drive on the front of the controller's queue.

Disksort

The *disksort*() routine is called by disk drivers to sort I/O requests into a drive's request queue using an *elevator sorting algorithm.* This algorithm sorts requests in a cyclic, ascending, cylinder order, so that requests can be serviced with a minimal number of one-way scans over the drive. This ordering was originally designed to support the normal read-ahead requested by the filesystem as well as to counteract the filesystem's random placement of data on a drive. With the improved placement algorithms in the current filesystem, the effect of the *disksort*() routine is less noticeable; it produces the largest effect when there are multiple simultaneous users of a drive.

The *disksort*() algorithm is shown in Fig. 8.8. A drive's request queue is made up of one or two lists of requests ordered by cylinder number. The request at the front of the first list indicates the current position of the drive. If a second list is present, it is made up of requests that lie before the current position. Each new request is sorted into either the first or second list according to the request's location. When the heads reach the end of the first list, the drive begins servicing the other list.

Disksort can also be important on machines that have a fast processor but that do not sort requests within the device driver. In this situation, if a write of several Kbyte is honored in order of queueing, it can block other processes from accessing the disk while it completes. Sorting requests provides some scheduling, which more fairly distributes accesses to the disk controller.

```
disksort(dq, bp)
    drive queue *dq;
    buffer *bp;
{
    if (drive queue is empty) {
        place the buffer at the front of the drive queue;
        return;
    }
    if (request lies before the first active request) {
        locate the beginning of the second request list;
        sort bp into the second request list;
    } else
        sort bp into the current request list;
}
```

Figure 8.8 Algorithm for disksort.

Drive-Positioning Algorithm

The algorithm used by the *upustart*() routine is shown in Fig. 8.9. The basic idea is clear: examine the next request on the drive's request queue. If the drive is not positioned near the location of the request, then initiate a positioning operation. Otherwise, the drive is positioned properly, so place the drive on the controller's queue so that the I/O operation will be done. The only interesting part of the algorithm to consider is the heuristic used in deciding when a drive should be positioned.

The *up* driver maintains two parameters, termed *sdist* and *rdist*, for each type of drive. These parameters are thresholds applied to the rotational distance from the current drive position to the position of the next I/O transfer. If the current position is in the same cylinder as the next transfer and is between *sdist* and *sdist* + *rdist* rotational distances, then no explicit positioning command is requested; instead, positioning is left to be done by the controller at the time the transfer takes place. Otherwise, a *search command* is issued to move the heads to the correct cylinder and then to wait for the sector at a distance of *sdist* from the desired sector.

The *sdist* and *rdist* parameters are chosen according to properties of the disk drive and controller. The goal is to ensure that the controller can complete the next I/O operation before the drive rotates the data past the position of the read–write heads. If the controller is told to initiate an I/O transfer after the starting point of the requested data has passed under the read–write heads, then the controller will be forced to wait for the data to rotate around until they are again under the read–write heads. This condition can be costly to performance, as the time spent waiting for the drive to revolve might have been used for other transfers. The *up* driver's heuristic attempts to ensure that this condition will not occur.

```
upustart(ui)
    unibus device *ui;
{
    if (no request on drive queue) return;
    if (controller is busy) {
        mark device as needing attention when controller is
            idle;
        return;
    }
    if (drive is not positioned over cylinder) {
        mark drive positioned over cylinder;
        if (controller has more than one drive &&
              heads are far from transfer point) {
            select drive;
            position drive at or near location of transfer;
            return;
        }
    }
    place drive on controller queue;
}
```

Figure 8.9 Algorithm for *up* driver unit start.

Many newer disk controllers provide the scheduling optimizations that the *up* driver provides internally. Having the controller make these calculations is a benefit for operating systems that do not directly support these facilities. However, since a disk controller cannot have all the information available to an operating system, there can be instances of anomalous behavior. For example, the controller cannot give synchronous requests a precedence higher than that it gives asynchronous ones.

Initiating an I/O Operation

When the driver decides that an I/O operation should be started, it invokes the *upstart*() routine, as shown in Fig. 8.10. The task of *upstart*() is straightforward: examine the next request on the controller queue and tell the controller to start the I/O operation. On machines where device controllers are directly attached to the main system bus, this is perhaps all that is needed. For the VAX, however, the device driver must call the UNIBUS adapter-resource routines to request resources needed in doing the transfer. The system allocates these resources dynamically, rather than statically at boot time, because many devices on a single bus adapter may together require more resources than are available in an adapter. Furthermore, certain I/O devices require exclusive use of the bus when doing data transfers because the device controller has insufficient data buffering. For these reasons, to initiate a DMA I/O operation, a device driver first sets up all the

```
upstart(ui)
    unibus device *ui;
{
    examine first request on controller queue;
    if (no request to process)
        return;
    mark controller busy and determine destination of request;
    select drive and check that it is ready and on-line;
    set up I/O transfer;
    call ubago to schedule adapter resources for transfer;
}
```

Figure 8.10 Algorithm for *up* driver controller start.

device-specific parameters for a transfer and then calls the *ubago*() routine to allocate resources in the UNIBUS adapter. When resources are available, the *ubago*() routine then calls back to the device driver to begin the I/O transfer. Once a transfer has been started, the work of the driver's strategy routine is complete. All that is left is for the controller to do the transfer and to deliver an interrupt to the host when the transfer is completed. Notice that queueing delays forced by the adapter routines can adversely affect the performance of a system. For this reason, tuning the performance of a VAX system requires careful consideration of the load that I/O devices will place on a UNIBUS.

Interrupt Handling

The *up* driver has a single interrupt service routine, *upintr*(). Interrupts are posted by the controller as each I/O or positioning operation completes. The interrupt-handling algorithm is shown in Fig. 8.11.

Interrupts may arrive for either I/O or positioning operations, but positioning interrupts that occur during a transfer operation will be deferred until the transfer operation is completed. So *upintr*() must check whether an I/O operation is pending, and if one is, must check the operation's completion status. Then, it scans for drives that have completed search operations. The *upustart*() routine is called to schedule the next operation on each drive that has completed its current request.

When an I/O request has been completed, *upintr*() notifies the process that requested the I/O operation by calling the *biodone*() routine. This routine wakes up the blocked process, frees the buffer for an asynchronous write, or, for a request by the *pagedaemon* process, invokes a procedure specified in the buffer structure.

Aside from the handling of successful I/O operations, the interrupt service routine is also responsible for handling the many types of errors that can occur. Although certain errors are unrecoverable, others may be handled by the device driver. Two errors in particular that the device driver will attempt to correct are requests that have a short error burst in the data transferred, and requests for

```
upintr(cntrl)
    controller *cntrl;
{
    if (controller was doing a transfer) {
        get buffer associated with transfer;
        select drive and check drive and controller status;
        process errors on either drive or controller;
        if (operation completed) {
            take request off controller queue;
            record transfer status;
            call biodone to notify I/O is complete;
            if (this drive has more operations pending)
                call upustart to start next
                    operation on drive;
        }
        release unibus resources used for transfer;
    }
    for (each drive with a completed seek)
        call upustart to start next operation on drive;
    if (devices are ready to transfer)
        call upstart to start next operation on controller;
}
```

Figure 8.11 Algorithm for *up* driver interrupt handling.

which the data have been placed in an alternate location on the drive. Recovery from the first type of error is done with an error-correction code (ECC) supplied by the controller to correct the data transferred by the controller. Recovery from the second type of error requires that the device driver look up the *bad sector* in a *bad-sector table* to locate the alternate sector. If the faulty sector is found in the bad-sector table, the driver initiates a transfer from the alternate location and returns those data as though they had been at the location originally requested.

The two error-recovery mechanisms described here are commonly termed *ECC correction* and *bad-sector forwarding*. Most current disk controllers provide both of these recovery schemes built into the controller. Bad-sector forwarding can be implemented in several ways. One scheme reserves a single region on a disk for mapping sectors with uncorrectable flaws. This region typically consists of several cylinders near the end of the drive. The problem with this method is that, when a bad sector is identified, the alternate sector may be located far away from the current position. Thus, accessing the alternate sector is a time-consuming positioning operation. To address this problem, a second scheme, termed *slip-sector forwarding*, is often used. Instead of one contiguous region being reserved, one sector on each track is reserved. In this scheme, an alternate *slip sector* can be used to replace a bad sector with at most a delay of a single disk revolution to reach the alternate sector. However, if more than one sector goes bad on a track, there is no way to remap the second sector that fails. Manufacturers commonly study the statistical failure properties of disk-drive media to determine, for example, how many slip sectors to allocate on a track and how many cylinders to reserve on a drive. Hybrid schemes that incorporate both approaches have been used as well; these tend to be the most effective, but can be costly to implement entirely within a controller. In general, bad-sector handling can have a noticeable effect on performance, but is preferable to discarding equipment (especially as current disk drives seldom have flawless media).

Adding raw access to the *up* driver is simple. All that is needed are two routines, *upread*() and *upwrite*(), and a set of buffers for doing raw I/O. The read and write routines simply invoke the *physio*() routine as described in Section 8.4.

UNIBUS Adapter Support Routines

The UNIBUS adapter routines provide two major functions in supporting drivers written for UNIBUS devices:

1. They manage each adapter's resources, dynamically allocating portions to drivers so the drivers can do DMA transfers.
2. They watch for adapter failures, resetting the adapter's state when the adapter reports a serious or recurrent error.

(The second function was required by the initial instability of UNIBUS adapters; this function is needed less frequently today.)

Each UNIBUS adapter has a set of registers that is used to map pages of memory into the address space of the UNIBUS. There are 496 such registers, each mapping one 512-byte page, enough to map 248 Kbyte of memory. The remaining 8 Kbyte of each UNIBUS address space is reserved for UNIBUS device registers. For a DMA transfer between main memory and a UNIBUS peripheral to be done, the I/O buffer must be mapped into the UNIBUS address space with a contiguous set of mapping registers, and a *buffered* or *unbuffered* data path must be allocated for use during the transfer. Buffered data paths cannot be shared by multiple devices doing DMA; thus, their use must be scheduled on a per-transfer basis.

I/O operations through a UNIBUS adapter are done in three steps:

1. Allocate resources for an operation
2. Initiate the operation
3. On notification that the operation has completed, release the resources allocated in step 1

The work of steps 1 and 3 is normally hidden inside the *ubago*() and *ubadone*() routines, respectively. The work of step 2 is device-specific and is carried out by a device driver's *go routine*, which is automatically invoked when resources have been allocated for an operation.

```
boolean ubago(ui)
    unibus device *ui;
{
    locate unibus adapter for device;
    raise priority to spluba;
    if (device needs exclusive use of adapter and other
        users exist || adapter is exclusively in use)
        goto resource_wait;
    call ubasetup to allocate unibus adapter resources for
        transfer (indicate no wait is to be done in the
            routine);
    if (not all resources were available)
        goto resource_wait;
    increment number of users of adapter;
    if (device needs exclusive use of adapter)
        mark adapter as exclusively in use;
    lower priority;
    if (this device was previously on adapter's waiting queue)
        remove device entry from adapter queue;
    call device's go routine to start operation;
    return (true);

resource_wait:
    place device on queue of devices awaiting adapter
        resources;
    lower priority;
    return (false);
}
```

Figure 8.12 Algorithm for scheduling a UNIBUS I/O operation.

The algorithm used by *ubago*() is shown in Fig. 8.12. Device drivers allocate resources implicitly through the call to the *ubasetup*() routine (the algorithm used by *ubasetup*() is shown in Fig. 8.13). If a device requires exclusive use of an adapter, or the adapter is currently in use by a device that requires exclusive access, then the device is placed on a queue of waiting devices maintained for each adapter. Similarly, if resources are currently unavailable, the device is placed on the adapter's queue.

When a driver receives an interrupt and releases resource through a call to *ubadone*() (see Fig. 8.14), the adapter's queue is scanned. Each device that is present on the queue is given another chance to allocate resources and to initiate its I/O operation. Processes that are blocked inside of *ubasetup*() awaiting resources are awakened to try again.

There is some subtlety in the implementation of these algorithms. The adapter routines must take care to guard against a bus reset that is caused by an

```
boolean ubasetup(number, bp, flags)
    unibus adapter number;
    buffer *bp;
    int flags;
{
    calculate number of adapter mapping registers needed for
        transfer;
    raise priority to spluba;
    while (mapping registers are unavailable) {
        if (flags indicate caller cannot wait) {
            lower priority;
            return (false);
        }
        increment count of waiters for mapping registers;
        block to await mapping registers;
    }
    allocate mapping registers required;
    if (a buffered data path is required) {
        while (no buffered data path is available) {
            if (flags indicate caller cannot wait) {
                release allocated
                    mapping registers;
                lower priority;
                return (false);
            }
            increment count of waiters for
                buffered data paths;
            block to await a buffered data path;
        }
        allocate a buffered data path;
    }
    lower priority;
    record allocated adapter resources;
    calculate physical location of data buffer;
    set up adapter mapping registers to point to data buffer;
    return (true);
}
```

Figure 8.13 Algorithm to allocate UNIBUS adapter resources.

unrecoverable adapter error or by a timeout on an I/O operation. When a reset occurs, any resources currently allocated for an I/O operation are reclaimed directly by the UNIBUS adapter reset routine. Thus, *ubarelse*() (see Fig. 8.15) must take care when freeing resources so that resources are not deallocated twice. To avoid this problem, *ubarelse*() raises the processor priority to *spluba* while it

```
ubadone(um)
    unibus controller *um;
{
    locate unibus adapter for controller;
    if (device required exclusive use of adapter)
        mark adapter as no longer in exclusive use;
    decrement number of users of adapter;
    call ubarelse to release resources used in transfer;
}
```

Figure 8.14 Algorithm for completing a UNIBUS I/O operation.

is releasing resources so it can block the bus-adapter reset routine that is invoked as the result of a UNIBUS adapter interrupt. Because the priority level during deallocation is raised, *ubarelse*() can do a consistency check on the resources it is freeing and can free them before the resources may be deallocated by the bus reset routine.

Figure 8.15 Algorithm for releasing UNIBUS adapter resources.

```
ubarelse(number, mapptr)
    unibus adapter number;
    mapping register pointer *mapptr;
{
    raise priority to spluba;
    if (buffered data path was used) {
        free data path;
        if (there are waiters for buffered data paths) {
            zero the count of waiters;
            wake up all processes waiting for a
                buffered data path;
        }
    }
    deallocate mapping registers used;
    lower priority;
    if (there are waiters for mapping registers) {
        zero the count of waiters;
        wake up all processes waiting for mapping registers;
    }
    while (there are requests queued for the adapter) {
        if (call ubago indicates operation could not be done)
            break;
    }
}
```

8.7 MASSBUS Devices

DEC designed the MASSBUS as an I/O bus for higher-speed mass-storage peripherals than could be supported by the UNIBUS. The MASSBUS has a greater bandwidth than does the UNIBUS, but it also has a more rigid structure. A MASSBUS can support at most eight devices, with only one at a time transferring data. The only devices available for a MASSBUS are disks and tapes. Tape formatters can each support up to eight tape transports. Each MASSBUS on a VAX is connected to the system bus via a *MASSBUS adapter*. Since the MASSBUS design supports higher transfer rates than those the UNIBUS supports, some vendors have designed device controllers that connect directly to the system bus and emulate a MASSBUS adapter.

The rigid structure of the MASSBUS permits a significant portion of each MASSBUS device driver to be isolated in a common set of *MASSBUS adapter-support routines*. These routines manage most of the I/O request queueing and interpose their own interrupt service routines between the devices and the device drivers. MASSBUS device drivers differ from UNIBUS device drivers in the way they schedule adapter resources for each DMA operation. The complicated resource scheduling required for a UNIBUS adapter is not needed, because the MASSBUS allows only one device to transfer data at a time. The use of a single data path simplifies I/O scheduling but can potentially add queueing delays.

Autoconfiguration

MASSBUS devices are probed and attached in a fashion similar to that used for UNIBUS devices. The major difference is that MASSBUS devices can be probed in a device-independent fashion because certain controller status registers in a MASSBUS adapter are defined with standard bit assignments. This means that a single MASSBUS probe routine can be written that identifies each of the eight possible devices on a MASSBUS adapter. Only the identification of tape transports must be handled on a per-device basis. Thus, autoconfiguration support in a MASSBUS device driver is reduced to an attach routine and, if the device is a tape controller, to a slave routine.

I/O Strategy

The only MASSBUS devices are tape and disk controllers. As these devices provide only raw and block-oriented interfaces, all I/O requests eventually pass through a device driver's strategy routine. Unlike scheduling in the *up* device driver, the I/O scheduling for MASSBUS devices is done mostly in the MASSBUS adapter-support routines. For example, the *htstrategy*() routine for the *ht* magnetic-tape device, shown in Fig. 8.16, is simple: It just places each request at the end of the transport's request queue and, if the transport is not currently active, calls the MASSBUS adapter-support routine *mbustart*() to start activity on the unit.

The I/O request scheduling algorithm is structured much like the algorithm used in the *up* driver. A MASSBUS adapter unit start routine, *mbustart*(), is called

```
htstrategy(bp)
    buffer *bp;
{
    raise priority to splbio;
    if (request queue for this tape transport is empty)
        place bp at the front of the queue;
    else
        place bp at the end of the queue;
    if (tape transport is not active)
        call mbustart to start an operation on transport;
    lower priority;
}
```

Figure 8.16 Algorithm for *ht* driver strategy.

by a device driver after one or more operations have been placed on the device's request queue. The *mbustart*() routine takes the operation at the head of the device's request queue and *calls back* to the device driver's *unit start routine* to initiate the operation. The unit start routine carries out whatever actions are needed for the specified request and then returns an indication that one of the following occurred:

- The request completed immediately (e.g., a *sense* operation on a tape drive).
- The request could not be completed because the device was busy (e.g., a dual-ported disk drive was servicing its other port at the time of the request).
- The request was started (for a non-data transfer operation).
- The request involved a data transfer and the device should be scheduled for access to the single data path on the MASSBUS adapter.

In the case of a data transfer, the device is placed on the MASSBUS adapter's data-transfer request queue and, if the adapter's data path is idle, the unit start routine starts the transfer immediately by calling the *mbstart*() routine.

The *mbstart*() routine is functionally similar to the *ubago*() routine described in the previous section. Unlike operations on UNIBUS adapters, however, the I/O operations are initiated in the *mbstart*() routine rather than in the device-driver start routine. This is possible because the register banks for all MASSBUS devices have a command register at a known location.

To begin a transfer, the driver's start routine is first invoked to fill in drive-specific registers and to determine the value to be placed in the device's command register. Then the data buffer is mapped into the MASSBUS address space so that the device can access the associated data buffer, and finally the command supplied by the driver's start routine is placed in the command register to initiate the operation.

Interrupt Handling

Interrupts by MASSBUS devices generate a single MASSBUS adapter interrupt to the CPU. The MASSBUS adapter interrupt service routine is invoked with the

```
mbintr(number)
    massbus adapter number;
{
    retrieve device status from massbus adapter;
    if (adapter was active doing a data transfer) {
        identify device that was transferring data;
        call device's data transfer complete interrupt
            routine;
        switch (status of data transfer) {
        case transfer done:
            remove request from device request queue;
            notify process that initiated operation;
            /* fall through... */
        case retry transfer because of error:
            remove request from adapter request queue;
            mark adapter not active doing data transfer;
            if (device's request queue is not empty)
                call mbustart to start device's next
                    operation;
            break;
        }
    }
    for (each device needing attention) {
        if (device has nondata transfer interrupt routine) {
            call device's nondata transfer interrupt routine;
            switch (status of nondata transfer) {
            case operation completed:
                remove request from device request queue;
                notify process that initiated operation;
                /* fall through... */
            case retry operation because of error:
                if (device's request queue is not empty)
                    call mbustart to start device's next
                    operation;
                break;
            }
        } else {
            call mbustart to start device's next operation;
        }
    }
    if ((the adapter request queue is not empty) &&
        (adapter is not marked as doing a data transfer))
        call mbstart to initiate next I/O operation;
}
```

Figure 8.17 Algorithm for MASSBUS adapter interrupt handling.

identity of the interrupting MASSBUS adapter, and must read a status register in the adapter to find out which devices require service. The interrupt-processing algorithm for a MASSBUS adapter is shown in Fig. 8.17. Each device driver may supply two interrupt service routines, one for operations that involve data transfer and one for operations that do not involve data transfer. Both types of routines must return a status code that indicates whether an operation has completed or needs to be retried because of an error (additional status codes exist that are not important to our discussion). The MASSBUS interrupt service routine uses these status codes to drive a *finite-state machine* that controls the scheduling of operations through the adapter.

Exercises

8.1 Would you expect a cartridge tape drive to have a block or character interface? Why?

8.2 Why do filesystem utilities such as **fsck** usually use the character-device interface to access disk drives?

8.3 Why are interrupt service routines running in the bottom half of the kernel precluded from calling the *sleep*() routine?

8.4 What responsibilities do device probe routines have during the autoconfiguration phase of system startup?

8.5 Explain the purpose and operation of the glue routines that 4.3BSD installs in the interrupt-vector table.

8.6 Why are two lists used by the *disksort*() routine in ordering I/O requests for a disk drive?

8.7 Adapter queueing of I/O requests destined for a UNIBUS or MASSBUS device can ruin disk-drive scheduling done by the device driver. What are the tradeoffs between doing seek optimization in device drivers and doing seek optimization in a disk controller?

8.8 Most hardware devices permit only one I/O operation at a time. How is this limit enforced by 4.3BSD?

8.9 Suppose you wanted to modify the *up* device driver for a disk controller that handles multiple simultaneous I/O requests. What assumptions in the I/O queueing structure of the driver would you have to change?

8.10 The device *open*() routine is called for each *open* system call, but the device *close*() routine is called on only the last close on a device. Why were these semantics chosen? Give an example of a device where these semantics cause problems.

8.11 What function does a UNIBUS adapter provide to support the connection of a UNIBUS on a VAX?

8.12 The *upprobe*() routine, shown in Fig. 8.3, waits for 10 milliseconds to allow the device to interrupt. How could you implement this delay? How would the CPU's performance affect the implementation that you have selected?

8.13 Why does 4.3BSD interpret the minor device number as a logical rather than as a physical device unit number?

8.14 Describe what a disk driver must do to support overlapped seeks. What is ECC correction? What is bad-sector forwarding? What is a slip sector?

8.15 Explain how the *sdist* and *rdist* parameters are used in the *up* disk driver.

8.16 Why does 4.3BSD require all UNIBUS device drivers to stage I/O operations through the UNIBUS adapter routines?

8.17 Why are the MASSBUS adapter routines able to do more work than are the UNIBUS adapter routines?

8.18 In the *physio*() routine shown in Fig. 8.1, the processor priority is raised to *splbio* before the content of the buffer header is used. Why is it necessary to raise the processor priority level?

*8.19 In the *physio*() routine shown in Fig. 8.1, the processor priority is raised and lowered several times. Could you instead raise the level once on entry and lower it on exit? Explain your answer.

*8.20 The disk label, containing the drive geometry and logical partitions, is read in by the disk driver when the first partition on a disk is opened. Where must the disk label be located? Why must it be in that place?

*8.21 Some operating systems allow device drivers to be loaded into a running system. What are the tradeoffs of this scheme?

*8.22 Suppose a device did not use vectored interrupts, but instead asserted the interrupt signal until it was told to stop. What implications would this have for the way 4.3BSD handles interrupts on the VAX? How would this affect the autoconfiguration scheme?

*8.23 Describe the interaction between the algorithms used by the filesystem to place data on a disk drive and the I/O scheduling algorithms embodied in the *disksort*() routine.

**8.24 Construct a model for disk-drive scheduling that you can use to calculate accurate values for the *sdist* and *rdist* parameters used by the *up* driver. How does the speed of the CPU affect your model?

**8.25 Describe an alternative scheme for managing UNIBUS resources during a bus reset.

**8.26 Consider a shared-memory multiprocessor architecture in which all devices are accessible on all processors. What changes to the I/O system and device drivers would be required to permit I/O operations to be managed by any processor?

CHAPTER 9

Terminal Handling

One of the most common types of hardware peripheral device found on UNIX systems is an interface supporting one or more terminals. The most common type of interface is a *terminal multiplexer*, a device that connects multiple asynchronous RS-232 serial lines, which may be used to connect terminals, modems, printers, and similar devices. Unlike the block storage devices described in Chapter 8 and the network devices to be considered in Chapter 11, terminal devices often process data one character at a time. Like other devices, terminal multiplexers are controlled by device drivers specific to the actual hardware.

Terminal interfaces interrupt the processor asynchronously to present input, which is independent of process requests to read user input. Data are processed when they are received, and then are stored until a process requests them, thus allowing *type-ahead*. Most terminal ports are used to attach local or remote terminals on which users may log in to the system. When used in this way, terminal input represents the keystrokes of users, and terminal output is printed on the users' screens or printers. We shall deal mostly with this type of terminal line usage in this chapter. Asynchronous serial lines are also used to connect modems for computer-to-computer communications or serial-interface printers. When serial interfaces are used for these purposes, they generally use a subset of the system's terminal-handling capability. In some cases, they use special processing modules for higher efficiency. We shall discuss alternate terminal modules later in this chapter.

9.1 Terminal Processing Modes

4.3BSD UNIX supports several modes of terminal processing. Much of the time, terminals are in *line mode* or *cooked mode*, in which input characters are echoed by the system as they are typed, and are collected until a carriage return is received. Only after the receipt of a carriage return is the entire line made available to the shell or other process reading from the terminal line. In line mode, the user may correct typing errors, deleting the most recently typed character with the *erase character*, deleting the last word with the *word-erase character*, or deleting the entire current line with the *kill character*. Other special characters generate signals sent to the current processes associated with the terminal; these signals may abort processing or may suspend it. Additional characters start and stop output, flush output, or prevent special interpretation of the succeeding character. The user can type several lines of input, up to an implementation-defined limit, without waiting for input to be read and then removed from the input queue. The user can select the special processing characters or even selectively disable them.

Screen editors and programs that communicate with other computers generally run in *character-at-a-time mode*. The system supports two such modes. In *cbreak mode*, the system makes each typed character available to be read as input as soon as that character is received, and thus erase and kill processing are not done. Other special characters are processed normally, allowing signals and flow control as in line mode. The other character-at-a-time mode is *raw mode*, in which all special character input processing is disabled; all characters are passed to the program reading from the terminal.

In addition to processing input characters, terminal interface drivers must do certain processing on output. Most of the time, this processing is quite simple. UNIX newlines are converted to a carriage return plus a line feed, and the interface hardware is programmed to generate appropriate parity bits on output characters. Some terminals require extra time to process characters that produce motion such as carriage return, newline, and tab; thus, the terminal driver may be set to insert a delay after each such character. In addition to character processing, the terminal output routines must manage flow control, both with the user (using stop and start characters) and with the process. As terminal devices are quite slow in comparison with other computer peripherals, a program writing to the terminal may produce output much faster than that output can be sent to the terminal. The process must thus be blocked when it has filled the terminal output queue, and must be restarted when sufficient output has drained.

9.2 Line Disciplines

Most of the character processing done for terminal interfaces is independent of the type of hardware device used to connect the terminals to the computer. Therefore, most of this processing is done by common routines in the *tty driver* or terminal handler. Each hardware interface type is supported by a specific device driver. The hardware driver is a device driver like those described in the previous chapter; it is responsible for programming the hardware multiplexer. It is responsible for receiving and transmitting characters and for handling some of the synchronization with the process doing output. The hardware driver is called by the tty driver to do output; in turn, it calls the tty driver with input characters as they

Table 9.1 Entry points of a line discipline.

Routine	Called from	Usage
l_open	above	initial entry to discipline
l_close	above	exit from discipline
l_read	above	read from line
l_write	above	write to line
l_ioctl	above	control operations
l_rint	below	received character
l_rend	none	unused
l_meta	none	unused
l_start	below	completion of transmission
l_modem	below	modem carrier transition

are received. Because serial lines may be used for more than just connection of terminals, a modular interface between the hardware driver and the tty driver allows either part to be replaced with alternate versions. The tty driver interfaces with the rest of the system as a *line discipline.* A line discipline is a processing module used to provide semantics on an asynchronous serial interface (or, as we shall see, on a software emulation of such an interface). It is described by a procedural interface, the *linesw* (line switch) structure.

The *linesw* structure specifies the entry points of a line discipline, much as the character-device switch *cdevsw* lists the entry points of a character device driver. Like all device drivers, a terminal multiplexer driver is divided into the top half, which runs synchronously when called to process a system call, and the bottom half, which runs asynchronously when device interrupts occur. The line discipline provides routines that do common terminal processing for both the top and bottom halves of a terminal hardware driver. The entry points of a line discipline are listed in Table 9.1.

Device drivers for serial terminal interfaces support the normal set of character-device-driver entry points specified by the character-device switch. Several of the standard driver entry points (*read*, *write*, and *ioctl*) immediately transfer control to the line discipline when called. (The standard tty select routine *ttselect*() usually is used as the device driver *select* entry in the character-device switch.) The *open* and *close* routines are similar; the line-discipline open entry is called when a line first enters a discipline, either at initial open of the line or when the discipline is changed. Similarly, the discipline close routine is called to exit from a discipline. All these routines are called from above, in response to a corresponding system call. The remaining line-discipline entries are called by the bottom half of the device driver to report input or status changes detected at interrupt time. The *l_rint* (receiver interrupt) entry is called with each character received on a line. The corresponding entry for transmit-complete interrupts is the *l_start* routine, which is called when output operations complete. This entry gives the line discipline a chance to start additional output operations. For the normal terminal line discipline, this routine simply calls the driver's output routine to start the next block of output. Transitions in modem control lines (see Section 9.7) may be detected by the hardware driver, in which case the *l_modem* routine is called with an indication of the new state.

The system includes several different types of line disciplines. Most lines use one of the two terminal-oriented disciplines described in the next section. Other disciplines in the system support graphics tablets on serial lines and asynchronous serial network interfaces.

9.3 User Interface

The terminal line discipline used by default on most terminal lines is derived from the discipline present in UNIX 32V and Seventh Edition UNIX. The user interface to this line discipline, known as the *old terminal driver*, is still present in 4.3BSD. An extension of the old driver was added to the system beginning with 4.1BSD to support new signals for job control and to provide logical line-editing facilities on CRT terminals. The extended driver, called the *new terminal driver*, retains the interface of the old driver but adds new options and modes to the previous set. Several of the options added in the new driver modify basic modes of the previously existing driver, thus creating a rather cluttered interface. Both new and old terminal line disciplines are implemented by the same terminal driver, which changes its behavior according to the current discipline.

The main user interface for control of the terminal line discipline is the *ioctl* system call. This call is used to change disciplines, to set and get values for special processing characters and modes, to set and get hardware serial line parameters and to do other control operations. Most *ioctl* operations require one argument in addition to a file descriptor and the command; the argument is the address of an integer or structure from which the system gets parameters, or into which return information is placed. The following set of *ioctl* commands apply specifically to the standard terminal line disciplines, although all line disciplines must support at least the first two. Other disciplines generally support other *ioctl* commands.

TIOCGETD	Get the identity of the line discipline for this line as an integer constant
TIOCSETD	Set the discipline for this line
TIOCGETP	Get the basic (old terminal driver) parameters for this line, including line speed, basic modes, and erase and kill characters
TIOCSETP	Set the basic parameters for this line
TIOCSETN	Set the basic parameters for this line without flushing input

TIOCGETC	Get values of the basic set of special characters (other than erase and kill)
TIOCSETC	Set the values of the special characters supported by the old terminal driver (other than erase and kill)
TIOCLGET	Get (set, add, delete) the *local* options—those used in only the new terminal driver
TIOCLSET	
TIOCLBIS	
TIOCLBIC	
TIOCGLTC	Get (set) the *local* special characters—those used by only the new terminal driver
TIOCSLTC	
TIOCGWINSZ	Get (set) the terminal or window size for the terminal line; the window size includes width and height in characters and (optionally, on graphical displays) in pixels
TIOCSWINSZ	

This set of terminal *ioctl* commands illustrates the gradual growth of the set of options supported by the terminal interface.

The parameters set by TIOCSETP and TIOCLSET include flags that modify the behavior of the terminal line. In particular, two flags (RAW and CBREAK) control the overall mode of the tty, and others control additional features or modify the overall mode. The RAW flag sets the terminal in *raw* mode; the CBREAK flag sets the terminal in *cbreak* mode; with neither flag set, the terminal is in *cooked* mode, the normal, line-at-a-time mode.

9.4 The *tty* Structure

Each terminal hardware driver contains a data structure to contain the state of each line that it supports. This structure, the *tty structure*, contains state information, the input and output queues, the modes and options set by the *ioctl* operations listed previously, and the line discipline number (see Table 9.2). The *tty* structure is shared by the hardware driver and the line discipline. The calls to the line discipline all require a *tty* structure as a parameter; the driver locates the correct *tty* according to the minor device number. This structure also contains information about the device driver needed by the line discipline.

The sections of the *tty* structure include

- State information about the hardware terminal line. The *t_state* field includes line state (open, carrier present, or waiting for carrier) and major file options

Table 9.2 The *tty* structure.

Type	Description
Character queues	Raw input queue
	Canonical input queue
	Device output queue
Hardware parameters	Device number
	Output procedure
	Terminal column number
Selecting	Process selecting for reading
	Process selecting for writing
State	Process group
	Flags
	Line discipline
	Number of rows and columns
	Input and output baud rates
	Special characters on input

(use of nonblocking I/O or signal-driven I/O). Transient state for flow control, delay processing, and synchronization also is stored here.

- Input and output queues. The hardware driver transmits characters placed in the output queue. Line disciplines generally use the *t_rawq* and *t_canq* (canonicalized queue) for input; in line mode, the canonical queue contains full lines, and the raw queue contains any current partial line. Line disciplines that do not use *t_rawq* and *t_canq* sometimes overlay this area with a different form of receive buffer.

- Hardware and software modes and parameters. The *t_flags* word contains modes set by both TIOCSETP and TIOCLSET. The line speeds set by TIOCSETP are placed in *t_ispeed* and *t_ospeed*.

- The line-discipline number (*t_line*).

- Special characters. The characters that require special actions are all stored in *t_tchars*. These characters are set with TIOCSETP (erase and kill), TIOCSETC (interrupt, quit, start, stop, end-of-file, and alternate end-of-line), and TIOCSLTC (suspend, delayed suspend, reprint-line, flush-output, word-erase, and escape-next-character).

- Hardware driver information. This information includes *t_oproc*, the driver procedure that starts transmissions after data are placed in the output queue; *t_addr*, the address of hardware-related data structures or registers; and *t_dev*, the device number of the terminal line.

- Terminal line-discipline software state. This includes the terminal column number and counts for tab and erase processing (*t_col*, *t_rocount* and *t_rocol*), the process group of the terminal (*t_pgrp*), and the identity of any processes selecting for input or output (*t_rsel* and *t_wsel*).
- Terminal or window size (*t_winsize*). This information is not used by the kernel, but it is stored here to present a consistent interface. In addition, 4.3BSD supplies the SIGWINCH signal (derived from Sun Microsystems' SunOS) that can be sent when the size of a window changes. This is useful for windowing packages such as X Window System [Scheifler & Gettys, 1986] that allow users to resize windows dynamically; programs such as text editors running in such a window need to be informed that something has changed and that they should recheck the window size.

The *tty* structure is initialized by the hardware terminal driver's open routine and by the line-discipline open routine.

9.5 Process Groups and Terminal Control

The process-control (job-control) facilities described in Chapter 4 depend on the terminal I/O system to control access to the terminal. Each job (a group of processes that are controlled together) is known by a process-group number. Each terminal structure contains a process-group number as well. The shell and the terminal are assigned to a process group (the shell's PID) when the terminal is first opened. Signals that are generated by characters typed at the terminal are sent to all the processes in the terminal's current process group. Some of those signals cause the process group to stop. The shell sets the process-group number for each job to be the PID of one of the group's members; each time it places a new job in the foreground, the shell sets the terminal process group to that of the new process group. Thus, the terminal process group is the identifier for the process group that is currently in control of the terminal—that is, for the process group running in the *foreground*. Other process groups may run in the *background*. If a process in such a group attempts to read from the terminal, its process group is sent another signal, which stops the process group. Optionally, background processes that attempt terminal output may be stopped as well. Each process holds a pointer to its controlling terminal (if it has one); these rules for control of input and output operations apply to only those operations on the controlling terminal.

Earlier systems without job control used the process group in a different way; similar behavior occurs in 4.3BSD when a login shell that does not support job control is used. The shell and the terminal are initially assigned to the same process group. New processes started by such a shell remain in the same group. A process group therefore identifies all the processes initiated from the same login shell when job control is not in use.

9.6 C-lists

The terminal I/O system deals with data in blocks of widely varying sizes. Most input and output operations deal with single characters (typed input characters and their output echoes). Input characters are usually aggregated with previous input to form lines of varying sizes. Some output operations involve larger numbers of data, such as screen updates or other command output. The data structures originally designed for terminal drivers, the character block, *C-block*, and character list, *C-list*, are still in use in 4.3BSD. Each C-block is a fixed-size, aligned buffer that contains a linkage pointer and space for buffered characters. Its size is always a power of two, so that the system can compute boundaries between blocks by masking off the low-order bits of a pointer. 4.3BSD uses 64-byte C-blocks storing 60 characters; earlier systems used buffers of 32 bytes. A queue of input or output characters is described by a C-list, which contains pointers to the first and last characters, and a count of the number of characters in the queue (see Fig. 9.1). Both of the pointers point to characters stored in C-blocks. When a character is removed from a C-list queue, the count is decremented and the pointer to the first character is incremented. If the pointer has advanced beyond the end of the first C-block on the queue, the pointer to the next C-block is obtained from the forward pointer at the start of the current C-block. After the forward pointer is updated, the empty C-block is placed on a free chain. A similar process is used to add a character to a queue. If there is no room in the current buffer, another buffer is allocated from the free list, the linkage pointer of the last buffer is set to point at the new buffer, and the tail pointer is set to the first storage location of the new buffer. The character is stored where indicated by the tail pointer, the tail pointer is incremented, and the character count is incremented. A set of utility routines manipulates C-lists: *getc*() removes the next character from a C-list and returns it; *putc*() adds a character to the end of a C-list. Groups of characters may be added to or removed from C-lists with *b_to_q*() and *q_to_b*(), respectively. The terminal driver also requires the abilities to remove a character

Figure 9.1 A C-list structure.

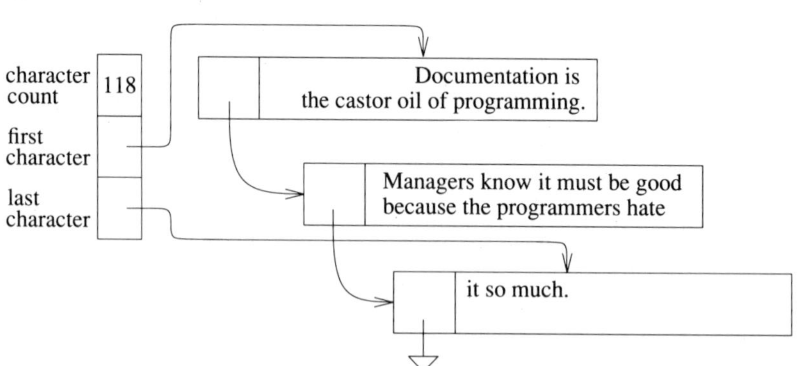

from the end of a queue with *unputc*(), to examine characters in the queue with *nextc*(), and to concatenate queues with *catq*().

When UNIX was developed on computers with small address spaces, the design of buffers for the use of terminal drivers was a challenge. The C-list and C-block provided an elegant solution to the problem of storing arbitrary-length queues of data for terminal input and output queues when the latter were designed for machines with small memories. On machines such as the VAX that have larger address spaces, it would be better to use a data structure that uses less CPU time per character at a cost of reduced space efficiency. The VAX still uses the original C-list data structure because of the high labor cost of converting to a new data structure; a change to the queue structure would require modification of all the line disciplines and all the terminal device drivers, which would be a substantial amount of work. One could just change the implementations of the interface routines, but the routines would still be called once per character unless the actual interface was changed, and changing the interface would require changing the drivers.

9.7 RS-232 and Modem Control

Most terminals and modems are connected via asynchronous RS-232 serial ports. This type of connection supports several lines in addition to those that transmit and receive data. UNIX usually supports only a few of these lines. The most commonly used lines are those showing that the equipment on each end is ready for data transfer. The RS-232 electrical specification is asymmetrical; each line is driven by one of the two devices connected and is sampled by the other device. Thus, one end in any normal connection must be wired as data terminal equipment (DTE), such as a terminal, and the other as data communications equipment (DCE), such as a modem. Note that *terminal* in DTE means *endpoint*: A terminal on which people type is a DTE, and a computer also is a DTE. The data terminal ready (DTR) line is the output of the DTE end that serves as a *ready* indicator. In the other direction, the data carrier detect (DCD) line indicates that the DCE device is ready for data transfer. VAX terminal interfaces are all wired as DTE (they may be directly connected to modems, or connected to local terminals with null modem cables). Therefore, the terminology used in the 4.3BSD terminal drivers and commands reflects this orientation, even though many computers incorrectly use the opposite convention.

When terminal devices are opened, the DTR output is asserted so that the connected modem or other equipment may begin operation. If *modem control* is supported on a line, the open does not complete, and no data are transferred until the DCD input *carrier* is detected. Thus, an open on a line connected to a modem will block until a connection is made, which commonly occurs when a call is received from a remote modem. Data may then be transferred as long as carrier remains on. If the modem loses the connection, the DCD line is turned off, and subsequent reads and writes fail.

Ports that are used with local terminals or other DTE equipment are connected with a *null modem* cable that connects DTR on each end to DCD on the other end.

Alternatively, the DTR output on the host port can be *looped back* to the DCD input. Finally, the driver may be configured to ignore modem-control inputs.

9.8 Terminal Operations

Now that we have examined the overall structure of the terminal I/O system and have described that system's data structures, as well as the hardware it controls, we continue with a description of its operation. We shall examine the operation of a generalized terminal hardware device driver and the normal terminal line discipline. We shall not cover the autoconfiguration routines present in each driver, as they function in the same way as do those described in Chapter 8.

Open

Each time the special file for a terminal-character device is opened, the hardware driver's open routine is called. The open routine checks that the requested device was configured into the system and was located during autoconfiguration, then initializes the *tty* structure. If the device was not yet open, the default modes and line speed are set. The *tty* state is set to TS_WOPEN, waiting for open. Then, if the device supports modem-control lines, the open routine enables the DTR output line, and blocks awaiting assertion of the DCD input line. Most drivers support *device flags* to override modem control; these flags are set in the system configuration file, and are stored in the driver data structures. If the bit corresponding to a terminal line number is set in a device's flags, modem control lines are ignored on input. When a carrier signal is detected on the line, the TS_CARR_ON bit is set in the terminal state. The driver then passes control to the initial (or current) line discipline through its open entry.

The default line discipline when a device is first opened is discipline 0, the *old* terminal driver. Its open routine, *ttyopen*(), checks to see whether the process opening the line has been assigned to a process group. If not, the process is assigned to the process group of the terminal, *t_pgrp*. If the terminal has no process group either, it uses the PID of the opening process. In this way, the initial open of a terminal line by the program accepting new logins sets the process groups of the process and of the terminal to the same value. If the line was not already open, the terminal-size information for the line is set to zero, indicating an unknown size. The line is then marked as open (state bit TS_OPEN).

Output Line Discipline

After a line has been opened, a write on the resulting file descriptor produces output to be transmitted on the terminal line. Writes to character devices result in calls to the device write entry, *d_write*, with a device number and a *uio* structure describing the data to be written. Terminal hardware drivers use the device number to locate the correct *tty* structure, then call the line discipline *l_write* entry with the *tty* structure and *uio* structure as parameters.

The line-discipline write routine does most of the work of output translation and flow control. It is responsible for copying data into the kernel from the user process calling the routine and for placing the translated data onto the terminal's output queue for the hardware driver. The terminal-driver write routine, *ttwrite*(), first checks that the terminal line still has carrier asserted; if not, an error is returned. Then, it checks whether the current process should be allowed to write to the terminal immediately. The user may set a *tty* option to allow only the foreground process to do output. If this option is in use, and if the terminal line is the controlling terminal for the process, then the process may do output immediately only if it is in the foreground process group (i.e., if the process groups of the process and of the terminal are the same). If the process is prevented from doing output, a signal (SIGTTOU) is sent to the process group of the process to suspend it. When the user moves the process group to the foreground, the write will be attempted again.

When it has confirmed that the write will be allowed, *ttwrite*() enters a loop that copies the data to be written into the kernel, checks for any output translation that is required, and places the data on the output queue for the terminal. It prevents the queue from becoming overfull by blocking if the queue fills before all characters have been processed. The limit on the queue size (the *high watermark*) is dependent on the output line speed. When it must wait for output to drain before proceeding, *ttwrite*() sets a flag in the *tty* structure state, TS_ASLEEP, so that the transmit-complete interrupt handler will awaken it when the queue is reduced to the *low watermark* (also dependent on line speed). The check of the queue size and subsequent sleep must be done such that the interrupt is guaranteed to occur after the sleep; see Fig. 9.2.

Once errors, permissions, and flow control have been checked, *ttwrite*() copies the user's data into a local buffer in chunks of at most 100 characters using *uiomove*(). If it is doing character mapping for single-case terminals, each character is translated and placed on the output queue with *ttyoutput*(); otherwise, the buffer is processed in sections. In raw mode, no translations are done, and the entire buffer is processed at once. The *new* terminal driver also provides an option (LITOUT) to allow a full eight-bit character output path. In other modes, groups of characters requiring no translation are located using *scanc*() with a lookup table that marks motion characters that might need translation or delay. Each group is placed into the output queue using *b_to_q*(). Trailing special

Figure 9.2 Checking the output queue in a line discipline.

```
struct tty *tp;

s = spltty();
if (tp->t_outq.c_cc > high-water-mark) {
     ttstart(tp);
     tp->t_state |= TS_ASLEEP;
     sleep(&tp->t_outq, TTOPRI);
}
splx(s);
```

characters are output with *ttyoutput*(). In either case, *ttwrite*() must check that sufficient C-list blocks are available; if not, it waits for a short time (by sleeping on *lbolt* for up to 1 second), then retries.

The routine that does output with translation is *ttyoutput*(), which accepts a single character, processes it as necessary, and places the result on the output queue. The following translations may be done, depending on the terminal mode:

- Tabs are expanded to spaces for terminals that do not support them.
- On upper-case-only terminals, backslashes are prepended to capital letters, and lower-case characters are replaced with capitals.
- Newlines are replaced with carriage return plus line feed if the CRMOD option is set. (This option also controls mapping of input carriage returns to newlines.)
- Delays are appended to characters that produce printhead motion. Delays are stored as characters outside of the ASCII character range, with the most significant bit set and the remaining bits specifying the amount of delay.

After data are placed on the output queue of a *tty*, *ttstart*() is called to initiate output. Unless output is already in progress, or has been suspended by receipt of a *stop* character or an output delay, *ttstart*() calls the hardware-driver start routine specified in the *tty*'s *t_oproc* field. If all the data have been processed and have been placed into the output queue, *ttwrite*() then returns an indication that the *write* completed successfully, and the actual serial character transmission is managed asynchronously by the device driver.

Output Top Half

The device driver handles the hardware-specific operation of character transmission, as well as synchronization and flow control for output. The structure of the *start*() routine varies little from one driver to another. There are two general classes of output mechanisms, depending on the type of hardware device. The first class operates on devices that are capable of direct-memory-access (DMA) output, which can fetch the data directly from the *C-list* block. (The DEC DH-11 terminal multiplexer is an example of this type of interface.) DMA interfaces supported by 4.3BSD on the VAX are all connected to the UNIBUS; thus, the output buffer must be mapped to UNIBUS address space with map registers in the UNIBUS adapter (see Chapter 8). To avoid the overhead of map allocation on each transmission, UNIX places the C-list blocks in a contiguous area of physical memory, then maps this area to the UNIBUS when the first terminal device is opened. The physical-memory base address of the transfer is computed from the UNIBUS address of the mapped area plus the offset of the data into the C-list area.

The driver start routine uses *ndqb*() to compute the number of contiguous characters in the first C-list block of the output queue that can be transmitted in one operation. If the terminal is in a mode that allows output delays, *ndqb*() is given a mask to distinguish delay characters. If a delay character is the first character to be transmitted, the terminal line is marked with TS_TIMEOUT, and *timeout*() is used to schedule the end of the delay, calling *ttrstrt*() to resume output when the delay ends. Otherwise, the UNIBUS address and the number of characters in the data block are computed, and the device is programmed with this information. The device fetches the data from main memory, transmits each of the characters in turn, and interrupts the CPU when the transmission is complete.

In the second class of terminal interfaces are those that transmit a single character at a time; the DEC DZ-11 terminal multiplexer is such a device. Each character is loaded into the device's output-character register for transmission. The CPU must then wait for the transmit-complete interrupt before sending the next character. Because of the large number of interrupts generated in this mode of operation, much of the information needed at interrupt time is computed in advance. The information needed is a pointer to the next character to be transmitted, to the extent of the block of characters to be transmitted, and to the address of the hardware device register to receive the next character. This strategy is known as *pseudo-DMA*; the precomputed information is stored in a *pdma* structure. A small assembly-language routine receives each hardware transmit-complete interrupt, transmits the next character, and returns. When there are no characters left to transmit, it calls a specified C-language interrupt routine with an indication of the line that completed transmission. The normal driver thus sees the illusion of DMA output, as it is not called until the entire block of characters has been transmitted.

After an output operation is initiated, the terminal state is marked with TS_BUSY so that new transmissions will not be attempted until the current one completes.

Output Bottom Half

When transmission of a block of characters has been completed, the hardware multiplexer interrupts the CPU; the transmit interrupt routine is then called with the unit number of the device. In most cases, the device has a register that the driver can read to determine which of the device's lines have completed transmit operations. For each line that has finished output, the interrupt routine clears the TS_BUSY flag. The characters that have been transmitted are removed from the output queue with *ndflush*(). These steps complete one section of output.

The line-discipline start routine is called to initiate the next operation; as noted, this routine generally does nothing but call the driver start routine specified in the terminal *t_oproc* field. The start routine now checks to see whether the output queue has been reduced to the low watermark, and, if it has been, whether the top half is waiting for space in the output queue. If the TS_ASLEEP flag is set, the output process is awakened; if a process is recorded in *t_wsel* as selecting for output, it is notified with *selwakeup*(). Then, if the output queue is not empty, the next operation is started as before.

Input Bottom Half

Unlike output, terminal input is not initiated by a system call, but arrives asynchronously when the terminal line receives characters from the keyboard or other input device. Thus, the input processing in the terminal system occurs mostly at interrupt time. Most hardware multiplexers interrupt each time a character is received on any line. They usually provide a *silo* that stores received characters, along with the line number on which the characters were received and any associated status information, until the device handler retrieves the characters. Use of the silo prevents characters from being lost if the CPU has not processed a received-character interrupt by the time the next character arrives. On many devices, the system can avoid per-character interrupts by programming the device to interrupt only after the silo is partially or completely full. However, the driver must then check the device periodically so that characters do not stagnate in the silo if additional input does not trigger an interrupt. Input flow-control characters must be processed without much delay, and users may notice delay in echoing of characters as well. If the device can also be programmed to interrupt a short time after the first character enters the silo, the driver may avoid periodic checks of the silo as well. The drivers in 4.3BSD for devices with such timers always use the silo interrupts. Other terminal drivers use per-character interrupts until the input rate is high enough to warrant the use of the silo alarm and a periodic scan of the silo.

When a device receiver interrupt occurs, or when a timer routine detects input, the receiver-interrupt routine reads each character from the input silo along with the latter's line number and status information. Normal characters are passed as input to the terminal line discipline for the receiving *tty* through its *l_rint* entry:

```
(*linesw[tp->t_line].l_rint)(input-character, tp);
```

Characters received with hardware-detected parity errors are discarded if only one parity is expected (either even or odd). When a *break* condition is detected (a longer-than-normal character with only 0 bits), an interrupt character or a null is passed to the line discipline, depending on the terminal mode.

The receiver-interrupt (*l_rint*) routine for the normal terminal line discipline is *ttyinput*(). The interpretation of terminal input described in Section 9.1 is done here. Input characters are echoed if desired. In raw mode, characters are placed into the raw input queue without interpretation. Otherwise, most of the work done by *ttyinput*() is to check for characters with special meanings and to take the indicated actions. Other characters are placed into the raw queue. In cooked mode, if the received character is a carriage return or another character that causes the current line to be made available to the program reading the terminal, the contents of the raw queue are added to the canonicalized queue, and *ttwakeup*() is called to notify any process waiting for input. In other modes, *ttwakeup*() is called when each character is processed. It will awaken any process sleeping on the raw queue awaiting input for a *read*, and will notify processes selecting for input. If the terminal has been set for signal-driven I/O using *fcntl* and the FASYNC flag, a SIGIO signal is sent to the process group controlling the terminal.

Ttyinput() must also check that the input queue does not become too large, exhausting the supply of C-list blocks; input characters are dropped when the limit (255 characters) is reached. If the TANDEM option is set, end-to-end flow control is invoked when the queue reaches half full by output of a stop character (normally XOFF or control-S).

Up to this point, all processing is asynchronous, and occurs whether or not a *read* call is pending on the terminal device. In this way, type-ahead is allowed to the limit of the input queues.

Input Top Half

Eventually, a *read* call is made on the file descriptor for the terminal device. Like all calls to read from a character-special device, this one results in a call to the device driver's *d_read* entry with a device number and a *uio* structure describing the destination for the data. Terminal device drivers use the device number to locate the *tty* structure for the device, then call the line discipline *l_read* entry to process the system call.

The *l_read* entry for the terminal driver is *ttread*(). Like *ttwrite*(), *ttread*() first checks that the terminal line still has carrier, returning an error if not. It then checks to see whether the current process is in the process group that currently controls the terminal. If the process group of the current process is not, that process group is stopped with the signal SIGTTIN until its process group receives control of the terminal. Finally, *ttread*() checks for data in the appropriate queue (the canonicalized queue in cooked mode, the raw queue in raw or cbreak mode). If no data are present, *ttread*() returns the error EWOULDBLOCK if the terminal is using nonblocking I/O; otherwise, it sleeps on the address of the raw queue. When *ttread*() is awakened, it restarts processing from the beginning, as the terminal state or process group might have changed while it was asleep.

When characters are present in the queue for which *ttread*() is waiting, they are removed from the queue one at a time with *getc*() and are copied out to the user's buffer with *ureadc*(). In raw mode, the characters are not examined as they are processed. In other modes, certain characters receive special processing as they are removed from the queue. Carriage returns are translated to newlines if the CRMOD flag is set, and the delayed-suspension character causes the current process group to be stopped with signal SIGTSTP. In addition, in cooked or cbreak modes, the end-of-file character terminates the read without being passed back to the user program. If there was no previous character, this condition results in the read returning zero characters, which is interpreted by user programs as indicating end-of-file. Characters are processed and returned to the user until the character count in the *uio* structure reaches zero, the queue is exhausted, or (in cooked mode) a line terminator is reached. When the call returns, the returned character count will be the amount by which the requested count was decremented as characters were processed.

After the read completes, if the terminal is in TANDEM mode and a stop character was sent because the queue was filling up, a start character (normally XON, control-Q) is sent if the queue is now less than 20 percent full.

The *stop* Routine

Character output on terminal devices is done in blocks as large as possible for efficiency. However, there are two events that should cause a pending output operation to be stopped. The first event is the receipt of a stop character, which should stop output as quickly as possible; in some cases, the device receiving output is a printer or other output device with a limited buffer size. The other event that stops output is the receipt of a special character that causes output to be discarded, possibly due to a signal. In either case, the terminal line discipline calls the character device driver's *d_stop* entry to stop any current output operation. Two parameters are provided, a *tty* structure and a flag that indicates whether output is to be flushed or suspended. If flushing output, the terminal discipline removes all the data in the output queue after calling the device stop routine.

The implementation of the *d_stop* routine is hardware-dependent. Different drivers stop output by disabling the transmitter, thus suspending output, or by changing the current character count to zero. Pseudo-DMA drivers may change the limit on the current block of characters so that the pseudo-DMA routine will call the transmit-complete interrupt routine after the current character is transmitted. Most drivers set a flag in the *tty* state, TS_FLUSH, when a stop is to flush data and the aborted output operation will cause an interrupt. When the transmit-complete interrupt routine runs, it notes the TS_FLUSH flag, and avoids updating the output-queue character count (the queue has probably already been flushed by the time the interrupt occurs). If output is to be stopped but not flushed, the TS_TTSTOP flag is set in the *tty* state; the driver must stop output such that the latter may be resumed from the current position.

The *ioctl* Routine

Section 9.3 described the user interface to terminal drivers and line disciplines, most of which is accessed via the *ioctl* system call. Most of these calls manipulate software options in the terminal line discipline; some of them also affect the operation of the asynchronous serial port hardware. In particular, the hardware line speed, word size, and parity are derived from these settings. Accordingly, *ioctl* calls are processed both by the current line discipline and by the hardware driver.

The device driver *d_ioctl* routine is called with a device number, an *ioctl* command, and a pointer to a data buffer when an *ioctl* is done on a character-special file. Like the read and write routines, most terminal-driver *ioctl* routines locate the *tty* structure for the device, then pass control to the line discipline. Depending on the return value from the line discipline, the driver may do additional processing, as shown in Fig. 9.3. The line-discipline *ioctl* routine does most of the common commands, including change of line discipline and change of terminal parameters. The *ioctl* routine returns an error number if an error is detected, or returns zero if the command has been processed successfully; it returns a minus one if the command is not recognized. In the first two cases, the hardware driver checks to see whether the command might affect the programming of the serial port parameters. If it might, the driver must reset the hardware parameters according to the new mode. The driver then returns the error indication from the line discipline. Some drivers implement additional *ioctl* commands that manipulate modem-control outputs. These commands are not recognized by the line discipline, and thus must be handled by the driver.

```
error = (*linesw[tp->t_line].l_ioctl)(tp, cmd, data, flag);
if (error >= 0) {
    if (cmd == TIOCSETP || cmd == TIOCSETN ||
        cmd == TIOCLBIS || cmd == TIOCLBIC ||
        cmd == TIOCLSET)
        dhparam(unit);    /* reset hardware parameters */
    return (error);
}
switch (cmd) {
    /* do hardware-specific commands */
}
```

Figure 9.3 Handling an error return from a line discipline.

Modem Transitions

The manner in which UNIX uses modem-control lines on terminal lines was introduced in Section 9.7. Most terminal multiplexers support at least the set of modem-control lines used by 4.3BSD; those that do not act instead as if carrier were always asserted. When a device is opened, the DTR output is enabled, and then the state of the carrier input is checked. If the state of the carrier input changes later, this change must be detected and processed by the driver. Some devices have a separate interrupt that reports changes in modem-control status; others report such changes along with other status information with received characters. One device used on the VAX (the DZ-11) does not interrupt when modem-control lines change, and the driver must check their status periodically. When a change is detected, the line discipline is notified by a call to its *l_modem* routine with the new state of the carrier input.

The normal terminal-driver modem routine, *ttymodem*(), maintains the state of the TS_CARR_ON flag in the *tty* structure, and processes corresponding state changes. When carrier establishment is detected, a wakeup is issued for any process waiting for an open to complete. When carrier drops on an open line, the process group controlling the terminal is sent a hangup signal, SIGHUP, as well as a continue signal (SIGCONT) for any processes that are stopped, and the terminal queues are flushed. The return value of *ttymodem*() indicates whether the driver should maintain its DTR output. If the value is zero, DTR should be turned off. *Ttymodem*() also implements an obscure terminal option to use the carrier line for flow-control handshaking, stopping output when carrier drops and resuming when it returns.

Closing Terminal Devices

When the last reference to a terminal device is closed, the device-driver close routine is called. Both the line discipline and the hardware driver may need to close down gracefully. The line-discipline close routine is called first. The standard line-discipline close entry, *ttylclose*(), waits for any pending output to drain if carrier is still on, then flushes the input queue and sets the terminal line discipline to the default. Note that the close may be interrupted by a signal while waiting for output to complete. The hardware driver may clear any pending operations, such as transmission of a break. If the state bit TS_HUPCLS has been set with the TIOCHPCL *ioctl*, DTR is disabled to hang up the line. Finally, *ttyclose*() flushes all the queues and clears all the terminal state.

9.9 Other Line Disciplines

We have examined the operation of the terminal I/O system using the standard terminal-oriented line-discipline routines, which implement both the *new* Berkeley line discipline and the *old* Seventh Edition UNIX line discipline. We now describe several other line disciplines in the system for completeness. Note that the preceding discussion of the operation of the terminal multiplexer drivers applies when these disciplines are used, as well as when the terminal-oriented disciplines are used.

Berknet

The first example of an alternate line discipline for alternate uses of serial lines is the Berknet line discipline. *Berknet* is an obsolete batch-oriented network that was used to connect PDP-11 and VAX UNIX systems using 9600-baud serial lines. Due to the overhead of input processing in the standard line discipline, a special reduced-function network discipline was devised. A seven-bit data path is provided for transfer of blocks of data terminated by newlines; acknowledgment and checksumming occur outside of the system. The Berknet discipline allocates a single buffer for each line, which it uses to buffer a single line of input at a time (the network software acknowledged each line before another could be sent). The *l_rint* received-character routine is expanded in-line in most of the multiplexer drivers to reduce the overhead as much as possible.

Serial Line IP Discipline

Another line discipline, *Serial Line IP* or SLIP, is used by more modern networking software to encapsulate and transfer Internet Protocol (IP) datagrams over asynchronous serial lines [Romkey, 1988]. (See Chapters 11 and 12 for information about IP.) The **slattach** program opens a serial line, sets the line's speed, and enters the SLIP line discipline. The SLIP line-discipline open routine associates the terminal line with a preconfigured network interface and prepares to send and receive network packets. Once the interface's network address is set with the **ifconfig** program, the network will route packets through the SLIP line to reach the system to which it connects. Packets are framed with a simple scheme; a framing character (0300 octal) is used to separate packets. Framing characters that occur within packets are quoted with an escape character (0333 octal) and are transposed (to 0334 octal). Escape characters within the packet are escaped and transposed (to 0335 octal).

The output path is started every time a packet is output to the SLIP interface. The SLIP discipline places the framing character and the data of the packet onto the output queue of the *tty*, escaping framing and escape characters as needed. It then starts transmission by calling *ttstart*(), which in turn calls the device's start routine referenced in the *tty t_oproc* field. It may place multiple packets onto the output queue before returning, as long as there is sufficient room in the queue and the system is not running short of C-list blocks. When transmission completes, the device driver calls the SLIP start routine, which continues to place data onto the output queue until all packets have been sent or the queue fills up again.

When characters are received on a line that is using the SLIP discipline, escaped characters are translated and data characters are placed into a network buffer. When a framing character ends the packet, the packet is presented to the network, and the buffer is reinitialized.

The SLIP discipline allows moderate-speed network connections to machines without specialized high-speed network hardware.

Graphics Tablet Discipline

The *tablet line discipline* is used to connect graphic devices such as digitizing tablets to the system using a serial line. Once the discipline is entered, it receives graphics data from the device continuously, and allows the application program to poll for the most recent information by reading from the line. The format of the information returned is dependent on that provided by the device; several different formats are supported.

9.10 Summary

We have examined the terminal I/O system in 4.3BSD. Terminal handling is split between the device drivers for the character devices to which terminals are connected and the line disciplines that are shared among all such drivers. The standard terminal line discipline supports both the *new* Berkeley terminal discipline and the *old* Seventh Edition UNIX discipline. Other line disciplines are used to support nonterminal uses of serial lines, such as network connections or connections to digitizing hardware. Planned future work, as mentioned in Chapter 1, includes support of a POSIX line discipline.

Exercises

9.1 What are the three possible modes of terminal input? Which mode is most commonly in use when users converse with an interactive screen editor?

9.2 Why are there two character queues for dealing with terminal input? Describe the use of each.

9.3 What do we mean when we say that modem control is supported on a terminal line? How are lines of this sort typically used?

9.4 What signals are sent to the processes associated with a terminal if a user disconnects the modem line in the middle of a session?

9.5 How is the high watermark on a terminal's output queue determined?

9.6 Why does a DH-11 terminal multiplexer have significantly less overhead than does a DZ-11?

*9.7 Consider a facility that allowed a tutor on one terminal to monitor and assist students working on other terminals. Everything the students typed would be transmitted both to the system as input, and to the tutor's terminal as output. Everything the tutor typed would be directed to the students' terminals as input. Describe how this facility might be implemented with a special-purpose line discipline. Describe further useful generalizations of this facility.

*9.8 The terminal line discipline supports logical erasure of input text when characters, words, and lines are erased. Remembering that other system activities continue while a user types an input line, explain what complications must be considered in the implementation of this feature. Name three exceptional cases and describe their effects on the implementation.

**9.9 What are the advantages of the use of line disciplines by device drivers for terminal multiplexers? What are the limitations? Propose an alternative approach to the current structure of the terminal I/O system.

**9.10 Consider the differences between the Berknet and SLIP disciplines. Although both use alternate line disciplines for efficiency, one of these uses would be extremely difficult to implement without modifications to the kernel, such as a specialized line-discipline module. Which use would be difficult to implement? Explain your choice.

References

Romkey, 1988.
J. Romkey, ''A Nonstandard for Transmission of IP Datagrams Over Serial Lines: SLIP,'' RFC 1055, SRI Network Information Center, Menlo Park, CA (June 1988).

Scheifler & Gettys, 1986.
R. W. Scheifler & J. Gettys, ''The X Window System,'' *ACM Transactions on Graphics* **5**(2), pp. 79–109 (April 1986).

PART 4

Interprocess Communication

CHAPTER 10

Interprocess Communication

Historically, UNIX has been weak in the area of *interprocess communication*. Prior to the release of 4.2BSD, the only standard interprocess-communication facility found in UNIX was the *pipe*, a reliable, flow-controlled, byte stream that could be established only between two related processes on the same machine. The limiting nature of pipes inspired many experimental facilities such as the Rand Corporation UNIX system's *ports* [Sunshine, 1977], *multiplexed files* that were an experimental part of Version 7 UNIX [UPMV7, 1983], and the Accent IPC facility developed at Carnegie-Mellon University [Rashid, 1980]. Some communication facilities were developed for use in application specific versions of UNIX; for example, the shared memory, semaphores, and message queues that were part of the *Columbus UNIX System*. The requirements of the DARPA research community, which drove much of the design and development of 4.2BSD, resulted in a significant effort to address the lack of a comprehensive set of interprocess-communication facilities in UNIX. The facilities designed and implemented in 4.2BSD were refined following that version's release. As a result, 4.3BSD provides a rich set of interprocess-communication facilities intended to support the construction of *distributed programs* built on top of communications primitives.

The interprocess-communication facilities are described in this chapter. The layer of software that implements these facilities is strongly intertwined with the network subsystem. The architecture of the network system is described in Chapter 11, and the networking protocols themselves are examined in Chapter 12. The reader will find it easiest to understand the material in these three chapters by first reading Chapter 10, and then Chapters 11 and 12. A section devoted to tying everything together appears at the end of Chapter 12.

10.1 Interprocess-Communication Model

There were several goals in the design of the interprocess-communication enhancements to UNIX. The most immediate need was to provide access to communication networks such as the DARPA Internet [Cerf, 1978]. Previous work in providing network access had focused on the implementation of the network protocols, exporting the transport facilities to UNIX applications via special-purpose, and often awkward, character-device interfaces [Cohen, 1977; Gurwitz, 1981]. As a result, each new network implementation resulted in a different application interface requiring most existing programs to be significantly altered or completely rewritten. The 4.2BSD interprocess-communication facilities were intended to provide a sufficiently general interface to allow network-based applications to be constructed independently of the underlying communication facilities.

The second goal was to allow multiprocess programs, such as distributed databases, to be implemented. The UNIX *pipe* requires all communicating processes to be derived from a common parent process. The use of pipes forced systems such as the Ingres database system to be designed with a somewhat contorted structure [Kalash *et al.*, 1986]. New communication facilities were needed to support communication between unrelated processes residing locally on a single host computer and residing remotely on multiple host machines.

Finally, the emerging networking and workstation technology required that the new communication facilities allow construction of local-area network services such as file servers. The intent was to provide facilities that could be easily used in supporting resource sharing in a distributed environment; the intention was not to construct a distributed UNIX system.

The interprocess-communication facilities were designed to support the following:

- **Transparency**: Communication between processes should not depend on whether or not the processes are on the same machine.
- **Efficiency**: The applicability of any interprocess-communication facility is limited by its performance. In 4.2BSD, interprocess communication is layered on top of network communication for performance reasons. The alternative is to provide network communication as a service accessed via the interprocess-communication facilities. Although this design is more modular, it would have required that network-communication facilities be accessed through one or more server processes. At the time 4.2BSD was designed, the prevalent hardware on which the system ran had such a slow process context-switch time that the performance of the communication facilities in a distributed environment would have been seriously constrained. Thus, the most efficient implementation of interprocess-communication facilities layers interprocess communication on top of network-communication facilities.
- **Compatibility**: Existing naive UNIX processes should be usable in a distributed environment without change. A *naive process* is characterized as a process that

performs its work by reading from the standard input file and writing to the standard output file. A *sophisticated process* is one that manages other processes or uses knowledge about specific devices, such as a terminal. A major reason why UNIX has been successful is its support for modularity through the use of naive processes that act as byte-stream filters. Although sophisticated applications such as shells and screen editors exist, they are far outnumbered by the collection of naive application programs.

In the course of designing the interprocess-communication facilities, the developers identified the following requirements to support these goals, and they developed a unifying concept for each:

- The system must support communication networks that use different sets of protocols, different naming conventions, different hardware, and so on.
  The notion of a *communication domain* was defined for these reasons. A communication domain embodies the standard semantics of communication and naming. Different networks almost always have different standards for specifying the name of a communication endpoint. Names may also vary in their properties. In one network, a name may be a fixed address for a communication endpoint, whereas in another it may be used to locate a process that can move between locations. The semantics of communication can include the cost associated with the reliable transport of data, the support for multicast transmissions, the ability to pass access rights or capabilities, and so on. By distinguishing communication properties, applications can select a domain appropriate to their needs.

- A unified abstraction for an endpoint of communication is needed that can be manipulated with a UNIX file descriptor.
  The *socket* is the abstract object from which messages are sent and received. Sockets are created within a communication domain much as files are created within a filesystem. Unlike files, however, sockets exist only as long as they are referenced.

- The semantic aspects of communication must be made available to applications in a controlled and uniform manner. That is, applications must be able to request styles of communication, such as virtual circuits or datagrams, but these styles must be provided in a manner that is consistent across all communication domains.
  All sockets are *typed* according to their communication semantics. Types are defined by the subset of properties a socket supports. These properties are

  1. In-order delivery of data
  2. Unduplicated delivery of data
  3. Reliable delivery of data
  4. Preservation of message boundaries

5. Support for out-of-band messages

6. Connection-oriented communication

Pipes have the first three properties, but not the fourth. An out-of-band message is one that is delivered to the receiver outside the normal stream of incoming, in-band data, and it usually is associated with an urgent or exceptional condition. A connection is a mechanism used to avoid having to transmit the identity of the sending socket with each packet of data. Instead, the identity of each endpoint of communication is exchanged prior to transmission of any data, and is maintained at each end so that it can be presented at any time. A *datagram socket* models potentially unreliable, connectionless packet communication; a *stream socket* models a reliable connection-based byte stream that may support out-of-band data transmission; and a *sequenced packet socket* models sequenced, reliable, unduplicated connection-based communication that preserves message boundaries. Other types of sockets are desirable and can be added.

- Processes must be able to locate endpoints of communication so that they may rendezvous without being related; for this reason, sockets can be *named.* A socket's name is meaningfully interpreted only within the context of the communication domain in which the socket is created.
  The names used by most applications are human-readable strings. However, the name for a socket that is used within a communication domain is usually a low-level *address.* Rather than placing name-to-address translation functions in the kernel, 4.3BSD provides functions for application programs to use in translating names to addresses. In the remainder of this chapter, we refer to the name of a socket as an *address.*

Using Sockets

Using sockets is reasonably straightforward. First, a socket must be created with the *socket* system call:

```
s = socket(domain, type, protocol);
int s, domain, type, protocol;
```

The type of socket is selected according to the characteristic properties required by the application. For example, if reliable communication is required, a stream socket might be selected. The *type* parameter is one of the socket types defined in a system header file. The *domain* parameter specifies the communication domain (or *protocol family*, see Section 10.4) in which the socket should be created; this domain is dependent on the environment in which the application is working. The most common domain for intermachine communication is the Internet communication domain, because of the large number of hosts that support the Internet communication protocols. The last parameter, the *protocol*, can be used to indicate a specific communication protocol to use in supporting the socket's operation.

Protocols are indicated by well-known constants specific to each communication domain. If the protocol is specified as zero, the system picks an appropriate protocol. The *socket* system call returns a file descriptor (a small integer number, see Section 6.2) that is then used in later socket operations. The *socket* call is similar to *open*, except that it creates a new instance of an object of the specified type, whereas *open* creates a new reference to an existing object, such as a file or device.

After a socket has been created, the next step depends on the type of socket being used. The most commonly used type of socket requires a *connection* before it can be used. Creation of a connection between two sockets usually requires that each socket have an address bound to it. Applications may explicitly specify a socket's address or may permit the system to assign one. A socket's address is immutable. Socket addresses may be reused if the communication domain permits, although domains normally ensure that a socket address is unique on each host, so that the association between two sockets is unique within the communication domain. The address to be bound to a socket must be formulated in a *socket address structure*. Applications find addresses of well-known services by looking up their names in a database. The format of addresses can vary among domains; to permit a wide variety of different formats, the system treats addresses as variable-length byte arrays, which are prefixed with a tag that identifies their format. The call to bind an address to a socket is

```
error = bind(s, addr, addrlen);
int error, s;
struct sockaddr *addr;
int addrlen;
```

where *s* is the descriptor returned from a previous *socket* system call.

For several reasons, binding a name to a socket was separated from creating a socket. First, sockets are potentially useful without names. If all sockets had to be named, users would be forced to devise meaningless names without reason. Second, in some communication domains, it may be necessary to supply additional, nonstandard information to the system before binding a name to a socket—for example, the ''type of service'' required when using a socket. If a socket's name had to be specified at the time the socket was created, supplying this information would not be possible without further complicating the interface.

In connection-based communication, the process that initiates a connection normally is termed a *client process*, whereas the process that receives, or responds to, a connection is termed a *server process*. In the *client process*, a connection is initiated with a *connect* system call:

```
error = connect(s, serveraddr, serveraddrlen);
int error, s;
struct sockaddr *serveraddr;
int serveraddrlen;
```

In the *server process*, the socket is first marked to indicate incoming connections are to be accepted on it:

```
error = listen(s, backlog);
int error, s, backlog;
```

Connections are then received, one at a time, with

```
snew = accept(s, clientaddr, clientaddrlen);
int snew, s;
struct sockaddr *clientaddr;
int *clientaddrlen;
```

The *backlog* parameter in the *listen* call is used to specify an upper bound on the number of pending connections that should be queued for acceptance. Processes can obtain the address of the client along with the new connected socket in the *accept* call by specifying the *clientaddr* and *clientaddrlen* parameters. Note that *accept* returns a file descriptor associated with a *new* socket. This new socket is the socket through which client–server communication can take place. The original socket *s* is used solely for managing the queue of connection requests in the server.

Sockets that are not connection-based may also use the *connect* system call to fix a peer's address, although this is not required. The system calls available for sending and receiving data (described later) permit connectionless sockets to be used without a fixed peer address via specification of the destination with each transmitted message. Likewise, connectionless sockets need not bind an address to a socket before using the socket to transmit data. However, in some communication domains, addresses are assigned to sockets when the latter are first used, if no specific address was bound.

A variety of calls are available for sending and receiving data. The usual *read* (*readv*) and *write* (*writev*) system calls, as well as the newer *send* and *recv* system calls, can be used with sockets that are in a connected state. *Send* and *recv* differ from the more common interface in that they both support an additional *flags* parameter. The *flags* can be used to *peek* at incoming data on reception (MSG_PEEK), to send or receive out-of-band data (MSG_OOB), and to send data without network routing (MSG_DONTROUTE). The *sendto* and *recvfrom* system calls have all the capabilities of *send* and *recv* and in addition permit callers to specify or receive the address of the peer with whom they are communicating; these calls are most useful for connectionless sockets, where the peer may vary on each message transmitted or received. Finally, the *sendmsg* and *recvmsg* system calls support the full interface to the interprocess-communication facilities. Besides scatter-gather operations being possible, an address may be specified or received, the optional flags described previously are available, and specially interpreted data, called access rights, may be transmitted and received (see Fig. 10.1).

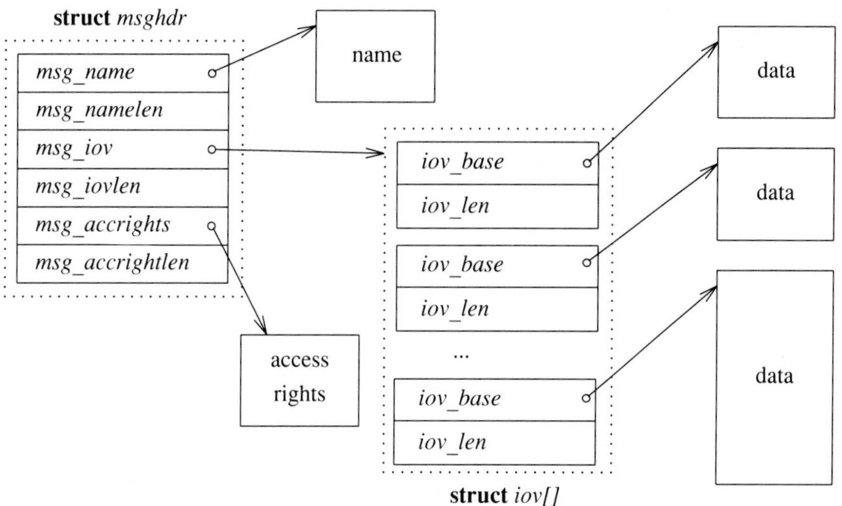

Figure 10.1 Data structures for the *sendmsg* and *recvmsg* system calls.

In addition to these system calls, several other calls are provided to access miscellaneous services. The *socketpair* call provides a mechanism by which two connected sockets may be created without binding addresses. This facility is almost identical to a pipe except for the potential for bidirectional flow of data. In fact, pipes are implemented internally as a pair of sockets. The *getsockname* call returns the locally bound address of a socket, whereas the *getpeername* call returns the address of the socket at the remote end of a connection. The *shutdown* call is used to terminate data transmission or reception at a socket, and two *ioctl*-style calls—*setsockopt* and *getsockopt*—can be used to set and retrieve various parameters that control the operation of a socket or of the underlying network protocols. These options include the ability to transmit broadcast messages, to set the size of a socket's send and receive data buffers, and to await the transmission of queued data when a socket is destroyed. Sockets are discarded with the normal *close* system call.

The interface to the interprocess-communication facilities was purposely designed to be orthogonal to the standard UNIX system interfaces—that is, to the *open*, *read*, and *write* system calls. This decision was made to avoid overloading the familiar interface with undue complexity. In addition, the developers thought that using an interface that was completely independent of the UNIX filesystem would improve the portability of software because, for example, UNIX pathnames would not be involved. Backward compatibility, for the sake of naive processes, was still deemed important; thus, the familiar read–write interface was augmented to permit access to the new communication facilities wherever it made sense (e.g., when connected stream sockets were used).

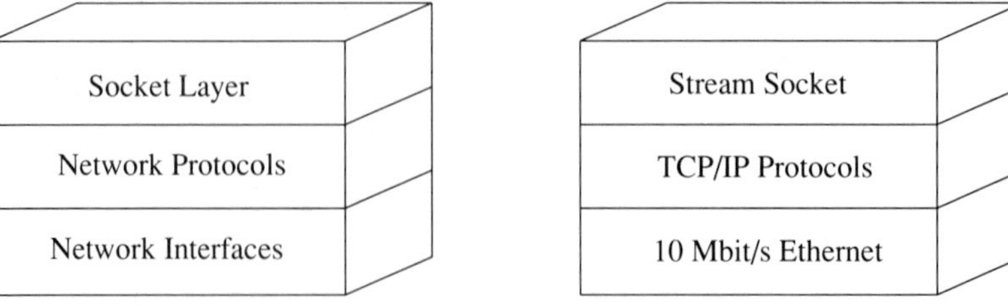

Figure 10.2 Interprocess-communication implementation layering.

10.2 Implementation Structure and Overview

The interprocess-communication facilities are layered on top of the networking facilities, as shown in Fig. 10.2. Data flows from the application through the socket layer to the networking support, and vice versa. State required by the socket level is fully encapsulated in the socket layer, whereas any protocol-related state is maintained in auxiliary data structures that are specific to the supporting protocols. Responsibility for storage associated with transmitted data is passed from the socket level to the network level. Consistent adherence to this rule assists in simplifying details of storage management. Within the socket layer, the socket data structure is the focus of all activity. The system-call interface routines manage the actions related to a UNIX system call, collecting the system-call parameters (see Section 3.2) and converting user data into the format expected by the second-level routines. Most of the socket abstraction is implemented within

Table 10.1 Socket-layer support routines.

Routine	Function
socreate()	create a new socket
sobind()	bind a name to a socket
solisten()	mark a socket as listening for connection requests
soaccept()	accept a pending connection on a socket
soconnect()	initiate a connection to another socket
soconnect2()	create a connection between two sockets
sosend()	send data
soreceive()	receive data
soshutdown()	shut down data transmission or reception
sosetopt()	set the value of a socket option
sogetopt()	get the value of a socket option

the second-level routines. All second-level routines have names with a *so* prefix, and directly manipulate socket data structures and manage the synchronization between asynchronous activities; these routines are listed in Table 10.1.

The remainder of this chapter focuses on the implementation of the socket layer. Section 10.3 discusses how memory is managed at the socket level and below in the networking subsystem; Section 10.4 covers the socket and related data structures; Section 10.5 presents the algorithms for connection setup; Section 10.6 discusses data transfer; and Section 10.7 describes connection shutdown. Throughout this chapter, references to the supporting facilities provided by the network-communication protocols are made with little elaboration; a complete description of the interaction between the network protocols and the socket layer appears in Chapter 11, and the internals of the network protocols are presented in Chapter 12.

10.3 Memory Management

The requirements placed on a memory-management scheme by interprocess-communication and network protocols tend to be very different from those of other parts of the operating system. Although all require the efficient allocation and reclamation of memory, communication protocols in particular need memory in widely varying sizes. Memory is needed for fixed-sized data structures, such as sockets and protocol state blocks, as well as for variable structures such as communication protocol packets. A special-purpose memory-management facility was created for use by the interprocess-communication and networking systems to address these needs.

Mbufs

The memory-management facilities revolve around a data structure called an *mbuf* (see Fig. 10.3). Mbufs, or memory buffers, are 128 bytes long, with 112 bytes of this space reserved for data storage. For large messages, up to 1 Kbyte of data may be associated with an mbuf by referencing a page from a private page pool. Data are stored either in the internal data area or in the external page, never in both. Data associated with an mbuf are accessed by the addition of an offset field in the mbuf structure to the base address of the mbuf. The offset is between 12 and 124 for data contained within the mbuf; for data located in a mapped page, the (unsigned) offset is greater than 124.

In addition to the offset field used to reference the data associated with an mbuf, a length field is also maintained. The length field indicates the number of bytes of valid data to be found at the offset. The offset and length fields allow routines to trim data efficiently at the start or end of an mbuf. In deletion of data at the start of an mbuf, the offset is incremented and the length is decremented. In deletion of data at the end of an mbuf, only the length need be decremented. When space is available within an mbuf, data can be added at either end. This

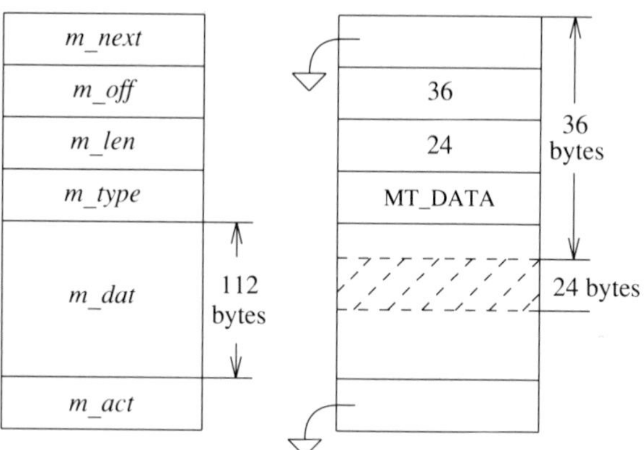

Figure 10.3 Memory-buffer (mbuf) data structure.

flexibility to add and delete space without copying is particularly useful in implementing communication protocols. Protocols routinely strip protocol information off the front or back of a message before the message's contents are handed to a higher-level processing module, or add protocol information as a message is passed to lower levels.

The provision for mapping pages into an mbuf permits data to be moved without a memory-to-memory copy operation. Instead, the page-table entries associated with the physical pages of memory can be changed to remap the memory from one mbuf to another. In addition, when multiple copies of a block of data are required, the same page can be mapped into multiple mbufs to avoid physical copies; an array of reference counts is maintained for the pool of mapped pages to support this style of sharing.

Multiple mbufs can be linked to hold an arbitrary number of data. This linkage is accomplished with the *m_next* field of the mbuf. By convention, a chain of mbufs linked in this manner is treated as a single object. For example, the communication protocols construct packets from chains of mbufs. A second field, *m_act*, is used to link objects constructed from chains of mbufs into lists of objects. Throughout our discussions, a collection of mbufs linked together with the *m_next* field will be called a *chain*; chains of mbufs linked together with the *m_act* field will be called a *list*.

The final component of the mbuf structure is the type field. Each mbuf is typed according to its use, with unused mbufs marked MT_FREE. The mbuf type serves two purposes. The only operational use of the type is to distinguish optional components of a message in an mbuf chain that is queued for reception on a socket data queue. Otherwise, the type information is used in maintaining statistics about storage use and, in case of problems, as an aid in tracking mbufs.

Mbufs have fixed-sized, rather than variable-sized, data areas for several reasons. First, the fixed size minimizes memory fragmentation. This was an important consideration at the time the networking software was originally designed, as one of the targeted machines was the BBN C70, a machine with a 20-bit physical address space. Second, communication protocols are frequently required to prepend or append headers to existing data areas, to split data areas, or to trim data from the beginning or end of a data area. The mbuf facilities are designed to handle such changes without reallocation or copying whenever possible. Finally, the *dtom*() function described later would be much more expensive if mbufs were not fixed in size.

The ease of use and efficiency with which the mbuf memory-management scheme operates has resulted in the use of mbufs for data structures other than those for which they were intended. Mbufs are used to hold everything from variable-sized protocol packets to a zombie process's status. Certain system routines even go so far as to impose a substructure on an mbuf's data-storage area to minimize wasted space. This overloading of the mbuf facility is due more to the weakness of the system's memory-allocation facilities than to the strength of the mbuf storage mechanism. Many vendors have addressed the lack of a general heap storage facility within the system, freeing them to eliminate many of the inappropriate uses of mbufs. Similar changes are also present in post-4.3BSD systems.

Storage-Management Algorithms

The mbuf store is composed of three central resources: a pool of pages allocated from the system memory allocator, a private page map for mapping pages into kernel address space, and an array of counters used in maintaining reference counts on mapped pages. Pages allocated to the mbuf store are divided into mbuf structures or are used for storage of data too numerous to fit in the mbuf structure's data array. Two free lists are maintained, one for mbuf structures and one for mapped pages. When the system is booted, the mbuf-allocation routines initialize the store by allocating 4 Kbyte of physical memory to create 32 mbuf structures, and four pages to initialize the pool of mappable pages. Further memory may be allocated as the system operates, up to a maximum of 256 Kbyte. Each page allocated to the mbuf store is recorded in the private page map *Mbmap*. Mbuf-allocation requests indicate that they must be fulfilled immediately or that they can wait for available resources. If a request is marked as "can wait" and the requested resources are unavailable, the process is put to sleep to await available resources. The nonblocking allocation request is necessary for code that executes at interrupt level. In the event that the mbuf store is exhausted and system resources are unavailable, or that the store has already been expanded to its limit, the mbuf-allocation routines ask the network-protocol modules to give back any available resources they can. Memory allocated to the mbuf store is never returned to the system.

An mbuf-allocation request is made through a call to *m_get*(), *m_getclr*(), or one of the equivalent macros used for efficiency purposes. If an mbuf is available on the free list, it is simply taken; otherwise, an attempt is made to expand the resource pool by one page. If the system has resources available and the mbuf store is not already at its limit, then the newly allocated page is divided into mbufs, which are placed on the free list. The caller then allocates the needed mbuf from the free list.

Releasing mbuf resources is straightforward; *m_free*() frees a single mbuf, and *m_freem*() frees a chain of mbufs. The system easily detects pages associated with mbufs when an mbuf is released by checking the offset field in the mbuf structure when the mbuf is freed. Pages are placed onto the free page list when their reference count reaches zero.

Mbuf Utility Routines

Many useful utility routines exist for manipulating mbufs. Those routines that will be used in Chapter 11 are described briefly here.

The *m_copy*() routine makes a copy of an mbuf chain starting at a logical offset, in bytes, from the start of the data. This routine may be used to copy all or only part of a chain of mbufs. If an mbuf is composed of mapped pages, the copy will reference the same pages by incrementing the reference counts on the pages; otherwise, the data portion is copied as well.

The *m_adj*() routine adjusts the data in an mbuf chain by a specified number of bytes, shaving data off either the front or back. No data are ever copied; *m_adj*() operates purely by manipulating the offset and length fields in the mbuf structures.

The *mtod*() routine takes a pointer to an mbuf header and a data type and returns a pointer to the data in the mbuf, cast to the given type. The *dtom*() function is the inverse: It takes a pointer to an arbitrary address in the data of an mbuf and returns a pointer to the mbuf header (not to the head of the mbuf chain). In 4.3BSD, this operation is done through simple truncation of the data address to an mbuf-sized boundary.

The *m_pullup*() routine is used to rearrange an mbuf chain so that a specified number of data resides in a contiguous data area within the mbuf (not page). This operation is used so that objects such as protocol headers are contiguous and can be treated as normal data structures, and so that *dtom*() will work when the object is freed. If there is room, *m_pullup*() will also add up to MPULL_EXTRA extra bytes to the contiguous region in an attempt to avoid being called in the future.

10.4 Data Structures

Sockets are the basic object used by communicating processes. A socket's type defines the communication semantics, whereas the communication domain defines auxiliary properties important to the use of the socket. Table 10.2 shows the four types of sockets currently supported by the system. To create a new socket, applications must specify the socket type and communication domain in which the socket is to be created. The request may also indicate a specific network protocol to be used by the socket. If no protocol is indicated, the system selects an appropriate protocol from the set of protocols supported by the communication

Table 10.2 Socket types supported by the system.

Name	Type	Properties
SOCK_STREAM	stream	reliable, sequenced, data transfer; may support out-of-band data
SOCK_DGRAM	datagram	unreliable, unsequenced, data transfer with message boundaries preserved
SOCK_SEQPACKET	sequenced packet	reliable, sequenced, data transfer with message boundaries preserved
SOCK_RAW	raw	direct access to the underlying communication protocols

domain. If the communication domain is unable to support the type of socket requested (i.e., no suitable protocol exists), the request will fail.

Sockets are described by a *socket* data structure that is dynamically created at the time of a *socket* system call. Communication domains are described by a *domain* data structure that is statically defined within the system based on the system's configuration (see Section 13.5). Communication protocols within a domain are described by a *protosw* structure that is also statically defined within the system for each protocol implementation configured. When a request is made to create a socket, the system uses the name of the communication domain to search linearly the list of configured domains. If the domain is found, the domain's table of supported protocols is consulted for a protocol appropriate for the type of socket being created, or for a specific protocol requested. (A wildcard entry may exist for a raw domain.) Should multiple protocol entries satisfy the request, the first is selected. We shall begin discussion of the data structures by examining the *domain* structure. The *protosw* structure is discussed in Section 11.1.

Communication Domains

The *domain* structure is shown in Fig. 10.4. The *dom_name* field is the ASCII name of the communication domain.[1] The *dom_family* field identifies the *protocol family* used by the domain; possible values are shown in Table 10.3. Protocol families refer to the suite of communication protocols of a domain used to support the communication semantics of a socket. The *dom_protosw* field points to the table of protocols supported by the communication domain, whereas the remaining entries contain pointers to domain-specific routines used in the management and transfer of access rights (described later).

[1] In the original design, communication domains were to be specified with ASCII strings; they are now specified with manifest constants.

dom_family	PF_UNIX
dom_name	"unix"
dom_init	...
dom_externalize	*unp_externalize*()
dom_dispose	*unp_dispose*()
dom_protosw	*unixsw*
dom_protoswNPROTOSW	*&unixsw[5]*
dom_next	

Figure 10.4 Communication-domain data structure.

Sockets

The *socket* data structure is shown in Fig. 10.5. A *socket* data structure resides in the data area of an mbuf. Whereas the use of an mbuf allows *socket* structures to be dynamically created, the size of the mbuf imposes a limit on the size of the

Table 10.3 Protocol families.

Name	Description
PF_UNIX	local communication; e.g., pipes
PF_INET	DARPA Internet (TCP/IP)
PF_IMPLINK	1822 Input Message Processor link layer
PF_PUP	old Xerox network
PF_CHAOS	MIT Chaos network
PF_NS	Xerox Network System (XNS) architecture
PF_NBS	National Bureau of Standards (NBS) network
PF_ECMA	European Computer Manufacturers network
PF_DATAKIT	AT&T Datakit network
PF_CCITT	CCITT protocols, e.g., X.25
PF_SNA	IBM System Network Architecture (SNA)
PF_DECnet	DEC network
PF_DLI	direct link interface
PF_LAT	local-area network terminal interface
PF_HYLINK	Network Systems Corporation Hyperchannel (raw)
PF_APPLETALK	AppleTalk network

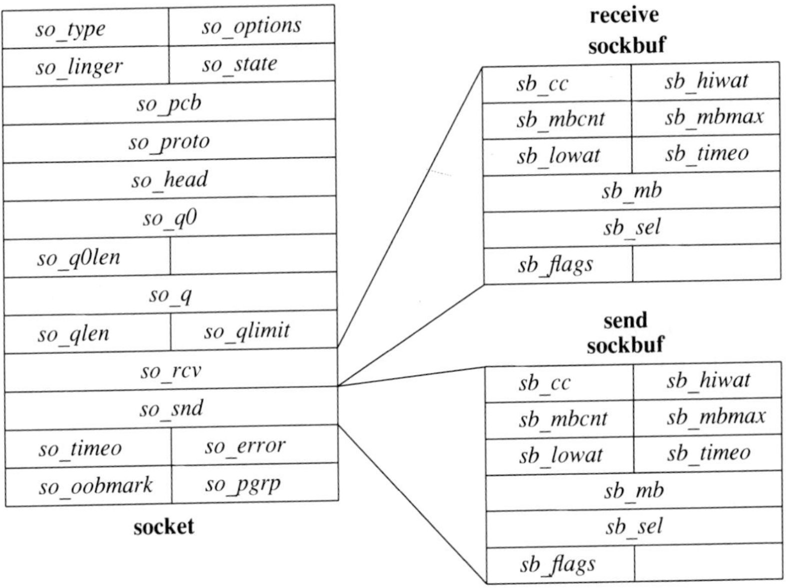

Figure 10.5 Socket data structure.

structure. Sockets contain information about their type, the supporting protocol in use, and their state (Table 10.4). Data being transmitted or received are queued at the socket in the form of a list of mbuf chains. Various fields are present for managing queues of sockets created during connection establishment. Each socket structure also holds a process-group identifier. The process-group identifier is used in delivering the SIGURG and SIGIO signals; SIGURG is sent when an urgent condition exists for a socket, and SIGIO is used by the asynchronous I/O facility (see Section 6.2). The socket contains an error field analogous to

Table 10.4 Socket states.

State	Description
SS_NOFDREF	no file-table reference
SS_ISCONNECTED	socket connected to a peer
SS_ISCONNECTING	in process of connecting to peer
SS_ISDISCONNECTING	in process of disconnecting from peer
SS_CANTSENDMORE	cannot send more data to peer
SS_CANTRCVMORE	cannot receive more data from peer

the error number in the user structure (Section 4.2); this field is needed for reporting asynchronous errors to the owner of the socket.

Sockets are located through a process's file descriptor via the file table. When a socket is created, the *f_data* field of the file structure is set to point at the socket structure, and the *f_ops* field to point to the set of routines defining socket-specific file operations. In this sense, the socket structure is a direct parallel of the *inode* structure used by the filesystem.

The socket structure acts as a queueing point for data being transmitted and received. As data enter the system as a result of system calls, such as *write* or *send*, the socket layer passes the data to the networking subsystem as a chain of mbufs for immediate transmission. If the supporting protocol module decides to postpone transmission of the data, or if a copy of the data is to be maintained until an acknowledgment is received, the data are queued in the socket's transmit buffer. When the network has consumed the data, it discards them from the outgoing queue. On reception, the network passes data up to the socket layer, also in mbuf chains, where they are then queued until the application makes a system call to request them. To avoid resource exhaustion, sockets impose upper bounds on the number of data that can be queued in a socket data buffer. This *high watermark* is initially set by the protocol, although an application can change the value up to a maximum of 56 Kbyte. The network protocols can examine the high watermark and use the value in flow-control policies, but they never alter it once it is set. A *low watermark* is also present in each socket data buffer, although it is not currently used. The low watermark is intended to allow applications to control data flow by specifying a minimum number of data to be present in the data buffer before a reception request is satisfied. For output, it would set the minimum amount of space available before transmission can be attempted.

Sockets used to accept incoming connection requests maintain two other queues. The list of sockets headed by the *so_q0* field represents a queue of connections that are incomplete at the communication protocol level, whereas the *so_q* field heads a list of sockets for which a completed connection exists at the protocol level. Like the data queue, the queue of completed connections also has an application-controllable limit on it. It is important to recognize that, although a connection may be established by the network protocol, the application may choose not to accept the established connection, or it may immediately close down the connection after discovering the identity of the client. Unlike some other systems, this system has no facility to allow an application to control the acceptance of a connection at the network level. We could consider this to be a deficiency, although in practice its principal effect is to require a higher-level handshake between the client and server processes before the server process will provide service. It is also possible for a network protocol to delay completion of a connection until after the application has obtained control with the *accept* system call.

Socket Addresses

Sockets may be labeled so that processes can connect to them. The socket layer treats an address as an opaque object. Applications supply and receive addresses

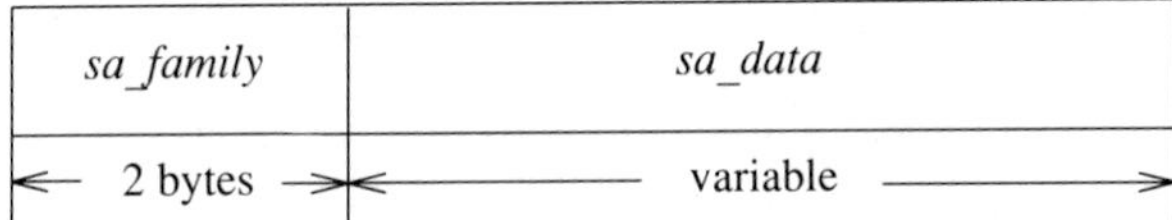

Figure 10.6 Socket address template structure.

as tagged, variable-length byte strings. Addresses always reside in an mbuf on entry to the socket layer. A structure called a *sockaddr*, shown in Fig. 10.6, may be used as a template for referring to the identifying tag of each address. Each address family implementation includes routines for address family-specific operations on addresses. When addresses must be manipulated—for example, to compare them for equality—a pointer to the address (a *sockaddr* structure) is used to extract the address family tag. This tag is then used to identify the routine to invoke for the desired operation.

It is common for addresses passed in by an application to reside in mbufs only long enough for the socket layer to pass them to the supporting protocol for transfer into a fixed-sized address structure. This occurs, for example, when a protocol records an address in a protocol state block. The *sockaddr* structure is the common means by which the socket layer and network-support facilities exchange addresses. The size of the generic data array was chosen to be large enough to hold most addresses directly. Communication domains that support larger addresses may ignore the array size. Only the routing data structures (discussed in Section 11.5) contain fixed-sized generic sockaddr structures. The UNIX communication domain, for example, stores filesystem pathnames in mbufs and allows socket names as large as 108 bytes, as shown in Fig. 10.7. The

Figure 10.7 Network system, Internet, and UNIX address structures.

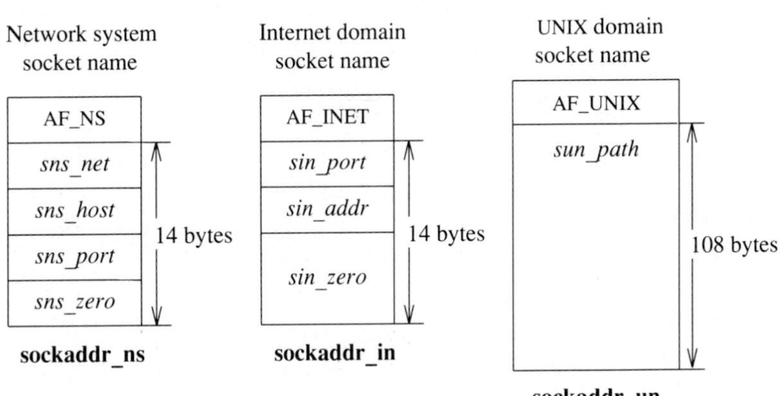

Internet communication domain, on the other hand, uses a structure that combines a DARPA Internet address and a port number. The Internet protocols reserve space for addresses in an Internet control-block data structure, and free up mbufs that contain addresses after copying their contents.

10.5 Connection Setup

For two processes to pass information between them, an *association* must be established. The steps involved in creating an association (*socket*, *connect*, *listen*, *accept*, etc.) were described in Section 10.1. In this section, we shall study the operation of the socket layer in establishing associations. As the state associated with a connectionless transfer of data is fully encapsulated in each message that is sent, our discussion shall focus on connection-based associations established with the *connect*, *listen*, and *accept* system calls.

Connection establishment in the client-server model is asymmetric. A client process actively initiates a connection to obtain service, whereas a server process passively accepts connections to provide service. Fig. 10.8 shows the state-transition diagram for a socket used to initiate or accept connections. State

Figure 10.8 Socket state transitions during process rendezvous.

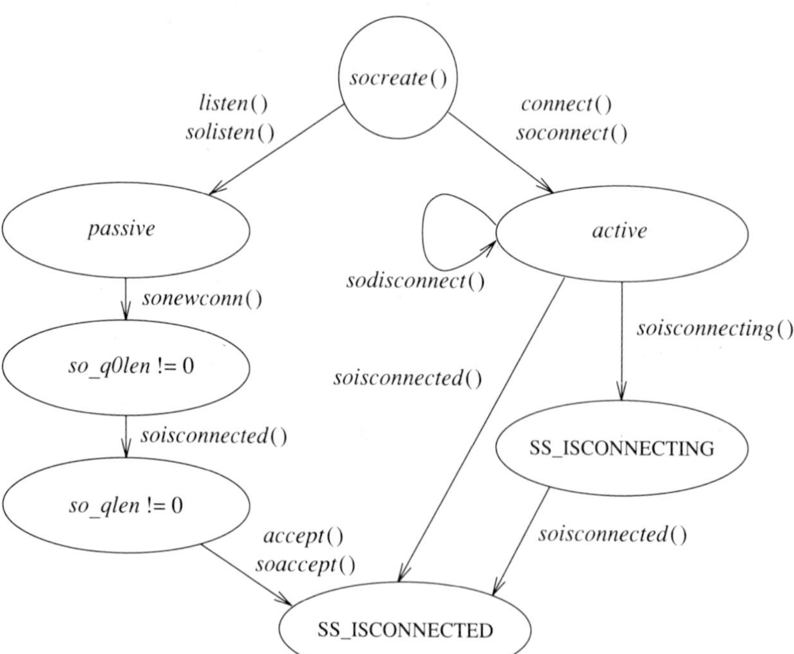

transitions are initiated either by user actions (i.e., system calls) or by protocol actions that result from receiving network messages or servicing timers that expire.

Sockets are normally used to send and receive data. When they are used in establishing a connection, they are treated somewhat differently. If a socket is to be used to accept a connection, a *listen* system call must be used. The *listen* call invokes *solisten*(), which notifies the supporting protocol that the socket will be receiving connections, establishes an empty list of pending connections at the socket (through the *so_q* field), and then marks the socket as *accepting connections*, SO_ACCEPTCON. At the time a *listen* is done, a backlog parameter is specified by the application. This parameter is used to set a limit on the number of incoming connections the system will queue awaiting acceptance by the application. (The system enforces a maximum on this limit.) Once a socket is set up to receive connections, the remainder of the work in creating connections is managed by the protocol layers. For each connection established at the server side, a new socket is created with the *sonewconn*() routine. These new sockets may be placed on the socket's queue of partially established connections while the connections are being completed, but once ready they are moved to the queue of connections completed and pending acceptance by an application (see Fig. 10.9). When an *accept* system call is made to obtain a connection, the system verifies that a connection is present on the socket's queue of incoming connections. If no pending connection is present, the system puts the process to sleep until one arrives (unless nonblocking I/O is being used with the socket, in which case an error is returned). When a connection is available, the associated socket is removed from the queue, a new file descriptor is allocated to reference the socket, and the result is returned to the caller. If the *accept* call indicates that the peer's identity is to be returned, the peer's address is copied into the supplied buffer.

On the client side, an application requests a connection with the *connect* system call, supplying the address of the peer socket to which to connect. The

Figure 10.9 Connections queued at a socket awaiting acceptance.

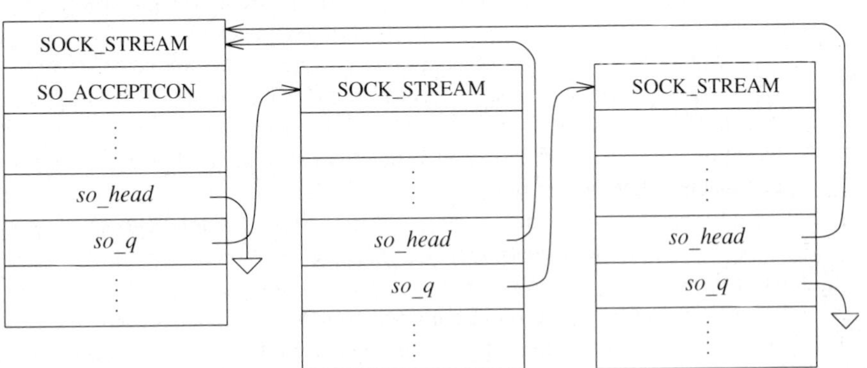

system verifies that a connection attempt is not already in progress for that socket, then invokes *soconnect*() to initiate the connection. The *soconnect*() routine first checks the socket to see whether the latter is already connected. If the socket is already connected, the existing connection is first terminated (this is done with only datagram sockets). With the socket in an unconnected state, *soconnect*() then marks the state as connecting, and makes a request to the protocol layer to initiate the new connection. Once the connection request has been passed to the protocol layer, if the connection request is incomplete, the system puts the process to sleep to await notification by the protocol layer that a completed connection exists. A nonblocking connect may return at this point, but a process awaiting a completed connection will awaken only when the connection request has been completed—either successfully or with an error condition.

A socket's state during connection establishment is managed jointly by the socket layer and the supporting protocol layer. The socket's state value is never altered directly by a protocol; to promote modularity, all modifications are performed by surrogate socket-layer routines, such as *soisconnected*(). Errors that are detected asynchronously are communicated to a socket in its *so_error* field. For example, if a connection request fails because the protocol layer detects that the requested service is unavailable, the *so_error* field usually is set to ECONNREFUSED before the requesting process is awakened. The socket layer always inspects the value of *so_error* on return from a call to *sleep*(); this is the standard method used in identifying errors detected asynchronously by the protocol layers.

10.6 Data Transfer

Most of the work performed by the socket layer is in sending and receiving data. It should be noted that the socket layer itself explicitly refrains from imposing any structure on data transmitted or received via sockets. This is in contrast to some interprocess-communication facilities available for UNIX today [Fitzgerald & Rashid, 1986]. Within the overall interprocess-communication model, any data interpretation or structuring is logically isolated in the implementation of the communication domain. An example of this logical isolation is the ability to pass file descriptors between processes using UNIX domain sockets.

Sending and receiving of data can be done with any one of several system calls. The system calls vary according to the amount of information to be transmitted and received and the state of the socket being used to perform the operation. For example, the *write* system call may be used with a socket that is in a connected state, as the destination of the data is implicitly specified by the connection; but the *sendto* or *sendmsg* system calls allow the process to specify the destination for a message explicitly. Likewise, when receiving data, the *read* system call allows a process to receive data on a connected socket without receiving the sender's address; the *recvfrom* and *recvmsg* system calls allow the process to retrieve the incoming message and the sender's address. The decision to provide many different system calls rather than to provide only a single general interface is debatable. It would have been possible to implement a single system-call interface and to provide simplified interfaces to applications via user-level library routines. Internally, all transmission and reception requests are converted to a uniform format and are passed to the socket-layer *sendit*() and *recvit*() routines, respectively.

Transmitting Data

The *sendit*() routine is responsible for gathering all system-call parameters that the application has specified into the kernel's address space (except the actual data), and then invoking the *sosend*() routine to perform the transmission. *Sosend*() handles most of the socket-level data-transmission options. This includes requests for transmission of out-of-band data and of data without network routing. In addition, *sosend*() is responsible for putting processes to sleep when their data transmissions exceed the buffering available in the socket's send buffer. The actual transmission of data is performed by the supporting communication protocol; *sosend*() moves data from the user's address space into mbufs in the kernel's address space, and then makes calls to the protocol to transfer the data.

Most of the work performed by *sosend*() is involved with breaking up an application's transmission request into one or more protocol transmission requests. This is necessary only when the number of data in the user's request plus the number of data queued in the socket's send data buffer exceeds the socket's high watermark. It is not permissible to break up a request if message boundaries are to be maintained in the user's data stream, as each request made by the socket layer to the protocol modules implicitly indicates a boundary in the data stream. Honoring each socket's high watermark ensures that a protocol will always have space in the socket's send buffer to queue unacknowledged data. It also ensures that no process, or group of processes, can monopolize system resources.

For sockets that guarantee reliable data delivery, a protocol will normally maintain a copy of all transmitted data in the socket's send queue until receipt is acknowledged by the receiver. Protocols that provide no assurance of delivery normally accept data from *sosend*() and directly transmit the data to the destination without keeping a copy. But *sosend*() itself does not distinguish between reliable and unreliable delivery.

Sosend() always ensures that a socket's send buffer has sufficient space available to store the next section of data to be transmitted. If a socket has insufficient space in its send buffer to hold all the data to be transmitted, *sosend*() uses the following strategy: If more than one page of data is present in the send queue, more than one page of data is awaiting transmission, and the process is not using nonblocking I/O, put the process to sleep until more space is available in the send buffer; otherwise, formulate a protocol transmit request according to the available space in the send buffer. This strategy tends to preserve the application-specified message size and helps to avoid fragmentation at the network level. The latter is very important, as system performance is significantly better when data-transmission units are a multiple of the machine's page size, because of the optimized support for mbufs with mapped pages. (*Sosend*() will copy data from the user's address space into pages allocated from the mbuf page pool whenever the data will fill at least one-half of a page.)

The *sosend*() routine, in manipulating a socket's send data buffer, takes care to ensure that access to the buffer is synchronized among multiple sending processes. It does this by bracketing accesses to the data structure with calls to *sblock*() and *sbunlock*(). Interlocking against asynchronous network activity is also a concern here, as the network-protocol modules that operate at network-interrupt level cannot wait for access to a data structure such as a socket data buffer. Thus, they do not honor the locking protocol used between processes. To block network-protocol modules, *sosend*() must raise the processor priority level to *splnet* to ensure that no protocol processing takes place that might alter the state of a socket being manipulated.

Receiving Data

The *soreceive*() routine is used to receive data queued at a socket. As the counterpart to *sosend*(), *soreceive*() appears at the same level in the internal software structure and performs similar tasks. Two types of data normally are queued for reception at a socket: in-band data and access rights. Out-of-band data are not normally placed in a socket's receive buffer, but instead are managed in the protocol layer and are retrieved through a special interface when requested by the user. (This special handling allows varying styles of urgent data transmission.)

Soreceive() checks the socket's state, including the receive data buffer, for incoming data, errors, or state transitions, and then processes queued data according to their type and the actions specified by the caller. A system-call request may indicate that only out-of-band data should be retrieved (MSG_OOB), or that data should be returned but not removed from the data buffer (by specifying the MSG_PEEK flag).

Data present in the receive data buffer are organized in one of two ways, depending on whether or not message boundaries are preserved. If the socket preserves message boundaries on incoming data, the buffer is organized as a list of messages. Each mbuf chain on a list represents a single message, and the boundary is implicit in the list structure (see Fig. 10.10). Protocols that supply the sender's address with each message place a single mbuf containing the address at the front of message. Immediately following any address is an optional mbuf containing access rights. Regular data mbufs follow the access rights. Names and access rights are distinguished by the type field in an mbuf; addresses are marked as MT_SONAME, whereas rights are tagged as MT_RIGHTS. When message boundaries are not preserved, the receive data buffer is simply a single chain of mbufs. As before, mbuf types are used to distinguish optional pieces of information. Note that the storage scheme used by sockets allows them to compact data of the same type into the minimal number of mbufs required to hold those data.

On entry to *soreceive*(), a check is made to see whether out-of-band data are being requested. If they are, the protocol layer is queried to see whether any such

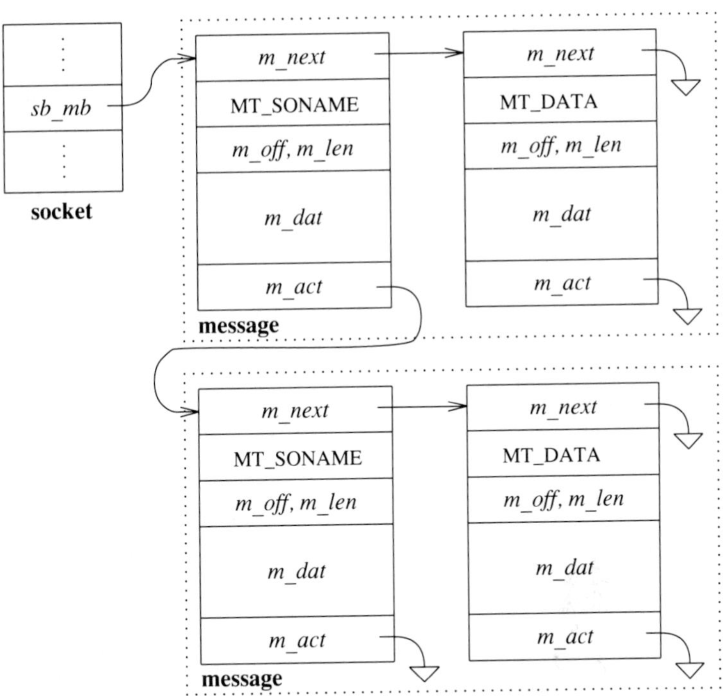

Figure 10.10 Data queueing for datagram socket.

data are available; if the data are available, they are returned to the caller. As regular data cannot be retrieved simultaneously with out-of-band data, *soreceive*() then returns. Otherwise, regular data have been requested, and *soreceive*() checks the receive data buffer character count to see whether data are available. If no data are present, the socket's state is consulted to find out whether data might be forthcoming. Data may no longer be received, because the socket is disconnected (and a connection is required to receive data), or because the reception of data has been terminated with a *shutdown* by the socket's peer. In addition, if an error from a previous operation was detected asynchronously, the error needs to be returned to the user; *soreceive*() checks the *so_error* field after checking for data. If no data or error exist, data might still arrive, and if the socket is not marked for nonblocking I/O, *soreceive*() puts the process to sleep to await the arrival of new data.

When data arrive for a socket, the supporting protocol notifies the socket layer by calling *sorwakeup*(). The contents of the receive buffer can then be processed, observing the data-structuring rules described previously. *Soreceive*() first removes any address that must be present, then optional access rights, and finally normal data. The removal of data is slightly complicated by the interaction between in-band and out-of-band data. The location of the next out-of-band datum is marked in the in-band data stream and is used as a record boundary during in-band data processing. That is, when an indication of out-of-band data is received by a protocol, the corresponding point in the in-band data stream is marked. Then, when a request is made to receive in-band data, only data up to the mark will be returned. This mark allows applications to synchronize the in-band and out-of-band data streams so that, for example, received data can be flushed up to the point at which out-of-band data are received. Each socket has a field, *so_oobmark*, that contains the character offset from the front of the receive data buffer to the point in the data stream at which the last out-of-band message was received. When in-band data are removed from the receive buffer, the offset is updated accordingly, so that data past the mark will not be mixed with data preceding the mark. The SS_RCVATMARK bit in a socket's state field is set when *so_oobmark* reaches zero to show that in-band and out-of-band data streams are synchronized. An application can test the state of this bit with the SIOCATMARK *ioctl* call to find out whether all in-band data have been read up to the point of the mark.

Once data have been removed from a socket's receive buffer, *soreceive*() updates the state of the socket and notifies the protocol layer that data have been received by the user. The protocol layer can use this information to release internal resources, to trigger end-to-end acknowledgment of data reception, to update flow-control information, or to start a new data transfer. Finally, if any access rights were received, *soreceive*() passes them to a communication domain–specific routine to convert them from their internal representation to the external representation.

Passing Access Rights

In addition to the transmission and reception of uninterpreted data, the system also supports the passage of data that have special meaning. These data normally represent the right to perform operations on associated objects. The data used to represent access rights, or capabilities, normally are meaningful only within the context of the process that created or obtained the right, so their transmission requires system support to make them meaningful in a receiving process's context. For example, in UNIX, access rights to files in the filesystem or sockets are encapsulated in the form of file descriptors. A file descriptor is a small integer number that is meaningful only in the context of the process that opened or created the associated file. To pass a file descriptor from one process to another, the system must create a reference to the associated file-table structure in the receiving process's user structure.

Access rights, or capabilities, are categorized as *internalized* or *externalized.* Internalized capabilities require the support of trusted agents to be useful. Keys associated with these capabilities are created by a trusted agent, and, when presented for the purpose of accessing a protected object, are deemed valid according to their interpretation in the context of the presenter.

Externalized capabilities, on the other hand, utilize keys that require no specific trusted agent for their use. That is, the validation of the right to access an object is based solely on the possession and presentation of the requisite key.

Systems that use externalized capabilities frequently utilize a public key-encryption algorithm. Keys for externalized capabilities normally have the property that they are long-lived and that they may be stored in locations such as a filesystem without losing their usefulness.

No specific system support is required to support externalized capabilities. To support internalized capabilities, however, the operating system, acting as a trusted agent, must verify and translate keys when transmitting them as messages between processes. The interprocess-communication system provides facilities, on a per-communication domain basis, to process all access rights transmitted and received in messages, and to dispose of rights that are not received.

Sending and receiving of access rights requires the internalization and externalization of these rights. Internalization converts a key held by a sending process into an internal form that can be passed as data in a message. Externalization reverses this process, converting the internal form into an external form that is meaningful in the context of the receiving process. Internalization of access rights is performed at the protocol layer when the *sosend*() routine requests transmission of data containing access rights. The access rights to be transmitted are passed as an mbuf chain separate from the regular data. When *soreceive*() encounters access rights on the receive data queue, it invokes the communication domain's *dom_externalize* routine to externalize the rights. The socket layer implicitly presumes that access rights stored in socket data queues will be valid as long as the system remains up. That is, there are no mechanisms to expedite the delivery of access rights, or to time out or invalidate rights stored on a socket data queue.

Access Rights in the UNIX Domain

In the UNIX domain, the internalization of file descriptors results in their conversion to system file-table pointers, whereas externalization requires allocation of new file descriptors for the receiving process. File descriptors passed in messages are actually duplicates of the ones held by the sending process (as though they had been created by *dup*). The sending process must explicitly close a file descriptor after that descriptor has been sent, in order to give it away.

A *garbage-collection* facility is provided to reclaim resources associated with access rights that are not delivered properly. Access rights may not be delivered for two reasons: either because the receiving socket has insufficient space, or because the user does not request them with the proper system call when receiving data from the socket. Garbage collection is used because normal message processing does not permit a protocol to access a message after it has passed on that message for delivery. This inability to access a message after it has been transmitted means that, if access rights in a message are not delivered, these rights will be discarded without being reclaimed.[2] In the UNIX domain, reclamation of access rights ensures that files associated with these rights are closed so that

[2] With hindsight, this problem would have been better handled with use of the per-domain disposal routine during freeing of an mbuf typed with MT_RIGHTS.

system resources such as file-table entries are not depleted.

For garbage collection to be implemented, each file-table entry must contain a count of references held by file descriptors present in socket receive queues, *f_msgcount*. Another variable, *unp_rights*, tracks the number of file descriptors held in all the UNIX domain sockets in use. When a file descriptor is internalized to a file-table pointer for the purpose of transmission, the *f_msgcount* for the file is incremented. On reception, when the file descriptor is externalized, *f_msgcount* is decremented. When a UNIX domain socket is reclaimed and *unp_rights* is nonzero, the garbage-collection routine, *unp_gc*(), is invoked to scan the file table and all UNIX domain sockets to reclaim unaccounted-for file-table references.

Unp_gc() uses a *mark-and-sweep algorithm* in performing its duties [Cohen, 1981]. The basic strategy is to locate all references to files that are present in UNIX domain sockets or in a process's user structure. Files that have existing references either in a user structure or in a socket's receive data buffer are *marked*, whereas those that are thought to be active, but for which no existing reference can be found, are not *marked*. The garbage collector can then reclaim lost references by searching the file table for un*marked* entries for which all references are indicated as being in socket receive queues.

Note that the garbage collector is invoked only when a UNIX domain socket is closed and file descriptors are known to be queued awaiting reception; thus, the overhead associated with the garbage collector is limited. Also, the garbage collector reclaims only those file-table entries that were lost while being passed in messages; references that might be lost in other parts of the system are not reclaimed.

10.7 Socket Shutdown

Although closing a socket and reclaiming its resources at first glance appears to be a straightforward operation, it can in fact be rather complicated. The complexity arises because of the implicit semantics UNIX attaches to the *close* system call. In certain situations (e.g., when a process exits), a *close* call is never expected to fail. However, when a socket promising reliable delivery of data is closed with data still queued for transmission or awaiting acknowledgment of reception, the socket must attempt to transmit the data, perhaps indefinitely, in order for the *close* call to maintain the socket's advertised semantics. If the socket discards the queued data to allow the *close* to complete successfully, it violates its promise to deliver data reliably. Discarding data can cause naive UNIX processes, which depend on the implicit semantics of *close*, to work unreliably in a network environment. However, if sockets block until all data have been transmitted successfully, in some communication domains a *close* may never complete!

The socket layer compromises in an effort to address this problem yet to maintain the semantics of the UNIX *close* system call. Figure 10.11 shows the possible state transitions for a socket from a connected to a closed state. In normal operation, closing a socket causes any queued but unaccepted connections to

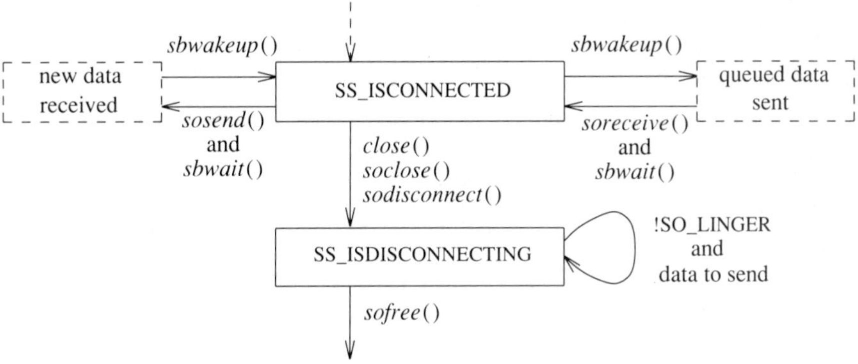

Figure 10.11 Socket-state transitions during shutdown.

be discarded. If the socket is in a connected state, a disconnect is initiated. The socket is marked to indicate that a file descriptor is no longer referencing it, and the close operation returns successfully. When the disconnect request completes, the network support notifies the socket layer, and the socket resources are reclaimed. The network layer may attempt to transmit any data queued in the socket's send buffer, although this is not guaranteed.

Alternatively, a socket may be marked explicitly to force the application process to *linger* when closing until pending data have drained and the connection has shut down. This option is marked in the *socket* data structure using the *setsockopt* system call with the SO_LINGER option. When an application indicates that a socket is to linger, it also specifies a duration for the lingering period. If the lingering period expires before the disconnect is completed, the socket layer forcibly shuts down the socket, discarding any data still pending.[3]

Exercises

10.1 What limitation in the use of pipes inspired the developers to design alternative interprocess-communication facilities?

10.2 Why are the 4.3BSD interprocess-communication facilities designed to be independent of the UNIX filesystem for naming sockets?

10.3 Why is interprocess communication layered on top of networking in 4.3BSD, rather than the other way around?

[3] Actually, lingering is only partly implemented; the lingering period is infinite and cannot be changed by users.

10.4 Would a screen editor be considered a naive or a sophisticated UNIX program, according to the definitions given in this chapter? Explain your answer.

10.5 What are out-of-band data? What type of socket supports the communication of out-of-band data? Describe one use for out-of-band data.

10.6 Give two requirements that interprocess communication places on a memory-management facility.

10.7 How many mbufs would be needed to hold a 3024-byte message? Draw a picture of the necessary mbuf chain and any associated memory pages.

10.8 Why does an mbuf have two link pointers? For what is each pointer used?

10.9 Why is the 4.3BSD socket data structure limited in size to at most 112 bytes?

10.10 Each socket's send and receive data buffers have high and low watermarks. For what are these watermarks used?

10.11 Consider a socket with a network connection that is queued at the socket awaiting an *accept* system call. Is this socket on the queue headed by the *so_q* or by the *so_q0* field in the socket structure? What is the use of the queue the socket is *not* on?

10.12 How does the protocol layer communicate an asynchronous error to the socket layer?

10.13 Sockets explicitly refrain from interpreting the data that they send and receive. Do you believe that this is the correct approach? Explain your answer.

10.14 Why does the *sosend*() routine ensure there is enough space in a socket's send buffer before making a call to the protocol layer to transmit data?

10.15 How is the type information in each mbuf used in the queueing of data at a datagram socket? How is this information used in the queueing of data at a stream socket?

10.16 Why does the *soreceive*() routine optionally notify the protocol layer when data are removed from a socket's receive buffer?

10.17 Describe an application where the ability to pass file descriptors is useful. Is there another way to simulate this facility in 4.3BSD?

10.18 What is the difference between an internalized capability and an externalized capability? Would UNIX descriptors be considered externalized or internalized capabilities according to the definitions given in this chapter?

10.19 What might cause a connection to linger forever when closing?

*10.20 What effect might storage compaction have on the performance of network-communication protocols?

**10.21 Why is releasing mbuf storage back to the system complicated? Is it desirable?

**10.22 In the original design of the interprocess-communication facilities, a reference to a communication domain was obtained with a *domain* system call,

```
int d; d = domain("inet");
```

(where *d* is a descriptor, much like a file descriptor), and sockets then were created with

```
s = socket(type, d, protocol);
int s, type, protocol;
```

What advantages does this scheme have over the one that is used in 4.3BSD? What effect does the introduction of a domain descriptor type have on the management and use of descriptors within the kernel?

References

Cerf, 1978.
V. Cerf, "The Catenet Model for Internetworking," Technical Report IEN 48, SRI Network Information Center, Menlo Park, CA (July 1978).

Cohen, 1977.
D. Cohen, "Network Control Protocol (NCP) Software," University of Illinois Software Distribution, University of Illinois, Champaign-Urbana, IL (1977).

Cohen, 1981.
J. Cohen, "Garbage Collection of Linked Data Structures," *Computing Surveys* **13**(3), pp. 341–367 (September 1981).

Fitzgerald & Rashid, 1986.
R. Fitzgerald & R. F. Rashid, "The Integration of Virtual Memory Management and Interprocess Communication in Accent," *ACM Transactions on Computer Systems* **4**(2), pp. 147–177 (May 1986).

Gurwitz, 1981.
R. F. Gurwitz, "VAX-UNIX Networking Support Project—Implementation Description," Technical Report IEN 168, SRI Network Information Center, Menlo Park, CA (January 1981).

Kalash *et al.*, 1986.
J. Kalash, L. Rodgin, Z. Fong, & J. Anton, "Ingres Version 8 Reference Manual," pp. 10:1–88 in *UNIX Programmer's Supplementary Documents,*

Volume 2, 4.3 Berkeley Software Distribution, Virtual VAX-11 Version, USENIX Association, Berkeley, CA (1986).

Rashid, 1980.
R. F. Rashid, ''An Inter-Process Communication Facility for UNIX,'' Technical Report, Carnegie-Mellon University, Pittsburgh, PA (August 14, 1980).

Sunshine, 1977.
C. Sunshine, ''Interprocess Communication Extensions for the UNIX Operating System: Design Considerations,'' Technical Report R-2064/1-AF, Rand Corporation, Santa Monica, CA (June 1977).

UPMV7, 1983.
UPMV7, *UNIX Programmer's Manual,* 7th ed, Volume 1 and 2, Holt, Rinehart & Winston, New York, NY (1983).

CHAPTER 11

Network Communication

In this chapter, we shall study the internal structure of the network subsystem provided in 4.3BSD. The networking facilities provide a framework within which many *network architectures* may coexist. A network architecture comprises a set of network-communication protocols, the *protocol family*, conventions for naming communication endpoints, the *address family* or *address format*, and any additional facilities that may fall outside the realm of connection management and data transfer. Networking facilities are accessed through the *socket* abstraction described in Chapter 10. The network subsystem provides a general-purpose framework within which to implement network services. These facilities include

- A structured interface to the socket level that allows the development of network-independent application software
- A consistent interface to the hardware devices used to transmit and receive data
- Network-independent support for message routing
- Memory management

We describe the internal structure of the network subsystem in Section 11.1. Then we discuss the interface between the socket layer and the network facilities, and examine the interfaces between the layers of software that make up the network subsystem. In Section 11.5, we discuss the routing database used by the network protocols; in Section 11.6, we describe the mechanisms provided to manage buffering and to control congestion. We present the *raw socket* interface that provides direct access to lower-level network protocols in Section 11.7. Finally, in Section 11.8 we discuss an assortment of issues and facilities, including out-of-band data, subnetwork addressing, the Address Resolution Protocol, trailer protocols, and support for network interfaces that reside on the VAX UNIBUS.

After we have discussed the framework in which the network protocols fit, we shall examine the implementations of existing network protocols in Chapter 12.

11.1 Internal Structure

The network subsystem is logically divided into three layers. These three layers manage the following tasks:

- Interprocess data transport
- Internetwork addressing and message routing
- Transmission-media support

The first two layers are made up of modules that implement communication protocols; the software in the third layer is structurally much like a device driver (see Chapter 8).

The topmost layer in the network subsystem is termed the *transport layer*. The transport layer must provide an addressing structure that permits communication between sockets and any protocol mechanisms necessary for socket semantics, such as reliable data delivery. The second layer, the *network layer*, is responsible for the delivery of data destined for remote transport or network-layer protocols. In providing internetwork delivery, the network layer must manage a private routing database or utilize the systemwide facility for routing messages to their destination host. The bottom layer, the *network-interface layer*, is responsible for transporting messages between hosts connected to a common transmission medium. The network-interface layer is mainly concerned with driving the transmission media involved and performing any necessary link-level protocol *encapsulation* and *decapsulation*.

The transport, network, and network-interface layers of the network subsystem most closely resemble the bottom three levels (2 through 0) of the Xerox Network System (NS) architecture. These layers correspond to the *transport*, *network*, and *link* layers of the ISO Open Systems Interconnection Reference Model [ISO, 1984], respectively. The internal structure of the networking software is not directly visible to users. Instead, all networking facilities are accessed through the socket layer described in Chapter 10. Each communication protocol that permits access to its facilities exports a user request routine to the socket layer. This routine is used by the socket layer in providing access to network services.

The layering described here is a *logical layering*. The software that implements network services may utilize more or fewer communication protocols according to the design of the network architecture being supported.

Data Flow

Data flow down to the network subsystem from the socket layer through calls to the transport-layer modules that support the socket abstraction. Data received at a network interface flow upward through communication protocols until they are placed in the receive queue of the destination socket. The downward flow of data typically is initiated by system calls. Data flowing upward are received asynchronously and are passed from the network-interface layer to the appropriate communication protocol through per-protocol input message queues (see Fig. 11.1). The system schedules network protocol processing from the network-interface layer by marking a bit assigned to the protocol in the system's network-interrupt status word and posting a *software interrupt* reserved for triggering network activity. Software interrupts are used to schedule asynchronous network activity, rather than protocols being run as independent UNIX processes, to avoid context-switching overhead. If a message received by a communication protocol is destined for a higher-level protocol, this protocol is invoked directly at software-interrupt level to process the message. Alternatively, if the message is destined for another host and the system is prepared to forward the message, the message will be returned to the network-interface layer for retransmission.

Figure 11.1 Upward data flow in the network subsystem. ETHER—Ethernet header; IP—Internet Protocol header; TCP—Transmission Control Protocol header.

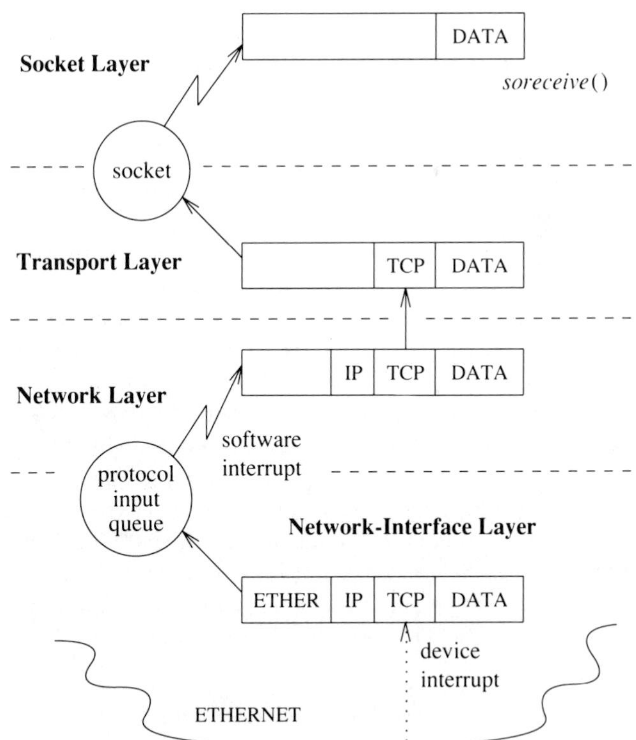

Communication Protocols

Each communication-protocol module is made up of a collection of procedures and private data structures. Protocols are described by a *protocol switch* structure that contains the set of externally visible entry points and certain attributes (see Fig. 11.2). The socket layer interacts with a communication protocol solely through the latter's protocol switch structure, recording the structure's address in a socket's *so_proto* field. This isolation of the socket layer from the networking subsystem is important in ensuring that the socket layer provides users with a consistent interface to all the protocols supported by a system.

Before a protocol is first used, the protocol's initialization routine is invoked. Thereafter, the protocol will be invoked for timer-based actions every 200 milliseconds if the *pr_fasttimo*() entry is present, and every 500 milliseconds if the *pr_slowtimo*() entry point is present. The *pr_drain*() entry is provided so that the system can notify the protocol if it is low on space and would like any noncritical data to be discarded.[1]

Protocols may pass data among themselves in chains of mbufs (see Section 10.3) using the *pr_input*() and *pr_output*() routines. The *pr_input*() routine is used to pass data *up* toward the user, whereas the *pr_output*() routine is used to pass data *down* toward the network. Similarly, control information passes up and down via the *pr_ctlinput*() and *pr_ctloutput*() routines. The *user request routine*, *pr_usrreq*(), is the interface between a protocol and the socket level; it is described in detail in Section 11.2.

In general, a protocol is responsible for storage space occupied by any of the arguments passed downward via these procedures and must either pass the space onward or dispose of it. On output, the lowest level reached must free space passed as arguments; on input, the highest level is responsible for freeing space passed up to it. Auxiliary storage needed by protocols is allocated from the mbuf store. This space is used temporarily to formulate messages or to hold data structures such as state control blocks. Mbufs allocated by a protocol for private use must be freed by that protocol when they are no longer in use.

The *pr_flags* field in a protocol's protocol switch structure describes the protocol's capabilities and certain aspects of its operation that are pertinent to the operation of the socket level (see Table 11.1). Protocols that are connection-based specify the PR_CONNREQUIRED flag so that socket routines will never attempt to send data before a connection has been established. If the PR_WANTRCVD flag is set, the socket routines will notify the protocol when the user has removed data from a socket's receive queue. This notification allows a protocol to implement acknowledgment on user receipt, and also to update flow-control information based on the amount of space available in the receive queue. The PR_ADDR field indicates that any data placed in a socket's receive queue by the protocol will be preceded by the address of the sender. The PR_ATOMIC flag specifies that each *user* request to send data must be performed in a single

[1] The protocol *pr_drain* routines were never called in the original release of 4.3BSD.

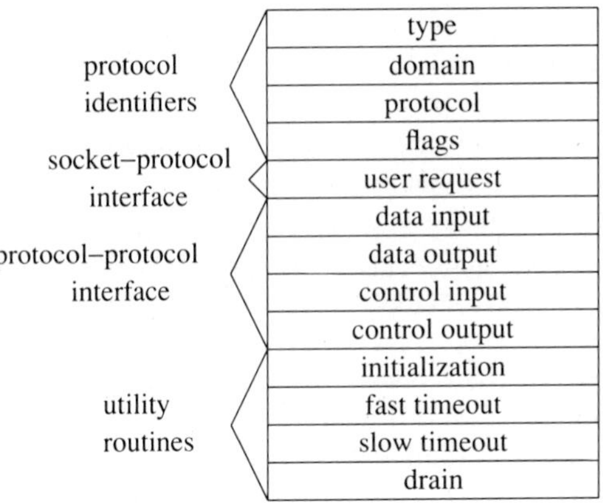

Figure 11.2 Protocol switch structure.

protocol send request; it is the protocol's responsibility to maintain record boundaries on data to be sent. The PR_RIGHTS flag indicates that the protocol supports the transfer of access rights; this flag is currently used only by the protocols in the UNIX communication domain (see Section 10.6).

Network Interfaces

Each network interface configured in a system defines a path through which messages can be sent and received. Normally, a hardware device is associated with this interface, although there is no requirement that one be (for example, all systems have a software *loopback* interface used for debugging and performance analysis). In addition to manipulating the hardware device, a network-interface module is responsible for encapsulation and decapsulation of any link-layer protocol header required to deliver a message to its destination. The selection of the interface to use in delivering a packet is a routing decision carried out at the

Table 11.1 Protocol flags.

Flag	Description
PR_ATOMIC	messages sent separately, each in a single packet
PR_ADDR	protocol presents address with each message
PR_CONNREQUIRED	connection required for data transfer
PR_WANTRCVD	protocol notified on user receipt of data
PR_RIGHTS	protocol supports passing access rights

network-protocol layer. An interface may have addresses in one or more address families. Each address is set at boot time using an *ioctl* system call on a socket in the appropriate domain; this operation is implemented by the protocol family after verifying the operation with an *ioctl* entry point provided by the network interface. The network-interface abstraction provides protocols with a consistent interface to all hardware devices that may be present on a machine.

An interface and its addresses are defined by the structures shown in Fig. 11.3. The network-interface module generally maintains the interface data structure as part of a larger structure that also contains information used in driving the underlying hardware device.

Each network interface has a queue of messages to be transmitted and routines used for initialization (*if_init*()), and output (*if_output*()). If the interface resides on a system bus, a reset routine will be invoked after a bus reset has been performed, so that it may reinitialize itself. An interface may also specify a timer routine and a timer value that (if it is nonzero) the system will decrement once per second, invoking the timer routine when the value expires. The timeout mechanism is typically used by interfaces to implement watchdog schemes for unreliable hardware and to collect statistics that reside on the hardware device.

The state of an interface and certain externally visible characteristics are stored in the *if_flags* field (see Table 11.2). The IFF_UP flag is set when the

Figure 11.3 Network-interface data structures.

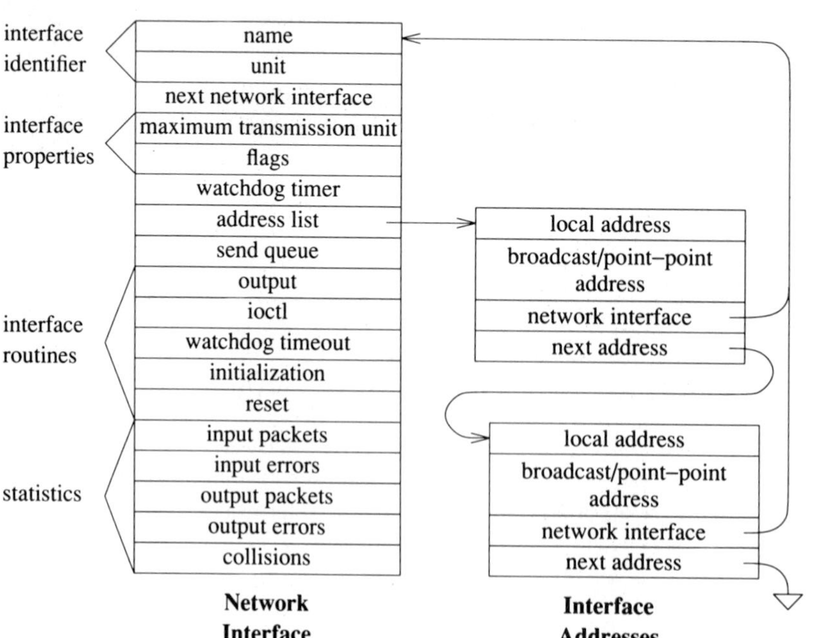

Table 11.2 Network interface flags.

Flag	Description
IFF_UP	interface is available for use
IFF_BROADCAST	broadcast is supported
IFF_DEBUG	enable debugging in the interface software
IFF_LOOPBACK	this is a software loopback interface
IFF_POINTOPOINT	interface is for a point-to-point link
IFF_NOTRAILERS	interface should not use trailer encapsulation
IFF_RUNNING	interface resources have been allocated
IFF_NOARP	interface should not use address-resolution protocol

interface is configured and ready to transmit messages. If an interface is connected to a network that supports transmission of *broadcast* messages, the IFF_BROADCAST flag will be set and the interface's address list will contain a broadcast address to use in sending and receiving such messages. If an interface is associated with a point-to-point hardware link (for example, a DEC DMR-11), the IFF_POINTOPOINT flag will be set and the interface's address list will contain the address of the host on the other side of the connection. (Note that the broadcast and point-to-point attributes are mutually exclusive, and the two addresses share storage in the interface address structure.) These addresses and the local address of an interface are used by network-layer protocols in filtering incoming packets. An interface sets the IFF_RUNNING flag after it has allocated system resources and posted an initial read on the device it manages. This state bit is used to avoid multiple allocation requests when an interface's address is changed. The IFF_NOTRAILERS flag indicates that an interface should refrain from using *trailer encapsulations* on outgoing packets, or (where per-host negotiation of trailers is possible) that trailer encapsulations should not be requested; trailer protocols are described in Section 11.8. The IFF_NOARP flag indicates that an interface should not use an *Address Resolution Protocol* in mapping internetwork addresses to link-layer addresses; it also is described in Section 11.8.

Interface addresses and flags are set with *ioctl* requests. The SIOCSIFADDR request is used initially to define each interface's addresses. The SIOCSIFFLAGS request can be used to change an interface's state and to perform site-specific configuration. The destination address of a point-to-point link is set with the SIOCSIFDSTADDR request. Corresponding operations exist to read each value. Protocol families also can support operations to set and read the broadcast address. Finally, the SIOCGIFCONF request can be used to retrieve a list of interface names and protocol addresses for all interfaces and protocols configured in a running system; this request permits network processes such as the routing daemon to be constructed without detailed knowledge of the system's internal data structures.

11.2 Socket-to-Protocol Interface

The interface from the socket routines to the communication protocols is through the user request, *pr_usrreq*(), and control output, *pr_ctloutput*()—routines defined in the protocol switch table for each protocol. When the socket layer requires services of a supporting protocol, it makes a call to one of these two routines. The control-output routine is used to implement the *getsockopt* and *setsockopt* system calls; the user-request routine is used for all other operations. Calls to *pr_usrreq*() specify one of the requests shown in Fig. 11.3. Calls to *pr_ctloutput*() specify PRCO_GETOPT to get the current value of an option, or PRCO_SETOPT to set the value of an option.

Protocol User-Request Routine

Given a pointer to a protocol switch entry, *pr*, a call on the user-request routine is of the form,

```
error = (*pr->pr_usrreq)(so, req, m, addr, rights);
    struct socket *so;
    int req;
    struct mbuf *m, *addr, *rights;
```

The mbuf data chain *m* is supplied for output operations and for certain other operations where a result is to be returned. The address *addr* is supplied for address-oriented requests such as PRU_BIND, PRU_CONNECT, and PRU_SEND (when an address is specified; e.g., *sendto*). The *rights* parameter is a pointer to an optional mbuf chain containing user-specified access rights (see Section 10.6). Each protocol is responsible for disposal of the data mbuf chains on output operations. A nonzero return value from the user-request routine indicates a UNIX error number that should be passed to higher-level software. A description of each of the possible requests follows.

- **PRU_ATTACH: Attach protocol to socket** When a protocol is first bound to a socket (with the *socket* system call), the protocol module is called with the PRU_ATTACH request. It is the responsibility of the protocol module to allocate any resources necessary. The *attach* request will always precede any of the other requests, and will not occur more than once.
- **PRU_DETACH: Detach protocol from socket** This operation is the antithesis of the attach request, and is used at the time a socket is deleted. The protocol module may deallocate any resources assigned to the socket.
- **PRU_BIND: Bind address to socket** When a socket is initially created, it has no address bound to it. This request indicates that an address should be bound to an existing socket. The protocol module must verify that the requested address is valid and is available for use.

Table 11.3 *pr_usrreq* routine requests.

Request	Description
PRU_ABORT	abort connection and detach
PRU_ACCEPT	accept connection from peer
PRU_ATTACH	attach protocol to socket
PRU_BIND	bind name to socket
PRU_CONNECT	establish connection to peer
PRU_CONNECT2	connect two sockets
PRU_CONTROL	control protocol operation (*ioctl*)
PRU_DETACH	detach protocol from socket
PRU_DISCONNECT	disconnect from peer
PRU_FASTTIMO†	service 200-millisecond timeout
PRU_LISTEN	listen for connections
PRU_PEERADDR	fetch peer's address
PRU_PROTORCV†	receive from below
PRU_PROTOSEND†	send to below
PRU_RCVD	have taken data; more room now
PRU_RCVOOB	retrieve out-of-band data
PRU_SEND	send these data
PRU_SENDOOB	send out-of-band data
PRU_SENSE	sense socket status (*fstat*)
PRU_SHUTDOWN	will not send any more data
PRU_SLOWTIMO†	service 500-millisecond timeout
PRU_SOCKADDR	fetch socket's address

† Request used only internally by protocols.

- **PRU_LISTEN: Listen for incoming connections** The *listen request* indicates that the user wishes to listen for incoming connection requests on the associated socket. The protocol module should perform any state changes needed to carry out this request (if possible). A listen request always precedes any request to accept a connection.

- **PRU_CONNECT: Connect socket to peer** The *connect request* indicates that the user wants to a establish an association. The *addr* parameter supplied describes the peer to which to connect. The effect of a connect request may vary depending on the protocol. Virtual-circuit protocols use this request to initiate establishment of a network connection. Datagram protocols simply record the peer's address in a private data structure and use it to tag all outgoing packets. There are no restrictions on how many times a connect request may be used after an attach.

- **PRU_ACCEPT: Accept pending connection** Following a successful listen request and the arrival of one or more connections, this request is made to indicate that the user is about to accept a socket from the queue of sockets with completed connections. The socket supplied as a parameter is the socket that is being *accepted*; the protocol module is expected to fill in the supplied buffer with the address of the peer connected to the socket.

- **PRU_DISCONNECT: Disconnect connected socket** Eliminate an association created with a connect request. This request is used with datagram sockets before a new association is created; it is used with connection-oriented protocols only when the socket is closed.

- **PRU_SHUTDOWN: Shut down socket data transmission** This call is used to indicate that no more data will be sent. The protocol may, at its discretion, deallocate any data structures related to the shutdown and/or notify a connected peer of the shutdown.

- **PRU_RCVD: Data were received by user** This request is made only if the protocol entry in the protocol switch table includes the PR_WANTRCVD flag. When the socket layer removes data from the receive queue and passes them to the user, this request will be sent to the protocol module. This request may be used by the protocol to trigger acknowledgments, to refresh windowing information, to initiate data transfer, and so on.

- **PRU_SEND: Send user data** Each user request to send data is translated into one or more PRU_SEND requests. A protocol may indicate that a single user send request must be translated into a single PRU_SEND request by specifying the PR_ATOMIC flag in its protocol description. The data to be sent are presented to the protocol as a chain of mbufs, and an optional address is supplied in the *addr* parameter. The protocol is responsible for preserving the data in the socket's send queue if it is not able to send them immediately or if it may need them at some later time (e.g., for retransmission).

- **PRU_ABORT: Abnormally terminate service** This request indicates an abnormal termination of service. The protocol should delete any existing associations.

- **PRU_CONTROL: Perform control operation** The *control request* is generated when a user performs an *ioctl* system call on a socket and the *ioctl* is not intercepted by the socket routines. This request allows protocol-specific operations to be provided outside the scope of the common socket interface. The *addr* parameter contains a pointer to a kernel data area where relevant information may be obtained or returned. The *m* parameter contains the actual *ioctl* request code. The *rights* parameter contains a pointer to a network-interface structure if the *ioctl* operation pertains to a particular network interface.

- **PRU_SENSE: Sense socket status** The *sense request* is generated when the user makes an *fstat* system call on a socket; it requests the status of the associated socket. This call returns a standard *stat* structure that typically contains only the optimal transfer size for the connection (based on buffer size, windowing information, and maximum packet size).

- **PRU_RCVOOB: Receive out-of-band data** Any *out-of-band* data presently available are to be returned. An mbuf is passed to the protocol module, and the protocol should either place data in the mbuf or attach new mbufs to the one supplied if there is insufficient space in the single mbuf. An error may be returned if out-of-band data are not (yet) available or have already been consumed. The *addr* parameter contains any options, such as MSG_PEEK, that should be observed while this request is carried out.

- **PRU_SENDOOB: Send out-of-band data** This request is like the send request, but is used for out-of-band data.

- **PRU_SOCKADDR: Retrieve local socket address** The local address of the socket is returned, if one has been bound to the socket. The address (in a domain-specific format) is returned in the mbuf passed in the *addr* parameter.

- **PRU_PEERADDR: Retrieve peer socket address** The address of the peer to which the socket is connected is returned. The socket must be in a connected state for this request to be made to the protocol. The address (in a domain-specific format) is returned in the mbuf pointed to by the *addr* parameter.

- **PRU_CONNECT2: Connect two sockets without binding addresses** The protocol module is supplied two sockets and is requested to establish a connection between the two without binding any addresses, if possible. This call is used in implementing the *socketpair* system call.

Internal Requests

The following requests are used internally by the protocol modules and are never generated by the socket routines. In certain instances, they are used solely for convenience in tracing a protocol's operation (e.g., the slow timeout request).

- **PRU_FASTTIMO: Service fast timeout** A fast timeout has occurred. This request is made when a timeout occurs in the protocol's *pr_fasttimo*() routine. The *addr* parameter indicates which timer expired.

- **PRU_SLOWTIMO: Service slow timeout** A slow timeout has occurred. This request is made when a timeout occurs in the protocol's *pr_slowtimo*() routine. The *addr* parameter indicates which timer expired.

- **PRU_PROTORCV: Receive data for protocol** This request is used between protocols, not by the socket layer; it requests reception of data destined for a protocol and not for the user. No protocols currently use this facility.

- **PRU_PROTOSEND: Send data to protocol** This request allows a protocol to send data destined for another protocol module, not for a user. The details of how data are marked *addressed-to-protocol* instead of *addressed-to-user* are left to the protocol modules. No protocols currently use this facility.

Protocol Control-Output Routine

A call on the control-output routine is of the form

```
error = (*pr->pr_ctloutput)(op, so, level, optname, mp);
    struct socket *so;
    int level, optname;
    struct mbuf **mp;
```

where *op* is PRCO_SETOPT when setting an option's value, and PRCO_GETOPT when getting an option's value. The *level* parameter indicates the layer of software that should interpret the option request. A *level* of SOL_SOCKET is specified to control an option at the socket layer. When the option is to be processed by a protocol module below the socket layer, *level* is set to the appropriate protocol number (the same number used in the *socket* system call.) Each level has its own set of option names; this name is interpreted only by the targeted layer of software. The last parameter is a pointer to a pointer to an mbuf chain; the preexisting chain contains an option's new value when setting, and the pointer is used to return an mbuf chain that contains an option's value when getting. Mbufs passed to the control-output routine when setting an option value must be freed by the protocol. When getting an option value, mbufs used to return an option value are allocated by the protocol and returned to the socket layer, where they are freed after data are copied to the user.

In supporting the *getsockopt* and *setsockopt* system calls, the socket layer always invokes the control-output routine of the protocol attached to the socket. To access lower-level protocols each control-output routine must pass control-output requests that are not for itself *downward* to the next protocol in the protocol hierarchy. Chapter 12 describes some of the options provided by the protocols in the Internet and XNS communication domains.

11.3 Protocol–Protocol Interface

The interface between protocol modules uses the *pr_usrreq*(), *pr_input*(), *pr_output*(), *pr_ctlinput*(), and *pr_ctloutput*() routines. The *pr_usrreq*() and *pr_ctloutput*() routines are used by the socket layer to communicate with protocols and have standard calling conventions. The remaining routines are not normally accessed outside of a protocol family, and therefore different calling conventions have evolved.

Although imposing a standard calling convention for all of a protocol's entry points might theoretically permit an arbitrary interconnection of protocol modules, it would be very difficult in practice. Crossing a protocol-family boundary would require a network address to be converted from the format of the caller's domain to the format of the callee's domain. Consequently, connection of protocols in different communication domains is not generally supported, and calling conventions for the routines listed in the preceding paragraph are typically standardized on a per-domain basis.

In the following sections, we briefly examine the general framework and calling conventions of protocols. In Chapter 12, we examine specific protocols to see how they fit into this framework.

pr_output

The protocol output routine often uses a calling convention designed to send a single message on a connection; for example,

```
error = (*pr_output)(pcb, m);
    struct pcb *pcb;
    struct mbuf *m;
```

Lower-level protocol output routines may not always have protocol control blocks, and thus may require more explicit parameters.

pr_input

Upper-level protocol input routines are usually called at software-interrupt level once the network-level protocol has located the protocol identifier. They are generally more stylized than are output routines because they are often called via a protocol switch. Depending on the nature of the protocol family, they may receive a pointer to a control block identifying the connection, or they may have to locate the control block from information in the received packet. A typical calling convention is

```
(void) (*pr_input)(m, ifp);
    struct mbuf *m;
    struct ifnet *ifp;
```

In this example, the interface from which the packet was received is passed as the second parameter, and the protocol does the connection-level demultiplexing.

pr_ctlinput

This routine is used to pass *control* information (i.e., information that might be passed to the user, but does not consist of data) *upward* from one protocol module to another. The common calling convention for this routine is

```
(void) (*pr_ctlinput)(req, addr);
    int req;
    struct sockaddr *addr;
```

The *req* parameter is one of the values shown in Table 11.4. The *addr* parameter is the address to which the condition applies. Many of the requests have been derived from the Internet Control Message Protocol (ICMP) [Postel, 1981], and from error messages defined in the 1822 host/IMP convention [BBN, 1978].

Table 11.4 Control-input routine requests.

Request	Description
PRC_IFDOWN	network interface transition
PRC_ROUTEDEAD	select new route if possible
PRC_MSGSIZE	message size forced packet to be dropped
PRC_HOSTDEAD	remote host is down
PRC_HOSTUNREACH	remote host is unreachable
PRC_UNREACH_NET	no route to network
PRC_UNREACH_HOST	no route to host
PRC_UNREACH_PROTOCOL	protocol not supported by destination
PRC_UNREACH_PORT	port number not in use at destination
PRC_UNREACH_NEEDFRAG	fragmentation needed but not allowed
PRC_UNREACH_SRCFAIL	source route failed
PRC_REDIRECT_NET	routing redirect for a network
PRC_REDIRECT_HOST	routing redirect for a host
PRC_REDIRECT_TOSNET	routing redirect for type of service and network
PRC_REDIRECT_TOSHOST	routing redirect for type of service and host
PRC_TIMXCEED_INTRANS	packet lifetime expired in transit
PRC_TIMXCEED_REASS	lifetime expired on reassembly queue
PRC_PARAMPROB	header-parameter problem detected

11.4 Protocol–Network-Interface Interface

The lowest layer in the set of protocols that constitutes a protocol family must interact with one or more network interfaces to transmit and receive packets. It is assumed that any routing decisions have been made before a packet is sent to a network interface; in fact, a routing decision is necessary to locate any interface at all unless one uses a single *hardwired* interface. There are two cases with which we should be concerned in the interaction between protocols and network interfaces: transmission of a packet and receipt of a packet. We shall consider each separately.

Packet Transmission

Assuming that a protocol has chosen an interface identified by *ifp*, a pointer to a network interface structure, the protocol transmits a fully formatted network-level packet with the following call,

```
error = (*ifp->if_output)(ifp, m, dst);
    struct ifnet *ifp;
    struct mbuf *m;
    struct sockaddr *dst;
```

The output routine for the network interface transmits the packet *m* to the protocol address specified in *dst*, or returns an error indication (a UNIX error number). In reality, transmission may not be immediate or successful; typically, the output routine validates the destination address, queues the packet on its send queue, and primes an interrupt-driven routine to transmit the packet. For unreliable media, such as the Ethernet, *successful* transmission simply means that the packet has been placed on the cable without a collision. In contrast, an ARPANET IMP interface guarantees proper delivery or an error indication for each message transmitted. The model employed in the networking system attaches no promise of delivery to the packets presented to a network interface, and thus corresponds most closely to the Ethernet. Errors returned by the output routine are only those that can be detected immediately and are normally trivial in nature (no buffer space, address format not handled, etc.). If errors are detected after the call has returned, the protocol is not notified.

In transmitting messages, each network interface usually must formulate a link-layer address for each outgoing packet.[2] The interface layer must understand each protocol address format that it supports to formulate corresponding link-layer addresses. The network layer for each protocol family selects a destination address for each message and then uses that address to select the appropriate network interface to use. This destination address is passed to the interface's output routine in the form of a *sockaddr* structure. Presuming that the address format is supported by the interface, the interface must map the destination protocol address into an address for the link-layer protocol associated with the transmission medium the interface supports. This mapping may be a simple algorithm, it may require a table lookup, or it may require more involved techniques such as using the Address Resolution Protocol described in Section 11.8.

Packet Reception

Network interfaces receive packets and dispatch them to the appropriate network-layer protocol according to information encoded in the link-layer protocol header. Each protocol family must have one or more protocols that constitute the network layer described in Section 11.1. In this system, each network layer protocol has an input-packet queue assigned to it. Incoming packets received by a network interface are queued in a protocol's input packet queue, and a software interrupt is posted to initiate network-layer processing (see Fig. 11.4). Similar queues are used to store packets awaiting transmission by network-interface modules.

Four macros are available for manipulating packet queues:

- **IF_ENQUEUE(ifq, m)** Place the packet *m* at the tail of the queue *ifq*.
- **IF_DEQUEUE(ifq, m)** Place a pointer to the packet at the head of queue *ifq* in *m* and remove the packet from the queue; *m* will be zero if the queue is empty.

---

[2] A link-layer address may not be required for a point-to-point link.

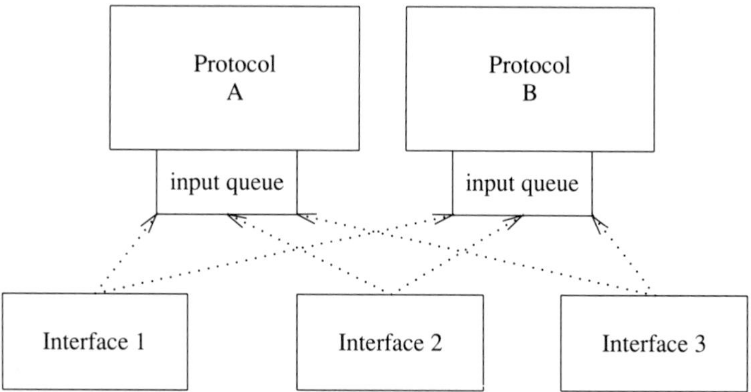

Figure 11.4 Input packets are dispatched to protocol input queues.

- **IF_DEQUEUEIF(ifq, m, ifp)** Remove the next packet from the head of a queue and return it in *m* and a pointer to the interface on which the packet was received in *ifp*.
- **IF_PREPEND(ifq, m)** Place the packet *m* at the head of the queue *ifq*.

Packet queues have a maximum length associated with them as a simple form of congestion control. The macro IF_QFULL() can be used to determine whether a queue is full, in which case another macro, IF_DROP(), can then be used to record the event in statistics kept for the queue. For example, the following code fragment is commonly found in a network interface's input routine:

```
if (IF_QFULL(inq)) {
    IF_DROP(inq);
    m_freem(m);        /* discard packet */
} else
    IF_ENQUEUE(inq, m);
```

On receiving a packet, a network interface decodes the packet type, strips the link-layer protocol header, attaches the identity of the receiving interface, and then dispatches the packet to the appropriate protocol. For example, packets are enqueued for the Internet domain with

```
schednetisr(NETISR_IP);   /* schedule IP input routine */
IF_ENQUEUE(&ipintr, m);   /* place message on IP's queue */
```

The *schednetisr*() macro marks a bit in a global status word and then posts a software interrupt. When the software interrupt occurs, the interrupt handler scans the status word, and for each preassigned bit that is set, invokes the associated protocol input routine. Bits in the status word are assigned according to the value of their protocol-family identifiers (see Table 11.5).

Table 11.5 Network-interrupt status-word bit assignments.

Status Bit	Value	Input Queue	Use
NETISR_RAW	PF_UNSPEC	*rawintrq*	unassigned/raw input
NETISR_IP	PF_INET	*ipintrq*	Internet IP protocol input
NETISR_IMP	PF_IMPLINK	*impintrq*	IMP/1822 error input
NETISR_NS	PF_NS	*nsintrq*	Xerox NS protocol input

Entries on a protocol's input queue contain both a packet and pointer to the network interface on which the packet was received. The pointer to the interface has many potential uses, such as deciding when to generate routing redirect messages. Input-handling routines that run at software-interrupt level are typically of the form

```
for (;;) {
    s = splimp();          /* block network from queue */
    IF_DEQUEUEIF(&xxintrq, m, ifp);
    splx(s);
    if (m == 0) break;     /* all packets processed */
    /* process packet and determine receiving protocol */
    (*pr_input)(m, ifp); /* invoke protocol */
}
```

While an entry is dequeued from an input queue, all network-interface input handling must be blocked by the processor's priority level being raised with *splimp*() to ensure that pointers in the queue data structure are not altered. Once a message is dequeued, it is processed and, if there is information in the packet for a higher-level protocol, the message is passed upward.

11.5 Routing

The networking system was designed for an internetwork environment in which a collection of local-area networks is connected at one or more points through hosts with multiple network interfaces (see Fig. 11.5). Hosts with multiple network interfaces, one on each local-area or long-haul network, are expected to act as gateways. In such an environment, issues related to gatewaying and packet-routing are important. Certain of these issues, such as congestion control, are handled in a simplistic manner (see Section 11.6). For others, the network system provides simple mechanisms on which more involved policies can be implemented. These mechanisms ensure that, as these problems become better understood, their solutions can be incorporated into the system.

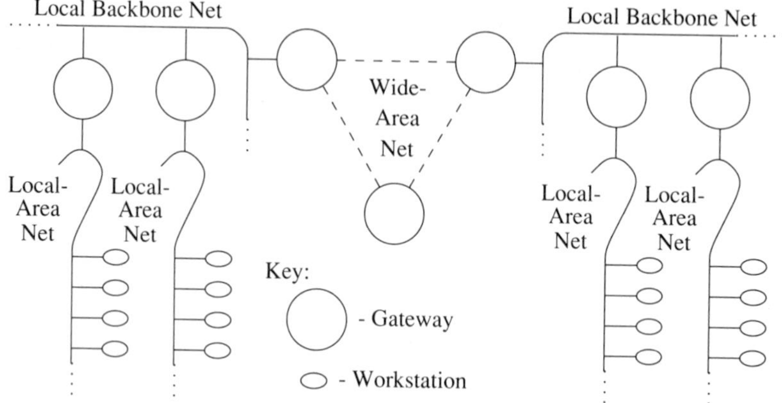

Figure 11.5 Example of the topology for which routing facilities were designed.

This section describes the facilities provided for message routing. Although there is nothing in the system that prevents protocols from managing their own routing information, the facilities described here were designed to support most needs. Note that the routing facilities included in the operating system do not impose *routing policies*, but instead support a *routing mechanism* by which externally defined policies can be implemented.

Routing Tables

The network system maintains a set of routing tables that is used by protocols in selecting a network interface to use in delivering a packet to its destination. These tables are composed of entries of the form shown in Fig. 11.6.

The routing information is organized in two separate tables, one for routes to a host and one for routes to a network. Hosts and networks are distinguished so that a single mechanism can be employed for broadcast and multidrop networks, and for networks built from point-to-point links (e.g., DECnet [DEC, 1980]).

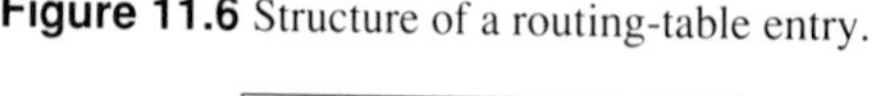

Figure 11.6 Structure of a routing-table entry.

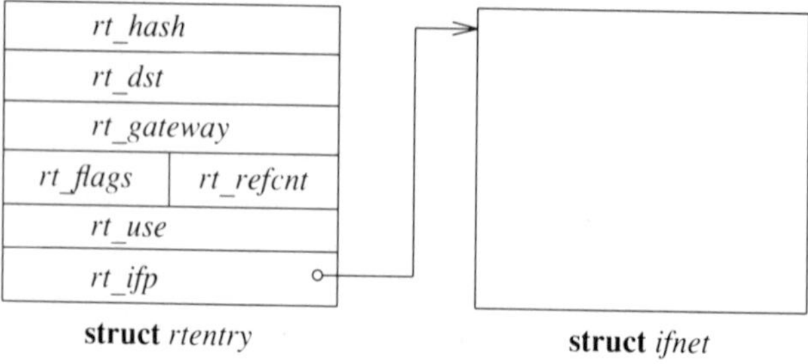

Each table is organized as a hashed set of linked lists. Two hash values are calculated by routines defined for each address family, one for the destination host and one for the network of the destination host. Each hash value is used to locate a hash chain to search (by taking the value modulo the hash-table size), and the entire value is used as a key in scanning the list of routes. Lookups are done first in the routing table for hosts, then in the routing table for networks. If both lookups fail, a final lookup is made for a *wildcard route* (by convention, *network* 0). The first appropriate route discovered is used. Use of this algorithm allows for the presence of specific routes to hosts, as well as routes to the network in general. Also, a fallback network route can be defined to an *intelligent gateway* that can then perform more informed routing decisions.

Each routing-table entry contains a destination (the desired final destination), a gateway to which to send the packet, and flags that indicate the route's status and type (host or network). A count of the number of packets sent using the route also is kept, along with a count of references held to the dynamically allocated structure to ensure that memory reclamation occurs only when the route is no longer referenced. Finally, a pointer to a network interface is kept; packets sent using the route are passed to this interface's output routine.

Routes are typed in two ways: as either *host* or *network*, and as either *direct* or *indirect*. The host–network distinction determines how to compare the destination address during lookup. If the route is to a network, only the packet's destination *network* is compared to that of the entry stored in the table. Otherwise, the route is to a host and the addresses must match *completely*.

The distinction between direct and indirect routes indicates whether the destination is directly connected to the source. This distinction is needed when the link-layer encapsulation is done. If a packet is destined for a peer at a host or network that is not directly connected to the source, the internetwork packet header will contain the address of the eventual destination, whereas the link-layer protocol header will address the intervening gateway. If the destination is directly connected, these addresses are likely to be identical, or a mapping between the two exists. The RTF_GATEWAY flag in a routing-table entry indicates that the route is to an *indirect* gateway agent, and that the link-layer header should be filled in from the *rt_gateway* field instead of from the final internetwork destination address.

It is assumed that multiple routes to the same destination will not be present. If more than one route is present, only the most recently installed route is used.

Routing Redirects

A *routing redirect* is a control request from a protocol to the routing system to modify an existing routing-table entry, or to create a new routing-table entry. Protocols usually generate such requests in response to routing-redirect messages they receive from gateways. Gateways generate routing-redirect messages when they recognize that a better route exists for a packet that they have been asked to forward. For example, if two hosts A and B are on the same network, and host A sends a packet to host B via a gateway C, then C will send a routing-redirect message to A indicating that A should send packets to B directly.

On hosts where exhaustive routing information is too expensive to maintain (e.g., workstations), the combination of wildcard routing entries and routing-redirect messages can be used to provide a simple routing-management scheme without the use of a higher-level policy process. Current connections may be rerouted after notification of the protocols by means of the protocols' *pr_ctlinput*() entries. Statistics are kept by the routing-table routines on the use of routing-redirect messages and on the latter's effect on the routing tables.

Routing-Table Interface

A protocol accesses the routing tables through three routines, one to allocate a route, one to free a route, and one to process a routing-redirect control message. The routine *rtalloc*() allocates a route; it is called with a pointer to a *route* structure that contains the desired destination (see Fig. 11.7). The route returned is assumed to be *held* by the caller until released with a call to *rtfree*(). Protocols that implement virtual circuits, such as Transmission Control Protocol (TCP), hold on to routes for the duration of the circuit's lifetime, whereas connectionless protocols, such as User Datagram Protocol (UDP), allocate and free routes whenever the routes' destination address changes.

The routine *rtredirect*() is called to process a routing-redirect control message. It is called with a destination address, the new gateway to that destination, and the source of the redirect. Redirects are accepted from only the current router for the destination. If a nonwildcard route exists to the destination, the gateway entry in the route is modified to point at the new gateway supplied. Otherwise, a new routing-table entry is inserted that reflects the information supplied. Routes to interfaces and routes to gateways that are not directly accessible from the host are ignored.

User-Level Routing Policies

The kernel routing facilities deliberately refrain from making policy decisions. Instead, routing policies are determined by user processes, which then add or

Figure 11.7 Data structures used in allocating routes.

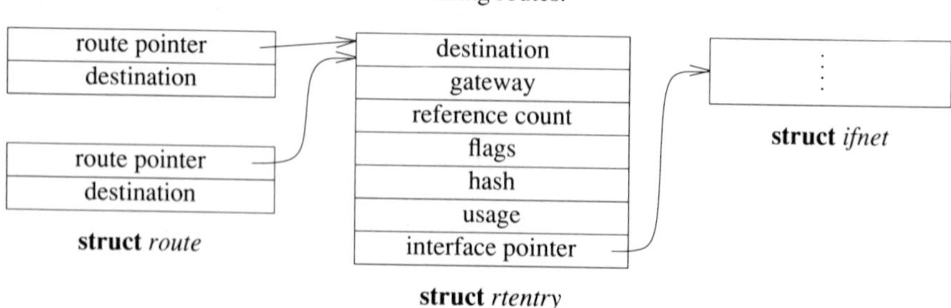

delete entries in the kernel routing tables through two *ioctl* system calls. The decision to place policy decisions in a user process implies that routing-table updates may lag a bit behind the identification of new routes, or the failure of existing routes. This period of instability is normally short, however, provided that the routing process is implemented properly. Internet-specific advisory information, such as ICMP error messages and IMP diagnostic messages, may also be read from raw sockets (described in Section 11.7).

Several routing-policy processes have been implemented. The system standard *routing daemon* uses a variant of the Xerox NS Routing Information Protocol [Xerox, 1981] to maintain up-to-date routing tables in a local environment. Interaction with other existing routing protocols, such as the Internet Exterior Gateway Protocol (EGP), has been accomplished using a similar scheme.

11.6 Buffering and Congestion Control

One of the major factors affecting the performance of a protocol is the buffering policy. Lack of a proper buffering policy can force packets to be dropped, cause false windowing information to be emitted by protocols, fragment host memory, and degrade the overall host performance. Due to problems such as these, most systems allocate a fixed pool of memory to the networking system and impose a policy optimized for *normal* network operation.

The 4.3BSD networking system is not dramatically different in this respect. At boot time, a small, fixed amount of memory is allocated by the networking system. At later times, more system memory may be requested as the need arises; at no time, however, is memory ever returned to the system. It would be possible to reclaim memory from the network; however, for this memory reclamation to be performed safely, some portion of the network would have to be disabled while data structures were updated. In the environments where the system has been used, storage use has not been an issue and thus storage reclamation has been left unimplemented.

Protocol Buffering Policies

Protocols reserve fixed amounts of buffering for send and receive queues at socket-creation time. These amounts define the high and low watermarks used by the socket routines in deciding when to block and unblock a process. The reservation of space does not currently result in any action by the memory-management routines.

Protocols that provide connection-level flow control base their decisions on the amount of space in the associated socket queues. That is, send windows are calculated based on the amount of free space in the socket's receive queue, whereas receive windows are adjusted based on the number of data awaiting transmission in the send queue.

Queue Limiting

Incoming packets from the network are always received unless memory allocation fails. However, each network-layer protocol input queue has an upper bound on the queue's length, and any packets exceeding that bound are discarded. It is possible for a host to be overwhelmed by excessive network traffic (for instance, if the host is acting as a gateway from a high-bandwidth network to a low-bandwidth network). As a *defense mechanism*, the queue limits can be adjusted to throttle network-traffic load on a host. Discarding packets is not always a satisfactory solution to a problem such as this (simply dropping packets is likely to increase the load on a network); the queue lengths were incorporated mainly as a safeguard mechanism. On the other hand, limiting *output* queue lengths can be valuable on hosts that gateway traffic from a high-bandwidth network to a low-bandwidth network.

11.7 Raw Sockets

A *raw socket* allows privileged users direct access to a protocol. Raw sockets are intended for knowledgeable processes that wish to take advantage of some protocol feature not directly accessible through the normal interface, or for the development of protocols built atop existing protocols. For example, the Internet EGP [Mills, 1984] is implemented as a user-level process utilizing a raw IP socket for delivery of packets. The raw IP socket interface attempts to provide an identical interface to the one a protocol would have if it were resident in the kernel.

The raw socket support is built around a generic raw socket interface, possibly augmented by protocol-specific processing routines. The next sections describe only the core of the raw socket interface; details specific to particular protocols are not discussed.

Control Blocks

Every raw socket has a protocol control block of the form shown in Fig. 11.8. All control blocks are kept on a doubly linked list for performing lookups during packet dispatch. Associations may be recorded in the control block and used by the output routine in preparing packets for transmission. The *rcb_proto* field contains the protocol family and protocol number with which the raw socket is associated. The protocol, family, and addresses are used to filter packets on input as described later. If any protocol-specific information is required, it can be attached to the control block through the *rcb_pcb* field. Protocol-specific options to be included in outgoing packets may be held with the *rcb_options* field.

A raw socket interface is datagram-oriented; each send or receive on the socket requires a destination address. Destination addresses may be supplied by the user or stored in the control block and automatically installed in the outgoing packet by the output routine. Since it is not possible to determine whether an address is present in the control block by inspection, two flags are used to indicate whether a local and foreign address are present. If routing is necessary, it must be performed by an underlying protocol.

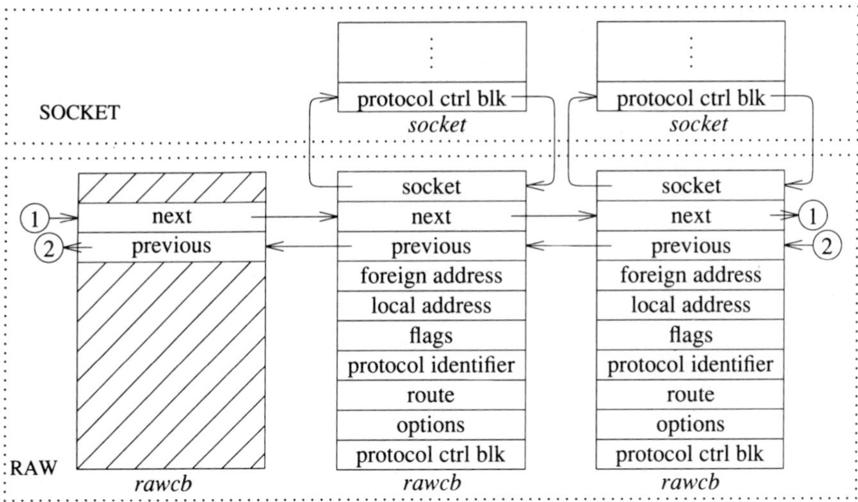

Figure 11.8 Raw socket control block.

Input Processing

Input packets are assigned to raw sockets based on a simple pattern-matching scheme. Each network interface or protocol gives unassigned packets to the raw input routine with the call[3]

```
raw_input(m, proto, src, dst)
    struct mbuf *m;
    struct sockproto *proto;
    struct sockaddr *src, *dst;
```

The data packet then has a generic header prepended to it of the form shown in Fig. 11.9, and it is placed in a packet queue for the raw input-protocol module. Packets taken from this queue are copied into all raw sockets that match the header according to the following rules:

1. The protocol family of the socket and header agree.
2. If the protocol number in the socket is nonzero, then it agrees with that found in the packet header.
3. If a local address is defined for the socket, the address format of the socket's local address is the same as the packet's destination address and the two addresses agree exactly.
4. Rule 3 is applied to the socket's foreign address and the packet's source address.

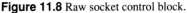

[3] In 4.3BSD, network interfaces do not pass unassigned packets to the raw input routine.

source
destination
protocol identifier

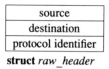

struct *raw_header*

Figure 11.9 Raw input packet header.

A basic assumption in the pattern-matching scheme is that addresses present in the control block and packet header (as constructed by the network interface and any raw input-protocol module) are in a canonical form that can be compared on a bit-for-bit basis.

Output Processing

On output, each send request results in a call to the raw socket's user request routine; this routine is common to all raw sockets. The user request routine passes the packet and a pointer to the raw control block to a protocol-specific output routine where any necessary processing is done before the packet is delivered to the appropriate network interface. The output routine is normally the only code required to implement a raw socket interface.

11.8 Additional Network Subsystem Topics

In the following sections, we shall discuss several aspects of the network subsystem that are not easy to categorize.

Out-of-Band Data

The ability to process out-of-band data is a facility specific to the stream-socket abstraction. Little agreement appears to exist as to what out-of-band data's semantics should be. TCP defines a notion called *urgent data*, in which in-line data are marked for *urgent delivery*; the NBS protocols [Burruss, 1980] and numerous other protocols provide a fully independent logical transmission channel along which out-of-band data are sent. In addition, the number of the data that can be sent in an out-of-band message varies from protocol to protocol, from 1 bit to 16 bytes or more.

A stream socket's notion of out-of-band data has been defined as the lowest reasonable common denominator. Out-of-band data are expected to be transmitted out of the normal sequencing and flow-control constraints of the data stream. A minimum of 1 byte of out-of-band data and one outstanding out-of-band message is expected to be provided by protocols supporting a stream socket. It is a protocol's prerogative to support larger-sized messages, or more than one outstanding out-of-band message at a time.

Out-of-band data are maintained by the protocol and usually are not stored in the socket's receive queue. A socket-level option, SO_OOBINLINE, is provided to force out-of-band data to be placed in the normal receive queue when urgent data are received. Placement of out-of-band data in the normal data stream can permit a protocol to hold several out-of-band messages simultaneously. This mechanism can avoid the loss of out-of-band messages caused by a user who responds slowly.

Address Resolution Protocol

The Address Resolution Protocol (ARP) is a link-level protocol that provides a dynamic address-translation mechanism for networks that support broadcast or multicast communication [Plummer, 1982]. ARP is used in 4.3BSD to map 32-bit Internet addresses to 48-bit Ethernet addresses. Although ARP is not specific either to Internet protocol addresses or to Ethernet, the 4.3BSD network subsystem supports only that combination. ARP is incorporated into the network-interface layer, although it logically sits *between* the network and network-interface layers.

The general idea of ARP is simple. A table of translations from network addresses to link-layer addresses is maintained. When an address-translation request is made to the ARP service by a network interface and the requested address is not in ARP's table of known translations, an ARP message is created that specifies the requested network address and an unknown link-layer address. This message is then broadcast by the interface in the expectation that one of the hosts attached to the network will know the translation—usually because the host is the intended target of the original message. If a response is received in a timely fashion, the ARP service uses the response to update its translation tables and to resolve the pending request, and the requesting network interface is then called to transmit the original message.

In practice, the simplicity of this algorithm is complicated by the necessity to minimize resources utilized by the name-translation tables and the network interfaces, to avoid stale translation data, and to deal with failed translation requests. The ARP translation tables are implemented as a cache of translations. Each entry in the cache maps a single Internet network address to its corresponding Ethernet address and has a timer associated with it. The entries are organized in a hash structure to speed lookups. A request is made to resolve an Internet address to an Ethernet address for an outgoing message by the call

```
result = arpresolve(ac, m, destip, desten, usetrailers);
    struct arpcom *ac;
    struct mbuf *m;
    struct in_addr *destip;
    u_char *desten;
    int *usetrailers;
```

ARP first checks its tables to see whether the Internet address, *destip*, is already present. If the address is known and the entry is *complete* (i.e., it is not waiting for a response), the Ethernet address is returned in *desten*. Otherwise, if the address was not found, ARP must allocate a new entry in the table, queue the outgoing message for future transmission, and broadcast a message requesting the Internet address translation. At the same time, a timer associated with the entry is initialized to ensure that the mbuf chain in which the message is stored will be reclaimed if no response is received for the translation. If another translation request is made before a reply is received, the queued message is discarded and only the newer one is saved.

At a later time—preferably before the timer has expired on the queued message—ARP will receive a response to its translation request. The received message is processed first by the *arpinput*() routine, as invoked from each network-interface device that supports ARP, and the ARP packet is processed to locate the translation entry. If the message completes a pending translation, the entry is updated and the original message is passed back to the network interface for transmission. This time, the resultant call to *arpresolve*() will succeed without delay.

ARP input handling must cope with requests for the host's own address as well as responses to translation requests the host generated. The input module also watches for responses from other hosts that advertise a translation for its own Internet address. This monitoring is done to ensure that no two hosts on the same network believe they have the same Internet address (although this error may be detected, ARP's only recourse is to log a diagnostic message).

ARP normally times out completed translation entries in its cache after 20 minutes and incomplete translation entries after 3 minutes. Entries may be marked *permanent*, however, in which case they are never removed from the cache. Entries may also be marked *published*, allowing one host to act as a surrogate for other hosts that do not support ARP.

The use of ARP is important to the smooth operation of an Ethernet network that uses the Internet protocols. However, it can pose compatibility problems when hosts that do not support ARP are also present. Published entries can be used for hosts that do not support ARP, but if these hosts do not support a complete 32-bit to 48-bit mapping between Internet and Ethernet addresses, this is insufficient. Fortunately, most Internet hosts now support ARP.

VAX UNIBUS Interfaces

All VAX hardware-based interfaces supported by 4.3BSD reside on the UNIBUS. UNIBUS interfaces fall into two categories, according to whether host–device communication is by DMA or through shared UNIBUS memory. For devices that support DMA, a common set of utility routines for dealing with the UNIBUS is used; their operation is described here.

Each network device has at least two packet buffers for transmitting and receiving messages. All DMA transfers pass through a UNIBUS adapter to the UNIBUS on which the hardware device is located. The UNIBUS I/O mapping registers must be set up to map an I/O buffer's memory pages into a UNIBUS's address space (see Fig. 11.10).

Each UNIBUS-based interface utilizes an *if_ubinfo* structure that contains the general information about the device's I/O buffers on one UNIBUS. In addition,

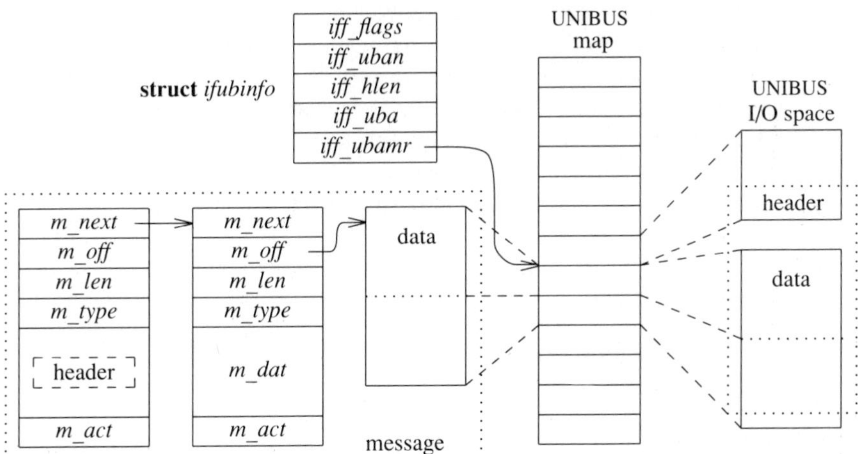

Figure 11.10 Mapping a message from VAX to UNIBUS address spaces.

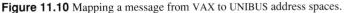

there is a structure describing each buffer, including UNIBUS resources held by the interface to map the buffer into the UNIBUS's I/O space. At system initialization, enough memory pages and UNIBUS map registers are allocated for each buffer to map a full-sized packet and header into the UNIBUS address space. The VAX virtual address of the buffer is held in *ifrw_addr*, and the map registers begin at *ifrw_mr*. UNIBUS map register *ifrw_mr*[−1] maps the link-layer protocol header ending on a page boundary (for the benefit of the trailer encapsulation, described later). Additional structures are associated with each receive and transmit buffer—normally one each per interface.

When transmitting a message, the interface software must transfer the contents of an mbuf chain to a region of memory that is mapped contiguously in the UNIBUS address space. It effects this transfer by copying the data or, when possible, by setting up the UNIBUS adapter's mapping registers to map data pages held by mbufs into the appropriate region of the UNIBUS address space. In the latter case, map registers that normally map pages of the transmit buffer are changed to point at the mbuf data pages temporarily. The map registers are restored to reference the reserved pages of the transmit buffer when they are next used. The mbufs containing pages mapped for transfer are placed on a queue to be freed after transmission. Mbufs whose contents were copied are reclaimed immediately.

When a message that has been transferred into VAX memory is received, a similar process must be performed. If a transfer contains at least one-half of a page of data, page frames are allocated from the mbuf page pool and are traded with the pages already containing the data. These new pages are mapped into the receive buffer to replace the pages just placed in mbufs, making the device ready for the next UNIBUS transfer.

The remapping of pages improves the network performance on machines where the CPU overhead for copying memory is higher than that for remapping pages of memory. This remapping is possible only when the message sizes are large enough to permit such operations (most commonly, when transmissions utilize a local-area network, such as the Ethernet). The use of a trailer encapsulation also interacts well with this scheme, potentially permitting data to be transferred from device input to a user's address space without copying.

Trailer Protocols

Memory-to-memory copies can represent a significant portion of the overhead associated with network data-transport services [Watson & Mamrak, 1987]. Consequently, the designers devoted a great deal of effort to minimizing such operations in the design of the network software. Many architectures provide virtual-memory hardware organized in page-sized units and permit I/O transfers to be mapped on a page basis. An attractive scheme for reducing copy operations is to keep data in page-sized units on page-aligned boundaries, so that the system can move data in memory by altering page-table entries rather than by physically copying the data. The socket software attempts to place user data in mbufs that have pages associated with them whenever possible (see Section 10.6). VAX UNIBUS devices that support DMA utilize routines that remap pages into the UNIBUS address space in preparation for DMA whenever possible. This potentially permits data transmission to be accomplished with only a single copy operation. Data must be copied into the kernel's address space under the existing memory-management scheme; the copying is not necessary in some other systems to which the networking software has been ported.

Unfortunately, performing a similar operation when receiving data from the network is difficult. Consider the format of an incoming packet. A packet typically contains a link-level protocol header followed by one or more headers used by higher-level protocols. Finally, the data, if there are any, follow these headers. As the header information may be variable in length, ensuring that data destined for a user's receive buffer are properly aligned in memory is impossible without a priori knowledge of the format of the protocol headers (e.g., the protocol header length would be known if the system supported only a single protocol header format).

To allow a variable-length protocol header to be present and still to ensure page alignment of data, a special local network encapsulation can be used. This encapsulation, termed a *trailer protocol* [Leffler & Karels, 1984], places variable-length header information after the data (see Fig. 11.11). The link-layer header contains a new trailer-specific protocol-type value that encodes the size of the data portion, and a new *trailer-protocol header* is inserted before the variable-length header information. The trailer protocol contains the original packet type and the size of the protocol information that follows it. If the link-layer protocol header is of fixed size (as is usually the case), input DMA may be offset by the size of this header to ensure that data land in a page-aligned region of memory.

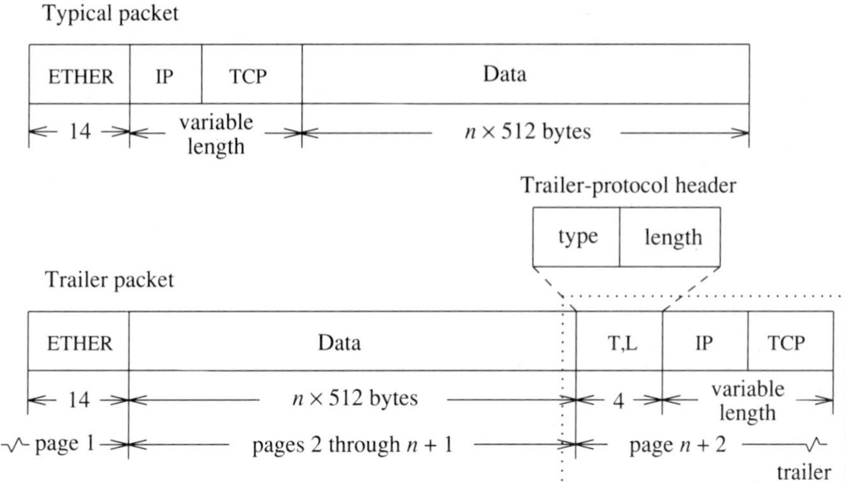

Figure 11.11 Trailer-protocol packet format.

The processing of a trailer protocol is simple. On output, the packet type in the link-layer header is set to indicate that a trailer encapsulation is being used. This type is selected from a set of types reserved for trailers according to the number of data pages in the message that precede the trailer-protocol header. The trailer-protocol header is initialized to contain the actual packet identifier and the size of the variable-length header, and is appended to the data along with the variable-length header information.

On input, the interface routines identify the trailer encapsulation by the packet type in the link-layer header and calculate the number of pages of data to find the beginning of the trailer. The trailing-protocol header information is then copied into a separate mbuf, and is linked to the front of the resultant packet. The data portion is left in the pages of the receive buffer, and new pages are allocated for the receive buffer.

Trailer protocols require cooperation between source and destination hosts. To permit trailers to be negotiated on a host-by-host basis, the ARP service includes negotiation of the use of trailer protocols. During the normal exchange of ARP request and response packets between a pair of hosts, each host may send an additional ARP response for the trailer-protocol type, indicating a desire to receive trailer-encapsulated packets.

For network interfaces that reside on an Ethernet and use ARP, each call to resolve an Internet address returns an indication of whether the receiving host wishes to receive trailer protocols. The system will send trailer encapsulations only if the host has indicated a willingness to receive them. Trailer-encapsulation packets are always accepted on networks that do not use ARP to negotiate the use of trailers; if hosts on a network are incapable of receiving trailers, a flag, IFF_NOTRAILERS, may be set in the interface structure to disable the use of trailers.

Exercises

11.1 Name two key data structures used in the networking subsystem that are important in ensuring that the socket-layer software is kept independent of the networking implementation.

11.2 Why are software interrupts used to trigger network protocol processing on receipt of data, rather than the protocol processing being encapsulated in separate processes?

11.3 What routines in the protocol switch are called by the socket layer? Explain why each of these routines is called.

11.4 Assume that a *reliably delivered message socket* (SOCK_RDM) is a connectionless socket that guarantees reliable delivery of data and that preserves message boundaries. Which flags would a protocol that supported this type of socket have set in the *pr_flags* field of its protocol-switch entry?

11.5 Give an example of a network interface that is useful without an underlying hardware device.

11.6 Give two reasons why the addresses of a network interface are *not* in the network-interface data structure.

11.7 Why is the name or address of a socket kept at the network layer and not at the socket layer?

11.8 Why does 4.3BSD not attempt to enforce a rigid protocol–protocol interface structure?

11.9 Describe two tasks performed by a network-interface output routine.

11.10 Why is the identity of the network interface on which each message is received passed upward with the message?

11.11 What routing *policies* are implemented in the kernel?

11.12 Why are two separate tables—one for hosts and one for networks—used in the routing facilities?

11.13 What routing facility is designed mainly to support workstations?

11.14 What is a routing redirect? For what is it used?

11.15 Why do the output-packet queues for each network interface have limits on the number of packets that may be queued?

11.16 What does the SO_OOBINLINE socket option do? Why does it exist?

*11.17 Explain why it is impossible to use the raw socket interface to support parallel protocol implementations—some in the kernel and some in user mode. What modifications to the system would be necessary to support this facility?

*11.18 Why are access rights provided to the user request routine at the same time as any associated data are provided, instead of being sent in a separate call?

*11.19 What is a trailer protocol? Should the use of trailer protocols improve the performance of a system that is I/O limited (e.g., a system with a slow hardware controller)? What about a system that is CPU-bound in its protocol processing?

References

BBN, 1978.
BBN, ''Specification for the Interconnection of Host and IMP,'' Technical Report 1822, Bolt, Beranek, and Newman, Cambridge, MA (May 1978).

Burruss, 1980.
J. Burruss, ''Features of the Transport and Session Protocols,'' Report No. ICST/HLNP-80-1, National Bureau of Standards, Washington, D.C. (March 1980).

DEC, 1980.
DEC, ''DECnet DIGITAL Network Architecture—General Description,'' Report No. AA-K179A-TK, Digitial Equipment Corporation, Maynard, MA (October 1980).

ISO, 1984.
ISO, ''Open Systems Interconnection—Basic Reference Model,'' ISO 7498, International Organization for Standardization (1984). Available from: American National Standards Institute, 1430 Broadway, New York, NY 10018.

Leffler & Karels, 1984.
S. J. Leffler & M. J. Karels, ''Trailer Encapsulations,'' RFC 893, SRI Network Information Center, Menlo Park, CA (April 1984).

Mills, 1984.
D. L. Mills, ''Exterior Gateway Protocol Formal Specification,'' RFC 904, SRI Network Information Center, Menlo Park, CA (April 1984).

Plummer, 1982.
D. Plummer, ''An Ethernet Address Resolution Protocol,'' RFC 826, SRI Network Information Center, Menlo Park, CA (September 1982).

Postel, 1981.
J. Postel, ''Internet Control Message Protocol,'' RFC 792, SRI Network Information Center, Menlo Park, CA (September 1981).

Watson & Mamrak, 1987.
R. W. Watson & S. A. Mamrak, ''Gaining Efficiency in Transport Services by Appropriate Design and Implementation Choices,'' *ACM Transactions on Computer Systems* **5**(2), pp. 97–120 (May 1987).

Xerox, 1981.
Xerox, ''Internet Transport Protocols,'' Xerox System Integration Standard 028112, Xerox Corporation, Stamford, CT (December 1981).

CHAPTER 12

Network Protocols

Chapter 11 presented the network communications architecture of 4.3BSD. In this chapter, we examine the network protocols implemented within this framework. The 4.3BSD system supports three communication domains: DARPA Internet, Xerox Network Systems (NS), and UNIX. The UNIX domain does not include network protocols, as it operates entirely within a single system. The DARPA Internet protocol suite was the first set of protocols implemented within the network architecture of 4.2BSD. Following the release of 4.2BSD, several proprietary protocol families were implemented by vendors within the network architecture. However, it was not until the addition of the Xerox NS protocols in 4.3BSD that the system's ability to support multiple network protocol families was visibly demonstrated. Although some parts of the protocol interface were previously unused and thus unimplemented, the changes required to add a second network protocol family did not substantially modify the network architecture.

In this chapter, we shall concentrate on the organization and implementation of the DARPA Internet protocols. This protocol implementation is widely used, both in 4BSD systems and in many other systems, because it was publicly available when many vendors were looking for tuned and reliable communication protocols. Developers have implemented other protocols, including Xerox NS, by following the same general framework set forth by the Internet protocol routines. After describing the overall architecture of the Internet protocols, we shall examine their operation according to the structure defined in Chapter 11. We shall also describe the significant algorithms used by the Internet protocols. We then shall present an overview of the Xerox NS protocols and their implementation.

12.1 DARPA Internet Network Protocols

The DARPA Internet network protocols were developed under the sponsorship of DARPA, for use on the ARPANET [McQuillan & Walden, 1977; DARPA, 1983].

They are commonly known as TCP/IP, although TCP and IP are only two of the many protocols in the family. Unlike earlier protocols used within the ARPANET (the ARPANET Host-to-Host Protocol, sometimes called NCP, Network Control Program [Carr *et al.*, 1970]), these protocols do not assume a reliable subnetwork that ensures delivery of data. Instead, the Internet protocols were devised for a model in which hosts were connected to networks with varying characteristics, and the networks were interconnected by gateways. Such a model is called a *catenet* [Cerf, 1978]. The Internet protocols are designed for packet-switching networks ranging from the ARPANET, which provides reliable message delivery or notification of failure, to pure datagram networks such as Ethernet that provide no indication of datagram delivery.

This model leads to the use of at least two protocol layers. One layer operates end-to-end between two hosts involved in a conversation. It is based on a lower-level protocol that operates on a hop-by-hop basis, forwarding each message through intermediate gateways to the destination host. In general, there exists at least one protocol layer above the other two, which is the application layer. This three-level layering has been called the ARPANET Reference Model [Padlipsky, 1985]. The three layers correspond roughly to levels 3 (network), 4 (transport), and 7 (application) in the ISO Open Systems Interconnection reference model [ISO, 1984].

The Internet communications protocols that support this model have the layering illustrated in Fig. 12.1. The Internet Protocol, IP, is the lowest-level protocol in the ARPANET Reference Model; this corresponds to the ISO network layer. IP operates hop by hop as a datagram is sent from the originating host to its destination via any intermediate gateways. It provides the network-level services of host addressing, routing and, if necessary, packet fragmentation and reassembly if intervening networks cannot send an entire packet in one piece. All the other protocols use the services of IP. The Transmission Control Protocol (TCP) and User Datagram Protocol (UDP) are transport-level protocols that provide

Figure 12.1 Internet protocol layering. TCP—Transmission Control Protocol; UDP—User Datagram Protocol; IP—Internet Protocol; ICMP—Internet Control Message Protocol.

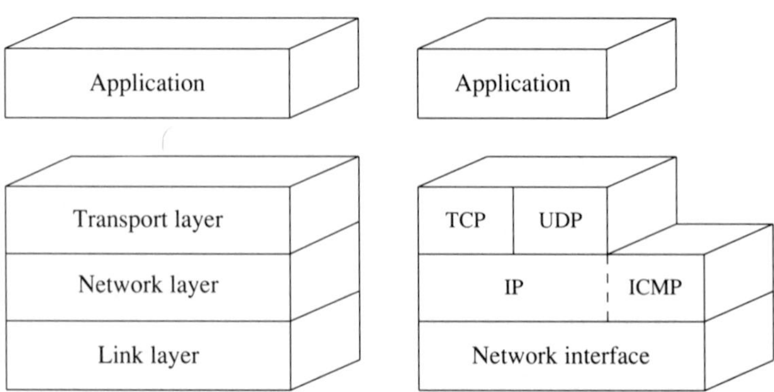

additional facilities to IP. Each protocol adds a port identifier to IP's host address so that local and remote sockets can be identified. TCP provides reliable, unduplicated, and flow-controlled transmission of data; it supports the stream socket type in the Internet domain. UDP provides an optional data checksum for checking integrity in addition to a port identifier, but otherwise adds little to the services provided by IP. UDP is the protocol used by datagram sockets in the Internet domain. The Internet Control Message Protocol (ICMP) is used for error reporting and for other network-management tasks; it is logically a part of IP, but like the transport protocols is layered above IP. It is usually not accessed by users. Raw access to the IP and ICMP protocols is possible through *raw sockets*; see Section 11.7 for information on this facility.

The Internet protocols were designed to support heterogeneous host systems and architectures. These systems use a wide variety of internal data representations. Even the basic unit of data, the *byte*, was not the same on all host systems; one common type of host supported variable-sized bytes. The network protocols, however, require a standard representation. This representation is expressed in terms of the *octet*, an eight-bit byte. We shall use this term as it is used in the protocol specifications to describe network data, although we continue to use the term *byte* to refer to data or storage within the system. All fields in the Internet protocols that are larger than an octet are expressed in *network byte order*, with the most significant octet first. The 4.3BSD network implementation uses a set of routines or macros to convert short and long integer fields between host and network byte order on hosts (such as the VAX) that have a different native ordering.

Internet Addresses

An *Internet host address* is a 32-bit number that identifies both the network on which a host is located and the host on that network. Network identifiers are assigned by a central agency, whereas host identifiers are assigned by each network's administrator. It follows that a host with network interfaces attached to multiple networks has multiple addresses. Figure 12.2 shows the original addressing scheme that was tied to the subnetwork addressing used on the ARPANET: Each host was known by the number of the ARPANET IMP to which it was attached and by its host port number on that IMP (Interface Message Processor; see Section 12.9). The IMP and host numbers each occupied one octet of the address. One of the remaining two octets was used to designate the network, and the other was available for uses such as multiplexed host connections—thus the name logical host. This encoding of the address limits the number of networks to 255, a number that quickly proved to be too small. Figure 12.2 shows how the network portion of the address was encoded such that it could be variable in size. The most significant bits of the network part of the address determine the class of an address. Three classes are defined, A, B and C, with high-order bits of 0, 10, and 110;[1] they use 8, 16, and 24 bits, respectively, for the network part of the

---

[1] A fourth class, D, has been defined with high-order bits 1110. It is used in experimental multicast facilities.

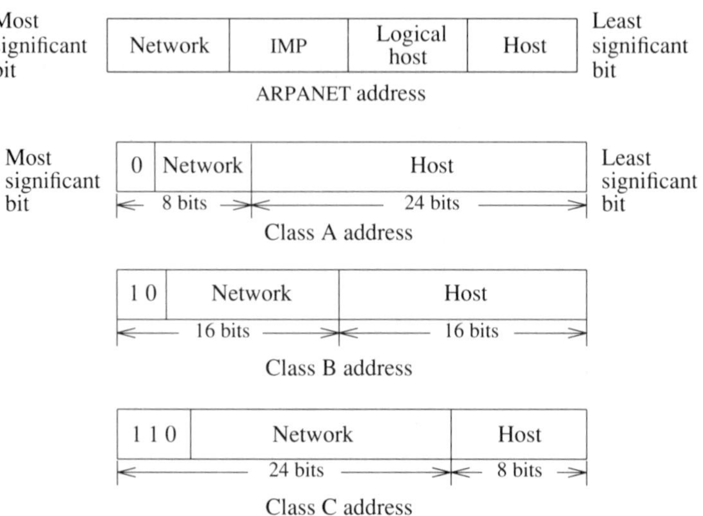

Figure 12.2 Internet addresses. IMP—Interface Message Processor.

address. Each class has fewer bits for the host part of each address and thus supports fewer hosts than do the higher classes. This form of frequency encoding supports a larger number of networks of varying size yet is compatible with the old encoding of ARPANET addresses.

Subnets

The basic Internet addressing scheme uses a 32-bit address that contains both a network and host identifier. All interconnected networks must be known to a central collection of routing agents for full connectivity. This scheme does not handle a large number of interconnected networks well because of the large amount of routing information necessary to ensure full connectivity. Furthermore, when networks are installed at a rapid pace, the administrative overhead is significant. However, many networks are installed at organizations such as universities, companies, and research centers that have a large number of interconnected local-area networks with only a few points of attachment to external networks. To handle these problems, the notion of a *subnet* addressing scheme was added [Mogul & Postel, 1985] that allows a collection of networks to be known by a single network number.

Subnets allow the addition of another level of hierarchy to the Internet address space. They partition a network assigned to an organization into multiple address spaces (see Fig. 12.3). This partitioning, each part of which is termed a *subnet*, is visible to only those hosts and gateways on the subnetted network. To hosts that are not on the subnetted network, the subnet structure is not visible. Instead, all hosts on subnets of a particular network are perceived externally as being on a single network. The scheme allows Internet routing to be performed

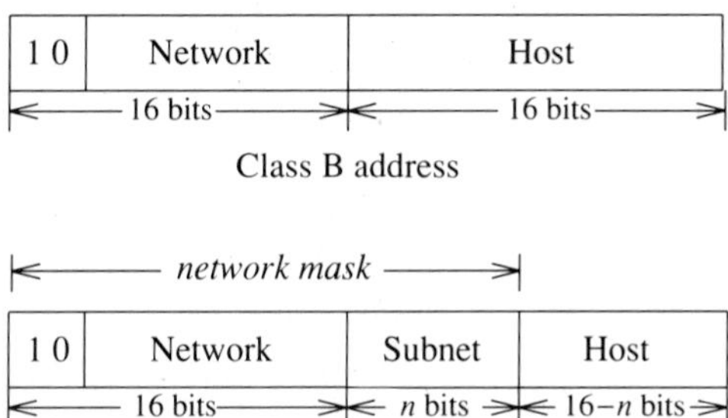

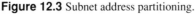

Figure 12.3 Subnet address partitioning.

on a site-by-site basis, as all hosts on a site's subnets appear to off-site hosts and gateways to be on a single Internet network. This partitioning scheme also permits sites to have greater local autonomy over the network topology at their site.

When a subnet addressing scheme is set up at a site, a partitioning of the assigned Internet address space for that site must be chosen. Consider Fig. 12.3. If a site has a class B network address assigned to it, it has 16 bits of the address in which to encode a subnet number and the identifier of a host on that subnet. An arbitrary subdivision of the 16 bits is permitted, but sites must balance the number of subnets they will need against the number of hosts that may be addressed on each subnet. To inform the system of the desired partitioning scheme, the site administrator specifies a *network mask* for each network interface. This mask shows which bits in the Internet address to include when extracting a network identifier from a local address. The mask includes the normal network portion as well as the subnet field. This mask also is used when the host part of an address is extracted. When interpreting an address that is not local, the system uses the mask corresponding to the class of the address.

The implementation of subnets is isolated, for the most part, to the routines that manipulate Internet addresses. Each Internet address assigned to a network interface is maintained in an *in_ifaddr* structure that contains an interface address structure and additional information for use in the Internet domain (see Fig. 12.4). When an interface's network mask is specified, it is recorded in the *ia_subnetmask* field of the address structure. The network mask, *ia_netmask*, is calculated based on the type of the network number (class A, B, or C) when the interface's address is assigned. For nonsubnetted networks, the two masks are identical. The system then interprets local Internet addresses using these values. An address is considered to be local if the field under the network mask matches the network field of an interface address. Thus, the subnet mask is assumed to be uniform throughout the subnetted network.

Broadcast Addresses

On networks capable of supporting broadcast datagrams, 4.2BSD used the address with a host part of zero for broadcasts. After 4.2BSD was released, the Internet broadcast address was defined as the address with a host part of all ones [Mogul,

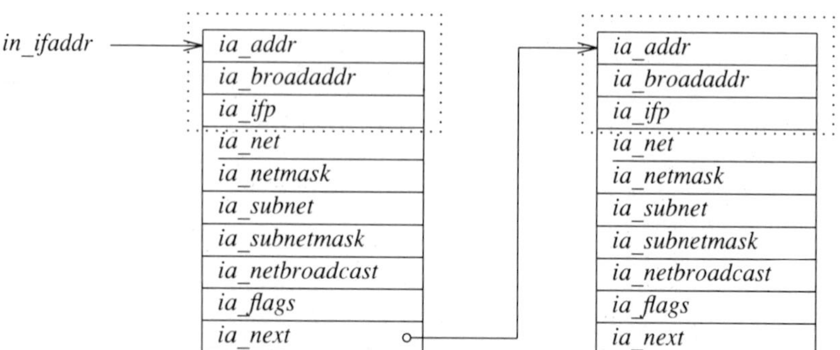

Figure 12.4 Internet interface address structure.

1984]. This change and the introduction of subnets both complicate the recognition of broadcast addresses. Hosts may use a host part of zero or ones to signify broadcast, and some may understand the presence of subnets, whereas others may not. For these reasons, 4.3BSD sets the broadcast address for each interface to be the host value of all ones, but allows the alternate address to be set for backward compatibility. If the network is subnetted, the subnet field of the broadcast address contains the normal subnet number. The *logical* broadcast address for the network also is calculated when the address is set; this would be the standard broadcast address if subnets were not in use. This address is needed by the IP input routine to filter input packets. On input, 4.3BSD recognizes and accepts subnet and network broadcast addresses with host parts of zeros or ones, as well as the address with 32 bits of one (''broadcast on this physical network'').

Internet Ports and Associations

At the IP level, packets are addressed to a host rather than to a process or communications port. However, each packet contains an eight-bit protocol number that identifies the next protocol that should receive the packet. Internet transport protocols use an additional identifier to designate the connection or communications port on the host. Most protocols (including TCP and UDP) use a 16-bit port number for this purpose. Each protocol maintains its own mapping of port numbers to processes or descriptors. Thus, an *association*, such as a connection, is fully specified by the tuple <source address, destination address, protocol number, source port, destination port>. Connection-oriented protocols such as TCP must enforce the uniqueness of associations; other protocols generally do so as well. When the local part of the address is set before the remote part, it is necessary to choose a unique port number to prevent collisions when the remote part is specified.

Protocol Control Blocks

For each TCP- or UDP-based socket, an *Internet protocol control block* (an *inpcb* structure) is created to hold Internet network addresses, port numbers, routing information, and pointers to any auxiliary data structures. TCP, in addition, creates a *TCP control block* (a *tcpcb* structure) to hold the wealth of protocol state information necessary for its implementation. Internet control blocks for use with TCP are maintained on a doubly linked list private to the TCP protocol module. Internet control blocks for use with UDP are kept on a similar list private to the UDP protocol module. Two separate lists are needed because each protocol in the Internet domain has a distinct space of port identifiers. Common routines are used by the individual protocols to add new control blocks to a list, to fix the local and remote parts of an association, to locate a control block by association, and to delete control blocks. IP demultiplexes message traffic based on the protocol identifier specified in its protocol header, and each higher-level protocol is then responsible for checking its list of Internet control blocks to direct a message to the appropriate socket. Figure 12.5 shows the linkage between the socket data structure and these protocol-specific data structures.

The implementation of the Internet protocols is rather tightly coupled, as befits the strong intertwining of the protocols. For example, the transport protocols send and receive packets including not only their own header, but also an IP pseudoheader containing the source and destination address, the protocol identifier, and a packet length. This pseudoheader is included in the transport-level packet checksum.

We are now ready to examine the operation of the Internet protocols. We begin with UDP, as it is far simpler than TCP.

Figure 12.5 Internet Protocol data structures.

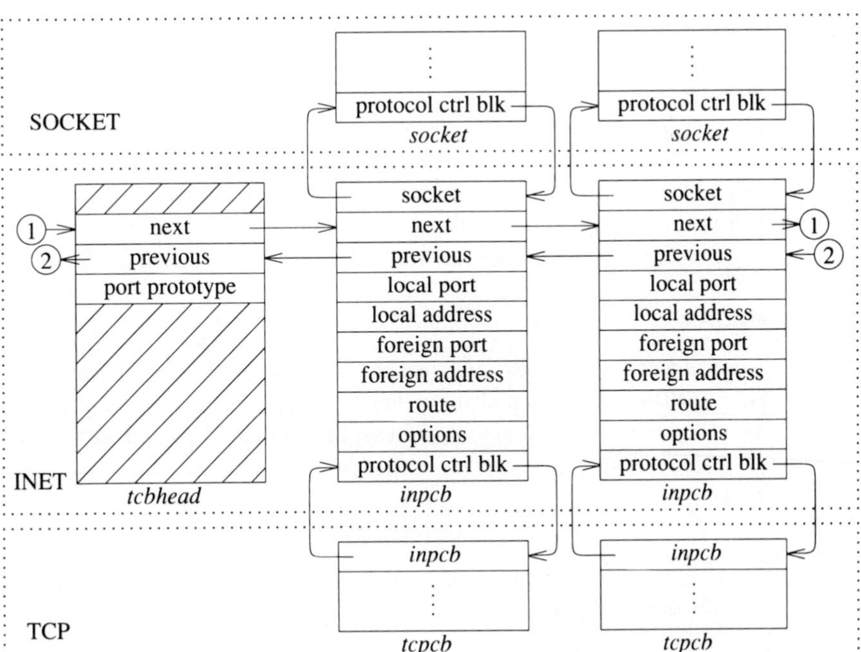

12.2 User Datagram Protocol (UDP)

The *User Datagram Protocol* (*UDP*) is a simple unreliable datagram protocol that provides only peer-to-peer addressing and optional data checksums.[2] Its protocol headers are extremely simple, containing only the source and destination port numbers, the datagram length, and the data checksum. The host addresses for a datagram are provided by the IP pseudoheader.

Initialization

When a new datagram socket is created in the Internet domain, the socket layer locates the protocol-switch entry for UDP and calls the *udp_usrreq*() routine PRU_ATTACH entry with the socket as a parameter. UDP uses *in_pcballoc*() to create a new protocol control block on its list of current sockets. It also sets the default limits for the socket send and receive buffers. Although datagrams are never placed in the send buffer, the limit is set as an upper limit on datagram size; the UDP protocol-switch entry contains the flag PR_ATOMIC, requiring that all data in a send operation be presented to the protocol at one time.

If the application program wishes to bind a port number—for example, the well-known port for some datagram service—it calls the *bind* system call. This request reaches UDP as the PRU_BIND request to *udp_usrreq*(). The binding may also specify a specific host address, which must be an address of an interface on this host. Otherwise, the address will be left unspecified, matching any local address on input, and with an address chosen as appropriate on each output operation. The binding is done by *in_pcbbind*(), which verifies that the chosen port number (or address and port) is not in use, then records the local part of the association.

To send datagrams, the system must know the remote part of an association. This address and port may be specified with each send operation using *sendto* or *sendmsg*, or the specification may be done ahead of time with the *connect* system call. In either case, UDP uses the *in_pcbconnect*() function to record the destination address and port. If the local address was not bound, and if a route for the destination is found, the address of the outgoing interface is used as the local address. If no local port number was bound, one is chosen at this time.

Output

A system call that sends data reaches UDP as a call to *udp_usrreq*() with the PRU_SEND request and a chain of mbufs containing the data for the datagram. If the call provided a destination address, the address is passed as well; otherwise, the address from a prior *connect* call is used. The actual output operation is done by *udp_output*(),

---

[2] In 4.3BSD, checksums are enabled or disabled by a per-system option and cannot be enabled or disabled on individual sockets.

```
error = udp_output(inp, m);
    struct inpcb *inp;
    struct mbuf *m;
```

where *inp* is an Internet protocol control block and *m* is an mbuf chain that contains the data to be sent. UDP simply prepends its header, fills in its fields and those of a prototype IP header, and calculates a checksum before passing the packet on to the IP module for output:

```
error = ip_output(m, opt, ro, flags);
    struct mbuf *m, *opt;
    struct route *ro;
    int flags;
```

The call to IP's output routine is more complicated than to UDP's because the IP routine cannot depend on having a protocol control block that contains information about the current sender and destination. The *m* parameter indicates the data to be sent, and the *opt* parameter may specify a list of IP options that should be placed in the IP packet header. IP options may be set for a socket with the *setsockopt* system call specifying the IP protocol level and option IP_OPTIONS. These options are stored in a separate mbuf, and a pointer to this mbuf is stored in the protocol control block for a socket; the pointer is passed to *ip_output*() with each packet sent. The *ro* parameter is optional; UDP passes a pointer to the route entry in the protocol control block for the socket. IP will determine a route and leave it in the route structure, so that it can be reused on subsequent calls. The final parameter, *flags*, indicates whether the user is allowed to transmit a broadcast message and if routing is to be performed for the message being sent (see Section 12.3). The broadcast flag may be inconsequential if the underlying hardware does not support broadcast transmissions.

Input

All Internet transport protocols that are layered directly on top of IP use the following calling convention when receiving input packets from IP:

```
(void) (*pr_input)(m, ifp);
    struct mbuf *m;
    struct ifnet *ifp;
```

Each mbuf chain passed is a single packet to be processed by the protocol module. The interface from which the packet was received is passed as the second parameter. The UDP input routine *udp_input*() is typical of protocol input routines. It first verifies that the length of the packet is at least as long as the IP plus UDP headers and uses *m_pullup*() to make the header contiguous. It then checks that the packet is the correct length and checksums the data if a checksum is present.

If any of these tests fail, the packet is simply discarded. Finally, the protocol control block for the socket that is to receive the data is located by *in_pcblookup*() from the addresses and port numbers in the packet. There might be multiple control blocks with the same local port number, but different local or remote addresses; if so, the control block with the best match is selected. An exact association matches best, but if none exists, a socket with the correct local port number but unspecified local address, remote port number, or remote address will match. A control block with unspecified local and/or remote addresses thus acts as a *wildcard* that receives packets for its port if no exact match is found. If a control block is located, the data and the address from which the packet was received are placed in the receive buffer of the indicated socket with *sbappendaddr*(). Otherwise, if no receiver is found and if the packet was not addressed to a broadcast address, an ICMP *port unreachable* error message is sent to the originator of the datagram.[3]

Control Operations

UDP supports few control operations. It supports no options in 4.3BSD, and passes calls to its *pr_ctloutput*() entry directly to IP. It has a simple *pr_ctlinput*() routine that receives notification of any asynchronous errors. Some errors simply cause cached routes to be flushed. Other errors are passed to any datagram socket with the indicated destination; only sockets with a destination fixed by a *connect* call may be notified of errors asynchronously. Such errors are simply noted in the appropriate socket, and socket wakeups are issued in case the process is selecting or sleeping while waiting for input.

When a UDP datagram socket is closed, the *udp_usrreq*() is called with the PRU_DETACH request. The protocol control block and its contents are simply deleted with *in_pcbdetach*(); no other processing is required.

12.3 Internet Protocol (IP)

Having examined the operation of a simple transport protocol, we continue with a discussion of the network-layer protocol [Postel, 1981a; Postel *et al.*, 1981]. The *Internet Protocol* (IP) is the level responsible for host-to-host addressing and routing, packet forwarding, and packet fragmentation and reassembly. Unlike the transport protocols, it does not always operate on behalf of a socket on the local host; it may forward packets, receive packets for which there is no local socket, or generate error packets in response to these situations.

[3] This error message generally has no effect, as the sender normally connects to this destination only temporarily, and destroys the association before new input is processed. However, if the sender still has a fully specified association, it may receive notification of the error. The host-name lookup routine in 4.3BSD uses this mechanism to detect the absence of a nameserver at boot time, allowing it to fall back to the local host file.

The functions performed by IP are illustrated by the contents of its packet header, shown in Fig. 12.6. The header identifies source and destination hosts and the destination protocol, and contains header and packet lengths. The identification and fragment fields are used when a packet or fragment must be broken into smaller sections for transmission on its next hop and to reassemble the fragments when they arrive at the destination. The fragmentation flags are *Don't Fragment* and *More Fragments*; the latter flag plus the offset are sufficient to assemble the fragments of the original packet at the destination.

IP options are present in an IP packet if the header length field has a value larger than the minimum. The *no-operation* option and the *end-of-option-list* option are each one octet in length. All other options are self-encoding, with a type and length preceding any additional data. Hosts and gateways are thus able to skip over options they do not implement. Examples of existing options are the *timestamp* and *record-route* options, which are updated by each gateway that forwards a packet, and the *source-route* options, which supply a complete or partial route to the destination.

Output

We have already seen the calling convention for the IP output routine, which is

```
error = ip_output(m, opt, ro, flags);
    struct mbuf *m, *opt;
    struct route *ro;
    int flags;
```

As described earlier, the parameter *m* is an mbuf chain containing the packet to be sent, including a skeletal IP header; *opt* is an optional mbuf containing IP options to be inserted after the header. If the route *ro* is given, it is a reference to a routing entry (*rtentry* structure), which may contain a route to the destination from a

Figure 12.6 Internet Protocol header. IHL is the Internet header length specified in units of four octets. Options are delimited by IHL.

0–3	4–7	8–15	16–31
version	IHL	type of service	total length
ID			fragment flags and offset
time to live		protocol	header checksum
source address			
destination address			
options			

previous call, and in which any new route will be left for future use. The *flags* may allow the use of broadcast or may indicate that the routing tables should be bypassed.

The outline of the work done by *ip_output*() is as follows:

- Insert any IP options
- Fill in the remaining header fields (IP version, zero offset, header length, and a new packet identification)
- Determine the route (i.e., outgoing interface and next-hop destination)
- Check whether the destination is a broadcast address, and, if it is, whether broadcast is permitted
- If the packet size is no larger than the maximum packet size for the outgoing interface, compute checksum and call interface output routine
- If the packet size is larger than the maximum packet size for the outgoing interface, break the packet into fragments and send each in turn

We shall examine the routing step in more detail. First, if no route entry is passed as a parameter, an internal routing entry is used temporarily. A route entry that is passed from the caller is checked to see that it is a route to the same destination, and that it is still valid. If either test fails, the old route is freed. After these checks, if there is no route, *rtalloc*() is called to allocate a route. The route returned includes a pointer to the outgoing interface information. This information includes the maximum packet size, flags including broadcast capability, and the output routine. If the route is marked with the RTF_GATEWAY flag, the address of the next-hop gateway is given by the route; otherwise, the packet's destination is the next-hop destination. If routing is to be bypassed because of a MSG_DONTROUTE option (see Section 10.1) or a SO_DONTROUTE option, a directly attached network shared with the destination is found; if there is no directly attached network, an error is returned. Once the outgoing interface and next-hop destination are found, enough information is available to send the packet.

As described in Chapter 11, the interface output routine normally validates the destination address and places the packet on its output queue, returning errors only if the interface is down, the output queue is full, or the destination address is not understood.

Input

In Chapter 11, we described the reception of a packet by a network interface and the packet's placement on the input queue for the appropriate protocol. The network-interface handler then schedules the protocol to run by setting a corresponding bit in the network status word and scheduling a *software interrupt*. The IP input routine is invoked via this software interrupt when network interfaces receive messages for an Internet protocol; consequently it is called without any parameters. The input routine, *ipintr*(), removes packets from its input queue one at a time and processes them to completion. A packet's processing is completed in one of four ways: it is passed as input to a higher-level protocol, it encounters an error which is reported back to the source, it is dropped because of an error, or it is forwarded along the path to its destination. In outline form, the steps in the processing of an IP packet on input are as follows:

1. Verify that the packet is at least as long as an IP header, and use *m_pullup*() to make the header contiguous.
2. Checksum the header of the packet and discard the packet if there is an error.
3. Verify that the packet is at least as long as the header indicates, and drop the packet if it is not. Trim any padding from the end of the packet.
4. Process any IP options in the header.
5. Check whether the packet is for this host. If so, continue processing the packet. If not, and if performing IP packet forwarding, try to forward the packet. Otherwise, drop the packet.
6. If the packet has been fragmented, keep it until all its fragments are received and reassembled or until it is too old to keep.
7. Pass the packet to the input routine of the next-higher-level protocol.

When the incoming packet is removed from the input queue, it is accompanied by an indication of the interface on which the packet was received. This information is passed to the next protocol, to the forwarding function, or to the error-reporting function. If any error is detected and is reported to the packet's originator, the source address of the error message will be set according to the packet's destination and the incoming interface.

The decision whether to receive a packet is not as simple as we might think. If a host has multiple addresses, the packet is received if its destination matches one of those addresses. If any of the attached networks support broadcast and the destination is a broadcast address, the packet is also received. (For reasons that are given in Section 12.1, there may be as many as five possible broadcast addresses for a given network.)

The IP input routine uses a simple and efficient scheme for locating the input routine for the receiving protocol of an incoming packet. The protocol field in the IP packet is eight bits long; thus, there are 256 possible protocols. Fewer than 256 protocols are actually defined or implemented, and the Internet protocol switch has far fewer than 256 entries. Therefore, IP input uses a 256-element mapping array to map from the protocol number to the protocol-switch entry of the receiving protocol. Each entry in the array is initially set to the index of a "raw" IP entry in the protocol switch. Then, for each protocol with a separate implementation in the system, the corresponding map entry is set to the index of the protocol in the IP protocol switch. When a packet is received, IP simply uses the protocol field to index into the mapping array, and uses the value at that location as the index into the protocol-switch table for the receiving protocol.

Forwarding

Implementations of the Internet Protocol traditionally have been designed for use by either hosts or gateways, not by both. That is, a system was either an endpoint for IP packets (as source or destination) or a gateway (which forwards packets between hosts on different networks, but uses upper-level protocols only for maintenance functions). Traditional host systems do not incorporate packet-forwarding functions; instead, if they receive packets not addressed to them, they simply drop the packets. 4.2BSD was the first common IP implementation that attempted to provide both host and gateway services in normal operation. This approach had advantages and disadvantages. It meant that 4.2BSD hosts connected to multiple networks could serve as gateways as well as hosts, reducing the requirement for dedicated gateway machines. Early gateways were neither inexpensive nor especially powerful. On the other hand, the existence of gateway-function support in ordinary hosts made it more likely for misconfiguration errors to result in problems on the attached networks. The most serious problem had to do with forwarding of a broadcast packet due to misunderstanding by either the sender or the receiver of the packet's destination. The compromise used in 4.3BSD is that packet-forwarding gateway functions are enabled only if multiple network interfaces are present on a host; these functions may always be disabled. Hosts with only one network interface never attempt to forward packets or to return error messages in response to misdirected packets unless they are explicitly configured as gateways (in which case they are considered to be gateways with broken interfaces). As a result, far fewer misconfiguration problems are capable of causing synchronized or repetitive broadcasts on a local network (''broadcast storms'').

The procedure for forwarding IP packets received at a host but destined for another host is the following:

1. Check that forwarding is enabled. If it is not, drop the packet.

2. Check that the destination address is one that allows forwarding. In particular, neither packets sent to network 0 or to network 127 (the official loopback network), nor those sent to addresses that are not on class A, B, or C networks, can be forwarded.[4]

3. Save at most 64 octets of the received message, in case an error message must be generated in response.

---

[4] Neither the use of class D addresses for multicast nor the implementation of multicast group agents were in existence when 4.3BSD was released. Forwarding of multicast datagrams is done by multicast agents rather than by standard packet-forwarding functions.

4. Determine the route to be used in forwarding the packet.

5. If the outgoing route uses the same interface as that on which the packet was received, and if the originating host is on that network, send an ICMP redirect message to the originating host. (ICMP is described in Section 12.8.)

6. Call *ip_output*() to send the packet to its destination or to the next-hop gateway.

7. If an error is detected, send an ICMP error message to the source host.

12.4 Transmission Control Protocol (TCP)

The major protocol of the Internet protocol suite is the *Transmission Control Protocol* (*TCP*) [Postel, 1981b; Cerf & Kahn, 1974]. TCP is the reliable connection-oriented stream transport protocol on which most application protocols are based. It includes several features not found in the other transport and network protocols described so far:

- Explicit and acknowledged connection initiation and termination
- Reliable, in-order, unduplicated delivery of data
- Flow control
- Out-of-band indication of urgent data

Because of these features, the TCP implementation is much more complicated than that of UDP or IP. These complications, along with the prevalence of the use of TCP, make the details of TCP's implementation both more critical and more interesting than are the implementations of the simpler protocols. We shall begin with an examination of the TCP itself, then continue with a description of its implementation in 4.3BSD.

A TCP connection may be viewed as a bidirectional, sequenced stream of data octets transferred between two peers. The data may be sent in packets of varying sizes and at varying intervals; for example, when they are used to support a login session over the network. The stream initiation and termination are explicit events at the start and end of the stream, and they occupy positions in the *sequence space* of the stream so that they can be acknowledged in the same manner as data are. Sequence numbers are 32-bit numbers from a circular space; that is, comparisons are made modulo 2^{32}, so that zero is the next sequence number after $2^{32}-1$. The sequence numbers for each direction start with an arbitrary value, called the *initial sequence number*. Each packet (*segment*) of a TCP connection carries the sequence number of its first datum and (except for messages during connection establishment) an acknowledgment of all contiguous data received. Acknowledgments are specified as the sequence number of the next datum not yet received. Acknowledgments are cumulative, and thus may

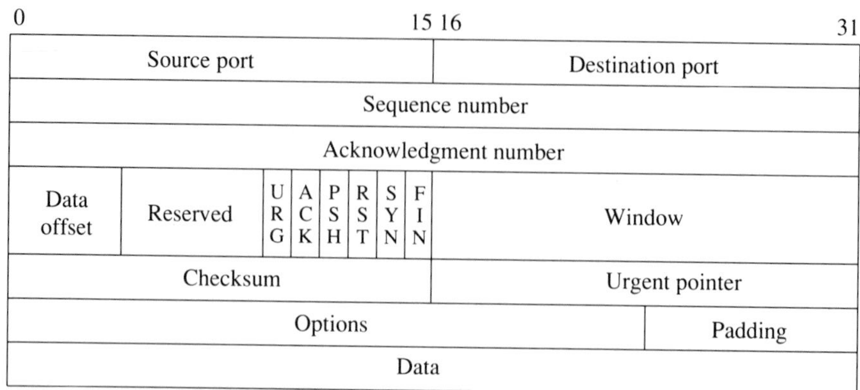

Figure 12.7 TCP packet header.

acknowledge data received in more than one (or part of one) packet. A packet may or may not contain data, but always contains the sequence number of the next datum to be sent.

Flow control in TCP is done with a *sliding-window scheme*. Each packet with an acknowledgment contains a window, which is the number of octets of data that the receiver is prepared to accept, beginning with the sequence number in the acknowledgment. Urgent data are handled similarly; if the flag indicating urgent data is set, the urgent-data pointer is used as a positive offset from the sequence number of the packet to indicate the extent of urgent data. Thus, TCP can send notification of urgent data without sending all intervening data, even if the flow control window would not allow the intervening data to be sent.

The complete header for a TCP packet is shown in Fig. 12.7. The flags include SYN and FIN, denoting the initiation (synchronization) and completion of a connection. Each of these flags occupies a sequence space of one. A complete connection thus consists of a SYN, zero or more octets of data, and a FIN sent from each peer and acknowledged by the other peer. Additional flags indicate whether the acknowledgment field (ACK) and urgent fields (URG) are valid, and include a connection-abort signal (RST). The header includes a header-length field so that the header can be extended with optional fields. Options are encoded in the same way as are IP options: the *no-operation* and *end-of-options* options are single octets, and all other options include a type and a length. The only option currently defined indicates the maximum segment (packet) size that a correspondent is willing to accept; this option is used only during initial connection establishment.

TCP Connection States

The connection-establishment and connection-completion mechanisms of TCP are designed for robustness. They serve to frame the data that are transferred during a connection, so that not only the data but also their extent are reliably communicated. In addition, the procedure is designed to discover old connections that have not terminated correctly because of a crash of one peer or loss of network connectivity. If such a half-open connection is discovered, it is aborted. Hosts choose new initial sequence numbers for each connection to lessen the chances that an old packet may be confused with a current connection.

The normal connection-establishment procedure is known as a ''three-way handshake.'' Each peer sends a SYN to the other, and each in turn acknowledges the other's SYN with an ACK. In practice, a connection is normally initiated by one of the two (the client) attempting to connect to the other (a server listening on a well-known port). The client choses a port number and initial sequence number and uses these in the initial packet with a SYN. The server creates a new connection block for the pending connection and sends a packet with its initial sequence number, a SYN, and an ACK of the client's SYN. The client responds with an ACK of the server's SYN, completing connection establishment. As the ACK of the first SYN is piggybacked on the second SYN, this procedure requires three packets, leading to the term ''three-way handshake.'' (The protocol still operates correctly if both peers initiate the connection simultaneously, although it requires four packets in that case.)

After a connection is established, each peer includes an acknowledgment and window information in each packet. Each may send data according to the window it receives from its peer. As data are sent by one end, the window becomes filled. As data are received by the peer, acknowledgments may be sent so that the sender can discard the data from its send queue. If the receiver is prepared to accept additional data, perhaps because the receiving process has consumed the previous data, it will also advance the flow-control window. Data, acknowledgments and window updates may all be combined in a single message.

If a sender does not receive an acknowledgment within some reasonable time, it retransmits data that it presumes were lost. Duplicate data are discarded by the receiver but are acknowledged again in case the retransmission was caused by loss of the acknowledgment. If the data are received out of order, the receiver generally retains the out-of-order data for use when the missing segment is received. Out-of-order data may not be acknowledged.

Each peer may terminate data transmission at any time by sending a packet with the FIN bit. A FIN represents the end of the data (like an end-of-file indication). The FIN is acknowledged, advancing the sequence number by one. The connection may continue to carry data in the other direction until a FIN is sent in that direction. The acknowledgment of that FIN terminates the connection. To guarantee synchronization at the conclusion of the connection, the peer sending the last ACK of a FIN must retain state long enough that any retransmitted FIN packets would have reached it or have been discarded; otherwise, if the ACK were lost and a retransmitted FIN were received, the receiver would be unable to repeat the acknowledgment. This interval is arbitrarily set to twice the maximum expected segment lifetime (2MSL).

The TCP input-processing module and timer modules must maintain the state of a connection throughout that connection's lifetime. Thus, in addition to

Table 12.1 TCP connection states.

State	Description
States involved in establishing a connection	
CLOSED	closed
LISTEN	listening for connection
SYN SENT	active, have sent SYN
SYN RECEIVED	have sent and received SYN
State in an established connection	
ESTABLISHED	established
States involved when the remote end initiates a connection shutdown	
CLOSE WAIT	have received FIN, waiting for close
LAST ACK	have received FIN and close; awaiting FIN ACK
CLOSED	closed
States involved when the local end initiates a connection shutdown	
FIN WAIT 1	have closed, sent FIN
CLOSING	closed, exchanged FIN; awaiting FIN ACK
FIN WAIT 2	have closed, FIN is acknowledged; awaiting FIN
TIME WAIT	in 2MSL† quiet wait after close
CLOSED	closed

† twice maximum segment lifetime

processing data received on the connection, the input module must process SYN and FIN flags and other state transitions. The list of states for one end of a TCP connection is shown in Table 12.1. Figure 12.8 shows the finite state machine made up by these states, the events that cause transitions, and the actions during the transitions. An earlier version of the TCP implementation was actually implemented as an explicit state machine.

If a connection is lost because of a crash or timeout on one peer but is still considered established by the other, any data sent on the connection and received at the other end will cause the half-open connection to be discovered. When a half-open connection is detected, the receiving peer sends a packet with the RST flag and a sequence number derived from the incoming packet to signify that the connection is no longer in existence.

Sequence Variables

Each TCP connection maintains a large set of state variables in the TCP control block. This information includes the connection state, timers, options and state flags, a queue that holds data received out of order, and several sequence number variables. The sequence variables are used to define the send and receive sequence space, including the current *window* for each. The window is the range of data sequence numbers that are currently allowed to be sent, from the first octet

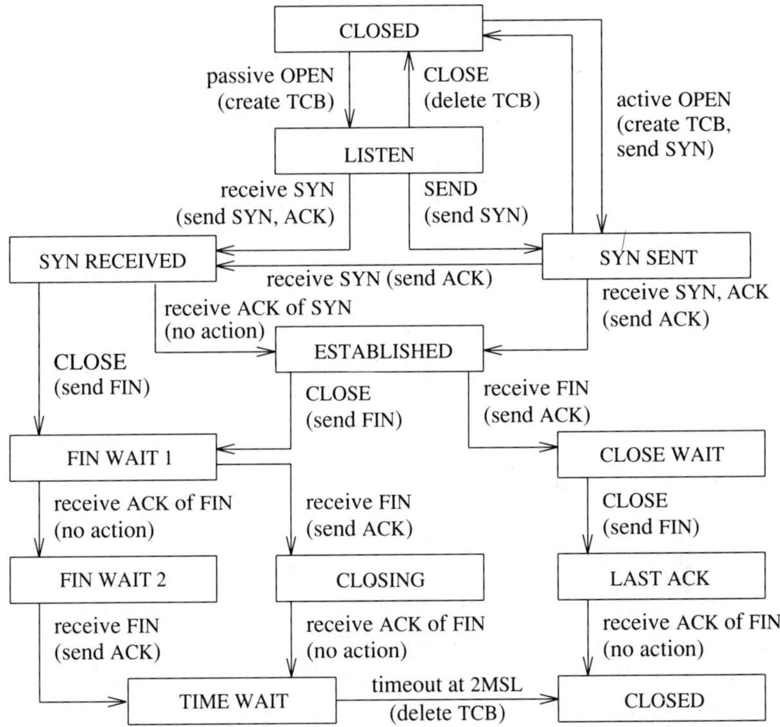

Figure 12.8 TCP state diagram. TCB—TCP control block; 2MSL—twice maximum segment lifetime.

of data not yet acknowledged up to the end of the range that has been offered in the window field of a header. The variables used to define the windows in 4.3BSD are a superset of those used in the protocol specification [Postel, 1981b]. The send and receive windows are shown in Fig. 12.9. The meanings of the sequence variables are listed in Table 12.2.

The area between *snd_nxt* and *snd_una* + *snd_wnd* is known as the *send window*. Data for the range *snd_una* to *snd_max* have been sent but not yet acknowledged, and are kept in the socket send buffer along with data not yet transmitted. The *snd_nxt* and *snd_max* values are normally maintained together except when retransmitting. The area between *rcv_nxt* and *rcv_nxt* + *rcv_wnd* is known as the *receive window*. These variables are used in the output module to decide whether data may be sent, and in the input module to decide whether data that are received may be accepted. When the receiver detects that a packet is not acceptable because the data are all outside the window, it drops the packet but sends a copy of its last acknowledgment. If the packet contained old data, the first acknowledgment may have been lost, and thus it must be repeated. The acknowledgment also includes a window update, synchronizing the sender's state with the receiver's state.

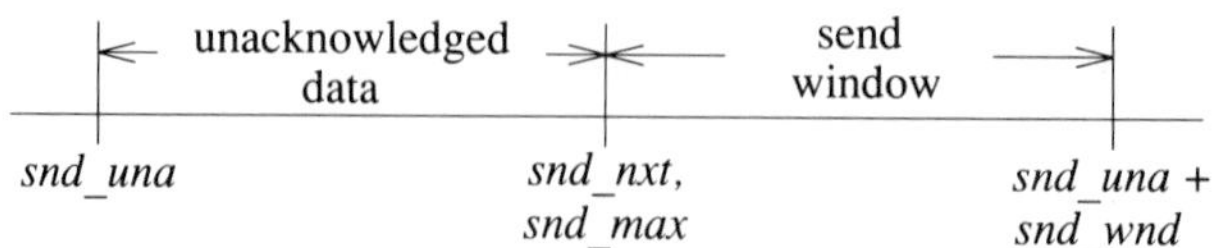

Send Sequence Space

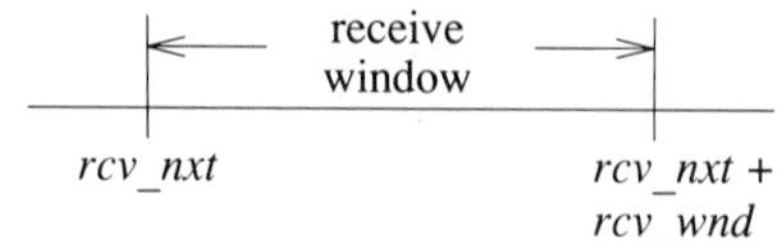

Receive Sequence Space

Figure 12.9 TCP sequence space.

12.5 TCP Algorithms

Now that we have introduced TCP, its state machine, and its sequence space, we can begin to examine the implementation of the protocol in 4.3BSD. Several aspects of the protocol implementation are global. The TCP connection state, output state, and state changes depend on external events and timers. TCP processing occurs in response to one of three events:

1. A request from the user, such as sending data, removing data from the socket receive buffer, or opening or closing a connection
2. The receipt of a packet for the connection
3. The expiration of a timer

Table 12.2 TCP sequence variables.

Variable	Description
snd_una	lowest send sequence number not yet acknowledged
snd_nxt	next data sequence to be sent
snd_wnd	number of data octets peer will receive, starting with *snd_una*
snd_max	highest sequence number sent
rcv_nxt	next receive sequence number expected
rcv_wnd	number of octets past *rcv_nxt* that may be accepted
rcv_adv	last octet of receive window advertised to peer

These events are handled in the routines *tcp_usrreq*(), *tcp_input*() and *tcp_timers*(), respectively. Each routine processes the current event and makes any required changes in the connection state. Then, for any transition that may require output, the *tcp_output*() routine is called to do any output that is necessary.

The criteria for sending a packet with data and/or control information are complicated, and therefore the TCP send policy is the most interesting and important part of the protocol implementation. For example, depending on the state- and flow-control parameters for a connection, any of the following may allow data to be sent that could not be sent previously:

- A user send call that places new data in the send queue
- The receipt of a window update from the peer TCP
- The expiration of the retransmission timer
- The expiration of the window-update timer

In addition, the *tcp_output*() routine may decide to send a packet with control information even if no data may be sent for any of these reasons:

- A change in connection state (e.g., open request, close request)
- Receipt of data that must be acknowledged
- A change in the receive window because of removal of data from the receive queue
- A send request with urgent data
- A connection abort

We shall consider most of these decisions in greater detail after we have described the states and timers involved. We begin with algorithms used for timing, connection setup, and shutdown, which are distributed through several parts of the code. We continue with the processing of new input and an overview of output processing and algorithms.

Timers

Unlike a UDP socket, a TCP connection maintains a significant amount of state information, and because of that state, some operations must be done asynchronously. For example, data might not be sent immediately when a process presents them, because of flow control. The requirement for reliable delivery implies that data must be retained after they are first transmitted so that they can be retransmitted if necessary. To prevent the protocol from hanging if packets are lost, each connection maintains a set of timers used to recover from losses or failures of the peer TCP. These timers are stored in the protocol control block for a connection. Whenever they are set, they are decremented every 500 milliseconds by the *tcp_slowtimo*() routine (called as the TCP protocol switch *pr_slowtimo* routine) until they expire, triggering a call to *tcp_timers*().

Two timers are used for output processing. One is the *retransmit timer* (TCPT_REXMT). Whenever data are sent on a connection, the retransmit timer is started, unless it is already running. When all outstanding data are acknowledged, the timer is stopped. If the timer expires, the oldest unacknowledged data are resent (at most one full-sized packet) and the timer is restarted with a longer value. The rate at which the timer value is increased (the *timer backoff*) is determined by a table of multipliers that provide a near-exponential increase in timeout values.

The other timer used for maintaining output flow is the *persist timer* (TCPT_PERSIST). This timer protects against the other type of packet loss that could cause a connection to constipate—the loss of a window update that would allow more data to be sent. Whenever data are ready to be sent, but the send window is too small to bother sending (zero, or less than a reasonable amount) and no data are already outstanding (the retransmit timer is not set), the persist timer is started. If no window update is received before the timer expires, the output routine sends as large a segment as the window allows. If that size is zero, it sends a *window probe* (a single octet of data) and restarts the persist timer. If a window update was lost in the network, or if the receiver neglected to send a window update, the acknowledgment will contain current window information. On the other hand, if the receiver is still unable to accept additional data, it should send an acknowledgment for previous data with a still-closed window. The closed window might persist indefinitely; for example, the receiver might be a network-login client, and the user might stop terminal output and leave for lunch (or vacation).

The third timer used by TCP is a *keepalive timer* (TCPT_KEEP). The keepalive timer monitors idle connections that might no longer exist on the correspondent TCP because of timeout or a crash. If a socket-level option is set and the connection has been idle since the last keepalive timeout, the timer routine will send a *keepalive packet* designed to produce either an acknowledgment or a reset (RST) from the peer TCP. If a reset is received, the connection will be closed; if no response is received after several attempts, the connection will be dropped. This facility is designed so that network servers can avoid languishing forever if the client disappears without closing. Keepalive packets are not an explicit feature of the TCP protocol. The packets used for this purpose by 4.3BSD set the sequence number to one less than *snd_una*, which should elicit an acknowledgment from the correspondent TCP if the connection still exists.[5]

The final TCP timer is known as the *2MSL timer* (TCPT_2MSL; ‘‘twice the maximum segment lifetime’’). TCP starts this timer when a connection is completed by sending an acknowledgment for a FIN (from FIN_WAIT_2 or CLOSING states, where the send side is already closed). Under these circumstances, the sender does

[5] In 4.3BSD, the keepalive packet contains no data unless the system is configured with a kernel option for compatibility with 4.2BSD, in which case a single null octet is sent. A bug prevents 4.2BSD from responding to a keepalive packet unless it contains data.

not know whether the acknowledgment was received. If the FIN is retransmitted, it is desirable that enough state remain that the acknowledgment can be repeated. Therefore, on entering the TIME_WAIT state, the 2MSL timer is started; on its expiration, the control block is deleted. To prevent this delay from blocking a process closing the connection, any process close request is returned successfully without the process waiting for the timer. Thus, a protocol control block may continue its existence even after the socket descriptor has been closed. In addition, 4.3BSD starts the 2MSL timer when FIN_WAIT_2 state is entered after the user has closed; if the connection is idle until the timer expires, it will be closed. Because the user has already closed, new data cannot be accepted on such a connection in any case. This timer is set because certain other TCP implementations (incorrectly) fail to send a FIN on a receive-only connection. Connections to such hosts will remain in FIN_WAIT_2 state forever unless the system times them out.

In addition to the four timers implemented by the TCP *tcp_slowtimo*() routine, TCP uses the protocol switch *pr_fasttimo* entry. The *tcp_fasttimo*() routine, called every 200 milliseconds, processes delayed acknowledgment requests. These will be illustrated in Section 12.6.

Estimation of Round-Trip Time

When connections must traverse slow networks that lose packets, an important decision determining connection throughput is the value to be used when the retransmission timer is set. If this value is too large, data flow will stop on the connection for an unnecessarily long time before the dropped packet is resent. Another round-trip time interval is required to receive an acknowledgment of the missing segment and a window update allowing new data to be sent. (With luck, only one segment will have been lost, and the acknowledgment will include the other segments that had been sent.) If the timeout value is too small, however, packets will be retransmitted needlessly. If the cause of the network slowness or packet loss is congestion, then unnecessary retransmission only exacerbates the problem. The traditional solution to this problem in TCP is to estimate the round-trip time, *rtt*, for the connection path by measuring the time required to receive acknowledgments for individual segments. An estimate of the round-trip time is maintained as a smoothed moving average, *srtt* [Postel, 1981b], using

$$srtt = (\text{ALPHA} \cdot srtt) + ((1-\text{ALPHA}) \cdot rtt).$$

The initial retransmission timeout is set to a multiple (BETA) of the current smoothed round-trip time. The version of TCP in the standard 4.3BSD tape distribution used this scheme, with a smoothing factor ALPHA of 0.9 (retaining 90 percent of the previous average) and a variance factor BETA of 2.

A newer version of TCP was included in the 4.3BSD Tahoe release that uses a somewhat more sophisticated algorithm. In addition to a smoothed estimate of the round-trip time, the new TCP keeps a smoothed variance (estimated as mean difference to avoid square-root calculations in the kernel). It employs an ALPHA value of 0.875 and a corresponding smoothing factor for the variance of 0.75. These values were chosen in part so that the smoothed averages could be computed using shift operations on fixed-point values, instead of using-floating point values, as in the earlier system. (On many hardware architectures, it is expensive to use floating-point arithmetic in interrupt routines, as doing so forces floating-point registers and status to be saved and restored.) The initial retransmission timeout is then set to the current smoothed round-trip time plus twice the smoothed variance. The new algorithm is substantially better on long-delay paths with little variance in delay, such as satellite links, as it computes the BETA factor dynamically [Jacobson, 1988].

Connection Establishment

There are two ways in which a new TCP connection can be established. An active connection is initiated by a *connect* call, whereas a passive connection is created when a listening socket receives a connection request. We consider each in turn.

The initial steps of an active connection attempt are similar to the actions taken during the creation of a UDP socket. The process creates a new socket, resulting in a call to *tcp_usrreq*() with the PRU_ATTACH request. TCP creates an *inpcb* protocol control block just as does UDP, then creates an additional control block (a *tcpcb* structure), as described in Section 12.1. Some of the flow-control parameters in the *tcpcb* are initialized at this time. If the process explicitly binds an address or port number to the connection, the actions are identical to those for a UDP socket. Then, a *connect* call initiates the actual connection. The first step is to set up the association with *in_pcbconnect*(), again identically to this step in UDP. A packet header template is created for use in constructing each output packet. An initial sequence number is chosen from a sequence-number prototype, which is advanced by a substantial amount. The socket is then marked with *soisconnecting*(), the TCP connection state is set to TCPS_SYN_SENT, the keepalive timer is set (to 45 seconds) to limit the duration of the connection attempt, and *tcp_output*() is called for the first time.

The output-processing module *tcp_output*() uses an array of packet control flags indexed by the connection state to determine which control flags should be sent in each state. In the TCPS_SYN_SENT state, the SYN flag is sent. Because there is a control flag to send, a packet is sent immediately using the prototype just constructed and with the current flow-control parameters. If the connection is to a destination on the local network (or a subnet of that network, see Section 12.1), a maximum-segment-size option is sent in this packet specifying a multiple of 512 bytes that is less than the maximum transmission unit of the outgoing interface. If the option is not sent, the other side must send packets no larger than the default (576 octets including headers). The retransmit timer is set to the default value (6 seconds), as no round-trip time information is available yet.

With a bit of luck, a responding packet will be received from the target of the connection before the retransmit timer expires. If not, the packet is retransmitted and the retransmit timer is restarted with a greater value. If no response is received before the keepalive timer expires, the connection attempt is aborted with a ''Connection timed out'' error. If a response is received, however, it is checked for agreement with the outgoing request. It should acknowledge the SYN that was sent, and should include a SYN. If it does both, the receive sequence variables are initialized and the connection state is advanced to TCPS_ESTABLISHED. If a maximum-segment-size option is present in the response, the maximum segment size for the connection is set to the minimum of the offered size and the maximum transmission unit of the outgoing interface; if the option is not present, the default size (512 data bytes) is recorded. The flag TF_ACKNOW is set in the TCP control block before the output routine is called, so that the SYN will be acknowledged immediately. The connection is now ready to transfer data.

The events that occur when a connection is created by a passive open are different. A socket is created and its address is bound as before. The socket is then marked by the *listen* call as willing to accept connections. When a packet arrives for a TCP socket in TCPS_LISTEN state, a new socket is created with *sonewconn*(), which calls the TCP PRU_ATTACH request to create the protocol control blocks for the new socket. The new socket is placed on the queue of partial connections headed by the listening socket. If the packet contains a SYN and is otherwise acceptable, the association of the new socket is bound, both the send and the receive sequence numbers are initialized, and the connection state is advanced to TCPS_SYN_RECEIVED. The keepalive timer is set as before, and the output routine is called after TF_ACKNOW has been set to force the SYN to be acknowledged; an outgoing SYN is sent as well. If this SYN is properly acknowledged, the new socket is moved from the queue of partial connections to the queue of completed connections. If the owner of the listening socket is sleeping in an *accept* call or does a *select*, the socket will indicate that a new connection is available. Again, the socket is finally ready to send data. Up to one window of data may already be received and acknowledged by the time the *accept* call completes.

Connection Shutdown

A TCP connection is symmetrical and full-duplex, so either side may initiate disconnection independently. As long as one direction of the connection can carry data, the connection remains open. A socket may indicate that it has completed sending data with the *shutdown* system call, which results in a call to the *tcp_usrreq*() routine with request PRU_SHUTDOWN. The response to this request is to advance the state of the connection; from the ESTABLISHED state, the state becomes FIN_WAIT_1. The ensuing output call will send a FIN, indicating an end-of-file. The receiving socket will advance to CLOSE_WAIT, but may continue to send. The procedure may be different if the process simply closes the socket; in that case, a FIN is sent immediately, but if new data are received, they cannot be delivered. Normally, higher-level protocols conclude their own transactions such that both sides know when to close. If they do not, however, TCP must refuse new data; it does so by sending a packet with RST set if new data are received after the user has closed. If data remain in the send buffer of the socket when the *close* is done, TCP will normally attempt to deliver them. If the socket option SO_LINGER was set with a linger time of zero, the send buffer is simply flushed; otherwise, the user process is allowed to continue, and the protocol waits for delivery to conclude. Under these circumstances, the socket is marked with the state bit SS_NOFDREF (no file-descriptor reference). The completion of data transfer and the final close can take place an arbitrary amount of time later. When TCP finally completes the connection (or gives up because of timeout or other failure), it calls *tcp_close*(). The protocol control blocks and other dynamically allocated structures are freed at this time. The socket is also freed if the SS_NOFDREF flag has been set. Thus, the socket remains in existence as long as either a file descriptor or a protocol control block refers to it.

12.6 TCP Input Processing

Although TCP input processing is considerably more complicated than is UDP input handling, the preceding sections have provided the background we need to examine the actual operation. As always, the input routine is called with parameters

```
(void) tcp_input(m, ifp);
    struct mbuf *m;
    struct ifnet *ifp;
```

The first few steps are beginning to sound familiar:

1. Locate the TCP header in the received IP datagram. Make sure that the packet is at least as long as a TCP header and use *m_pullup*() if necessary to make it contiguous.
2. Compute the packet length, set up the IP pseudoheader, and checksum the TCP header and data. Discard the packet if the checksum is bad.
3. Check the TCP header length; if it is larger than a minimal header, make sure that the whole header is contiguous, allocate an extra mbuf, and copy the TCP options into it.
4. Locate the protocol control block for the connection with the port number specified. If none exists, send a packet containing the reset flag RST and drop the packet.
5. Check whether the socket is listening for connections; if it is, follow the procedure described for passive connection establishment.
6. Process any TCP options from the packet header.
7. Clear the idle time for the connection and set the keepalive timer to its normal value.

At this point, the normal checks have been made, and we are prepared to deal with data and control flags in the received packet. There are still many consistency checks that must be made during normal processing; for example, the SYN flag must be present if we are still establishing a connection, and must not be present if the connection has been established. We shall omit most of these checks from our discussion, but the tests are important to prevent wayward packets from causing confusion and possible data corruption.

The next step in checking a TCP packet is to see whether the packet is acceptable according to the receive window. It is important that this step be done before control flags, in particular RST, are examined, as old or extraneous packets should not affect the current connection unless they are clearly relevant in the current context. A segment is acceptable if the receive window has nonzero size, and if at least some of the sequence space occupied by the packet falls within the receive window. If the packet contains data, some of the data must fall within the window; portions of the data that precede the window are trimmed, as they have already been received, and portions that exceed the window also are discarded, as they have been sent prematurely. If the receive window is closed (*rcv_wnd* is zero), then only segments with no data and with a sequence number equal to *rcv_nxt* are acceptable. If an incoming segment is not acceptable, it is dropped after an acknowledgment is sent.

The way in which these tests are applied in the 4.3BSD Tahoe release version of TCP is somewhat different from the way they are done in the original 4.3BSD tape distribution. We shall use the tests used in the Tahoe release here, as they are more correct. The older version performed similar tests, but in a slightly different order. The processing steps are as follows:

1. Check whether the packet begins before *rcv_nxt*. If it does, ignore any SYN in the packet, and trim any data that fall before *rcv_nxt*. If no data remain, send a current acknowledgment and drop the packet. (The packet is presumed to be a duplicate transmission.)

2. If the packet still contains data after trimming, and the process that created the socket has already closed the socket, send a reset (RST) and drop the connection. This reset is necessary to abort connections that cannot complete; it typically is sent when a remote-login client disconnects while data are being received.

3. If the end of the segment falls after the window, trim any data beyond the window. If the window was closed and the packet sequence number is *rcv_nxt*, the packet is treated as a window probe; TF_ACKNOW is set to send a current acknowledgment and window update, and the remainder of the packet is processed. If SYN is set and the connection was in TIME_WAIT state, this is really a new connection request, and the old connection is dropped; this procedure has been called *rapid connection reuse*. Otherwise, if no data remain, send an acknowledgment and drop the packet.

The remaining steps of TCP input processing check the following flags and fields and take the appropriate actions: RST, ACK, window, URG, data, and FIN.

As the packet has already been confirmed to be acceptable, these actions can be done in a straightforward manner:

4. If RST is set, close the connection and drop the packet.

5. If ACK is not set, drop the packet.

6. If the acknowledgment-field value is higher than previous acknowledgments, new data have been acknowledged. If the connection was in SYN_RECEIVED state and the packet acknowledges our SYN, enter ESTABLISHED state. If the sequence range that was newly acknowledged includes the sequence number for which the round-trip time was being measured, average the time sample into the smoothed round-trip time estimate for the connection. If all outstanding data have been acknowledged, stop the retransmission timer; otherwise, set it back to the current timeout value. Finally, drop the data that were acknowledged from the send queue in the socket. If a FIN has been sent and was acknowledged, advance the state machine.

7. Check the window field to see whether it advances the known send window. First, check whether this is a new window update. If the sequence number of the packet is greater than that of the previous window update, or the sequence number is the same but the acknowledgment is higher, or if both sequence and acknowledgment are the same but the window is larger, record the new window.

8. If the urgent-data flag URG is set, compare the urgent pointer in the packet to the last-received urgent pointer. If it is different, new urgent data have been sent. The urgent pointer is used to compute *so_oobmark*, the offset from the beginning of the socket receive buffer to the urgent mark (Section 10.6), and the socket is notified with *sohasoutofband*(). If the urgent pointer is less than the packet length, the urgent data have all been received. TCP normally removes the data octet sent in urgent mode (the last octet before the urgent pointer[6]) and places it in the protocol control block until it is requested with a PRU_RCVOOB request. A socket option may request that urgent data be left with the normal data.

9. At long last, examine the data field in the received packet. If the data begin with *rcv_nxt*, then they can be placed directly into the socket receive buffer with *sbappend*(). Otherwise, the packet is retained in a per-connection queue until the intervening data arrive. The flag TF_DELACK is set in the protocol control block to indicate that an acknowledgment is needed, but the latter is not sent immediately in hope that it can be piggybacked on any packets sent soon (presumably in response to the incoming data) or combined with acknowledgment of other data received soon. The next time that the *tcp_fasttimo*() routine runs, it will change the flag to TF_ACKNOW and call the *tcp_output*() routine to send the acknowledgment.

---

[6] The actual position of the ''urgent'' octet is a subject of disagreement; the 4.2BSD and 4.3BSD interpretation follows the original TCP specification.

10. As the final step in processing a received packet, check for the FIN flag. If it is present, the connection state machine may have to be advanced, and the socket is marked with *socantrcvmore*() to convey the end-of-file indication. If the send side has already closed (a FIN was sent and acknowledged), the socket is now considered closed, and it is so marked with *soisdisconnected*(). The TF_ACKNOW flag is set to force immediate acknowledgment.

Step 10 completes the actions taken when a new packet is received by *tcp_input*(). However, as noted earlier, receipt of input may require new output. In particular, acknowledgment of all outstanding data or a new window update requires either new output or a state change by the output module. Also, several special conditions set the TF_ACKNOW flag. In these cases, *tcp_output*() is called at the conclusion of input processing.

12.7 TCP Output Processing

We are finally ready to investigate the most interesting part of the TCP implementation—the send policy. As we saw earlier, a TCP packet contains an acknowledgment and a window field as well as data, and a single packet may be sent if any of these three change. A naive TCP send policy might send many more packets than necessary. For example, consider what happens when a user types one character to a remote-terminal connection that uses remote echo. The server-side TCP receives a single-character packet. It might send an immediate acknowledgment of the character. Then, milliseconds later, the login server would read the character, removing it from the receive buffer; the TCP might immediately send a window update noting that one additional octet of send window was available. After another millisecond or so, the login server would send an echoed character back to the client, necessitating a third packet sent in response to the single character of input. It is obvious that all three responses (the acknowledgment, the window update, and the data returns) could be sent in a single packet. However, if the server were not echoing input data, the acknowledgment could not be withheld for too long a time, or the client-side TCP would begin to retransmit. The algorithms used in the send policy to minimize network traffic yet to maximize throughput are the most subtle part of a TCP implementation. The send policy used in 4.3BSD includes several standard algorithms as well as some approaches suggested by the network research community. We shall examine each part of the send policy.

As we saw earlier, there are several different events that may trigger the sending of data on a connection; in addition, packets must be sent to communicate acknowledgments and window updates (consider a one-way connection!).

Sending Data

The most obvious reason that the tcp output module *tcp_output*() is called is that the user has written new data to the socket. Write operations are done with a call to *tcp_usrreq*() with the PRU_SEND request. (Recall that *sosend*() waits for enough space in the socket send buffer if necessary, then copies the user's data into a chain of mbufs that is passed to the protocol with the PRU_SEND request.) The action in *tcp_usrreq*() is simply to place the new output data in the socket's send buffer with *sbappend*() and to call *tcp_output*(). If flow control permits, *tcp_output*() will send the data immediately.

The actual send operation is not very different from one for a UDP datagram socket; the differences are that the header is more complicated, and additional fields must be initialized, and that the data sent are simply a copy of the user's data.[7] A copy must be retained in the socket's send buffer in case of retransmission. Also, if the number of data octets is larger than the size of a single maximum-sized segment, multiple packets will be constructed and sent in a single call.

The *tcp_output*() routine allocates an mbuf to contain the output packet header and copies the contents of the header template into that mbuf. The data to be sent are added as a separate chain of mbufs obtained with an *m_copy*() operation from the appropriate part of the send buffer. The sequence number for the packet is set from *snd_nxt*, and the acknowledgment is set from *rcv_nxt*. The flags are obtained from an array containing the flags to be sent in each connection state. The window to be advertised is computed from the amount of space remaining in the socket's receive buffer; however, if that amount is small (less than one-fourth of the buffer and less than one segment), it is set to zero. The window is never allowed to end at a smaller sequence number than it did in previous packets. If urgent data have been sent, the urgent pointer and flag are set accordingly. One other flag must be set: The PUSH flag on a packet indicates that data should be passed to the user, something like an end-of-record mark or buffer-flush request. This flag is generally considered obsolete, but is set whenever all the data in the send buffer have been sent; 4.3BSD ignores this flag on input. Once the header is filled in, the packet is checksummed. The remaining parts of the IP header are initialized, and the packet is sent with *ip_output*(). The retransmission timer is started if it it is not already running, and the *snd_nxt* and *snd_max* values for the connection are updated.

Avoidance of the Silly-Window Syndrome

Silly-window syndrome is the name given to a potential problem in a window-based flow-control scheme in which a receiver sends several allocations rather than waiting for a reasonable-sized window to become available [Clark, 1982]. For example, if a network-login client program has a total receive buffer size of 4096 octets, and the user stops terminal output during a large printout, the buffer will become nearly full as new full-sized segments are received. If the remaining buffer space dropped to 10 bytes, it would not be useful for the receiver to volunteer to receive an additional 10 octets. If the user then allowed a small

[7] However, for send operations large enough for *sosend*() to place the data in external mbuf clusters, the copy is done by creation of a new reference to the data cluster.

number of characters to print and stopped output again, it still would not be useful for the receiving TCP to send a window update allowing another 14 octets. Instead, it is desirable to wait until a reasonably large packet can be sent, as the receive buffer already contains enough data for the next several pages of output. Avoidance of the silly-window syndrome is desirable in both the receiver and the sender of a flow-controlled connection, as either end can prevent silly small windows from being used. Receiver avoidance of the silly-window syndrome has been described already; when a packet is sent, the receive window is advertised as zero if it is less than one packet and less than one-fourth of the receive buffer. For sender avoidance of the silly-window syndrome, an output operation is delayed if at least a full packet of data is ready to be sent, but less than one full packet can be sent because of the size of the send window. Instead of sending, the output state is set to persist state by the persist timer being started. If no window update has been received by the time the timer expires, the allowable data are sent in the hope that the acknowledgment will include a larger window. If not, the connection stays in persist state, sending a window probe periodically until the window is opened.

An initial implementation of sender avoidance of the silly-window syndrome produced large delays and low throughput over connections to hosts using TCP implementations with tiny buffers. Unfortunately, those implementations *always* advertised receive windows less than 512 octets, which was considered silly by this implementation. As a result of this problem, the 4.3BSD TCP keeps a record of the largest receive window offered by a peer in the protocol-control-block variable *max_sndwnd*. When at least one-half of *max_sndwnd* may be sent, a new segment is sent. This technique improved performance when a 4.3BSD system was communicating with these primitive hosts.

Avoidance of Small Packets

Network traffic exhibits a bimodal distribution of sizes. Bulk data transfers tend to use the largest possible packets for maximum throughput. Network-login services tend to use small packets, however, often containing only a single data character. On a fast local-area network such as an Ethernet, the use of single-character packets generally is not a problem, as the network bandwidth usually is not saturated. On slower long-haul networks such as the ARPANET or on networks interconnected by slow links, it is desirable to collect input over some period and then to send it in a single network packet. Various schemes have been devised for collecting input over a fixed time, usually about 50 to 100 milliseconds, and then sending it in a single packet. These schemes noticeably slow character echo times on fast networks, however, and often save few packets on slow networks. In contrast, a simple and elegant scheme for reducing small-packet traffic was suggested by Nagle [Nagle, 1984]. This scheme allows the first octet output to be sent alone in a packet with no delay. Until this packet is acknowledged, however, no new small packets may be sent. If enough new data arrive to fill a maximum-sized packet, another packet is sent. As soon as the outstanding data are acknowledged, the input that was queued while waiting for the first packet may be sent. Only one small packet may ever be outstanding on a connection at one time. The net result is that small numbers of data are queued during one round-trip time. If the round-trip time is less than the intercharacter arrival time, as with a remote-terminal session on a local-area network, transmissions are never delayed, and response time remains low. When a slow network intervenes, input after the first character is queued, and the next packet contains the input received during the preceding round-trip time. This algorithm is attractive both because of its simplicity and because of its self-tuning nature.

Eventually, people discovered that this algorithm did not work well for certain classes of network clients that sent streams of small requests that could not be batched. One such client was the network-based X Window System [Scheifler & Gettys, 1986], which required immediate delivery of small messages to get real-time feedback for user interfaces such as rubber-banding to sweep out a new window. Hence an option, TCP_NODELAY, was added to TCP to defeat this algorithm on a connection. This option can be set with a *setsockopt* call, which reaches TCP via the *tcp_ctloutput*() routine.

Window Updates

TCP packets must be sent for reasons other than data transmission. On a one-way connection, the receiving TCP must still send packets to acknowledge received data and to advance the sender's send window. The time at which these packets are sent is a determining factor for network throughput. For example, if the receiver simply set the TF_DELACK flag each time data were received on a bulk-data connection, acknowledgments would be sent every 200 milliseconds. Using 4096-octet windows on a 10-Mbit/s Ethernet, this would result in a maximum throughput of 160 Kbit/s, or 1.6 percent of the physical network bandwidth. Clearly, once the sender has filled the send window that it has been given, it must stop until the receiver acknowledges the old data (allowing them to be removed from the send buffer and new data to replace them) and provides a window update (allowing the new data to be sent).

Because TCP's window-based flow control is limited by the space in the socket receive buffer, TCP has the PR_RCVD flag set in its protocol-switch entry so that the protocol will be called (via the PRU_RCVD request of *tcp_usrreq*()) when the user has done a receive call that has removed data from the receive buffer. The PRU_RCVD entry simply calls *tcp_output*(). (In 4.2BSD, *tcp_output*() was also called after each packet was received by *tcp_input*(); that call is eliminated under most circumstances in 4.3BSD.) Whenever *tcp_output*() determines that a window update sent under the current circumstances would provide sufficient new send window to the sender to be worthwhile, it sends an acknowledgment and window update. If the receiver really had to wait until the window was full, the sender would already have been idle for some time when it finally received a window update. Therefore, the window-update strategy in 4.3BSD is based on a fraction of the receive window. Whenever a new window update would expose at least 35 percent of the total receive buffer, the window update is sent. Using the default 4096-byte buffers and 1024-octet segments on an Ethernet, this criterion causes every other segment to be acknowledged. This window-update strategy produces a two-fold reduction in acknowledgment traffic and a two-fold reduction in input processing for the sender. This strategy assumes that the sender in each connection has a send buffer of a similar size to the receiver's receive buffer. Unfortunately, this assumption was not always correct, and if the sender's buffer was less than 35 percent of the size of the receiver's receive buffer, window updates were never triggered except when *tcp_fasttimo*() forced out delayed acknowledgments. Therefore, in the 4.3BSD Tahoe release of TCP, the strategy was changed to send a window update if at least twice the segment size was added to the sender's window.

Retransmit State

When the retransmit timer expires while a sender is awaiting acknowledgment of transmitted data, *tcp_output*() is called to retransmit. The retransmit timer is first set to the next multiple of the round-trip time in the backoff series. The variable *snd_nxt* is moved back from its current sequence number to *snd_una*. A single packet is then sent containing the oldest data in the transmit queue. Unlike some other systems, 4.3BSD does not keep copies of the packets that have been sent on a connection, but retains only the data. Thus, although only a single packet is retransmitted, that packet may contain more data than does the oldest outstanding packet. On a slow connection with small numbers of data, this may mean that a single-octet packet that is lost may be retransmitted with all the data queued since they were first transmitted.

If a single packet was lost in the network, the retransmitted packet will elicit an acknowledgment of all data yet transmitted. If more than one packet was lost, the next acknowledgment will include the retransmitted packet and possibly some of the intervening data. It may also include a new window update. Thus, when an acknowledgment is received after a retransmit timeout, any old data that were not acknowledged will be resent, and some new data may be sent as well.

Source-Quench Processing and Congestion Control

If a gateway along the route used by a connection receives more packets than it can send along this path, it may be forced to drop packets. When this happens, the gateway may send an ICMP *Source Quench* error message to hosts whose packets have been dropped to indicate that the senders should slow their transmissions. Although this message indicates that some change should be made, it provides no information on how much of a change must be made or for how long the change should take effect. One algorithm for handling source quench was proposed by Nagle [Nagle, 1984] and implemented in 4.3BSD. As the receipt of a source quench indicates that too many packets are outstanding in the network, the host receiving a source quench must reduce the number of packets it sends at one time. The algorithm uses a second window, like the send window but maintained separately, called the congestion window (*snd_cwnd*). Initially, the congestion-window size is set to some large amount. When a source quench is received for some destination, the congestion-window size is set to a fraction of the data outstanding, but to no less than the maximum segment size; in 4.3BSD, the fraction is 0.8. The send policy is then modified so that new data are sent if allowed by both the normal and congestion send windows. As the network congestion might be reduced with time, the congestion window is opened by a small amount (e.g., 10 percent), whenever a new acknowledgment is received. If this opening results in too large a congestion window at some point, a new source quench should be received. Thus, the number of data outstanding should modulate slowly around the limit that can be tolerated by the network.

The implementation of this scheme in 4.3BSD suffered from two flaws. First, although the congestion window needed to be kept in bytes to maintain significance, the send policy should have truncated this limit to a multiple of the segment size. The original implementation would send a smaller segment at the end of the congestion window. This produced no less congestion on the network, but fragmented buffers at the receiver and led to the use of odd packet sizes for some time. This problem was corrected in the 4.3BSD Tahoe release, as described in the following two sections. Second, many gateways do not send source-quench messages for each packet dropped.

Slow Start

Many TCP connections traverse several networks between source and destination. When some of the networks are slower than others, the entry gateway to the slowest network often is presented with more traffic than can be handled. It may buffer some number of input packets to avoid dropping packets due to sudden changes in flow, but eventually its buffers will fill and it must begin dropping packets. When a TCP connection first starts sending data across a fast network to a gateway to a slower network, it may find that the gateway's buffers are already nearly full. In the original send policy used in 4.3BSD, a bulk-data transfer would start out by sending a full window of packets once the connection was established. These packets could be sent at the full speed of the network to the bottleneck gateway, but that gateway could transmit them at only a much slower rate. As a result, the initial burst of packets was highly likely to overflow the gateway's buffers, and some of the packets would be lost. If such a connection used an expanded window size in an attempt to gain performance—for example, when traversing a satellite-based network with a long round-trip time—this problem would be even more severe. However, if the connection could once reach steady state, a full window of data often could be accommodated by the network if the packets were spread evenly throughout the path. At steady state, new packets would be injected into the network only when previous packets were acknowledged, and the number of packets in the network would be constant. In addition, even if packets arrived at the outgoing gateway in a cluster, they would be spread out when traversing the network by at least their transmission times in the slowest network. If the receiver sent acknowledgments when each packet was received, the acknowledgments would return to the sender with approximately the correct spacing. The sender would then have a self-clocking means for transmitting at the correct rate for the network without sending bursts of packets that the bottleneck could not buffer.

An algorithm named slow-start brings a TCP connection to this steady state [Jacobson, 1988]. It is called *slow start* because it is necessary to start data transmission slowly when traversing a slow network. The scheme is simple; a connection starts out with a limit of just one outstanding packet. Each time an acknowledgment is received, the limit is increased by one packet. If the acknowledgment also carries a window update, two packets can be sent in response. This process continues until the window is fully open. During the slow-start phase of the connection, if each packet was acknowledged separately, the limit would be doubled during each exchange, resulting in an exponential opening of the window. Delayed acknowledgments might cause acknowledgments to be coalesced if more than one packet could arrive at the receiver within 200 milliseconds, slowing the window opening slightly. However, the sender never sends bursts of more than two or three packets during the opening phase, and sends only one or two packets at a time once the window has opened.

The implementation of the slow-start algorithm uses the same congestion-window field in the connection block that was originally used for source-quench handling in 4.3BSD, *snd_cwnd*. This field is set to the size of one packet whenever the connection comes to a halt. It is initialized to one packet for any connection to a destination not on a shared network, and is set to one packet whenever transmission stops due to a timeout. Otherwise, once a dropped packet was acknowledged, the resulting window update might allow a full window of data to be sent, which would once again overrun intervening gateways. This slow start after a retransmission timeout eliminates the need for a test in the output routine to limit output to one packet on the initial timeout. In addition, the timeout may indicate that the network has become slower due to congestion, and temporary reduction of the window may help the network recover from its condition. The connection is forced to reestablish its clock of acknowledgments after the connection has come to a halt, and the slow start accomplishes this as well.

The use of the slow-start algorithm after retransmission timeouts allows a connection to respond correctly to a dropped packet, whether or not a source quench is received to indicate the loss. The action on receipt of a source quench in this version of TCP is simply to anticipate the timeout due to the dropped packet, setting the congestion window to one packet. This action prevents new packets from being sent until the dropped packet is resent at the next timeout. At that time, the slow start will begin again.

Avoidance of Congestion with Slow Start

The addition of the slow-start algorithm to TCP allows a connection to send packets at a rate that the network can tolerate, reaching a steady state at which packets are sent only when another packet has exited the network. A single connection may reasonably use a larger window without flooding the entry gateway to the slow network on startup. For some paths, using slow start and a large window can lead to much better performance than could be achieved previously. For example, paths that traverse satellite links have long intrinsic delay, even though the bandwidth may be high, but the throughput is limited to one window of data per round-trip time. Even with such a path, gateways with limited buffering, such as most ARPANET gateways, between the source and the satellite uplink would be flooded without slow start. It is highly desirable for a TCP connection to be self-tuning, however, as the characteristics of the path are seldom known at the end-points. A window size large enough to give good performance when a long-delay link is in the path will overrun the network when most of the round-trip time is in queuing delays. As a connection opens the window during a slow start, it injects packets into the network until the network links are kept busy, and then additional widening of the window will simply increase the size of the queues in the gateway. Opening the window past the point at which all the transmission links are kept busy does not increase throughput, but it does increase the delay seen by the connection. If a connection expands to too large a window for a path, or if additional load on the network collectively exceeds the capacity, gateway queues will build until packets must be dropped. At this point, the connection will close the congestion window to one packet and will initiate a slow start. If the window is simply too large for the path, however, this process will repeat once the window is opened too far.

The connection can learn from this problem, and adjust its behavior accordingly with another algorithm installed at the same time as slow start was. This algorithm keeps a new state variable for each connection, *t_ssthresh* (slow-start threshold), which is an estimate of the usable window for the path. When a packet is dropped, as evidenced by a retransmission timeout, this window estimate is set to one-half the number of the outstanding data octets. The current window is obviously too large at the moment, and the decrease in window utilization must be large enough that congestion will decrease rather than stabilizing. At the same time, the slow-start window (*snd_cwnd*) is set to one segment to restart. The connection starts up as before, opening the window exponentially until it reaches the *t_ssthresh* limit. To test for improvement in the network, it continues to expand the window slowly; as long as this expansion succeeds, the connection can continue to take advantage of reduced network load. The expansion of the window in this phase is linear, adding one additional full-sized segment to the current window for each full window of data transmitted. This slow increase allows the connection to discover when it is safe to resume use of a larger window while reducing the loss in throughput due to the wait after the loss of a packet before transmission can resume. Note that the increase in window size during this phase of the connection is linear as long as no packets are lost, but the decrease in window size when signs of congestion appear is exponential (it is divided by 2 on each timeout). With the use of this dynamic window-sizing algorithm, it is possible to use larger default window sizes for connection to all destinations without overrunning networks that cannot support them.

12.8 Internet Control Message Protocol (ICMP)

The *Internet Control Message Protocol (ICMP)* [Postel, 1981c] is the control- and error-message protocol for IP. Although it is layered above IP for input and output operations much like UDP, it is really an integral part of IP. Unlike those of UDP, most ICMP messages are received and implemented by the kernel. ICMP messages may also be sent and received using a raw IP socket (see Section 11.7).

ICMP messages fall into three general classes. One class includes various errors that may occur somewhere in the network and that may be reported back to the originator of the packet provoking the error. Such errors include routing failures (network or host unreachable), expiration of the time-to-live field in a packet, or a report by the destination host that the target protocol or port number is not available. The second message class may be considered as gateway-to-host control messages. The two instances of such messages are the source-quench message that reports excessive output and packet loss, and the routing redirect that informs a host that a better route is available for a host or network via a different gateway. The final message class includes network management, testing, and measurement packets. These include a network address request and reply, a network mask request and reply, an echo request and reply, and a timestamp request and reply.

All the actions and replies required by an incoming ICMP message are done by the kernel ICMP layer. ICMP packets are received from IP via the normal protocol-input entry point, as ICMP has its own IP protocol number. The ICMP input routine formulates responses to any requests and passes the reply to *ip_output*() to be returned to the sender. When error indications or source quenches are received, a generic address is constructed in a *sockaddr* structure, and the address and error code are reported to each network protocol's control-input entry *pr_ctlinput*() by *pfctlinput*().

Routing changes indicated by redirect messages are processed by the *rtredirect*() routine. It verifies that the gateway from which the message was received was the next-hop gateway in use for the destination, and it checks that the new gateway is on a directly attached network. If these tests succeed, the kernel routing tables are modified accordingly. If the new route is of equivalent scope to the previous route (e.g., both are for the destination network), the gateway in the route is changed to the new gateway. If the scope of the new route is smaller than that of the original route (either a host redirect is received when a network route was used, or the old route used a wildcard route), a new route is created in the kernel table. Routes that are created or modified by redirects are marked with the flags RTF_DYNAMIC and RTF_MODIFIED, respectively. Once the routing tables are updated, the protocols are notified by *pfctlinput*(), using a redirect code rather than an error code. TCP and UDP simply flush any cached route from the protocol control block when a redirect is received. The next packet sent on the socket will thus reallocate a route, choosing the new route if it is now the best route.

Once an incoming ICMP message has been processed by the kernel, it is passed to *raw_input*() for any ICMP raw sockets. The raw sockets can also be used to send ICMP messages. The low-level network test program **ping** works by sending ICMP echo requests on a raw socket and listening for corresponding replies.

ICMP is also used by other Internet network protocols to generate error messages. UDP sends only ICMP Port Unreachable error messages, and TCP uses other means to report such errors. However, many different errors may be detected by IP, especially on systems used as IP gateways. The *icmp_error*() function constructs an error message of a specified type in response to an IP packet. Most error messages include a portion of the original packet that caused the error as well as the type and code for the error. The identity of the interface on which the original packet was received is also passed to *icmp_error*() in case the destination of the original packet was a different host, as occurs when forwarding is done; the source address of the error message can then be set to the address of the gateway on the network closest to (or shared with) the originating host. Also, when IP forwards a packet via the same network interface on which that packet was received, it may send a redirect message to the originating host if that host is on the same network. The *icmp_error*() routine accepts an additional parameter for redirect messages—the address of the new gateway to be used by the host.

12.9 ARPANET Host Interface

The protocols we have described so far were designed for use in an Internet environment centered on the ARPANET. The ARPANET (and similar networks, including the Milnet) are packet-switched networks consisting of minicomputers interconnected by 56-Kbit/s trunks. Hosts and gateways are connected to the switching nodes, which receive packets from a host, forward them via some number of intermediate nodes if necessary, and deliver them to the destination host or gateway. The *Packet Switch Node* (*PSN*), previously known as an *Interface Message Processor* (IMP) [Heart *et al.*, 1970], provides the host interface and packet-switching functions. It supports reliable message delivery with flow control. Messages are presented to the receiving PSN with a header containing the destination host (as a PSN number and the host's number on the PSN). The PSNs use a dynamic routing protocol to determine the route to the destination PSN [McQuillan *et al.*, 1980]. Messages may be fragmented into subnetwork packets of at most 128 octets, then reassembled by the destination PSN. The end-to-end protocol used by the PSNs manages buffer allocation, message delivery, and acknowledgment. Once a message is accepted by the source PSN, the source host will receive either an acknowledgment or a failure message within a specified time (30 seconds). Flow control is implemented by hosts being limited to a maximum of eight outstanding messages to each other host. Thus, the acknowledgment of one message allows another message to be sent, and the acknowledgment is known as *Ready for Next Message* (RFNM).

Two major types of host connections to PSNs are in current use. The original host interface to the IMP is known as an 1822 interface, after the number of the report containing the specification for its message protocol and electrical signaling [BBN, 1978]. The other interface now used for connection to a PSN is X.25, which we shall describe later.

The *ARPANET Host Access Protocol* (AHIP), is the newer name for the 1822 host protocol. This protocol is implemented by common routines in the **netimp** directory of the kernel source. Several types of hardware interfaces supply connections to a PSN using the 1822 protocol. The packet formatting and interpretation, as well as the per-host flow control, are done by the common layer, whereas the drivers are responsible for only sending and receiving messages. The AHIP protocol uses a simple header containing a message type, destination IMP and host numbers, and a link type. Some messages are exchanged with the local PSN, for example the initialization messages. The link type is used in data messages to identify the protocol that is to receive the message, and thus corresponds with the type field of an Ethernet header. There are several message types for control information, including the RFNM message, the failure message (*Incomplete Message*), and messages that indicate that destination hosts are down or unreachable.

The IMP interface software maintains a list of entries for hosts with which it is communicating. This host entry contains a count of messages that have been sent to the host for which RFNM (or Incomplete Message) messages have not been received. When packets in excess of the limit are received for transmission to the same host, up to eight additional packets are enqueued in the host entry for transmission when RFNMs are received. Messages beyond this limit are dropped, returning the error that indicates buffer space has been exhausted. On gateways this error causes an ICMP source-quench message to be generated for the originating host. If a *Host Dead* or a *Host Unreachable* message is received, indicating that a destination is down, the host entry is marked with this information and a timer is set. Until the timer expires, attempts to send to that destination will produce errors of the appropriate type, and the packets are dropped with no attempt made to send them. Gateways may thus send appropriate ICMP error messages to hosts attempting to send packets to unreachable destinations.

The other type of host interface that may used for connection to a PSN is X.25 [CCITT, 1980], similar to the connection to a public packet-switched data network. An X.25 interface to the Milnet (Defense Data Network, DDN) may be used to connect a host to a PSN for use with the Internet protocols. In this mode, the X.25 interface is used to create virtual circuits to the local PSN for communications with other hosts, rather than to make X.25 virtual circuits terminating at the destination hosts. Hosts with X.25 connections may communicate with hosts that have 1822 connections; the PSNs map both access protocols onto the internal end-to-end protocol, and each host uses the flow-control mechanism appropriate to its access method. 4.3BSD does not include drivers for hardware using an X.25 interface to a PSN, although such drivers are available.

12.10 Xerox Network Systems Communication Domain (XNS)

The Xerox Network Systems (NS) communication domain supports three communication protocols. *IDP* is the *Internetwork Datagram Protocol*, which forms the basis for the level-1 transport protocol in the NS architecture. IDP is responsible for the internet packet format, internet addressing, and routing. The

Sequenced Packet Protocol (SPP), is a level-2 transport protocol layered on top of IDP. SPP provides reliable, unduplicated, and flow-controlled transmission of messages. The third protocol is the *Error Protocol*, which reports errors; this protocol is used as a diagnostic tool as well as as a means of improving performance; it is not normally accessed by users.

SPP is used to support the operation of both stream and sequenced packet sockets created in the NS domain. The standard datagram service, called *Packet Exchange* (*PEX*), is implemented by a user-level library using IDP datagram sockets. Raw access to the Error Protocol and IDP protocols is possible through *raw sockets*.

For each SPP- or IDP-based socket, an *NS protocol control block* is created to hold NS information similar to that found in the Internet protocol control block. Also like TCP, SPP creates an *SPP control block* to hold the protocol state information necessary for its implementation. Unlike those in the Internet domain, the NS protocol control blocks for all protocols are maintained on *one* doubly linked list. In the NS domain, packet demultiplexing at the network-protocol level is done first according to the network address and port numbers and then according to the communication protocol. The linkage between the socket data structure and the protocol-specific data structures is identical to that found in the Internet communication domain.

The NS and Internet protocol implementations are similar. Consequently, understanding the data structures, organization, and algorithms of one protocol family makes understanding the other much easier.

The SPP protocol output routine uses the following convention:

```
error = spp_output(spcb, m);
    struct sppcb *spcb;
    struct mbuf *m;
```

where the *spcb* is an SPP protocol control block and *m* is the mbuf chain that contains the data to be sent.

The IDP protocol uses a similar convention:

```
error = idp_output(nsp, m);
    struct nspcb *nsp;
    struct mbuf *m;
```

which differs only in the use of an NS protocol control block. Both SPP and IDP pass packets to the common NS module used for packet transmission with

```
error = ns_output(m, ro, flags);
    struct mbuf *m;
    struct route *ro;
    int flags;
```

As in the previous example, the *m* parameter is an mbuf chain containing the message to be transmitted. The *ro* parameter is used in making routing decisions (for IDP, this will always be zero, as it does not hold routing information between packets transmitted). The *flags* parameter indicates whether the user is allowed to transmit a broadcast packet and whether routing is to be performed. As noted before, the broadcast flag may be inconsequential if the underlying hardware does not support the notion of broadcasting.

All output routines return 0 on success and a UNIX error number if a failure is detected immediately.

All NS protocol input is received by the NS interrupt routine, *nsintr*(), which is invoked at software-interrupt level when a network interface receives a message to be processed by an NS protocol module. The interrupt routine performs consistency checks on the packet, and then determines whether to receive, forward, or discard the packet. If the packet is to be received, *nsintr*() locates the NS protocol control block for the receiving socket according to the sender's address and the destination port number. It then passes the packet to the receiving protocol.

Both IDP and SPP use the following calling convention:

```
(void) (*pr_input)(m, nsp, ifp);
    struct mbuf *m;
    struct nspcb *nsp;
    struct ifnet *ifp;
```

Each mbuf chain is a single packet to be processed by the protocol module. The interface from which the packet was received is passed as the last parameter.

The IDP *pr_ctlinput*() routine is mainly used to pass control information to the IDP and SPP protocol modules from the Error protocol's input routine. (It may also be invoked from the Internet ICMP module if NS is being encapsulated inside IP.) The common calling convention for this routine is

```
(void) (*pr_ctlinput)(req, arg);
    int req;
    caddr_t arg;
```

The *req* will usually be a value shown in Table 11.4, although only a restricted subset of these requests is mapped from Error Protocol codes in *ns_err_input*(). The *arg* parameter is a pointer to an Error Protocol packet when a mapped request is supplied. Otherwise, the *arg* is a pointer to a socket address structure.

XNS Control Operations

The SPP and IDP *pr_ctloutput*() routines provide access to NS-specific options that control the behavior of SPP and/or IDP in processing data transmitted and received through a socket. Options usable with both SPP and IDP protocols are SO_HEADERS_ON_INPUT, to have protocol headers returned on each message with data; SO_MTU, to set the maximum size of a message that will be sent or received; and SO_DEFAULT_HEADERS, to establish a default header for outgoing messages.

12.11 Summary

In this section, we shall tie together much of the material presented in the last three chapters. To do this, we shall describe the operation of the socket and network layers during normal use.

There are three stages in the lifetime of a socket. Initially, the socket is created and is associated with some communication domain. During its lifetime, data passes through it to one or more other sockets. When the socket is no longer needed, it must go through an orderly shutdown process in which its resources are freed.

Creating a Communication Channel

Sockets are created by users with the *socket* system call and internally with the *socreate*() routine. To create a socket, the user must give a communication domain and socket type, and it also may request a specific communication protocol within that domain. The socket routines first locate the domain structure for the communication domain from a global list initialized at boot time for each configured domain. The table of protocols that constitute the domain's protocol family is located in the domain structure. This table of protocol-switch entries is then scanned for an appropriate protocol to support the type of socket being created (or for a specific protocol, if one was specified). The socket routine performs this search by examining the *pr_type* field, which contains a possible socket type (e.g., SOCK_STREAM), and the *pr_protocol* field, which contains the protocol number of the protocol, normally a well-known value. If a suitable protocol is found, a reference to the protocol's protocol-switch entry is then recorded in the socket's *so_proto* field, and all requests for network services are made through the appropriate procedure identified in the structure.

After locating a handle on a protocol, *socreate*() allocates an mbuf and creates the socket data structure with the socket's initial state. To complete the creation process, *socreate*() makes a PRU_ATTACH request to the protocol's user request routine so that the protocol may *attach* itself to the new socket.

Next, an address may be bound to a socket. Binding of an address is done internally by *sobind*(), which makes a PRU_BIND request to the socket's supporting protocol. The Internet and XNS domains each provide a routine that manages their address spaces. Addresses in the UNIX domain are names in the filesystem name space, and consequently name requests go through the filesystem name-lookup routine, *namei*().

For a socket to be ready to accept connections, the socket layer must inform the protocols with a PRU_LISTEN request. This request obviously has no meaning for connectionless protocols such as UDP and IDP. For connection-oriented protocols such as TCP and SPP, however, a listen request causes a protocol state transition. Before effecting this state change, protocols verify that the socket has an address bound to it; if it has none, the protocol module chooses one for it.

In the UNIX domain a listen request causes no state change, but a check is made to ensure that the socket has a name. Unlike the other protocols, however, the UNIX domain will not select a name for the socket.

Soconnect() is invoked to establish a connection, generating a PRU_CONNECT request to the protocol. For connectionless protocols, the address is recorded as a default address to be used when data are sent on the socket (i.e., the process does a *write* or *send*, instead of a *sendto*). Setting the address does not require any peer communication, and the protocol module returns immediately.

For a connection-based protocol, the peer's address is verified, and a local address is assigned for unbound sockets. Instead of entering a *connected* state immediately, the socket is marked as *connecting* with *soisconnecting*(). The protocol then initiates a handshake with the peer by transmitting a connection-request message. When a connection request of this sort is completed, usually on receipt of a message by the protocol input routine, the socket's state is changed with a call to *soisconnected*().

From a user's perspective all connection requests appear synchronous because the *connect* system call invokes *soconnect*() to initiate a connection and then, at the socket level, puts the calling process to sleep if the connection request has not been completed. Alternatively, if the socket has been made nonblocking with *fcntl*, *connect* returns the error EINPROGRESS once the connection has been initiated successfully. The caller may test the completion of the connection with a *select* call testing for ability to write to the socket.

For connection-based communication, a process must accept an incoming connection request on a listening socket by calling *accept*, which in turn calls *soaccept*(). This call returns the next completed connection from the socket receive queue.

Sending and Receiving Data

Once a socket has been created, data can begin to flow through it. A typical TCP/IP connection is shown in Fig. 12.10. The *sosend*() routine is responsible for copying data from the sending process's address space into mbufs. It then presents the data to the network layer with one or more calls to the protocol's PRU_SEND request. The network may choose to send the data immediately, or to wait until a more auspicious time. If the protocol delays, or if it must retain a copy of the data for possible retransmission, it may store the data in the socket's send buffer. Eventually, the data are passed down through TCP and IP to the appropriate interface driver as one or more packets; at each layer, an appropriate header is added. Each packet is sent out over the network to its destination machine.

On receipt at the destination machine, the interface driver's receiver-interrupt handler verifies and removes its own header and places the packet onto an appropriate network-protocol input queue. Later, the network-level input processing module (e.g., IP or IDP) is invoked by a software interrupt; it runs at a lower

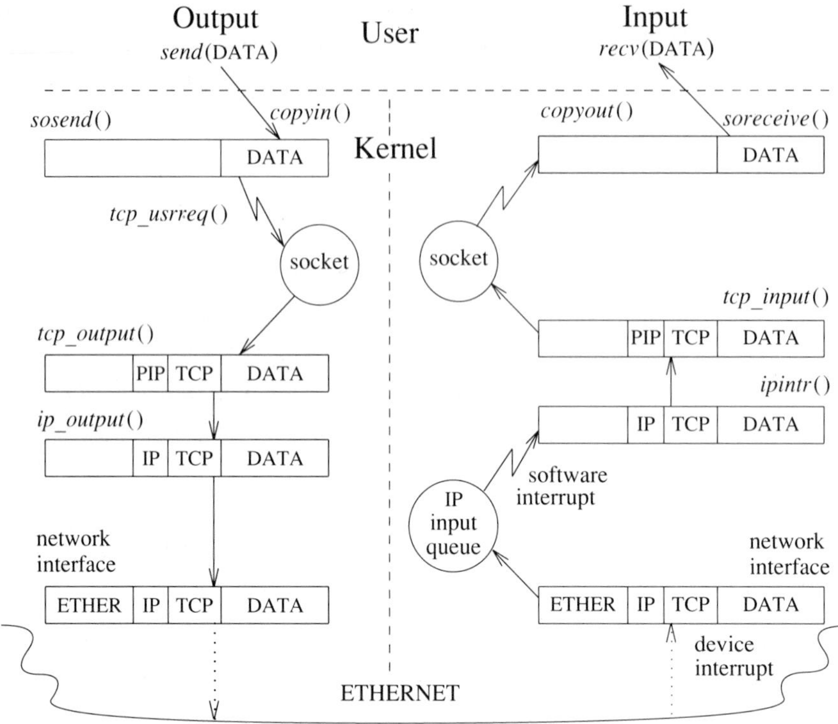

Figure 12.10 Data flow through a TCP/IP connection over an Ethernet. ETHER—Ethernet header; PIP—pseudo IP header; IP—IP header; TCP—TCP header.

interrupt priority level than that of the hardware network interface interrupt. In this example, the packets on the input queue are processed first by IP and then by TCP, each of which verifies and removes its header. If received in order, the data are then placed on the appropriate socket's input queue, ready to be copied out by *soreceive*() on receipt of a *read* request.

Terminating Data Transmission and/or Reception

The *soshutdown*() routine stops data flow at a socket. Shutting down a socket for reading is a simple matter of flushing the receive queue and marking the socket as unable to receive more data; this is done with a call to *sorflush*(), which in turn invokes *socantrcvmore*() to change the socket state, and then releases any resources associated with the receive queue. Shutting down a socket for writing, however, involves notifying the protocol with a PRU_SHUTDOWN request. For reliable connections, any data remaining in the send queue must be drained before the connection can finish shutting down. If a protocol supports the notion of a *half-open* connection (i.e., a connection in which unidirectional data flow is possible), the socket may continue to be usable; otherwise, the protocol may start a disconnect sequence. Once a socket has been shut down in both directions, the protocol starts a disconnect sequence. When the disconnect completes, first the resources associated with the network and then those associated with the socket are freed.

Exercises

12.1 Is TCP a transport-, network-, or link-layer protocol?

12.2 How does IP identify the next-higher-level protocol that should process an incoming message? How does this dispatching differ in the Xerox NS architecture?

12.3 How many hosts can exist on a class C Internet network? Is it possible to use subnet addressing with a class C network?

12.4 What is a broadcast message? How are broadcast messages identified in the DARPA Internet?

12.5 Why are TCP and UDP protocol control blocks kept on separate lists?

12.6 Why does the IP output routine check the destination address of an outgoing packet to see whether it is a broadcast address instead of the socket-layer send routine (*sosend*())?

12.7 Why does 4.3BSD not forward broadcast messages?

12.8 Why does the TCP header include a header-length field even though it is always encapsulated in an IP packet that contains the length of the TCP message?

12.9 What is the flow-control mechanism used by TCP to limit the rate at which data are transmitted?

12.10 How does TCP recognize messages from a host that are directed to a connection that previously existed, but that has since been shut down (such as after a machine is rebooted)?

12.11 When is the size of the TCP receive window for a connection not equal to the amount of space available in the associated socket's receive buffer? Why are these values not equal at that time?

12.12 What are keepalive messages and for what does TCP use them? Why are keepalive messages implemented in the kernel rather than, say, in each application that wants this facility?

12.13 Why is calculating a *smoothed* round-trip time important, rather than, for example, just averaging calculated round-trip times?

12.14 Why does TCP delay acknowledgments for received data? What is the maximum period of time that TCP will delay an acknowledgment?

12.15 Explain what the silly-window syndrome is and give an example in which its avoidance is important to good protocol performance. How does the 4.3BSD TCP avoid this problem?

12.16 What is meant by *small-packet avoidance*? Why is small-packet avoidance bad for clients that exhibit one-way data flow and that require low latency for good interactive performance (e.g., the X Window System)?

*12.17 A *directed broadcast* is a message that is to be broadcast on a network one or more hops away from the sender. Describe a scheme for supporting directed-broadcast messages in the Internet domain.

*12.18 Why is the initial sequence number for a TCP connection selected at random, rather than being, say, always set to zero?

*12.19 In the TCP protocol, why do the SYN and FIN flags occupy space in the sequence-number space?

*12.20 Describe a typical TCP packet exchange during connection setup. Assume an active client initiated the connection to a passive server. How would this scenario change if the passive server tried simultaneously to initiate a connection to the client?

*12.21 Sketch the TCP state transitions that would take place if a server process accepted a connection and then immediately closed it before receiving any data. How would this scenario be altered if 4.3BSD supported a mechanism whereby a server could refuse a connection request before the system completed the connection?

*12.22 At one time, the 4BSD TCP used a strict exponential backoff strategy for transmission. Explain how this nonadaptive algorithm can adversely affect performance across networks that are very *lossy*, but that have high bandwidth (e.g. some networks that utilize satellite connections).

*12.23 Why does UDP match the completely specified destination addresses of incoming messages to sockets with incomplete local and remote destination addresses?

*12.24 Why might a sender set the *Don't Fragment* flag in the header of an IP packet?

*12.25 The *maximum segment lifetime* (MSL) is the maximum time a message may exist in a network; that is, the maximum time that a message may be in transit on some hardware medium or queued in a gateway. What does TCP do to ensure that TCP messages have a limited MSL? What does IP do to enforce a limited MSL [Fletcher & Watson, 1978]?

**12.26 Describe a protocol for calculating a bound on the maximum segment lifetime of messages in an internet environment. How might TCP use a bound on the MSL (see Exercise 12.25) for a message to minimize the overhead associated with shutting down a TCP connection?

References

BBN, 1978.
BBN, "Specification for the Interconnection of Host and IMP," Technical Report 1822, Bolt, Beranek, and Newman, Cambridge, MA (May 1978).

CCITT, 1980.
CCITT, "Recommendation X.25: Interface between Data Terminal Equipment (DTE) and Data Circuit-Terminating Equipment (DCE) for Terminals Operating in the Packet Mode on Public Data Networks," in *Public Data Networks, Orange Book, vol. VIII.2* (1980).

Carr *et al.*, 1970.
S. Carr, S. Crocker, & V. Cerf, "HOST–HOST Communication Protocol in the ARPA Network," *Proceedings of the AFIPS Spring Joint Computer Conference*, pp. 589–597 (1970).

Cerf, 1978.
V. Cerf, "The Catenet Model for Internetworking," Technical Report IEN 48, SRI Network Information Center, Menlo Park, CA (July 1978).

Cerf & Kahn, 1974.
V. G. Cerf & R. E. Kahn, "A Protocol for Packet Network Intercommunication," *IEEE Transactions on Communications* **22**(5), pp. 637–648 (May 1974).

Clark, 1982.
D. D. Clark, "Window and Acknowledgment Strategy in TCP," RFC 813, SRI Network Information Center, Menlo Park, CA (July 1982).

DARPA, 1983.
DARPA, "A History of the ARPANET: The First Decade," Technical Report, Bolt, Beranek, and Newman, Cambridge, MA (April, 1983).

Fletcher & Watson, 1978.
J. Fletcher & R. Watson, "Mechanisms for a Reliable Timer-Based Protocol," pp. 271–290 in *Computer Networks 2*, North-Holland, Amsterdam, The Netherlands (1978).

Heart *et al.*, 1970.
F. E. Heart, R. E. Kahn, S. Ornstein, W. Crowther, & D. Walden, "The Interface Message Processor for the ARPA Computer Network," *Proceedings of the AFIPS Spring Joint Computer Conference*, pp. 551–567 (1970).

ISO, 1984.
ISO, "Open Systems Interconnection—Basic Reference Model," ISO 7498, International Organization for Standardization (1984). Available from: American National Standards Institute, 1430 Broadway, New York, NY 10018.

Jacobson, 1988.
V. Jacobson, "Congestion Avoidance and Control," *Proceedings of the ACM SIGCOMM Conference*, pp. 314–329 (August 1988).

McQuillan & Walden, 1977.
J. M. McQuillan & D. C. Walden, "The ARPA Network Design

Decisions,'' *Computer Networks* **1**(5), pp. 243–289 (1977).

McQuillan *et al.*, 1980.
J. M. McQuillan, I. Richer, & E. Rosen, ``The New Routing Algorithm for the ARPANET,'' *IEEE Transactions on Communications* **28**(5), pp. 711–719 (May 1980).

Mogul, 1984.
J. Mogul, ``Broadcasting Internet Datagrams,'' RFC 919, SRI Network Information Center, Menlo Park, CA (October 1984).

Mogul & Postel, 1985.
J. Mogul & J. Postel, ``Internet Standard Subnetting Procedure,'' RFC 919, SRI Network Information Center, Menlo Park, CA (August 1985).

Nagle, 1984.
J. Nagle, ``Congestion Control in IP/TCP Internetworks,'' RFC 896, SRI Network Information Center, Menlo Park, CA (January 1984).

Padlipsky, 1985.
M. A. Padlipsky, *The Elements of Networking Style,* Prentice-Hall, Englewood Cliffs, NJ (1985).

Postel, 1980.
J. Postel, ``User Datagram Protocol,'' RFC 768, SRI Network Information Center, Menlo Park, CA (August 1980).

Postel, 1981a.
J. Postel, ``Internet Protocol,'' RFC 791, SRI Network Information Center, Menlo Park, CA (September 1981).

Postel, 1981b.
J. Postel, ``Transmission Control Protocol,'' RFC 793, SRI Network Information Center, Menlo Park, CA (September 1981).

Postel, 1981c.
J. Postel, ``Internet Control Message Protocol,'' RFC 792, SRI Network Information Center, Menlo Park, CA (September 1981).

Postel *et al.*, 1981.
J. B. Postel, C. A. Sunshine, & D. Cohen, ``The ARPA Internet Protocol,'' *Computer Networks* **5**(4), pp. 261–271 (July 1981).

Scheifler & Gettys, 1986.
R. W. Scheifler & J. Gettys, ``The X Window System,'' *ACM Transactions on Graphics* **5**(2), pp. 79–109 (April 1986).

PART 5

System Operation

CHAPTER 13

System Startup

When a computer is powered on, there is nothing running on the CPU. For a program to be set running, the binary image of the program must first be loaded into memory from a storage device. Many microprocessor systems automatically start programs that reside in nonvolatile storage devices such as programmable read-only memories (PROMs). Once the image of the program is loaded, the CPU must be directed to start execution at the first memory location of the loaded program. This process of *bootstrapping* a program into execution is used to start any program running on a CPU.

In this chapter, we examine how the UNIX kernel, or any other similar program, is bootstrapped. We then study the operation of the system during the initialization phase, which takes the system from a *cold start* to the point at which user-mode programs can be run. A final section examines topics that are related to the startup procedure. These topics include configuring the kernel load image, shutting down a running system, and debugging system failures.

13.1 Overview

The UNIX kernel is only a program, albeit a large one. Like any UNIX program, its binary image resides in a file in the filesystem until it is loaded and set running. 4.3BSD presumes the executable image of the kernel resides in a file named **vmunix** on the filesystem that is designated as the *root filesystem*. When UNIX is bootstrapped on a machine, a special program, named **boot**, is first loaded and is started running. The **boot** program's task is to load and initialize the executable image of a program and to start it running. **Boot** may come from the same storage device as the file it bootstraps, or it may be loaded from a storage device supported by the machine's console processor specifically for bootstrapping purposes.

The **boot** program reads the binary image of a program to be bootstrapped into main memory and then initializes the CPU so that the loaded program can be started. Programs loaded by **boot** are set running with virtual-address translation and hardware interrupts disabled. The loaded program is responsible for enabling these facilities and any additional hardware, such as I/O devices, that it intends to use.

When the UNIX kernel is loaded by the **boot** program, the kernel goes through several stages of hardware and software initialization in preparation for normal system operation. The first stage is responsible for initializing the state of the CPU, including the run-time stack and virtual-memory mapping. Memory mapping, including virtual-address translation, is enabled early in the startup procedure to minimize the amount of special-purpose assembly-language code that must be written. Once virtual-memory mapping is enabled, the system does machine-dependent initializations and then machine-independent initializations. The machine-dependent operations include setting up virtual-memory page tables and configuring I/O devices; the machine-independent actions include mounting the root filesystem and initializing the myriad system data structures. This order is necessary because many of the machine-independent initializations depend on the I/O devices being initialized properly.

Following the setup of the machine-independent portions of the kernel, the system is in operational status. System processes are created and made runnable and user-level programs are brought in from the filesystems to execute. At this point, the system is ready to run normal applications.

13.2 Bootstrapping

Bootstrapping a program is a machine-dependent operation. On most machines, this operation is supported either by a secondary processor termed the *console processor*, or by a *console monitor*. The console-monitor program is resident in nonvolatile storage and is invoked automatically when the CPU is reset. The console facilities are expected to support the bootstrap of standalone programs. Most console processors and monitors also execute diagnostic operations when a machine is reset to ensure that the hardware is functioning properly.

The boot Program

The console processor or console monitor often does not understand the format of the 4.3BSD filesystem. Instead, a vendor's proprietary filesystem format, or some other filesystem format, is interpreted by the software that supports bootstrapping operations. For this reason, the UNIX kernel historically has been bootstrapped through the **boot** program. This program is a general-purpose *standalone* program that can be used to load and execute other standalone programs. A *standalone program* is a program that is capable of operating without the assistance of the UNIX kernel. Standalone programs usually are linked with the *standalone I/O library*, a library that supports a UNIX-like I/O interface on a variety of hardware devices. The standalone I/O library provides these facilities through a collection of *standalone device drivers* and a library of routines that support reading of files from UNIX filesystems that reside on the devices.

Once the **boot** program has been loaded and started, it must load the file containing the executable image of the program to be bootstrapped and then start the loaded program running. To load the appropriate file, **boot** must know the pathname of the file to be loaded and the hardware device on which the file resides. This information is communicated to **boot** in one of two ways. On the VAX, two hardware registers are initialized to contain values that specify how **boot** should operate and which device should be used when program images are loaded. Other machines communicate the bootstrapping information to the **boot** program by initializing the run-time stack and then placing the parameters on the stack in the same way the UNIX kernel passes arguments to programs.

The registers used on the VAX are called the *boothowto register* and the *bootdevice register*. The boothowto register is interpreted by **boot** when the latter starts running; depending on the register's value, **boot** will either load the file **vmunix** from a device specified in the bootdevice register, or will prompt at the console terminal for the name of a file to load and a device from which to obtain the specified file. The value placed in the boothowto register is defined from the flags shown in Table 13.1. The value placed in the bootdevice register to identify the hardware device to use for bootstrapping is dependent on the configuration of the standalone I/O library with which **boot** is linked. Since the composition of this library is dependent on the hardware devices available on a machine, the contents of the bootdevice register can vary among different types of machines. For our discussion, it is sufficient to know that the register's contents specify a default device and filesystem partition from which to read programs.

Boot always loads programs at memory location 0. Since **boot** is initially loaded in memory at location 0, it must copy its own image to another place in

Table 13.1 Flags passed to the **boot** program and to the *reboot* system call.

Flag	Description
RB_ASKNAME	prompt for a filename to bootstrap
RB_SINGLE	bootstrap a system to single-user operation
RB_NOSYNC†	do not sync before rebooting
RB_HALT†	do not reboot, just halt
RB_INITNAME	use the name given instead of **/etc/init**
RB_DFLTROOT	use the compiled-in root device
RB_KDB	give control to the kernel debugger
RB_RDONLY	mount the root filesystem read-only
RB_DUMP†	dump kernel memory before rebooting

† Meaningful to only the *reboot* system call.

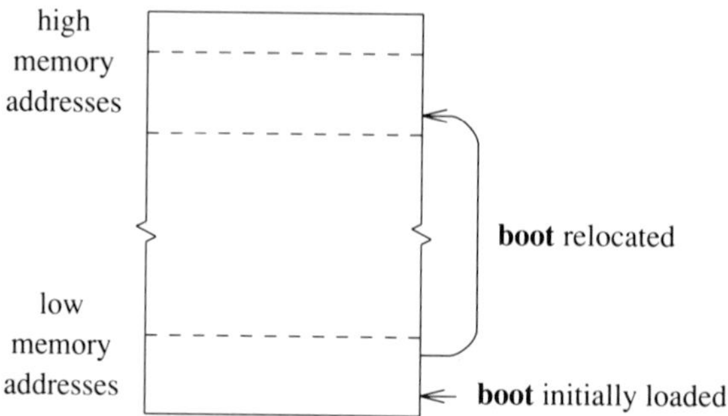

Figure 13.1 Placement of the **boot** program in memory.

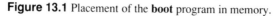

memory to avoid loading the image of the program it bootstraps on top of itself (see Fig. 13.1). This *relocation* implies that the **boot** program must be created with its starting address set to the memory location at which it will be copied; otherwise, references to data structures in the **boot** program will access the wrong memory locations after **boot** is copied (remember that **boot** operates with virtual-address translation disabled).

VAX Console Media

Most VAX computers include a console processor and some form of secondary storage that is accessible from the console processor. The VAX–11/780 console subsystem includes a floppy-disk drive, whereas the VAX–11/750 and VAX–11/730 console subsystems include a small cartridge-tape drive.

The exact sequence of steps taken during bootstrapping a VAX varies from machine to machine. In normal operation, the VAX console processor searches for a file called **DEFBOO.CMD** on its console media. This file contains commands that the console processor should interpret in order to bootstrap the CPU. The commands in this file typically reset the CPU and I/O subsystems, initialize registers to known values, and then load a file from the console storage device and start it running. The user can request alternative actions on some VAX machines by setting front panel switches, or by typing special commands on the console terminal.

When the console storage device is used in the bootstrapping process, the **boot** program must reside on this storage device. 4.3BSD supports two utility programs that manipulate the filesystem format used by the console processor—**arff** and **flcopy**. These programs are used to place programs such as **boot** on VAX console storage media.

13.3 Kernel Initialization

When the UNIX kernel is started by the **boot** program, it does an initialization in preparation for the execution of application programs. The initialization process is roughly divided into three stages. The first stage is written entirely in assembly language and does the work necessary for non–assembly-language code to operate. The second stage does machine-dependent operations including the configuration and initialization of the I/O devices on the machine. The third stage does machine-independent operations, completing its work by starting up the system-resident processes that compose the foundation for the normal UNIX run-time environment.

Assembly-Language Startup

The first steps taken by the system during initialization are carried out by assembly-language code. This work is very machine-dependent; it includes

- Setting up the run-time stack
- Identifying the type of CPU on which the system is executing
- Calculating the amount of physical memory on the machine
- Enabling the virtual-address–translation hardware
- Initializing the memory-management hardware
- Crafting the hardware context for process 0
- Invoking the initial C-based entry point of the system

Our discussion of these steps will concentrate on the work required to support the VAX; similar actions are necessary for any machine on which 4.3BSD runs.

When the **boot** program starts the UNIX kernel running, it sets up only two components of the machine state:

1. The interrupt priority is set at its highest level so that all hardware interrupts are blocked.
2. The hardware address-translation facility is disabled so that all memory references are to physical memory locations.

The UNIX kernel presumes nothing else about the state of the machine on which it is running.

The kernel is loaded into physical memory at location 0. In normal operation, the VAX address-translation hardware is enabled and the kernel image is mapped into virtual memory starting at hexadecimal location 80000000. In preparation for enabling address translation, the physical memory used by the kernel is mapped into the identical virtual locations. This *double mapping* is necessary because the VAX will not enter mapped mode until address translation is enabled *and* a branch instruction is executed. Double mapping of the physical memory associated with the kernel ensures that a branch instruction to a succeeding instruction (specified as a virtual address) will go to the correct physical location.

A second task of the startup code is to identify the type of VAX on which the system is executing. Although all VAX computers support a common instruction set, the I/O architecture varies among machines. Furthermore, some microprocessor implementations of the VAX architecture directly support only a subset of the complete VAX instruction set. For these machines, the kernel must *emulate* the missing hardware instructions in software.

The kernel identifies the type of VAX on which it is executing by interrogating the contents of the *system identification register* (SID). The contents of this register includes a well-known constant that uniquely identifies the type of VAX. 4.3BSD uses the system type

- To distinguish among the different types of console storage media and console processor interfaces
- To decide which hardware devices and I/O interfaces might be configured on a machine
- To handle exceptional machine conditions (*machine checks*)
- To calculate real-time delays implemented with *spin loops*
- To decide how to set up interrupt handlers

4.3BSD can be configured such that a single kernel load image can support a number of different VAXes.

Machine-Dependent Initialization

After the assembly-language code has completed its work, it calls the first kernel routine written in C, the *main*() routine. One parameter is passed to this routine—the number of the first available page of memory. The system calculates this value, taking into account the size of the kernel's load image and any pages allocated to run-time stacks and to other data structures. The *main*() routine immediately calls the *startup*() routine to do machine-dependent initializations. *Startup*() is supplied the same value *main*() received from the assembly-language code.

The tasks of the machine-dependent startup code include

- Initialization of the *error-message buffer*
- Allocation of memory for system data structures
- Initialization of the kernel's memory allocator
- Autoconfiguration and initialization of I/O devices

A few other hardware-specific parts of the machine are initialized after the call to *startup*() returns; these operations are described later, in our discussion of the machine-independent startup code.

Message Buffer

The *message buffer* is a 4 Kbyte circular buffer located at the top of physical memory. Diagnostic messages displayed on the console with the *printf*() routine (or one of its variants) are kept in this buffer as an aid in tracking problems. Prior to 4.3BSD, the message buffer was accessible only through the **/dev/kmem** special device. Furthermore, utilities such as the **dmesg** program that read the message buffer and copy the buffer's contents to an administrative log file were unable to synchronize their activities properly with the generation of new diagnostic messages. For these reasons, 4.3BSD added a special device, **/dev/log**. This device provides a read-only interface to the message buffer that supports the *select* system call. In addition, most system diagnostics are now generated in a format that is interpreted by the **syslogd** program. These changes ensure that system diagnostics are saved reliably in log files.

Initialization of the message buffer is straightforward. First, the system allocates memory for the buffer by deducting the size of the message buffer from the size of physical memory calculated by the assembly-language code. Then, a private page map, *msgbufmap*, is initialized to reference the physical pages just allocated.

System Data Structures

Allocation of memory for the system data structures is easy at this point in the startup procedure. The *startup*() routine is supplied the identity of the first available page of physical memory that follows the resident kernel, *firstaddr*. In addition, the kernel is known to reside in virtual memory starting at hexadecimal location 80000000. Thus, to allocate space for contiguous data structures, the system simply assigns the virtual address of the next available block of physical memory to each data structure,

```
base = 0x80000000 | (firstaddr * NBPG)
```

and then increments the value of *firstaddr* by the size of the data structure. Memory allocated to data structures in this way is not necessarily initialized to zero; initialization routines called from *main*() ensure that the contents of each data structure are set up properly.

The technique just described is used to allocate memory for each contiguous system data structure. Most of these data structures are sized at the time the system is configured, with the sizes based on the peak number of users expected (see also Section 13.5). The buffer cache and core map, however, are sized according to the amount of physical memory available on the machine. The buffer-cache size is calculated as 10 percent of the first 2 Mbyte of physical memory and 5 percent of the remaining memory. The system ensures that there are a minimum of 16 buffers, although this lower limit should never be a problem unless the system is configured with very large filesystem block sizes. In addition to the buffers dedicated to the buffer cache, the system must also allocate buffer headers for swapping operations: one-half of the number of file I/O buffer headers is allocated for use in swap and paging operations. The system must calculate the size of the core map after allocating the buffer cache and static data structures, because that value is used to map all physical memory not otherwise allocated to the system. Once the core-map and system-memory allocator have been initialized (described in the following section), the normal system memory-allocation mechanisms must be used.

Memory Allocator

The last step in the machine-dependent startup procedure prior to autoconfiguration is the initialization of the system's memory allocator. The kernel has already allocated all the physical memory it requires to hold system data structures; any remaining memory is made available for general use. The memory allocator is initialized by a call to the *meminit*() routine with the first and last available pages of memory. The core map structure is initialized to reference this memory and the *firstfree*, *maxfree*, *freemem*, and *avefree* variables used by the memory-management system (see Section 5.12) are set up based on the available memory.

Autoconfiguration

Autoconfiguration is the procedure carried out by the system to recognize and enable the hardware devices present in a system. This process was introduced in Section 8.5, where the requirements it places on device drivers were described. In this section, we shall concentrate on the central workings of the autoconfiguration process. In particular, we shall study the data structures that are used to describe a system's hardware topology and the way in which devices are accessed by the system.

To understand the autoconfiguration process, we must first gain some familiarity with the structure of a VAX computer. The *VAX architecture* is a specification that pertains mostly to the operation of the CPU. That is, each VAX computer supports a common instruction set, memory-management facilities, mechanisms for handling traps and interrupts, and so on. A common subset of the instruction set is implemented in hardware, with any remaining instructions emulated in software. I/O devices for a VAX reside on I/O buses that have well-defined specifications that are *not* part of the basic architectural specification. Each *VAX system* combines an *implementation* of a VAX CPU with a *system bus*. I/O devices may be directly connected to the computer's system bus or, more commonly, to existing I/O buses that are connected to the system buses through hardware *bus adapters* (see Fig. 13.2). Each physical connection to the system bus of a VAX, including the bus adapters, is made through a *nexus*. A nexus does any system-bus arbitration that devices need to access the system bus. Each nexus also provides an 8-Kbyte bank of registers on the system bus through which the CPU can access and control the associated device. The registers associated with a nexus are located in the I/O portion of the *system region*. Nexuses are

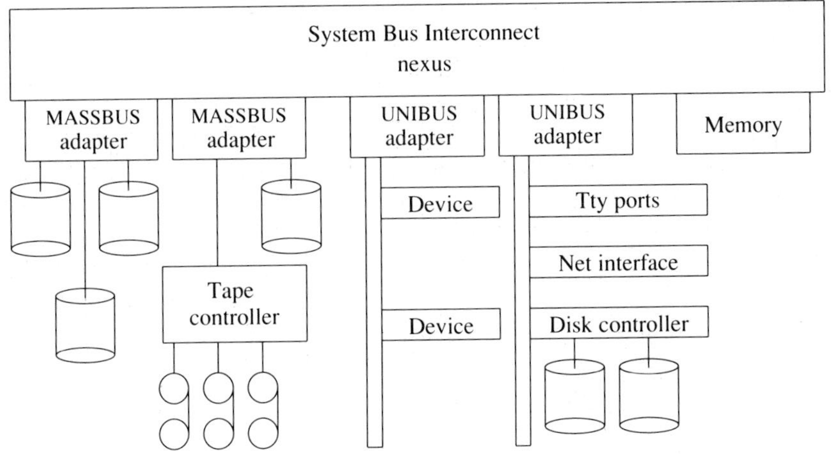

Figure 13.2 Basic VAX computer architecture.

self-describing; one register in each nexus register bank contains a value that uniquely identifies the type of device attached to that nexus.

Autoconfiguration works by systematically probing the possible nexuses on a VAX looking for active connections to the system bus. For each nexus that is in use, the type of device attached to the nexus is interpreted and, depending on this type, the necessary actions are taken to initialize and configure the device. For memory controllers attached to a nexus, the system must initialize the controller and enable the reporting of memory errors. For bus adapters, the configuration routines must probe for I/O devices that might be present on the associated I/O buses.

To configure an I/O device, the system requires that the device be specified at *configuration time* as potentially present in the system (see Section 13.5). The set of possible devices is organized into two *initialization tables*, one for devices that might reside on a MASSBUS and one for devices that might be present on a UNIBUS. When an I/O adapter is encountered at autoconfiguration time, the system searches the initialization tables for devices that might be configured on that adapter. For each matching device, a probing operation is made either by the device driver (for UNIBUS devices) or by the autoconfiguration code (for MASSBUS devices) and, if the probe is successful, the device is recorded in the system data structures as a *configured device* (see Section 8.5).

Aside from the work involved in probing for devices, the configuration process must also identify where I/O devices will interrupt, and then must install the appropriate interrupt service routines so that future interrupts from the devices will be handled by the supporting device drivers. The dynamic configuration of I/O devices and interrupt handlers permits a single kernel to be configured for a number of different hardware configurations; this flexibility is important in minimizing system maintenance.

To configure interrupt handlers dynamically, the system initializes all the possible interrupt vectors for an I/O adapter to point to a special-purpose routine. This routine simply records the interrupt vector and the interrupt priority level at which an interrupt occurs in well-known registers, and then returns. The device-driver probe routines are written such that they define a usage for these registers, but they never actually load a value into the registers. At boot time, the system modifies the probe routines such that they will not save the affected registers on entry. This permits values placed in the registers before a probe routine is called to be altered by an invocation of the special-purpose interrupt handler. To probe for a device and to configure its interrupt vectors, the system can simply initialize the registers to known values, call the device driver to probe the device and to generate an interrupt, and then check the values in the registers to see whether the device has interrupted. For example, the probe routine for the *up* device driver is

```
upprobe(reg)
    caddr_t reg;
{
    register int br, cvec;          /* must be r11, r10 */

                    /* probe device and generate interrupt */
    ((struct updevice *)reg)->upcs1 = UP_IE|UP_RDY;
    DELAY(10);
                        /* disable interrupt */
    ((struct updevice *)reg)->upcs1 = 0;
    return (sizeof (struct updevice));
}
```

On the VAX, the declaration of the variables *br* and *cvec* cause the C compiler to reserve registers R11 and R10 for use within the routine. Normally, these registers would be saved on entry to the routine, but alteration of the VAX *register save mask* for the *upprobe*() routine allows this action to be defeated. When *upprobe*() is called and the device interrupts, the registers will be set to contain the interrupt priority level and interrupt vector for the device. Because the save mask has been altered to prevent R10 and R11 from being restored to their previous values, these registers will still contain the interrupt priority level and interrupt vector for the device in the routine that called *upprobe*().

The technique used to configure interrupt vectors depends on the 4.3BSD C compiler's implementation of the *register* declaration. If instead register declarations were interpreted as *advisory*, or the registers allocated to the variables were assigned in an indeterminate fashion, then this scheme would not work. When an ANSI C compiler is used, it is impossible to force a particular variable to be in a register. However, it is possible to force a variable to be allocated to memory with use of the *volatile* keyword. When this feature is used, the calling routine has to arrange to pass the address of a volatile variable in which to place the result.

Interrupt vectors that are not assigned to devices configured at boot time remain pointing to the initial interrupt handler. A global variable, *cold*, is set to 1 by the system until after the autoconfiguration phase of the startup procedure is completed. The interrupt handler checks this variable, and, if the value is nonzero, it takes the actions described; otherwise, the handler generates a diagnostic on the console.

Although VMS can load device drivers after the system is completely booted, 4.3BSD cannot load device drivers because

- 4.3BSD device drivers use some shared global data structures
- Some buses, such as the UNIBUS, are not globally addressable
- A new device might interrupt at the same location as an existing device, leading to confusion

MASSBUS devices do not have these problems, and could be loaded later. The developers did not implement specific support for this capability in 4.3BSD because they did not think it would be useful.

Machine-Independent Initialization

With the static system data structures allocated and the I/O devices configured and initialized, the system is ready to complete the initialization procedure and to start up the first few processes. The first action of the *main*() routine on return from *startup*() is to set up the context for process 0; the process that will eventually implement the swapping policy of the virtual-memory system. The first entry in the process table is allocated for process 0, and the process is marked runnable and is installed as the currently running process (see Chapter 4). The user structure, run-time stack, and process control block for this process were initialized in the assembly-language startup code, so only minor work is required to complete the initialization. The last page of the run-time stack is marked read-only to act as a *red zone*; this ensures that the process will not expand its stack beyond the fixed space allocated to it without causing a system trap. Various pointers in the user structure are initialized, and system default parameters in the user structure that are inherited across a *fork* system call are established. The latter include the resource limits, the file-creation mask, and the group identifier array.

When process 0 has been crafted, various routines are called to initialize each system data structure:

- The *vminit*() routine sets up the parameters used by the paging system. These parameters are dependent on the amount of available physical memory and the number of I/O devices that will be used for paging and swapping. The resource limits on a process's stack and data segments, as well as the resident-set size, are installed in the user structure of process 0. These limits will then be automatically inherited by all other processes, since they are descendents of process 0.

- The disk quota resource-control system is initialized; it includes the cache of quotas for resident processes as well as the cache of per-user data structures.
- The real-time clock is started through a call to *startrtclock*(). This routine primes the necessary hardware that supplies regular interrupts to the system. The clock rate, if programmable, is set up according to the *hz* variable that is defined at the time the system is configured. By default, 4.3BSD runs with a 100-hertz real-time clock. This value can be altered, but selecting a frequency of less than 50 hertz degrades the system's response time to I/O devices that are polled. For some hardware terminal multiplexers, lowering the clock frequency can permit high data-flow rates to swamp input buffers. A poorly chosen clock frequency can also cause roundoff errors in certain calculations. For example, with a 60-hertz clock rate, integer calculations involving the clock frequency will skew. The system normally avoids this problem by maintaining timeout values in terms of clock ticks. A final consideration in choosing a clock frequency is that the frequency defines the minimal observable time interval in the system. This is important for statistical calculations, such as program profiling and accounting, where *entire* clock ticks are charged to a process- or program-counter value at the time a real-time clock interrupt is serviced. In general, the clock frequency should be selected to be as high as possible without too much system overhead being incurred.

Following the initialization of the clock, the network memory-management system is initialized with a call to *mbinit*() (see Chapter 10). The character list data structures used by the terminal I/O facilities are set up through a call to *cinit*(), and subsequent calls are then made to initialize

- The network interfaces
- The communication domains and network communication protocols
- The process-management data structures
- The text table
- The hashed inode cache and inode table
- The swap-space management data structures
- The systemwide filesystem name cache

Before the system can reach single-user operation, it must still mount the root filesystem, and create process 1 (the process that executes **/etc/init**) and process 2 (the process that copies pages of memory to secondary storage in support of the virtual-memory system). The identity of the root filesystem is defined by the value of the *rootdev* variable. This value is initially defined at configuration time, although users may change it at boot time by bootstrapping the system from a device other than the configured one (see the previous discussion of autoconfiguration).

The root inode of the mounted root filesystem is needed to initialize the current working directory and root directory for process 0. In addition, the last modification date in the superblock of the root filesystem is used in initializing the system's time of day. The timestamp from the superblock is compared to any current value for the time of day available in hardware, and the current time of day is constrained to be within 6 months of the time in the filesystem (unless the filesystem time is completely unbelievable). This consistency check ensures that the system will be bootstrapped with a reasonably accurate time of day. User-level facilities—such as the *timedaemon*, **timed**—support time synchronization and recalibration in a network environment.

Finally, the system is ready to execute user-mode programs. Process 1 is created with a call to *newproc*(), then the contents of a small assembly-language program that is compiled into the kernel are copied into the process's user address space and the process is set executing. The contents of this program are basically as follows:

```
main() {
    char *argv[2];

    argv[0] = "init";
    argv[1] = 0;
    exit(execv("/etc/init", argv));
}
```

That is, the program starts up the **/etc/init** program, exiting if the call to *execv* fails. This makes **/etc/init** critical to operation: If it does not run correctly, if it is not there, or if the parts of the filesystem necessary to reach it are damaged, the system cannot be booted from that filesystem. This error is more serious than is an incorrect **/vmunix**, because the bootstrap allows naming of a different object file for the kernel, but there is no direct way to specify a different **init** program. When enough disk space is available, the usual backup is to keep a different filesystem available for such pathological cases.

The second process to be started is the *pagedaemon*, with process identifier 2. This process executes entirely in kernel mode by invoking the *pageout*() routine, a procedure that never returns. Like process 0, the *pagedaemon* marks its process structure to ensure that that structure will not be removed from memory. The *pagedaemon* also expands its data segment to provide itself room to map pages of memory it will be writing to secondary storage (see Section 5.12).

The last action of *main*() is to call the *sched*() routine within process 0. Like the *pagedaemon*, this process executes entirely in kernel mode, and the call to *sched*() never returns. The *sched*() routine implements the swapping policy of the virtual-memory system; it is described in Section 5.13.

13.4 User-Level Initialization

With the start of execution of process 1, most of the system is operating and functional. There are several additional steps taken between this point and the time a user sees a prompt to sign on to the system. All these actions are done by user-level programs that use the standard UNIX system-call interface that has been described in previous chapters. We shall briefly examine the steps that take place in a typical 4.3BSD system; be aware, however, that these steps can vary drastically among UNIX systems.

/etc/init

The **/etc/init** program is invoked as the last step in the bootstrapping procedure. The parameters specified at the time UNIX was boostrapped are passed to **init** in a machine-dependent fashion. On the VAX, the flags passed to the **boot** program are passed to **init** in the same hardware register as that in which they were passed to the kernel. **Init** uses the values of these flags to determine whether it should bring the system up to single- or to multiuser operation. In single-user operation, **init** forks a process that invokes the standard UNIX shell, **/bin/sh**. The standard input, output, and error descriptors of the process are directed to the system's console terminal, **/dev/console**. This shell then operates normally, but with superuser privileges, until it terminates.

In multiuser operation, **init** first spawns a shell to interpret the commands in the file **/etc/rc**. These commands do filesystem consistency checks, start up system processes, and initialize database files, such as the **/etc/mtab** file that contains the list of mounted filesystems. If the **/etc/rc** script completes successfully, **init** then forks a copy of itself for each terminal device that is marked for use in the file **/etc/ttys**. These copies of **init** invoke other system programs, such as **/etc/getty**, to manage the standard sign on procedure. Process 1 always acts as the master coordinating process for system operation. It is responsible for spawning new processes as terminal sessions are terminated, and for managing the shutdown of a running system.

/etc/rc

The **/etc/rc** command script first checks the integrity of the filesystems. This check is necessary to ensure that any damage that might have occurred from a previous system failure is repaired. The filesystem support within the kernel is concerned solely with reading and writing existing filesystems. Any inconsistencies in a filesystem are repaired by user-level programs.

The program **/etc/fsck** is the major tool used in checking filesystem consistency and in repairing damaged filesystems. Normally, **fsck** is invoked from the **/etc/rc** script to examine and repair each filesystem before it is mounted. If the root filesystem, mounted by the kernel before **/etc/rc** is invoked, requires repairs, 4.3BSD must reboot itself to ensure consistency between the data in the buffer cache and the data in the filesystem. This reboot operation is done automatically, as described later.

Following the filesystem checks, the filesystems are mounted and any devices that are to be used for swapping and paging are enabled. Disk quotas are then checked and enabled, and the system starts the background processes that implement various system services. These processes include **/etc/update**, the program that flushes the disk writes from the buffer cache every 30 seconds; **/etc/cron**, the program that executes commands at periodic time intervals; **/etc/accton**, the program that enables system accounting; and **/etc/syslogd**, the system error-logging process. Some of these processes are started from the command script **/etc/rc.local**. The commands in **/etc/rc.local** are tailored according to the needs of each host, whereas the commands in **/etc/rc** are common to all hosts. For example, processes that provide network services are typically started up from the **/etc/rc.local** command file.

/etc/getty

The **/etc/getty** program is spawned by **/etc/init** for each hardware terminal line on a system. This program is responsible for opening and initializing the terminal line. Opening the terminal causes the system to assign a process group (if the process already had a process group, **getty** uses the *vhangup* system call first to zero it). The **getty** program sets the initial parameters for a terminal line and establishes the type of terminal attached to the line. For lines attached to a modem, **getty** can be directed to accept connections at a variety of baud rates. **Getty** selects this baud rate by changing the speed of the terminal line in response to a break character or a framing error, typically generated as a result of the user hitting a break key. Successive break keys can be hit by a user to cycle through a number of line speeds until the proper one is found. **Getty**'s actions are driven by a terminal-configuration database that is located in the file **/etc/gettytab**.

Getty finally reads a login name, and invokes the **/bin/login** program to complete a login sequence.

/bin/login

The **login** program is responsible for signing a user onto the system; it is usually invoked by **/etc/getty** with the name of the user who wishes to log in to the system. **Login** prompts the user for a password (after turning off terminal echoing if possible). If the password supplied by the user encrypts to the same value as that stored in the master password file **/etc/passwd**, **login** writes a record of the sign on in various accounting files, initializes the user and group identifiers to those specified in the password and **/etc/group** files, and changes to the user's login directory. Finally, **login** uses *exec* to overlay itself with the user's shell.

The **login** program is also invoked when a user enters the system through a network connection; **getty** and **init** are bypassed for such connections. Before this complication was added (in 4.2BSD), the system could recognize a login shell by noticing that the shell's parent process was **init**. This was useful for accounting and for limiting the number of simultaneous logins. The flag SLOGIN was added to the proc structure for **login** to set to mark a login shell. The 4.3BSD **login** does not set or use this flag, but the flag has been used elsewhere [Elz, 1984].

13.5 System Startup Topics

In this section, we consider topics that are related to the system startup procedure.

Kernel Configuration

The software that makes up a 4.3BSD kernel is defined by a *configuration file* that is interpreted by the **/etc/config** program. Configuration files specify the hardware and software components that should be supported by a kernel. The **config** program uses the configuration file to generate a set of data files and an input file for the **make** program that are used to compile and link a kernel load image.

A sample configuration file for a VAX computer is shown in Fig. 13.3. Among the most important *global* configuration parameters are

- The type of machine on which the system is run; *vax* in our example.
- The type of CPU to be supported. Many CPU types may be specified, and the system will attempt to support the one on which it has been bootstrapped. The CPU types specified in our example are *VAX780* and *VAX750*.
- The time zone in which the system will operate and, optionally, a daylight-saving-time correction algorithm. The system normally runs on Universal Coordinated Time (UTC); the time zone and daylight-saving-time correction algorithm are used by applications in calculating the local time of day. In Fig. 13.3, the Pacific standard time zone is specified as 8 hours past UTC, and the standard daylight-saving-time algorithm is requested (see also Section 3.5).
- The maximum expected number of simultaneously active users on the system. This value is used to calculate the sizes of numerous data structures.

Additional parameters can be specified to enable the inclusion of optional code.

Figure 13.3 A sample configuration file for a VAX.

```
machine         vax
cpu             "VAX780"
cpu             "VAX750"
timezone        8 dst
maxusers        16

config          vmunix          root on hp0

controller      mba0            at nexus ?
controller      uba0            at nexus ?
controller      uba1            at nexus ?
disk            hp0             at mba? drive 0
disk            hp1             at mba? drive 1
controller      hk0             at uba? csr 0177440             vector rkintr
disk            rk0             at hk0 drive 0
device          dz0             at uba? csr 0160120 flags 0xff  vector dzrint dzxint
controller      zs0             at uba? csr 0172520             vector tsintr
device          ts0             at zs0 drive 0
```

For example, the filesystem disk-quota support is not normally included in a system; to force it to be compiled into the system, the line ''options QUOTA'' would be specified.

The *config* specification in Fig. 13.3 indicates that **/etc/config** should arrange to create a kernel load image in the file **vmunix** that has its root filesystem on the disk drive named *hp0*. The remainder of the configuration file describes the hardware devices that may be present on the machine. Specifications that include question marks act as *wildcards*. For example, *uba?* specifies that a device might be present on either of the two UNIBUS adapters described in the configuration file.

Disks and tapes are configured in terms of controllers and devices. This division reflects the actual hardware topology present on a machine. The *csr* specifications identify the base address of a controller's bank of registers. The *vector* specification identifies the name and number of interrupt handlers (or vectors) for a device. These names are actually the names of the interrupt service routines in the device drivers that have been written to support the hardware.

The configuration file is used by **/etc/config** to generate a number of output files, several of which are compiled and linked into the kernel's load image:

- A file that describes the hardware device topology and the devices that might be present on the machine
- A file that includes assembly-language routines that connect the hardware interrupt-vector entry points to the device-driver interrupt handlers specified in the configuration file
- A file that defines the devices to use for the root filesystem and for swapping and paging
- A number of small header files that control conditional compilations of source code
- A file for the *make* program that is used to compile and link the kernel load image

A complete description of the configuration process and **/etc/config** can be found in [Leffler & Karels, 1986].

System Shutdown and Autoreboot

4.3BSD provides several utility programs to halt, reboot, or bring a system from multiuser to single-user operation. Safe halting and rebooting of a system requires support from the kernel. This support is provided by a *reboot* system call.

The *reboot* system call is a privileged call. A single parameter specifies how the system should be shut down and rebooted. This parameter is a superset of the flags passed by the **boot** program to the system when the latter is initially bootstrapped (see Table 13.1). A system can be brought to a halt (typically by its being forced to execute an infinite loop), or it can be rebooted to single- or multiuser operation. There are additional controls that can be used to force a crash dump before rebooting (see the next section for information about crash dumps), and to disable the writing of data that are in the buffer cache to disk (in case the information in the buffer cache is wrong).

On most hardware, rebooting requires support from the console processor or monitor. Typically, a reboot operation is initiated by a command being passed to the console processor. This command causes the system to be rebooted as though someone had typed the appropriate commands on the console terminal. Automatic rebooting is also commonly done by the console processor when a catastrophic failure is recognized. The system will automatically reboot itself if it recognizes an unrecoverable failure during normal operation. Failures of this sort, termed *panics*, are all handled by the *panic*() subroutine. 4.1BSD was one of the first UNIX systems to be able to recover *automatically* from catastrophic failures by rebooting, repairing any filesystem damage, and then restarting normal operation. Facilities to *checkpoint* the state of active processes and automatically to resume the processes' execution after a system reboot have been added by some vendors, such as Cray Research.

System Debugging

4.3BSD provides several facilities for debugging system failures. The most commonly used facility is the *crash dump*, a copy of memory that is saved on secondary storage by the kernel in the event of a catastrophic failure. Crash dumps are created by the *doadump*() routine. They occur if a reboot system call is made in which the RB_DUMP flag is specified, or if the system encounters an unrecoverable, and unexpected, error.

The *doadump*() routine disables virtual-address translation, raises the processor priority level to its highest value to block out all device interrupts, and then invokes the *dumpsys*() routine to write the contents of physical memory to secondary storage. The precise location of a crash dump is configurable; most systems place the information at the back of the primary swap partition. The device driver's dump entry point is used to do this operation.

A crash dump is retrieved from its location on disk after the system is rebooted and the filesystems have been checked. The **/etc/savecore** program exists solely for this purpose. It creates a file into which the crash-dump image is copied. **Savecore** also makes a copy of the initial kernel load image, **/vmunix**, for use in debugging. Crash dumps can be examined with either of the 4.3BSD debugging programs, **adb** or **dbx**. Both debuggers can also be used to examine and modify a running system through the **/dev/mem** special file. More information about the use of **adb** for kernel debugging can be found in [Leffler & Joy, 1986].

Exercises

13.1 What is the purpose of the **boot** program?

13.2 What is the job of the machine-language startup? Why is this program written in machine language?

13.3 What is the purpose of the kernel's message buffer?

13.4 What are the first three processes started when the system is booted?

13.5 Assume that **/boot** is read in from the console media. Name the three other files that must be present to boot the system to single-user mode.

13.6 Why are kernel data structures sized when the system boots, instead of when the kernel is compiled?

13.7 What information is supplied in a configuration file that cannot be determined at the time the system is booted?

13.8 The *reboot* system call causes the system to halt or reboot. Give three reasons why this system call is useful.

*13.9 Suppose a machine does not have a battery-backup time-of-day clock. Propose a method for determining that the time-of-day clock is incorrect and describe a way to initialize its time of day. What are the limitations of your method?

References

Elz, 1984.
K. R. Elz, ''Resource Controls, Privileges, and Other MUSH,'' *USENIX Association Conference Proceedings*, pp. 183–191 (June 1984).

Leffler & Karels, 1986.
S. J. Leffler & M. J. Karels, ''Building Berkeley UNIX Systems with Config,'' pp. 2:1–32 in *UNIX System Manager's Manual, 4.3 Berkeley Software Distribution, Virtual VAX-11 Version*, USENIX Association, Berkeley, CA (1986).

Leffler & Joy, 1986.
S. J. Leffler & W. N. Joy, ''Using ADB to Debug the UNIX Kernel,'' pp. 3:1–11 in *UNIX System Manager's Manual, 4.3 Berkeley Software Distribution, Virtual VAX-11 Version*, USENIX Association, Berkeley, CA (1986).

Glossary

absolute pathname *See* pathname.

access rights In an operating system, the rights of processes to access system-maintained objects. For example, the ability to write data into a file. Rights are recognized and enforced by the system and typically are associated with capabilities. The passing of access rights in messages is supported by the 4.3BSD interprocess-communication facilities. For example, the UNIX communication domain supports the transmission of file descriptors and their associated access rights.

adb A program debugger that was first introduced in the Seventh Edition UNIX system.

address family A collection of related address formats, as found in a communication domain.

address format A set of rules used in creating network addresses of a particular format. For example, in the Internet communication domain, a host address is a 32-bit value that is encoded using one of four rules according to the type of network on which the host resides.

Address Resolution Protocol (ARP) A communication protocol used to map one network address to another dynamically. For example, ARP is used in 4.3BSD to map DARPA Internet addresses into Ethernet addresses dynamically.

address translation A mechanism, typically implemented in hardware, that translates memory addresses supplied by a program into physical memory addresses. This facility is important in supporting multiprogramming because it allows an operating system to load programs into different areas of memory, and yet to have each program execute as though it were loaded at a single, fixed memory location.

advisory lock A lock that is enforced only when a process explicitly requests its enforcement. An advisory lock is contrasted with a hard lock, the enforcement of which is mandatory.

AGE buffer list A list in the filesystem buffer cache. This list holds buffers whose contents have not yet proven useful—for example, read-ahead blocks.

ARP *See* Address Resolution Protocol.

ARPANET The Advanced Research Projects Agency Network. A packet-switching network established in December 1969 by DARPA.

ARPANET Host Access Protocol A protocol used to communicate between a host and an ARPANET PSN.

association In the interprocess-communication facilities, a logical binding between two communication endpoints that must be established before communication can take place. Associations may be long-lived, such as in virtual-circuit–based communication, or short-lived, such as in a datagram-based communication paradigm.

AST *See* asynchronous system trap.

asynchronous system trap (AST) On the VAX, a software-initiated interrupt to a service routine. ASTs enable a process to be notified of the occurrence of a specific event asynchronously with respect to its execution. In 4.3BSD, ASTs are used to initiate process rescheduling.

attach routine A device-driver routine that is used during the autoconfiguration phase to establish the software state for a device. Attach routines are called for each device that the system has probed successfully.

autoconfiguration phase A phase of operation the system goes through when bootstrapping itself into operation. In the autoconfiguration phase, the system probes for hardware devices that might be present in the machine, and attaches each device that it locates. *See also* attach routine; probe routine; slave routine.

background process In job-control–oriented process-management systems, a process whose process group is different from that of its controlling terminal, and thus, is currently blocked from most terminal access. Otherwise, a background process is one for which the command interpreter is not waiting; that is, the process was set running with the ''&'' operator. The opposite of a background process is a *foreground process*.

backing storage Storage that is used to hold objects that are removed from main memory during paging and swapping operations. *See also* secondary storage.

bad sector A sector with an uncorrectable media defect.

bad-sector forwarding A facility whereby bad sectors on a disk are transparently replaced with good sectors. The system does this replacement by *forwarding* requests for each bad sector to the replacement good sector. The good sectors are taken from reserved areas of a disk. Bad-sector forwarding can be done on the host in the device driver, or, as is becoming commonplace, in the disk controller. *See also* slip-sector forwarding.

bad-sector table A table used in bad-sector forwarding. During bad-sector forwarding, the system looks up the location of the good (forwarded) sector in the bad-sector table, using the bad-sector number as a key.

Berknet An obsolete network developed at the University of California, Berkeley that used serial lines for communication.

block In the filesystem, a unit of allocation. The filesystem allocates space in block-size units, or in fragments of block-size units.

block device A random-access mass-storage device that supports a block-oriented interface; for example, a disk drive.

block-device interface The conventions established for accessing block devices within the kernel. These conventions include the set of procedures that can be called to perform I/O operations, as well as the parameters that must be passed in each call.

block-device table A table within the kernel in which the device-driver routines that support the block-device interface for each device are recorded. The ordering of entries in the block-device table is important, since it defines the major-device number for block devices.

block I/O I/O to a block device.

block size The natural unit of space allocated to a file (*filesystem block size*), or the smallest unit of I/O that a block device can perform (for disk devices, usually the sector size). In 4.3BSD, the filesystem block size is a parameter of the filesystem that is fixed at the time the filesystem is created.

bootdevice register The register in which the first-level bootstrap passes the identity of the device from which the system should be bootstrapped. On the VAX, the bootdevice register is R10.

boothowto register The register in which the first-level bootstrap passes a code that indicates whether the system should be bootstrapped to multiuser or to single-user operation, and whether or not to prompt for the name of the file to bootstrap. On the VAX, the boothowto register is R11.

bootstrapping Bringing a system up into an operational state. When a machine is first powered on, it is typically not running any program. Bootstrapping initializes the machine, loads a program from secondary storage into main memory, and sets that program running.

bottom half With regard to system operation, the collection of routines in the kernel that are invoked as a result of interrupts. These routines cannot depend on any per-process state and, as a result, cannot block by calling the *sleep*() routine. *See also* top half.

breakpoint fault A hardware trap that is generated when a process executes a breakpoint instruction.

broadcast To transmit to all parties. In a network, a *broadcast message* is transmitted to all stations attached to a common communication medium.

bss segment The portion of a program that is to be initialized to zero at the time the program is loaded into memory. The name *bss* is an abbreviation for ''block started by symbol.''

buffered As in ''buffered I/O''; a technique whereby data are held, or buffered, to minimize the number of I/O operations that are performed. For example, the standard I/O library buffers output to files by accumulating data to be written until there is a full filesystem block to write, or until a flush request is made by the application.

buffered data path A data path in a UNIBUS adapter that buffers data transfers between the UNIBUS and a VAX's system bus during DMA operations. *See also* unbuffered data path.

bus A standardized electrical and mechanical interconnection for components of a computer.

bus adapter A hardware device that permits one style of I/O bus to be connected to another. *See also* MASSBUS adapter and UNIBUS adapter.

byte A unit of measure applied to data. A byte is almost always 8 bits. *See also* octet.

C-block The data buffer that holds the actual data in a C-list data structure.

C-list A linked-list data structure used by the system in supporting terminal I/O.

capability Data presented by a process to gain access to an object. *See also* access rights.

catenet A network in which hosts are connected to networks with varying characteristics, and the networks are interconnected by gateways. The DARPA Internet is an example of a catenet.

cathode ray tube (CRT) A screen-display device commonly used in computer terminals. A terminal that includes a CRT is often called a CRT.

caught signal A signal is said to be ''caught'' if the delivery of the signal to a process results in a signal-handler procedure being invoked. A signal handler is installed by a process with the *sigvec* system call.

cbreak mode A mode of operation for a terminal device whereby processes reading from the terminal receive input immediately as it is typed. This mode differs from raw mode in that certain input processing, such as interpreting the interrupt character, is still performed by the system. *See also* cooked mode and raw mode.

central processing unit (CPU) The primary computational unit in a computer. The CPU is the processing unit that executes applications. Additional processing units may be present in a computer for handling, for example, I/O.

character A datum that represents a single printable or control symbol. Characters are usually 8 or 16 bits long. *See also* byte and octet.

character device A device that provides either a character-stream oriented I/O interface or, alternatively, an unstructured (raw) interface. For example, a terminal multiplexer is a character device that exhibits a character-oriented I/O interface, whereas all magnetic-tape devices support a character-device interface that provides a raw interface to the hardware. Devices that are not character devices are usually block devices.

character-device interface The conventions established for accessing character-oriented devices within the kernel. These conventions include the set of procedures that can be called to do I/O operations, as well as the parameters that must be passed in each call.

character-device table A table within the kernel in which the device-driver routines that support the character-device interface for each device are recorded. The ordering of entries in the character-device table is important, since it defines the major-device number for character devices.

checksum The value of a mathematical function computed for a block of data used to detect corruption of the data block.

child process A process that is a direct descendent of another process as a result of being created with a *fork* system call.

client process In the client-server model of communication, a process that contacts a server process to request services. A client process is usually unrelated to a server process; the client process's only association with the server process is through a communication channel.

CLOCK algorithm *See* global CLOCK algorithm.

clock hand An abstraction used in describing the global CLOCK algorithm used by the virtual-memory system in its page-replacement strategy. In this algorithm, all the pages of main memory are envisioned in a circular loop, and two pointers shuttle through the pages in the loop as clock hands move on the face of a clock.

cluster The logical grouping of contiguous physical pages of memory. In 4.3BSD, this grouping is used by the virtual-memory system to simulate memory pages with sizes larger than the physical page size supported by the hardware.

cold start The initial phase of a bootstrap procedure. The term is derived from the fact that the software assumes nothing about the state of the machine—as though the machine had just been turned on and were cold.

communication domain An abstraction used by the interprocess-communication facilities to organize the properties of a communication network or similar facility. A communication domain includes a set of protocols, termed the *protocol family*; rules for manipulating and interpreting names; the *address family*; and, possibly, other intrinsic properties, such as the ability to transmit access rights. The facilities provided by the system for interprocess communication are defined such that they are independent of the communication domains supported by the system. This design makes it possible for applications to be written in a communication-domain–independent manner.

communication protocol A set of conventions and rules used by two communicating processes.

configuration file A file that contains parameters for the system-configuration program **/etc/config**. This file describes the hardware devices and topology that the system should be able to support, as well as miscellaneous parameters, such as the maximum number of users that are expected to be using the system simultaneously.

configuration procedure The procedure followed by a system administrator in configuring a kernel for a machine, or for a collection of machines. The configuration procedure involves defining a configuration file, which is then supplied to the **/etc/config** program to create the necessary data files for building a kernel.

connect request A request passed to the user-request routine of a communication-protocol module as a result of a process making a *connect* system call on a socket. The request causes the system to attempt to establish an association between a local and a remote socket.

console monitor The terminal attached to a console-terminal interface.

console processor An auxiliary processor to the main CPU that allows an operator to start and stop the system, to monitor system operation, and to run hardware diagnostics.

context switching The action of interrupting the currently running process and switching to another process. Context switching occurs as one process after another is scheduled for execution. On the VAX, an interrupted process's hardware context is saved in that process's process-control block using the *svpctx* instruction, and another process's hardware context is loaded with the *ldpctx* instruction.

continue signal Signal 19 (SIGCONT). A signal that, when delivered to a stopped or sleeping process, causes that process to resume execution.

control request A request passed to the user-request routine of a communication-protocol module as a result of a process making an *ioctl* system call on a socket.

controlling terminal The terminal device for a process from which keyboard-related signals may be generated. The controlling terminal for a process is normally inherited from the process's parent. If the parent process has no controlling terminal, the controlling terminal is the first terminal device a process opens.

cooked mode A mode of operation for a terminal device whereby processes reading from the terminal receive input only after a special end-of-line character, usually a carriage-return, is typed. Cooked mode is the normal mode of operation for a terminal. It is used, for example, by most command interpreters. *See also* cbreak mode and raw mode.

copy-on-write A technique whereby multiple references to a common object are maintained until the object is modified (written). Before the object is written, a copy is made and the modification is made to the copy, rather than to the original. In virtual-memory management, copy-on-write is a common scheme used to manage pages shared by multiple processes. All the PTEs mapping a shared page are set such that the first write reference to the page causes a page fault. In servicing the page fault, the faulted page is replaced with a private copy, which is writable.

core file A file (named **core**) that is created by the system when certain signals are delivered to a process. The file contains a record of the state of the process at the time the signal occurred. This record includes the contents of the process's virtual address space and, on most systems, the user structure.

core map The data structure used by the 4.3BSD kernel to manage main memory. The core map contains one entry for each cluster of main memory.

CPU *See* central processing unit.

crash Among computer scientists, an unexpected system failure.

crash dump A record of the state of a machine at the time of a crash. This record is usually written to a place on secondary storage that is thought to be safe, to be saved until the information can be recovered.

CRT *See* cathode ray tube.

current working directory The directory from which relative pathnames are interpreted for a process. The current working directory for a process is set with the *chdir* system call.

cylinder The tracks of a disk that are accessible from one position of the head assembly.

cylinder group In the filesystem, a collection of cylinders on a disk drive that are grouped together for the purpose of localizing information. That is, the filesystem allocates inodes and data blocks on a per–cylinder-group basis.

daemon A long-lived process that provides a system-related service. There are daemon processes that execute in kernel mode (e.g., the *pagedaemon*), and daemon processes that execute in user mode (e.g., the *routing daemon*). The old English term, *daemon*, means ''a deified being'', as distinguished from the term, *demon*, which means an ''evil spirit.''

DARPA Defense Advanced Research Projects Agency. An agency of the U.S. Department of Defense that is responsible for managing defense-sponsored research in the United States.

data path In a UNIBUS adapter, a pathway between the UNIBUS and the VAX's system bus through which data are transferred during a DMA operation.

data segment The segment of a process's address space that contains the initialized and uninitialized data portions of a program.

datagram socket A type of socket that models potentially unreliable connectionless packet communication.

dbx The name of a program debugger that was first introduced in 4.2BSD.

decapsulation In network communication, the removal of the outermost header information on a message. The inverse of encapsulation.

demand paging A memory-management technique in which memory is divided into pages and the pages are provided to processes as needed—that is, *on demand*. *See also* pure demand paging.

descriptor An integer assigned by the system when a file is referenced by the *open* system call, or when a socket is created with the *socket*, *pipe*, or *socketpair* system calls. The integer uniquely identifies an access path to the file or socket from a given process, or from any of that process's children. Descriptors can also be duplicated with the *dup* and *fcntl* system calls.

descriptor table A per-process table that holds references to objects on which I/O may be performed. I/O descriptors are indices into this table.

device In UNIX, a peripheral connected to the CPU.

device driver A software module that is part of the kernel and that supports access to a peripheral device.

device flags Data specified in a system configuration file and passed to a device driver. The use of these flags varies between device drivers. Device drivers for terminal devices use the flags to indicate the terminal lines on which the driver should ignore modem-control signals on input.

device number A number that uniquely identifies a device within the block or character device classes. A device number comprises two parts: a major-device number and a minor-device number.

device special file A file through which processes can access hardware devices on a machine. For example, a tape drive is accessed through such a file.

direct memory access (DMA) A facility whereby a peripheral device can access main memory without the assistance of the CPU. DMA is typically used to transfer contiguous blocks of data between main memory and a peripheral device.

directed broadcast A message that is to be broadcast on a network to which the sender is not connected directly.

directory In UNIX, a special type of file that contains entries that are references to other files. By convention, a directory contains at least two entries, dot (.) and dot-dot (..). Dot refers to the directory itself; dot-dot refers to the parent directory.

directory entry An entry in a directory that is represented by a variable-length record structure in the directory file. Each structure holds an ASCII string that is the filename, the number of bytes of space provided for the string, the number of bytes of space provided for the entry, and the number of the inode associated with the filename. By convention, a directory entry with a zero inode number is treated as unallocated, and the space held by the entry is available for use.

dirty In computer systems, an object that has been modified is said to be "dirty." A system usually tracks whether or not an object is dirty because it needs to save the object's contents before reusing the space held by the object. For example, in the filesystem, a buffer in the buffer cache is dirty if its contents have been modified. Dirty buffers must eventually be written back to the disk.

disk partition A contiguous region of a disk drive that is used as a swap area or to hold a filesystem.

distributed program A program that is partitioned among multiple processes, possibly spread across multiple machines.

DMA *See* direct memory access.

double indirect block *See* indirect block.

ECC correction A procedure whereby corrupted data are detected and corrected through the use of a redundant error-correction code (ECC). ECC correction is common in disk subsystems. The ECC is recorded with each disk sector and is used to identify and correct bit errors in the recorded data.

effective GID *See* effective group identifier.

effective group identifier (effective GID) The GID that the system uses, with the GIDs in the groups array, to check filesystem group access permission. The effective GID is set when a set-group-identifier program is executed. *See also* group identifier and real group identifier.

effective UID *See* effective user identifier.

effective user identifier (effective UID) The UID that the system uses to check many user permissions. For example, the effective UID is used by the filesystem when checking owner access permission on files. The effective UID is set when a set-user-identifier program is executed. *See also* user identifier and real user identifier.

elevator sorting algorithm An algorithm used by the device drivers for I/O requests for moving head disks. The algorithm sorts requests into a cyclic ascending order based on the cylinder number of the request. The algorithm's name is derived from the fact that it orders disk requests in a manner similar to the way ride requests would best be handled for an elevator.

emulate To simulate.

encapsulation In network communication, the procedure by which a message is created that has an existing message enclosed in it as data. A protocol normally encapsulates a message by crafting a leading protocol header that indicates the original message is to be treated as data. The inverse of *decapsulation.*

erase character The ASCII character that is recognized by the terminal handler in cooked mode to mean ''delete the last character in the line of input.'' Each terminal can have a different erase character, and that erase character can be changed at any time with an *ioctl* system call. The terminal handler does not recognize the erase character on terminals that are in raw or cbreak mode. *See also* word-erase character and kill character.

errno The global variable in C programs that holds an error code that indicates why a system call failed. On the VAX, the value placed in errno is returned by the kernel in register R0; it is moved to *errno* by code in the C run-time library.

error-message buffer *See* message buffer.

fault rate The rate at which a process generates page faults. For a reference string, the fault rate is defined to be time-independent by its being specified as the number of page faults divided by the length of the reference string.

fetch policy The policy used by a demand-paged virtual-memory–management system in processing page faults. Fetch policies differ primarily in the way they handle prepaging of data.

ffs An instruction on the VAX that locates the first bit that is set to one in a string of bits.

FIFO In the UNIX filesystem, a type of file that can be used for interprocess communication. Data written by one process to a FIFO are read by another in the order in which they were sent. The name refers to the fact that data are transferred in a first-in-first-out fashion.

file An object in the filesystem that is treated as a linear array of bytes. A file has at least one name, and it exists until all its names are deleted explicitly.

file offset A byte offset associated with an open file descriptor. The file offset for a file descriptor is set explicitly with the *lseek* system call, or implicitly as a result of a *read* or *write* system call.

file structure The data structure used by the kernel to hold the information associated with one or more open file descriptors that reference a file. In most cases, each open file descriptor references a unique file structure. File structures may be shared, however, when open descriptors are duplicated with the *dup* and *dup2* system calls, inherited across a *fork* system call, or received in a message through the interprocess-communication facilities.

filename A string of ASCII characters that is used to name an ordinary file, special file, or directory. The characters in a filename cannot include null (0) or the ASCII code for slash ('/'). (On 4.3BSD the eighth bit, or parity bit, must also be 0.)

filesystem A collection of files. The UNIX filesystem is hierarchical, with files organized into directories, and filesystems, in most cases, restricted to a single physical hardware device such as a disk drive. Filesystems typically include facilities for naming files and for controlling access to files.

fill-on-demand klustering A technique used by the virtual-memory system for prepaging data. When a page fault is encountered for a fill-on-demand page, the page-fault handler attempts to read in the desired page together with adjacent pages on either side of the page for which the fault occurred. *See also* kluster.

fill-on-demand page fault The first page fault for an individual page; it must be resolved by retrieval of data from the filesystem or by allocation of a zero-filled page.

fill-on-demand page-table entry A PTE for a page whose reference will generate a fill-on-demand page fault.

finite-state machine A technique for expressing a set of decision-making rules that is based solely on a *current state* and one or more input variables.

first-level bootstrap The initial code that is executed in a multilevel bootstrapping operation. Usually, the first-level bootstrap is limited in size and does little more than bootstrap into operation a larger, more intelligent, program. For example, the first-level-bootstrap on the VAX-11/750 is limited to 512 bytes; its sole task is to bootstrap the **boot** program so that **boot** can, in turn, bootstrap the kernel.

foreground process In job-control–oriented process-management systems, a process whose process group is the same as that of its controlling terminal; thus the process is allowed to read from and write to the terminal. Otherwise, a foreground process is one for which the command interpreter is currently waiting. The opposite of a foreground process is a *background process*.

fragment In the filesystem, a part of a block. The filesystem allocates new disk space to a file as a full block or as one or more fragments of a block. The filesystem uses fragments, rather than allocating space in only full block-size units, to reduce wasted space when the size of a full block is large.

fragment-descriptor table A data structure in the filesystem that describes the fragments that are free in an entry of the allocation map. The filesystem uses the fragment-descriptor table by taking a byte in the allocation map and using the byte to index into the fragment-descriptor table. The value in the fragment-descriptor table indicates how many fragments of a particular size are available in the entry of the allocation map. By doing a logical AND with the bit corresponding to the desired fragment size, the system can determine quickly whether a desired fragment is contained within the allocation-map entry.

free list In the memory-management system, the list of available clusters of physical memory (also called the *memory free list*). There are similar free lists in the system for many data structures: inodes, file-table entries, disk-quota structures, and so on.

free-space reserve A percentage of space in a filesystem that is held in reserve to ensure that certain allocation algorithms used by the filesystem will work well. By default, 10 percent of the available space in a filesystem is held in reserve.

garbage collection A memory-management facility in which unused portions of memory are reclaimed without an application having to release them explicitly.

GID *See* group identifier.

global CLOCK algorithm An algorithm used by the virtual-memory–management system in selecting candidate pages for replacement. The algorithm treats all the pages of main memory as though they were organized in a circle. Two logical hands (in the modified algorithm used in 4.3BSD) then sweep through the pages, with each page at the front hand being marked unreferenced and each page at the back hand checked to see whether it was referenced since the front hand passed over it. If a page is found to be unreferenced when it is checked by the back hand, it is treated as a candidate for replacement; otherwise, it is ignored.

go routine A routine supplied by a device driver for a UNIBUS device. The routine is expected to initiate an I/O operation on a device after necessary resources have been allocated by the UNIBUS adapter-support routines.

group identifier (GID) A 16-bit integer value that uniquely identifies a collection of users. GIDs are used in the access-control facilities provided by the filesystem. *See also* effective group identifier and real group identifier.

half-open A connection that is thought to be open by only one of the two endpoints is said to be ''half-open.''

handler A procedure that is invoked in response to an event such as a signal.

hard limit A limit that cannot be exceeded. *See also* soft limit.

hard link A directory entry that directly references an inode. If there are multiple hard links to a single inode and if one of the links is deleted, the remaining links still reference the inode. By contrast, a symbolic link is a file that holds a pathname that is used to reference a file.

hard lock A lock that cannot be ignored or avoided. *See also* advisory lock.

heap In UNIX, the region of a process that can be dynamically expanded with the *sbrk* system call. Its name is derived from the disorderly fashion in which data are placed in the region.

high watermark A data-flow control that specifies an upper bound on the number of data that may be buffered. In the interprocess-communication facilities, each socket's data buffer has a high watermark that specifies the maximum number of data that may be queued in the data buffer before a request to send data will block the process (or will return an error if nonblocking I/O is being used).

hole In a file, a region that is part of the file, but that has no associated data blocks. The filesystem returns zero-valued data when a process reads from a hole in a file. A hole is created in a file when a process positions the file pointer past the current end-of-file, writes some data, and then closes the file.

home directory The current working directory that is set for a user's shell when the user logs into a system. This directory is usually private to the user. The home directory for a user is specified in a field in the password-file entry for the user.

Host Dead message A message from an ARPANET PSN that indicates that the host to which a previous message was directed is unavailable because the host is *down*.

host identifier A 32-bit value that is intended to identify uniquely a host within a network of machines. This value is set with the *sethostid* system call at the time the system is bootstrapped. A process may retrieve the value of the host identifier with the *gethostid* system call. Host identifiers are intended for use in constructing networkwide unique identifiers for objects such as files, processes, and users.

Host Unreachable message An ICMP message that indicates that the host to which a previous message was directed is unavailable because there is no known path to the desired host.

ICMP *See* Internet Control Message Protocol.

IDP *See* Internetwork Datagram Protocol.

IMP *See* Interface Message Processor.

indirect block In the filesystem, the first 12 blocks of the file are pointed to directly by the inode. Additional data blocks are described with a pointer from the inode to an *indirect data block*; the system must first fetch the indirect block that holds the number of the data block. In 4.3BSD, as many as two indirect blocks may have to be fetched to locate the desired data block. An indirect block that contains data block numbers is termed a *single-level indirect block*; an indirect block that contains block numbers of single-level indirect blocks is called a *double level indirect block*. 4.3BSD has provision for, but does not use, an indirect block that contains block numbers of double-level indirect blocks; such a block is termed a *triple-level indirect block*.

init The first user program that is started up when the system is bootstrapped. This program (**/etc/init**) is mainly responsible for managing the terminal lines attached to a machine.

initial sequence number *See* sequence space.

inode A data structure used by the filesystem to describe a file. The contents of an inode include the file's type, the UID of the file's owner, and a list of the disk blocks and fragments that make up the file. Note that inodes do not have names; directory entries are used to associate a name with an inode.

inode table The data structure used by the kernel to hold the active inodes in the system. The inode table is always resident in main memory. Inactive entries in the table are reused on an LRU basis.

Input/Output (I/O) The transfer of data between the computer and its peripheral devices.

intelligent gateway A gateway machine that is capable of making intelligent decisions about routing network data. Such machines usually participate in a scheme whereby routing information is updated dynamically to reflect changes in network topology. An intelligent gateway is also expected to respond to hosts that make poor routing decisions with routing redirect messages.

interactive program A program that must periodically obtain user input to do its work. A screen-oriented text editor is an example of an interactive program.

Interface Message Processor (IMP) The original name for a hardware device used in the construction of packet-switched networks such as the ARPANET. *See also* Packet Switch Node.

Internet Control Message Protocol (ICMP) A host-to-host communication protocol used in the DARPA Internet for reporting errors and controlling the operation of IP.

internet domain A communication domain in the interprocess-communication facilities that supports the DARPA Internet architecture. This architecture supports both stream and datagram-oriented styles of communication between processes on machines in an internet.

internet host address In the DARPA Internet, a 32-bit number that identifies both the network on which a host is located and the host on that network.

Internet Protocol (IP) The network-layer communication protocol used in the DARPA Internet. IP is responsible for host-to-host addressing and routing, packet forwarding, and packet fragmentation and reassembly.

Internetwork Datagram Protocol (IDP) In the Xerox Network Systems architecture, a communication protocol that serves as the level-1 protocol. IDP is responsible for the internet packet format, internet addressing, and routing.

interprocess communication (IPC) The transfer of data between processes. Most facilities for interprocess communication are designed such that data are transferred between objects other than processes. An interprocess-communication model that is not directly process-oriented is advantageous because it is possible to model scenarios in which communication endpoints are location-independent and, possibly, dynamically migrated. For example, in 4.3BSD, communication is between sockets, not processes.

interrupt In computer systems, an event external to the currently executing process that causes a change in the normal flow of instruction execution. Interrupts usually are generated by hardware devices that are external to the CPU.

interrupt priority level The priority that is associated with a device interrupt. This value is usually defined by switches or jumpers located on a device controller and transmitted with each interrupt request made by the hardware device. *See also* processor priority level.

interrupt stack A run-time stack that is used by procedures that are invoked to respond to interrupts and traps. On the VAX, a systemwide interrupt stack is provided that is independent of the normal kernel–run-time stack located in the user structure of each process.

interrupt vector A storage location known to the system that contains the starting address of a procedure to be executed when a given interrupt or exception occurs. The system defines separate vectors for each interrupting device controller and for classes of exceptions.

interrupt-vector table A table of interrupt vectors. On most machines that support vectored interrupts, the vector supplied by the interrupting device is used to index into an interrupt-vector table. The VAX uses several interrupt-vector tables; for example, each UNIBUS adapter has its own interrupt-vector table. *See also* vectored interrupt.

I/O *See* Input/Output.

I/O page A section of an address space in which I/O device control registers are accessible. On the VAX, the last 8 Kbyte of the address space of each UNIBUS adapter is reserved as an I/O page through which UNIBUS-device control registers are accessed. *See also* memory-mapped I/O architecture.

I/O redirection The redirection of an I/O stream from its default assignment. For example, all the standard shells permit users to redirect the standard output stream to a file or process.

I/O stream A stream of data directed to, or generated from, a process. Most I/O streams in UNIX have a single common data format that permits users to write programs in a tool-oriented fashion and to combine these programs in pipelines by directing the standard output stream of one program to the standard input stream of another.

I/O vector *See* iovec.

iovec A data structure used to specify user I/O requests made to the kernel. Each structure holds the address of a data buffer and the number of bytes of data to be read or written. Arrays of such structures are passed to the kernel in *readv* and *writev* system calls.

IP *See* Internet Protocol.

IPC *See* interprocess communication.

job In UNIX, a set of processes that all have the same process-group identifier. Jobs that have multiple processes are normally created with a pipeline. A job is the fundamental object that is manipulated with job control.

job control A facility for managing jobs. With job control, a job may be started, stopped, and killed, as well as moved between the foreground and the background. The terminal handler provides facilities for automatically stopping a background job that tries to access the controlling terminal, and for notifying a job's controlling process when such an event occurs.

keepalive packet A type of packet used by TCP to maintain information about whether or not a destination host is up. Keepalive packets are sent to a remote host, which, if it is up, must respond. If a response is not received in a reasonable period of time to any of several keepalive packets, then the connection is terminated. Keepalive packets are used only on TCP connections that have been created for sockets that have the SO_KEEPALIVE option set on them.

keepalive timer A timer used by the TCP protocol in conjunction with keepalive packets. The timer is set when a keepalive packet is transmitted. If a response to the packet is not received before the timer expires several times, then the connection is shut down.

kernel The central controlling program that provides basic system facilities. The UNIX kernel creates and manages processes, provides functions to access the filesystem, and supplies communication facilities. The UNIX kernel is the only part of UNIX that a user cannot replace.

kernel map The resource map that is used by the 4.3BSD kernel in allocating the PTEs that are used to map the virtual address spaces of user processes.

kernel mode The most privileged processor-access mode. The UNIX kernel operates in kernel mode.

kernel process A process that executes with the processor in kernel mode. The *pagedaemon* and *swapper* processes are examples of kernel processes.

kernel state The run-time execution state for the kernel. This state, which includes the program counter, general-purpose registers, and run-time stack, must be saved and restored on each context switch.

kill character The ASCII character that is recognized by the terminal handler in cooked mode to mean ''delete everything typed on this terminal after the last end-of-line character.'' Each terminal can have a different kill character, and that kill character can be changed at any time with an *ioctl* system call. The terminal handler does not recognize the kill character on terminals that are in raw or cbreak mode. *See also* erase character and word-erase character.

kluster A group of pages related by their locality in a process's virtual address space. This grouping is performed by the virtual-memory system when servicing certain page faults for the purpose of prepaging. The name is spelled with a 'k' to distinguish it from the clustering of pages. *See also* fill-on-demand klustering.

ldpctx A VAX instruction that causes the current VAX process state to be loaded from the process-control block pointed to by the PCBB register. *See also* svpctx.

least recently used (LRU) A policy of reuse whereby the least recently used items are reused first. For example, in the filesystem, there are a fixed number of data buffers available for doing I/O. Buffers that hold valid data are reallocated in an LRU order in the hope that the data held in the buffer may be reused by a subsequent read request.

line discipline A processing module in the kernel that is used to provide semantics on an asynchronous serial interface or on a software emulation of such an interface. Line disciplines are described by a procedural interface whose entry points are stored in a *linesw* data structure.

line mode *See* cooked mode.

link layer Layer 2 in the ISO Open Systems Interconnection Reference Model. In this model, the link layer is responsible for the (possibly unreliable) delivery of messages within a single physical network. The link layer corresponds most closely to the network-interface layer of the 4.3BSD network subsystem.

listen request A request passed to the user-request routine of a communication-protocol module as a result of a process making a *listen* system call on a socket. This request indicates that the system should listen for requests to establish a connection to the socket. Otherwise, the system will reject any connection requests it receives for the socket.

load average A measure of the CPU load on the system. The load average in 4.3BSD is defined as an average of the number of processes ready to run or waiting for disk I/O to complete, as sampled over the previous 1-minute interval of system operation.

locality of reference A phenomenon whereby memory references of a running program are localized within the virtual address space over short periods of time. Most programs tend to exhibit some degree of locality of reference. This locality of reference makes it worthwhile for the system to prefetch pages that are adjacent to a page that is faulted, so as to reduce the fault rate of a running program.

logical block A block defined by dividing a file's linear extent by the underlying filesystem block size. Each logical block of a file is mapped into a physical block. This additional level of mapping permits physical blocks to be placed on disk without concern for the linear organization of the logical blocks in a file.

logical drive partitions A software scheme that is used to divide a disk drive into one or more linear extents or partitions.

logical unit An integer that specifies the unit number of a hardware device. The hardware device and unit number are specified in terms of logical devices and units as discovered by the system during the autoconfiguration phase of its bootstrap sequence. For example, a reference to partition 1 on disk drive 2 typically refers to partition 1 on the third disk drive identified at boot time (devices are numbered starting at 0). The actual mapping between logical unit numbers and physical devices is defined by the configuration file that is used to build a kernel. For flexibility, most systems are configured to support a reasonably dynamic mapping between physical and logical devices. This dynamic mapping permits, for example, system administrators to move a disk drive from one controller to another without having to reconfigure a new kernel or to reconstruct the associated special files for the device.

long-term–scheduling algorithm *See* short-term–scheduling algorithm.

loop In the virtual-memory system, the circular collection of pages that make up the part of main memory that is used by pageable processes. A global CLOCK algorithm is used by the virtual-memory system to manage pages in the loop.

lossy A communication medium that has a high rate of data loss is said to be "lossy."

low watermark A data-flow control that specifies the minimum number of data that must be present before an action can be taken. In the interprocess-communication facilities, each socket's data buffer has a low watermark that specifies the minimum number of data that must be present in the data buffer before a reception request will be satisfied.

LRU *See* least recently used.

machine check On the VAX, an exceptional machine condition that indicates that the CPU detected an internal error in itself. For example, a machine check is generated if a parity error is detected in a cache memory.

magic number The number located in the first few bytes of an executable file that specifies the type of executable file that file is. On the VAX, the magic number is present in the first four bytes of each executable file.

main memory The primary memory system on a machine.

major-device number An integer number that uniquely identifies the type of a device. This number is defined as the index into the array of device-driver entry points for the device and is used, for example, when a user creates a device special file with the *mknod* system call.

mapped An object is said to be mapped into the virtual address space of a process when page tables have been set up that map the pages of the object into the process's address space.

mark and sweep algorithm A garbage-collection algorithm that works by sweeping through the set of collectable objects, marking each object that is referenced. If, after this marking phase, there are any objects that are unmarked, they are reclaimed.

masked A signal is said to be "masked" if it has been specified in a *sigblock* or *sigsetmask* system call. When a signal is masked, its delivery is delayed until it is unmasked. In addition, in 4.3BSD, the system automatically masks a caught signal while that signal is being handled.

MASSBUS An I/O bus designed by DEC for higher-speed mass-storage peripherals than could be supported by the UNIBUS. The MASSBUS is found mainly on older models of PDP-11 and VAX computers.

MASSBUS adapter A hardware device that permits a MASSBUS to be attached to the system bus of a VAX.

MASSBUS-adapter support routines The set of routines in the kernel that are used in implementing device drivers for MASSBUS peripherals. These routines schedule the use of MASSBUS-adapter resources: the memory-mapping registers and the data paths.

MASSBUS unit number An integer number used by a device driver to identify a MASSBUS adapter. The MASSBUS unit number used by a device driver is a logical number that is mapped into a physical unit number by a table that is constructed at the time the system is bootstrapped. This mapping is done to provide flexibility in the configuration of devices on a machine.

master device *See* slave device.

maximum segment lifetime (MSL) The maximum time a segment of data may exist in the network. *See also* 2MSL timer.

mbuf A data structure that describes a block of data; mbufs are used in the interprocess-communication facilities. ''Mbuf'' is shorthand for ''memory buffer.''

memory address A number that specifies a memory location. Memory addresses are often categorized as *physical* or *virtual* according to whether they reference *physical memory* or *virtual memory*.

memory free list *See* free list.

memory-management system The part of the operating system that is responsible for the management of memory resources available on a machine.

memory-management unit A hardware device that implements memory-management–related tasks such as address translation and memory protection. Most contemporary memory-management units also provide support for demand-paged virtual-memory management.

memory-mapped I/O architecture An architecture where the data structures associated with hardware devices are accessed as part of the physical address space of a machine. Such devices are said to be memory mapped. This style of architecture is contrasted with one in which special machine instructions are used to access hardware devices. *See also* I/O page.

message buffer A circular buffer in which the system records all kernel messages directed to the console terminal. The device **/dev/klog** can be used by a user program to read data from this buffer in a manner that ensures that no data will be lost. On the VAX, the message buffer is allocated early in the bootstrapping of the system, and it is placed in high memory so that it can be located after a reboot, allowing messages printed out just before a crash to be saved.

minor-device number An integer number that uniquely identifies a subunit of a device. For example, the minor-device number for a disk device specifies a subunit termed a *partition*, whereas the minor-device number for a terminal multiplexer identifies a specific terminal line. The minor-device number is interpreted on a per-device basis and is used, for example, when a user creates a device special file with the *mknod* system call.

modem control For data-communication equipment, the support of a set of signals used to ensure reliable initiation and termination of connections over asynchronous serial lines governed by the RS-232 standard. Support for modem control is normally important only for serial lines that are accessed via dialup modems.

MSL *See* maximum segment lifetime.

multilevel feedback queue A queueing scheme in which requests are partitioned into multiple prioritized subqueues, with requests moving between subqueues based on dynamically varying criterion. The 4.3BSD kernel uses a multilevel feedback queueing scheme for scheduling the execution of processes.

multiplexed file A type of file used for interprocess communication that was supported in the Seventh Edition UNIX system.

network address A number that specifies a host machine.

network architecture The collection of protocols, facilities, and conventions (such as the format of a network address) that define a network. Like machine architectures, network architectures may be realized in different ways. For example, some network architectures are specifically designed to permit their implementation in hardware devices.

network byte order The order defined by a network for the transmission of protocol fields that are larger than one octet. In the DARPA Internet protocols, this order is "most significant octet first."

network-interface layer The layer of software in the 4.3BSD network subsystem that is responsible for transporting messages between hosts connected to a common transmission medium. This layer is mainly concerned with driving the transmission media involved and performing any necessary link-level protocol encapsulation and decapsulation.

network layer The layer of software in the 4.3BSD network subsystem that is responsible for the delivery of data destined for remote transport or network-layer protocols.

network mask A value that is used in the subnet addressing scheme of the DARPA Internet. A network mask specifies which bits in a local Internet address the system should include when extracting a network identifier from a local address.

network virtual terminal A terminal device that receives and transmits data across a network connection.

new terminal driver The terminal line discipline that extends the old terminal driver to support job control and logical line-editing facilities.

nexus On the VAX, a physical connection to the main system bus that supports the transfer of data and control information (such as interrupt vectors).

nice In UNIX, a user-controllable process scheduling parameter. The value of a process's *nice* variable is used in calculating that process's scheduling priority. Positive values of *nice* mean that the process is willing to receive less than its share of the processor. Negative values of *nice* mean that the process should be given more than its share of the processor.

nonblocking I/O A mode in which a descriptor may be placed, whereby the system will return an error if any I/O operation on the descriptor would cause the process to block. For example, if a *read* system call is performed on a descriptor that is in nonblocking I/O mode, and no data are available, the system will return the error code EWOULDBLOCK rather than block the process until data arrive. *See also* signal-driven I/O.

nonlocal goto A transfer in control that circumvents the normal flow of execution in a program across routine boundaries. For example, if procedure A calls procedure B, and B calls C, then a direct transfer of control from C back to A (bypassing B) would be a nonlocal goto.

nonresident An object that is not present in main memory is said to be "nonresident." For example, a page in the virtual address space of a process may be nonresident if the page has never been referenced.

octet A basic unit of data representation; an eight-bit byte. The term *octet* is used instead of *byte* in the definition of many network protocols because some machines use other byte sizes.

old terminal driver The terminal line discipline present in UNIX 32V and the Seventh Edition UNIX. This interface supports only a very simple line-editing facility based on erase and kill characters. More advanced line-editing facilities, such as the word erase and literal characters, as well as support for job control, are present in the new terminal driver.

Optimal Replacement Policy A replacement policy that optimizes the performance of a demand-paging virtual-memory system. In this book, the Optimal Replacement Policy refers to the policy in which advanced knowledge of the full reference string of a program is known, and pages are selected such that the number of page faults is minimized.

out-of-band data Data transmitted and received out of the normal flow of data. Stream sockets support a logically separate out-of-band data channel through which at least one message of at least one byte of data may be sent. The system immediately notifies a receiving process of the presence of out-of-band data, and out-of-band data may be retrieved out of the received order of data.

overlay In computer systems, a region of code or data that may be replaced with other such regions on demand. Overlays are usually loaded into a process's address space on demand, possibly on top of another overlay. Overlays are a commonly used scheme for programs that are too large to fit in the address space of a machine that does not support virtual memory.

P0 base register (P0BR) On the VAX, the processor register, or its saved value in a process-control block, that contains the virtual address of the page table for a process's P0 region. (The P0 region maps a process's text, data, and heap.)

P0 length register (P0LR) On the VAX, the processor register, or its saved value in a process-control block, that contains the number of entries in the page table for a process's P0 region.

P0BR *See* P0 base register.

P0LR *See* P0 length register.

P1 base register (P1BR) On the VAX, the processor register, or its saved value in a process-control block, that contains the virtual address of a process's P1 region page table. (The P1 region maps a process's stack and user area.)

P1 length register (P1LR) On the VAX, the processor register, or its saved value in a process-control block, that contains the number of nonexistent page-table entries for pages in a process's P1 region.

P1BR *See* P1 base register.

P1LR *See* P1 length register.

Packet Exchange (PEX) The standard datagram service in the Xerox Network Systems architecture. This facility is implemented in 4.3BSD by a user-level library using IDP datagram sockets.

Packet Switch Node (PSN) A hardware device used in the construction of packet-switched networks such as the ARPANET. Each PSN utilizes a protocol that provides reliable, flow-controlled, packet-switching functionality. *See also* Interface Message Processor.

page In memory-management, the fixed-sized unit of measure used to divide a physical or virtual address space. *See also* demand paging.

page fault An exception generated by a process reference to a page of its virtual address space that is not marked as resident in memory.

page push A pageout of a dirty page.

page reclaim A page fault, where the page that was faulted is located in memory, usually on the memory free list.

page-table entry (PTE) The data structure that identifies the location and status of a page of a virtual address space. When a virtual page is in memory, the PTE contains the page frame number needed to map the virtual page to a physical page. When it is not in memory, the PTE contains the information needed to create the page or to locate the page on secondary storage.

pagedaemon In 4.3BSD, the name of the process that is responsible for writing parts of the address space of a process to secondary storage to support the paging facilities of the virtual-memory system. *See also* swapper.

pagein An operation performed by the virtual-memory system in which the contents of a page are read from secondary storage.

pageout An operation performed by the virtual-memory system in which the contents of a page are written to secondary storage.

pageout in progress A pageout operation that has been started, but has not yet been completed. In 4.3BSD, the system tracks the number of pageouts for each shared text segment, to ensure there are no other references when it reclaims the resources associated with such a segment.

paging The actions of bringing pages of an executing process into main memory when they are referenced, and removing them from memory when they are replaced. When a process executes, all its pages are said to reside in virtual memory. Only the actively used pages, however, need to reside in main memory. The remaining pages can reside on disk until they are needed.

panic In UNIX, an unrecoverable system failure detected by the kernel. 4.3BSD automatically recovers from a panic by rebooting the machine, repairing any filesystem damage, and then restarting normal operation. *See also* crash dump.

parent process A process that is a direct relative of another process as a result of a *fork* system call.

partition *See* disk partition.

pathname A null-terminated character string starting with an optional slash (''/''), followed by zero or more directory names separated by slashes, and optionally followed by a filename. If a pathname begins with a slash, the pathname is said to be an *absolute pathname* and the path search begins at the root directory. Otherwise, the pathname is said to be a *relative pathname* and the path search begins at the current working directory of the process. A slash by itself names the root directory. A null pathname refers to the current working directory.

PCB *See* process control block.

PCBB *See* Process Control Block Base.

persist timer A timer used by TCP for maintaining output flow on a connection. This timer is started whenever data are ready to be sent, but the send window is too small to bother sending and no data are already outstanding. If no window update is received before the timer expires, a window probe is sent.

PEX *See* Packet Exchange.

physical block One or more contiguous disk sectors to which the system maps a logical block.

physical unit number An integer that is recognized by a device controller as specifying a particular hardware unit. For example, a tape transport has a physical unit number that a user must use in referring to the device when making requests to an associated tape controller. The physical unit number is often different from the logical unit number used by the system.

PID *See* process identifier.

pipe An interprocess-communication facility that supports the unidirectional flow of data between related processes. Data transfer is stream-oriented, reliable, and flow controlled. A pipe is specified to the shell with the ''|'' symbol. For example, to connect the standard output of a program named **a** to the standard input of a program named **b**, the command ''a | b'' would be used.

pipeline A collection of processes in which the standard output of one process is connected to the standard input of the next with a pipe.

placement policy The policy used by the virtual-memory system to place pages in main memory when servicing a page fault.

POSIX The portable operating-system interface standards group, P1003, established by the IEEE. Their first established standard was the kernel interface,

1003.1, which was ratified in 1988.

post a signal To notify a process that a signal is pending for it. Since most of the actions associated with a signal are performed by the receiving process, posting a signal usually does little more than to record the pending signal in the process's proc structure and to arrange for the process to be run.

prefetching The retrieval of data before they are needed. Many machines prefetch machine instructions so that they can overlap the time spent fetching instructions from memory with the time spent decoding instructions.

prepaging The prefetching of pages of memory. Prepaging is a technique used by virtual-memory systems to reduce the number of page faults.

probe routine A device-driver routine is responsible for deciding whether or not a hardware device is present on a machine and for attempting to make the device interrupt.

probing The operation of checking to see whether a hardware device is present on a machine. Each different type of hardware device usually requires its own technique for probing.

/proc filesystem A filesystem-based interface to active processes that can be used to construct process-debugging facilities. Each process is represented by a directory entry in a pseudo-directory named **/proc**. Applications access the virtual address space of a process by opening the file in **/proc** that is associated with the process, and then using the *read* and *write* system calls as though the process were a regular file. This facility is part of the Eighth Edition UNIX system.

proc structure A data structure maintained by the kernel for each active process in the system. The proc structure for a process is always resident, as opposed to the user structure, which is moved to secondary storage when the process is swapped out.

process In operating systems, a task or thread of execution. In UNIX, user processes are created with the *fork* system call.

process control block (PCB) A data structure used to hold process context. On the VAX, the hardware PCB contains the hardware portion of this context. The software PCB contains the software portion, and is located in memory immediately after the hardware PCB.

Process Control Block Base (PCBB) On the VAX, a register that holds the physical address of the process-control block for the currently running process.

process group A collection of processes on a single machine that all have the same process-group identifier. This grouping is used to arbitrate between multiple jobs contending for the same terminal.

process-group identifier A positive integer used to identify uniquely each active process group in the system. Process-group identifiers are typically defined to be the PID of the process-group leader. Process-group identifiers are used by command interpreters in implementing job control, when broadcasting signals with the *killpg* system call, and when altering the scheduling priority of all processes in a process group with the *setpriority* system call.

process-group leader The process in a process group whose PID is used as the process-group identifier. This process is typically the first process in a pipeline.

process identifier (PID) A nonnegative integer used to identify uniquely each active process in the system.

process open file table *See* descriptor table.

process priority A parameter used by the kernel to schedule the execution of processes. The priority for a process changes dynamically according to the operation of the process. In addition, the *nice* parameter can be set for a process to weight the overall scheduling priority for the process.

process table The collection of proc structures that describe all the active processes that exist in the system. The process table is always resident in main memory.

processor priority level A priority that is used to control the delivery of interrupts to the CPU. Most machines support multiple priority levels at which the processor may execute. Similarly, interrupts also occur at multiple levels. When an interrupt is posted to the processor, if the priority level of the interrupt is greater than that of the processor, then the interrupt is recognized by the processor and execution is diverted to service the interrupt. Otherwise, the interrupt is not acknowledged by the CPU, and it is held pending until the processor priority drops to a level that permits the interrupt to be acknowledged. Changing the processor priority level is usually a privileged operation that can be done only when the processor is executing in kernel mode.

Processor Status Longword (PSL) On the VAX, a processor register that consists of a word of privileged processor status and the *Processor Status Word* (PSW). The privileged processor status information includes the current processor priority level, the current and previous access modes, and the interrupt stack bit. The PSW contains unprivileged processor status information, such as the condition codes, the arithmetic trap-enable flags, and the trace-trap–enable bit.

protocol family A collection of communication protocols that are related by being part of a single network architecture. For example the TCP, UDP, IP, and ICMP protocols are part of the protocol family for the DARPA Internet.

protocol switch structure A data structure that holds all the entry points for a communication protocol supported by the kernel.

pseudo-DMA A technique in which DMA is simulated in software. This technique is usually used by device drivers that need to receive data from or send data to a device that has real-time constraints that cannot be met under normal operating circumstances.

PSL *See* Processor Status Longword.

PSN *See* Packet Switch Node.

PTE *See* page-table entry.

pure demand paging Demand paging without prepaging.

raw-device interface The character-device interface for block-oriented devices such as disks and tapes. This interface provides raw access to the underlying device, arranging for direct I/O between a process and the device.

raw mode A mode of operation for a terminal device whereby processes reading from the terminal receive input immediately as it is typed and without an interpretation of the input characters. *See also* cooked mode and cbreak mode.

raw socket A socket that provides direct access to a lower-level communication protocol.

Ready for Next Message (RFNM) A type of message in the protocol used between a host and a PSN. This type of message is sent from a PSN to the local host to which it is connected when the PSN receives an acknowledgment for an outstanding message. The message from the PSN to the local host indicates that the PSN is ready to accept a new message for transmission to the remote host. RFNM messages are part of the host-to-host flow-control facility provided by PSNs.

real GID *See* real group identifier.

real group identifier (real GID) The GID that is recorded in the accounting record when a process terminates. The real GID for a process is initially set at the time a user logs into a system, and is then inherited by child processes across subsequent *fork* and *execve* system calls (irrespective of whether or not a program is set-group-identifier). The real GID can be made the effective GID with the *setregid* system call. *See also* effective group identifier and real group identifier.

real UID *See* real user identifier.

real user identifier (real UID) With respect to a process, the true identity of the user that owns the process. The real UID for a process is initially set at the time a user logs into a system, and is then inherited by child processes across subsequent *fork* and *execve* system calls (irrespective of whether or not a program is set-user-identifier). The real UID is recorded in the accounting record when a process terminates. The real UID can be made the effective user identifier with the *setreuid* system call. *See also* effective user identifier and real user identifier.

receive window In TCP, the range of sequence numbers that defines the data that the system will accept for a connection. Any data with sequence numbers outside this range that are received are dropped. *See also* sliding-window scheme.

reclaim *See* page reclaim.

reclaim from free A page-reclaim operation from the memory free list. This scenario can take place if a page is reclaimed by the page-replacement algorithm, but the page is not reassigned before a process faults on it.

red zone A read-only region of memory immediately below the last page of the per-process run-time stack (on the VAX). The red zone is set up by the system so that a fault will occur if a process overruns its kernel-mode run-time stack.

reference bit A bit in a PTE that indicates whether a process has accessed the associated page. The VAX architecture does not support a reference bit, so the bit is simulated in software.

reference string A dataset that describes the pages referenced by a process over the time of the process's execution. This description represents the memory-related behavior of the process at discrete times during its lifetime.

referenced In the virtual-memory system, a page that is read from or written to is considered to have been referenced.

register save mask On the VAX, a word that describes the registers to be saved on entry to a procedure that is called using a VAX call instruction.

relative pathname *See* pathname.

reliably delivered message socket A type of socket that guarantees reliable data delivery and preservation of message boundaries, and that is not connection-based.

relocation The copying of a program's contents from one place in an address space to another. This copying may be accompanied by modifications to the image of the program, so that memory references encoded in the program remain correct after that program is copied. Code that is not bound to a particular starting memory address is said to be *relocatable*.

replacement policy The policy that a demand-paged virtual-memory–management system uses to select pages for reuse when memory is otherwise unavailable.

resident An object that is present in main memory is said to be ''resident.'' For example, a page in the virtual address space of a process is resident if its contents is present in main memory.

resource map A data structure used by the system to manage the allocation of a resource that can be described by a set of linear extents.

retransmit timer A timer used by TCP to trigger the retransmission of data. This timer is set each time data are transmitted to a remote host. It is set to a value that is expected to be greater than the time it will take the receiving host to receive the data and return an acknowledgement.

RFNM *See* Ready for Next Message.

root directory The directory used in resolving absolute pathnames. Each process has a root directory that can be set with the *chroot* system call, and the system has a unique root directory, the identity of which is set at the time the system is bootstrapped.

root filesystem The filesystem containing the root directory that is considered the root of all filesystems on a machine. The identity of a default root filesystem is compiled into a kernel, although the actual root filesystem used by a system may be set to some other filesystem at the time a system is bootstrapped.

rotational-layout table A per-filesystem data structure that describes the rotational position of blocks in a filesystem. The filesystem uses the rotational-layout table for a filesystem in selecting rotationally optimal blocks for allocation to a file.

round robin In queueing, an algorithm in which each requester is serviced for a fixed period of time in a first-come-first-served order; requests are placed at the end of the queue if they are incomplete after service.

route In packet-switched–network communication, a route to a destination specifies the host or hosts through which data must be transmitted to reach the destination.

routing daemon The process in 4.3BSD that provides a routing-management service for the system. This service uses a protocol that implements a distributed database of routing information that is dynamically updated to reflect changes in topological connectivity.

routing redirect message A message generated by a gateway when the latter recognizes that a message that it has received can be delivered with a more direct route.

run queue The queue of processes that are ready to execute.

SBR *See* system base register.

scatter loading A memory-management technique used in UNIX 32V. With scatter loading, when a process is loaded into memory, the contents of its address space are loaded into (possibly) discontiguous regions of memory. Scatter loading tends to be more space-efficient than is loading into a single contiguous region, but can result in memory fragmentation.

scheduling In operating systems, the planning used to share a resource. For example, process scheduling is used to share the CPU and main memory.

scheduling priority A per-process parameter maintained by the kernel that specifies the priority with which the latter will schedule the execution of a process. When a process is executing in user mode, the system periodically calculates the scheduling priority, using the process priority and the *nice* parameter.

secondary storage Storage that is used to hold data that do not fit in main memory. Secondary storage is usually located on rotating magnetic media, such as disk drives. *See also* backing storage.

sector The smallest contiguous region on a disk that may be accessed with a single I/O operation.

segment A contiguous range of data defined by a base and an extent. In memory management, a segment is defined by a contiguous range of memory addresses, and is used to describe a portion of a process's address space or a portion of main memory. In communication protocols, a segment is defined by a contiguous range of sequence numbers for which there are associated data.

send window In TCP, the range of sequence numbers that defines the data that the system may transmit on a connection and be assured that the receiving party has space to hold them on receipt. Any data with sequence numbers prior to the start of the send window have already been sent and acknowledged. Any data with sequence numbers after the end of the window will not be sent until the send window changes to include them. *See also* sliding-window scheme.

sense request A request passed to the user-request routine of a communication-protocol module as a result of a process making a *stat* system call on a socket.

sequence space The range of sequence numbers that are assigned to data transmitted over a TCP connection. In TCP, sequence numbers are taken from a 32-bit circular space that starts with an arbitrary value called the *initial sequence number*.

Sequenced Packet Protocol (SPP) In the Xerox Network Systems architecture, a communication protocol that serves as a level-2 protocol. SPP is layered on top of IDP and provides reliable, unduplicated, and flow-controlled transmission of messages.

sequenced packet socket A type of socket that models sequenced, reliable, unduplicated, connection-based communication that preserves message boundaries.

Serial Line IP (SLIP) An encapsulation used to transfer IP datagrams over asynchronous serial lines. Also, the line discipline that implements this encapsulation.

server process A process that provides services to client processes via an interprocess-communication facility.

session In job control, all the processes started during a single login session.

set-group-identifier program A program that runs with an additional group privilege. Set-group-identifier programs are indicated by a bit in the inode of the file. When a process specifies such a file in an *execve* system call, the GID of the file is made the effective GID of the process.

set-priority-level A request that sets the current *processor priority level*. In 4.3BSD on the VAX, all such requests are made with calls to routines that have a name with the prefix ''spl''. For example, to set the processor priority level high enough to block interrupts that cause terminal processing, the *spltty*() routine would be called.

set-user-identifier program A program that runs with an UID different from that of the process that started it running. Set-user-identifier programs are indicated by a bit in the inode of the file. When a process specifies such a file in an *execve* system call, the UID of the file is made the effective UID of the process.

shadow swap map A data structure in the user structure of each process that is used temporarily to record new swap space allocated to a process while that process is holding existing space.

shared text segment A text segment that is shared by more than one process. Shared text segments can be created only from certain types of programs.

Such programs are identified by their magic number. These programs are created with a text segment that is rounded to a size that makes sharing possible. *See also* text segment.

shell A program that interprets and executes user commands. When a user logs into a UNIX system, a shell process is normally created with its standard input, standard output, and standard error descriptors directed to the terminal or network virtual terminal on which the user logged in.

short-term–scheduling algorithm The algorithm used by the system to select the next process to run from among the set of processes that are deemed runnable. The *long-term–scheduling algorithm*, on the other hand, can influence the set of runnable processes by swapping processes in and out of main memory (and thus in and out of the set of runnable processes).

signal In UNIX, a software event; in 4.3BSD, this event is modeled after a hardware interrupt.

signal-driven I/O A mode in which a descriptor may be placed, whereby the system will deliver a SIGIO signal to a process whenever I/O is possible on the descriptor. *See also* nonblocking I/O.

signal handler A procedure that is invoked in response to a signal.

signal-trampoline code The piece of code located in the user structure of each process that is used to invoke a signal handler. The signal-trampoline code contains instructions that set up parameters for calling a signal handler, do the actual call to the signal handler, and, on return, do a *sigreturn* system call to reset kernel state and resume execution of the process after the signal is handled.

silly-window syndrome A condition observed in window-based flow-control schemes in which a receiver sends several small (i.e., silly) window allocations rather than waiting for a reasonable-sized window to become available.

single indirect block *See* indirect block.

slave device A hardware device that is controlled by a *master device*. For example, a disk drive is a slave device to a disk controller. The distinction between master and slave devices is used by the autoconfiguration system. A slave device is assumed to be accessible only if its corresponding master device is present.

slave routine A device-driver routine that is responsible for deciding whether or not a slave device is present on a machine. Slave routines are never called unless the master device for the slave has been probed successfully.

sleep queue The queue of processes that are blocked awaiting an event. The name is derived from the *sleep*() routine that places processes on this queue.

sliding-window scheme A flow-control scheme in which the receiver limits the number of data it is willing to receive. This limit is expressed as a contiguous range of sequence numbers termed the *receive window* and is periodically communicated to the sender, who is expected to transmit only data that are within the window. As data are received and acknowledged, the window *slides* forward in the sequence space. *See also* sequence space; receive window; send window.

SLIP *See* Serial Line IP.

slip sector A sector that is used to replace a bad sector on the same track.

slip-sector forwarding The procedure of retargeting a bad sector to a *slip sector*.

SLR *See* system length register.

small-packet avoidance Avoiding the transmission of packets that are so small that they are inefficient.

socket In the 4.3BSD interprocess-communication model, an endpoint of communication. Also, the data structure that is used to implement the socket abstraction, and the system call that is used to create a socket.

soft limit A limit that may be temporarily exceeded, or exceeded a limited number of times. A soft limit is typically used in conjunction with a hard limit.

soft link *See* symbolic link.

software interrupt A software-initiated interrupt. The VAX supports 15 prioritized software interrupts. The kernel can request these interrupts by setting bits in the Software Interrupt Request Register (SIRR).

software-interrupt process A process that is set running in response to a software interrupt. In 4.3BSD, input processing for each transport-layer communication protocol is embodied in a software-interrupt process.

special file *See* device special file.

spin loop A sequence of instructions that causes the processor to do a specific operation repeatedly. Standalone device drivers use spin loops to implement real-time delays.

SPP *See* Sequenced Packet Protocol.

stack An area of memory set aside for temporary storage, or for procedure and interrupt-service linkages. A stack uses the last-in first-out (LIFO) concept. On the VAX, the stack grows from high memory addresses to low memory addresses. As items are added to (''pushed onto'') the stack, the stack pointer decrements; as items are retrieved from (''popped off'') the stack, the stack pointer increments.

stack segment A segment that holds a stack.

stale translation A translation or mapping that was true at some time, but that is no longer valid. For example, on machines that have a translation lookaside buffer, if a PTE in memory is changed to alter the mapping, any address translation for that page that is present in the TLB must be flushed to avoid a stale translation.

standalone Software that can run without the support of an operating system is said to be capable of ''standalone'' operation.

standalone device driver A device driver that is used in a standalone program. A standalone device driver usually differs from a device driver used in an operating system in that it does not have interrupt services, memory management, or full support for virtual-memory mapping. In the UNIX standalone I/O library, for example, a standalone device driver polls a device to decide when an operation has completed, and is responsible for setting up its own memory mapping when doing DMA.

standalone I/O library A library of software that is used in writing standalone programs. This library includes standalone device drivers that are used to do I/O.

standard error The I/O stream on which error messages are conventionally placed. This stream is usually associated with descriptor 2 in a process.

standard input The I/O stream on which input is conventionally received. This stream is usually associated with descriptor 0 in a process.

standard output The I/O stream to which output is conventionally directed. This stream is usually associated with descriptor 1 in a process.

start routine A device-driver routine that is responsible for starting a device operation after the system has acquired all the resources that are required for the operation.

sticky bit The bit in an inode that indicates that the text segment of the program is to be treated as a *sticky text*.

sticky text A text segment that is saved in the swap area for future reuse, rather than its being reloaded from the file from which it is was originally obtained. *See also* sticky bit.

stream I/O system A facility in the Eighth Edition UNIX system that permits the flexible configuration of processing for streams of data. In this system, it is possible to connect kernel-resident modules dynamically in a stack-oriented fashion, and to have these modules process data sent and received on an I/O stream.

stream socket A type of socket that models a reliable, connection-based, byte stream that may support out-of-band data transmission.

subnetwork A physical network that is a part of a larger logical network with a single shared network address. The subnet is assigned a subset of the logical network's address space.

superblock A data structure in the filesystem that gives the basic parameters of the filesystem.

superuser The user whose UID is 0. Processes owned by the superuser are granted special privileges by UNIX. The superuser's login name is usually *root*.

svpctx A VAX instruction that causes the current VAX process state to be loaded into the process-control block pointed to by the PCBB register. *See also* ldpctx.

swap area A region on secondary storage that is used for swapping and paging.

swap device A device on which a swap area resides.

swap map The data structure that describes available space in the swap area.

swap space *See* swap area.

swapper In 4.3BSD, the name of the process that implements the swapping portion of the memory-management facilities. Historically, the swapper is process 0. *See also* pagedaemon.

swapping A memory-management policy in which entire processes are moved to and from secondary storage when main memory is in short supply.

symbolic link A file whose *contents* are interpreted as a pathname when it is supplied as a component of a pathname. Also called a *soft link*.

synchronous Synchronized with the current process. For example, in UNIX all I/O operations appear to be synchronous: the *read* and *write* system calls do not return until the operation has been completed. (For a *write*, however, the data may not actually be written to their final destination until some time later—for example, in writing to a disk file.)

system activity An entry into the kernel. System activities can be categorized according to the event or action that initiates them: system calls, hardware interrupts, hardware traps, and software-initiated traps or interrupts.

system base register (SBR) On the VAX, the processor register that contains the physical address of the base of the system page table.

system bus The central bus in a machine. On many machines, the system bus is used to connect the CPU to main memory and to peripheral devices. On some machines, such as the VAX, many peripheral devices are not directly connected to the system bus, but instead are connected to an *I/O bus*, which is connected to the system bus through a bus adapter; see, for example, *UNIBUS* and *MASSBUS*.

system call In operating systems, a request to the system for service; also called a *system service request*.

system clock The device that is used to maintain the system's notion of time-of-day. On most systems, this device is an interval timer that periodically interrupts the CPU. The system uses these interrupts to maintain the current time-of-day, as well as to perform periodic functions such as process scheduling.

system identification register On the VAX, a processor register that contains the processor type and serial number.

system length register (SLR) On the VAX, the processor register that contains the number of PTEs in the system page table.

system mode *See* kernel mode.

system page table The page table used to map the virtual address space of the kernel. *See also* system base register and system length register.

system region On the VAX, the third quarter of the virtual address space of a process. Virtual addresses in the system region are shareable between processes.

TCP *See* Transmission Control Protocol.

terminal In computer systems, a device used to enter and receive data interactively from a computer. Most terminals include a CRT, which is used display data that is received from a computer. In the Electrical Industry Association (EIA) standard RS-232-C for connecting computers and Data Terminal Equipment (DTE), a terminal is a device that is placed at the other end of a wire that is connected to Data Communications Equipment (DCE). In this standard, a terminal might be any kind of device, not just the kind of device on which people type.

terminal multiplexer A hardware device that connects multiple serial lines to a computer. These serial lines may be used to connect terminals, modems, printers, and similar devices.

text segment The segment of a program that holds machine instructions. The system usually makes a program's text segment read-only and shareable by multiple processes when the program image is loaded into memory. *See also* shared text segment.

text structure A data structure used by the kernel to manage shared text segments.

thrashing A condition where requested memory utilization far exceeds the availability of memory. When a machine is thrashing, it usually spends more time performing system-related tasks than executing application code in user mode.

tick An interrupt by the system clock.

time quantum In a timesharing environment, the period of time that the process scheduler gives a process to run before it preempts that process so that another process can execute. Also called a *time slice*.

time slice *See* time quantum.

timer backoff The rate at which a timer value is increased. For example, in TCP, the value of the retransmit timer is determined by a table of multipliers that provide a near-exponential increase in timeout values.

TLB *See* translation lookaside buffer.

top half With regard to system operation, the collection of routines in the kernel that are invoked synchronously as a result of a system call or trap. These routines, the top half of the kernel, depend on per-process state and can block by calling *sleep*(). *See also* bottom half.

trace trap On the VAX, a trap caused by setting the *trace* bit in the PSL. This trap is used by the system to implement single-stepping in program debuggers. The kernel sets the trace bit in the PSL of the process being debugged so that a trace trap will be generated after the process executes one instruction. This trap is fielded by the kernel, which stops the process and returns control to the debugging process.

track In computer systems, the sectors of a disk that are accessible by one head at one of its seek positions.

trailer protocol A protocol in which control information is placed *after* the data. 4.3BSD uses a trailer protocol for transmitting packets on an Ethernet when a packet contains at least 512 bytes of data and the data size of the packet is a multiple of 512 bytes (and when the receiving host is willing to accept the protocol). This protocol is designed to permit the receiving host to receive data in page-aligned areas of memory and, thereby, to avoid memory-to-memory copy operations.

translation lookaside buffer (TLB) A processor cache containing translations for recently used virtual addresses.

translation-not-valid fault On the VAX, a fault generated when a process references a page in memory whose PTE is not marked valid—that is, the valid bit in the PTE is zero.

Transmission Control Protocol (TCP) A connection-oriented transport protocol used in the DARPA Internet. TCP provides for the reliable transfer of data, as well as the out-of-band indication of urgent data.

transport layer The layer of software in the network subsystem that provides the addressing structure required for communication between sockets, as well as any protocol mechanisms necessary for socket semantics such as reliable data delivery.

triple indirect block *See* indirect block.

tty driver The software module that implements the semantics associated with a terminal device. In 4.3BSD, the terminal-handling software is implemented in several line disciplines.

2MSL timer A timer used by the TCP protocol during connection shutdown. The name refers to the fact that the timer is set for twice the maximum time a segment may exist in the network. This value is chosen to ensure that future shutdown actions on the connection are done only after all segments associated with the connection no longer exist.

type-ahead The ability to transmit data to a system, usually by a user typing at a keyboard, before they are requested by a process.

u-dot *See* user structure.

UDP *See* User Datagram Protocol.

UID *See* user identifier.

uio A data structure used by the system to describe an I/O operation. This structure contains an array of *iovec* structures, the file offset at which the operation should start, the sum of the lengths of the I/O vectors, a flag showing whether the operation is a read or a write, and a flag showing whether the source and destination are both in the kernel's address space, or whether the source and destination are split between user and kernel address spaces.

unbuffered data path A data path in a UNIBUS adapter that has no buffering. Transfers through a UNIBUS adapter that use an unbuffered data path generate one or more system-bus data transfers for each UNIBUS transfer. *See also* buffered data path.

UNIBUS An I/O bus designed by DEC for medium- and low-speed peripherals.

UNIBUS adapter A hardware device that permits a UNIBUS to be attached to the system bus of a VAX.

unit start routine A device-driver routine that is responsible for initiating an operation on a unit. This routine typically does any preparatory work necessary for the operation, and then asks the system to allocate resources for the operation and schedule a call to the device driver's *go routine* that will tell the hardware device to do the operation.

UNIX domain A communication domain in the interprocess-communication facilities that supports stream and datagram-oriented styles of communication between processes on a single machine.

urgent data In TCP, data that are marked for urgent delivery.

user area *See* user structure.

User Datagram Protocol (UDP) A simple, unreliable, datagram protocol used in the DARPA Internet. UDP provides only peer-to-peer addressing and optional data checksums.

user identifier (UID) A 16-bit nonnegative integer that uniquely identifies a user. UIDs are used in the access-control facilities provided by the filesystem. *See also* effective user identifier; real user identifier; set-user-identifier program.

user mode On the VAX, the least privileged processor access mode. User processes run in user mode.

user page table The page table used to map the virtual address space of a process. On the VAX, user page tables reside in the virtual address space of the kernel. Therefore, the translation of virtual addresses by a process executing in *user mode* requires two page tables: the user page table for the process and the kernel or system page table.

user-request routine A routine provided by each communication protocol that directly supports a socket (a protocol that indirectly supports a socket is layered underneath a protocol that directly supports a socket). This routine serves as the main interface between the layer of software that implements sockets and the communication protocol. The interprocess-communication facilities make calls to the user-request routine for most socket-related system calls. *See also* connect request; control request; listen request; sense request.

user structure A data structure maintained by the kernel for each active process in the system. The user structure contains, among many things, the UID and GIDs of the process, the table of open descriptors, and the kernel mode runtime stack. Unlike the proc structure, the user structure for a process is moved to secondary storage if the process is swapped out. Also referred to as the *u-dot area* and *user area*.

VAX architecture The functionality found in all VAX machines, no matter what implementation technique is used. This functionality is usually defined by the attributes visible to the machine-level programmer and can be characterized by the VAX instruction set.

VAX system A particular implementation of the VAX architecture. The implementation includes the actual hardware structure used in realizing the architecture; for example, the algorithms used in controlling the machine as it interprets the architecture. The implementation also encompasses all the details associated with the physical aspects of a machine; for example, the kind of logic and how that logic is packaged and interconnected.

vectored interrupt A type of interrupt. When a device generates a vectored interrupt, it transmits a value to the CPU that is used to select an interrupt handler from an *interrupt vector table.*

virtual address An address that references a location in a *virtual address space.*

virtual address space A contiguous range of virtual-memory locations.

virtual machine A machine whose architecture is emulated in software.

virtual memory A facility whereby the effective range of addressable memory locations provided to a process is independent of the size of main memory; that is, the virtual address space of a process is independent of the physical address space of the CPU.

wait The UNIX system call that is used to wait for the termination of a descendent process.

wait channel A value used to identify an event for which a process is waiting. In most situations, a wait channel is defined as the address of a data structure related to the event for which a process is waiting. For example, if a process is waiting for the completion of a disk read, the wait channel is specified as the address of the data structure supplied to the block I/O system.

wildcard route A route that is used if there is no explicit route to a destination.

window probe In TCP, a message that is transmitted when data are queued for transmission, the send window is too small for TCP to bother sending data, and no message containing an update for the send window has been received in a long time. A window probe message contains a single octet of data.

word-erase character The ASCII character that is recognized by the terminal handler in cooked mode to mean ''delete the last word typed on this terminal,'' where a word is defined as a consecutive string of characters that does not include a space or horizontal tab. Each terminal can have a different word-erase character and that character can be changed at any time with an *ioctl* system call. The terminal handler does not recognize the word-erase character on terminals that are in raw or cbreak mode. *See also* erase character and kill character.

working directory *See* current working directory.

working set The set of pages in a process's virtual address space to which memory references have been made over some period of time. Most processes exhibit some locality of reference and the size of their working set is typically less than one-half of their total virtual memory size.

XNS domain A communication domain in the interprocess-communication facilities that supports the Xerox Network System (XNS) architecture. This architecture supports both stream and datagram-oriented styles of communication between processes on machines in an internet.

zombie process A process that has terminated but whose exit status has not yet been received by its parent process (or by *init*).

Index

#!, 56

A

absolute pathname, 35, 413, 435
Accent operating system, 20, 281, 300
accept system call, 286, 296, 298–299, 308, 367, 385
access control, filesystem, 36
access rights, 39, 283, 293, 302, 413
  passing, 304–306
  receiving, 304
accounting, process resource, 51, 62–63, 93
address family, 311, 413
address format, 311, 413
Address Resolution Protocol, 317, 325, 335–336, 339, 413–414
  implementation of, 335–336
  purpose of, 335
address, socket, 296–298
address space. *See* virtual address space
address structure
  internet, 297
  socket, 284–285
  UNIX domain, 297
  XNS, 297
address translation, 110, 413
  VAX, 120–122
adjtime system call, 54
AGE buffer list, 211–213, 222, 414
algorithm
  CLOCK, 150–153, 163, 417, 429
  daylight saving time, 54
  for *disksort*(), 245
  elevator sorting, 244
  mark-and-sweep garbage collection, 306
  MASSBUS adapter interrupt handling, 255
  for physical I/O, 232
  TCP slow-start, 376–378
Alliant, 86
alloc(), 217–218
allocation
  descriptor, 299
  directory space, 188
  file block, 193–195, 199, 207–208, 218–219
  filesystem fragment, 218–219
  inode, 194
  kernel memory, 28–29
  swap space, 129
  user page table, 131
allocbuf(), 212–213
ANSI C compiler, 402
argdev, 141
ARP. *See* Address Resolution Protocol
ARPANET, 7, 11, 14, 325, 343–346, 373, 377, 380, 414, 425–426, 434
  Host Access Protocol, 380, 414
  host interface, 380–381
  Reference Model, 344

arpinput(), 336
arpresolve(), 336
assembly-language startup, 397–398
assembly language in the kernel, 22, 46–47, 90, 229, 405
AST. *See* asynchronous system trap
asynchronous I/O, 174
  in *pageout*(), 155
asynchronous system trap, 44, 90, 101, 414
  use in context switching, 90
attach routine, 236, 239, 414
autoconfiguration, 41, 400–403
  alternative schemes for, 403
  contribution of, 9
  device driver support for, 227, 234–237
  of interrupt vector, 236, 401–403
  of MASSBUS device, 253
  operation of, 401–403
  phase, 234–235, 414
  up device driver, 239–242, 402
avefree, 400

B

B programming language, 3–4
Babaoğlu, Özalp, 7
background process, 103, 265, 414, 423
backing storage, 109, 414
bad sector handling, 248, 414–415
bawrite(), 210
BCPL, 4
bdwrite(), 210
Bell Laboratories, 3–4, 13, 115
Berknet, 276, 415
/bin/login, 59, 407
/bin/sh, 56, 406
bind system call, 350
biodone(), 247
blkpref(), 217
block device, 37, 171–172, 226, 229–230, 415
  table, 227, 415
block-device interface, 169, 226–227, 229, 233, 238, 415
block I/O, 171, 192–193, 415
block size, 196, 227, 415
bmap(), 142, 206–208, 213, 217
Bolt Beranek and Newman, 7, 40, 291
boot, 393–397, 406, 409, 423
  flags, 395
  operation of, 394–396
bootdevice register, 395, 415
boothowto register, 395, 415
bootstrapping, 22, 40, 124, 230, 234, 393–396, 415
  setting time when, 53
  see also initialization, **boot**
bottom half of, 44, 415
  device driver, 228
  kernel, 44–45, 85
  terminal driver, 261
  terminal driver input, 271–273
  terminal driver output, 271
Bourne shell, 56
bread(), 209, 212, 230
break character, 272
breakpoint fault, 104, 415
brealloc(), 212
brelse(), 210
broadcast message, 317, 351–352, 356, 388, 415
  address, 317, 347–348
  IP handling of, 354
bss segment, 56, 416
b_to_q(), 266, 269
buffer cache, 130, 147, 171–172, 195, 226–227, 231
  consistency, 212
  effectiveness, 208
  implementation of, 211–213
  interface, 209–210
  management, 208–213
  memory allocation, 212–213
  structure of, 210–211
buffer list
  AGE, 211–213, 222, 414
  EMPTY, 211, 213
  LOCKED, 211
  LRU, 211, 222
buffered data path, 237, 249, 416
buffering
  filesystem, 171–172, 208–209
  network, 331–332
  terminal, 266–267
bus adapter, 225, 400, 416
bus architecture, VAX, 225
bwrite(), 210, 230

C

C-block, 266, 416
C library, 54
  system calls in the, 47
C-list, 170, 228, 266, 270, 416
C programming language, 3–4, 15, 23, 47
C++ programming language, 4
C shell, 102
C70, 291
cache
  buffer, 130, 147, 171–172, 195, 226–227, 231
  directory offset, 220
  filesystem name, 220–221
  inode, 205–206
  text-page, 127, 148
callout queue, 51–53
capability, 220, 304, 416
Carnegie-Mellon University, 281
Case Western Reserve University, 115
castor oil, 266
catq(), 267
caught signal, 25, 95, 416
cbreak mode, 38, 260, 263, 416
character device, 37–38, 170–171, 226, 230–234, 416
  table, 227, 417
character-device interface, 169, 226–227, 230, 233, 238, 261, 417
chdir system call, 36, 419
checksum, 345, 349–351, 354, 368, 372, 417
child process, 24, 75, 91, 417
chmod system call, 32
chown system call, 32
chroot system call, 36, 439
cinit(), 404
cleanup(), 155
client process, 285, 417
CLOCK algorithm, 150–153, 163, 417, 429
  changes in 4.3BSD, 153
  clock hand, 150, 417
clock, alternate, 55
clock initialization, real-time, 404
clock interrupt handling, 50–53
clock interrupt rate, 50, 404
clock, real-time, 43
close-on-exec, 175–176
close system call, 30, 32, 175, 189, 261, 287, 306, 367
closedir(), 189
cluster, 117, 417
  synchronization, 125
cold start, 393, 417
communication domain, 38, 283, 293, 417
  data structures, 293
communication protocol. *See* protocol
Computer Consoles, Inc., 12
Computer Systems Research Group, vii, 8–12, 14–15, 40, 54
configuration
  device, 234, 409
  file, 408, 418
  kernel, 408–409
  procedure, 234, 418
  time, 401
  time zone, 408
congestion control
  network, 331–332
  TCP, 376–378
  see also network buffering
connect request, 319, 418
connect system call, 285–286, 298–299, 350, 352, 366, 385, 418
connection
  queueing, socket, 296, 299
  setup, TCP, 359, 366–367
  shutdown, TCP, 359, 367–368
  states, TCP, 360
console
  media, VAX, 396
  monitor, 394, 418
  processor, 394, 418
context switching, 49, 70, 79–86, 129, 418
  AST use in, 90
  intraprocess, 83–84
  involuntary, 79, 90
  process state, 80
  during swapping, 84
  VAX influence on, 90
  voluntary, 79, 81–83
control-output routine, protocol, 322
control request, 320, 418
controlling terminal, 26, 103, 418
cooked mode, 38, 259, 263, 418
copy-on-write, 6, 28, 138, 162, 418
copyin(), 119
copyout(), 119
copyseg(), 138

core(), 101
core file, 25, 94, 419
core map, 124–128, 148–149, 419
Cornell University, 40
crash, 172, 419
crash dump, 228, 230, 410, 419
creat system call, 32
CSRG. *See* Computer Systems Research Group
CTSS operating system, 3
current working directory, 35, 190, 419
cylinder group, 197–198, 419

D

DARPA, 7, 9–11, 40, 281–282, 298, 343, 387, 413–414, 416, 419, 426, 432, 437, 447–448
  Internet, 7, 39
  steering committee, 7
data path, 237, 419
  buffered, 237, 249, 416
  unbuffered, 237, 249, 447
  UNIBUS, 237–238
data segment, 26, 55–56, 142, 419
  expansion, 142
data structures
  communication domain, 293
  filesystem, 203–208
  interprocess communication, 292–298
  socket, 294–296
datagram socket, 284, 419
daylight saving time algorithm, 54
DCD, 267–268
DCE, 267, 446
deadlock avoidance
  in file locking, 178
  during *fork* system call, 137
  when locking resources, 85–86
debugging
  information in exec header, 56
  process, 100, 103–105
  system, 410
  see also ptrace system call
decapsulation, 312, 315, 419, 421
DECnet, 328
DEFBOO.CMD, 396
Defense Data Network, 381
deficit, 157
demand paging. *See* paging
descriptor, 30, 420
  allocation, 299
  duplication, 176
  locking, 177–179
  management, 172–177
  multiplexing, 179–181
  passing, 175
  table, 30, 173, 420
desfree, 152, 157
design
  4.2BSD, 11
  4.2BSD IPC, 9, 282–283
  4.2BSD network, 13, 39–40
  mbuf, 290–291
  memory-management, 27–28
/dev/console, 406
/dev/klog, 431
/dev/kmem, 186, 399
/dev/log, 399
/dev/mem, 170, 410
/dev/null, 170
device, 37–38, 225
  configuration, 234, 409
  flags, 268, 420
  interrupt, 49–50, 226
  interrupt handler, 49
  MASSBUS, 253–256
  naming, 236–237
  number, 170, 227, 420
  slave, 236, 442
  special file, 33, 420
  swap, 114, 127, 445
  UNIBUS, 237–252
device driver, 37, 49, 169–171, 225–256, 420
  attach routine, 236
  autoconfiguration, *up*, 239–242, 402
  bottom half of, 228
  I/O strategy, MASSBUS, 253–254
  I/O strategy, *up*, 244
  internal interface to, 225
  interrupt handling, MASSBUS, 254–256
  interrupt handling, *up*, 247–249
  maximum transfer size, 171
  probe routine, 235–236
  sections of a, 227
  seek optimization in *up*, 245–246

slave routine, 236
support for autoconfiguration, 227, 234–237
support for *select* system call, 181–183
top half of, 228
use of disk geometry, 241
Digital Equipment Corporation, 7
direct memory access, 147, 232, 234, 237–239, 246, 249, 253, 270–271, 274, 336, 338, 416, 419–421, 437, 444
directed broadcast, 388, 420
directory, 34, 187, 420
entry, 35, 195, 420
offset cache, 220
operations, 32–33, 189
space allocation, 188
structure, 187–189
dirty, 420
disk geometry, device driver use of, 241
disk geometry, filesystem use of, 201
disk labels, 241–242
disk partition, 187, 230, 241, 421, 431
disksort(), 243–244, 256–257
algorithm for, 245
distributed filesystem, 13, 32
DMA. *See* direct memory access
dmesg, 399
dmmax, 128, 135
dmmin, 135, 154
dmtext, 136
doadump(), 410
domain. *See* communication domain
double indirect block, 194, 421, 425
dquot table, 214–216
DTE, 267, 446
dtom(), 291–292
DTR, 267–268, 275–276
dumpsys(), 410
dup system call, 31, 174–176, 305, 420, 422
implementation of, 176
dup2 system call, 31, 176, 422

E

ECC correction, 238, 248, 257, 421
effective GID. *See* effective group identifier
effective group identifier, 59, 421
effective UID. *See* effective user identifier
effective user identifier, 59, 421
EGP. *See* Exterior Gateway Protocol
Eighth Edition UNIX, 6, 13, 39, 104
elevator sorting algorithm, 244, 421
Elz, Robert, 10, 191
EMPTY buffer list, 211, 213
Emulex SC-21V, 238–239, 243
encapsulation, 312, 315, 317, 338, 421. *See also* trailer protocol
Encore, 86
environment, location of process, 57
erase character, 260, 421
errno, 23, 47–48, 422
error-message buffer, 398, 422
Error Protocol, 382
/etc/accton, 407
/etc/config, 234, 408–409, 418
files generated by, 409
/etc/cron, 407
/etc/fsck, 196, 231, 256, 406
/etc/getty, 406–407
/etc/gettytab, 407
/etc/group, 407
/etc/init, 404–407, 425
initial startup of, 405
/etc/mknod, 236
/etc/mtab, 406
/etc/passwd, 407
/etc/rc, 406–407
/etc/rc.local, 407
/etc/savecore, 410
/etc/syslogd, 399, 407
/etc/timed, 405
/etc/ttys, 406
/etc/update, 406
Ethernet, 7, 11, 39–40, 313, 344
exec header, 56
exec system call, 31, 59, 63, 69, 136–142, 144, 159–162, 175, 405, 407
execve system call, 24, 79, 104, 140, 438, 441
operation of, 140–142
swap space allocation during, 141
exit(), 93, 101, 144, 159
exit system call, 24, 93, 118, 139, 144–145, 159–160
operation of, 93–94, 144
status, 24–25, 75, 93
Exterior Gateway Protocol, 331–332

F

fault rate, 112, 422
fchmod system call, 32
fchown system call, 32
fcntl system call, 9, 174–176, 272, 385, 420
Federal Information Processing Standard, 9
fetch policy, 112, 422
ffs, 90, 422
FIFO, 33, 422
file, 30, 187, 422
  access validation, 58–59
  executable, 56
  hole in, 36, 424
  offset, 31, 174, 422
  permission bits, 58
file block
  allocation, 193–195, 199, 207–208, 218–219
  allocation, implementation of, 217–219
  extension, 217
  locality of reference, 202
  lookup, 206–207
  mapping, 206
  numbers for paging, precomputing, 132
  reading, 207
  writing, 207
file locking, 174, 177–179
  deadlock avoidance in, 178
  implementation of, 178–179
file structure, 31, 173, 296, 422
file table, 173–175
  flag, 174, 176, 272
  handling during *fork* system call, 175
  implementation of, 174–175
  object oriented, 173–174, 176
  operations, 173
filename, 34–35, 422
filesystem, 169, 422
  abstraction, 191–193
  access control, 36
  buffering, 171–172, 208–209
  comparison with other systems, 200
  data structures, 203–208
  disk structure, 187–191
  distributed, 13, 32
  fragment allocation, 218–219
  fragmentation, 198–200
  implementation of, 191–195
  initialization, 404, 406
  interaction with virtual memory, 141
  layout policies, 201–203
  limits, 127
  links, 189–191
  local allocation routines, 202–203
  name cache, 220–221
  name length, 37
  name translation, 36, 203–205, 219–221
  old, 196
  organization, 196–198
  overview, 34–37
  parameterization, 200–201
  /proc, 104–105, 436
  quotas, 9, 191, 213–217, 404, 408
  redesign, 195–203
  redundant information in, 197
  resource locking, 86
  storage optimization, 198–200
  use of disk geometry, 201
  see also buffer cache, quotas
fill-on-demand
  klustering, 146–147, 422
  page fault, 132, 146, 423
  page table entry, 132–133, 423
First Edition UNIX, 69
firstaddr, 399
firstfree, 124, 400
floating point in the kernel, use of, 366
flow control in TCP, 358
fodkluster(), 146
foreground process, 103, 265, 414, 423
fork system call, 3, 24, 31, 63, 69, 74, 81, 91–92, 104, 136–139, 151, 162, 175, 186, 403, 417, 422, 435–436, 438
  deadlock avoidance during, 137
  file-table handling during, 175
  implementation of, 136–138
  implementation issues, 138
  see also process creation
Forkmap, 137, 139
Fortran programming language, 15, 32
4.0BSD, 7
4.1aBSD, 14
4.1BSD, 7–8
  memory management in, 117–118
4.2BSD, 7–8
  design, 11
  IPC design, 9, 282–283
  network design, 13, 39–40
  virtual-memory interface, 8

4.3BSD, 4, 7–8
compatibility of, 12
kernel, division of software in, 21
memory management in, 118
network additions in, 40
portability of, 21
Tahoe release, 7, 10, 12, 29, 54, 119–120, 150, 232, 241–242, 365, 369, 375
virtual-memory system deficiencies, 12
fragment-descriptor table, 218, 423
fragmentation
filesystem, 198–200
system page table, 155, 157
free(), 29
free list, 195, 423
memory, 125–126, 423, 431
free-space reserve, 200, 423
freemem, 128, 149, 157, 400
fseek(), 15
fstat system call, 32, 320
fsync system call, 172, 210

G

garbage collection, 305, 423
gateway handling, 329
GENIE operating system, 3
getblk(), 212
getc(), 266, 273
gethostid system call, 425
getpeername system call, 287
getrusage system call, 61
getsockname system call, 287
getsockopt system call, 287, 318, 322
gettimeofday system call, 53–54
GID. *See* group identifier
go routine, 249, 424, 448
Greenwich time. *See* Universal Coordinated Time
group identifier, 58–60, 62, 421, 424, 438, 441, 448
use in file-access validation, 59
gsignal(), 99

H

hard limit, 62, 424
hard link, 189, 424
hardclock(), 51–52, 55, 61–62, 88–89
Harris, Guy, 10
Harvard University, 7
heap, 57, 424
high watermark on, 424
socket, 296, 301, 331
terminal, 269
history of
4.3BSD memory management, 115–118
job control, 8, 103
process management, 69
UNIX, 3–8
home directory, 36, 424
Host Dead message, 381, 425
host identifier, 60, 425
host name, 60
Host Unreachable message, 381, 425
ht device driver, 253
htstrategy(), 253
Hyperchannel, 11
hz, 404

I

I/O, 425, 427
asynchronous, 174
nonblocking, 175, 180, 299–301, 303, 432
physical, 126, 158, 231
queueing, 228
redirection, 31, 427
scatter/gather, 34, 185
signal driven, 176, 180, 442
types of kernel, 169–170
I/O buffer, 228, 230
I/O page, 237, 427
I/O stream, 30, 427
I/O strategy
MASSBUS device driver, 253–254
up device driver, 244
I/O vector, 184, 427
ICMP. *See* Internet Control Message Protocol
icmp_error(), 380
IDP. *See* Internetwork Datagram Protocol
IEEE, 8–9, 435
if_init(), 316
if_output(), 316
IMP. *See* Interface Message Processor
implementation of
ARP, 335–336
buffer cache, 211–213

dup system call, 176
file block allocation, 217–219
file locking, 178–179
file table, 174–175
filesystem, 191–195
fork system call, 136–138
ioctl system call, 176–177
pipe, 30
quotas, 191, 213–217
select system call, 181–184
trailer protocol, 338–339
uiomove(), 184–185
UNIBUS network interface, 336–338
Ingres database system, 282
init, 25, 46, 76, 151, 405, 425, 450
initial sequence number, 357, 425, 441
initial startup of **/etc/init**, 405
initialization
filesystem, 404, 406
kernel, 396–405
machine-dependent, 398–403
machine-independent, 403–405
memory allocator, 400
pagedaemon, 405
paging system, 403
real-time clock, 404
system data structures, 399–400
system processes, 403, 405
user-level system, 405–407
see also bootstrapping
inode, 187–208, 213–217, 219–223, 236, 296, 404, 425
allocation, 194
cache, 205–206
contents, 195
definition, 194–195
locality of reference, 202
management, 205–206
table, 205, 425
in_pcballoc(), 350
in_pcbbind(), 350
in_pcbconnect(), 350, 366
in_pcbdetach(), 352
in_pcblookup(), operation of, 352
intelligent gateway, 329, 425
interactive program, 71, 426
Interdata 8/32, 6
interface
buffer cache, 209–210
capabilities, network, 316–317
line switch, 261, 428
network, 315–317
protocol, 293
protocol–network-interface, 324–327
protocol-protocol, 322–323
socket-to-protocol, 318–322
Interface Message Processor, 323, 325, 331, 345–346, 380–381, 425–426
interleaving, swap space, 128
International Organization for Standardization, 9, 13, 312, 344, 429
protocol suite, 40
internet addresses
broadcast, 347–348
host, 345–348, 426
packet demultiplexing, 348
structure, 297
subnet, 346–347
Internet Control Message Protocol, 331, 344–345, 352, 357, 375, 378–381, 383, 425–426, 437
interaction with routing, 379
port unreachable message, 352
internet domain, 39, 426
Internet Protocol, 40, 276, 313, 332, 344–345, 348–357, 368, 372, 378–380, 387–388, 426–427
handling of broadcast message, 354
input processing, 354–357
options, 353
output processing, 353–354
packet demultiplexing, 349
packet forwarding, 356–357, 380
protocol header, 353
responsibilities of, 352
Internetwork Datagram Protocol, 381–385, 425–426
interprocess communication, viii, 6, 12–13, 19, 30, 33, 38–40, 61, 172, 281–307, 426–427
connection setup, 298–300
data structures, 292–298
data transfer, 300–306
design, 4.2BSD, 9, 282–283
facilities, interface design, 287
memory management in, 289–292
model of, 282–287
receiving data, 302–304
reliable delivery, 301
socket shutdown, 306–307

transmitting data, 301–302
interrupt, 426
device, 49–50, 226
priority level, 45, 85, 426
software, 50, 313, 354, 443
stack, 45, 50, 78, 96, 426
interrupt handling, 49–50, 226, 229
algorithm, MASSBUS adapter, 255
clock, 50–53
MASSBUS device driver, 254–256
up device driver, 247–249
interrupt vector, 226, 427
autoconfiguration of, 236, 401–403
table, 226, 427, 449
interrupted system call, 47–48, 98
involuntary
context switching, 79, 90
swapping, 157–158
ioctl system call, 33, 97, 103, 173, 176, 261–263, 274, 276, 304, 316–317, 320, 331, 418, 421, 428, 449
implementation of, 176–177
iovec, 184–185, 427, 447
IP. *See* Internet Protocol
IPC. *See* interprocess communication
ipintr(), operation of, 354–357
ip_output(), 351, 354, 357, 372, 379
operation of, 353–354
ISO. *See* International Organization for Standardization
issig(), operation of, 101
ITS operating system, 8

J

job, 427
job control, 26, 76, 97, 102–103, 427
history of, 8, 103
signals in 4.3BSD, 25
terminal driver support for, 265, 269, 273
use of process group, 26
Joy, William, 7

K

keepalive packet, 364, 427
keepalive timer, 364, 428
kernel, 20, 428
assembly language in the, 22, 46–47, 90, 229, 405
bottom half of, 44–45, 85
configuration, 408–409
I/O, types of, 169–170
initialization, 396–405
memory allocation, 28–29
mode, 69, 114, 428
organization, 20–23
partitioning, reason for, 20
preemption, 45
process, 45–46, 428
state, 70, 428
top half of, 44–45, 85
kernel stack, 50
growth of, 78
location of, 57, 78
size of, 78
kernelmap, 130, 137, 145, 428
initialization of, 130
kill character, 260, 428
kill system call, 96
killpg system call, 76, 96, 103, 436
klustering, 149, 428
Korn shell, 102
Kulp, Jim, 103

L

lbolt, 270
ldctx(), 84, 92
ldpctx, 81, 418, 428
least recently used, 117, 126, 150, 205–206, 211, 425, 428, 430
buffer list, 211, 222
lightweight process, 107
limits in system, 127, 191
line discipline, 260–262, 268, 276–277, 428
Berknet, 276
close(), 275–276
output(), 268–270
SLIP, 276–277
tablet, 277
line mode, 259, 429
line switch interface, 261, 428
link layer, 312, 429
link system call, 32. *See also* filesystem links
LISP programming language, 7, 115
listen request, 319, 429
listen system call, 286, 298–299, 367, 429
load average, 87–88, 429

locality of reference, 113, 146, 201–202, 429
LOCKED buffer list, 211
locking
descriptor, 177–179
on page, 126
resources on a shared-memory multiprocessor, 86
resources, deadlock avoidance when, 85–86
socket data buffer, 302
logical
block, 192, 429
device unit, 236–237
drive partitions, 243, 429
unit, 242, 429
longjmp(), 83–84, 160
loop, 150, 429
lotsfree, 152, 154
low watermark on, 430
socket, 296, 331
terminal, 269, 271
LRU. *See* least recently used
lseek system call, 31, 174, 189, 422
lstat system call, 191

M

Mach operating system, 20
machine check, 398, 430
machine-dependent initialization, 398–403
machine-independent initialization, 403–405
m_adj(), 292
magic number, 56, 430
main(), 398–399, 403, 405
main memory, 109, 430
major device number, 170, 227, 236, 430
malloc(), 29, 57
mark-and-sweep algorithm, 306, 430
Massachusetts Institute of Technology, 3, 8
MASSBUS, 225–227, 403, 416, 430, 445
device, 253–256
device, autoconfiguration of, 253
device driver I/O strategy, 253–254
device driver interrupt handling, 254–256
unit number, 229, 430
MASSBUS adapter, 253, 430
interrupt handling algorithm, 255
support routines, 253, 430
maxfree, 124, 400
maximum segment lifetime, 359, 361, 388, 431–432. *See also* 2MSL timer
maximum-segment-size option, TCP, 366
maxslp, 158
mbinit(), 404
Mbmap, 291
mbstart(), 254
mbuf, 172, 289–291, 431
allocation of, 291
design, 290–291
utility routines, 292
mbustart(), 253–254
MC68000, 119
m_copy(), 292, 372
memall(), 127, 131
memfree(), 127
meminit(), 400
memory allocation
buffer cache, 212–213
kernel, 28–29
routines, 127–128
memory allocator initialization, 400
memory free list, 125–126, 423, 431
memory management, 109–161
in 3BSD, 116–117
in 4.1BSD, 117–118
in 4.3BSD, 118
design, 27–28
evolution of 4.3BSD, 115–118
hardware, use of, 70
hardware, VAX, 27, 118–124
in IPC, 289–292
portability of, 21, 27
in Seventh Edition UNIX, 115–116
system, 109, 431
unit, 111, 431
in UNIX/32V, 116
memory-mapped I/O architecture, 226, 431
memory overlay, 111
memory size limit, 127
message buffer, 399, 431
m_free(), 292
m_freem(), 292
m_get(), 291
m_getclr(), 291
Microsoft Corporation, 7
Milnet, X.25 interface to, 381
minfree, 152, 157
MINIX operating system, 8
minor device number, 170, 227, 236, 431

minphys( ), 231
mkdir system call, 9, 32, 41
mknod system call, 33, 430–431
mmap system call, 27–28, 234
modem control, 267–268, 431
mount system call, 229
m_pullup( ), 292, 351, 355, 368
MS-DOS operating system, 189
msgbufmap, 399
MSL. *See* maximum segment lifetime
mtod( ), 292
MT XINU, 10
Multics operating system, 3, 8
multilevel feedback queue, 86, 432
multiplexed file, 281, 432
multiprocessor
  locking resources on a shared-memory, 86
  virtual memory for a shared-memory, 27
multiprogramming, 69–71

N

Nagle, John, 373, 375
name cache, filesystem, 220–221
name length, filesystem, 37
name translation, filesystem, 36, 203–205, 219–221
namei( ), 86, 206, 219–221, 384
National Bureau of Standards, 9, 334
NCP. *See* Network Control Program
ndflush( ), 271
ndqb( ), 270
network
  additions in 4.3BSD, 40
  architecture, 311, 432
  buffering, 331–332
  byte order, 345, 432
  congestion control, 331–332
  data flow, 172, 312–313
  design, 4.2BSD, 13, 39–40
  layer, 312, 432
  layering, 312
  mask, 347, 432
  protocol capabilities, 314–315
  queue limiting, 332
  time synchronization, 53–54
  timer, 52, 314
  virtual terminal, 13, 432
Network Control Program, 344
Network File System, Sun Microsystems, 13
network interface, 315–317
  capabilities, 316–317
  layer, 312, 432
  UNIBUS, 336–338
new terminal driver, 262, 269, 276, 432
newbuf( ), 212–213
newproc( ), 405
nextc( ), 267
nexus, 400, 432
nice, 25, 60, 156, 432, 437, 440
Ninth Edition UNIX, 6
nodev( ), 239
nonblocking I/O, 175, 180, 299–301, 303, 432
nonlocal goto, 48, 83–84, 92, 433
noproc, 90, 93
notavail( ), 212
ns_err_input( ), 383
NSFnet, 39
nsintr( ), 383
null modem connection, 267
nulldev( ), 238–239

O

object oriented file table, 173–174, 176
octet, 345, 433
old filesystem, 196
old terminal driver, 262, 268, 276, 433
Olson, Arthur, 10
open system call, 30–32, 174, 189–190, 205–206, 229, 256, 261, 285, 287, 420
opendir( ), 189
Optimal Replacement Policy, 113, 433
out-of-band data, 302, 321, 334–335, 433
  receipt of, 303
  transmission of, 301
overlay, 22, 115, 433

P

P0 base register, 122–123, 433–434
P0 length register, 122–123, 433–434
P0BR. *See* P0 base register
P0LR. *See* P0 length register
P1 base register, 122, 434
P1 length register, 122, 434
P1BR. *See* P1 base register
P1LR. *See* P1 length register

packet
  forwarding, IP, 356–357, 380
  queue, 325–327
  reception, 325–327
  transmission, 324–325
packet demultiplexing
  internet addresses, 348
  IP, 349
  XNS, 382
Packet Exchange, 382, 434–435
Packet Switch Node, 380–381, 425, 434, 437
page fault, 111, 120, 123, 126, 434
  fill-on-demand, 132, 146, 423
  on the VAX, 122–124
page, locking on, 126
page push, 154, 434
page reclaim, 148, 434
page replacement, 7, 112–113, 149–155
  in the VMS operating system, 151
  VAX influence on, 149
page table, 79
  allocation, user, 131
  expansion, 143
  layout of process, 131
  paging of, 131
  text, 134, 148, 159–161
  VAX, 119–120
page table entry, 119, 122, 131, 419, 423, 428, 434, 437, 439, 443, 445, 447
  fill-on-demand, 132–133, 423
  format of a VAX, 120
  normal, 132
  types, 131–133
  valid bit, 119, 132
page in-transit, 126, 149
pagedaemon, 45–46, 151–152, 154, 157, 162, 247, 405, 419, 428, 434
  initialization, 405
  operation of the, 151
pagein(), 61, 126, 145–146, 148–149, 434
  operation of, 145–149
  of swapped pages, 147–149
pageout(), 62, 148, 151, 153–155, 405, 434
  asynchronous I/O in, 155
  operation of, 153–155
pageout in progress, 155, 434
paging, 7, 27, 57, 112, 114, 145–149, 420, 434
  of page table, 131
  parameters, 151–152
  system initialization, 403
  systems, characteristics of, 112
panic(), 410
panic, 410, 435
parent directory, 36
parent process, 24, 75, 91, 435
partition. *See* disk partition
pathname, 35, 435
PCB. *See* process control block
PCBB. *See* Process Control Block Base
PDP-11, vii, 6, 8, 48, 69, 103, 115–116, 171, 226, 237, 276, 430
PDP-7, 3, 69
performance. *See* system performance
Perkin Elmer, 45
persist timer, 364, 435
PEX. *See* Packet Exchange
pfctlinput(), 379
physical block, 193, 435
physical I/O, 126, 158, 231
  algorithm for, 232
  restrictions on, 231
physical unit number, 229, 435
physio(), 231, 233, 249, 257
  operation of, 231
PID. *See* process identifier
pipe, 30, 281–282, 435
  implementation of, 30
  system call, 30–31, 420
pipeline, 26, 31, 435
placement policy, 112, 435
portability of
  4.3BSD, 21
  memory management, 21, 27
  Seventh Edition UNIX, 6
POSIX, viii, 8–9, 12–13, 33, 96, 99, 103, 277, 435
  signal handling, 99
pr_ctlinput(), 314, 322–323, 330, 352, 379, 383
pr_ctloutput(), 314, 318, 322, 352, 383
pr_drain(), 314
preemption
  kernel, 45
  process, 85, 90
prefetching, 146, 436
prepaging, 112, 118, 436
pr_fasttimo(), 314, 321
pr_input(), 314, 322–323

printf(), 399
priority level, interrupt, 45, 85, 426
probe routine, 235–236, 239, 436
probing, 227, 235, 436
/**proc** filesystem, 104–105, 436
proc structure, 70, 72–77, 80, 131, 436
procdup(), 92
process, 23, 69, 436
  checkpoint a, 410
  creation, 91–92, 136–140
  debugging, 100, 103–105
  flags, 74, 104
  kernel, 45–46, 428
  lightweight, 107
  limit, 127
  open file table, 205, 437
  page table, layout of, 131
  preemption, 85, 90
  profiling, 49, 55
  queues, 74
  resource accounting, 51, 62–63, 93
  scheduling, 43, 53, 58, 71–72, 83, 86–91
  state, 74, 80
  state, change of, 83, 93, 100–101, 104
  synchronization, 83
  table, 57, 437
  termination, 93–94, 144–145
process control block, 77–81, 92, 122, 131, 435–436
Process Control Block Base, 81, 435–436
process group, 26, 76, 96–97, 102, 436
  hierarchy, 75
  identifier, 76, 96, 176, 295, 436
  job-control use of, 26
  socket, 97, 295
  terminal, 97, 265, 268, 272–273, 275
process identifier, 24–26, 74–75, 91, 103, 265, 268, 435–437
  allocation during process creation, 91
process management, 23–26, 55–58, 69–105
  history of, 69
process priority, 25, 48, 60–61, 74, 76, 81, 437
  calculation of, 51, 83, 87–88
  ordering of, 77
  while sleeping, 76, 82
processor priority level, 45, 437, 441
Processor Status Longword, 46–47, 78, 437, 446
profil system call, 64
profiling
  process, 49, 55
  timer, 51, 55
program relocation, 396, 439
programming language
  B, 3–4
  BCPL, 4
  C, 3–4, 15, 23, 47
  C++, 4
  Fortran, 15, 32
  LISP, 7, 115
protocol, 39, 314–315, 418
  capabilities, network, 314–315
  control-output routine, 322
  interface, 293
  network-interface interface, 324–327
  protocol interface, 322–323
  remote procedure call, 13
  switch structure, 314, 437
protocol family, 284, 293–294, 311, 437
pr_output(), 314, 322–323
pr_slowtimo(), 314, 321
pr_usrreq(), 314, 318, 322
pseudo-DMA, 271, 437
psig(), 100–101
  operation of, 101
psignal(), 99–101
  operation of, 100–101
PSL. *See* Processor Status Longword
PSN. *See* Packet Switch Node
PTE. *See* page table entry
ptrace system call, 83, 103–104
  limitations of, 104
Purdue University, 7, 115
pure demand-paging, 112, 437
Pushmap, 154
putc(), 266

Q

q_to_b(), 266
queue limiting, network, 332
quota table, 216–217
quotachk(), 213–215
quotas
  configuration of, 404, 408
  contribution of, 9
  format of record, 214
  implementation of, 191, 213–217
  limits, 191

R

Rand Corporation, 7, 281
raw device interface, 170, 438
raw mode, 38, 260, 263, 438
raw socket, 37, 311, 332–334, 345, 379, 382, 438
  control block, 332
  input processing, 333–334
  output processing, 334
raw_input(), 379
read system call, 30, 32, 34, 39, 97, 103–104, 172, 174, 185, 189, 261, 272–273, 286–287, 300, 386, 422, 433, 436, 445
readdir(), 189
readv system call, 34, 184, 286, 427
Ready for Next Message, 380–381, 438–439
real GID. *See* real group identifier
real group identifier, 59, 438
real-time clock, 43
  initialization, 404
real-time system, UNIX as a, 90
real-time timer, 51, 55, 74
real UID. *See* real user identifier
real user identifier, 59, 438
realloccg(), 217
reboot, 409–410
reboot system call, 395, 409, 411
receive window, 361, 438, 442
reclaim, 438
  from free, 148, 438
recv system call, 34, 172, 286
recvfrom system call, 34, 286, 300
recvit(), 301
recvmsg system call, 34, 286, 300
  data structures for, 287
red zone, 72, 403, 438
reference bit, 120, 149, 439
  simulation of a, 133, 150
reference string, 112, 439
register save mask, 402, 439
relative pathname, 35, 435, 439
release engineering, 14–15
reliably delivered message socket, 340, 439
remote procedure call protocol, 13
remque, 90
remrq(), 89
rename system call, 9, 32
  addition of, 32
replacement policy, 112, 439
resident set size, 73, 151
resource accounting, process, 51, 62–63, 93
resource limit, 24, 60–62
resource map, 130, 439
resume(), 80–81, 90, 92, 160
retransmit timer, 364, 366, 439
return from interrupt instruction, 47
rewinddir(), 189
RFNM. *See* Ready for Next Message
Ritchie, Dennis, 3–4, 8
rmalloc(), 130
rmdir system call, 9, 32
rmfree(), 130, 145
root directory, 35, 439
root filesystem, 36, 393, 439
root user, 58, 444
rotational delay, 201
rotational-layout table, 218, 439
round robin, 86, 440
round-trip time, 365
  TCP estimation of, 365–366
roundrobin(), 88, 90
routing, 327–331
  daemon, 331, 419, 440
  interaction with ICMP, 379
  mechanism, 328
  policy, 328, 330–331
  redirect, 329–330, 440
  tables, 328–330
  types of, 329
RS-232 serial line, 259, 267, 446
rtalloc(), 330, 354
rtfree(), 330
rtredirect(), 330, 379
run queue, 74, 86, 440
  management of, 89–91
  VAX influence on, 89
runrun, 90
rwip(), 206–207

S

savecore, 410
savectx(), 84, 92
sbappend(), 370, 372
sbappendaddr(), 352
sblock(), 302
SBR. *See* system base register
sbrk system call, 57, 142, 424

sbunlock( ), 302
SC-21V, Emulex, 238–239, 243
scanc( ), 269
scatter/gather I/O, 34, 185
scatter-loading, 116, 440
sched( ), 156, 405
schedcpu( ), 88, 90
schednetisr( ), 326
schedpaging( ), 152
scheduling, 70, 440
  parameters, 24
  priority, 76, 440
  process, 43, 53, 58, 71–72, 83, 86–91
secondary storage, 109, 440
seek optimization, 241, 256
  in *up* device driver, 245–246
seekdir( ), 189
segment, 110, 357, 440
  bss, 56, 416
  data, 26, 55–56, 142, 419
  stack, 26, 55, 142, 443
  text, 26, 55–56, 127, 446
select system call, 12, 181–183, 186, 233, 261, 367, 385, 399
  device driver support for, 181–183
  implementation of, 181–184
seltrue( ), 234
selwait, 182–183
selwakeup( ), 181–183, 271
send system call, 34, 39, 172, 286, 296, 385
send window, 361, 440
sendit( ), 301
sendmsg system call, 34, 286, 300, 350
  data structures for, 287
sendsig( ), 101–102
sendto system call, 34, 286, 300, 318, 350, 385
sense request, 320, 441
sequence numbers, TCP, 357
sequence space, 357, 441
sequence variables, TCP, 360–361
Sequenced Packet Protocol, 381–384, 441, 443
sequenced packet socket, 284, 441
Sequent, 86
Serial Line IP, 276–278, 441, 443
server process, 285, 441
session, 103, 441
set-group-identifier program, 59, 441
set-priority-level, 85, 441
set-user-identifier program, 59, 441
sethostid system call, 425
setjmp( ), 83–84
setpgrp system call, 96
setpri( ), 88–90
setpriority system call, 96, 436
setrq( ), 89
setrun( ), 89–90, 100
setsockopt system call, 287, 307, 318, 322, 351, 374
settimeofday system call, 54
Seventh Edition UNIX, 6–8, 12, 281
  memory management in, 115–116
  portability of, 6
shadow swap map, 141, 441
shared text segment, 6, 73, 79, 441
  limit, 127
shell, 20, 442
  Bourne, 56
  C, 102
  Korn, 102
short-term scheduling algorithm, 87, 442
shutdown system call, 287, 303, 367
SIGALRM, 55
sigblock system call, 96, 98, 430
SIGBUS, 123
SIGCHLD, 100, 104
SIGCONT, 96, 100, 275, 418
SIGHUP, 275
SIGIO, 174, 272, 295, 442
SIGKILL, 25, 95–96, 101
signal, 25–26, 73, 94–103, 442
  checking for a pending, 48
  comparison with other systems, 97–98
  delivering, 57, 101–102
  driven I/O, 176, 180, 442
  handler, 25, 94, 442
  handling, POSIX, 99
  posting, 96, 99–101
  problems addressed by 4.3BSD, 97
  restrictions on posting, 96
  stack, 25, 96
  trampoline code, 78, 102, 129, 442
sigpause system call, 96
SIGPROF, 55, 64
sigreturn system call, 96, 102, 442
SIGSEGV, 123
sigsetmask system call, 96, 98, 430
sigstack system call, 96, 98
SIGSTOP, 25, 95–96

SIGTRAP, 104
SIGTSTP, 106, 273
SIGTTIN, 273
SIGTTOU, 100, 269
SIGURG, 295
sigvec system call, 94, 97–98, 101, 416
SIGVTALRM, 55
SIGWINCH, 265
SIGXCPU, 51
silly-window syndrome, 372, 442
  TCP handling of, 372–373
single indirect block, 194, 425, 442
Sixth Edition UNIX, 4, 6, 8, 12, 77
slave device, 236, 442
slave routine, 236, 239, 442
sleep(), 77, 79, 81–86, 88, 90, 96, 99, 106, 151, 228, 256, 300, 415, 442, 446
  operation of, 82
sleep queue, 74, 442
sliding-window scheme, 358, 442
slip sector, 248, 443
  forwarding, 248, 443
SLIP. *See* Serial Line IP
slow-start algorithm, TCP, 376–378
SLR. *See* system length register
small-packet avoidance, 388, 443
  TCP implementation of, 373–374
soaccept(), 385
sobind(), 384
socantrcvmore(), 371, 386
socket, 30, 33, 39, 169, 172–173, 283, 293, 311, 443
  address, 296–298
  address structure, 284–285
  connection queueing, 296, 299
  data buffer locking, 302
  data buffering, 296, 301, 303
  data structures, 294–296
  error handling, 300
  options, 318
  process group, 97, 295
  shutdown, 306–307
  state transitions during rendezvous, 298
  state transitions during shutdown, 307
  states, 295
  types, 283, 293
  using a, 284–287
socket system call, 9, 13, 30–31, 39, 284–285, 293, 298, 318, 322, 384, 420
socket-to-protocol interface, 318–322
socketpair system call, 287, 321, 420
soconnect(), 300, 385
socreate(), 384
soft limit, 62, 443
soft link, 190, 443, 445
softclock(), 51–52, 55
software interrupt, 50, 313, 354, 443
sohasoutofband(), 370
soisconnected(), 300, 385
soisconnecting(), 366, 385
soisdisconnected(), 371
solisten(), 299
sonewconn(), 299, 367
soreceive(), 302–305, 308, 386
sorflush(), 386
sorwakeup(), 303
sosend(), 301–302, 305, 308, 372, 385, 387
soshutdown(), 386
source-quench processing, TCP, 375–376
special file, 33, 37, 173, 443
spin loop, 398, 443
splbio(), 228, 257
splimp(), 327
splnet(), 302
spltty(), 228, 441
SPP. *See* Sequenced Packet Protocol
stack, 443
  growth on VAX, 57
  kernel, 50
  location of kernel, 57
  segment, 26, 55, 142, 443
  segment expansion, 142
  zero filling of user, 57
stale translation, 124, 443
standalone, 443
  device driver, 395, 444
  I/O library, 394, 444
  program, 394–396
standard error, 31, 444
standard input, 31, 444
standard output, 31, 444
Stanford University, 14
startrtclock(), 404
startup(), 398–399, 403
stat system call, 32, 190–191, 320, 441
statistics collection, 51, 55, 61
sticky bit, 118, 148, 162, 444
sticky text, 148, 444

stop character, 234, 270
stream I/O system, 6, 13, 444
stream socket, 284, 444
subnet, 12, 346
  internet addresses, 346–347
Sun Microsystems, 119, 265
  Network File System, 13
superblock, 196, 444
superuser, 58, 177, 444
svpctx, 81, 418, 444
swap(), 154
swap area, 114, 444
swap device, 114, 127, 445
swap map, 135, 445
swap space, 114, 445
  allocation, 129
  allocation during *execve* system call, 141
  allocation during *fork* system call, 136
  expansion, 135
  interleaving, 128
  management, 128–129, 134–136
swapin(), 83
  operation of, 159–160
swapon system call, 129
swapout(), operation of, 158–159
swapper, 45, 156–159, 428, 445
  operation of, 156
swapping, 27, 58, 113, 137, 151, 155–161, 445
  in 4.3BSD, reasons for, 155
  context switching during, 84
  involuntary, 157–158
  a text segment, 160–161
swdone(), 154
swtch(), 80–82, 90, 94
  operation of, 90
symbolic link, 190–191, 445
sync system call, 172, 186, 207
synchronization, 84–86
  cluster, 125
  network time, 53–54
syscall(), 46
Sysmap, 130
system activity, 43–44, 445
system base register, 120–121, 440, 445
system bus, 400, 445
system call, 20, 23, 44–45, 445
  handling, 28, 46–49, 80
  interrupted, 47–48, 98
  result handling, 47–48
system calls
  accept, 286, 296, 298–299, 308, 367, 385
  adjtime, 54
  bind, 350
  chdir, 36, 419
  chmod, 32
  chown, 32
  chroot, 36, 439
  close, 30, 32, 175, 189, 261, 287, 306, 367
  connect, 285–286, 298–299, 350, 352, 366, 385, 418
  creat, 32
  dup, 31, 174–176, 305, 420, 422
  dup2, 31, 176, 422
  exec, 31, 59, 63, 69, 136–142, 144, 159–162, 175, 407
  execve, 24, 79, 104, 140, 438, 441
  exit, 24, 93, 118, 139, 144–145, 159–160
  fchmod, 32
  fchown, 32
  fcntl, 9, 174–176, 272, 385, 420
  fork, 3, 24, 31, 63, 69, 74, 81, 91–92, 104, 136–139, 151, 162, 175, 186, 403, 417, 422, 435–436, 438
  fstat, 32, 320
  fsync, 172, 210
  gethostid, 425
  getpeername, 287
  getrusage, 61
  getsockname, 287
  getsockopt, 287, 318, 322
  gettimeofday, 53–54
  ioctl, 33, 97, 103, 173, 176, 261–263, 274, 276, 304, 316–317, 320, 331, 418, 421, 428, 449
  kill, 96
  killpg, 76, 96, 103, 436
  link, 32
  listen, 286, 298–299, 367, 429
  lseek, 31, 174, 189, 422
  lstat, 191
  mkdir, 9, 32, 41
  mknod, 33, 430–431
  mmap, 27–28, 234
  mount, 229
  open, 30–32, 174, 189–190, 205–206, 229, 256, 261, 285, 287, 420

pipe, 30–31, 420
profil, 64
ptrace, 83, 103–104
read, 30, 32, 34, 39, 97, 103–104, 172, 174, 185, 189, 261, 272–273, 286–287, 300, 386, 422, 433, 436, 445
readv, 34, 184, 286, 427
reboot, 395, 409, 411
recv, 34, 172, 286
recvfrom, 34, 286, 300
recvmsg, 34, 286, 300
rename, 9, 32
rmdir, 9, 32
sbrk, 57, 142, 424
select, 12, 181–183, 186, 233, 261, 367, 385, 399
send, 34, 39, 172, 286, 296, 385
sendmsg, 34, 286, 300, 350
sendto, 34, 286, 300, 318, 350, 385
sethostid, 425
setpgrp, 96
setpriority, 96, 436
setsockopt, 287, 307, 318, 322, 351, 374
settimeofday, 54
shutdown, 287, 303, 367
sigblock, 96, 98, 430
sigpause, 96
sigreturn, 96, 102, 442
sigsetmask, 96, 98, 430
sigstack, 96, 98
sigvec, 94, 97–98, 101, 416
socket, 9, 13, 30–31, 39, 284–285, 293, 298, 318, 322, 384, 420
socketpair, 287, 321, 420
stat, 32, 190–191, 320, 441
swapon, 129
sync, 172, 186, 207
truncate, 32–33
unlink, 32
vfork, 91, 134, 136, 138–139, 144, 162
vhangup, 407
wait, 25, 69, 93–94, 104, 139, 145
wait3, 25, 93–94, 104
write, 30, 32–34, 39, 97, 103–104, 172, 174, 185, 199, 261, 270, 286–287, 296, 300, 385, 422, 436, 445
writev, 34, 184, 286, 427
system debugging, 410
system identification register, 398, 445
use of the, 398
system length register, 120–121, 443, 445
system page table, 120, 129, 445
allocation, 130
fragmentation, 155, 157
layout, 130
system performance, 12, 47, 50–52, 54, 57, 70, 90, 301, 404
system processes initialization, 403, 405
system region, 119, 445
system shutdown, 409–410
system startup, 393–394
initial state, 397

T

Tahoe release. *See* 4.3BSD Tahoe release
TCP. *See* Transmission Control Protocol
tcp_close(), 368
tcp_ctloutput(), 374
tcp_fasttimo(), 365, 370, 375
tcp_input(), 363, 371, 374
operation of, 368–371
tcp_output(), 363, 366, 370–372, 374–375
operation of, 372
tcp_slowtimo(), 363, 365
tcp_timers(), 363–364
tcp_usrreq(), 363, 366–367, 372, 374
telldir(), 189
TENEX operating system, 8, 103
terminal, 38, 446
buffering, 266–267
multiplexer, 226, 259, 446
terminal driver, 234, 260, 262, 447
bottom half of, 261
close(), 275–276
data queues, 264, 266–267, 269–274
hardware state, 263–264
input, 271–273
input, bottom half of, 271–273
input silo, 271–272
input, top half of, 273
ioctl(), 262–263, 274
modem control, 267–268
modem transitions, 275
modes, 259–260, 264, 272
open(), 268
output, 270–271
output, bottom half of, 271
output, *stop*(), 273–274
output, top half of, 270–271

software state, 265
special characters, 259–260, 264
start(), 270
top half of, 261
user interface, 8, 262–263
window size, 265, 268
terminal process group, 97, 265, 268, 272–273, 275
text-page cache, 127, 148
text page table, 134, 148, 159–161
initialization, 141
text segment, 26, 55–56, 127, 446
swapping a, 160–161
see also shared text segment
text structure, 72, 79–80, 446
Thompson, Ken, 3–4, 8, 20
thrashing, 71, 446
3BSD, memory management in, 116–117
tick, 50, 446
time, 53–55
algorithm, daylight saving, 54
of day, 43
of day register, 53
quantum, 86, 446
representation, 54–55
slice, 71, 86, 446
synchronization, network, 53–54
time zone, 53–54
configuration, 408
handling, 10, 54
timeout(), 51–53, 270
timer
2MSL, 364–365, 447
backoff, 364, 446
network, 52, 314
profiling, 51, 55
real-time, 51, 55, 74
resolution of, 54
virtual-time, 55
watchdog, 52
TLB. *See* translation lookaside buffer
top half of, 44, 446
device driver, 228
kernel, 44–45, 85
terminal driver, 261
terminal driver input, 273
terminal driver output, 270–271
TOPS-20 operating system, 8
trace trap, 104, 446
traced process, 100, 104
trailer protocol, 317, 338–339, 447
implementation of, 338–339
negotiation, 339
translation lookaside buffer, 124, 446–447
translation-not-valid fault, 120, 447
Transmission Control Protocol, viii, 12, 40, 313, 330, 334, 344–345, 348, 357–379, 384, 387–388, 446–447
congestion control, 376–378
connection setup, 359, 366–367
connection shutdown, 359, 367–368
connection states, 360
delayed acknowledgements in, 370
estimation of round-trip time, 365–366
features of, 357
flow control in, 358
handling of silly-window syndrome, 372–373
handling of urgent data, 370
implementation of small packet avoidance, 373–374
implementation, use of 4BSD, 9
input processing, 368–371
maximum-segment-size option, 366
options, 358
output processing, 371–378
packet header, 358
retransmission handling, 375
send policy, 363, 371–378
sequence numbers, 357
sequence variables, 360–361
slow-start algorithm, 376–378
source-quench processing, 375–376
state diagram, 361
timers, 363–365
window updates, 374–375
transport layer, 312, 447
trap(), 46
trap handling, 44, 46–47, 49–50, 80
trap type code, 46
triple indirect block, 194, 425, 447
truncate system call, 32–33
addition of, 32
ttread(), 273
ttrstrt(), 271
ttselect(), 234, 261
ttstart(), 270, 277
ttwakeup(), 272
ttwrite(), 269–270, 273
tty driver. *See* terminal driver

tty structure, 263–265
ttyclose(), 276
ttyinput(), 272
ttylclose(), 275
ttymodem(), 275
ttyopen(), 268
ttyoutput(), 269–270
Tunis operating system, 8, 20
2MSL timer, 364–365, 447. *See also* maximum segment lifetime
type-ahead, 259, 447

U

u-dot. *See* user structure
ubadone(), 249–250
ubago(), 247, 249–250, 254
ubarelse(), 251–252
ubasetup(), 250
UDP. *See* User Datagram Protocol
udp_input(), 351
udp_output(), 350
udp_usrreq(), 350, 352
UID. *See* user identifier
uio, 184–185, 231–232, 268, 273, 447
uiomove(), 185, 233, 269
  implementation of, 184–185
Ultrix operating system, 23
unbuffered data path, 237, 249, 447
UNIBUS, 225–227, 270–271, 403, 416, 445, 448
  data path, 237–238
  device, 237–252
  network interface, 336–338
UNIBUS adapter, 237, 448
  support routines, 249–252
Universal Coordinated Time, 53–54, 64, 408
University of California at Berkeley, 7, 115
University of Illinois, 7
University of Maryland, 40
UNIX/32V, 6–7, 11
  memory management in, 116
UNIX as a real-time system, 90
UNIX domain, 38, 448
  address structure, 297
  passing access rights in the, 305–306
UNIX, history of, 3–8
UNIX Programmer's Manual, 4
UNIX Support Group, 6
UNIX System III, 6–9, 39
UNIX System V, 4, 6–9, 177, 195
  Release 3, 6, 13, 103
unlink system call, 32
unp_gc(), 306
unputc(), 267
unselect(), 182
up device driver, 236, 238–249, 253, 256–257
  autoconfiguration, 239–242, 402
  I/O strategy, 244
  interrupt handling, 247–249
  seek optimization in, 245–246
update, 172, 186, 207
updatepri(), 89
ureadc(), 273
urgent data, 334, 448
  TCP handling of, 370
  transmission, styles of, 302
USENET, 10
user area. *See* user structure
User Datagram Protocol, 330, 344–345, 348–352, 366, 372, 379, 384, 387–388, 447–448
user identifier, 58–60, 62, 64, 92, 421, 425, 438, 441, 444, 447–448
  use in file-access validation, 58
user-level system initialization, 405–407
user mode, 69, 114, 448
user page table, 129, 448
  allocation, 131
user request routine, 314, 318–321, 448
  operations, 318–321
user structure, 44, 57, 70, 72, 77–78, 131, 448
  contents of, 77
  location of, 57
  mapping on VAX, 78
Usrptmap, 130–131
UTC. *See* Universal Coordinated Time

V

V Kernel operating system, 20
valid bit, PTE, 119, 132
VAX, vii, viii, 6–7, 11–12, 21, 45
  VAX-11/750, 117
  VAX-11/780, 6, 116
  address translation, 120–122